FRANK MCLYNN

Marcus Aurelius

Warrior, Philosopher, Emperor

VINTAGE BOOKS

London

Published by Vintage 2010

2 4 6 8 10 9 7 5 3 1

Copyright © Frank McLynn 2009

Frank McLynn has asserted his right under the Copyright, Designs
and Patents Act 1988 to be identified as the author of this work

First published in Great Britain in 2009 by
The Bodley Head

Vintage
Random House, 20 Vauxhall Bridge Road,
London SW1V 2SA

www.vintage-books.co.uk

Addresses for companies within The Random House Group Limited
can be found at: www.randomhouse.co.uk/offices.htm

The Random House Group Limited Reg. No. 954009

A CIP catalogue record for this book
is available from the British Library

ISBN 9781844135271

The Random House Group Limited supports The Forest
Stewardship Council (FSC), the leading international forest
certification organisation. All our titles that are printed on
Greenpeace approved FSC certified paper carry the FSC logo.
Our paper procurement policy can be found at:
www.rbooks.co.uk/environment

MARCUS AURELIUS

Frank McLynn is the author of many critically acclaimed books, including *Napoleon, 1066, Villa and Zapata, Wagons West, Stanley, 1759* and *Lionheart and Lackland*.

CONTENTS

CONTENTS

ILLUSTRATIONS

Section Two

15. Richard Harris in *Gladiator* (*Dreamworks/Universal/The Kobal Collection/Buitendijk, JAAP*)

16. Alec Guinness the *The Fall of the Roman Empire* (© *Rank Organisation/Samuel Bronston Productions/The Ronald Grant Archive*)

17. Lucius Verus (*Alinari Archives-Anderson Archive, Florence*)

18. Parthian warrior (*The Art Archive/Archaeological Museum Teheran/Gianni Dagli Orti*)

19. *The Triumph of Marcus Aurelius* by Giandomenico Tiepolo (*Galleria Sabauda, Turin, Italy/The Bridgeman Art Library*)

20. Man being eaten by lions (*The Art Archive/Archaeological Museum El-Jem Tunisia/Gianni Dagli Orti*)

21. Persecution of Christians (*akg-images*)

22. Marcus Aurelius departing for war (*Alinari Archives-Anderson Archive, Florence*)

23. Marcus Aurelius receives defeated Barbarians (*akg-images/Nimatallah*)

24. Marcomannic prisoners before Marcus Aurelius (*akg-images/Erich Lessing*)

25. Romans in battle against the Barbarians (© *The Print Collector/Heritage-Images/Imagestate*)

26. 'Rain Miracle' (*akg-images/Museo della Civiltà, Rome*)

27. Transport of German prisoners and the spoils of war (*Alinari/The Bridgeman Art Library*)

28. The beheading of German nobles (*Piazza Colonna, Rome, Italy, Alinari/The Bridgeman Art Library*)

29. Marcus Aurelius enters Rome in his triumphal chariot (*akg-images/Erich Lessing*)

30. Commodus as Hercules (*Photo Scala, Florence*)

31. *The Death of Marcus Aurelius* by Eugene Delacroix (© *Photoservice Electa/Leemage*)

PREFACE

Most of my historical work has been archive-based, so it was both a change and a shock to operate in an historical field where the primary sources, apart from the classical authors, tended to be in the fields of archaeology, numismatics and epigraphy. Nevertheless, the change proved both refreshing and interesting. Since it is nearly fifty years since I went to Oxford as a classical scholar, it was a particular pleasure to renew acquaintance with many old friends (Tacitus, Cicero, Juvenal, Pliny the Younger, etc) and to read for the first time others who, from the standpoint of classical literature, had always been considered below the salt (Pliny the Elder, Aurelius Victor, Cassius Dio, Strabo, etc). At first bewildered and bemused by the plethora of learned journals devoted to ancient history – and the vast numbers of academics still engaged in this 'esoteric' pursuit – I soon learned that a thorough knowledge of German was almost more important than a command of Latin and Greek. Fortunately I had my daughter Julie, an expert in the German tongue, to guide me through some of the more taxing scholarly articles.

The literary sources for a life and times of Marcus Aurelius must always centre on the emperor's own *Meditations*, his correspondence with his tutor Fronto, the invaluable history of Rome by Cassius Dio and the controversial *Historia Augusta*, a series of biographies of Roman emperors by different ancient hands. I am aware of the massive scholarly debates still conducted about the authenticity of the *Historia Augusta* but can only report that, by the technique of 'compare and contrast' and what J.S. Mill would call 'the method of difference', I have found it reliable enough for the reign of Marcus Aurelius. The later sources, such as Eutropius, Aurelius Victor and Orosius, are best cited only as back-up to contemporary accounts. Much valuable, but often maddeningly incomplete, information comes from the work of Marcus's great contemporaries, such as Lucian, Apuleius, Tertullian, Justin Martyr and, above all, Galen. Scepticism is sometimes expressed as to whether one can write a biography of figures in the ancient world but I would rate Marcus as fourth in terms of such plausible candidates, behind Julius Caesar, Cicero and Julian the Apostate but well ahead of the Julio-Claudian emperors, Hannibal or Alexander the Great. If I convince the reader of the historical importance and enduring significance of this singular personality, I will not have written in vain. My especial thanks for helping me to write the book go to Julie (as mentioned), to my wife Pauline for listening to reams of Marcusiana, to Tony Whittome at Random House and to Will Sulkin at the Bodley Head, who remains an author's dream editor.

Frank McLynn, Farnham 2008

INTRODUCTION

Why should we be interested in a Roman emperor who lived 2,000 years ago? We can scarcely summon up any interest in the presidents, prime ministers and rulers of yesteryear unless they were political giants or monsters of evil. There can be many answers to this question, and not just in terms of the validity of studying history in general. Marcus Aurelius is the one figure of antiquity who still speaks to us today. We may thrill to the exploits of Alexander the Great, Hannibal or Caesar, and historical novelists may beguile us for a while with their reconstructions of Cicero or Julian (the only other figures from ancient history, apart from Caesar and Marcus Aurelius whose mental processes we know well), but the only voice from the Greco-Roman world that still seems to have contemporary relevance is that of the man who ruled the Roman empire from 161 to 180 A.D. The continuing sales of his book of reflections – the *Meditations* – alone prove that, but other evidence is not hard to find. We continue to use the tag 'Marcus Aurelius' for a ruler who is wise. A reviewer surveying a series of interviews with King Juan Carlos of Spain remarked that he was very far from being Marcus Aurelius; the radical right-wing U.S. commentator and politician Pat Buchanan famously remarked that George W. Bush was 'no Marcus Aurelius'. Meanwhile Bush's predecessor in the White House, Bill Clinton, claimed to have read and reread Marcus's book during his presidency. The nineteenth-century writer Samuel Butler claimed that no one is really dead if they are still widely remembered, and on this basis Marcus Aurelius is more alive than most people living. His survival as a major influence has puzzled and even embarrassed some people, who have attempted to deal with the phenomenon by facetiousness.[1]

Another exit avenue for those irritated or perplexed by Marcus's fame and immortality has been to claim that Marcus is of interest only to philosophers and contemplatives, and that the other famous Stoic, Epictetus, is the one who appeals to men of action. James Stockdale, an American fighter pilot shot down over Vietnam and then held by the Vietcong as a prisoner of war for seven and a half years, during which time he endured torture and four years' solitary confinement, later explained that it was the inspiration of Epictetus that enabled him to survive.[2] Epictetus was for a while taken up as the new hero, and the model for self-help books; he gained extra kudos for having been an influence on the black Haitian revolutionary of the nineteenth century, Toussaint L'Ouverture, who is increasingly coming to the fore as a patron saint of Third World revolutionary movements.[3] But the attempt to ghettoise Marcus Aurelius as a 'mere' influence on thought, but irrelevant to action, immediately breaks down when we contemplate the number of adventurers who have testified to the Stoic emperor's influence. We shall have much more to say about Marcus's impact down the ages later, but for now we will rest content with just two examples. Captain John Smith, he of Pocahontas fame, was deeply impressed by the example of a ruler who was both a thinker and a warrior, albeit a reluctant one. He carried with him on his adventures in Virginia just two books: the works of Machiavelli and the *Meditations* of Marcus Aurelius.[4] In some ways even more impressive is the example of Cecil Rhodes, multimillionaire, politician and would-be empire builder. As his biographer writes: 'He carried a well-thumbed, personally marked-up copy of this last book with him everywhere, favouring such aphorisms as 'Can any man thinks he lives for pleasure and not for action or execution?' 'Go to the ant, thou sluggard, consider her ways and be wise.' There were exactly one hundred and one passages in his copy of the book heavily underlined by Rhodes, with four propositions especially prominent. These were: Death is an aspect of life, so live the latter as if the former is imminent; the intellect should always prevail over the emotions; do what is serious, not frivolous, do what is right, not popular, do what you do for others first and yourself second; be self-reliant but also tolerant, flexible and prepared to change your views.[5]

Marcus Aurelius's widespread popularity today can be seen at a number of levels, some apparently trivial, others deadly serious. He is the only Roman emperor the movies have taken seriously and also the best represented on the screen. Roman emperors usually function as 'footnotes' in films set in imperial Rome (one thinks of Ivan Triesault as Nero in *Barabbas* or George Relph as Tiberius in *Ben-Hur*) or are presented in melodramatic turns, as with Jay Robinson as Caligula in *The Robe* or Peter Ustinov's famous comico-tyrannic turn as Nero in *Quo Vadis*. Yet in *Gladiator* and *The Fall of the Roman Empire*, (played respectively by Richard Harris and Alec Guinness), Marcus Aurelius appears as a serious figure in all senses. But it is not just through celluloid presentations that Marcus has lived on. I would like to suggest that his current eminence has five main sources. In the first place, he satisfies the thirst for philosophical guidance which ancient philosophers thought they had a duty to perform but which their modern counterparts have largely abandoned. With the exception of a handful of lone wolves like Karl Jaspers, Jean-Paul Sartre and George Santayana, modern philosophy has retreated from the hurly-burly of everyday life to concern itself with technical issues of ever more esoteric import. In Europe the taste was for logical positivism and phenomenol-ogy, in the United States for symbolic logic, pragmatism or abstruse philosophy of science, while Britain retreated into the inane and scholastic cul-de-sac of linguistic philosophy. Faced with this abdication of respon-sibility from professional philosophers, the man and woman in the street turned either to Oriental mysticism or to the ancients. Academic special-ists and desiccated pedants sneer that ordinary people use the *Meditations* as 'a bran-tub of aphorisms for all seasons' and object that wisdom should not be obtained from tea-chest mottoes and that no philosophy worthy of the name should be of the cracker-barrel variety. Yet those who can find no consolation in organised religion are deeply attracted to Marcus's oracular utterances, of which dozens have attained popularity.

It is worth reminding ourselves of some of them. 'The universe is change; or life is what our thoughts make it.' 'Nothing happens to anyone that he is not fitted by Nature to bear.' 'Do not despise death, for even death is one of the things that Nature wills.' 'By a tranquil mind I mean a well-ordered one.' 'It is the act of a madman to pursue impossibilities.' 'How much more grievous are the consequences of anger than the cause of it.' 'How ridiculous and unrealistic is the man who is astonished at anything that happens in life.' 'Loss is nothing else but change, and change is Nature's delight.' 'Life is warfare, and the sojourn of a stranger, and after fame comes oblivion.' 'To the wise, life is a problem; to the fool a solution.' 'If you are distressed by anything, the pain is not due to the thing itself but to your own estimate of it; and this you have power to revoke at any moment.' 'Remember that there is a proper dignity and proportion to be observed in the performance of every act in life.' 'The object in life is not to be on the side of the majority but to escape finding oneself in the ranks of the insane.' 'You will get relief from vain fancies if you perform every act in life as though it were your last.' 'What is beautiful has the source of beauty in itself; praise forms no part of it. So it is none the worse or the better for being praised.' 'The happiness of your life depends on the quality of your thoughts. Therefore guard accordingly and take care you entertain no notions unsuitable to virtue and reason.' 'Never esteem anything as an advantage to yourself that will make you break your word or lose your self-respect.' 'How much time he saves who does not look to see what his neighbour says or does or thinks.' 'Get into yourself; there is a source of strength that will always spring up if you look there.' 'Waste no more time talking about great souls and how they should be. Become one yourself.' 'Never let the future disturb you. You will meet it, if you have to, with the same weapons of reason which today arm you against the present.'[6]

A second reason for Marcus's continuing prominence could be that his embrace of Stoicism when a ruler chimes with a similar embrace by Americans of the philosophy of pragmatism, the ideas of judging truth by its consequences. Just as Stoicism was the Roman philosophy *par excellence*, could anything be more American than a creed one of whose leading practitioners (William James) could speak of the 'cash value' of an idea? There is also a ternary motif at work, and we shall see that triads were an obsession of Marcus. The three chief Stoics of the Roman era, Seneca, Epictetus and Marcus Aurelius, find an echo in the three American pragmatists: C.S. Pierce, William James and John Dewey. Students of philosophy, incidentally, will be able to link Dewey's quasi-Hegelian holism with similar ideas in Marcus's thought. Pragmatism is one of the hidden factors behind the dominance of the law and lawyers in U.S. society, because of the tendency to dissolve all philosophical and ethical issues into legal ones, or the indeterminate into the determinate. If there is a conflict between two equal and opposite values, as there often is in liberal and 'open' societies, the Supreme Court will solve the dilemma for you. Naturally, this will always be done in a rough-and-ready *ad hoc* manner, since the Supreme Court is composed of individuals, each with his her own political principles, prejudices and predilections; the idea of a supra-human Chief Justice, totally 'objective', may be a necessary political and social myth but it is an illusion for all that. The beauty of pragmatism is that it enables one to make judgements based on supposed consequences, which always lie in the future and are thus immediately unverifiable. In its own way, then, pragmatism in the U.S.A. functions as an ideological 'support' for the social and political system, just as Stoicism did in Roman society. Stoicism was a primitive form of pragmatism, in that one knew in advance that the value of duty would always overrule that of pleasure, and strenuous virtue that of lazy idolence or apathy. It is tempting to push the analogy farther than it will really go, by arguing that Stoicism and pragmatism are both 'imperial' ideologies, both suited to world powers at the moment of their greatest dominance. It is even more tempting to link the similarities between the Roman and American work with the well-known enthusiasm of Bill Clinton for Marcus Aurelius, though this has triggered a host of 'backlash' commentators, led by the Catholic right-wing commentator Gary Wills, sceptical that Clinton could ever have derived anything of value from Stoicism. As one critic wrote: 'If Bill Clinton ever read from the man who praised virtuous behaviour over political outcomes, he cannot have been concentrating too hard. Marcus Aurelius preached the irrationality of sexual passion. Bill Clinton practised it.'[7]

A third reason for Marcus's favourable reception in the modern world is his feeling for Nature, which at times comes close to Wordsworth's position in the *Prelude* and the ode *Intimations of Immortality* – a deep appreciation of sensuousness tinged with melancholy. Here is Marcus's paean to the beauties of Nature: 'The way loaves of bread split open on top in the oven, with the ridges just by-products of the baking but nonetheless mysteriously pleasing, arousing our appetites without our knowing why. The way ripe figs begin to burst or when olives are on the point of falling, when the shadow of decay gives them a special beauty. Or when stalks of wheat bend under their own weight. Or the furrowed brow of a lion, or the flecks of foam on a boar's mouth . . . If you look at things in isolation there's nothing particularly beautiful about them, yet by adding to Nature they enrich us and draw us in. And anyone with a feeling for Nature – anyone with deep sensitivity – will find it all gives pleasure, even when it is inadvertent. You will find the jaws of animals as beautiful as painted ones or sculptures . . . And other things like that will call out to the observer constantly, things unnoticed by others, but things available to those who are at home with Nature and its works.'[8] The sentiments, albeit expressed in a kind of oracular prose and lacking metrical poetry, are not very dissimilar from those of Wordsworth, especially when we place them in their proper context of overall melancholia.[9] As Matthew Arnold, himself a fine poet, pointed out, Marcus's appreciation of Nature has 'a delicate penetration, a sympathetic tenderness, worthy of Wordsworth.'[10]

Perhaps linked with this is a fourth main reason for Marcus's favourable reception in the modern world. The decline of organised religion in the

West has led to a massive upsurge of interest in New Age ideas and the thought and philosophy of the Orient, with which Marcus's *Meditations* have an obvious affinity. The classic doctrines of Hinduism in the *Upanishads* (dating from the 6th century B.C.) similarly stress the inferiority of pleasure to 'the good', the illusion of selfishness, the desirability of self-knowledge and the holistic interpenetration of all things in the universe, in short, pantheism. The texts share Marcus's contempt for the body and stress that he who finds spirit becomes spirit and becomes, in a sense, everything. 'I am this world and I eat this world. Who knows this, truly has knowledge.' And: 'Death said, "The good is one thing, the pleasant another; these two, having different objects, chain a man. It is well with him who clings to the good; he who chooses the pleasant misses his end."' [11] Buddha, in the following century, while retaining most of this, broke away from Hinduism through his 'heresy' of Karma and Nirvana and proposed an eightfold way to wisdom. This consists of the following: Right View, or understanding the origins of suffering; Right Resolve, or choosing to avoid self-indulgence; Right Speech, or refraining from gossip; Right Action, not murdering or (which in Buddha's view was the same thing) soldiering; Right Livelihood, or not making money in socially harmful ways; Right Effort, avoiding unwholesome thoughts; Right Mindfulness, or achieving control of mental states; and Right Concentration, the attainment of inner serenity.[12] The third great source of Eastern philosophy, apart from the *Upanishads* and Buddha's 'bible' the *Dhammapada*, is the *Bhagavad-Gita* or 'Song of God', itself part of the Hindu epic (analogous to the *Iliad*), the *Mahabharata*.[13] Probably composed in the second century B.C., this offers a head-on challenge to Buddha's doctrines, stressing the immortality of the soul, a personal God and the fallacy of pacifism. Again, there are many pre-echoes of Marcus, as in the following: 'For that which is born, death is certain, and for the dead, birth is certain. Therefore grieve not over that which is unavoidable.'[14] It is easy to understand why Marcus has sometimes been called 'the Roman Buddha.' Not until Schopenhauer and C.G. Jung were there personalities in Western thought who were so much in sympathy with the wisdom of the East.[15]

The Wordsworthian feeling for Nature and the affinities with Oriental thought come together in the final Aurelian theme, explaining Marcus's perennial popularity: his role as an apostle of solitude. This notion alone links him strongly with doyens of the Romantic movement, most notably Rousseau, Byron and Wordsworth.[16] The Elizabethan thinker Francis Bacon stated that: 'Whosoever is delighted in solitude is either a wild beast, or a god.'[17] Marcus was in no doubt that the solitude he sometimes felt even in palaces engendered godlike thoughts, and the perception that to be alone can trigger the numinous insight and the mystical inspiration is widespread in literature. It is more than just curious that the great solitaries of history have always entertained thoughts not unlike those in the *Meditations*, and that such feelings can be precipitated even by artificial solitude.[18] What all this shows is that, despite his huge influence, Marcus is a hard act to follow. His actual lesson was that one has a duty to involve oneself in everyday life while seeing it for what it is and holding it at bay with mental reservations; this is not the same thing at all as reclusive withdrawal or the life of the artificial solitary. Marcus will probably never be hugely popular with committed Christians, if only because he persecuted them. But for others he holds out the prospect of spirituality for atheists, happiness without God, joy without heaven and morality without religion. As we shall have occasion to say over and over again, he truly was a man for all seasons, and those seasons include the twenty-first century. Marcus's career was beset with ironies and contradictions. There was the conflict between what reason and Stoic doctrine told him the world should be like (which necessarily entailed Panglossian optimism) and how he instinctively perceived it (which engendered pessimism). There was the obvious contradiction between his philosophical stance on the unreality of evil and his jaundiced comments on the world which showed that he thought it only too real. And there was that between his contempt for the external world and the duty he owed it as a Roman emperor, between his desire to be a philosopher/hermit and his destiny as a warrior. Yet perhaps the greatest irony is that Marcus despised fame and the opinion of posterity – he often speaks of the absurdity of posthumous fame – but has survived as an influence, an example and an inspiration for two millennia.

The Roman Empire
Lifetime of Marcu...

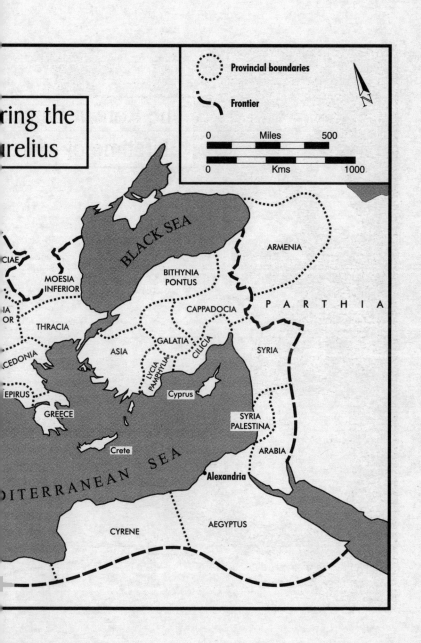

ring the
urelius

Provincial boundaries

Frontier

| 0 | Miles | 500 |
| 0 | Kms | 1000 |

N

BLACK SEA

ARMENIA

...CIAE

MOESIA
INFERIOR

BITHYNIA
PONTUS

...IA
...OR

P A R T H I A

THRACIA

CAPPADOCIA

...CEDONIA

ASIA

GALATIA

CILICIA

SYRIA

LYCIA
PAMPHYLIA

EPIRUS

GREECE

Cyprus

SYRIA
PALESTINA

Crete

ARABIA

...DITERRANEAN   SEA

Alexandria

...OITERRANEAN

CYRENE

AEGYPTUS

I

Just as we refer to, say, John F. Kennedy as the thirty-fifth president
of the United States, so we may call Marcus Aurelius the sixteenth
ruler of the Roman empire (that is, if we include the three short-lived
incumbents of the 'year of the four emperors' in AD 68–9).[1]
Conventionally the emperors from AD 14 to 69 are called the Julio-
Claudian dynasty, Vespasian and his sons Titus and Domitian are the
Flavians, the childless Trajan and Hadrian are usually termed the
Spanish emperors, and then Antoninus Pius initiated the era of
the Antonines, which ended with Marcus Aurelius's son Commodus.
The story of Marcus Aurelius ideally requires a knowledge of all the
emperors who preceded him, but the biographer would then be
involved in an endless quasi-Hegelian task, since an understanding of
Augustus in turn requires an understanding of Julius Caesar, and he
can be understood only in terms of the class war under the Roman
republic stretching back at least as far as the Gracchus brothers in the
second century BC. The obvious temptation is to start Marcus Aurelius's
life at his birth in 121 without any preamble, but such an approach
would be severely one-dimensional. Self-contained biographies are fine
in eras we know well, but to understand a Roman emperor, of all
people, we need to know something of the wider world in which
he operated, his historical context and milieu, as well as the scope
and limitations of his power.

When Marcus Aurelius was born, Rome was approaching the 900th
anniversary of its founding (traditionally in 753 BC). For centuries this

undistinguished town on the Tiber had warred with its Etruscan neighbours, principally the city of Veii. Some time in the sixth century BC
the Romans threw out the last of their kings and declared themselves
a republic, ruled by a body of oligarchs known as the Senate. Rome
became an expansionist military power from the late fourth century
(around the time Alexander the Great was completing his conquests
in the East). The Romans' first target was the powerful Samnite confed-
eracy of central Italy, but the Samnites proved almost a match for
them and succumbed only in the decade of the 290s. Next Rome came
into collision with the Greek colonies of southern Italy, which famously
called in one of Alexander the Great's descendants, Pyrrhus of Epirus,
to help them, but in vain. Rome went on to vanquish Syracuse, the
great power in Italy, and then became involved in a titanic struggle
for mastery in the western Mediterranean with the North African
state of Carthage (in modern Tunisia). The so-called Punic Wars,
lasting sixty years, were the result. Rome nearly went under to the
brilliant generalship of the Carthaginian general Hannibal, but its
superior resources eventually ground the Carthaginians down at the
beginning of the second century BC. From the western Mediterranean,
Rome expanded east, sweeping into its maw Greece, North Africa,
Spain, France, Egypt and the whole of the modern Middle East. Britain,
vanquished in AD 43, was the last significant conquest. But by the first
century BC victorious Rome had become the victim of endemic civil
strife, internal rebellions by its Italian allies, slave revolts and a vicious
class war within the city itself, which threatened to destabilise the
entire Roman state. In these circumstances salvation was sought in
the 'man on horseback'. Julius Caesar, conqueror of Gaul and victor
in a bloody civil war, became a one-man ruler. Suspected of wishing
to make himself king, he was assassinated by a senatorial conspiracy
on the Ides of March in 44 BC. But the Senate had merely gained a
breathing space. Caesar's nephew Octavian took a mere dozen years
to make himself ruler of the Roman world, and in 27 BC proclaimed
himself a new kind of autocrat, an emperor.

The Roman emperors ruled a vast stretch of territory, from Scotland
to the Sahara Desert and from the Atlantic to the River Euphrates in
present-day Iraq; the total land area has been estimated as 3.5 million
square miles in the reign of the emperor Trajan, or about half the
size of the United States. The northern border in Europe followed

the course of the Rhine and Danube rivers all the way to the Black
Sea. Outside the empire were Scotland, Ireland, the Baltic countries,
Germany, Poland and the former Czechoslovakia. Inside the magic
cordon of empire were the present-day England, France, Spain,
Portugal, Greece, the former Yugoslavia, Romania, Turkey, Israel,
Lebanon, Syria, Egypt and the northerly parts of what are today the
nation-states of Morocco, Tunisia, Algeria and Libya. Today's Switzerland,
Austria and Hungary lay on either side of disputed territory, a kind
of no-man's-land between the Roman empire and the ferocious
German tribes to the north. Most importantly for transport and
communication, the entire coastline of the Mediterranean lay within
the Roman empire; truly it was, as the Romans said, *mare nostrum*
(our sea). Since demography is an esoteric science, where inexact or
incomplete data have to be 'guesstimated', using sometimes controversial models, it is not surprising to find that the exact population
of the Roman empire has always been a subject of intense academic
debate. But the most likely estimate for the reign of Marcus Aurelius
is somewhere between seventy and eighty million.[2] There is little justification for histories that insinuate a 'quantum jump' in population
between the reigns of Augustus and Marcus Aurelius, for over these
150 years the population grew at a fairly constant rate of about 0.15 per
cent a year. It can at least be stated with confidence that the Roman
empire contained the highest level of population in the Mediterranean
until the sixteenth century. By the time of Marcus's accession the
empire embraced about one-fifth of the entire population of the then
world, acting as a kind of mirror image to the Han empire in distant
China, where a census of AD 156 registered nearly sixty million people.[3]

At least one million of the Roman empire's population lived in
Rome itself. There is a fairly general consensus that Rome's population was 750,000 in AD 14 and rose to one million by the year 100,
although some observers would put the figure as high as 1,250,000 by
the reign of Antoninus Pius; as always, the demography of the ancient
world is an inexact science, and full certainty is precluded by our
ignorance of such key variables as the extent of the slave population,
the size of households, the average number of people residing in each
house, what extrapolations we should make from the free corn issue
(the *annona*), and so on.[4] The slave population of the empire is estimated at somewhere between seven and ten million, though it is thought

that about half the population of the city of Rome – or at least 500,000
– were slaves; in general, the proportion of slaves to free-born was
always much higher in Italy than in Egypt or North Africa. The population of Italy itself has been estimated at anywhere between seven
and fourteen million, though the smaller figure is the more probable.
The Italian peninsula contained between 430 and 450 cities, depending
on the exact definition of 'city', and this urban population accounted
for about one-third of Italy's people.[5] In the empire as a whole the
total urban population has been estimated at anywhere between six
and nineteen million, with the most likely scenario being that cities
accounted for about 20 per cent of the population, or fifteen million
if we assume that the total figure of 70–80 million is correct. Outside
Rome, the largest city in the empire was Alexandria, with more than
300,000 inhabitants, closely followed by Carthage with almost the same
number and Antioch close up in third place. Ephesus and Pergamum
may each have contained 180,000 inhabitants.[6] Yet in general, apart
from North Africa, which was more densely populated in antiquity
than it is today, the Roman empire was sparsely peopled by modern
standards. All large pre-industrial urban populations were incapable
of reproducing themselves and required constant immigration from
the more thinly peopled but more healthy rural areas.

The Roman economy was underdeveloped. The mass of the people
lived in poverty, technology was backward, agricultural labour was
predominant and land was *the* source of wealth and power; the
associated ethos, ideology and values of a landed aristocracy were
therefore paramount. Since the Mediterranean area is not suited for
pastoralism in the way that areas of vast rich plains are (only sheep
and goats can deal with the summer water shortage), agriculture was
the single most important item in the Roman economy.[7] Vines, olives
and cereals – the so-called 'Mediterranean triad' – were by far the
most important product, and Cato the Elder, the most famous agron-
omist of the Roman republic, went to great lengths to show that they
were also the most profitable. Dry legumes – broad beans, peas, chick-
peas and lentils – came a poor fourth, while poultry farming and the
rearing of pigs and sheep were worthwhile only if the farmer lived
near a large town.[8] Mining of gold, silver, lead and other minerals was
also important, but perhaps the most dynamic feature of Roman
economics was long-distance trade and commerce. Very similar in

its structure and limitations to the trade of early modern Europe
c. 1400–1750, Rome's riverine and seaborne commerce linked the
Mediterranean with the Black and Red Seas and with the Indian Ocean.
The importance of the Rivers Nile, Rhône, Rhine, Tiber, Ebro and
Guadalquivir, to say nothing of lesser Italian streams like the Anio,
Nera, Topino and Chiani, can hardly be overstated.[9] Although the
Mediterranean was considered supremely dangerous in winter
(November–February), and the cautious avoided it also in March–April
and September–October, greed made people willing to risk storm and
shipwreck even in the depths of winter. To some extent the risk was
a calculated one, since Roman trading ships were large and comparable
to European vessels in the period 1550–1750, and the dangers of the
Mediterranean were moderate and even picayune compared with
those faced by the captains of ocean-going freighters on the Atlantic
and Pacific in the Age of Discovery. But the greatest overall consideration was cost, and profit. It has been calculated that the ratio of
land, river and maritime costs in the Roman empire was an
astonishing 55:6:1.[10]

Rome was not entirely non-industrial, since there were brick, marble,
pottery, glass and textile industries (the last-named estimated on its
own to have employed 4 per cent of the population), not to mention
primitive lumber mills. Banks, such as they were, were local and there
were no empire-wide credit-granting facilities. Because of the aristocratic prejudice against trade, much commerce was ostensibly in the
hands of slaves and former slaves (freedmen), though it is usually
considered that this was largely a front behind which the Roman upper
classes conducted profitable enterprises.[11] The most sober view is that
the Roman empire resembled a Third World economy today.
Technology was primitive, largely because of the institution of slavery,
and agriculture predominated, absorbing the labour of three-quarters
of the population. Meanwhile the contribution of commerce and
industry to the overall wealth of the economy amounted to no more
than 5 per cent. The Gross National Product was low for such a vast
empire: it has been estimated at 17 billion sesterces by the end of
Augustus's reign, or the equivalent of 1,400 tonnes of gold.[12]
Productivity was poor: having risen in the era of the Punic Wars in
the third century BC, it peaked under the Julio-Claudian emperors and
began to decline around the time of Marcus Aurelius's principate.

The growth rate of the economy was only about 0.1 per cent a year. Nevertheless, the view that the Roman empire was a primitive economy has recently been challenged by a group of economists seeking to show that it was really a proto-capitalist enterprise. It is true that the 'pro-marketeers' can identify many distinct market exchanges that seem unlike the features of a slave or command economy. Roman economic transactions are indeed unique, resembling neither the trade of a modern or even an early modern economy, nor the simple exchange system of a primitive society. The empire had a large market for food, textiles and metals and the social and institutional mechanisms to sustain such a system. The question remains: how many market exchanges does it take to make a genuine market economy? And the Roman economy cannot have been truly commercial because most people were engaged in agriculture, lived at subsistence level and had no surplus for consumer goods; in a word, the economy was bedevilled by a low level of *effective demand*.[13] Fortunately, perhaps, the exact nature of the Roman economy is not an issue that need detain any longer a biographer of Marcus Aurelius.

The Roman empire was above all an empire of conquest, and this simple fact had profound consequences for society at every level. The main sources of income for the empire were tribute paid by the conquered, indirect taxes on the sale of slaves, customs duties, and revenue from estates, mines and other properties. The level of Roman taxation was always relatively low, partly because taxation was levied mainly to recover the costs of war and defence and partly because the taxpayers were the defeated. From 167 BC until the fourth century AD the citizen inhabitants of Italy paid no land tax.[14] The system was inherently unfair, as taxpayers in the provinces received peace and security as their only return from their taxes, whereas Italians got a proper system of law and order, justice and good roads (to say nothing of the special privileges enjoyed by the citizens of Rome, to be discussed later). Since Rome was an empire of conquest, it is not surprising to find the tax yields rising astronomically during the classic era of conquest under the republic. In 250 BC Roman tax revenues were between four and eight million sesterces a year, but by 150 BC this figure was 50–60 million, by 50 BC 340 million and by AD 50 at the end of Claudius's reign 800 million.[15] Tax revenues rose one hundredfold in 300 years, but then remained at roughly the same level until the third century AD. Low as a proportion of Gross National Product (perhaps 5 per cent), per capita taxation has been estimated at thirteen sesterces per head of population, or 11 per cent of minimum subsistence. To put this in a historical context, the tax load was more than the French and English governments raised in the sixteenth and seventeenth centuries, but much less than they levied in the eighteenth.[16]

The truly distinctive thing about the Roman economy was that it rested on slavery, which is seen by many historians as the principal barrier to technological breakthrough: in short, the Romans did not innovate technically because they could derive an economic surplus from slaves. Depending on the figures we adduce for the overall population and slaves, maybe one in six of the inhabitants of the Roman empire was a slave. They were particularly numerous in Italy, where the ratio of slave to free may have been as high as 1:3; and in certain cities scattered throughout the empire, such as Pergamum, where every third person was a slave.[17] Although very few advanced societies in history have depended on slavery as an economic base (obvious examples being nineteenth-century Brazil and the American South before 1861), Roman slavery had little in common with these other models and in some ways is best understood by the tribal slavery of Africa as discovered by the Victorian explorers; both systems were bewilderingly complex. To simplify, one might say that Roman slaves were of three main kinds: those in urban households, those who worked in the fields in the country, and the chained slaves employed on great estates (*latifundiae*) and in the mines.[18] The lot of domestic slaves, as might be expected, was more privileged and pampered than that of their unfortunate counterparts involved in heavy manual labour, and this was not just because of the lighter duties. The more slaves a wealthy Roman possessed, the greater his prestige; some had 400 or more in their household.[19] There were thus more slaves than jobs for them to do, and to compensate a ludicrous division of labour arose, whereby one slave would buy groceries, another would cook, another put on his master's shoes, another dress him, another massage him, and another follow him around to attend to his every need. The Stoic philosopher Epictetus, *the* great intellectual influence on Marcus Aurelius, pointed out the absurdity of all this – and he knew, because he had been a slave himself.[20]

In Rome slaves could be found in a bewildering variety of occupa-
tions: as street cleaners, builders of baths and temples, factory workers,
navvies on roads and aqueducts; as shop workers, cooks, barbers, hair-
dressers, nurses, tutors, secretaries, butlers, laundry women, house
cleaners, seamstresses and schoolteachers.[21] Roman patricians were often
in a kind of competition with their wealthy neighbours to see if they
could buy better-looking or more accomplished slaves, and the over-
supply of labour thus generated meant that male slaves were often
found doing household chores that females could easily do.[22] It will
be clear, then, how different Roman slavery was from that of the ante-
bellum American South, quite apart from the consideration that
American slaves were always black and those in the Roman empire
could be any colour. Roman slaves were often talented, clever and
educated, occupying positions of responsibility and with a real prospect
of freedom. Some slaves in large households had de facto control of
great wealth, supervised other workers (both free and slave) and (and
here the similarity to African tribal slavery is most marked) were themselves served by other slaves.[23] Yet despite their managerial powers and
often sumptuous lifestyle, they owned nothing legally and were subject
to the arbitrary whim of their masters. There were severe penalties
for running away, including branding on the forehead. Intense hostility
of owners to slaves, and vice versa, lay only just under the surface
and is a pervasive motif in instructive literature like the life of Aesop.[24]

Under the Roman republic, slaves were acquired largely by war and
piracy. The slave population thus consisted of conquered and defeated
people, the children of slaves and the products of the slave trade. In
addition there were abandoned children, and in some provinces destitute peasants sold their offspring into slavery; there were even some
races, like the Phrygians, who did not consider slavery dishonourable.[25]
But with the coming of the famous Roman peace (*pax Romana*) the
question arose: how were the Romans to acquire fresh slaves? Here
we encounter one of the perennial problems of ancient Rome: that
an empire based on conquest has a built-in momentum that cannot
be arrested without system failure. One answer might be that the slave
population could constantly reproduce itself, but this did not happen.
Certainly slaves were encouraged to propagate and even procreate
within the sacred confines of marriage,[26] but, as in imperial Brazil in
the nineteenth century, the slave population failed to keep up its

numbers. Many of the reasons are obvious. Three-quarters even of the household slaves were male. Only household slaves (*vilici*) were allowed female partners; those employed in agriculture, mining, dock work, porterage, transport, and so on, were not. On the other hand, many female slaves were set free (manumitted) so as to be marriageable and bear free children; emancipation of these nubile slaves removed the very individuals who were essential for the maintenance of numbers. Moreover, all the evidence is that female slaves were not particularly prolific. Finally, even free people found it hard to keep up their population levels, given the menace from war, famine, plague and poor diet, medicine and obstetrics. The average life expectancy of Romans at birth is a much-disputed subject, but even if we allow an optimistic figure of twenty-five to thirty years, the corresponding figure for slaves was at most twenty.[27]

By the time Marcus Aurelius became emperor, more than half a million new slaves were required annually. Where were they to come from in an era of *pax Romana*? The occasional large-scale provincial revolt and intermittent new war of conquest provided part of the answer. The historian Josephus estimated that one result of the great Jewish revolt of AD 66–70 was 97,000 Jewish slaves.[28] Trajan's conquest of Dacia (modern Romania) in the early second century injected many tens of thousands more, and the great Jewish revolt of Bar-Kochba in Hadrian's reign (see pp. 33–35) was said to have produced another 100,000. Roman forays into Scotland and other outposts of Britain put more slaves on the market. But there were other supplies to satisfy the constant demand. Slaves could be obtained from outside the Roman empire, from Germany or Parthia, most obviously.[29] The sale of children by parents and kidnapping was one avenue.[30] The use of criminals in the mines released other slaves, while possibly the most important source of all was the enslavement of foundlings or abandoned children – a custom not abandoned until AD 374. Child exposure and infanticide were common in the Roman empire, and females, particularly, were abandoned at birth by poor parents.[31] In this hideous way supply and demand in slavery remained at equilibrium. The consequence was that there was no serious drop in the number of slaves until the reign of Marcus Aurelius. It was his misfortune, as we shall see, to confront a general manpower shortage caused largely by plague.

Society in the Roman empire was one of the most rigidly stratified there has ever been, with grotesque levels of inequality. At the top of the steep social pyramid was the senatorial class, its membership determined solely by wealth and limited in number to 600. To be a senator it was a necessary condition to be worth at least one million sesterces.[32] The next class down was the equestrian, and again membership was determined by wealth, with the minimum figure this time being 400,000 sesterces; there were perhaps 2,000 knights or equestrians in Rome and some 30,000 empire-wide. Below them again would be members of the bourgeoisie, mainly landowners; their role was measured financially by possession of 200,000 sesterces and socially by the status of juryman, to which such wealth entitled them. At 100,000 sesterces one qualified to be a town councillor: in short, property qualifications determined one's entry into every single social sphere. Below the bourgeoisie in the pyramid would come the shop-owners, retail traders, money-changers, artisans, doctors, teachers and other members of the liberal professions, the salaried classes, minor municipal officers and that vast range of people connoted by the term petty bourgeoisie. Finally there was the proletariat of free wage earners and below them the slaves. This was a society where heredity was all-important; without the advantages of birth, and in the absence of a business culture, it was impossible to rise through the social ranks through mere money-earning. Moreover, meritocracy was almost totally absent.[33] There was no administrative class of civil servants providing a meritocratic route, as in modern societies, and the dominant ideology was hostile to all such notions: the landed aristocracy who monopolised all the top government positions thought it natural and proper that these should be filled by men of birth. The only real avenue for social mobility was that of the freedman, for the manumitted slave could rise higher in Rome than in any other slave society. It takes an effort of imagination to conceive of a society where vast wealth was concentrated in so few hands; perhaps the nearest modern equivalent would be Saudi Arabia.[34]

It is worth emphasising that the senatorial class in the Roman empire (to which Marcus Aurelius belonged) literally lived like kings. Private wealth was not subject to progressive taxation and the rates of tax were not heavy. Private property in Italy was exempt from taxation until the end of the third century AD, death duties remained at 5 per cent until the early third century, and in the provinces the basic rates of tribute were only 5–10 per cent. There were few restraints on the accumulation of wealth in the case of those who already had capital, and the large aristocratic fortunes were furthermore the result of surpluses maintained over the generations and concentrated in fewer and fewer hands because of a declining elite birthrate,[35] not to mention slavery itself – slaves retained only that portion of what they produced that would keep them alive. The wealthy lived a charmed life, for economic policy was framed around them. Public taxes were set so low precisely so that the private incomes of the rich (mainly rent from estates) could be higher. The route to wealth was invariably investment in land and agriculture, which was a cornucopia, since the vast population of Rome created a huge demand for products such as wheat, olive oil, wine, meat and cloth.[36] Three main types of landowner can be identified: local gentry with land in their region of origin; middle-ranking senators and equestrians of municipal background with properties additional to their local estates; and the elite, with a complex of properties in Italy and abroad. In the second century AD they were usually required to own one-third (later reduced to one-quarter) of their estates in Italy.[37]

The incomes of the landed aristocracy probably doubled or trebled in the first century AD and rose sixfold in the years 100–400. Meanwhile the plight of the mass of the people was desperate.[38] Since the state quite literally fulfilled the Marxist definition of an institution for the benefit of the ruling classes, the only possible route upwards for an ambitious free man was a career in the army, since the aristocracy had perforce to share the benefits of empire with its military protectors. The generally low level of income made a legionary's life look attractive since, after the emperor Domitian's 33 per cent pay rise, the common soldier received 1,200 sesterces a year, plus a big retirement bonus and occasional *ex gratia* payments or donatives; retired veterans were usually prosperous members of their local community. Yet of the thousands of hopefuls recruited into the army each year, only a handful was ever heard from again, not surprisingly, since mathematical probability was against them. Only one or two of the thousands of retiring veterans each year made it to the coveted rank of procurator.[39] And even within the army the Roman mania for glaring inequality manifested itself. A cavalryman had a salary twenty times greater than an infantryman.

Pay scales varied by a factor of sixty-seven, with elite troops (*primi pili*) receiving 90,000 sesterces a year.[40]

How wealthy were the members of the senatorial elite? Pliny the Younger, living at the beginning of the second century AD, had a fortune of twenty million sesterces – twenty times the wealth needed to be a senator – but regarded himself as only moderately rich. In his time the wealthiest man was estimated to have a fortune ten times greater than Pliny's, with an income equivalent to that of 25,000 subsistence farmers. In the last days of the republic, Cicero reckoned that a rich Roman needed an annual income of 100,000–600,000 sesterces – an era when the wealth of the richest, such as Marcus Crassus, was legendary.[41] A middling senator, defined as one who had the capital necessary for maximisation of his estates, had by Marcus Aurelius's era an income of between six and nine million sesterces a year. The largest ever fortunes were seen in the first century AD, when a handful of men had wealth estimated at 400 million sesterces each – the equivalent of between 750,000 and 1,500,000 tonnes of wheat. The emperor Nero confiscated the fortunes of six men who between them owned all Tunisia. By contrast, the largest private fortunes in Tudor and Stuart England *c.* 1550–1650 were worth roughly 21,000–42,000 tonnes of wheat. With a population at least twenty times as great, the biggest fortunes in the Roman empire exceeded those of Tudor and Stuart England by a factor of 18–72.[42]

Roman aristocrats believed in conspicuous consumption and flaunting their wealth; the notion of the rich miser would have been incomprehensible to them. A freedman named C. Caecilius Isidorus left, at his death in 8 BC, 3,600 pairs of oxen, 257,000 other stock, 4,116 slaves and sixty million sesterces in cash.[43] One of Augustus's admirals lost 100 million sesterces through risky investment in viticulture.[44] By the time of Marcus Aurelius the great fortunes were declining in sheer size. Apuleius, author of *The Golden Ass*, writing in 158–9 (just before Marcus's accession), recorded that his father's fortune was two million sesterces, but that, on his own marriage to Pudentilla of Oea, he had added another four million to the family portfolio.[45] He also wrote that Pudentilla had 600 slaves – which seems slightly above average in the light of a persuasive hypothesis that the normal ratio of slaves to wealth was 400 slaves to three million sesterces of wealth.[46] Slaves were an important item in the wealth ledger. Although for legal

purposes they were often assumed to have a value of 2,000 ses[blank]
one would normally expect to pay in the hundreds rather[blank]
thousands of sesterces.[47] Figures of 100,000 and more, which are
sometimes mentioned in ancient literature, would be considered
extravagant, but the highest known price paid for a slave was an
astonishing 700,000 sesterces.[48]

Aristocrats liked to compete in the wealth stakes and agonise about
the proper definition of the truly rich man: was it, as was often said,
the man who could afford to keep an entire legion of 6,000 men on
his yearly income; or was it, as Seneca thought, one who farmed land
in every single province of the empire (Seneca himself was worth
300 million sesterces)?[49] By the time of Marcus Aurelius, the largest
private fortune was less than 288 million sesterces, as compared with
the 400 million of men like Cornelius Lentulus (d. AD 25) and others
in the first century. A moderate fortune in Marcus's time was around
twenty million sesterces.[50] But the figures were still staggeringly high,
given that average wages were just four sesterces a day. Naturally the
issue of wages was determined by the brute facts of a slave economy,
where the cost of free labour was inevitably driven down to the point
of bare subsistence and reproduction, where it would be no more
expensive than hiring a slave. In Cicero's time a moderately wealthy
man had an income 714 times that of a pauper – Cicero, with his
annual earnings from legal work of about 555,555 sesterces, was in this
former class – while the very rich had an income 10,476 times greater.
Yet in the early empire the super-rich were 17,142 times wealthier. To
put this in proportion, the ratio for rich and poor in Victorian England
– where the gulf between the two was considered obscenely wide –
was 'only' 1:6,000: a gap just one-third the size of that in the Roman
empire.[51]

Such was the world into which the future emperor Marcus Aurelius
was born on 26 April in the year AD 121. It was, with hindsight, an
auspicious birthday, shared with a number of other notable thinkers:
Shakespeare, David Hume, Ludwig Wittgenstein, the Scots 'common-
sense' philosopher Thomas Reid and (at least according to the Shia
branch of Islam) Mohammed. From his earliest moments he was the
recipient and heir of immense wealth and privilege for, next to the
obvious factor of wealth, kinship decided life chances in the Roman
empire. Marcus was supremely well connected. He was a member of

the influential Annius clan, or *gens*, which originated in Spain. The Annii first appear in the historical record during the civil war between Pompey and Julius Caesar, domiciled in the town of Ucubi, south-west of modern Córdoba in what was then the province of Baetica in Roman Spain, but it was with Marcus's great-grandfather that the family early emerged into clear daylight.[52] The great-grandfather grew rich from the trade in olive oil and achieved senatorial rank, but it was only in the career of his ambitious and go-getting son Marcus Annius Verus (Marcus's grandfather) that real consolidation occurred: Vespasian recognised him as a patrician. He went on to become prefect of the city of Rome and to hold three consulships (AD 97, 121, 126) – a rare honour.[53] Perhaps even more importantly, he married well, to Rupilia Faustina, daughter of Libo Rupilius Frugi, a man of consular rank. It did him no harm that he thereby became linked by kinship to a future emperor – for his mother-in-law Matidia was the mother (by another husband) of Vibia Sabina, wife of the emperor Hadrian.[54] Annius Verus had four children with Rupilia – Verus, Libo, Anna Galeria Faustina and a fourth child, a girl of unknown name – and remarkably all survived, but then the Annius clan had a reputation both for being fertile and prolific and for producing healthy issue. The eldest son Verus married Domitia Lucilla, and thus came into untold riches. His mother-in-law (Marcus Aurelius's maternal grandmother) was an immensely wealthy woman also called Domitia Lucilla, and she bequeathed most of her fortune to her namesake daughter.[55] One of the items in the portfolio was a vast brickworks on the outskirts of Rome, which generated super-profits during the building boom that had gone on almost continuously since the reign of Nero.

The union of Verus with Domitia Lucilla produced two children: Marcus (b. 121) and Anna Cornificia Faustina (b. 123). The boy Marcus had dozens of wealthy and influential relatives, for on his mother's side he was descended from the famous orator Cnaeus Domitius Afer (d. 59). Unfortunately Marcus's father Verus died when the boy was three; it was a young death by the standards of the Roman aristocracy, because he was not yet a consul, a rank usually reached by the age of thirty-two, and Verus was only a praetor, the second of the great offices (quaestor, praetor, consul) that a Roman oligarch habitually filled as part of a traditional senatorial career structure (the so-called *cursus honorum*). Marcus had no clear memory of his father, but later referred to his 'integrity and manliness' – which he admitted were nouns derived mainly from his father's general reputation.[56] Perhaps in tribute to Verus's memory, or perhaps because she had no real interest in men, Marcus's mother did not remarry. She seems to have been a somewhat puritanical lady, but was evidently a person of some importance and attracted envy because of her influence. The future emperor Didius Julianus was her protégé, as was the wealthy Greek orator Herodes Atticus, who was a guest at her house near the present site of St John Lateran on one of his visits to Rome.[57] It was perhaps from Atticus that she got her well-known love of all things Greek. She was nearly fifty when she died, some time in the closing years of the reign of Antoninus Pius (155–61), but remained an important factor in her son's life. Marcus referred to 'her reverence for the divine, her generosity, her inability not only to do wrong but even to conceive of doing it. And the simple way she lived – not in the least like the rich.'[58] This was unusual, for the imperial Romans, while paying lip-service to the spartan austerity of republican Rome, were not notable for their self-denial; they also believed in conspicuous consumption and, by living thus while possessing such a great fortune, Domitia Lucilla was in effect distancing herself from her class's dominant ethos.

The salient influences in Marcus's early life were all male. His grandfather Annius Verus took over the responsibility of bringing him up after the death of Verus junior, but the greatest day-to-day contact with an adult mentor seems to have been with Lucius Catilius Severus, his maternal great-grandfather or, more likely, his step-great-grandfather (if, as seems probable, he married the widow of Domitius Tullus, whose daughter Domitia Lucilla the elder was Marcus's grandmother). Catilius Severus was from an Italian family living in Bithynia who 'married up'. His career was slow to take off, but he became prominent in the later years of the emperor Trajan and gave crucial support to Hadrian during the controversial accession period, when Severus commanded one of the eastern armies. In the final days of Hadrian's reign, he incurred the displeasure of Hadrian, as did so many, and was demoted from his position as city prefect.[59] The presence of Catilius Severus, alongside the already complex genealogy of Marcus's father and mother, was not the only complicating factor in the family galaxy of the extended Annius family. A fourth child was born to

Annius Verus and Rupilia Faustina, a daughter, and this girl went on to be the wife of C. Ummidius Quadratus, scion of an old Naples family, whose fortunes dated back to the days of Augustus; Quadratus was suffect consul (a kind of deputy) in 118 and governor of Moesia Inferior province early in Hadrian's reign.[60] Originally a friend of Hadrian's, he inevitably fell foul of him and, in the last years of his reign, was in mortal danger from the wrath of that unpredictable emperor, who saw him as a threat to his succession plans. He probably died in the year 139, but by then Antoninus Pius had become emperor and the storm clouds had passed. In even greater jeopardy in the perilous last years of Hadrian was Quadratus's son (b. 114), Ummidius Quadratus Ammianus Verus, who eventually married Marcus's sister Anna Cornificia; Anna was thus marrying her first cousin.[61]

At birth, Marcus's mother immediately handed him over to a wet-nurse. The practice of handing over children to wet-nurses was by now universal among the upper classes, to the disgust of writers like Tacitus and Quintilian, who contrasted the 'decadent' practice with the great tradition of motherhood championed by Roman matrons under the republic.[62] Wet-nurses cared for the child in slave quarters until it reached school age, when it was returned to the parents. The system had several advantages for the pampered oligarchs: it saved aristocratic women from the chore of breast-feeding, which most saw as inimical to their beauty and well-being; it enabled the parents to be available for the full range of social activities and political engagements; and, most of all, in an era of very high child mortality, it warded off the worst aspects of grief by diluting the affective and emotional bond between parents and children.[63] The psychological effects of wet-nursing are usually thought pernicious by modern experts, but it must be remembered that the Romans had a much more diffuse notion of family than that in the post-Industrial Revolution West. Child-minders were a fact of life in a culture that regarded marrying for love as eccentric, even deviant, and whose kinship boundaries were constantly shifting; divorce and remarriage among aristocratic families may have reached 50 per cent.[64] Any given marriage might bring together children from several previous unions, each of whom also had ties to the home of their biological mother. The consequence was that children were looked after by a wide range of people: slaves, elderly dependants and nannies of all kinds.

Additionally, the relative lack of privacy in a modern sense – Romans habitually copulated in front of slaves – made family bonds looser.[65] At the same time it would be a mistake to suggest that Romans had no interest in their infants. It is a reasonable inference that after his birth in April 121, Marcus's parents would have indulged in all the usual rituals dear to Roman oligarchs. It was customary for a pater-familias to acknowledge his son by lifting him from the hearth and then, after nine days, purifying him. It was at this ceremony that the forename of Marcus was bestowed, but Roman superstition necessi-tated other odd customs. Two presents were given to children: a rattle, and a golden amulet to be worn around the neck until the boy was inducted into the official roll of manhood – supposedly a charm to ward off the evil eye and dark spirits.[66]

Marcus was initially brought up in his parents' villa on the Caelian, one of the seven hills of Rome. Under the empire it was *the* fashion-able area of Rome, a sparsely inhabited residential district where the aristocrats had their city mansions. Among the many splendid build-ings were the Lateran Palace (later the site of the church of St John Lateran), the temple of Claudius, the barracks of the Imperial Horse Guards and the palace owned by Marcus's grandfather (close to Marcus's parents' house). Standing on the Caelian in those days, one could enjoy an uninterrupted view of the grandeur that was Rome and its great sights: the Forum, the Palatine, the Colosseum (built by Vespasian), the Circus Maximus and the new Baths of Trajan.[67] Although Marcus had an uncle, Annius Libo (consul in 128 and married into the venerable Fundania family), he was a shadowy figure who does not seem to have impinged greatly on his nephew's life. Grandfather Annius Verus, however, was a constant presence. In his *Meditations* Marcus mentions that his grandfather taught him the virtue of good character and self-control – not giving vent to bad temper. Yet he appears to have had doubts about the man's moral example. When his wife Rupilia Faustina died, the old man took a mistress with whom he lived openly, and this woman seems to have been at the hub of a raffish social circle that the priggish young Marcus disliked as 'bad company': in the *Meditations* he thanks the gods that he was raised by his grandfather's 'girlfriend' for only a short time.[68] Possibly the most salient role-model for the lad was the emperor himself. From an early age the boy would have been aware of the presence of Hadrian, who from the start took an interest in him and called him 'verissimus' – a pun on his family name and the superlative adjective meaning 'most truthful'; some observers think that the waspish Hadrian was exercising his vespine humour and insinuating that he thought the lad a prig.[69]

Certainly it was Hadrian who showered favours on the boy. The Roman elite liked to go through the pretence that their sons had ascended to the highest position through merit and, in accordance with this ideology, Hadrian 'promoted' Marcus to the equestrian class at the age of six – rather as some later potentates would make their sons cardinals at a similar age; the idea was that the boy would enter the senatorial order 'by merit' when he officially became a man. It should be stressed that, although not unprecedented, the favours Hadrian showered on him were extremely rare honours for one so young.[70] Having made his protégé a knight, Hadrian next considered that he should have some training in the Roman priestly classes. Roman religion was an esoteric business and some of its rituals were only partially understood, even by the elite. There was a Commission of Fifteen in charge of the Sibylline books, said to foretell the future of Rome. There was a College of Vesta or the Vestal Virgins, charged with caring for the sacred fire at the temple of Vesta. Girls aged six to ten with both parents living were chosen to serve for thirty years: ten years as apprentices, ten years as fully fledged priestesses and ten years as teachers, training the new intake.[71] There were the Salii Colini, devoted to the worship of Quirinus (the deified Romulus, founder of Rome). And there were the twelve priests of the Salii proper, one of the three top-ranking priestly colleges, among whom Hadrian enrolled young Marcus at the age of eight. The Salii worshipped Mars, and the qualifications for priesthood were that you should hail from patrician stock and have both parents living; clearly the 'divine' Hadrian took it upon himself to waive the latter rule. The Salii were the 'jumping priests' (Latin salire, to jump) who purified the sacred trumpets that the Romans carried into battle, and their job was to keep Rome safe in wartime. Their priestly vestments were old-fashioned Italian battle dress or outfits supposedly worn by ancient warriors: an embroidered tunic, a breastplate, a short red cloak, a sword and a very pointed or conical helmet made of felt.[72]

On their left arm the Salii carried sacred figure-of-eight shields or *ancilia* – or, strictly speaking, they carried the sacred shield that was said to have fallen from heaven in days of yore, sent down from heaven to King Numa by Jupiter himself, and eleven copies: one shield per priest. In its origins a crop fertility rite, the sacred ritual of the Salii was most in evidence in March – the month of Mars when the god of war was especially worshipped. The festival of Mars ran from 1 to 24 March, with red-letter days being the 1st, 9th and 24th.[73] During this time the Salii danced through the streets of Rome, carrying poles with the shields mounted on them held in the left hand; with the right hand they banged the shields with a drumstick. Each night they stopped in a different locality, were feasted free of charge and moved on again in the morning. The songs they sang were not understood (probably not even by the singers) and were a frequent source of comment and speculation in the taverns. One thing was understood: that the names of deified emperors were inserted into the 'standards' that the Salii sang, for an emperor was above all an *imperator* or military commander.[74] The priests received special treatment, for the last nine days of the festival of Mars were meant to be fast-days except for priests; the breaking of the fast on 25 March is thought by some scholars to be the origin of Mardi Gras, instead of the 'fat Tuesday' before Christian Lent. During fast-days, as if by compensation, the feasts laid on for the Salii were more and more lavish: the feast in the temple of Mars on the Palatine Hill at the end of the festival was so opulent that the emperor Claudius, determined to establish himself as a 'heavy grubber', disguised himself as a priest to get in on the trencherman act.[75] Whatever the exploits of a past emperor, one future emperor certainly made his mark among the Salii. It was reported that when the young priests were casting their crowns on the banqueting couch of Mars, Marcus's happened to fall on the brow of the god's statue – the best possible omen. The suspicion of priggishness and ultra-seriousness seems borne out by the report that young Marcus quickly asserted his ascendancy in the college, became master and leader of dance and song and even took it upon himself to dismiss priestly veterans and to initiate promising newcomers.[76]

Around the age of seven or eight Marcus also commenced his education in earnest. There are two views on his early childhood so far. One is that it was excessively lonely and cramping, with a distant mother and no obvious parent or parent substitute with whom to bond.

On this model, his early years would have been remarkably similar to
other famous figures with a quasi-solipsistic childhood, such as
Nathaniel Hawthorne; the obvious difference is that Hawthorne's
mother was left financially impoverished by the loss of her husband.[77]
The other perspective stresses the over-bonding with older men, especially his grandfather and Catilius Severus; on this view, the later
adoption by Antoninus Pius would simply have added a third old man
to the pantheon. So, far from being damaged by an unhappy or dysfunc-
tional childhood (like Hawthorne with his half-crazed mother), perhaps
Marcus's infancy was *too* serene and mollycoddled, perhaps he was an
over-pampered child. These are matters of speculation, but what is
hard fact – strengthening the inference of 'autistic' tendencies in young
Marcus – is that his family insisted on having him educated at home
with private tutors instead of sending him to school. Marcus acknowledged a particular debt to Catilius Severus as follows: 'Avoiding public
schools, hiring good teachers, and accepting the resulting costs as
money well spent.'[78]

Many oligarchic Roman families, the Annius clan among them,
insisted that their children be educated at home rather than at school,
and it is worth asking why. In the first place it was thought that schools
were likely to corrupt the morals of the young, partly because they
would come into contact with rougher, more depraved elements, and
partly because there was little effective discipline in the public schools,
with teachers either being martinets or pussycats, but seldom striking
the right balance, and their charges being idle, ill-behaved, conceited
or self-willed.[79] Upper-class youths (*iuvenes*) were like Oxbridge under-
graduates of the 1920s and 1930s in their riotousness. This in turn
connected with the lesser levels of parental control and discipline
under the Roman empire, as opposed to the strict standards of the
republic. Parents both spoiled their children and delegated them to
nurses and slaves, where they ran wild. Beyond this, educational standards in general declined under the empire, and this in turn related
to the unresolved tensions in second-century society between the official ethos of spartan discipline associated with Cato the Elder and the
great figures of the republic, and the vulgar, decadent money-
mindedness and conspicuous consumption that had come in with the
emperors. Many parvenu and arriviste families, impressed by the showmanship and fluency of star advocates, who commanded huge fees,

wanted their sons to enjoy an accelerated education that would get them to the gravy-trough earlier; there was no place for the liberal education of rhetoric and philosophy in their world view. By educating Marcus at home, his grandparents could ensure that he imbibed the old values of austerity and stoicism.[80]

By the time of the Flavian and Antonine emperors the craze in upper-class circles was for employing tutors from abroad, usually Greeks, for the process of home education.[81] Marcus's first teacher was probably a slave, who encouraged the notion of austerity: 'to put up with discomfort and not make demands'. He taught the boy that only lesser minds supported the factions (Blues, Greens, Whites and Reds) in chariot-racing or had favourite gladiators, and that the wise man was he who got on with his job, minded his own business and did not listen to gossips or slanderers.[82] Soon there was also a painting master, Diognetus, who exhorted him similarly not to waste time on nonsense and to give up unworthy pastimes like cock-fighting (which the Romans usually did with quails); the objection was not the cruelty involved (it could scarcely be that, in the Roman world of all places), but because it was a pastime indulged in by 'low-lives'. Diognetus also advised him to take with a pinch of salt all maguses, exorcists and others claiming a channel to the supernatural and to turn to philosophy and a self-denying lifestyle.[83] Marcus went slightly overboard on this and chose to ape the 'Greek way of life' – which meant sleeping on a camp-bed wrapped only in a cloak or an animal skin. When he was twelve, his mother made a rare appearance in his life. Finding him sleeping on the ground in a philosopher's cloak or *pallium*, she remonstrated with him and finally persuaded him to give up 'this nonsense' and sleep in a bed.[84] Marcus's spartan sacrifice was all the more remarkable since he always had problems sleeping and was a natural 'owl', where most Romans were 'larks'. One of the advantages to him of home education was that he could lie in and not be up betimes, as most Romans were; the Roman schoolboy making his bleary-eyed way to school was usually up before dawn.[85]

The names of many of Marcus's early teachers are extant. Andron taught him geometry, Gemimus drama and music, and Euphorion literature. Two teachers of Latin are mentioned: Trosius Aper from Pola in the extreme north-east of Italy, and Tuticius Proculus of Sicca Veneria in Africa. Diognetus seems to have been an unusual

gogue, for in general the Roman attitude to philosophy was that
immed up in a line from one of Ennius's plays: 'We must philosophise
a bit but we don't like a lot of it.'[86] In literature, pupils made their
first acquaintance with Greek and Latin poetry by copying out and
learning by heart selected passages. Virgil's *Aeneid* was *the* book every
pupil had to know, as it was Rome's own epic; the school textbook
par excellence, it held pride of place for several centuries. Of the three
famous Greek dramatists, Euripides was the most widely read in the
Roman empire, and Marcus soon rote-learned huge chunks; the art
of reading aloud and reciting from memory was much prized in antiquity.[87] Apart from Diognetus, the teacher from this period who seems
to have made the most impression on young Marcus was Alexander,
a Greek from Cotiaeum in Syria, who had other distinguished pupils,
such as the future orator Aelius Aristides, and was nicknamed 'the
literary critic' to distinguish him from another Alexander in Marcus's
life, a Platonist philosopher. Alexander of Cotiaeum was an expert in
Homer, and moralising interpretations of the blind Greek poet were
much in vogue. Marcus summed up Alexander's advice as follows:
you should not appear a pedant, constantly correcting people, or jump
on them for errors in grammar, syntax or pronunciation, but just
answer their question, bring up another example or debate the substantive issue itself, as opposed to its wording; the clever educator moves
the discussion away from the error onto another plane, but then subtly
and unobtrusively introduces the correct expression (of grammar,
syntax or pronunciation), so that the pupil learns his error without
being humiliated for having made it.[88]

It was Juvenal, a Roman satirist, who popularised the notion so
beloved of Romans (and taken over by the Victorians) that the ideal
of education was a sound mind in a healthy body. Since Marcus
Aurelius was notably frail as an adult, it has been argued that he was
not physically robust as a youth, yet the evidence does not seem to
bear this out. He was fond of boxing, wrestling, running, ball games
and fowling, from the last two of which we can infer that he did not
always take his tutors' advice on what was seemly for a male of his
class; to judge from his later tolerance of religious charlatans and
hucksters, neither did he heed Diognetus's warnings about those who
dabbled in the occult. Vigorous as a youth, he rode and hunted with
gusto. But he was never a natural athlete, and probably forced himself

to take part in strenuous physical activity as a point of principle rather than for pleasure, much as he steeled himself to attend chariot races and gladiatorial shows (which he detested) just to show that he was a 'regular guy' and not a prig.[89] It is possible, therefore, that he enjoyed normal health as a very young man, but later suffered largely psycho-somatic complaints resulting from the stress of high office. It would, however, be an exaggeration to say that he was carefree until his late teens. He was always over-serious, even if not gloomy or austere. Never a hedonist in the days of adolescence or early adulthood, he took a positive satisfaction in having largely avoided the tugs of the flesh. Two entries in the *Meditations* are significant. First, he thanks the gods that he didn't lose his virginity too early and didn't enter adulthood until it was due time – he even says that he consciously deferred the passage to manhood. Second, he remarks delphically that he is glad he did not lay a finger on Benedicta or Theodotus and that, even later, when he was overcome by passion, he soon recovered from it.[90] Benedicta and Theodotus were presumably attractive slaves of either sex – Roman mores allowed males up to eighteen a bisexual period. And the tone of Marcus's many asides on sex in the *Meditations* suggests that libido was never a particular problem for him. Like many people who are not highly sexed, Marcus could never really under-stand what all the fuss was about when it came to Eros.

2

Around the time of his fifteenth birthday Marcus underwent a significant rite of passage when he donned the *toga virilis* – the visible manifestation of a male's enrolment in the ranks of men. Discarded were the striped toga and gold amulet of childhood, and on went the white robe of the Roman citizen. Moreover, hitherto named Marcus Catilius Severus, he reverted to his true family name of Marcus Annius Verus.[1] The old men (including the emperor) who had taken such an interest in the boy's education could be pleased with the results so far, for here was an exemplar of the old Roman virtues, an almost perfect meld of Greek sophistication and Stoic sensibility. The more thoughtful emperors had already become concerned about certain trends in social life, especially the cult of conspicuous consumption and the consequent mass import of luxury goods. Vespasian was one of the first to express such concerns, but all the Flavian and Antonine emperors were unhappy with the rising nouveau-riche class, who liked to educate their sons in a narrow money-oriented way, cutting out all liberal studies.[2] Hadrian, a Spanish emperor himself, saw Marcus as almost the quintessence of Roman Spain, and his partiality for the young man was such that in some quarters it elicited the ludicrous rumour that Marcus was actually his natural son.[3] But Marcus was a kind of lodestone with which Hadrian hoped to guide the future of the empire. Almost immediately after Marcus assumed the toga of manhood, Hadrian expressed the wish (that is, the command) that Marcus should be betrothed to the daughter of Ceionius Commodus.

The main reason for this was that Ceionius Commodus was Hadrian's choice of successor, but was in poor health and came from a short-lived family. The extended Ceionius clan originated in three marriages made a generation or so earlier by a woman named Plautia, who married Ceionius Commodus, Avidius Nigrinus and Vettuleus Ceralius. By fusing the feeble Ceionius genes with the prolific Annius genes, Hadrian was combining two of the most powerful clans in Rome – the Montagues and Capulets as it were – one Spanish, one Italian, and advancing his own long-term plans for the succession.[4]

In so many ways, then, young Marcus Aurelius lived under the shadow of Hadrian. Three aspects of the emperor impressed everyone who studied his twenty years of the principate (117–38). First, there was his open and predatory homosexuality. Roman culture accepted bisexuality and expected youths to pass through a phase of 'Greek love' – either male-on-male infatuation or actual physical consummation. But it was expected that, after about the age of eighteen, a man would be publicly heterosexual, marry and raise a family; if he continued to take male lovers, well and good, as long as it was done in private and he did not 'debauch' adult males. Hadrian violated this principle in two ways: he did not restrict himself by age in his choice of male partners and he practised his 'deviant' sexuality openly. This may or may not have been the hidden meaning behind the sibylline judgement of the Christian apologist Tertullian when he called Hadrian 'an explorer of all the world's curiosities'.[5] Hadrian's most famous lover was Antinous, who was twenty at the time of his mysterious death by drowning in the Nile. Some said that Antinous was drowned by Hadrian's agents as a sacrificial victim. Others claimed that he drowned himself, knowing that the ageing Hadrian was concerned about his own health and needed a sacrifice to appease the gods. Yet others think he developed a death wish, feeling that, once an adult, he could no longer honourably be Hadrian's lover, but that the emperor wanted the relationship to continue. In short, Antinous's position had become untenable and intolerable, and he took the only way out.[6]

Controversial as Hadrian's sexual profile was, he alienated even more elite Romans by his peace policy. His predecessor Trajan had won martial glory in Dacia (modern Romania) and Mesopotamia, but immediately on coming to the throne, Hadrian abandoned all these eastern conquests and announced that he intended to consolidate the empire on an 'as is' basis; there would be no more forward policies, no more expansionism. The subterranean murmur of criticism on this score would have been a vociferous rant, had people not feared Hadrian's deadly viciousness so much. Later Roman writers liked to compare his 'cowardly' peace policy with the abandonment of the conquest of Germany by Tiberius and Germanicus. As one cynically remarked: 'Having obtained peace from many kings by means of secret gifts, he used to boast openly that he had achieved more in peacetime than others by warfare.'[7] It is a common criticism of Hadrian that he failed to grasp that the Roman empire was always a dominion of conquest and, like the shark, needed to keep swimming continually, and that he had no obvious solutions to the problems that inevitably accrued once Rome stopped expanding. His defenders tend to say two things. One is that his predecessor Trajan had given him an impossible hand to play, since Trajan himself was a 'one-off', the first emperor since Augustus who knew how to harness traditional Roman ideals to his own ends and make his ambitions seem the natural ones of Rome.[8] This is what the poet Martial meant when he said that if Julius Caesar and his old enemy Cato the Younger could be raised from the dead to live in Antonine Rome, they would no longer be enemies, since the ancient conflicts of the republic had all been resolved.[9] Trajan had somehow managed to reconcile the reality of war and conquest with an ideology of peace and good faith by his personal charisma as emperor and 'god', instead of using the traditional flummery of the 'just war'. Anyway, said other defenders, Hadrian had not abandoned expansionism, but was going about it in a more subtle way. When he pulled Roman troops back from the Euphrates, he had in mind the withdrawal from Macedonia in the second century BC by Cato the Elder – in other words, he was aiming at indirect rule, not the complete abandonment of Roman ambitions in the East.[10]

The third noteworthy aspect of the reign of Hadrian was the emperor's tireless travels through the length and breadth of the empire. In the year 121 (when Marcus was born) he visited Gaul and the Danube frontier (Raetia, Noricum, Upper Germany). In 122 his travels took him to Gaul, Spain, Lower Germany and Britain, where he commissioned the famous wall between the Solway Firth and the North Sea. The year 123 saw him concentrating on the Mediterranean coast of Africa and the Middle East; in a very busy year he swept through the provinces of Africa and Mauretania, taking in Libya and Cyrene, then proceeded to Crete, Asia Minor, Pontus, Bithynia and the frontier as far as the Euphrates. In 124 he began his love affair with Greece, touring the country, spending much time in Athens and also heading north to take in Thrace, Moesia, Pannonia and Dacia. Returning to Greece in 126, he spent a relatively quiet year, heading back to Rome via Sicily and then remaining in the Eternal City until 128, when he made further visits to Africa and his beloved Athens. In 129 he was again in the East, touring successively Asia Minor, Pamphylia, Phrygia, Pisidia, Cilicia, Syria, Samosata, Cappadocia, Pontus and Antioch. 130 was a year for the desert, for the imperial itinerary took him through Judaea, Palestine, Arabia, Egypt, Alexandria and the Nile (where Antinous drowned). In 131 he was in the Libyan desert and then again in Asia and Syria, before coming to rest again in his favourite city, Athens. Compelling affairs of state forced him back to Rome in 132, but the following year he was on the road again, this time limiting himself to Judaea, Egypt and Antioch. Most of 135 was spent in Syria, but finally ill-health and the need to ensure the imperial succession drove him back in 136 to Rome, where he spent his final miserable two years.[11]

Although month-by-month details of the reign of Hadrian may elude us because of the paucity of ancient sources, we nonetheless know a great deal about the personality of this enigmatic emperor. According to Julian the Apostate (who is usually ranked alongside Hadrian and Marcus Aurelius as one of three hyper-intellectual emperors), he was an austere-looking man with a long beard, 'an adept in all arts but especially music, one who was always gazing at the heavens and prying into hidden things'.[12] The full beard is confirmed from a number of sources; he pioneered this fashion, which became a staple of the Antonine emperors, although Hadrian originally favoured the hirsute style simply to hide pockmarks and other blemishes on his face. He was tall and elegant in appearance, with bright, piercing eyes, strongly built and wore his hair curled. He originally spoke Latin with a Spanish accent, but corrected this by diligent study. A fitness freak, he rode and walked a great deal, prided himself on his skill in arms, liked hunting and was particularly fond of killing lions with a javelin.[13] Energy was his most obvious characteristic – not just the globe-trotting kind that took him round and round the perimeter of his empire, but the kind that necessitates constant action and a plethora of fresh projects. And so it was that Hadrian changed the physical face of Rome, rebuilding the Pantheon, adding the Roman Forum and erecting a mausoleum (now the Castel Sant'Angelo).[14] Always impatient and in a hurry, he was the subject of a famous anecdote that conveyed his restlessness. While on his journeys, he passed through a village and a woman approached him with a request. 'I don't have the time,' he replied. 'Then stop being emperor' was the devastating riposte. It is said that Hadrian was so nettled that he turned back and gave the audacious woman a hearing.[15]

Hadrian's character and personality can usefully be summed up in a threefold analysis. In the first category are his attitudes and actions, which appear neither good nor evil on the surface (but which can doubtless be worked up either way by admirers and detractors). He possessed both total recall and a photographic memory, and could remember anyone's face, once glimpsed. He knew as much of the detail of the state's budget as the ordinary person knows of his or her household accounts. He was also what would be called in modern parlance a 'multitasker': he could dictate, listen and converse at the same time and not miss a trick. He could be very witty: when he refused a request to a grey-haired man, the man simply dyed his hair and returned with the same request, thinking the emperor would not recognise him. Hadrian looked at him witheringly and said, 'I have already refused this request to your father.'[16] Many of his actions were simple prudence, but others showed a shrewd insight into the techniques of political management. He wrote off the debt of 900 million sesterces owing to the state treasury, and burned the tax documents in the Forum, to the predictable joy of all debtors; and he kept the army on side by declaring a double donative to the troops.[17] He was fanatically philhellene, besotted with Athens and a devotee of the Eleusinian mysteries – indeed, he liked all things Greek so much that his enemies called him (behind his back) 'Greekling' – but balanced this by painstakingly carrying out his duties as high priest (*pontifex maximus*) and keeping all foreign cults at arm's length in Rome itself. He could affect the common touch when he needed to and rough it with the troops, eating homely fare, but had his gourmet side in private: a favourite dish was tetrapharmacum, a mixture of pheasant, sow's udders, ham and pastry, and he liked to make a laboured joke about it, to the effect that it fulfilled the formula of Epicurus and his 'fourfold medicine'.[18]

Second, we must consider the evidence for a 'good' Hadrian. His refusal of the title of 'Father of His Country' offered by the Senate, on the grounds that Augustus had not been voted the honour until late in life, sounds like pleasing humility, but may simply have been a clever ploy to humour the Senate. His handling of it, except at the beginning and end of his reign, was usually astute, and his insistence on traditional standards won him plaudits, especially his requirement that senators and knights should never be seen in public without the togas denoting their rank. Although he differed from Trajan in almost every respect (except the shared Spanish ancestry), he insisted on divine honours for his predecessor – a man who had been a trial to him, not least by insisting that he take part in mammoth drinking sessions. But there seems no arguing the fact that, after his third consulship in 119, he did not hold that office again, in contrast to Trajan, who held five consulships when emperor; to say nothing of the earlier Flavian emperors, who were notorious for 'hogging' consulships.[19] With all his faults, Hadrian's intellectual talents were undeniable, and he particularly showed his mental calibre in his realisation that the roots of the prosperity of the Roman empire were to be found in the rural areas of Africa and Asia. He tried valiantly to revive agricultural life, attempted to deal with the scandal of the sky-high taxes levied by farmers-general and tax-gatherers (*conductores*) in Africa, and reversed the process of peasant apathy and alienation that had resulted in a switch to pastoralism with consequent decay of the cornfields and vineyards.[20] Unfortunately he undid most of the benefit of his economic reforms by spending on his lavish building programmes, by the cost of his ceaseless journeying and by the huge expansion of bureaucracy in his reign. Moreover, in his building programme he alienated the crowd in Rome by destroying the theatre that Trajan built in the Campus Martius, compounding his error by claiming that all his unpopular measures were those enjoined on him by Trajan on his death-bed; this simply won him the accolade of humbug.[21]

But there is much more evidence of a 'bad' Hadrian. His record towards the Senate was patchy. All Roman emperors supposedly ruled on a separation-of-powers system whereby they had to work closely with the Senate, but this was an elaborate fiction. The more brutal emperors simply executed and expropriated as they wished, cowing and terrifying senators. The more intelligent ones liked to obfuscate and camouflage their naked use of power by humouring the Senate, flattering it and even truckling to it. Hadrian was in this tradition.[22] He also won over the equestrian class by giving them privileges at the expense of freedmen. Whereas previously court offices had been held by freedmen as private posts, Hadrian changed them into official civil-service positions by stipulating that they had to be occupied by knights. The opening to the equestrian class of a great new career led to the rise of this social sector, to the point where by the end of the third century knights held a virtual monopoly in the civil service. Keen on running a tight ship in the areas of auditing and administration, Hadrian found this easier to do in partnership with the equestrians. Naturally cruel, he affected generosity because he remembered what had happened to the emperor Domitian.[23] He was almost modern in his interest in what we would now call social control, and studied closely the mood both of the mob and of the army. Concluding that the common people could be kept quiet by lavish shows in the arena, he specialised in providing them with wild-beast shows and some-times had a hundred lions killed in a single spectacle (Hadrian always had something of an obsession with lions).[24] As for the army, he liked to pretend to be one of the men, going on route-marches in full armour, sharing hardships, but at the same time stealthily increasing discipline and identifying possible troublemakers and (among the ranks of generals) pretenders to the purple. He had an efficient spy system, turning the *frumentarii* or secret service into paid agents, and in some ways anticipated modern communist systems by having people inform on each other, even encouraging wives to write to him with complaints about their husbands.[25]

Overwhelmingly the evidence on Hadrian that has come down to us suggests a very dark character indeed. Superficially austere, digni-fied, genial, straightforward, generous, decisive and merciful, he slowly revealed to the more perceptive that this was a mere carapace, 'character armour', which masked autocratic and even psychopathic tendencies. A rehearsal of the epithets than can warrantably be applied to him is profoundly disconcerting: unpredictable, irascible, capricious, wilful, changeable, fickle (his critics said he was more volatile than any woman), envious, lustful, ambitious, meddlesome, jealous, micro-managing – all these express only part of a thoroughly dislikeable personality. A lover of display while claiming the Greek virtues of moderation, he feigned the Athenian qualities of self-restraint and mildness and, under a mask of affability, concealed his lust for glory. Here is one estimate of him: 'changeable, manifold, fickle, born as if to be a judge of vices and virtues, controlling his passionate spirit by some kind of artifice, he expertly concealed his envious, unhappy and wanton character, immoderate in his urge for ostentation'.[26] Seemingly averse to pomp and national pride, and ostensibly hostile to the claims of wealth, birth and class, favouring only the cultivated urban aristocracy, under his sophisticated veneer Hadrian was a deep-dyed reactionary, who was particularly incensed at the progress made by the social class of freedmen and was determined to put these upstarts back in their box, as it were. Frighteningly ambitious, he was one of those people who always has to be first or best, combative, with a relish for scoring points off genuine experts or professionals. He liked to dispute with philosophers, professors and scholars (than whom, in his own opinion, he always knew better), and if he could not gain the day by argumentation or logic, did so by the glint in his eye that warned his adversary not to press the point. On one occasion he argued with the sophist Favorinus, and it was quite obvious to all that Favorinus had the better of the debate. Prudently Favorinus then said that the emperor had converted him to his way of thinking and was quite right. When reproached for cowardice by his friends afterwards, Favorinus said, 'You advise me badly, friends, since you do not permit me to believe that he who commands thirty legions is the most learned of all. Just remember that. The most learned man is always the one who commands thirty legions.'[27]

Hadrian regarded himself as the greatest polymath of all time. Those who knew him well said that he had a fair grasp of arithmetic, geometry and painting and could sing and play the flute well. But this was not enough for the emperor: he wanted to be acclaimed as an original genius, across the board and in all fields. He regarded himself as an expert astrologer, studied star signs and the attributes of the 'houses', and liked to remind people that his great-uncle had been an acknowledged adept in astrology. He claimed to be able to outpoint everyone in his knowledge of architecture, etymology and military science.

He yearned for literary fame, composed poetry and wrote his own autobiography (alas, lost).[28] A maddening 'know-all', Hadrian always had to be one up. The poet Florus, writing about the emperor's tour of Britain in 122, penned these lines:

> I don't want to be emperor, please
> To tramp around among Britons,
> Or in Scythian frosts to freeze.

Hearing of this, Hadrian at once composed an answer:

> And I don't want to be Florus, please
> To tramp around pubs and bars
> And get myself infested with fleas.[29]

Holding himself forth as an expert in literature, he let it be known that he disliked Homer and Plato (he was speaking with authority, he said, as he was the world's leading authority on them), scouted Tacitus and Suetonius, preferred Cato to Cicero, Ennius to Virgil and Coelius Antipater to Sallust. That all this went beyond simple eccentricity in literary criticism to outright bad taste is most clearly evinced by his preference for Antimachus of Colophon to Homer.[30] Hadrian bestowed honours and riches on tragedians, grammarians, comedians and rhetoricians, but in return it was clearly understood that one had to take his ignorant criticisms and his affectation of intellectual superiority.[31] Maddeningly omniscient (at least in his own mind), superior, patronising and condescending, Hadrian and his 'superiority complex' might have been no more than an embarrassing irritant, but the desire to be top dog also masked genuinely homicidal tendencies: Hadrian was a man one crossed at one's mortal peril. Always on a notoriously short fuse, he once stabbed a slave in the eye with a pen in one of his rages. The unfortunate lost his eye, and Hadrian later felt remorse and asked the slave to choose a gift in recompense. The one-eyed victim did not reply. Hadrian then pressed him, whereupon the slave said that all he wanted was his eye back.[32]

Yet blindings and strikings were not the worst of it. At the limit, this man who is usually classed among the 'good emperors' could be as vicious as Nero or Caligula. He ruthlessly killed off all the likely successors he did not approve of – Severianus, Fruscus, Platorius Nepos, Terentius Gentianus – and his murder of senators at the beginning and end of his reign made him a hate-figure for the Senate. Towards the end of his life, he even turned on his beloved Greeks and conceived a poisonous hatred for the city of Antioch.[33] His natural taste for violence is clear from his love of gladiators; anticipating Commodus, he even fought in the arena himself to demonstrate his expertise with arms. Vengeful, brooding and vindictive, Hadrian would nurse grudges for ever and then suddenly take revenge for ancient slights, having even common soldiers and freedmen executed for petty insults.[34] His worst fault was a paranoid hyper-suspicion, even of close friends. He compelled his brother-in-law Severianus to commit suicide even though he was ninety, drove two 'bosom buddies' to suicide, reduced another to poverty, destroyed the reputation of yet another, and outlawed and persecuted most of the rest who were on intimate terms with him.[35] In the year of his death, he dreamed he had been overcome by a lion, and this may be the most significant clue to the inner Hadrian.[36] Even those who reject the insights of modern depth psychology, when applied to the ancient world, can scarcely deny the relevance of an ancient interpreter of dreams who stressed a gap between the manifest and latent content of them. Artemidorus tells us that all dreams of wild animals indicate sickness, and particularly those where a lion features.[37] Hadrian's 'lion complex' may tell us something significant about his inner demons, for his true sickness was surely mental.

Such was the man in whose shadow the young Marcus grew up. In the period just before adopting the *toga virilis*, Marcus would have been transfixed, as all elite Romans were, by the third and most horrible of all Rome's Jewish wars. Although it is conventional to regard Hadrian's reign as a period of peace after the strenuous wars of Trajan, the Roman empire was in fact rarely undisturbed by one or other invasion, incursion or uprising. There was armed conflict in Spain with the Moors of Africa, with the Sarmatians along the Danube and in Britain, Libya and Egypt.[38] In the year 132 the thunderbolt of war hit Palestine. The Jews – on paper Roman subjects for some 200 years – had never reconciled themselves to their fate. A great rebellion in the year 66 had managed to prolong itself because of the crisis caused by the final years of Nero and, in particular, by the year of the four emperors in 68–9. Vespasian ordered his son Titus to stifle the core of the rebellion in Jerusalem, which he did efficiently in 70, but the last embers of revolt did not die down until the mass suicide of Jewish defenders at the fortress of Masada in 73. Trajan's Parthian war provided another opportunity for the discontented in Palestine. There is clear evidence of collusion between Parthia and the Jews who, in Roman eyes, treacherously stabbed them in the back while they were occupied on the Euphrates.[39] But the 'second front' failed as ignominiously as the main front in Mesopotamia, and a Jewish rising was again put down, this time with terrible loss of life, which Cassius Dio, like all ancient historians with a mania for exaggerated numbers, estimated at 460,000; this is an impossible figure, but we may nonetheless assume casualties large enough to shock even the ancients.[40]

The so-called Bar-Kochba revolt of 132–5 was the most serious threat yet to the Roman position in Palestine, as for the first time the Jews had mastered their fatal flaw of factionalism and united under a common leader, the mysterious Simon Bar-Kochba. What triggered the third great uprising is disputed. The Romans were never anti-Semitic in any significant sense, but they distrusted the Jews as a potential fifth column and remembered with bitterness the 'stab in the back' during Trajan's Parthian campaign. Some say that Hadrian's strict ban on circumcision was the trigger, but it is more likely that greater offence was given by his rebuilding of Jerusalem as a Roman settlement and, perhaps especially, given the sequence of events, by the new cult of the deified Antinous, which the emperor, for obvious reasons, was promoting in the East.[41] At any rate, the sudden Jewish eruption took the Romans by surprise and they reacted with anger and incredulity when they realised the meticulous planning that had gone into the rebellion. Like the Vietcong more than 1,800 years later, Jewish guerrillas had constructed a nationwide network of tunnels, and had shown masterly ingenuity in arming themselves for the struggle. Knowing of Hadrian's micromanaging control of the army, and aware that he always rejected arms and armour that were substandard, Jewish craftsmen deliberately turned out defective weapons, knowing that the interfering emperor would reject them. The rejects were then officially dumped, but secretly reworked ready for use when the time came. Caught unawares, the Romans were soon on the back foot, despite the presence of two legions and more than a dozen auxiliary regiments. The fighting was desperate and bloody from the beginning, and the Egyptian Legion 22 *Deiotariana* appears to have been wiped out. Soon most of

Palestine was in Bar-Kochba's hands. A terrifying figure animated by zealotry, he is said to have slaughtered the land's Christians when they refused to help him against the Romans.[42]

Hadrian responded as all the most able emperors did when faced by military crisis: he rushed all his best generals and elite units to the scene of trouble. Replacing Tinaeus Rufus, the bogeyman in the Jewish tradition, he brought his best general, Sextus Julius Severus, over from Britain together with crack units from that island. On their travels to the theatre of war, Severus and his men swept up other units from along the Rhine–Danube frontier; it is probable that Hadrian, then on his way back to Rome, conferred with him on the Danube.[43] Severus was given nothing but the best and took to Palestine with him all the rising military stars: M. Statius Priscus, M. Censorius Cornelianus and Q. Lollius Urbicus. Severus, who does not seem to have been ready to open his campaign until 134, waged a clever war of attrition, never engaging the enemy in strength, but slowly and relentlessly closing the noose around Bar-Kochba by cutting off food supplies, severing communications, intercepting stragglers and ambushing rearguards. In the course of a ruthless scorched-earth policy, he gutted fifty Jewish outposts and razed 985 villages, so that a crow flying overhead would have had to carry its own provisions. Countless bloody skirmishes and mini-battles ensued, with Severus careful never to commit his troops to a single decisive battle, before Bar-Kochba was finally besieged in the fortress of Bethar, six miles south-west of Jerusalem.[44] After a desperate resistance, the Jewish defenders were undone by famine and thirst. Late in 135 (or possibly early 136) the Romans took the stronghold and killed the fanatical rebel leader. His severed head was taken to Severus, and legend has it that it had a snake coiled around it when he viewed it. Severus, making a point of humiliating the Jews who had cost him so many men, said scathingly, in mockery of Yahweh, 'If his God had not slain him, who would have overcome him?'[45] The triumphalism masked a desperate and hard-fought campaign. Casualties on both sides were terrific, and Cassius Dio this time outdid himself by claiming that no fewer than 580,000 Jews were slain in battle.[46]

There may have been echoes of this slaughterous experience in Hadrian's mind during the last two years of his reign, when the mask of affability was thrown off and the emperor was revealed in his full homicidal fury. His determination to arrange the imperial succession as he wanted it became an obsession, in which all obstacles had to be destroyed. It was fortunate indeed for Marcus that he was such a favourite and that Hadrian saw him as a key link in the union of the Ceionius and Annius clans. The man Hadrian initially chose to succeed him was one of the consuls of the year 136, a thirty-four-year-old named L. Ceionius Commodus, and the choice has always puzzled scholars because he was highly unsuitable, being a dilettante of uncertain health, good-looking, but probably already seriously tubercular. The man he originally wanted as the next emperor in line was Avidius Nigrinus (it will be remembered that he was one of the three husbands of Plautia, and that Ceionius Commodus married his daughter), but Hadrian had executed him in 118 on a trumped-up charge of conspiracy. Ceionius Commodus, husband of Nigrinus's daughter, made sense if Hadrian was going to continue promoting the Ceionius clan, and perhaps the choice was also some kind of acknowledgement that the execution of Nigrinus had been a bad error.[47] Hadrian renamed Ceionius Commodus as Aelius Caesar, declared him the heir to the throne and ordered all other possible claimants to commit suicide so that there would be no pretenders to the imperial purple; both Nigrinus and Commodus had stronger claims to succeed than either Aelius or Marcus.[48] Inevitably, the suspicion has arisen that the newly styled Aelius Caesar was Hadrian's own illegitimate son from a union with Plautia (wife of L. Ceionius Commodus the elder), but we should beware of giving the idea too much credence; after all, the emperor's partiality for Marcus had been implausibly explained in the same way. An even more absurd idea was that Ceionius was Hadrian's lover, but after the scandal of Antinous, anything was considered possible.[49]

Having adopted Aelius Caesar as his son and heir, Hadrian then made the inexplicable decision to send a man of such uncertain health to serve for a year in Carnuntum on the Danube frontier, where the climate was notoriously harsh. The idea that he sent his designated successor to impress the flaky German tribe, the Quadi, whose rising power was causing concern, fails to convince, as does the linked notion that by adopting Aelius, Hadrian signalled that he in turn wanted *his* son, the future Lucius Verus (see below *passim*) to succeed.[50] Lucius Verus was at this time only six, and there was no guarantee that Aelius Caesar would live long enough to hand over to a son who had achieved adulthood. On the other hand, if as is usually alleged Hadrian was simply using Aelius as a stopgap until his real choice as successor, young Marcus, was old enough, then all becomes clear. Yet another view is that the impulsive Hadrian made another of his wild decisions (probably because someone was advising a contrary course of action on him) and then regretted it, but could not go back on his word once he had made the choice public, so decided to give Nature a helping hand in polishing off Aelius. Whatever the case, the climate on the Danube did the trick, and Aelius died shortly after his return to Rome, on 1 January 138, expiring from the kind of haemorrhage associated with tuberculosis.[51] The idea of Aelius as someone who would keep the throne warm for Marcus is the most appealing of the rival hypotheses. A great deal of fuss is made in the official histories of Marcus about his apparent generosity to his sister. The surface story is that Marcus's mother asked him to give Anna Cornificia Faustina part of the fortune he had inherited from his father; Marcus then replied that he was quite content with the bequest from his *grandfather*, so made the whole of the paternal fortune over to his sister, adding the recommendation that his mother should bequeath all her property in the same manner.[52] But the probable reality is that Hadrian had dynastic plans of his own for Anna Cornificia and 'leaned on' Marcus to make the transfer.

The circumstantial evidence that Hadrian wanted Marcus to succeed him, possibly around the time the young man was twenty-one, is overwhelming.[53] Soon after being officially entered on the rolls of manhood, Marcus was made prefect of the city during the Latin Festival. Originally an office of real significance under the republic – for the prefect administered Rome whenever the two consuls were absent – the prefecture had been kept on under the empire as a formality: a sinecure given to young members of the senatorial class on the make or to princes of the imperial family.[54] Marcus did with this office what he had done as a young priest with the Salii, making something out of an empty ritual and impressing by his administrative skills, both when dealing with magistrates and when attending Hadrian's banquets.[55] It did Marcus's prospects no harm at all that he also became the favourite of the empress Sabina. But the year 136 was a black one for many. First, Sabina died in mysterious circumstances, and it was rumoured that Hadrian had poisoned her because she opposed his plans for the succession – not his favouritism for Marcus, but the elevation of the Ceionius clan. Then the emperor entered one of his most paranoid phases. He nearly died from a haemorrhage and was seriously ill at his magnificent villa at Tivoli to the East of Rome, but during his convalescence he brooded over reports that his spies had brought him about the less-than-correct behaviour of his ninety-year-old brother-in-law Julius Severianus and his grandson Pedanius Fuscus Salinator. He at once ordered the two to commit suicide. Severianus did not go quietly. He made a public declaration of his innocence, offered incense to the gods and then opened his veins, but not before pronouncing a solemn curse on Hadrian: 'May he long for death but be unable to die.'[56] His death and that of his grandson were deeply unpopular with the Senate, but the emperor simply responded to the underground murmurings with a wider purge, involving even more deaths. His supporters claimed, sycophantically, that there were precedents for the emperor's murder of Pedanius Fuscus, citing the way Claudius had dumped his son Britannicus in favour of Nero.[57]

With his critics temporarily silenced by early 138, but with Aelius Caesar dead, Hadrian had still not settled the succession and his health grew worse by the day. On his sixty-second birthday, 24 January, he once again surprised and dismayed the senators by announcing his new choice as successor: it would be Aurelius Antoninus, a relatively unknown senator with limited experience of government. Lying on his invalid's couch, Hadrian explained the reasons for his choice: in brief, it was Antoninus's very lack of distinction and his middle age, for an older man might be senile and make grievous mistakes, while a younger one might be rash and headstrong. From Hadrian's point of view, Antoninus was a perfect blank slate: he was a steady character, had no real enemies or ongoing feuds, had no siblings and just one daughter surviving from five children; his two sons had both died young. To satisfy all the legal requirements, Hadrian formally 'adopted' Antoninus, but made it a condition of the succession that Antoninus should in turn adopt the seventeen-year-old Marcus and the seven-year-old son of Aelius Caesar, the future Lucius Verus.[58] Although the movement into new families for dynastic reasons was a special form of adoption, the practice in general was common in Rome, particularly in the senatorial class. There were many reasons for its popularity. For those childless against their will, it provided an heir, and it was always a condition of being named as the heir in Roman wills that the adopted 'son' would assume the name of the benefactor. For the willingly childless, adoption was an ingenious way of perpetuating the family name without incurring the expenses of child-rearing, which were considerable. Large families were financially burdensome: daughters had to be provided with dowries, and sons put through the expensive senatorial career hoops – the *cursus honorum*.[59]

Even philoprogenitive families tried to avoid having more than three, but planning a family (in the literal, non-contraceptive sense) was fraught with risks. If you decided to opt for a large family, given the high levels of infant mortality and the possibility that all the children could be girls, you could still fail to perpetuate your line. On the other hand, if you had too many boys, you could end up having to put *them* up for adoption. Roman law allowed a paterfamilias to give children in adoption, and it was usually the eldest son for whom this fate was reserved, provided he was of good health and above-average intelligence. A sum of money was exchanged, the boy assumed the new father's name and a secondary name (*cognomen*) that indicated his original family.[60] Apart from being a crafty way to maintain the hereditary principle, which might otherwise collapse through lack of male heirs, the adoption system enabled the childless to play manipulative games with their clients. In the Roman world, where an aristocrat was judged by the number of his clients, a rich elderly man (or woman) would typically have lots of cronies, clients and hangers-on, always hoping to inherit in the absence of a clear heir. The devious would enjoy stringing all these hopefuls along until failing health indicated the approach of death, when there would be a sudden adoption. In general, adoption made sense both in financial terms and because important families could thereby cement kinship alliances with other elite members. In the case of emperors, even more important considerations weighed, since adoption ensured a smooth succession.[61] Typically, Hadrian aimed not just at the succession of Antoninus, but at the subsequent principate of the new son of the emperor-in-waiting, who from this moment on officially took the name Marcus Aurelius.

Antoninus took a long time to accept the crown offered by Hadrian, confirming the dying emperor's opinion that he was not ambitious

and had thus been a wise choice. There is some evidence that
Antoninus was genuinely reluctant to take up the imperial burden, but
simple prudence obliged him to accept. If he turned down the offer
and still lived when a new emperor emerged, he would be a marked
man – not so much a king over the water, but an emperor on the water
of the Tiber; no man could feel secure on the throne knowing that he
was second choice and that the first choice was still extant, ready at
any moment to be used as a rallying point by rebellious senators or
praetorians.[62] The formal ceremony of adoption took place on 25
February. In addition to adopting Marcus and the son of Aelius Caesar,
Antoninus also pledged himself to marry his daughter Faustina to the
eight-year-old boy (the future Lucius Verus) when they were of age.
Antoninus was not yet emperor and could not style himself Augustus,
but he received the title *imperator* and the traditional powers given to
a Caesar, the tribunician and proconsular powers and privileges.[63] His
elevation distressed and disconcerted many, but especially Marcus's
step-great-grandfather Catilius Severus, who was angry that he had
been passed over for a man with (in his view) lesser claims. They had
been consuls together in 120, but it was Antoninus's first consulship
and Severus's second, making him clearly the senior man. He had been
proconsul of Africa, had commanded one of the German legions, served
in three junior prefectures in Rome and had governed Cappadocia and
finally Armenia in Trajan's Parthian war (in 117); he was one of that
emperor's favourites and had been decorated by him. Hadrian had used
him in a senior position in the Syrian army, and most recently he had
been prefect of the city of Rome. How could Antoninus, a man of
undistinguished record compared to his, be elevated above him? Hadrian
knew of Severus's feelings and acted with his usual ruthlessness. He
dismissed him from his post as prefect and shortly afterwards had him
liquidated. He also cropped anyone else he thought could be a danger
to Antoninus, just as he had felled the opposition to Aelius earlier.
During these years Ummidius Quadratus and his namesake son were
in mortal peril, especially the son who had married Marcus's sister. It
is surprising that in his clean sweep of potential pretenders Hadrian
did not eliminate them too, but it has been speculated that Quadratus
the younger made it clear that he did not want the crown.[64]

Given that Antoninus was already an old man and, in normal
circumstances, Marcus would not have long to wait before he assumed

the purple, it might be supposed that he was ecstatic at his adoption as, in effect, heir apparent. Nothing could be further from the truth. So far from being overjoyed by his elevation, he was appalled. He told his friends and intimates that royal adoption meant he must leave the realm of innocence behind, to assume the cares of office and experience the evil of mankind.[65] The worst part of the promotion was that he had to leave his mother's villa to move into Hadrian's private home. Marcus made a point of living as austerely and frugally there as he had at home and insisted on acting towards his family as a dutiful son, despite his elevation as heir apparent. Living with a near-madman cannot have been easy, for Hadrian was now fading fast, demanding that his doctors kill him by euthanasia and issuing fresh death-warrants when they refused. Patiently Antoninus explained to the dying emperor that it was his duty to endure pain rather than be put out of his misery, as this would make him (Antoninus) a parricide.[66] But still the madness went on, with Hadrian identifying fresh enemies every day: those who allegedly opposed his peace policies, mere traitors who wanted the principate for themselves, and dog-in-the-manger senators who opposed his plans for the succession.[67] Marcus's state of mind, given the liquidation of his mentor Severus and the danger in which his sister and brother-in-law stood, can be imagined. Yet we have even better evidence for his mental world at this time, for he tells us that on the night after his adoption he dreamed he had ivory shoulders. According to Artemidorus, to dream of ivory was an auspicious sign denoting eloquence in the dreamer.[68] Yet some modern observers have suggested, more cogently, that the dream reinforced Marcus's own stated feelings that he was entering a world of madness, evil and illusion; simply put, Marcus was suffering an identity crisis arising from the chasm between the studious, ivory-tower world he had hitherto inhabited and the brutal public world of the Roman empire that he was now forced to enter.[69]

Hadrian's last public act was to appoint next year's magistrates. He designated Antoninus as consul for the second time and overrode the law that prohibited anyone from becoming quaestor before the age of twenty-four by insisting that the Senate confirm the seventeen-year-old Marcus in that position for the year 139.[70] But his illness and ravings grew worse, exacerbated by his abandoning the diet his doctors had put him on. Feeling that the end was near, he ate and drank as the fancy took him, and finally left Rome for Baiae on the Campanian coast. It was not long before Antoninus was summoned to this death-bed. Self-deluding to the end, Hadrian composed a maudlin poem:

> Little soul, wandering and pale,
> Guest and companion of my body,
> Now go off to places, pale, stiff and barren
> Nor will you make jokes, as was your wont.[71]

On this two comments are in order. Roman emperors had a bad habit of leaving somewhat tacky final messages. According to legend, Nero said, 'What an artist dies here', while Vespasian remarked donnishly that he seemed to be turning into a god. And the reference to making jokes is a bit steep from Hadrian, a man totally devoid of real humour (laughing with others) as opposed to lacerating wit (laughing at others). Another quoted last remark was 'Many doctors have killed a king.'

Hadrian died with Antoninus at his side on 10 July 138, aged sixty-two. The *Historia Augusta* records that he expired 'hated by all', by which of course it meant 'all the Senate' – hardly surprisingly, in light of the way he had culled their number both at the beginning and end of his reign.[72] The one encouraging thing about Hadrian's death was that it showed Antoninus and his heir, the young Marcus Aurelius, collaborating smoothly, raising hopes that the bad old days might be at an end. Antoninus arranged for Hadrian's funeral and his interment in the imperial vault at Castel Sant'Angelo. While he was away at Baiae and doing all this, Marcus, as quaestor-designate, presented a gladiatorial spectacle from his own funds, as a private citizen.[73]

Hadrian was long-lived by the standards of the day, and Antoninus, at fifty-one, should have had at most a decade to live. Marcus, then, could reasonably expect to be emperor by the age of thirty. In the light of that, it is disconcerting to find what (at first glance), looks like a total lack of gratitude on his part towards the departed prince. It has been noted by many that, in a long list in Book One of the *Meditations*, of all the people to whom Marcus Aurelius owes a debt of gratitude, Hadrian is conspicuously absent.[74] The liquidation of Severus and the nightmare period that Marcus spent in Hadrian's resi-dence in 138 may have something to do with this, but there were deeper reasons. His long pen-portrait of Antoninus, his adoptive father, clearly implies criticism of Hadrian, for Antoninus was his predecessor's polar opposite in almost every way. Antoninus, Marcus recalls, put an end to the cult of sex with young boys – an obvious hit at the lover of Antinous and a string of others. Hadrian never found defenders for this aspect of his life, and was explicitly censured for it by another intellectual emperor, Julian the Apostate, who felt (with Marcus and Antoninus) that sexual licence of such a blatant kind actually endangered the security of the state.[75] Although Marcus and Hadrian are often bracketed as examples of cerebral princes, they had little in common in their mental predilections. Hadrian was obsessed with all things Greek, but the revival of Hellenistic culture known as the Second Sophistic did not draw Marcus, as it had drawn the older emperor. When he calls Antoninus 'no sophist', this is most easily construed as an indirect criticism of Hadrian, a notorious supporter of Sophists – indeed, Julian the Apostate expressly dubbed him 'the Sophist'.[76] The idea of Marcus as a philhellene is suspect: he wrote in Greek mainly to steep himself in the idiom of Epictetus, and it is significant that the philosophy of Epictetus was the one taste he did share with Hadrian. Beyond that, he thought that the project of trying to re-create the world of Periclean Athens – Hadrian's apparent objective – was self-evidently absurd.[77]

Hadrian often boasted about his peace policy: 'I have achieved more by peace than others by war' was his proud boast. Fanaticism about his pacific approach, both for and against, probably underpinned at least some of his murders of the senatorial class.[78] Marcus's teacher of rhetoric, Cornelius Fronto, was remarkably bitter towards Hadrian, partly because he had been in danger during the unpredictable last two years of his reign, and partly because Hadrian was someone who neglected the interests of the empire in favour of globe-trotting. Instead of providing leadership and discipline and addressing the deep problems of empire, Fronto thought, Hadrian spent his time building monuments and sucking up to his soldiers. As for the famous peace policy, what about the fact that Hadrian lost far more men in the Bar-Kochba revolt – itself the result of his ineptitude – than all the 'warlike' emperors had in their campaigns?[79] Fronto thought Hadrian a great one at empty speechifying, haranguing soldiers with banalities and clichés even though his real enthusiasm for the military was skin-deep;

his real motive was fear of the army. What was one to make of a man, Fronto said tauntingly, who abandoned all Trajan's hard-won gains and then allowed his troops to grow stale through lack of real combat while he insisted they perform technical manoeuvres; why train men with wicker weapons when he could have got them to fight with a real sword and shield? Marcus was never one for allowing Fronto to get away with what he considered his wilder statements, but it is significant that he allowed all these animadversions to pass without a word of demur.[80]

As for the travels, Marcus praised Antoninus particularly for staying in Rome and running the empire from the centre; once again the implicit criticism of Hadrian is obvious. He also spoke of Antoninus's frugality – in obvious contrast to Hadrian's lavish building programmes and general prodigality – and of his respect for Roman traditions, again in contrast to Hadrian's over-hasty innovations. Yet beyond all this, it is legitimate to infer in Marcus a visceral dislike of Hadrian and all his works. Hadrian had himself portrayed on his coins with grandiose titles: Clement, Indulgent, Just, Tranquil, Patient in Illness. Marcus made it clear that he despised such boastful imperial titles; the epithets he aspired to were those denoting a philosopher or a good man. And he loathed Hadrian for using murder and terror as an instrument of policy; Hadrian, it was clear, was a man who had no proper idea of friendship and knew neither its value nor its limits.[81] It was for the precocious quaestor, now emerging from the dark days of Hadrian, to show by example that, though still a young man, he already knew better.

3

When Antoninus became emperor, with Marcus as his deputy, one of his first tasks was to complete the young's man 'formation' in traditional learning. The transitional figures in Marcus's education appear to have been the two Alexanders. Alexander the Platonist, a native of Seleucia, seems to have taught the elements of rhetoric and philosophy, and Marcus always liked him immensely at the personal level; when he was emperor, Marcus made Alexander his secretary for Greek correspondence – a controversial appointment, as will be seen later. Alexander taught him conscientiousness and duty, that it was not good enough to say that one was too busy to reply to correspondence or to claim 'urgent business' to get out of unpleasant chores.[1] Marcus was not so fond personally of Alexander of Cotiaeum, the grammarian, also the tutor of Lucius Verus, possibly because he suspected him of moral unsoundness. In contrast to other grammarians like Apollonius Dyscolus, who lived in learned poverty and austere obscurity (mainly in Alexandria), Alexander of Cotiaeum was a devotee of the high life, who liked the luxury of palace living, was money-minded and charged high fees. Marcus forgave him, partly because, as already mentioned, he learned from Alexander how to reprimand people without angering or alienating them, instead making them aware of their faults indirectly; and partly because Alexander was generous to his friends and to his native city and benefited the Greek world in general by his eminence.[2] Other figures from the intermediate stage of Marcus's education were Caninius Celer, who taught Greek and elementary rhetoric and was the author of a romance entitled *Araspes the Lover*; and Aninius Macer, of whom nothing is known.[3]

Marcus also attended lectures on law by Lucius Volusius Maecianus. It may have been at these lectures that he met the young men he later mentioned as his favourite fellow-students: Seius Fuscianus and Aufidius Victorinus from the senatorial order, and Baetius Longus and Calenus from the equestrian; to the latter two Marcus was generous with money, as lack of funds often destroyed a promising career for those less well-off, like the knights.[4] Around the beginning of the reign of Antoninus, Marcus was also a regular attender at the lectures of Sextus of Chaeronea, nephew of the famous biographer Plutarch. Sextus was a professional teacher of philosophy who made a deep impression on the young man. He taught Marcus a variety of useful lessons: what it meant to be a true father; how to live according to Nature; how to achieve gravitas without pomposity; how to use logic to investigate and analyse the world; how to avoid anger and other negative emotions and to be free of passion while full of love; how to praise without bombast and to display expertise without being pretentious. Above all Marcus imbibed human lessons from Sextus: how to get on in company and so act that everyone wanted to be your friend and was pleased and honoured by your presence; part of this involved developing intuitive sympathy for friends, and tolerance for all amateurs, sloppy thinkers, barrack-room lawyers and saloon-bar philosophers.[5] Another influence was Cinna Catulus, a Stoic philosopher, from whom he learned the following: 'Not to shrug off a friend's resentment – even if it is unjustified – but to try to put things right. To show your teachers ungrudging respect and your children unfeigned love.'[6]

Of all the Greeks who were brought in to tutor him, Marcus seems to have valued Apollonius of Chalcedon most. He probably first met him in 136 and attended some of the classes he gave in Rome, but then Apollonius returned to his native city. When Antoninus became emperor and Marcus mentioned the Greek's qualities, the emperor sent for him to return to Rome and be the young man's personal tutor. An arrogant prima donna, Apollonius was said by his critics to have come to Rome as if he were Jason in search of the Golden Fleece – a reference to the high fees he charged, which raised imperial eyebrows. Told to report to the palace for his duties, Apollonius replied that it was not right for the master to go to the pupil; the pupil should rather seek out the master and sit at his feet. Such impudence might not have gone down so well with Hadrian, but Antoninus laughed it off: 'It seems it was easier for Apollonius to come from Colchis to Rome than from his lodgings in Rome to the Palatine,' he remarked waspishly.[7] Marcus ignored Apollonius's massive self-regard and instead focused on the wisdom he imparted, later remarking that he was one of three people whom he especially thanked the gods for having known. Apollonius taught that nothing mattered except the purity of Stoic doctrine, and that a man should be the same in all circumstances, indifferent both to worldly success and to pain, illness or the loss of a child. From him Marcus learned that the truly generous man knew how to receive as well as give, and came to realise that you could accept favours from friends without losing self-respect or appearing ungrateful.[8] Cynics (in the modern sense) said that the virtue of receiving was a very convenient doctrine for one so interested in receiving largesse, and that Apollonius rationalised his greed by asserting that his teaching was far more valuable than any 'mere' material object he received from grateful students.

Antoninus took a very liberal attitude to the education of his heir apparent, but never had the tolerance for Greek philosophers and (especially) sophists that Marcus had – or, in the latter case, taught himself to have. Antoninus thought that a training in rhetoric was the most important aspect of an aristocrat's education, and that the teachers of an emperor-in-waiting should be not just masters of their disciplines but also well versed in politics and the problems of running the state. That is why he made sure that five men of consular rank or close to their consulships were also appointed as Marcus's tutors (Claudius Severus, Claudius Maximus, Cornelius Fronto, Herodes Atticus and Junius Rusticus). The first of these, Claudius Severus Arabianus, consul in 146, was an Aristotelian philosopher who instructed Marcus in the entire philosophical tradition of resistance to tyranny. A devotee of republican virtue and ancient Roman liberties, Severus's main theme was the importance of reconciling imperial authority with liberty. There is a minority view that he was as important a rhetorician as Aelius Aristides (of whom more later) and as libertarian a thinker as the Christian apologist Athenagoras (ditto).[9] Only about nine years older than Marcus, he was from the city of

Pompeiopolis in Asia Minor, and the title Arabianus referred to his birth in Trajan's new province of Arabia, where his father had been the first governor. He was another of Marcus's special favourites (though not in the top three), and his son would later marry one of Marcus's daughters. From him Marcus learned about the famous heroes of republican Rome who gave everything for liberty – Thrasea, Helvidius, Cato, Dion, Brutus. Severus believed in freedom of speech, equality before the law and enlightened rulers. He preached the love of family, truth and justice, the value of helping others, the joys of sharing and the merits of optimism. He advised Marcus always to be straightforward with people and to let them know exactly where they stood, never dissembling or harbouring long-term grudges as Hadrian used to do. A friend should always be quite clear what your attitude was on any subject, there should be no prevarication, and if people offended you or merited your disapproval, you should be utterly frank with them.[10]

An even greater influence on Marcus (and ranked by him as the second most important person for whose acquaintanceship he had to thank the gods) was Claudius Maximus. About twenty years older than Marcus, Maximus was consul in 144 and went on to a distinguished career in imperial administration, being governor or proconsul of Upper Pannonia and Africa in the 150s. He is probably best known for being the presiding judge at the trial of Apuleius, author of *The Golden Ass*, who flattered him shamelessly in the process of getting a favourable verdict.[11] Another Stoic, Maximus inculcated the following lessons: you must master your self, keep your personality in balance and combine dignity and grace; you should be cheerful in all circumstances, particularly when ill, and do your job without whining; you should be generous, charitable, honest, sincere and forgiving. Marcus said that by common consent Maximus was a man who always spoke without malice, but who said exactly what he thought. He was imperturbable and unshockable, was never apprehensive and never taken aback; he was never rash, hesitant, bewildered or at a loss, never hung back from a task, was never downcast or fawningly hypocritical, never obsequious, but not aggressive or paranoid either. Unlike the men who could not lie straight in bed, Maximus seemed a man of natural probity and integrity – there was nothing forced or bogus about his rectitude – and he gave the sense of staying on the straight and narrow by his own choice rather than keeping on it by external duress. Nobody could ever patronise him, but, by the same token, no one would ever feel patronised by him. Like so many others of Marcus's mentors, he also preached affability and geniality in social life.[12]

It would be invaluable to know more about all these men and their influences on young Marcus, but the historian and biographer is at the mercy of his sources and, unlike the historical novelist, cannot simply make things up. It is all the more regrettable, then, that the largest cache of primary material that has come down to us concerns Marcus's relations with his teacher of rhetoric, Cornelius Fronto, a man he did not hold in particularly high regard. The greatest rhetorician and advocate of his age, Fronto was at one time thought of as a second Cicero. Born in Cirta, North Africa and probably from the equestrian class, he migrated to Rome at an early age and made his name as a lawyer; perhaps the African background was significant, for Juvenal the satirist claimed that that province was the nursery of advocates.[13] By the time he taught Marcus, Fronto was a rich man with three estates, one on the Esquiline Hill, a country villa on the Via Aurelia and a seaside home on the Bay of Naples. The opinion of posterity is that he was both fatuous and pedantic, and the verdict certainly receives support from his extant letters. A fusspot and extreme hypochondriac, Fronto was the leader of an antiquarian movement encouraged by Hadrian, which took its inspiration from the writers of the pre-Augustan period. Over-addicted to far-fetched similes and metaphors, Fronto was a philistine who thought poetry pointless; for him its only use was as a storehouse to be ransacked for archaisms that could be introduced into oratory. Fronto's notion of rhetoric was that of creating a narrative landscape full of clichés, leading the listener along the proper path to a pre-ordained conclusion. Stereotypes of thought and explanation and lack of analysis were masked by the use of novel and unfamiliar words, and Fronto's speeches induced the same sort of irritation that a modern reader feels when confronted by the trite formulae of Cicero. Truth was always the last consideration in Roman oratory: the object was to manipulate a familiar arsenal of cosmological and psychological explanations to take the listener with you to a predestined end.[14]

Something of the flavour of Fronto can be conveyed by the first letter he wrote to Marcus in 139, shortly after being appointed tutor

in rhetoric. The main theme of the epistle is the thought far better
summed up in later years by Alexander Pope:

> A little learning is a dangerous thing,
> Drink deep, or taste not the Pierian spring.

The implicit rebuke to his charge arises because (we may infer) Marcus
thought that his teacher's excessive concentration on word order and
exact phraseology was pedantic (as indeed it was). Fronto then set out
his stall by saying what he thought was wrong with his great predecessor, Cicero: in short, it was because he took insufficient care to
find the *mot juste*.[15] Cicero (like Simenon in the twentieth century)
worked from a restricted palette of words, but Fronto (like the
Victorian explorer and polymath Sir Richard Burton) believed in
seeking out unusual words and then using them to prevent their
obsolescence. His attitude was that famously attributed to Flaubert:
spend the morning putting a comma in, and then the afternoon taking
it out. Marcus could not understand all the fuss about altering a single
syllable, but Fronto hit back by accusing his student of imprecision
and (worse) pleonasm.[16] Yet Fronto soon had to acknowledge Marcus's
brilliance: he remarked that his invented maxims (one of the rhetorical exercises that masters regularly set their pupils) were as good as
anything in the great Roman writer Sallust: 'Whatever you venture
on, such are your abilities, you will be successful.'[17] As it develops, the
correspondence makes it clear that Marcus was far more intelligent
than Fronto and knew how to handle him. He often used Fronto's
rebukes to make an unrelated point of his own, as all good politicians
do. Replying to the first extant letter, he claimed that scolding gave
him greater pleasure than praise; he valued Fronto's commitment to
the truth and valued those who were not mealy-mouthed, but said
straight out what was right and what was wrong. Having paid a
graceful compliment, Marcus then launched into the hobby-horse that
really interested him: the equivocation and ambiguity of oracles.[18]

The Roman elite thought that rhetoric was the most important part
of an aristocrat's education, and in Fronto's training of Marcus we can
see many of the themes common to the general training of Roman
orators. The most straightforward part was the descriptions of battles,
storms and scenes in Nature that pupils were made to write. Then came

exercises in so-called balance: a typical example would be a point-by-point comparison of the characters of Ajax and Odysseus as they disputed over the armour of the dead Achilles – one of the most famous incidents in classical mythology. Other exercises were what we might call counterfactual. What sort of speech would Homer's heroes have made in contexts where they are not reported as having made any? The student had to imagine what Ajax would have said when he lost the arms of Achilles to Odysseus, or what Achilles would have said when the high king Agamemnon deprived him of the slave girl Briseis. Then there were the eccentric exercises in praising the inert or disgusting aspects of Nature: a paean to dust, laziness or snakes were typical examples; the comic writer Lucian famously wrote an encomium on a fly.[19] Since the orator Quintilian had famously eulogised sleep, Fronto set Marcus to compose an oration dispraising it. Fronto insisted that all these essays be composed in Latin. Even though all Roman intellectuals were supposed to be bilingual, and oligarchic children were put to Greek composition even before writing in their own language, Fronto distrusted Greek as the language of philosophy; for the first three centuries of the Christian era no philosopher wrote exclusively in Latin.[20] He therefore 'leaned on' Marcus whenever the younger man wrote in Greek, but the quicker-witted Marcus was able to catch the master out in instances where Fronto himself had written in the older language.[21] Fronto believed that even demotic Latin was better than Greek, and he was not alone in this prejudice: Juvenal the satirist famously tore into Roman women who thought it clever to converse in Greek.[22]

Much of the correspondence of Fronto to Marcus shows the teacher only too aware of his charge's eminence. The letters have been compared to those of Pliny the Younger to Trajan, but Fronto's were even more wheedling and sycophantic. Typical is this: 'You were formed by Nature, before you were fitted by training, for the exercise of all the virtues. For before you were old enough to be trained, you were already perfect and complete in all noble accomplishments, before adolescence a good man, before manhood a practical speaker. But of all your virtues, this even more than the others is worthy of admiration, that you unite all your friends in harmony.'[23] Marcus, for his part, claimed more affection for his teacher than he obviously felt. An early letter reads as follows:

Go on, threaten as much as you like and attack me with loads of arguments, yet you shall never drive me, your lover, I mean me, away. Nor shall I any the less assert that I love Fronto or love him the less because you prove with reasons so various and so vehement that those who are less in love must be more helped and indulged . . . This I can without any rashness affirm: if that Phaedrus of yours ever really existed, if he was ever away from Socrates, Socrates never felt for Phaedrus a more passionate longing than I for the sight of you all these days.[24]

There is no record of any reply to this, but four years later we find Fronto writing archly that his wife has said (albeit teasingly) that she envies Fronto for being so loved by Marcus. He continued in the same vein: he was lucky to have Marcus's affection, as Fortuna was a goddess while reason was man-made: in other words, there was no rational motive for Marcus's affection, so it must be a gift from the goddess Fortuna. 'Let men doubt, discuss, dispute, guess, puzzle over the origin of our love as over the fountains of the Nile.'[25]

There is much more in the same vein in the correspondence. 'Like all your friends,' writes Fronto, 'I take in deep draughts of love for you.' Marcus is even more euphuistic: 'Your letter had the effect of making me feel how much you loved me . . . beyond question you have conquered in loving all lovers that have ever lived . . . So passionately, by heaven, am I in love for you . . . I will love you while I have life and health . . . I will love you more than anyone else loves you, more in fact than you love yourself . . . I can never love you enough' – these are just some of the expressions of affection in the correspondence.[26] These high-flown sentiments have seduced the unwary into thinking that what is being described here is carnal, homosexual love.[27] But this is to misunderstand an idiom of the Roman world of the second century, a conceit, admittedly tiresome to modern ears. To buttoned-up modern sensibilities, it seems inconceivable that two men could express love without sexuality, but the Romans were in this sense more liberated. Marcus and Fronto used the word 'love' in a ludic way, and both knew what the other was doing and what it meant; it was a kind of elaborate charade or game, in its way part of the very rhetorical hyperbole that Fronto was supposed to be teaching his pupil.[28] To labour the issue would seem to protest against wrongful interpretations too much and to give them too much credit. Three points are salient. All Marcus's pronouncements were hostile to homosexuality and he praised the emperor Antoninus for clamping down on the practice.[29] Even the easygoing Romans regarded same-sex intercourse with a man aged more than eighteen as a serious offence – which was one of the reasons Hadrian caused such outrage – and the dutiful Marcus Aurelius lacked the rebellious or 'deviant' personality needed to defy this code.[30] Finally, despite all the verbal conceits, Marcus simply did not rate Fronto that highly and does not include him in the 'top three' he thanks the gods for having known – inconceivable if he had actually been his physical lover. All Marcus has to say about Fronto in his *Meditations* is that his tutor taught him to recognise the malice, cunning and hypocrisy that power produces and the peculiar ruthlessness and lack of affection evinced by the Roman aristocracy; by implication he does not even consider that his tuition in rhetoric was outstanding.[31] No true physical lover could ever be so offhand and dismissive, for even if the 'affair' had turned sour, we would expect to discern some bitterness or bile.

It is the banality of the Fronto–Marcus correspondence that most impresses, not its passion. Much of it is technical advice on similes, metaphors, tropes and other rhetorical devices – a kind of early attempt to teach creative writing. Like all true hypochondriacs, Fronto spends a lot of time moaning about his ailments and is simply overjoyed if his pupil has anything wrong with him and so can be inducted into the magic circle of valetudinarians. Fronto complains of a bad knee, an injured arm, insomnia and other mystery ailments, and Marcus comforts him with verbal bromides, telling him that he would rather see him well again than master all the Catos, Ciceros and Sallusts there ever were.[32] Sometimes we can detect a certain weariness in Marcus at having to deal with the constant illnesses and complaints thereof. Sending him birthday greetings some time in the period 140–3, Marcus makes a fourfold appeal to the gods on behalf of his teacher. He wishes that Aesculapius, the god of healing, will bring him good health; that Minerva will ensure that all his wisdom comes from Fronto; that the tutelary deities will watch over him; and that, as he journeys to Rome, the god of travel will ensure that his tutor is with him in spirit.[33] Meanwhile Fronto continues as didactic and tiresome as ever. 'Unless speech is graced by the dignity of language, it becomes downright impudent and indecent. In sum, you too, when you have had to speak in the Senate or harangue people, have never used a far-fetched word, never an unintelligible or unusual figure, knowing that a Caesar's eloquence should be like the clarion and not like the clarionet, in which there is less resonance and more difficulty.'[34] Only occasionally are Fronto's thoughts more interesting, as when he suddenly announces that the so-called Golden Age in history was really a time of laziness and lotus-eating. He muses that even good-looking women can never really trust their physical beauty and feel the need for make-up to enhance their charms. And he announces that small is beautiful: lions are not as diligent in tracking down their prey as ants, and spiders weave their webs more meticulously than Penelope (Odysseus's wife) wove hers.[35]

The complacent tenor of the Fronto–Marcus relationship was broken up in the year 140 when Antoninus decided to employ yet another teacher of rhetoric for his heir apparent. This was none other than Herodes Atticus, well known already to the young man from his early friendship with Marcus's mother. Born in Marathon, Attica (famously twenty-six miles from Athens), into a fabulously wealthy family (his grandfather was worth 100 million sesterces), Herodes made a name for himself as an orator and also acquired administrative experience under Hadrian, who appointed him prefect in charge of the free cities of Asia Minor in 125. Since his father had been consul under Trajan, he had an effortless entrée into elite circles, but he was tactless and insensitive, making many enemies throughout his career.[36] Antoninus fell foul of him when he was proconsul of Asia under Hadrian. One particular incident, described later on page 78, is said to have led to Antoninus's ire. Even Herodes's biographer Philostratus, who was always prepared to give his hero the benefit of the doubt, tacitly admitted that Herodes was in the wrong.[37] Since Antoninus later became emperor, Herodes could have considered himself lucky that it was not his brooding, vengeful predecessor he had insulted. He then retired to Athens and was elected chief magistrate or archon, but alienated many by his high-handed methods, patronising attitude and intolerance of criticism. Although generous in funding the building of great public edifices and monuments, Herodes was not one to do good by stealth. As an orator, he was considered the most naturally talented of all, a man whose speciality was understatement, subtlety and irony. He found learning easy, but could not resist showing off his talents by studying while drinking and by making a virtue of doing with very little sleep.[38] Marcus always found the prima donna-ish antics of the arrogant Herodes a trial, especially later when he was emperor, and as a teacher either found him deficient or decided that he could learn nothing from him; this is the explanation for the total absence of any mention of Herodes in the *Meditations*, when he thanks the gods for his teachers.

However, Herodes was by no means negligible, even if Marcus did not care for him. A dislike of philosophy did not prevent Herodes from using the works of Epictetus to put a bumptious, self-regarding young philosophy student in his place by citing a telling passage of Stoicism that decisively refuted the would-be genius's stance.[39] In general, though, Herodes despised Stoicism and its doctrine that emotions should he held in check, and declared that such an attitude was like that of benighted and ignorant barbarians who, learning that pruning was a good thing, proceeded to chop down all their vines and olives; or, as we might say, threw out the baby with the bath water. 'These disciplines of devotees of the unemotional,' he said, 'who want to be considered calm, brave and steadfast because they experience neither desire nor grief, neither anger nor pleasure, are people who strangle the vitality of the spirit and gradually live out their days in a torpor of bloodless, enervated negativity.'[40] It may have been such sentiments as these that earned him Marcus's displeasure. But it is hard not to sympathise with Herodes's contempt for idlers and drones who affected a 'philosophic' stance while demanding handouts. Like modern hippies who claimed to be 'artists', many lazy Romans turned to panhandling while dressed in the traditional philosopher's cloak, bearded and with hair hanging down to their waist. On one occasion such a man stopped Herodes in the street and asked for money. When Herodes asked him what he did for a living, the hirsute man answered that he was a philosopher; 'Isn't that obvious?' he added aggressively, as if talking to an idiot. 'I can see a man and a beard,' Herodes replied, 'but I don't see a philosopher.' One of Herodes's entourage then came up and recognised the man as a well-known tramp with an ugly reputation, one of those beggars who demands money as of right. After delivering a pithy lecture on the deplorable practice of layabouts posing as philosophers, Herodes was munificent enough to give the man sufficient money for thirty days' subsistence.[41]

Although there are not that many overt references to Herodes in the Fronto–Marcus correspondence, it is clear that Fronto found the presence of a rival unsettling; from 140 onwards there is far less explicit didacticism in the letters from master to pupil and more anxiety to please. Marcus's divided loyalties soon found expression in a strange letter to Fronto, where he asked him to back-pedal on a case involving Herodes: 'I know that you have often said to me, "What can I do that will please you most?" Now is the time. If my love for you *can* be increased, you can increase it now . . . It is a favour I am asking you and, if you grant it, I promise to put myself in your debt in return.'[42] It seems that Herodes Atticus was to appear in court, and Fronto had been retained for the other side. Much about the trial Marcus refers to is obscure; we do not even know its eventual result. Either Herodes was being accused by the Athenians, who seemed to do this periodically as they got tired of his high-handedness, and Fronto was the prosecutor; or, as seems marginally more likely, this is the case that Fronto's speech *De Demostrativo* refers to, in which case Herodes was the prosecutor and Fronto the defending counsel. It is known that the Athenians were especially angry with Herodes, as they claimed he had defrauded them of a bequest to the city of Athens from his father Atticus, but this was probably the substantive issue in a much later trial.[43] Whichever of these scenarios we opt for – and scholars disagree vehemently – it was clearly going to be necessary for Fronto to pitch into Herodes and discredit him. Marcus was essentially asking Fronto to pull his punches, as he did not want his two tutors falling out in public. He acknowledged that Fronto's position was difficult. 'But you will say, "What! If I am attacked may I not repay him in like coin?" But you will win yourself greater praise if you do not reply when attacked. Still, if he is the first to attack, it will be pardonable for you to answer as best you can. But I have asked him not to start a slanging match and I think I have persuaded him. For I love both of you, each for his own merits. I remember that he was brought up in the house of my grandfather Publius Calvisius, and that I have been educated with you.'[44]

Fronto's diplomatic powers were stretched to the limit in replying to this difficult request. He claimed (disingenuously?) not to know that Herodes Atticus was one of Marcus's friends and that he had somehow blundered into the position where he was on the opposing side in a lawsuit.

> I agree that I ought not to say anything harmful about Herodes that does not bear on the case itself. But how am I supposed to deal with the facts of the case, which are grim and sordid? This is where I need your advice. Don't forget we're dealing with a case involving men grievously beaten up and robbed, and one even killed, to say nothing of Herodes's unfilial attitude to his father. Cruelty and avarice must always be denounced, and additionally in this trial a murderer has to be identified. If you think I ought to press hard on these charges, please advise me. If not, and you think I ought to throttle back on Herodes himself, I shall take your advice on what you think is the best thing to do. At least you may be assured that I won't say anything about his character or the other episodes in his life unless they are directly relevant to this case.

Fronto warned Marcus that he might have to use the kind of supercharged language that all lawyers have to employ to win cases. 'If I happen to call him an uneducated little Greek, it will not mean war to the death. Farewell, my Caesar, and see that you love me to the utmost. I even love your handwriting – so when you write to me I would be glad if you would do so in your own hand.'[45] This last was something of a Parthian shot. Fronto made it clear that he knew Marcus was annoyed with him and for this reason had got a secretary to write the letter, instead of inditing it in his own hand, his usual practice. He was also hinting that he thought this ploy somewhat unworthy of his friend.

Perhaps thinking he had overplayed his hand, Fronto sent another after it, saying that he had seen some of the witness statements and depositions and the trial was going to be unavoidably rough on Herodes. Marcus obviously thought he had made and gained his point, for his reply was emollient.

I must thank you, dearest Fronto, for not just taking my advice seriously but actually agreeing with it. As to what you say in your most affable letter, my opinion is this. Everything relevant to the case obviously must be mentioned but, as far as your own private feelings are concerned, however much you are provoked and however justified you feel, it's best to let them go unsaid . . . Herodes loves you, and I am doing my best in that quarter, and assuredly he who does not love you neither sees with his eyes nor understands with his heart.[46]

For such a young man, Marcus was, from his own point of view, exhibiting statesmanship and getting the notorious prima donnas in his inner circle to collaborate. His attitude was that of Edward the Fourth in Shakespeare's *King Richard the Third*:

> Hastings and Rivers, take each other's hand
> Dissemble not your hatred, swear your love . . .
>
> Madam, yourself is not exempt from this;
> Nor you, son Dorset; Buckingham, nor you,
> You have been factious one against the other.
> Wife, love Lord Hastings, let him kiss your hand;
> And what you do, do it unfeignedly.[47]

But Fronto was secretly annoyed that Marcus wanted to protect Herodes from the consequences of his own delinquency. He capitulated unwillingly, allowing his concern for Marcus's continuing favour to override his interest in abstract justice; to put it in modern parlance, he had been 'leaned on'. It did not help that Marcus later piled on the misery by insisting that Fronto write to Herodes to commiserate with the 'uneducated little Greek' for the loss of his son.[48] But whenever there was dissension among his friends, Marcus tended to blame Fronto – an attitude inconceivable if they had really been, as some eccentric modern critics allege, sexual lovers.

After the excitement over the Herodes Atticus affair, Marcus and Fronto resumed a more normal teacher–pupil relationship. We cannot follow all the stages in the higher education of the heir apparent, but the veils lift again in the year 143, when Fronto became suffect consul (a kind of deputy who replaced consuls who died or resigned in office), which meant that he remained in Rome during the summer while Marcus spent time at the seaside resort of Baiae on the Campanian coast – a favourite retreat for emperors and imperial families.[49] For Fronto to have been given even this modified form of consular office was a great honour, which he owed almost entirely to the favour of Marcus Aurelius. He conceded the point himself in a letter to Marcus in this year, when he played devil's advocate: 'What benefit has your Fronto conferred on you that you have so much affection for him? Has he given his life to you or your parents? Has he undergone dangers in your place? Has he successfully administered some province? Has he commanded an army? None of these things?'[50] One of the reasons Marcus gave his tutor the position was to balance his status with that of Herodes, who was ordinary consul in 143, having just made a dynastic marriage to an aristocratic Roman lady named Annia Regilla. As the son of a man who had been consul (Atticus), Herodes was doing no more than occupy a post that was clearly his in the normal course of a senatorial career (*cursus honorum*), but Fronto was an equestrian, and even Marcus dared not defy class-bound convention by making such a man an ordinary consul; the position of suffect consul, which Fronto held in July–August 143, was the best consolation prize he could find for him.[51] Fronto used his time alone in Rome to cosy up to Marcus's mother Domitia Lucilla. He sent his wife Gratia to celebrate Domitia Lucilla's birthday, utilising some heavy-handed humour in a letter to Marcus to the effect that Gratia would cost his mother nothing, as she had a birdlike appetite.[52] Fronto obviously enjoyed being suffect consul and able to address the Senate, but, in yet another of those tiresome conceits that he and Marcus used, claimed to be bored by it. His flattery of Domitia Lucilla was downright shameless. After lauding her as the acme of womanhood, he went on to contrast her with the normal run of women, who tended to be insincere and mask their true feelings with laughter: 'This goddess, true woman that she is, who gets most worship from women, is Deceit, offspring, truly, of Aphrodite and a meld of many and various traits of womankind.'[53]

From Baiae, and later Naples, Marcus continued dutifully to send his rhetorical exercises back to the master. He was now concentrating on the so-called 'epideictic' or 'show oratory' – encomiastic, panegyric, eulogistic and denunciatory, in which the usual subjects were episodes from Greek and Roman history or praise and censure of characters in Homer.[54] Set the task of refuting Quintilian's famous oration in praise of sleep by composing one entitled 'Of Wakefulness', Marcus sent Fronto an essay predictably cherry-picking certain passages from the *Odyssey* and making the risible argument that Odysseus would not have spent twenty years roaming around the Mediterranean except that he kept falling asleep at critical moments, as when his sailors released the caged winds of Aeolus. There followed the usual tiresome examples from elsewhere in Homer, from Ennius and from Hesiod (truly the Romans liked to cite a precedent for everything they did or thought), with Marcus almost visibly yawning and admitting that even he did not find his arguments convincing and that he would always prefer to sleep than to be awake. 'Now, after soundly abusing sleep, I am off to slumber, for I have spun all this out for you in the evening. I hope sleep will not pay me out.'[55] Needless to say, any attempt at humour was wasted on Fronto, who sent back a pedantic, nitpicking screed of practical criticism. Curiously, though lacking humour himself, Fronto knew only too well that it was the most effective weapon in propaganda and persuasion, pointing out that anger, spleen and invective were rarely as effective as irony, as Socrates, the great master of this technique, demonstrated. 'For the race of mankind is by nature stiffnecked against the high-handed but responds readily to coaxing.'[56] Here Fronto was on the verge of the important insight, doubtless commonplace to us, that the greatest humourists are deep down usually angry men, who know that human nature ignores tirades, but is responsive to laughter.

The extant correspondence for the year 143 alternates Fronto's po-faced hints and tips for oratorical success with a degree of mutual back-scratching that the modern reader is bound to find arch, insinuating and even maudlin. Fronto warns his pupil to be careful never to alienate the all-important masses when making a speech. Echoing the deep fear of the Roman mob entertained by the elite, he reveals himself as the disenchanted patrician by reflecting gloomily that the people always get what they want; an emperor even has to release felons or criminals if the crowd clamours for it.[57] He claims to have spent a sleepless night worrying about whether his partiality for Marcus has blinded him to defects that a detached observer could clearly see, only to conclude that, no, he is on the right track. There is continuing

praise for Marcus's great eloquence, far beyond anything norm
expected in a man of his age, but a warning that verse is better than
prose as an aid to writing speeches and some advice not to waste time
reading Ennius, who has nothing to teach orators.[58] Marcus replied to
all this by saying that he could see through his teacher; that Fronto,
unable to win credit for his praise because he was so partial to him,
has decided to make it more credible by throwing in some abuse.
Archly he added that he was 'nervous in mind and a little depressed
lest I have said something in the Senate today such that I should not
deserve to have you as a master'.[59] There were signs that Marcus was
already confident enough to reject the parts of Fronto's teaching he
did not care for. A particular bone of contention seems to have been
the orator Marcus Antonius Polemo, then at the height of his fame
as a rhetorician. Marcus responded to Fronto's praise of him by brack-
eting Polemo and Horace as the two writers he most disliked.[60] Polemo,
famously described as conversing with emperors with condescension
and only with gods as equals, once evicted the future emperor
Antoninus from his house in Smyrna – and at midnight – saying that
he was a mere proconsul of Asia and therefore could not compare
with him.[61] Antoninus thus had the dubious distinction of having been
insulted by two Greek egomaniacs in Asia Minor, if we bear in mind
his altercation with Herodes Atticus on the road to Mount Ida.

The real value of the Fronto–Marcus correspondence, when the
pupil was on the Campanian coast and the teacher in Rome, is the
rare insight it gives us into Marcus's everyday life as a young man.
Admitting that his observations are 'banalities', Marcus nonetheless
conveys an easy sybaritism in his impressions of summer on the coast:

> The climate of Naples is decidedly pleasant, but violently variable.
> Every two minutes it gets colder or warmer or rawer. To begin with,
> midnight is warm, as at Laurentum, then, however, the cockcrow watch
> chilly, as at Lanuvium; soon the hush of night and dawn and twilight
> till sunrise cold, for all the world like Alfidus; anon the forenoon sunny,
> as at Tusculum; following that a noon as fierce as at Puteoli; but indeed
> when the sun has gone to his bath in Ocean, the temperature at last
> becomes more moderate, such as we get at Tibur; this continues the
> same during the evening and first sleep of night.[62]

A more interesting letter reveals the famous quick-tempered, 'short fuse' side of Marcus, but what is intriguing is that we cannot really discern his true attitude to the incident. As he cantered along the main highway from Laurentum to Rome[63] with his bodyguard, he met two shepherds with four dogs and a flock of sheep blocking the road. As they came within earshot, Marcus heard one of the shepherds say to the other: 'Watch out for these mounted fellows, they're a dab hand at pillaging.' Angered by this, Marcus dug his spurs into his horse and galloped straight into the middle of the flock, stampeding them in all directions. One of the shepherds was so angry at all the unnecessary work caused that he threw his crook at the offenders, and it hit Marcus's equerry. The headstrong young heir to the throne remarked drily: 'Thus he who feared to lose his sheep, lost his crook instead.'[64] Is this the typical arrogance of the young blood temporarily inconvenienced by one of the lesser breeds? Or is Marcus telling the story against himself? The tone and timbre of the letter do not permit a definite answer. However, to set this incident in context, it is worth pointing out that in the year 144, when he was twenty-three, Marcus told Fronto of the delightful afternoon he spent picking grapes. As we see from Odysseus in Homer's poem, from Cincinnatus and other examples in the ancient world, aristocrats in classical times did not consider agricultural labour beneath them; there was none of that horrible anti-manual work snobbery that so disfigured the culture of the Spanish conquistadores. On the very same grape-picking day Marcus joined the emperor Antoninus in the oil-press room of a country villa after their bath; it was an unusual venue, but they chose it so that they could listen to the badinage and banter of the local yokels, who were quite unaware that their emperor was eavesdropping.[65]

By the year 144 the relationship between Marcus and Fronto, which had begun with all those euphuistic expressions of 'love', was becoming much cooler. Perhaps by now Marcus had learned all he needed from Fronto; perhaps he had begun to tire of the older man's pedantic ways; and, probably most of all, he was by now bored with rhetoric and wanted to switch full time to philosophy. The two of them continued to send each other speeches, each one trying to claim he was more 'shameless' than the other in so doing.[66] Marcus revealed that he was a classic 'night owl', giving the following account of a typical day: 'By a satisfactory arrangement of meals I worked from

3 a.m. till 8. Then, from 8–9 paced about in slippers. Then put on boots and went hunting but did not find any wild boar, though plenty are reported hereabouts. My main exercise was climbing a steep hill. Returned home in the afternoon and read a speech by Plato on the property of Pulchra.' He then complained that he had caught a chill, whether from his nocturnal writing or walking in slippers was uncertain. He concluded: 'So I will pour oil on my head and go off to sleep, for not a drop of it do I intend to pour into my lamp today, so tired am I with riding and sneezing.'[67] After 143, Fronto had less and less to say for himself, and there is something almost pathetic in one letter from this period, which breathes a sense that the teacher is losing his hold on his pupil. First, Fronto declares that his love for Marcus means far more than the consulship of the previous year. Then he compares their relationship to that between Philoctetes and Hercules or Patroclus and Achilles, but adds, fawningly, that of course Marcus is even more illustrious than the two great mythical heroes he has mentioned.[68] There is no reciprocal gushing from Marcus. He was at that time (144) attending a course in comedy by a Roman comic writer named Geminus, but it does not seem to have done much for his sense of humour. There is something almost cruel in the way Marcus forces Fronto to write a letter of condolence to Herodes Atticus, who had just lost the first son he had with Annia Regilla and was in a state of inconsolable grief – Herodes's emotions, whatever the subject, were always larger than life.[69] Gritting his teeth, Fronto wrote to Herodes and tried to find something comforting to say: you're still young and can have more children was the best he could come up with. Again there is pathos in his words when he mentions Marcus: 'I confess and make no secret of it, that I am your rival in his love – everything else is remediable and of infinitely less importance than this.'[70]

Sensing that whatever hold on Marcus he once had was slipping away, Fronto was overjoyed if ever he could bring his student back to his favourite subject: illness, hypochondria and the swapping of symptoms. Sick with constant mysterious ailments in shoulder, elbow, knee and ankle (surely at least some of them psychosomatic), and forever suffering from insomnia, Fronto pounced in gratitude if Marcus ever mentioned an ache, pain or malady.[71] Marcus was already becoming something of a food fad (the physician Galen would have much to say about this at a later date) and boasted of gargling with honey and eating a single slice of bread for lunch, while all around him were gorging and guzzling on beans, onions and herrings full of roe.[72] He alternated between keeping strange hours through sleeplessness – he once read Cato's primer on agriculture between the hours of 5–9 a.m. – and sleeping late on the grounds that he had a heavy cold. Consciously or unconsciously (for the delight certainly shows in his letters), Fronto was overjoyed that Marcus was joining the ranks of the creaking gates and compulsive valetudinarians. At times the Fronto–Marcus correspondence bids fair to become an essay-writing contest between *malades imaginaires*; the only thing to be said in Marcus's favour is that he was always a model patient and exhibited scrupulous humility in following his doctors' prescriptions.[73] Typical is this from Marcus: 'As far as my strength is concerned, it is certainly beginning to come back. The pain in my chest, too, is quite gone; but the ulcer in the trachea is still there.'[74] Fronto may have experienced, in addition to his own ailments, 'biter bit syndrome', for by the year 145 Marcus's tales of woe sound indistinguishable from the master's: Socrates is right, says Marcus, the greatest pleasure is cessation from pain, and he then goes on to draw a typical Fronto-like analogy between the ending of pain and absence making the heart grow fonder. In so far as there was an organic explanation for Marcus's ailments, his doctors should at least have prevented him from dictating thirty letters a day, which he mentions as a fair average.[75]

The year 144 marked the moment when Marcus began to turn away from Fronto and reject many of his ideas, so perhaps a judicious summary of his real influence is in order. As a writer, Marcus never entirely jettisoned the lessons taught by Fronto, who instilled the idea of using ornate language in which to clothe philosophical thoughts: 'Every time you conceive of a paradoxical thought, turn it over within yourself, vary it with diverse figures and nuances, make trial of it and dress it in splendid words.'[76] This is why the basic Stoic philosophy of Epictetus (of which more later) becomes richly orchestrated by Marcus in his *Meditations*. It cannot be said that Fronto's views were altogether coherent, for he appears at one time to dissuade Marcus from favouring either Green or Blue horse-race factions in the arena or different types of gladiator in the amphitheatre, while at the same time cautioning him not to be stand-offish or fastidious about games and circuses in general.[77] But it seems clear that Marcus's later excessive deference for the Senate was due to Fronto's teaching; the older man always preached reverence and respect: 'You are mistaken if you think that an opinion blurted out in the Senate in the language of Thersites [the famous demagogue in the *Iliad*] would carry equal weight with a speech by Menelaus and Homer.'[78] Yet Fronto's greatest gift to Marcus was to teach him the importance of 'affectionateness' – the key to humanity and so signally lacking in the Roman upper classes. As a provincial equestrian and 'new man', Fronto deeply resented the snobbery and hardness of the old Roman aristocracy, and Marcus readily agreed with him that the old ruling class lacked compassion and tenderness.[79]

The occasion for Fronto's demotion to the second rank as a person of importance in Marcus's life was the wholehearted conversion of the heir apparent to the philosophy of Stoicism; like many converts, Marcus became more zealous and more committed to the doctrine than some of his teachers. By far the greatest influence of all his tutors was the Stoic philosopher Quintus Junius Rusticus; Marcus says that of all the boons the gods gave him, knowing Rusticus was the greatest. In the *Meditations* Marcus devotes thirteen lines to Rusticus, as against three somewhat inconsequential ones to Fronto. Rusticus, he says, made him realise that he needed to train and discipline his character, to read texts closely and not just skim to get the gist, and to abandon the pointless subject of rhetoric, as also poetry and belles-lettres.[80] There was no point, Rusticus argued, in those ludicrous treatises on abstract subjects or homilies and moralising, which he burlesqued as 'The Simple Life' or 'The Man Who Lives Only for Others'. To live the life of a philosopher was not a matter of showy austerity, wearing hair shirts, sleeping rough or wearing a philosopher's cloak, as Diognetus had taught him when he was young, but simply knowing how to live well; in theory an emperor could do that as well as a shepherd. Like most Stoics, Rusticus stressed simplicity of style, lucidity as against verbal fireworks.[81] If we contrast simplicity with ostentation, clarity with orotundity and brevity with prolixity, we can immediately grasp the chasm that separated Rusticus from Fronto. Rusticus brilliantly turned one of the key points of Fronto's teaching against him. Fronto forever dinned into Marcus the need for an emperor not to be a tyrant; but, said Rusticus, the last thing a trainee emperor needed was a training in oratory – what was the point of rhetoric under the empire when political decision-making no longer occurred as a result of great speeches in the Senate, as under the republic, but according to the will, and even the whim, of an emperor?[82]

Some scholars think the turning point in Marcus's mental formation, the moment when he broke decisively with Fronto and with rhetoric in favour of Rusticus and Stoicism, occurred sometime in 145–6 when Marcus suddenly told Fronto that he had been neglecting the study of Cicero and Plautus in favour of a new discovery called Aristo: 'Aristo's books are a joy for me and at the same time a torture. They are a joy, in that they teach me better things, but when they show me to what extent my inner dispositions are distant from these better things, then all too often your disciple blushes and is angry because, at the age of twenty-five, I have not yet assimilated into my soul any of the salutary dogmas and purest reasonings. This is why I am tormented, angry and jealous, and I no longer eat.'[83] Scholars have picked over this letter for other clues, and the issue is not helped by the fact that Aristo's writings have not survived. This has allowed wrangles to develop about what exactly Aristo's doctrines were, and even about who he was, with some opting for Aristo of Chios, a minor philosopher, and others for the lawyer and theorist of jurisprudence Titus Aristo.[84] But it is unnecessary, and surely implausible, to imagine a sudden light-on-the-road-to-Damascus conversion. The psychologist C.G. Jung cautions that such conversions are rare and actually coined the word 'enantiodromia' to describe the gradual birth of ideas long gestated in the mind; in the case of Marcus, the germination of Stoicism clearly began at the age of twelve when he came under the influence of Diognetus, but it needed the personality of Rusticus to effect the final breakthrough. Marcus tells us that the single key event was that Rusticus introduced him to the works of the Stoic philosopher Epictetus, whom he always preferred to Seneca as a guide to Stoicism, even though Seneca enjoyed by far the greater fame.[85]

There is no doubt that Fronto suffered grievously over the defection of his star pupil, especially as Rusticus delighted in putting the great rhetorician's nose out of joint. It did not take much guessing whom Rusticus had in mind when he advised Marcus 'not to run off into zeal for the sophistic, or to write on speculative themes, or to discourse on edifying texts, or to exhibit in fanciful colours the ascetic or the philanthropist. To avoid rhetoric, poetry and urbanity . . . to write letters in a simple style.'[86] Fronto, it seems, ever jealous about his position on the inside track of Marcus's emotions, had been looking for jeopardy in the wrong direction: worried about the rivalry with Herodes Atticus, he did not see the real danger looming from Rusticus. His bitterness at his student's apostasy found expression later in many jibes and snide asides. He told Marcus that an emperor had to be eloquent, willy-nilly, and philosophy would not help him: 'Even if you attain the wisdom of Cleanthes or of Zeno, you will still be obliged, like it or not, to wear the purple pallium, and not that of the philosopher, made of coarse wool.' He condemned Stoicism as the arch-enemy of common sense, and urged Marcus to relax and forget about it: 'Even your Chrysippus himself [the founder of Stoicism], they say, used to get drunk every day.'[87] Elsewhere we find Fronto going to the very brink of the permissible in his bitterness. On one occasion Marcus was ill and Fronto wrote to say that, given his principles, he doubtless felt nothing when his life was threatened.[88] He reported minor triumphs over Rusticus, as when the philosopher changed his previous opinion and said that Marcus really had been a great loss to the legal profession: 'My dear Rusticus . . . who would give his life or sacrifice it willingly to save your little finger, was then forced to concede – much against his will and with a disgusted look on his face – that what I used to say about your rhetorical talents was right.'[89] Given Fronto's sensitivity about status, baubles and gongs, what probably upset him most was Marcus's political favouritism for Rusticus. Once Marcus was emperor he rewarded Rusticus with a consulate (in 162) and later with a second one. Marcus thanked the gods that he was able to advance such a teacher to honours and distinctions, although he was implicitly critical of him for wanting such glittering prizes – rightly, as they contradicted everything the Stoics allegedly stood for.[90] The final irony about the break with Fronto was that, at a personal level, Marcus always got on better with him than with Rusticus, who had the knack of making him furiously angry. Indeed, Marcus claimed that it was from Rusticus that he learned not to flare up when people irritated and annoyed him, as Rusticus did constantly.[91]

It is deeply sad that Marcus Aurelius should have subscribed to such a bleak and ultimately nihilistic view of the universe and mankind's place in it.[92] Stoicism was an arid doctrine that tried, in D.H. Lawrence's phrase, to 'do the dirt on life'. It is a world view in which nothing unexpected can happen, and noble things like desire, fantasy, adventure, initiative, creativity, hope, cultural life and, ultimately, civilisation itself all disappear. That it should have any modern adherents is almost incredible.[93] Even the most perceptive of the ancients could see through to the fallacy at its core. As Sextus Empiricus pointed out, hunger will never convince the hungry that it is not an ordeal, and those who suffer will always rail against the injustice of the world.[94] Cicero, another Stoic fellow-traveller, made a very mild criticism: 'What the Stoics say may be true, it is certainly important, but the way they say it is all wrong.'[95] It is a supreme irony that a 'unitary' theory of the world should have produced, in its most famous initiate, a 'divided self'. Marcus Aurelius never apostatised from this creed that made such an impression on him as a young man, but Stoicism did not help him in his role as emperor. As ruler of an empire, he had to accept mundane standards of what was good and bad, for Stoic forbearance would not stop barbarians crossing the frontier or the Roman crowd rioting if the grain ships did not arrive from Africa. In dealing with his subjects who were not Stoic or sage material, he accepted conventional definitions of right and wrong. He did his duty, but the duty collided with the philosophy he held so dear, since that very duty was deduced from moral standards he did not accept as valid. The ultimate paradox of Stoicism is that it enjoins the would-be sage to do his duty as part of the higher morality, but that very duty is based on standards that the ethics of Stoicism itself reject.[96] That sounds like the very definition of unhappiness. The young man so captivated by this strange doctrine would never again be the carefree horse-riding and grape-treading youth of yesteryear.

4

Hadrian had appointed Antoninus as his successor thinking that, at fifty-one, Antoninus would not have long to live and that Marcus would take over in five years at most. But Antoninus defied the actuarial statistics and lived for another twenty-three years. An enigmatic figure, in many accounts of Roman history he features virtually as the 'man who never was' – neither outstandingly brilliant nor egregiously evil, and with no major achievements to his credit. Hadrian had selected him as the proverbial safe pair of hands, a good bet from a number of standpoints, having no major enemies, no brothers and sisters and just one child surviving from five born to his wife Faustina.[1] Old, tranquil, averse to innovation or caprice, popular with the Senate, where he had served for twenty-five years, he had a solid senatorial career behind him. From a family that originally came from Narbonese Gaul, and with paternal and maternal grandfathers who had both been consuls, Antoninus had an idyllic childhood at Lorium on the Via Aurelia, enjoying all the privilges of a massively wealthy family. He had gone through the usual *cursus honorum* – quaestor in 112, praetor in 117, consul in 120 – had been appointed by Hadrian as one of his consular administrators in 130 and had also served as proconsul in Asia. Hadrian thought he was a rare example of a man who was both an excellent administrator and an outstanding human being; the fact that Antoninus shared Hadrian's vision of limited empire and peace at almost any price further commended him. In one of those cryptic signals in which the Roman ruling class specialised, Hadrian sent out a coded message that Antoninus was dear to him by appointing him joint *pontifex maximus* – an office rarely shared by any emperor.[2]

Antoninus began his reign by overseeing the funeral obsequies of the late emperor and having him deified. After making Marcus Aurelius the youngest quaestor in imperial history and encouraging him to keep the people happy with a gladiatorial spectacle presented at his (Marcus's) expense, Antoninus departed for Baiae to bring back Hadrian's remains. He then oversaw the burial of the late emperor in the new imperial tomb of Castel Sant'Angelo.[3] But getting the Senate to accept the deification of the hated Hadrian was an unhappy struggle. Antoninus had to lean very hard on that august body to get his way on this issue, succeeding only when he pointed out that to refuse divine honours would in effect nullify Hadrian's succession settlement: this in turn meant that he himself would have no legitimacy as emperor and the regime itself would immediately be in peril from ambitious pretenders. The Senate took the point – better a phoney god than the chaos principle – and acquiesced. They voted for deification partly out of respect and deference for Antoninus and partly because they were afraid of the possible reaction of the army, whose darling Hadrian had been.[4] Antoninus went to great lengths to conciliate the Senate, promising them that Hadrian's system of spies and informers would be dismantled immediately. In a histrionic gesture, he also produced alive and well the senatorial colleagues arrested by Hadrian, whom the other 'Conscript Fathers' thought long since dead. Antoninus made a point of trying to convince the senators that he would merely be 'chairman of the board' and not a despot. At first he refused the title of 'Father of His Country' voted him by the Senate, but consented to accept it in 139. But he was shrewd enough to decline the offer to have the months of September and October renamed after his wife.[5]

It was partly his bending over backwards to the Senate, combined with the courageous manner in which he had held out to get Hadrian deified, that won him the accolade 'Pius' that ever afterwards dignified his name. However, it must be conceded that theories on how he became Antoninus Pius were legion. Some singled out the lavishing of honours on a very difficult predecessor; others emphasised the way he had declared an immediate amnesty for all condemned by Hadrian and had rescued many senators from his cruelty. Still others said the title was a reward for his rare human qualities. 'Pious' in the Roman sense, meaning having a sense of duty, seemed the only appropriate epithet for a man who had made such a careful distinction between what the stability of the state required (the deification of Hadrian) and his own personal opinion, which was obviously that Hadrian had indeed been a tyrant. Others pointed to Antoninus's rare human qualities, such as the way he habitually gave his arm to his ancient father-in-law when they walked to the Senate together.[6] In general, though, the title 'Antoninus Pius' symbolised that the emperor and the Senate were now working hand in hand, and that Antoninus had extra moral authority and gravitas because he had accepted the (at least nominal) sovereignty of the Senate. The senatorial order was also deeply relieved that Antoninus was rigidly conservative and had no inclination to tinker or experiment. Antoninus indeed believed that the empire was poised on a delicate equilibrium and that the slightest change might bring disaster, like removing an individual card from a house of cards. Rome, for better or worse, was about to experience twenty-three years of changelessness, despite some cosmetic rearrangement.[7] Like Lampedusa's *Leopard* prince, Antoninus essentially believed in change only so that everything would remain the same.

The man himself was more complex than appeared at first sight. Frugal and careful with money, he had a reputation for meanness: he was, said Cassius Dio, 'the man who splits a cumin seed' – that is, a byword for stinginess. Others, however, said that this canard was unfair: the truth was that he was generous to his close friends and to the army.[8] In pointed contrast to the globe-trotting Hadrian, he refused to travel on the grounds of expense, and his determination to stay in Italy and govern there was (rightly) read as an implicit criticism of his deified predecessor.[9] He returned all the Italian share of the *aurum coronarium* – the money raised in honour of his accession – and remitted half of that contributed by the provinces, a clear indication of the favouritism for Italy that would characterise his reign. His economic and financial policies were austere and conservative, always working against exploitation and heavy taxation. Although personally very wealthy, he was determined that his private fortune would not be swallowed up by the demands of the imperial throne, and deliberately created a so-called *res privata*, a government department to administer his private wealth and keep it distinct and separate from the money in the imperial treasury, the *patrimonium*.[10] He was obsessive on this point and, when reproached by his wife for not being sufficiently generous to his household, replied, 'Foolish woman, now that we have gained an empire, we have lost even what we had before.'[11]

Despite all his financial caution, he was obliged to provide regular gifts of money to the people and to the soldiers, as well as lavish games and entertainments. The money he gave to the people was always termed largesse, while that to the army was known as donatives. He distributed eight different rounds of largesse: in 139 to celebrate his ascent to the purple; in 142 and 145 to keep the system ticking over; in 148 to celebrate the 900th anniversary of the founding of Rome; and then again in 151, 152, 158 and in January 161, right at the end of his reign. In twenty-three years he doled out largesse worth 800 denarii a head, an average of thirty-five denarii a year, or rather less than most second-century emperors: Hadrian had given forty-eight a head, Marcus Aurelius would provide forty-five a head, while in the reign of Septimius Severus the per capita rate went up to sixty-one.[12] He gave donatives to the army on his accession, in 140 and again in 148. Additionally, in 148 he cancelled individual debts to the state and had the records of the arrears destroyed. He also lent money at interest, charging a rate of 4 per cent when the market rate fluctuated between 6 and 12 per cent.[13] Finally, he used his own funds to distribute free oil, grain and wine in periods of famine, relieved the devastation caused by fire and floods (in Rome) and by fires and earthquakes (in the provinces), to say nothing of relief payments to victims when the stands in the Circus Maximus collapsed.[14]

Antoninus Pius carried his spartan attitude to money into his private life, taking frugal meals and reducing the pomp on state occasions to republican simplicity. Apart from suffering migraines, he enjoyed robust health and proselytised for the health-giving qualities of dry bread.[15] Tall and good-looking, he had a slightly raucous but sonorous and generally pleasant speaking voice, though from the silence of Marcus and Fronto on the matter, we may infer he was not much of an orator. Most ancient observers described him as intelligent, genial, kind, honest, hard-working, dutiful and dedicated to the affairs of the state.[16] Vain about his looks, Antoninus also realised the importance of image and tried hard to ensure that Roman iconography would reflect his own self-image. He modelled himself on Vespasian, encouraging images and statuary that showed him as a shrewd, benevolent man of the people, his face corrugated with laughter lines and, most of all, down-to-earth, eschewing both the humourlessness of Hadrian and the severe, scowling, ferocious, disciplinarian appearance of an emperor like Galba or the over-dreaminess of Augustus.[17] The only real criticism of Antoninus in his own time – the charge of stinginess apart – was that he was not wise in matters of sex and had made an unfortunate marriage (around AD 110) with Faustina the Elder, a beautiful woman with large eyes, but with whom he did not get on.[18] Modern scholars have been more critical. Some think that beneath the mask of 'just folks' affability, Antoninus had a mighty opinion of himself and his merits. To judge from the 'Health' and 'Well-Being' mottoes on his coins, he was one of those men who thought it a personal merit that he enjoyed the luck of good health, and there was something smug and self-regarding about his evident pride in his longevity.[19] Others point out that under his principate the titles of the emperor became more grandiloquent and that this apparently modest man went in for showy titles – such as *optimus ac sanctissimus omnium saeculorum princeps* ('the best and most holy emperor of all ages').[20] One modern critic regards Antoninus as a kind of modernised Cato, with all the austerity, but with added sexual licence, 'a blend of Italian landowner and petty bourgeois, unambitious, unelastic and uncreative'.[21] The doyen of modern Roman historians, Sir Ronald Syme, thought that, as evinced by his edicts and letters, he was 'subtle, ironical and crafty'.[22]

In the first book of his *Meditations* Marcus Aurelius provided a lengthy character sketch of his 'adopted father', which is more than just interesting, in the light of the foregoing. He praises Antoninus for his compassion and gentleness, for hard work, persistence and for constancy to his friends, never tiring of them, manipulating them or playing the game of imperial favourites. 'He had unshakeable adherence to decisions once he had made them . . . listened to anyone who could contribute something worthwhile, treated people according to their merits, had a sense of when to press on and when to back off.' Marcus praised him for his indifference to outward show and superficial honours, and for putting a stop to the Hadrianic cult of homosexual liaisons with young boys. Antoninus did not insist that his friends had to attend all his banquets or travel with him to the countryside if they did not want to, and he did not necessarily treat those who were always at his side with more esteem than those he excused to attend to necessary business. He was a good committee man: he asked searching questions at meetings, was single-minded in his determination to cut through to the nub of the matter and was never content with first impressions; nor did he provide those so-called proofs of toughness and efficiency at meetings by racing through them or ending discussions prematurely. He was good at advanced planning and had an eye for detail. He had a keen sense of the needs of the empire and, especially, of the treasury and was willing to take full responsibility (and blame if need be) for policies. Self-reliant and cheerful, he hated flattery and bogus acclamations, demagoguery and passing fads; by the same token, he detested sycophants and those who attempted to curry favour or pander to his supposed whims.[23]

Marcus found him devoutly religious, but not superstitious. Antoninus had a casual attitude to privilege and wealth, treating them both without arrogance and without apology; if there was good food and fine wine around, he took them; but if not, he did not miss them. He was not glib, shameless or pedantic; it was very much a case of: what you saw was what you got. He was, Marcus thought, what we would nowadays call a 'people person'. He felt at ease with other people and could put them at their ease. His good health and good looks were remarkable, but he was never vain or hypochondriacal. 'He could have one of his migraines and then go right back to what he was doing – refreshed and at the height of his powers.' Marcus also admired 'his willingness to yield precedence to experts – whether in oratory, law, psychology or whatever – and to support them robustly so that each maximised his potential.' That was an obvious hit at Hadrian, who always thought he knew better and saw deeper than any expert, even a lifetime professional – exactly the kind of arrogance that so irked Marcus.

Antoninus also respected tradition without feeling the need for constant self-congratulation as 'The Man Who Supports Traditional Values'. Two of his salient characteristics were reliability and predictability. He saw life steady and saw it whole, tended to stick to the same ways of doing things and the tried and tested formulae; he hated going off at tangents. Marcus liked his pragmatic approach to public works and state spending, giving the nod to building projects,

gladiatorial games and largesses only when he thought them necessary for the social good or stability, not because of the fame and glory
that would accrue to him personally. 'He had few secrets – only state
secrets, and not many of those.' There was nothing self-indulgent
about him: he was not a *bon vivant* or a gastronome, did not bathe at
strange hours, wear colourful clothes or try to set new sartorial fash-
ions or have a household of attractive slaves, as so many upper-class
Romans did. 'He was never rude or violent and never lost self-control.
No one ever saw him sweat . . . You could say of him what was said
of Socrates, that whereas normal people find pleasure easy and
abstinence difficult, he knew both how to enjoy things and to abstain
from them if he thought that necessary. He was strong enough both
to endure self-denial and not go over the top in his pleasures – the
sign of a man of perfect, invincible spirit, an indomitable personality
with a soul in perfect equilibrium.'[24]

Beneath this blizzard of praise we can discern a few subtle criticisms. Clearly the subtext of some of Marcus's observations is that
Antoninus was too much in a rut, lacked initiative, preferred life to
continue unchanged even to the point of being in the same places –
Rome, Loricum and Lanuvium (in Campagna), Tusculum (in Latium),
Signia or occasionally Tuscany. When away from Rome (which he
liked to leave as often as possible) he liked to fish with a rod, hunt
wild boar, read from his vast library or simply talk with friends and
cronies.[25] Nevertheless, there can be no doubting the warmth of the
entente between Antoninus and his heir. The emperor insisted that
Marcus reside in the House of Tiberius, the imperial palace on the
Palatine Hill, and that his imperial status be recognised with the full
pomp of a court. Marcus disliked all this ostentation and protested,
but Antoninus insisted, arguing that the common people would not
understand Marcus's fastidious philosophical objections and would
think the less of him. Remembering his own Stoic prescriptions, Marcus
reflected that life for a Roman was duty rather than pleasure, so he
took up the poisoned chalice of court life. In his *Meditations* he thanked
Antoninus for making him realise that 'even at court you can live
without a troop of bodyguards and gorgeous clothes, lamps, sculpture – the whole charade'.[26] Meanwhile Antoninus showered him with
honours. Having made him quaestor at seventeen (when the minimum
age was supposed to be twenty-four), in which capacity he was

consulted by the Senate on high policy, the emperor designated Marcus as his co-consul in 140 ('at the demand of the Senate') and gave him the title of Caesar. Marcus was also inducted into the four priestly colleges of which the emperor was always a member (the *pontifices*, *augures*, *quindecimviri sacris faciundis* (keepers of the Sibylline books) and the *septemviri epulonum*. Since it was clear that Antoninus would not beget children, Marcus was heir presumptive verging on heir apparent, and to reinforce this he was made head of the equestrian order. It made a very favourable impression that, at the ceremony when he became honorary leader of the knights, Marcus entered the Forum with the other equestrians, although he was Caesar and could have insisted on special pomp to underline his rank.[27]

All of this represented accelerated promotion. As quaestor, his main duties had been to represent Antoninus in the Senate when he was absent and to be a kind of parliamentary private secretary. As consul in 140, he chaired meetings of the Senate, oversaw its administration and performed religious ceremonies. Soon he was on the imperial council, the real decision-making body in Rome, where the so-called 'friends' (*amici*) of the emperor met in conclave. As the 140s wore on and Marcus confirmed that Antoninus's choice had been supremely wise, more and more honours came his way. He was appointed consul for a second time, received the traditional tribunician power, proconsular authority outside the city and the right to represent Antoninus in the Senate. He also received the unprecedented privilege of being able to introduce five different pieces of legislation in the Senate – the most any emperor was allowed – with the proviso that imperial legislation always took precedence.[28] Soon coins showing Marcus as Caesar were struck. Fronto proudly reported to Marcus that wherever he went there were portraits of the young Caesar on view – at bookstalls, booths, money-changers' bureaux, in the porches and windows of houses.[29] Yet there were limits to Antoninus Pius's promotion of his protégé. He was never given the title of Augustus or *imperator*, and in some ways appeared at a disadvantage when compared with Aelius Caesar and Antoninus himself when they were Caesars under Hadrian. Unlike them, Marcus had no personal cabinet, was not sent on any missions to the provinces, and signed no official documents emanating from the Chancellery unless it had to do with personal matters. Marcus was above all a privileged councillor and it was in this capacity that Fronto was forever asking him to intervene to plug the merits of one person or another.[30]

Antoninus's longevity was a severe test of Marcus's patience and moral fibre. A lesser man would certainly have turned to poisoning or assassination to get rid of the elderly obstacle to the purple. Can one imagine a Caligula, Nero, Commodus or Elagabalus waiting patiently for more than twenty years to become emperor? Additionally, Antoninus did not make things easy for his heir in small ways, for his micromanaging, controlling personality was itself a trial. In the twenty-three years of Antoninus's reign Marcus spent just two nights away from him.[31] This was another severe test of his patience and stoical character. What he saw of Italy was heavily dependent on Antoninus's travels to his favourite holiday lairs. We catch glimpses of Marcus on the road to Signia in the correspondence with Fronto. Sometime during the years 144–5 we find him at Trajan's villa at Centumcellae (modern Civitavecchia), famously described in Pliny's letters.[32] Marcus tells Fronto that the journey out from Rome by carriage was ruined by heavy rainfall, but that, before reaching Antoninus's country estate at Signia, they turned off the road to Anagnia and inspected this ancient township full of antiquities, bookshops, chapels and shrines. Typically the letters show Marcus by far the more interesting person of the two. While he wants to talk about the local wines and the Etruscan book of the dead, Fronto is in characteristically pedantic and didactic mood. Hearing that Marcus intends to establish a 'royal forest' or game reserve, Fronto patronisingly 'reminds' him that it is best to strike a wild boar at full gallop when out hunting.[33] The boredom Marcus undoubtedly felt while on attendance on Antoninus at Lorium and his other haunts was doubtless assuaged by the obvious personal regard that Antoninus had for him. When he mourned the death of his old tutor Alexander, the palace retinue complained to the emperor that the young Caesar's grief was excessive. Antoninus immediately took Marcus's side. 'Let him be a human being for once,' he said, 'since neither philosophy nor the empire can extinguish feelings.'[34]

Although Antoninus tolerated philosophers and was quite happy to see his young protégé as a paid-up member of the Stoic fraternity, he never had Marcus's patience for the foibles and pretensions of the sophists. We have already remarked on his scathing witticism at the

expense of the prima donna Apollonius of Chalcedon (see pp. 46–7),
a venal humbug described by Lucian, when he set out to be Marcus
Aurelius's tutor, as like a new Jason sailing in search of the Golden
Fleece. Another of Marcus's favourites, Alexander the Platonist, who
later served as Marcus's secretary (*ab epistulis Graecis*) in the 170s, also
fell foul of him. When making a plea on behalf of his native Seleucia,
Alexander (another prima donna) decided that the emperor was not
listening with the required rapt attention and remarked impertinently,
'Pay attention to me, Caesar.' Marcus testified that no one ever saw
Antoninus angry, but on this occasion he was at the very least extremely
cross: 'I *am* paying attention,' he said severely, 'and I know you well.
You are the fellow who is always arranging his hair, cleaning his teeth
and polishing his nails, and who always smells of perfume.'[35]

There was particular bad blood between Antoninus Pius and
Herodes Atticus, maybe partly because of the emperor's dislike of
homosexuality, but mainly because of Herodes's overweening arrogance. Antoninus's ire was said to derive from an incident when he
was on a rare foreign foray, as proconsul of the province of Asia. A
dispute arose about who had the right of way on a narrow road around
Mount Ida. Herodes, regarding himself as the uncrowned king of the
eastern Roman empire, claimed precedence over a 'mere' proconsul,
drove on and nearly tipped Antoninus into a ditch.[36] Antoninus tried
to get his revenge by bringing an alleged case of corruption to Hadrian's
notice. Herodes Atticus had received three million drachmas from
Hadrian to improve the water supply of Alexandria in the Troad, but
spent seven million, getting credit for the four million balance.
Antoninus wrote to Hadrian to accuse Herodes of peculation, malfea-
sance, misfeasance and nonfeasance. Hadrian could not ignore this
and complained to Herodes's father, who replied with a classic of
'dumb show'. 'Don't concern yourself with trifles, Caesar. All amounts
over the three million drachmas I have given as a present to my son,
and he's given them to his favourite city.'[37]

Even worse was the behaviour of the sophist Polemon, another of
Marcus's favourites. A tragic actor once complained to the emperor
that Polemon had sacked him in the middle of a play. 'What time of
day was that?' asked Antoninus. 'Around midday,' the actor replied.
'You're lucky,' said Antoninus. 'That man had me thrown out of the
house in the middle of the night and I didn't complain.'[38] Again the

reference was to an incident during his Asian procuratorship. Part of the problem was that Antoninus had given hostages to fortune by his 'just folks' persona. Like many people who affect simplicity and the common touch, he was secretly touchy and expected deference. The sophists, always up for the main chance, quickly saw an opportunity to get away with things that a despotic emperor would not have tolerated for a second. Caught in the consequences of his would-be common touch, Antoninus was forced to put up with a high degree of familiarity from his intimates and from those who considered themselves equal to him; all he could do in compensation was boast that he allowed free criticism, as opposed to Trajan and, particularly, Hadrian.[39] A man named Homullus invited Antoninus to his home but, when the emperor became lyrical about the quality of porphyry in the house, remarked cuttingly, 'When you go to another person's house, you should be deaf and dumb.'[40] That this same Homullus was a malignant 'stirrer' became apparent from another incident. Seeing Marcus's mother Lucilla at prayer by a statue of Apollo in her private garden, the malevolent Homullus told Antoninus it was obvious that she was praying he would die soon so that her son could take over; Antoninus swatted this aside as obvious troublemaking.[41] The thing that Antoninus most deeply resented was the sophists' presumption that they were on a level of equality with the emperor. But he had to tread warily, for even emperors hesitated to overrule or humiliate powerful members of the local elite in the Greek world, like Herodes Atticus, as we have seen. Antoninus's resentment continued to simmer, and his contemptuous attitude to philosophers and sophists is clear from the following wording in a decree, an obvious hit at Herodes Atticus and his ilk: 'I feel that those who are wealthy will give financial assistance voluntarily to their cities. And if they quibble about the size of their estates, they will thereby make it clear that they are not philosophers.'[42]

An important part of Marcus's apprenticeship under Antoninus was learning the techniques of crowd control, so to speak, for all Roman emperors feared the unruly nature of the mob. The classic recipe for social control – Juvenal's 'bread and circuses'[43] – expressed a literal truth. Rome, with its one million population, had too many drones in the hive, hence the chronic food shortages, overcrowding, tenement housing, frequent fires, endemic violence and disease. The Roman proletariat was as much part of a dependency culture as those who live on welfare in Western societies today. To keep these restless spirits tranquil, successive Roman emperors had opted for the distribution of free grain, whereby the state guaranteed a supply of wheat to its registered free male citizens (no women, slaves or foreigners received the dole); this was a crucial fact about Rome, since in pre-modern societies at least 60 per cent of household income was spent on food. In Augustus's time around 250,000 people received this dole. Each adult was given seventy-two pounds of wheat per month gratis, enough to supply an adult with a staple diet, but not enough for a family; the emperor Septimius Severus added free oil in the early third century, and in the fourth century the handout expanded to include a ration of pork and wine.[44] Augustus agonised about whether to abolish the wheat dole, first introduced by his 'father' Julius Caesar, but decided against it, fearing it would become a political football, with every pretender to the throne promising to restore it. His successor Tiberius kept it on but, as a quid pro quo, abolished the people's participation in elections. Needless to say, the import, storage and distribution of at least 200,000 tonnes of wheat – authorities differ on the amount needed.[45] – was a huge task, and the stretch of the Tiber between Rome and the port of Ostia was almost permanently jammed with grain ships.

The total cost of supplying wheat to Rome may have amounted to 135 million sesterces or 15 per cent of state revenue. There were spin-offs, of course, since the supply of wheat also helped the rich economically, by providing an income surplus with which ordinary people could buy the wine produced on their estates, and by holding down the price of labour in the capital. The real curiosity of the Roman economy was that the state organised production in the grain-growing areas and paid for the finished product in Rome, but left its transportation in the hands of private enterprise, which was the backbone of the grain supply. A single 400-tonne wheat ship arriving in Ostia or Puteoli was worth one million sesterces – the minimum qualifying fortune needed for senatorial rank, so the incentives for entrepreneurship were clear.[46] Over 100 million sesterces were invested in ships to feed the one million population of Rome, or about 1 per cent of the total capital owned by Roman senators. Egypt was the key location, to the point where some historians have alleged that Egypt was a socialist system within a wider market economy.[47] On the private market wheat cost four times as much in Rome as in Egypt, and two or three times the price of wheat in Sicily or elsewhere in Italy, so the free grain distribution was crucial to social stability. Even so, no family could live on the free allocation alone, and it is estimated that only 15 per cent of the grain imported into Rome was for free distribution.[48] If we posit that Rome probably needed to import 300,000 tonnes of grain, oil and wine a year at a minimum, the fragile and brittle nature of the economic and political system can be appreciated.[49] All grain ships had to cross the Mediterranean – from Sardinia, Sicily, Egypt and North Africa – and oil likewise was shipped from Spain and Africa. When it is realised that the Mediterranean was 'closed' for four months a year from November to March and was considered dangerous for another two months on either side, the risks of famine and dearth in Rome were very high. All Roman emperors had a high official, a prefect of the *annona* (corn supply), whose work was crucial.[50]

Additionally, male citizens in Rome received cheap wine – another state subsidy to offset market forces, since the market price of wine at Rome was sixty-one sesterces per amphora as opposed to forty-eight sesterces at Pompeii.[51] Since cheap wine was not available elsewhere in the Roman empire, it is not surprising that Roman drunkenness was much commented on. Romans were essentially pampered, and they expected a high standard of bread and wine as of right, in contrast to, say, Asia Minor, where the peasants produced and ate a horrible black bread.[52] Another perk for the urban poor in Rome was the system of public baths, again discounted for citizens. The baths (like modern hospitals) may have acted as a focus and breeding ground for disease, as Roman doctors tended to recommend the baths as a panacea – for people suffering from malaria, cholera, dysentery, diarrhoea, gonorrhoea and worm-infestation. Indeed, Hadrian allowed the sick to use the baths in the morning before the healthy.[53] Those slightly higher in the social scale could benefit from *sportulae* – handouts from rich patrons who kept a flock of 'clients' at their beck and call. Although the *sportula* is sometimes called a 'dole', this is misleading, as it implies a regular state-backed system of welfare benefits. The *sportula* was more in the nature of a modern 'freebie' for the well connected (like modern all-expenses paid trips for Members of Parliament or journalists). Nero really introduced it by suppressing

public dinners in favour of cash handouts, although Domitian made
a vain attempt to reverse the process in his reign. By the end of the
first century clients typically received six to seven sesterces for each
daily visit: one in the morning at the patron's house and another in
the evening at the public baths. The poets Martial and Juvenal particularly despised those who made their living from *sportulae*.[54]

The Roman proletariat also benefited from free theatrical shows,
chariot races, gladiatorial combats and animal-slaughtering shows.
Neither Marcus Aurelius nor Antoninus Pius was personally keen on
public spectacles (though Antoninus enjoyed well-made plays at the
theatre), but, like all emperors, they had to placate the mob.[55] Like
the modern social elite when faced with mass enthusiasm for football
or reality television shows, they deplored the phenomena and despised
those who enjoyed them, but could see no alternative. But in Rome
public spectacles were always a time of tension, since this was the
moment when the mob tended to get out of hand.[56] For the tenth
and twentieth anniversaries of his accession Antoninus arranged games
featuring tigers, rhinoceroses, crocodiles and hippopotami, and
provided 100 lions for Rome's anniversary in 148.[57] Theatrical presentations took place in the Campus Martius, but these were dwarfed in
popularity by the animal and gladiator shows in the Colosseum, which
could seat 50,000–80,000 spectators and, above all, by the chariot races
in the Circus Maximus, which could seat 150,000–200,000. The rival
factions of Whites, Blues, Greens and Reds attracted fanatical
supporters, and the public exploits and private lives of the charioteer
'stars' were as much a subject of general interest as the exploits of
movie and rock stars today. Antoninus kept up a constant flow of
entertainment, offering yearly games for his birthday, for religious
festivals and for elite marriages or other important occasions. Marcus
praised his cleverness in this area, saying that he managed to satisfy
the mob without overplaying this aspect of social control, once again
showing himself a master at hitting the equilibrium point.[58]

Free games and circuses, free wheat, cheap wine, cheap baths,
largesses, *sportulae* and all the other fringe benefits of life in Rome
engendered a consumer surplus that made Rome something of a
cornucopia, but also produced steep inflation. Galen said that the great
thing about living in Rome was that all the seasonal crops from every
nation were sent there, so that one was surrounded by an embarrassment

of riches.[59] There was a bewildering variety of imports: herbs from the Greek islands, pepper from south India, fish-pickle from Spain, nine types of papyrus from Egypt, even mastiffs from Britain. Olive oil – used in food, for indoor lighting, in soaps, medicines, perfumes and cosmetics – was another staple much in demand; consumption was maybe two litres a head per year.[60] The demand for wine, estimated as at least 1.5 million hectolitres a year, was insatiable, with the Campanian vintages being the most prized, and fine wines marketing for as much as 1,000 sesterces an amphora.[61] Peaches were particularly prized at Rome and could fetch up to thirty sesterces each, while mullet could command prices as high as 10,000 sesterces each.[62] Goats' milk was so highly sought-after that owners of goats could make four sesterces a day from each animal. The permanent demand for luxuries in Rome led farmers in the environs to raise a different kind of poultry (the equivalent of our organic chicken, perhaps), sold at enormous prices.[63] The Roman food market was so inexhaustible that it was profitable to drive geese to Rome from the other side of the Alps and to ship produce from Italian farms 150 miles away.[64] The inevitable result was hyper-inflation in Rome. The basic cost of living there was so much higher than elsewhere in the empire partly because of huge demand and partly because Romans were so obsessed with keeping up appearances – wearing the right sort of toga, and so on.[65] Both Varro and Columella, experts in the economy of the Italian countryside, mentioned the high incomes of Italian landowners catering for the capital city's demand for luxury foodstuffs.[66] Not only did the cost of basic foodstuffs rise, but housing became so dear in Rome that the annual rent of a dingy hole in the city would buy the freehold of a fine house and garden in a town in the countryside.[67]

The ordinary people of Rome not only demanded that the authorities bail them out of the worst consequences of this, with largesses, doles, handouts, free wheat, cheap wine, cheap baths and free entertainment, but also insisted that a high level of social investment and infrastructure be maintained. Roman aqueducts have been much admired, and it was only their effect that reduced some of the public-health problems.[68] The snag was that much of Rome's water supply went for display in public places. Ironically, water was Rome's enemy in another sense, apart from the shortage of good drinking liquid. The Cloaca Maxima had been built to deal with torrential rains and was thus more like a storm drain in the modern sense than a nineteenth-century sewage system.[69] The Tiber regularly flooded the low-lying areas of the city, being particularly prone to bursting its banks in spring and winter, when houses collapsed into the freezing, filthy water; the fact that the river was also a sewer merely compounded the problems. It is true that Roman building programmes were impressive, but only because slave and convict labour could be used and local populations drafted into compulsory work gangs. Within Rome the authorities financed building programmes carried out by private contractors with a large permanent labour force. Marcus Crassus, for instance, the man who defeated Spartacus, was a property developer with his own gang of 500 navvies.[70] All these multitudinous aspects of social control in Rome had to be absorbed by the young Marcus.

Antoninus bound Marcus even more closely to him by giving him his daughter Faustina as wife. The complex kinship systems binding the Roman elite have already been mentioned. Before Antoninus adopted Marcus as his son, he was already in any case his uncle, since around the year 110 Antoninus had married Anna Galeria Faustina, sister of M. Annius Libo and M. Annius Verus, Marcus's father. Meanwhile Domitia Lucilla, Marcus's mother, was the product of a second marriage between Hadrian's mother Domitia and P. Calvisius Ruso. Since Antoninus married the sister of M. Annius Verus (husband of Domitia Lucilla), he was Hadrian's brother-in-law and Marcus was Hadrian's half-nephew.[71] Antoninus's marriage to Anna Galeria Faustina (Faustina the Elder, as she is usually called, to distinguish her from her daughter Faustina the Younger) was stormy. Although a beautiful woman with large eyes, she did not conform to the expectations of an aristocratic Roman matron. Instead of being deferential and subservient, she was known for her 'excessive frankness and levity'. Apparently the charges against her were that she was very flirtatious, if not worse, and was a meddlesome 'power devil', intervening in spheres that did not concern her.[72] Faustina bore Antoninus four children: two boys and two girls. The two sons died young – which of course was why Antoninus adopted Marcus – and the elder daughter, Aurelia Fadilla, died in 135. Immediately on becoming emperor, Antoninus sent his wife (Marcus's aunt) to see if the young man was willing to change Hadrian's marriage arrangements. He suggested that the arranged marriage between Marcus and Ceionia Fabia be cancelled and that instead he should be betrothed to Faustina the Younger, who would not be of marriageable age until 145. This of course also meant the cancellation of the proposed marriage between Lucius, Ceionia's brother, and the younger Faustina. Marcus agreed with his usual affability. The losers from the new arrangement were the Ceionius clan.[73]

The death of Faustina the Elder in October 140 alerts us to important aspects of oligarchic Roman marriage. She was placed in the mausoleum of Hadrian alongside the three children who had died before Antoninus became emperor. The Senate granted her exceptional honours, including deification. Immediately we can understand that the honours granted to empresses tell us nothing whatever about the true state of private relations between an emperor and his wife; the honours and the deification were simply a political imperative to maintain the credibility of the regime.[74] Elite Romans did not have high expectations of their wives' loyalty or good behaviour, and did not expect much in the way of emotional fulfilment from their marriages. Even adultery by a wife does not seem to have been viewed as a particularly grave offence.[75] Although women were in many respects second-class citizens under the Roman empire – and even the philosophical Marcus Aurelius did not regard a woman as his equal – nonetheless they enjoyed legal and property rights that were remarkable when set aside the lot of women in most traditional agrarian societies.[76] Many elite women had large fortunes they could dispose of as they pleased; powerful both by their individual wealth and their potential as child-bearers, upper-class women were assiduously courted as valuable political and economic assets. The more intelligent females fully played up to this.[77] Marcus's aunt Matidia had a huge fortune and kept a string of hangers-on slavering in anticipation of possible benefaction; there were vociferous complaints from the sycophants when her will was read and it emerged that they had all been duped.

After his wife's death, Antoninus maintained his dignity by refusing to remarry. Instead he took one of his wife's freedwomen, Galeria Lysistrata, as his mistress. This, plus his promise of his daughter to Marcus, showed very clearly that there would be no obstacle to the young man's eventual ascent to the purple. In April 145 the marriage between Marcus and Faustina was celebrated with all due pomp.

Antoninus made both a donative to the army and a cash payment to the people of Rome to celebrate the great event, and lavished money on games and public spectacles. Marcus was given all imperial powers short of the title of Augustus, but Antoninus did confer the title of Augusta on his daughter.[78] Coinage issued to commemorate the wedding stressed Faustina's piety, chastity, fecundity and family-mindedness. It would be absurd to imagine the marriage as a love match; such unions were acts of cold dynastic calculation.[79] Also far-fetched is the notion, touted in some quarters, that Marcus may have been a male virgin at marriage. The supreme unlikelihood of this is matched only by the opposite suggestion: that Benedicta and Theodotus, explicitly mentioned in the *Meditations* as temptations to which Marcus did *not succumb*, were his first lovers.[80] The plain truth is that there are vast chunks of Marcus Aurelius's life about which we know nothing, and it is not surprising that the sex life of this self-effacing man features as one of them. The idea of a honeymoon in the modern sense was also unknown, but we do know that Marcus and Faustina spent much of the years 145–7 by the seaside, at Caieta in Latium and at Lorium. The early omens for Faustina did not seem propitious, as Marcus soon reported her ill and feverish. The correspondence with that notable hypochondriac Fronto shortly degenerated into a 'swap the symptom' contest.[81] With Fronto wittering on about cold and pains in the knee, Marcus hit back with a 'grand slam': 'This is how I have spent the last few days. My sister was suddenly attacked with such a violent pain in her private parts that her face was dreadful to look at. Then my mother, in her worry, accidentally hit her side on the angle of a wall, which caused a great deal of pain to us as well as to her. As for me, when I went to lie down I found a scorpion in my bed – but I managed to kill it before lying on it.'[82]

Marcus married at twenty-four, exactly the right age for a member of the senatorial class, and Faustina at fourteen, a little earlier than the usual age for aristocratic girls.[83] After a slow start in the child-rearing stakes – women were expected to conceive immediately on marriage – which at first caused Antoninus to think his children might be infertile, Marcus and Faustina soon became almost machine-like in their ability to procreate, and produced fifteen children, of whom six survived to early adulthood. In this they were superb oligarchic role-models, for the Roman elite was deeply anxious about its ability to reproduce itself. Despite the tens of thousands of drones in Rome itself, the governors of the empire suffered from an ongoing and pervasive fear that the population might decline to the point where the *pax Romana* was no longer viable; or, better put, they feared that the numbers in the *elite* would decline.[84] There were three main aspects to this 'birth neurosis'. One was that the death rate itself was so high; another was that child mortality wiped out significant numbers in all families; finally, there was the disturbing but well-known phenomenon whereby it is affluent groups above all that practise contraception. There was an abiding tendency in the aristocracy to attempt to avoid 'life's tasks', even though such an attitude was considered distinctly un-Roman.[85] Where the poor were deterred from producing large families through sheer poverty or dislike of children as a burden, among the rich it may well have been simply that such people were not philoprogenitive just because they were not prepared to face the sorrow that was almost inevitable in an era of high infant mortality; whether the culture of eschatology in Rome made this easier or harder to bear is not clear.[86]

The issue of the death rate is reasonably clear-cut. The life expectancy at birth for members of the senatorial class was thirty years and about twenty-five for others, though some authorities would downsize this to an average life expectancy of twenty-two for men and twenty for women.[87] In Egypt the figure was 23.78 years at birth, with the average age at death thirty-two to thirty-three; in other words, the death ratios in the Roman empire were comparable to those in England in the years 1200–1450.[88] One-third of the population died by the age of twenty-eight months, and 40–50 per cent by the age of eight. Even if one survived the perilous years of infancy and adolescence, there was little security. Of 100 soldiers who enlisted at the age of twenty, it is estimated that seventy-eight would survive to the age of thirty-five, sixty-nine of those to the age of forty, and just sixty to the age of forty-five; even in peacetime roughly one-third would die in a typical twenty- to twenty-five-year career. Of course if one more realistically factors in actual fighting and exposure to disease in high-risk areas of the empire and its frontiers, the truer figure would be that about 55 per cent would perish over twenty-five years.[89] Death rates in the Roman empire were so high largely because of disease, poor nutrition and the low level of real wages (not to mention other perils such as lead poisoning).[90] Conditions in Rome were particularly bad, with overcrowding in high-rise tenement blocks enabling infectious diseases to take hold. The dreadful sanitary and drainage situation in Rome has already been mentioned, with the Tiber having to deal with thirty-five million cubic feet of human waste a year. The under-bureaucratised Roman state meanwhile either could not or would not take the tough measures needed to quarantine the population and eradicate pestilence.

The toll on women and children was particularly severe. Uterine haemorrhage, inflammation and puerperal sepsis killed maybe twenty-five in every thousand women at childbirth. Children tended to die of gastric disorders, diarrhoea and dysentery.[91] Infant mortality rates of around 30 per cent seem standard for the ancient world, as do deaths in infancy and puberty of upwards of 40 per cent.[92] It was for this reason that wet-nursing was so popular in the Roman empire: parents handed over their children to nurses because they did not want to invest emotion in those likely to die. Consequently, for most children, mothers were figures as remote as fathers.[93] There were sociological factors too, in an increasing disinclination to breed among wealthy Romans. During the late republic, wealth from conquered territories flowed into Rome and made rich Romans philoprogenitive. When the flow of loot and treasure came to an end under the empire, even members of the elite started restricting their families, mainly by contraception.[94] In the lower orders infanticide was the preferred method of birth control, but attitudes towards this swung sharply negative under the Antonines, in contrast to the tolerance in the late republic and first century of the empire.[95] Avoiding reproduction out of financial meanness, or the desire to avoid the pain and suffering of child mortality, produced a distinctive mindset in the second century AD. Many Romans came to take a highly individualistic and even nihilistic attitude to life, and ceased to care about family, lineage or male heirs.[96] Those who tried to balance the pleasures of parenthood with cynicism tended to opt for adoption, which avoided the considerable costs of rearing and educating a child, involved no sorrows over lost children and exposed the 'form' of an adolescent. One could adopt an heir when the character of the young man in question was plain to see, thus avoiding disappointment and heartache.[97] The popularity of adoption helps to explain why the Roman aristocracy, with the same death rate as medieval and early modern societies, nevertheless failed to reproduce itself on their scale.[98]

Various emperors had tried various methods to increase the birthrate among the elite. Augustus passed laws trying to ensure a hereditary caste by requiring aristocratic marriages to produce three children. But apart from the intrinsic unworkability of such schemes, even the modest goal of three children did not fit the bill because of the high level of infant mortality – it has been estimated that one-third of all couples would still have no child of either sex to inherit the family name and estate.[99] Later emperors tried to increase the birthrate by paying a primitive form of family allowance, the *alimenta*. The basic idea was that landowners would be given a loan from the imperial treasury of 8 per cent of the value of their lands; they would then have to pay interest on the loan at 5 per cent a year to provide the funds for the *alimenta* scheme. Trajan's government scheme paid sixteen sesterces a month to legitimate boys and ten a month to illegitimate girls; later schemes were more generous, paying out twenty and sixteen sesterces respectively.[100] In some of the later schemes, gifts from wealthy individuals were invested in land, which provided the capital for *alimenta* foundations. It was important that neither money nor land fell into the hands of the municipal authorities, which were notoriousy corrupt and would almost certainly try to embezzle it. The scheme was thus a partnership between the emperor and private landowners, and inevitably a certain amount of arm-twisting or other subtle pressure was needed by the emperor to keep it in being, for the payment of interest in perpetuity reduced the value of estates.[101]

Again and again in classical literature we encounter the constant exhortation to Romans to breed and raise children and to avoid the evils of abortion, child exposure and infanticide.[102] Writing to one of his friends who had just missed becoming a great-grandfather because his granddaughter had had a miscarriage, Pliny the Younger opined that the Roman way was to consider that there would be other opportunities for childbirth and that at least the life of the granddaughter was saved.[103] It is in this context that the philoprogenitive effort of Marcus and Faustina should be judged. The average woman who reached the menopause had borne five or six children, but larger families were difficult to produce since the reproductive life of most Roman women seems to have been less than in the modern era and may in some cases have lasted no more than fifteen years. Add to that the fact that stillbirths and spontaneous miscarriages occurred in about 20 per cent of all pregnancies, and the very high level of natural infant mortality, and it can readily be understood that only 40 per cent of families giving birth to three children would have a son who lived long enough to inherit from his father.[104] As one authority comments cryptically: 'Couples with as many as eight children are attested but large numbers of surviving children are infrequent.'[105] Yet another consideration is salient: a man of twenty-five marrying a girl of fifteen (or of twenty-four marrying one of fourteen, as in Marcus's case) had statistics against him, for there was a one-in-four chance that one or both spouses would die within five years.[106] Given all this, Marcus and Faustina, with fifteen children and six surviving into adulthood, were the ancient equivalent of those heroes of the revolution and those heroine mothers who used to be celebrated under the old Soviet system.

The birth of Marcus's first child, Domitia Faustina, on 30 November 147 was an occasion for private joy and public celebration, with another round of largesses and games being authorised by the proud Antoninus.[107] But Faustina's amazing powers as a child-bearer may have been offset by Marcus's frail constitution. The letters between Marcus and Fronto for 147 are full of the usual valetudinarian complaints. Marcus went down with a fever and took a long time to return to solid food, as the letters to Fronto confirm. 'I have had a bath and today even done a little walking and taken a little more food, but not as yet without discomfort . . . Thanks be to the gods and your prayers, I have bathed today and taken sufficient food, and wine too I have used with relish.'[108] Much more serious, however, were the maladies that were soon afflicting the infant Domitia Faustina. Marcus wrote to Fronto that although the child had recovered from diarrhoea and fever, there was still a lot of coughing and her emaciation was extreme.[109] Fronto replied tactlessly, 'How shocked I was when I read the beginning of your letter. The way it was written made me think that some danger to *your* health was meant. Then when you made it clear that the danger which I had taken to be yours at the beginning of the note was to your daughter Faustina, how my apprehension was transformed.' Marcus wrote back to rebuke him for his insensitivity, and Fronto had to backtrack frantically. We can almost hear the wheels in motion when he remarks disingenuously that the things that seem worst are the first thing one hears. He tried to excuse himself for his seeming lack of compassion for Domitia Faustina by attempting to preach a parable. It was like carrying a heavy weight and transferring it from the right shoulder to the left, he explained. It was not that the weight was any the less, but simply that the mere fact of transferring it brought momentary relief.[110]

Sensing that he had given offence, Fronto proceeded to dig himself deeper into the hole as he wrote. He admitted that he loved Marcus more than he loved his daughter: 'You are more likely to know the cause of this, since you have learned more about the nature and feelings of men, and learned it better.' (A modern reader might take this as a snide reference to Marcus's philosophical studies, except that Fronto always seemed incapable of irony.) He asked Marcus not to upset little Faustina by telling her of his preference for her father. The 'proof' he adduced of his love for Marcus again has a strange ring to modern ears.

I have sometimes criticised you behind your back in quite strong terms, in front of a very few of my intimate friends. This was in the days when you used to go about in public with too serious a face and used to read books at the theatre or at banquets – I still used to go to the theatre and to banquets myself in those days – and it was on occasions like this that I used to call you a hard and unreasonable person, even a hateful character, when I had been roused to anger. But if anyone else found fault with you in my hearing I could not listen with patience.[111]

Fronto added that he sometimes criticised Marcus to pre-empt criticism from others, which he would have found unbearable. A lesser man might have used this opportunity to jettison the tiresome Fronto once and for all. But Marcus, never more a Stoic than when he endured the unendurable (whether Antoninus's nitpicking or Fronto's boring blather), ignored the further effusions, concentrating on the important issue. He told Fronto in the next letter that little Faustina was now almost permanently ill, to which the egregious orator replied with another litany of his own ailments – pains in the elbow, neck and groin.[112] Marcus stopped writing regularly to him, which produced a masterpiece of effrontery from Fronto. He said he himself was lazy about writing to his Caesar, but this was a sign of his love, as it would spare Marcus the chore of writing back to him.[113] He spoke truer than he knew.

Little Domitia Faustina finally succumbed to her illness, and died around 151. In 149 twin sons were born to Marcus and Faustina, but did not survive the year and were buried with sadness in the mausoleum of Hadrian.[114] On 7 March 150 a sturdier child came into the world: Annia Aurelia Galeria Lucilla (the Lucilla referring to Marcus's mother Domitia Lucilla); she was destined to survive and be married twice. In 151 there was another short-lived girl and in 152 a boy (T. Aelius Antoninus), but he too did not survive long. In 153, however, another survivor was born: Annia Galeria Aurelia Faustina. In 157 a son was born, but he did not survive and was dead by March 158. Having now borne eight children of whom only two survived, Faustina fared better with the next two daughters, who both lived into adulthood: Fadilla, born in 159, and Cornificia, born in 160.[115] By the time of her father's death in 161, Faustina had produced three daughters from ten live births, not quite what Antoninus had had in mind when he betrothed her to Marcus; the marriage was supposed to engender sons who would assure the stability of the imperial succession for generations to come, and for this reason Antoninus had associated Marcus and his children with himself on altars dedicated to Jupiter (*Iovi Optimo Maximo pro salute*).[116] In addition to losing six children in the decade of the 150s, Marcus also had to endure the deaths of his mother and sister. Still alive in 155, Domitia Lucilla died some time before 161; Marcus says in the *Meditations* that she did not have a long life.[117] Marcus had always treated his sister Cornificia well. She and her husband Ummidius Quadratus had a son (born in 138–9) whom Marcus later took under his wing. The younger Ummidius Quadratus served as a legate to the proconsul of Africa and died of the plague in the late 160s. Marcus was as generous to him as he had been to his sister.[118] The loss of Cornificia in 152 – she can have been thirty at most – was a severe blow, coming as it did in the same year as the death of his son Aelius Antoninus.

It has perhaps been too readily assumed that because even rich Romans killed or exposed newborn babies, and tried to detach themselves emotionally by farming out their offspring to wet-nurses, they were unaffected by the death of their children. But it has been well said that cynicism and detachment about infanticide or normal infant mortality tell us nothing about the attitudes of Romans to those children they did choose to rear, and with whom they forged an affective bond.[119] There are several passages in the *Meditations* where Marcus Aurelius refers to the grief caused by the loss of children. He himself was in a kind of double bind, for he not only had to practise the normal level of detachment common to those who lived with the fact of high infant mortality, but also had to be true to the doctrine of Stoicism, which on this point was brutal and even inhuman.[120] He twice quotes a fragment from Euripides's *Antiope*: 'If I and my pair of children are forgotten by the gods, then even this must have a reason.' His remarks are worth quoting, evincing as they do a soul in human denial. 'Stick with first impressions. Accept the fact that your son is sick. But don't extrapolate from that to the conclusion that he might die.'[121] 'Pray not for some way to save your child but for a way to lose your fear of this.'[122] 'Your children are leaves. The wind scatters some of them on the ground; such are the children of men.'[123] 'As you kiss your son goodnight, whisper to yourself that he may be dead in the morning. Don't tempt fate, you may say. By talking about a natural event? Is fate tempted when we speak of grain being reaped?'[124]

Not surprisingly, Marcus has been much criticised for these attitudes, and certainly the idea of children as corn to be harvested does not chime with a modern sensibility. Some have speculated that the coldness and inhumanity may not derive exclusively from Stoicism, but may be a reflection of a general Roman cast of mind – anti-Wordsworthian, one might say – whereby childhood was thought to contain nothing of value. Marcus and Romans in general were uninterested both in their own childhood and in the world of the child.[125] Not only did Marcus not consider women and children to be of equal value to the adult male, but he was unable to see infancy from the child's point of view. Yet some of his remarks, like that about a spinning top, show clearly that the ancients were perfectly capable of imagining the world from a child's point of view, if only they thought there was some point in so doing. Other commentators think that in the world of late antiquity attitudes were slowly starting to change. Certainly Fronto's strange and eccentric remark, that he would be willing to be a boy again if that would gain him Marcus's presence, would have made no sense to Cicero or his contemporaries in the late republic. Yet others detect an ambivalence in Marcus's remark about children. Some have translated the passage about kissing your son goodnight to read 'whisper to yourself that *you* may be dead in the morning' – implying true Stoicism rather than cold-heartedness. Others say that the ambiguity in some of the remarks denotes a fundamental tension in Marcus's thinking, observable elsewhere in the *Meditations*, between his feelings as a Roman and his putative duty as a member of the world community.[126]

The Stoic sense of duty kept Marcus at his post on the imperial council – which under Hadrian and Antoninus Pius evolved into something like a council of state – for more than twenty years. Indeed, he was seldom permitted to leave Antoninus's side.[127] What he really thought of the pedantic, control-freak, parsimonious and narcissistic emperor must for ever remain a matter of speculation, both because Marcus always adopted a Thumper-like attitude to people (if he really disliked them, he simply said nothing) and because he was role-playing as an emperor even in the privacy of his own diaries. It is reasonable to infer that he really did approve of many of Antoninus's initiatives and policies. Antoninus liked to boast that he allowed free speech and liberal criticism, and this was a cause dear to Marcus's heart.[128] Similarly, he backed the emperor's generosity to the *alimenta* schemes for orphaned Italian girls and accepted, albeit reluctantly, that a munificent provision of games was a necessary evil, to avoid social turmoil.[129] When Marcus praises Antoninus for his contempt for empty military glory, we know from a wealth of other such remarks that he is being sincere.[130] Improving the lot and status of aliens, especially in the Greek part of the empire, was another project with which Marcus would have sympathised.[131] But the endless precisian nitpicking must have grated, perhaps especially the mania for fixing clear provincial boundaries, particularly in Thrace, one of Antoninus's hobby-horses.[132] And there was much worse. Antoninus's neglect of the army and his peace policy, coming after Hadrian's similarly long period of appeasement, meant that when multiple military crises later rained down on Marcus, he was ill prepared.[133] Even with his high degree of forbearance he must have considered it intolerable that by the age of forty he had never commanded an army or governed a province (or even seen anything of 'abroad'). Antoninus was the last emperor who enjoyed the luxury of never stirring from Rome and its environs, and being entirely focused on Italy. It must have irked Marcus that, despite all his labours, Antoninus never gave him the title of Augustus. He had no personal cabinet, went on no missions to the provinces and did not even sign official letters emanating from the Chancellery, unless it was to do with personal matters, as when he wrote to the Dionysiac Society of Smyrna in 158 when they had congratulated him on the birth of a son.[134] The way Antoninus treated his heir apparent was generous and well-meaning, but ultimately mindless and absurd.

Marcus has many claims to greatness, but his stoicism during the long 'let sleeping dogs lie' reign of Antoninus was surely the ultimate test of a character and moral fibre. His summing up on twenty-two years before the mast, as it were, as the faithful first mate to Captain Antoninus was as follows:

Take Antoninus as your model always. Think of his qualities: energy in pursuit of the rational, steadiness, calmness, gentleness, modesty, sense of reverence, his intellectual curiosity and his lust for life. He never nodded things through but always examined issues meticulously, tolerated unfair criticism and did not hit back, was contemptuous of informers, never made snap judgements, was patient and unhurried, an unrivalled judge of character. He did not go in for jealousy, back-biting or character assassination, disdained empty rhetoric, knifed through to the essentials, lived in a spartan way, worked hard (often until dusk), ate sparingly. He was a good friend who knew his own mind and was not swayed by the last person to speak. He was constant and was not forever changing his mind or lacking a fixed set of values or ideas. He was not a prima donna, could tolerate criticism and was even pleased if his ideas or suggestions could be improved upon. He was deeply religious, with a keen sense of the numinous, but did not go in for base superstition. Think on all this, so that when your time comes your conscience will be as clear as his.[135]

High praise indeed, but we should remember that it is a list of praise-worthy qualities. There is no corresponding list of deficiencies. From discrete remarks elsewhere in the *Meditations* it is possible to assemble a more nuanced, critical view of Antoninus. Marcus thought he lived too much in the past, put his head in the sand, was too conservative and always wanted the same things – to be in the same place and for everything to go on as before.[136] The cynic would say that Antoninus was a great one for hair-splitting and logic-chopping, picking away at legal minutiae, but he lacked the vision to deal with the fundamental problems of the empire. People who hate change with a passion, as Antoninus did, are a constant in human history, but are rarely effective in politics. The empire's problems he left for Marcus to solve and got himself an inflated reputation by doing as little as possible. Like Philip II of Spain in the sixteenth century, Antoninus knew his empire only from the paperwork on his desk.[137]

As Antoninus grew older, in the decade of the 150s (he reached the age of seventy in 156), he delegated more and more of the onerous tasks of administering the empire to Marcus. For the biographer, this decade is a frustrating one, as we catch only occasional glimpses of the Stoic heir apparent, both as a public figure and in his private life. Sorrow for the children who died young was balanced by the never-ending sense of duty as the senior imperial counsellor. The correspondence with Fronto continued, though at a much lower level, with the ex-tutor's hypochondria still very much to the fore.[138] Fronto lobbied Marcus continually for favours, places and advancement, but, when he finally got his big chance, he muffed it. Sometime after 155 he was successful in the ballot for the two senior proconsulships (Asia and Africa). But having set his heart on Africa, he was cast down to discover that he had been assigned to Asia. Immediately he claimed that 'broken health' prevented him from taking up his post.[139] Whether his health really was impaired, or whether this was a fit of the sulks because he could not have the African post he desired, is difficult to establish conclusively, but from the voluminous correspondence that he sent Marcus's way, detailing meticulously the reforms he would have carried out had he been able to return in triumph to his native Africa, we may infer that the 'illness' was a convenient excuse. There is some evidence that the disillusionment Marcus had been feeling towards Fronto ever since his 'conversion' to philosophy in around 144 was accelerated by his tutor's inability or unwillingness to take up the Asian proconsulship. Marcus had put himself out on Fronto's behalf, laying the groundwork for a successful tour in Asia by energising all his contacts there.[140] Certainly from about 155–8 the correspondence seems almost to peter out, and when it continues it is one-sided, with Fronto making all the running.

A further contretemps arose when the prefect of the guard, Gavius Maximus, died in 156–7 after twenty years in the post – an unprecedented incumbency. Widely unpopular, Maximus was denounced in splenetic terms by an oligarch named Censorius Niger in his will, and there was implicit criticism of Antoninus for tolerating such a man in such a position for such a long time. The problem was that Niger's major beneficiary was Fronto, to whom he bequeathed half of an enormous estate. Fronto was in a quandary. To accept the legacy might seem like an endorsement of Niger's animadversions and, moreover, Fronto knew that Marcus disapproved of the late benefactor. In his best Uriah Heep manner, Fronto wrote Marcus a letter of apology, making a distinction between a man who does not love Marcus – an offence that would instantly make him Fronto's enemy – and one whom Marcus does not like; the latter, surely, is irrelevant, argues Fronto, for no friendship is transitive in this way.[141] Maybe Fronto was fortunate in that Marcus's full attention was taken up at this time with the egregious Herodes Atticus, who made another of his ill-judged splashes into scandal. When his wife Regilla died at the end of a pregnancy, her brother Bradua accused Herodes of murder. A trial became necessary, but the jury acquitted Herodes, who then alienated the stiff-upper-lipped Roman oligarchs with a public and effusive display of grief for his late wife.[142] Thus let off the hook, the brazen Fronto went on to lobby Antoninus assiduously on behalf of his friend Arrian of Alexander; his persistence paid off and Alexander got a procuratorship, even though the emperor felt that such an appointment would simply encourage more lobbyists to try their luck.[143] It is significant of the state of relations between Marcus and Fronto in the late 150s that Marcus refused to get involved in any of Fronto's patronage requests and simply referred him on to Antoninus.

By the year 160 it was obvious that even the ascetic, long-lived Antoninus could not last much longer. Perhaps as a deliberate insurance policy, he appointed Marcus and Lucius Verus as joint consuls for the following year (Marcus's third consulate and Lucius's second). At the beginning of March 161 he suffered a short illness, brought on by one of his rare gastronomic indulgences at his country house at Lorium. Cassius Dio tells that he tucked into some alpine cheese with gusto at dinner one night (this does not sound like the man who used to make a virtue of eating dry bread), vomited in the small hours and next day was found to have a fever. In a delirium, he spoke of a number of foreign kings with whom he was angry.[144] Feeling worse and worse and with fewer lucid moments occurring, and gradually convinced that he was at the point of death, Antoninus summoned Marcus and the other members of the imperial council and formally commended him to them as the next emperor, expressing the wish that he would treat the empire as well as he had always treated his daughter Faustina. He gave the watchword 'Serenity' to the tribune of the guard, then turned over in bed as if to go to sleep and breathed his last, on 7 March 161. Dio recorded that it was a good death, 'sweet and like the softest sleep'.[145] Fronto somewhat retrieved his position with a well-judged funeral panegyric, which Marcus praised. For once Fronto struck the right note, replying that Antoninus's merits were so obvious that a Parthian orator could have done just as well with such raw material.[146] For Marcus, the long apprenticeship was now over and he prepared to ascend the throne as the sixteenth emperor of Rome.

5

Marcus was forty when he became emperor – a ripe old age by normal Roman standards, though naturally all elite members benefited from better diet, doctoring and general lifestyle than the man in the street.[1] Julian the Apostate later recalled that Marcus was careless of his appearance, wore plain clothes and had a kind of transfigured look, deriving from his severe diets and 'picky' attitude to food. The giant marble statue recently unearthed by archaeologists at Sagalassos, Turkey, shows his bulging eyes, which were thought peculiarly appropriate for a contemplative, and a dreamy, far-away look. For all that, he usually conveyed imperial gravitas and appeared supremely dignified, his eyes lined and his brows furrowed from excessive study; his basic demeanour was poker-faced, expressionless in both happiness and grief.[2] His long beard intrigued many observers, and this is reflected in his portraits, where both hair and beard grow longer as the reign progresses, though the general image, with a smooth and confident face, remains consistent, with only two main variants. Beards were thought by the Romans to convey an impression of wisdom and profundity, recalling as they did both the famous Greek philosophers and the heroes of old, to say nothing of the hirsute Olympians like Zeus (or Jupiter).[3] But some say, more cynically, that Hadrian pioneered the fashion for beards not because of his love of all things Greek, but simply to cover his own facial blemishes.[4] In Marcus's case there was an additional reason for loving the bearded look. Epictetus taught that the Roman habit of shaving was inferior to the Greek fashion for facial hair, since Nature had endowed men with beards to distinguish them clearly from women; in the ancient world anything smacking of 'unisex' or androgyny was regarded as 'against Nature'.[5] Yet Marcus did not always impress onlookers as a paragon of gravitas and authority. The historian Herodian reported that he had a low voice and a ponderous manner.[6]

Both Marcus's own writings and the biographical sketches of him written by others agree that he always enjoyed very poor health. The *Meditations* are full of references to physical pain and the necessity of the true Stoic to disregard this.[7] The origin and nature of all his many maladies is mysterious, but there are occasional pointers in the sources. At the simplest level, Marcus was an insomniac who hated getting out of bed in the morning – a serious fault in the culture of Rome where people considered it a virtue to be up betimes.[8] There is a famous passage at the beginning of Book Five of the *Meditations*, as so often in the form of an internal dialogue, that makes this clear.

> At dawn, when you have trouble getting out of bed, tell yourself, As a human being I have to go to work. Why am I complaining if I'm going to do what I was born to do – the things I was brought into the world to do? Is this really what I was created for – to snuggle under the blankets and stay warm? But, you say, it's nicer here. I see, so you were born to feel nice, is that it? Not to do things and experience them? Don't you see the plants, the birds, the ants and spiders and bees all going about their individual tasks, putting the world in order as best they can? And you mean you're not willing to do your part as a human being? Why aren't you jumping up to do what your nature demands? But we have to sleep sometime, you say. I agree. But Nature set a limit on that – just as it did with eating and drinking. And you're over the limit. You've had more than enough of that. But when it comes to working, you're still below your quota.[9]

Elsewhere Marcus develops this into the thesis that even animals know how to sleep, but only humans know how to work in the true sense. He condemns sloth as a cardinal sin and suggests that when one wakes up is the perfect time for reflection.[10]

Physically frail, Marcus was hypersensitive to cold and probably accentuated his debility by taking little food, and then only at night.

When he was young he could fight in armour and kill wild boars on horseback, but already in early middle age he was complaining that many physical feats were now beyond him, and there are constant laments about pains in his stomach and chest, about blood-spitting, vertigo, sudden spasms of acute pain and other chronic ailments.[11] So what exactly was the matter with him? Many possible causes have been suggested: pulmonary tuberculosis, migraine, a gastric ulcer or some form of blood disease. Inevitably, perhaps, it has been suggested that he was a *malade imaginaire*, a hypochondriac reacting to stress.[12] But he was a man who did not believe in pampering himself and certainly did not get the sleep he needed, out of his fastidious Stoic refusal to allow pain to have the upper hand.[13] Instead, he thanked the gods for letting him live longer than he expected: 'I am grateful that my body has held out, especially considering the life I've led.'[14] One ingenious theory is that an objective stomach ulcer triggered other psychosomatic manifestations and affected his entire personality. On one model of behaviour, the ulcerous man will withdraw into himself, be permanently worried and preoccupied and will employ the carapace of hypertrophied self-investigation to hide himself from others. Conscientious to the point of pedantry, he is likely to be fascinated with administrative detail rather than human behaviour. Such a reading can be squared with Marcus in certain moods, but is perhaps overly dependent on an explicit or implicit theory of psychological types. Here is one such modern assessment of the alleged Marcus type: 'If he is a thinking man, he will incline to seek for justification, to compose superior personalities, and to adopt Stoic or Pharisaic attitudes. In the area of ethics, he will be virtuous by effort, good by application and a believer by force of will.'[15]

One of the most controversial aspects of Marcus's illnesses was his use of the drug theriac to relieve the pain in his chest and stomach. The famous physician Galen, who later became Marcus's personal doctor, was a great believer in this drug's efficacy. Consisting of one part seed of bituminous clover (*Aristolochia rotunda*), one of birthwort (*Aristolochiaceae*), one of wild or mountain rue (*Ruta chalepensis*) and one of pounded pulse or ground vetch (*Vicia ervilia*), the whole made into a pill and taken with wine, theriac was supposed to have marvellous qualities as a painkiller, sleeping pill and an antidote to poisoning – not just the venom of snakebite, but also the toxic potions that would-be assassins were known to try to get emperors to drink.[16] Marcus at first mixed varying amounts of poppy juice in the theriac, but, when he got drowsy, stopped adding this to the mixture. Then he found he could not sleep, so returned to the compound *with* the poppy juice. The first disputed issue is whether the emperor's drowsiness was a one-off event that did not recur once *aged* poppy juice was used, or whether, as seems more likely, the insomnia was so deep-seated that Galen had to resort to tougher measures. Researches into Galen's pharmacopoeia reveal that at one time he tried three different remedies for Marcus, some of which utilised poppy juice and others did not. An ancient antidote he had taken over from the physician Andromachus contained no fewer than sixty-four ingredients, only one of which was poppy juice. On the other hand, Galen also used an antidote of 100 ingredients, which seems to have contained little or no poppy juice. However, the key piece of evidence is that Galen added mandrake or opium in the theriac.[17]

Opium was a drug well known to the ancients, used as a soporific by the Egyptians, Greeks and Romans. Principally an anodyne, it had (or was thought to have) many other valuable properties, particularly in the sexual arena, where it could act as an aphrodisiac, prolong erection and delay ejaculation. Most of all, it could transport the user to another dimension, most famously described by Thomas de Quincey, who spoke of an 'abyss of divine enjoyment'.[18] The burning issue is whether Galen's prescription that added opium to the theriac turned Marcus into an opium addict, and thus added him to a distinguished list of such addicts throughout history that has included Avicenna, Linnaeus, Paracelsus, Robert Clive of India, Alexandre Dumas, Edgar Allan Poe, Coleridge, Keats, Wilberforce, Baudelaire, Elizabeth Barrett Browning, Wilkie Collins and André Malraux. The proponents of the 'emperor as addict' theory argue that this would explain both Marcus's odd detachment from domestic and everyday realities and the bizarre visions in the *Meditations*, especially those concerned with a racing sensation of the over-rapid passage of time.[19] Those sceptical of the opium-addiction idea contend that all the 'sensational' material in Marcus's writings is well within the idiom of Stoicism, where the notion of a supernatural passage of time is a constant motif. They draw a contrast between de Quincey's famous feelings of the unreality of space and time, which clearly *were* the result of an addiction, and the allegedly fevered *imagination* of Marcus as he laboured to procure for Stoicism an Olympian viewpoint, *au dessus de la mêlée*. It is argued, further, that similar dream imagery can be found in the work of the Neoplatonist philosopher Plotinus and others, none of whom were known to take opium.[20] Since we do not know how much opium Galen gave the emperor, the debate must perforce remain inconclusive. The 'certainty' that Marcus's visions are of the same type as de Quincey's may be overdone, but so too is the scepticism, which rests far too much on an *a priori* conviction that Marcus Aurelius 'cannot have been' an opium addict. Circumstantial evidence that Galen might have overplayed his hand when treating his famous patient is provided by Commodus's forthright rejection of the theriac/opium brew; it did not again become a popular prescription drug in the Roman empire until the reign of Septimius Severus.[21]

Elucidation of Marcus and opium might be possible if we had detailed descriptions of the emperor's dreams, but in this area, in the *Meditations*, he is disappointingly vague. He tells us, as do so many philosophers, that it is difficult to distinguish dreams from the waking state, raises the possibility that all our experience might be a dream, or at the very least that one of the ways to deal with the external world is to treat it as if it were a dream.[22] It is frustrating that we know more about the dreams of lesser figures, such as Galen or Aelius Aristides, than we do about those of Marcus Aurelius. Aelius, for example, dreamed that he was captured by Parthians who were about to brand him when he suddenly woke up.[23] Galen claimed that the god Asclepius regularly contacted him in dreams and gave him advice, about letting blood and other technical matters.[24] It is no exaggeration to say that educated people in the second century were obsessed with dreams, and Marcus's contemporary, the Greek Artemidorus, produced a book of dream interpretation that partly anticipated Freud in the important place it gave to sexuality and partly pre-empted Jung, in that it saw dreams as a guide to the future.[25] Artemidorus distinguished between *euhypnion* – a routine dream whereby the mind sorted, processed and computerised the previous day's events – and the more important *oneiros* – the dream relating to the future.[26] He adumbrated an inchoate form of the distinction between latent and manifest content that Freud later made famous, but tended to interpret symbols more broadly in the Jungian way, seeing a bird, for example, not as a phallic

, but as the sign of a soul yearning to fly free.[27] An interpret-
of imperial dreams by Artemidorus would have been invaluable,
especially as it would sidestep all the notorious problems about
transcultural dream interpretation. Scholars of the ancient world tend
to claim that ancient dreams can be interpreted only within the cultural
parameters in which the dreamer operated, whereas those of a psychoanalytical persuasion would say that the unconscious is universal across
space and time.[28] Writers who have ventured into the disputed territory of Marcus's dreams have usually regretted it.[29]

We are on safer ground with Marcus's conscious personality, for
here we have not only his own confessions in the *Meditations*, but also
the verdict of contemporary biographers and historians. He concedes
that he is not quick-witted and needs time to get his intellect into
gear, or as we might say, he was like a tank – a powerful weapon once
fully deployed, but not useful in short, quick, exchanges.[30] It was
perhaps as well that a man not able to think on his feet did not pursue
a career as a lawyer. Marcus himself thought that his ponderous lack
of quicksilver was no great matter: it was a trait he was born with,
like the colour of his eyes. The only important thing, he considered,
parroting the usual Stoic pieties, was his freedom to act in a moral
way. What mattered, he thought, were the things that *were* within his
control, and he prided himself on the following characteristics: lack
of duplicity, being serious, putting up with suffering, feeling contempt
for pleasure, having few needs, not complaining about Destiny, avoiding
gossip and idle chatter, being benevolent and possessing greatness of
soul[31] – though a critic would doubtless say that the last is not a quality
to be self-assigned. As when accepting the appellation 'author', this is
a case where it is for others to bestow the title. But Marcus did show
genuine self-awareness. He knew he was quick-tempered and had a
short fuse, but at the same time he knew that anger was a signal weakness and so worked hard to conquer it; the *Meditations* are full of
reminders to himself never to indulge his propensity for ire and rage.[32]
'Anger,' he wrote, 'is just as much a weakness as abandoning life's
struggle. Both the man who runs away and the man who lets himself
be alienated from his fellow-man are essentially deserters.'[33]
Noteworthy in his list of qualities is the commitment to truth.[34] His
detestation of lying and liars pervades his writings, and it has been
pointed out that this is more unusual than it might seem to a modern

reader. Neither the Greeks nor the imperial Romans had the same black-and-white feeling about veracity and mendacity, and Marcus's attitude is in some ways a throwback to the ethos of early Rome and ascetics like Cato the Elder.[35]

Again and again in his writings Marcus stresses straightness, plain dealing, integrity and simplicity, though he knew he did not make himself popular thereby. He bore 'with unruffled temper the insolence of not a few'.[36] Like Henry V, Marcus liked to find out what the man in the street really thought of him and then go away and ponder the possible truth of negative opinions; if he thought the criticism justified, he would amend his behaviour accordingly.[37] He also thought that the philosophy of Stoicism made consideration for the opinion of others a moral imperative: 'It is fairer for me to follow the advice of so many and such good friends than for my many and good friends to obey my single wishes.'[38] It is quite clear that, despite his frequent protestations that he did not care what other people's opinion of him was, as long as he was doing the right thing, he was remarkably sensitive on this score. He particularly feared that his countrymen disliked him and thought of him as a pedantic pedagogue.[39] There are many revealing slips in his writings which indicate that, if anything, he was over-sensitive to what people thought.[40] In his *Meditations* Marcus frequently tests himself to see whether there is any truth in the derogatory canards that circulated. It was said, for example, that he was mean, though this was an accusation routinely made by whingers and malcontents against all Roman emperors, no matter how open-handed they were; we have already encountered the accusation in the case of Antoninus Pius.[41] In fact Marcus was remarkably generous with money, not only showering largesse on his friends but also granting lavish and extravagant donatives and *congiaria* (periodic cash handouts) on the army and the people.[42] In the case of his sister, who married Ummidius Quadratus, Marcus not only settled on her a larger share of the family estate than she was entitled to, but, on her death in 152, secured for their son Ummidius Quadratus junior a share in the property of his mother Domitia Lucilla, the extremely wealthy owner of brickworks all over Italy.[43]

Yet Marcus was, perhaps predictably, the victim of one of the oldest human syndromes, whereby no good deed goes unpunished or, as he put it cynically in his own notebook, 'Kingship: to earn a bad

reputation by good deeds'. His very simplicity, lack of 'side' and ostentation, his commitment to the truth and his generosity were all thought
by his critics just too good to be true. As the *Historia Augusta* puts it:
'There were some who complained that he was affected and not so
simple as he seemed, or as Antoninus Pius and Verus had been.'[44]
Others said that his *sancta simplicitas* was an example of 'false consciousness': he was out of place as a man looking for tenderness, affection,
warmth, sincerity and authenticity in a Roman world permeated by
cruelty and dominated by an arrogant patrician caste; it was said that
his dislike of the circus and the arena showed that he was not really
the right man to lead the Roman empire.[45] Still others continued to
sneer at him for his commitment to philosophy. As emperor, he
attended lectures given by Sextus of Chaeronea, and was taunted for
this by a certain Lucius, a sophist known for his blunt rudeness. Marcus
replied, 'Learning is a good thing, even for one who is growing old.
From Sextus the philosopher I shall learn what I do not yet know.'
The acidulous Lucius replied, 'O Zeus! The ageing emperor of the
Romans is laying tablets round his neck in order to go to school,
while my king Alexander [the Great] died at the age of thirty-two.'[46]
The historian Cassius Dio provided a full-blooded rebuttal of all these
critics, pointing out that Marcus did nothing out of affectation, but
everything out of virtue; he remained always the same, did not change
and did not act on what the last person to speak to him said or advised.
'Nothing could force him to do anything alien to his own character:
not the idea of making an example of someone nor the magnitude
of the crime.'[47]

Among the many complexities, ambiguities and self-contradictions
in Marcus's character was the conflict between doctrines to which he
was naturally bound by his adherence to Stoicism and the underlying
thrust of his personality. While committed philosophically to the idea
of constant change and metamorphosis and to the notion that everything is in a state of flux, Marcus was at heart a deeply conservative
man who loathed change. Whenever there was a choice between the
old and the new, he opted for the old. This preference was obvious
in his theatre-going, where he liked the 'old comedy' of Aristophanes,
with its directness and blunt criticism of the 'great and the good', over
the so-called New Comedy of Plautus and Terence, which he considered mere technique and facile realism or, at best, the pointlessness

of art for art's sake.[48] This preference for Greek over Latin emerges not just from the fact that he wrote the *Meditations* in Greek, considering his native tongue an inadequate vessel for philosophical thought, but also in his overwhelming predilection for Greek tragedy. The four separate lines of tragedy that he quotes in the *Meditations* are all classical Greek (one from Sophocles and the other three from Euripides).[49] Marcus was incurious in artistic matters, had a narrow range of interests and thought music and dancing pointless.[50] He was not interested in mathematics, astronomy, poetry, art or sculpture and, even within his chosen discipline of philosophy, his scope was narrow when compared with people like Cicero, although in compensation Herodian claimed that Marcus was devoted to the literature of the past in a way that surpassed the interest of any previous Greek or Roman.[51] In social matters he was equally conservative, and he considered it axiomatic that women's minds and souls were inferior to men's.[52] Some critics think that the turbulence and upset of his early life – being put under the tutelage of Annius Verus when his father died, living with his mother Domitia Lucilla under the direction of her grandfather Catilius Severus and then finally being adopted by Antoninus at Hadrian's orders – left him with a loathing of change and a desire that things should always remain the same. Marcus was aware of the conflict between his deep character and disposition and the requirements of Stoicism and sometimes tried to rationalise it in a somewhat flippant manner, remarking that, having surmounted so many changes, he would not fear death, which was merely another change.[53]

The most obvious aspect of Marcus's personality is the contrast between the easy-going, grape-treading, hunting and fishing young oligarch, who enjoyed antiquarianism, hill-walking, gossiping with his mother and listening to the prattle of rustics, and the grim, severe adult he came to be – a man with few, if any, real friends. A modern diagnosis of the middle-aged to elderly Marcus might be that he suffered from some form of clinical depression, and the phrase 'mournful resignation' has often been used to denote his mindset.[54] Since the classic defence against depression is humour, it is significant and noteworthy that most authorities concur in finding Marcus notably humourless.[55] Ernest Renan, the great nineteenth-century scholar and commentator, was particularly severe on this aspect of a man he otherwise admired; he claimed that the last of the great Antonines lacked what he called 'the kiss of a fairy' (the gift of laughter and gaiety at birth).[56] The evidence suggests that Marcus was the type of man – like, say, Earl Haig, the First World War general – who knew that there was something called humour and that people enjoyed laughter, but could never see what the joke was supposed to be; the sole reference to laughter in the *Meditations* is a disparaging reference to bad lines in a play placed there for laughs by an inept playwright.[57] Some have defended Marcus on the spurious grounds that no great man (allegedly) ever had a sense of humour or the absurd, but this (in turn risible) proposition is amply refuted by the examples of Churchill and Abe Lincoln, to go no further.[58] Indeed Renan, contrasting Marcus's po-faced melancholy with his 'father' Antoninus Pius's ready wit, was led to declare, 'In some respects Antoninus was the greater of the two. His goodness of heart did not lead him into indiscretions; he escaped the torment of the inward malady which pitilessly gnawed at the heart of his adoptive son.'[59] Some have used Marcus's lack of wit and humour as a springboard to question his intelligence in general and have coupled it with his inability to read the characters of men – most notably Lucius Verus, Avidius Cassius and his own son Commodus – and his gullibility in matters of magic and religion (of which more later) to indict him for a general lack of intellect.[60] This is an unjustifiable inference. Marcus's deep problem was his need to be faithful to the inhuman creed of Stoicism, which frowned on laughter as an activity for lesser minds. His hero Epictetus preached that one should always avoid raising a laugh, as that automatically diminished people's respect for you.[61]

Perhaps more surprising than the lack of a sense of humour is the ultra-censorious attitude to sex and sexuality. There are two aspects to this, one common to Marcus and Epictetus, the other peculiarly Marcus's own. From Epictetus comes a quasi-Gnostic contempt for the body and the physical world, and a corresponding obsession with the mind and the otherworldly prescriptions of Stoicism. Epictetus regarded the body as a prison or fetter for the soul, echoing the words of Socrates in *Phaedo*; but this has no real precedent in the history of Stoicism until then.[62] Marcus took over this notion and built on it, frequently describing the body as 'meaningless'; he was particularly exercised by its rebarbative smells, by other's people's body-odour, halitosis, flatulence, and so on.[63] In the later books of the *Meditations* the detached Gnostic contempt for the body and the physical becomes something like Swift's savage indignation, and Marcus works himself into a lather: even taking a bath means coming into contact with 'oil, sweat, dirt, greyish water, all of it disgusting'. The body is 'a mess of blood, pieces of bone, a woven tangle of nerves, veins, arteries'. Later he expresses 'disgust at what things are made of: liquid, dust, bones, filth. Marble as hardened dirt, gold and silver as residues, clothes as hair, purple dye as shellfish blood'.[64] Yet it is important to be clear that Epictetus does not transfer his contempt for the physical world into a hatred of sexuality and never advocated mortification or asceticism.[65] His general exhortation on how to live is one of his best-known sayings: 'Eat like a man, drink like a man, get dressed, get married, have children, lead the life of a citizen . . . Show us all this so that we can see whether or not you have really learned something from the philosophers.'[66] Although there are passages in his lectures where Epictetus inveighs against sexual lust – and he remarks witheringly that an adulterer is as useless *qua* man as a cracked saucepan[67] – in general he takes the matter-of-fact stance of a man of the world. He recommends avoidance of sexual intercourse before marriage, but cautions against any hint of boasting about one's chastity or taking a holier-than-thou attitude towards unregenerate sensualists, and concedes that if the demands of the flesh become too great, a man is justified in going to prostitutes.[68] Such liberalism did not appeal at all to Marcus Aurelius. For one thing, he *did* boast about the sexual temptations he had overcome.[69] For another he was full of loathing for 'prostitutes and perverts'.[70] The disgust for sexuality is most keenly expressed in some life-denying comments on sexual intercourse: 'Something rubbing against your penis, a brief climax, and a little cloudy liquid.' Parallelling the Church Fathers' famous contempt for the body and sexuality – *inter urinam et faeces nascimur* – Marcus puts 'mating' in the same category as defecation. 'He deposits his sperm and leaves.'[71]

He frequently states his conviction that sexual lust is a form of 'false consciousness', that the way to deal with libido is not to find a way to sleep with women, but to control and conquer the appetite.[72] His fastidious disdain is all the more surprising since Antonine Rome was unquestionably a 'permissive' society; doubtless all societies are obsessed with sex under the surface, as Freud famously argued, but few have been as candid as the Romans in the second century AD. This emerges clearly from Artemidorus's famous work on dream interpretation, where most of the dreams analysed are sexual. Some of the interpretations are banal, as when we are told that a good dream is one of having sex with one's wife or a beautiful woman not one's wife, but a bad dream is having sex with an old woman or a prostitute. The Oedipus complex is prefigured in the statement that sex with one's mother in the missionary position means that the father and son will be enemies. If a sick man dreams of sex with a dead mother, Artemidorus continues, this means the man will soon die and be united with 'mother earth'. But it is apparently good to dream of sex with a dead mother when one is in the middle of a lawsuit, though bad if the intercourse is in a standing position or from the rear. The worst dream of all is to be given fellatio by the mother, as this presages disaster. On the other hand, fellatio with a wife or mistress means hatred and this is particularly the case if it is the dreamer who is providing oral intercourse. To be an active partner in a dream about bestialism is fine, but to be the passive partner again presages catastrophe.[73] Clearly the dominant Roman culture was highly sexualised until Christianity changed public attitudes, and in such a context, Marcus seems noticeably out of step with the mainstream. Was he perhaps protesting too much when he asserted that his dreams simply provided him with antidotes against spitting blood and dizziness?[74] It has been suggested that Marcus found it difficult even in his private writing to be completely frank about his feelings and secret thoughts.[75] At all events a certain prudery, to put it no stronger, is evident in his utterances. It is perhaps not surprising that Marcus was so keen to praise Antoninus Pius for restricting homosexual behaviour and, as we have remarked, the deep subtext of his distaste for Trajan and Hadrian may be their promiscuous same-sex intercourse.[76]

It has sometimes been suggested that Stoicism has an organic link with psychoanalysis, but this would be hard to sustain from an examination of Marcus's brand of the doctrine. There is a certain philosophical contradiction between the remorseless self-examination from the Stoic viewpoint in which Marcus indulges and his hostility to any idea of 'depth psychology' or probing into the motives of others.[77] His most explicit statement of distaste for 'alienists' or soul doctors (one shudders to think what he would have made of

Artemidorus) is as follows: 'Nothing is more pathetic than people who run around in circles "delving into the things that lie beneath" and conducting investigations into the souls of the people around them, never realising that all you have to do is to be attentive to the power inside you and worship it sincerely.'[78] But psychoanalysis is above all an 'extrovert' discipline, to use the Jungian term, concentrating on the relationship of the subject with objects and the external world. Marcus's concerns were, in Jungian terms, wholly 'introvert' and indeed at times verged on solipsism. Far from pondering the deep forces that might be propelling him, Marcus's gloomy introspection was almost entirely devoted to self-criticism: he laments that he has not yet succeeded in living like a philosopher, or in living according to Nature and Reason. He lists his faults and admits his mistakes and even concedes that he is no better than those he criticises severely.[79] On the other hand, there is none of the masochistic self-flagellation and the constant consciousness of being a corrupt entity that we encounter in, say, St Augustine's *Confessions*. Marcus tells us, 'I don't deserve to be ashamed of myself, for I have never voluntarily harmed anyone.'[80] Occasionally, indeed, his self-criticism can come across as arrogance. Take this, for example: 'There is a sense in which a man of forty, if he is slightly intelligent, has seen everything there has been and everything that will be, because of the uniformity of things.'[81] This hardly squares with the views of his hero Socrates, who declared that every day he lived he realised how much less he knew.[82]

Yet another contradiction in Marcus's tortured, complex personality is that between the positive view of human beings to whom he is committed by the doctrines of Stoicism and his own Swiftian disgust for *Homo sapiens*. Here are some of the 'public' utterances, significantly recorded not in the *Meditations* but by the historian Cassius Dio. 'He used to say that it was impossible to create people as one would like them to be, but that each one had to be utilised in whatever task he was capable of accomplishing . . . He used to praise them for the service they had rendered, and he paid no attention to the rest of their behaviour.'[83] Or again: 'He bore the faults of others, neither inquiring too closely into them nor chastising them' – and this included insults and injuries to himself, which most other emperors would have construed as lese-majesty.[84] But sometimes the Stoic role-playing and the inauthenticity of his public persona became too much for Marcus, and he revealed his true feelings: 'Let people see and discover what a man who truly lives in accordance with Nature is like! If they can't put up with you, then let them kill you! That would be better than living like them.'[85] Or again: 'How worthless, shortlived and cheap are the objects of our experience and desire, things that can be possessed by a sodomite, a whore or a brigand. Think next of the characters of those with whom you live; even the best of them can hardly be borne, not to mention that a man can hardly stand himself.'[86] Most of all, he detested the flatterers and sycophants who clustered around an emperor like moths to the flame.[87] Herodian claimed that Marcus created a vogue for philosophy, but Cassius Dio, more shrewdly, saw that a host of phoneys and charlatans arose, claiming to be devotees of philosophy simply to win favour with the emperor and thus gain places, pensions and perquisites; Marcus himself provides hints that he was well aware of this situation.[88] Given that he had a very low opinion of his fellow-humans and that all his best friends were dead by the late 160s, even while he, the would-be full-time philosopher, had to devote so much time to the affairs of state, it is not surprising that Marcus in late-middle and old age manifested all the symptoms of the classically alienated man: isolated, lonely, melancholic, quasi-solipsistic, hating his life at court (he likened it to a termagant stepmother) and the intrusion of the detested world of the quotidian. The more he got involved in the management of the empire, the more he felt himself alone and alienated.[89] On the other hand, his Stoicism required that he had to conceal this repugnance and rationalise it as the quest for Plato's Republic.[90] One gnomic utterance on this point is particularly striking: 'Live as if you were on a mountain. It doesn't matter whether one lives in one place or another, as long as one lives everywhere as within one's own City, which is the world.'[91]

Yet Marcus never knowingly short-changed the empire, bored and disgusted though he was with matters of state, high politics and diplomacy. Few individuals in history can ever have had a keener sense of duty. He had something of an obsession with being a 'good' emperor and frequently noted with horror and contempt the antics of the evil men who had worn the purple. Caligula, Domitian, Tiberius and Nero are often mentioned as egregious tyrants, and Marcus was particularly good at avoiding the Neronian trap into which Julian the Apostate was later to fall – that of the posturing emperor-artist.[92] Nero especially appalled Marcus, who always contrasted Antoninus Pius's moderation in all things with Nero's excesses. There was the contrast between the sensible ordinances on bathing and the deranged ones of Caligula and Nero; to say that Antoninus was 'not fond of building' is clearly a coded criticism of both Hadrian and Nero, whose expansive building programme was notorious.[93] Trajan and Hadrian, sometimes classed as 'good emperors', fell foul of Marcus because of their open and promiscuous homosexuality.[94] But above all Marcus was consistently on the side of all the brave souls in Roman history who had challenged imperial tyrants, even at the lowly level of abstract advocacy, and paid for their 'insolence' with their lives.[95] The relations between emperors and subjects had particularly interested Epictetus and in his work he frequently imagines hypothetical circumstances where an individual is relating to Caesar – and this in turn reinforced Marcus's determination never to do a despotic act.[96] He liked to quote the saying of Antisthenes, also a favourite of Epictetus's: 'A king's role is to act well and be spoken ill of in return.'[97] And he was especially fond of Epictetus's teachings on the limits of imperial power. Even an emperor could not provide 'security from fever, shipwreck, fire, earthquake, lightning . . . or from love, sorrow and envy', because only God could do that.[98]

The avoidance of tyranny for Marcus meant following the example of Antoninus and locating sovereignty in the Senate.[99] He thanked the gods that his 'father' had made him indifferent to, and contemptuous of, pomp, processions and pageantry.[100] He also continually reminded himself that while living in a palace one could lead a good and virtuous life. His conception of empire was that one should enhance security, peace, trade and Roman glory while promoting the Stoic view of the perfect society, envisaging the empire not as a thing in itself, but as a community designed for the general good.[101] With no sympathy for modern flag-waving, Marcus nonetheless appears a modern figure in his dual role as thinker and ruler – though in fairness it must be conceded that most of the modern thinker-leaders have been a disaster: Lenin, Hitler, Mao, and so on. This in itself made Marcus unlike most of the great figures of the past: Alexander the Great, Hannibal, even Julius Caesar. He himself theorised that to become a good and benevolent ruler one had to ascend the various stages in the hierarchy of social being – man, adult, citizen, Roman, emperor – and master each in turn; this was one obvious reason why the Caligulas and Neros had been deficient.[102] Marcus advocated a kind of practical version of Kant's categorical imperative: act in such a way that what is good for Rome will be good for the entire world. He said that Destiny had marked him down for this role: he was brought into the world to be the guardian of the people, as the ram is of the flock and the bull of the herd.[103] Yet he realised that the whispers at Rome were that he had failed, and on two main counts. He had lamentably failed to achieve Plato's Republic and he had not emulated the conquests of men like Demetrius Poliorcetes, Philip of Macedon and Alexander the Great. On the second charge, Marcus replied that these so-called illustrious men had no philosophical understanding and were therefore not to be taken seriously. On the first, he remarked that there was an intrinsic absurdity in believing that everything could be changed overnight or even in one person's lifetime.[104] Posterity has largely vindicated him. Cassius Dio recorded this verdict: 'He not only possessed all the other virtues but also was a better ruler than anyone else who had ever been emperor.'[105] In the nineteenth century Renan suggested that Marcus outpointed all the three great Mogul emperors in India: Babar, Humaioun and Akbar.[106]

Throughout his reign Marcus emphasised collegiality and consultation with his cabinet and the Senate. This has led the unwary to claim that he was essentially a weak man, who cared more for the appearance of consensus than for taking the tough decisions an effective emperor had to take. It is true that he constantly emphasised tolerance, and his leniency towards charlatans is often cited. There was one notable instance involving a 'preacher' who made speeches in the Campus Martius prophesying the imminent end of the world. Marcus was no stranger to the millenarianism and eschatology of the second century, but many rulers would have taken the line that such alarmist preachings constituted a threat to public morale and order, to say nothing of the implied insult to the present incumbent on the imperial throne, and would have executed him instantly. The prophet foretold that the sign of Armageddon would be when he fell from a tree and was turned into a stork. He then set it up that he fell from a tree (without of course injuring himself) and, by sleight of hand, released a stork from a voluminous cloak. It was the most obvious conjuring trick, and the prestidigitator was hauled before the emperor for sentencing. Marcus took the line that the man was a harmless lunatic and instantly pardoned him.[107] But it would be a grave mistake to extrapolate from this and other similar examples, and his oft-professed credo of tolerance, to the proposition that he was a soft touch. He was prepared to overrule his cabinet colleagues when he was convinced that he was in the right, even if he was only in a majority of one. The best-known instance was when he opted to continue the northern campaign against the Germans, despite their opposition (see Chapter Fourteen).[108] As for tolerance, this did not extend to mercy to allies or foes who broke treaties or failed to keep their word. The good press that Marcus has received down the centuries has blindsided many historians and critics to the numerous instances where his behaviour could be considered harsh – his use of torture as an instrument of judicial examination, or his execution of prisoners simply because they were a drain on his army's food supplies.[109]

Marcus's ruthlessness most clearly manifested itself in his attitude to his in-laws. Commodus was the only one of his sons to survive to adulthood, but the girls fared much better. Those who became women acquired husbands, but Marcus made sure they were nonentities who could never challenge Commodus; if they showed any sign of ambition they were liable to meet with a sudden 'accident'. Only those who think of Marcus Aurelius as some kind of modern liberal should be surprised by this. In almost all dynasties throughout history, rulers have murdered children, mothers and spouses for *raison d'état*, and the murder of brothers was considered so self-evidently prudential as almost to be a mathematical axiom.[110] Roman history was no exception, and so we find that to control the succession Nero killed Britannicus, Tiberius slew Agrippa Postumus and Caligula disposed of Tiberius Gemellus. Rulers always ruthlessly killed off members of clans who married into their families, to prevent pretenders from arising. Of all the clans with sons who married the daughters of Marcus Aurelius, only the Claudii Severi remained out of harm's way, and then only because they displayed not a scintilla of political ambition.[111] And all this after the initial winnowing process to ensure that none of his sons-in-law was in any way meritorious. The historian Ronald Syme euphemistically referred to the emperor's in-laws as 'a notable and heterogeneous company',[112] but the truth is that they were talentless members of the senatorial class, carefully chosen exemplars of high social birth and low intelligence. Marcus's daughter Annia Galeria Faustina was married to C. Claudius Severus in 163, son of Marcus's tutor of philosophy, but a man who had evidently not inherited his father's gifts. The Severi were originally a Greek family from Paphlygonia, but were sufficiently established by this time that the clan could boast of having produced three consuls.[113] Fadilla (born 159) later married Lucius Verus's nephew Plautius Quintillus, son of Ceionia Fabia and descended through his father from the Avidii and Plautii of Trebula Safenas. Cornificia (b. 160) would marry Petronius Sura Mamertinus, either grandson or grand-nephew of Antoninus Pius's praetorian prefect Petronius Mamertinus, a kinsman of Fronto. While Marcus had ensured the dignity of his daughters by marrying them into senatorial and consular families, Commodus – the emperor after Marcus – was not so punctilious. He had Marcus's last-known child, Vibia Aurelia Sabina, married off to L. Antistius Burrus, the son or nephew of a mere garrison commander.[114]

Although Marcus showed considerable solicitude for his daughters when they were little girls, it seems that once they were women he regarded them as mere pawns in the dynastic mating game. It is possible, as some have alleged, that his real favourite among his children was his son Marcus Annius Verus (b. 162). In 169 disaster struck when the child was found to have a tumour under his ear; the operation to save him was a miserable failure. Steeling himself against this supreme trial, Marcus allowed himself just five days of mourning. He argued that because the games of Jupiter Optimus Maximus were in progress, he did not want them interrupted by a show of ostentatious public mourning. Instead he ordered that statues be erected for his son and that a golden image of him be carried in procession at the Circus, and that his name be inserted in the songs of the Salii.[115] The real reason Marcus did not mourn his son any longer was because of the brutal and inhuman teaching of the Stoics on this point.[116] It is true that Romans tried to anaesthetise themselves against grief for lost children, because they did not want to invest emotion in those likely to die. It is also true that the normal Roman ethos frowned on hysterical grief at the death of loved ones, as unmanly and unnatural, not just because of the normally low life expectancy, but because life taught the lesson that all human organisms, and especially children, were appallingly vulnerable. Herodes Atticus, who made a point of lengthy public lamentation whenever he lost a family member, was explicitly censured for this by Lucian.[117] But Stoicism went beyond this and provided a plethora of arguments against excessive mourning, all of which Marcus deployed at various times. First, one only had to look at the fate of certain clans and families who had died off entirely. Second, death was part of the natural order, as much an aspect of the cosmos as childbirth. He instanced all those who were 'relicts' after the death of loved ones. Third, the gods must have their reasons for the sorrow and tragedy they visit on us. It was no accident that one of Marcus's favourite quotes from tragedy was from Euripides: 'If I and my two children cannot move the gods, the gods must have their reasons.'[118] Above all, there were two terrible recipes that strike a modern sensibility as inhuman heartlessness. Talking of 'representations', Marcus says, 'The fact that my son is sick – that I can see. But that he might die of it – no.' And again: 'As you kiss your son goodnight, says Epictetus, whisper to yourself, "He may be dead in the morning."'[119] It is perhaps fortunate for human sanity that a greater genius than Marcus Aurelius has adequately refuted this stance.[120]

The East
and

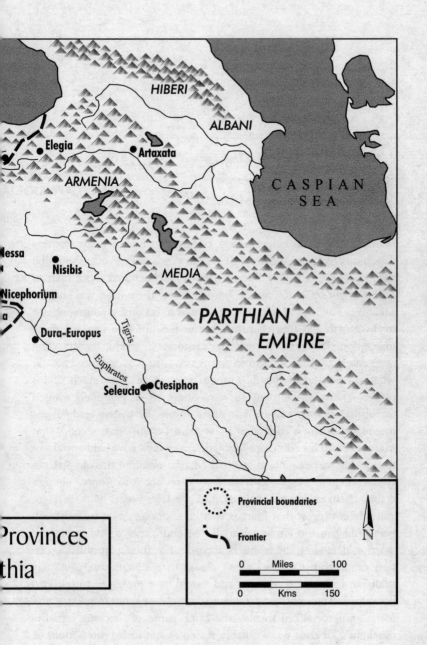

HIBERI

ALBANI

Elegia

Artaxata

ARMENIA

CASPIAN
SEA

essa

Nisibis

MEDIA

Nicephorium

PARTHIAN
EMPIRE

a

Tigris

Dura-Europus

Euphrates

Seleucia Ctesiphon

Provinces

thia

Provincial boundaries

Frontier

N

0	Miles	100

0	Kms	150

6

Marcus's first act as emperor was to insist that Lucius Verus, the boy Antoninus had also adopted at Hadrian's insistence in 138, should be named as his co-ruler. Nothing whatever had been said about such an arrangement by Antoninus on his death-bed; the notion was entirely Marcus's. The idea of joint emperors was to become a commonplace in the fourth and fifth centuries, but at this juncture was a definite innovation. Even in the modern 'democratic' world, leaders cling desperately to their autocratic prerogatives, so we are bound to ask: whatever possessed Marcus Aurelius to give away so much of his power? There can be many answers. Some say he genuinely wanted to fulfil Hadrian's wishes,[1] but this assumes, first, that Hadrian *did* intend Verus to be co-emperor (far from certain) and, second, that Marcus – with his contempt for Hadrian – would have paid any attention to his wishes. Others say that Marcus admired the old Spartan system of joint kings and wanted to introduce it to Rome. Though it may be an *ex post* rationalisation of the later events of their reign, still others suggest that Marcus wanted a kind of 'dyarchy' whereby he would run the empire from Rome and Verus would act as the warrior, defending the frontiers abroad.[2] The most plausible suggestion came from Cassius Dio, who said that Marcus was genuinely reluctant to become emperor and would have preferred to retire to his studies. The reluctant president is a cliché of modern politics, and some emperors liked to play the same game of 'backing into the limelight' (Tiberius was a notable example), but their protestations of reluctance were always bogus. Only in Marcus's case is there reason to believe that he might have been genuinely unwilling to take up the burdens of office. But, in that case, it is reasonable to ask why he stayed at his post with Antoninus for twenty-two years instead of asking for permission to be a modern Cincinnatus and retiring to his estates. Moreover, it hardly made sense for Marcus to devolve impe-rial duties to a 'more vigorous man' if his choice of that man was Lucius Verus. The Ceionii were notoriously short-lived: Verus's great-grandfather, grandfather and father all died within a few years of their consulships.[3] When we have sifted through all the possible reasons for Marcus's apparent act of self-negation, the overwhelming probability remains that he made Lucius Verus co-emperor to co-opt him and head off the possibility of a coup by the Ceionius clan jealous that their putative rights to the throne had been ignored.[4] Having Verus at his side as a comrade-ruler was an act of statesmanship.

Born in December 130, Lucius was the son of Hadrian's first choice as successor, Lucius Aelius Caesar; all we know of his mother was that she was called Avidia. He did not receive the name by which history knows him – Lucius Verus – until 161 when, as co-emperor, Marcus transferred his own surname to his colleague to establish a family connection.[5] He was not a precocious youth like Marcus; no one would have regarded him as 'one to note'. Although he had different teachers for elementary education, at the higher level Antoninus gave him most of the same tutors and teachers that Marcus had enjoyed, but none of them discerned great signs of intellectual promise; what he did have was an appealing and charming person-ality, which made him something of a teacher's pet. One of the few details of his education we possess is that he liked to compose verses. When he assumed the *toga virilis* in 145 he was promoted into the predictable tutelage of Fronto and Herodes Atticus. He also studied philosophy with Apollonius of Chalcedon and Sextus of Chaeronea. Fronto thought him a reasonably good speaker, but was later dismayed to find that the best passages in his speeches had been written by his friends. Lucius Verus always had an amused contempt for learning and academia, but used his charm to bluff his way out of most situ-ations. He was indulged by all around him, especially his day-to-day 'minder' the freedman Nicomedes, a faithful retainer of Lucius's father; yet Nicomedes was no fool, and eventually achieved the unheard-of feat for a freedman of rising to the position of *procurator summarum rationum*.[6]

Antoninus usually had little time for Lucius, correctly intuiting that he was no Marcus. He was largely kept in the background and marginalised. He never received the same marks of imperial favour as Marcus. Whereas Marcus always travelled with the emperor in the imperial carriage, Lucius had to find his berth in the carriage of the praetorian prefect. Most of the time Antoninus made it plain that he tolerated Lucius only because of his promise to adopt him as the price of being nominated Hadrian's successor. Lucius received no other title than 'son of Augustus', did not bear the appellation 'Caesar', as Marcus did, and had no coins struck bearing his image. But Antoninus took care not to humiliate him, by giving him a seat on the imperial council.[7] Only occasionally did Antoninus succumb to the young man's seductive charm. On one occasion he rebuked Marcus mildly for his earnestness, saying that he could learn something from Lucius's attitude to life.[8] Although Lucius was a lesser star in Antoninus's galaxy, the emperor treated him well and gave him accelerated promotion, though not on the scale of privilege he had accorded to Marcus. In 152 Lucius was appointed quaestor for the next year, at the age of twenty-two, two years below the official age for quaestorships (though it should be remembered that Marcus had been a quaestor at seventeen). Two years later he became consul without ever having been praetor – a most unusual step, as the tripartite *cursus honorum* was usually rigidly adhered to – and served with a venerable greybeard (T. Sextius Lateranus) as his consular colleague. At twenty-three, Lucius was nine years below the usual minimum age. Once again, though, we should remember the contrast with Marcus, who was consul for the first time at eighteen and for the second time at twenty-three.[9] Lucius was consul for the second time with Marcus in 161, but was everywhere perceived to be his junior in every sense. Even when Marcus co-opted him as joint emperor, he made it clear that he himself was the senior partner by retaining for himself the title of high priest (*pontifex maximus*) with Lucius as a simple *pontifex*.[10]

Lucius Verus was one of those popular, charismatic, yet ultimately empty-headed and second-rate personalities either in power or close to power that we encounter throughout history; many of the contemporary descriptions make him seem an uncanny pre-echo of Henry

II's son, Henry the Young King, a charming hedonist, spendthrift and profligate. He was extremely good-looking, tall and stately in appearance, with a forehead that projected over his eyebrows. Such was his vanity that he used gold tint to highlight his hair. Halting in speech and no intellectual, he was notoriously unpredictable: some Romans compared him to Nero, but the comparison did not really hold, for Verus was neither cruel nor interested in acting on the stage.[11] An unregenerate sybarite, as a youth he was known for his affairs with young men. Favoured with an excellent digestion and needing little sleep, yet cursed with the short life expectancy of all members of the Ceionius clan, he comes across as a basically nice guy who was weak, easily led astray and could see no meaning in anything but pleasure.[12] Debauchery, carnality, carousing and gambling were his fortes. He liked to trawl the taverns and low dives of Rome in disguise, getting into scrapes and revelling in his incognito, though on at least one occasion he was recognised. He often returned to his quarters at dawn, black and blue after some ferocious donnybrook, often caused by his peculiar habit of smashing the cups in taverns by hurling coins at them.[13] At chariot races he was a fanatical supporter of the Greens against the Blues, Reds and Whites – unfortunately the circus faction most often associated with tyrants like Caligula and Nero,[14] and was the particular bête noire of the Blue faction, which detested him cordially. He bred horses for the races and had an attachment to his horse Volucer, which some said recalled Alexander the Great and Bucephalus; the unkind said Caligula and Incitatus. He liked to spoil Volucer, put raisins and nuts in his manger instead of barley and, when the horse died, insisted on a solemn burial on the Janiculum Hill.

His banquets at his villa on the Via Cassia – near modern Acqua Traversa, north of the *Pons Mulvica*, off the Clodian Way running from Rome to central Tuscany (the Clodian Way branched off from the Via Cassia near Veii) – were also notorious. No expense was spared: there was gold and silver in abundance, the finest glass, flowers out of season, precious ointments, and carriage mules and muleteeers waiting to take the revellers home.[15] Verus pioneered the idea of having couches for twelve at his banquets, which was considered a particular eccentricity. There was an old Roman saying that 'seven make a dinner, nine a din', based on the ancient principle that the numbers at a banquet should not be less than the Graces (three) or more than the

Muses (nine).[16] Verus dispensed with this principle, as with all other guidelines to Roman etiquette. He liked to offer his young male waiters as presents for the guests and, whatever meat was being served, gave a gift of the corresponding live animal to the departing rioters.[17] The costs of his feats were astronomical, with six billion sesterces being quoted for one particular escapade. Marcus was said to have groaned when he learned the cost of this 'noble dinner' and told his associates that he feared for the fate of the empire.[18] He and Lucius Verus maintained separate courts, as different as could be: one a salon for thinkers and intellectuals, the other a haven for debauchees, satyrs, pederasts, voyeurs, perverts and simple drunkards. At Marcus's court it was the fashion to have the head shaved, in the style of the Stoics. At Verus's it was the fashion to wear the hair long: indeed, Verus was notorious for his shaggy barbarian-style locks, which he wore as long as possible to underline the point that he was not in competition with Marcus and had no desire to emulate him.[19]

Attempts have sometimes been made to rehabilitate Lucius Verus, and it must be stressed that he was a profligate, sensualist, drunkard, pansexualist, hedonist and sybarite, rather than a psychopath in the manner of Nero, Caligula or Elagabalus. It may be that the negative portrait of him in the *Historia Augusta* is overdone, and his champions, clutching at straws, point out that Galen, for one, says nothing about Verus's dissolute character.[20] Others point out that the Christian theorist Justin Martyr referred to him as a 'philosopher and lover of culture', though this was probably just routine flattery from a Christian apologist seeking favours.[21] Some say that Lucius Verus had a very hard hand to play, being younger brother (by adoption), junior partner and ultimately son-in-law of Marcus, as well as clearly his intellectual inferior. Nonetheless, the negative picture of him can be sustained from the letters of one of his supporters, none other than Fronto himself, who is usually cited in defence.[22] Beneath all Fronto's flattery we can discern the same careless, luxury-loving *fainéant* of the other sources. Verus habitually took no notice of the views of an elderly valetudinarian, and Fronto was often hard put to it to remain civil. At one of Verus's riotous banquets, Fronto had to struggle to show deference to the host while vehemently protesting at the behaviour of one of Verus's thuggish friends. The unnamed reprobate insulted one of Fronto's friends and then, sensing that he had gone too far, asked

Tranquillus, a mutual associate, to patch up the quarrel. At first Fronto was inclined to stand on his dignity and rebuffed the offender's offer of apology, but was then compelled to accept it grudgingly when Verus insisted that there had to be harmony within his circle. Fronto then wrote to Verus to put his side of the dispute, fully aware that the offender, having made a token apology, had subsequently gone behind his back to Verus and attempted to blacken him.[23]

Marcus may have gained something from making Verus co-emperor, since the younger man was charismatic and popular with the mob, and thus helped to offset the perception of Marcus as a rather cold, dry and detached ruler. The coinage issued by the joint emperors stresses the harmony between them, and Marcus clearly indulged the young man's foibles, including the almost childish estimate he had of his own merits.[24] Verus lusted after glory, but was too ingenuous to keep anything hidden; with him it was very much a case of 'what you saw was what you got'. That there were often tensions between the two men is clear, but there is no evidence that Verus plotted against Marcus. He seems to have been genuinely fond of him, while amusedly contemptuous of his liking for philosophy. He genuinely despised Marcus's entourage, thinking they were all sycophants, playing at being philosophers in order to toady and cosy up to Marcus; it was a common perception that all Marcus's followers were phoneys, going through the philosophical motions in the hope of winning imperial favour.[25] Marcus, for his part, was often exasperated by Verus and particularly disliked the unscrupulous freedmen (Coedes, Eclectus, Geminus, Apolaustus, Agaclytus and Pergamus) who battened off him. In public, though, he always expressed approbation and, following his invariable custom, praised Verus in the *Meditations* as 'a brother whose natural abilities were a standing challenge to my own self-discipline, provoking me to improve my own character, and whose love and affection moved my heart and enriched my life'.[26]

Marcus and Verus began their reign cautiously. Almost their first act was to visit the camp of the praetorian guard in the north-eastern suburbs of Rome and award a donative of 20,000 sesterces a man (and even more to officers). All Roman emperors had to do this on ascending the throne, to make sure the key component of their power was kept loyal and happy. This unprecedentedly generous bounty was a shrewd move, for emperors usually handed over large sacks of money only when they were already in trouble or faced a military crisis. By putting money in the bank, as it were, Marcus hoped to be able to draw on funds of goodwill if and when a genuine crisis did arise. Having received predictable acclamation from the troops for this largesse, the two emperors then distributed a handsome *congiarium* to the mob.[27] Next Marcus supervised the funeral and deification of Antoninus Pius. He and Verus transported the corpse to the mausoleum of Hadrian, where the funerary urn was placed in the burial chamber with all the usual rites and obsequies, alongside the ashes of Hadrian, Aelius Caesar, Faustina the Elder and other notables. Antoninus's epitaph read: 'In his twenty-fourth tribunician potentiate, twice saluted emperor and four times consul, father of his country.'[28] Following the public funeral, Marcus moved quickly to deify his predecessor. This time there was no opposition from the Senate to the apotheosis of the late emperor, such as Antoninus had faced over Hadrian; more than twenty years of ostensible deference to the 'Conscript Fathers' had done their work.

The ceremony of deification was held in the Campus Martius, and a funeral pyre lit, from which the soul of Antoninus was thought to have flown into the empyrean. Marcus and Lucius pronounced a panegyric and ordered funeral games; the Senate chipped in with a gift of chariot races in the Circus Maximus. The emperors issued coinage in Antoninus's honour and organised the cult of the divine Antoninus Pius.[29] Then Marcus announced the betrothal of his eleven-year-old daughter Lucilla to Lucius Verus. There is something of a mystery about Verus's bachelor status, for a Roman nobleman should have married and begotten children by his age (thirty-one). It is of course possible that he had already married and been widowed, but in that case we should expect the sources to have something to say about the matter. It has been speculated, more probably, that Marcus always had such a match in mind and had over the years encouraged Verus to remain single until his daughter was of nubile age.[30] Others claim that Antoninus Pius expressly vetoed any marriage for Verus, on the grounds that any children so produced might be pretenders to Marcus's throne. Whatever the reason, Marcus now bound Verus closer to him by new kinship ties. Wags in the Forum muttered about the 'irregularity' whereby Verus, destined by Hadrian to be Faustina the Younger's husband, was now marrying her daughter. To celebrate the engagement and show the continuity with his adopted father, Marcus announced a fresh injection of funds into the *alimenta* scheme.[31]

Further good omens occurred when Faustina gave birth to male twins on 31 August. They were given the names of T. Aurelius Fulvius Antoninus (after Faustina's father the emperor) and Lucius Aurelius Commodus (to honour Lucius Verus). The occasion was marked by a triumphant coinage issue and the official astrologers provided suitably ecstatic horoscopes.[32] The muttering sceptics were not appeased: some pointed out that the twins had the same birthday as Caligula, scarcely a propitious sign. More significant than the fawning predictions of the tame astrologers was a dream that Faustina had during her pregnancy, when she saw herself giving birth to serpents, one fiercer than the other.[33] Yet in the spring and summer of 161 both rulers and ruled went through a halcyon, honeymoon period. To show that the liberal policies of Antoninus regarding censorship would be continued, both Marcus and Verus pointedly ignored a savage lampoon on their personalities by the comedian Marullus; under any emperor before Antoninus such lése-majesty would certainly have incurred the death-penalty.[34] Lucius Verus, doubtless surprised by his sudden elevation, was in particularly good spirits. Writing to Fronto, he rebuked him in half-serious, half-joking mode for having gone to the imperial palace to see Marcus without calling in to see him. Fronto predictably put the blame on the officiousness of Verus's freedmen, but already there were clear signs of a change in his attitude.[35] Relations between him and Verus had been cool at the end of the 150s, but now that his more malleable ex-pupil wore the purple, Fronto may have calculated that he could manipulate him; he had already given up on such tactics with the much shrewder Marcus. As his modern biographer notes of the period after 161: 'Fronto appears in a new guise, the intriguer outmanoeuvering his rivals at court, and as unctuous a flatterer as any.'[36]

The tranquillity of the first six months of the reign of the new emperors was abruptly shattered in the autumn of 161 by the first of the crises that would thereafter rain down on the principate with depressing regularity. First, Rome sustained one of the worst ever floodings of the Tiber. Rome's sacred river was an abiding nightmare for Romans for, as Pliny the Elder noted, the worst inundations always happened in the Eternal City itself.[37] There had been severe flooding in 193 BC, 60 BC, 54 BC, 27 BC, 22 BC, AD 15, AD 36, AD 69 as well as during the reigns of Nerva and Trajan. The low-lying areas around the Campus Martius were always worst affected.[38] The problem had been recognised for centuries, but successive initiatives in the Senate were always shelved. The Romans liked to rationalise their idleness in this regard by claiming that floods were simply a wake-up call from the gods, angry at human laxness, and never presaged an outright disaster. Tiberius had (appropriately enough) appointed a Tiber Commission, but this seems to have been a toothless body, regarded by the commissioners as a sinecure. Ironically, right at the end of his reign Antoninus had ordered a general review of defences against the Tiber, but he died before anything could be achieved.[39] The extensive flooding of late 161 destroyed many buildings, drowned large numbers of animals, severely damaged crops and left famine in its wake; even more seriously, it triggered a serious outbreak of malaria, a perennial scourge in ancient Rome.[40] Marcus worked doggedly to improve the city's defences against the ravages of the swollen river, and by the end of his reign there was a senior curator based in Rome with an assistant at Ostia to give advance warning of flooding.[41] But the problem was never really solved. There were serious floods again in 217 and 374.[42] For Marcus, the problems of relief were compounded by disasters elsewhere in the empire. He had no sooner allocated money for famine relief and the building of new river barriers than word came in of a massive earthquake at Cyzicus, requiring a simultaneous drain on the treasury.[43]

But the flooding of the Tiber was a bagatelle alongside the shocking news that was next to reach Rome. For the first time in forty years Rome was at war with her arch-enemy Parthia, and this time the hostilities were not of Roman choosing. To make sense of this major development in the first years of Marcus's reign, we have to go back in time 200 years to the first Roman contacts with Parthia. The kingdom of Parthia, in the north-east of modern Iran, was orginally part of the Seleucid empire – the realm founded in Persia by Alexander the Great's successors when they divided up his empire after his death. In the second century BC the Arsacid kingdom of Parthia overthrew the Seleucids and became the dominant power in Persia and the Middle East.[44] The Parthian empire that was acquired by continual conquest throughout the second century eventually embraced the whole of modern Iran, as well as significant chunks of present-day Armenia,

Iraq, Georgia, eastern Turkey, eastern Syria, Turkmenistan, Afghanistan, Tajikistan, Pakistan, Kuwait, Saudi Arabia, Bahrain, Qatar and the UAE. Parthia covered 648,000 square miles – the rough equivalent of Great Britain, France, Spain and Germany rolled together, or the United States east of the Mississippi, but excluding New England. Geographically heterogeneous, it contained four main habitats: the mountains, the desert, the Khuzestan plain and the Caspian sea coast between the Alburz mountains and the sea.

As Rome expanded eastwards in the first century BC, a collision between the two power blocs became inevitable.[45] But it must be said that the personal ambitions of Roman leaders, rather than fear of Parthia or geopolitical imperatives, account for most of the wars in the first 150 years of contact between the powers: the cause of war, in short, was Roman imperialism.[46] The proconsul Marcus Crassus, the conqueror of Spartacus, was widely viewed in the decade of the 50s BC as very much the weak partner in the famous triumvirate that he formed with Julius Caesar and Pompey to rule Rome. To compensate, in an evil hour he decided to invade Parthia, to win a martial glory that would equal that of Caesar and his conquest of Gaul. Crassus invaded Mesopotamia with seven legions. Once at Zeugma, he unaccountably neither followed the Euphrates and tried to assail the Parthian capital at Ctesiphon nor headed north to Edessa and Armenia at the foot of the hills, but instead marched his army across open plains, where the Parthians annihilated it at Carrhae (Harran) in 53 BC. Fully two-thirds of the legions were killed or captured, and more than 10,000 were taken prisoner.[47] Legend and tradition say that most of these were taken to the Margiana oasis in the Kara Kum desert (in the north-east of Iran) and put to slave labour in the fields. Thence several hundred were said to have escaped and joined the nomadic Hsiung-Nu (whom some identify with the Huns) under the chieftain Jzh-Jzh in a campaign against the Chinese in 36 BC; in the course of this war they taught the nomads the Roman turtle, or *testudo*, defensive formation.[48]

After this military catastrophe the Romans cried foul. It was, they said, unsportsmanlike for the Parthians to have lured them out into open country, where they were at a severe disadvantage. For their part, their easy victory bred contempt in the Parthians for Roman arms and led them into over-confidence.[49] Yet time would show that the Parthian achievement was no fluke. In 44 BC just before his assassination, Julius Caesar was planning a massive war of revenge in the East: he assembled sixteen legions and 10,000 cavalry for the task. Caesar envisaged a campaign that would place him on a par with Alexander the Great. Having defeated the Parthians, he would continue to India or circumnavigate the Caspian, before returning to Gaul via southern Russia and Germany.[50] The events of the Ides of March put paid to such oriental dreams, but his immediate military heir Mark Antony revived them six years later. Using an army of the same size planned by Caesar (100,000), Antony forced the Parthians to strain every last military muscle. Where they had put just 10,000 heavily armed cavalry into the field against Crassus, this time they called out their full strength (50,000).[51] It should have been a duel of the titans. But Antony made every mistake in the book. He started his campaign too late in the year, and took it for granted that he could spend the winter in a captured city. He had not worked out the logistics and commissariat for feeding his immense army. He did not have adequate siege engines to invest the cities he intended to blockade. And he evinced a fundamental uncertainty of objective. Finding the Parthians waiting for him at the Euphrates crossing at Zeugma, he turned north towards Armenia without rethinking his strategy and campaigned for a year in Upper Media. In the only large-scale engagement that he fought he was forced to retreat, and was saved from encirclement only by the strength of his cavalry screen.[52]

What should have been Antony's secret weapon – the endemic factionalism of the Parthians – did not help him very much. The accession of the Parthian ruler Phraates IV to the throne in 37 BC was followed by a bloodbath that forced many of the empire's nobles to flee west; many ended up in Antioch, where Mark Antony had just arrived from Rome. As a would-be proconsul of the East, Antony was easy prey for the lies and cajolery of the exiles, especially as he wanted to be the man who avenged Carrhae. Once in Armenia, he put together a force of 70,000 fighting men for the coming offensive, which – allied to the 30,000 from friendly rulers of the Near East and 13,000 from his ally King Artavasdes of Armenia, to say nothing of 300 wagonloads of weapons and siege engines – made up the largest army ever seen in this part of the world, including even Alexander's.[53] In 36 BC he penetrated deep into western Persia and besieged the Parthian winter palace at Vera, south-east of Lake Urmia in Azerbaijan. Unaccountably, but presumably because they were delaying his rate of march, Antony then decided to leave behind all his siege engines; reading the runes correctly, the Armenians promptly deserted. When Antony proceeded to the siege of Praaspa, a Parthian royal residence in the mountains, fiasco ensued. Only the Armenians knew about mountain warfare and they were gone, yet without siege engines the Romans could not put a dent in the walls.[54] Harassed by guerrillas, with food running low and winter coming on, caught between a doughty defence from Praaspa and ever more confident irregulars buzzing on his flanks, Antony made the classic military blunder: he opted for a winter retreat, and not across plains and easy ground, but through the mountain passes of Azerbaijan and Armenia. The retreat turned into an awful pre-echo of Napoleon's withdrawal from Moscow in 1812. The toll from famine, cold and ambuscade rapidly whittled down Roman numbers. Their morale plummeted as a result of the frequent ambushes, into many of which they were led by treacherous local guides, and in the end the proud Roman army was reduced to a panic-stricken rabble.[55] When the few survivors limped into Artavasdes's capital, Antony had his work cut out just to keep the Armenian king friendly and loyal. He survived only by receiving money from his lover Cleopatra and by kidnapping Artavasdes (whom Cleopatra later had tortured to death). Altogether he lost 32,000 dead from a force of 85,000–90,000 – a disaster, but not quite at the level of Carrhae.[56] The scale of the setback was concealed at Rome, but Antony's defeat was decisive. It was his rival's military failure in the East that led Octavian (the future emperor Augustus) to make his bid for supreme power.[57]

For about 150 years after Antony's ill-judged venture, Rome and Parthia were basically at peace, though relations were always tense and uncertain. Elated by his defeat of Antony, Phraates IV indulged his despotic tendencies and, as a consequence, had to fight a long civil war against the pretender Tiridates and his powerful supporters – a revolt put down in the end only with the help of the savage Scythian horsemen of the steppes. Tiridates fled to Syria, where the emperor Augustus protected him and kept him on ice as a possible pawn to play later, in case Phraates did not remain quiet; but the Parthian king, exhausted by civil conflict, recognised Roman suzerainty over Armenia and sent five sons to Rome as hostages. He was eventually murdered by his Italian concubine and their son in 4 BC.[58] In the reign of Tiberius, Parthia was again riven by revolt, this time when the Greek cities of Seleucia rebelled. The kings of Parthia had always allowed their subject Greeks to retain their ancient rights, but from time to time the Greeks found the pretensions of the Parthian oligarchy too much to take.[59] Roman policy towards Parthia was predicated on their dominance in Armenia: they insisted that the kings there be their clients and were prepared to back this requirement by force if necessary. Under the surface, tensions continued to seethe, for on the one hand successive Roman generals dreamed of emulating Alexander and conquering Asia as far as the Indus, while, in flat contradiction to this, some Parthian 'hawks' wanted to restore the old Persian empire, which in turn meant throwing Rome out of the East.[60] But there were also signs of a more nuanced attitude from the emperors and from elite Roman opinion in general towards Parthia; there was no longer the knee-jerk reflex reaction that Parthians were benighted barbarians.[61]

The reign of Nero saw violent oscillations in Roman policy towards Parthia. At first Nero showed signs of the familiar 'Alexander complex' and seemed to be planning a major expedition in the East; he even formed a new, specially raised legion that he called 'the phalanx of Alexander'. Under his general Corbulo, the Romans campaigned in Armenia and treated contemptuously the Parthian offer of a secure frontier along the Euphrates.[62] Then, in a major volte-face, Nero conceded hegemony in Armenia to the Parthians, thus reversing traditional Roman policy in the area. The Parthians were overjoyed and praised Nero as the wisest of the wise. Indeed, there were many in Rome who agreed with them; the historian Cassius Dio, always an opponent of Roman expansionism, gave Nero high marks for his pacific attitudes in the East, whatever his reservations about the rest of his reign.[63] The ruler who emerged from the maelstrom of the 'year of the four emperors' in 68–9, Vespasian, did not reverse Nero's policy, but contemptuously rejected the Parthian request for an alliance against the warlike and dangerous nomads, the Alans. Vespasian's son Domitian, emperor from 81 to 96, entertained wild ambitions to campaign down the River Araxes to India; on the way he intended to subdue Colchis and the Caucasus and turn the Black Sea into another Roman lake. But he got no further than sending raiding parties as far as the Caspian.[64] Nonetheless, there was a gradual return to the pre-Nero policy of demanding supremacy in Armenia and building up complex networks of nominally independent client kings.[65]

Under Trajan, the warrior-emperor, Rome finally returned to the out-and-out aggression of Crassus and Mark Antony and undertook a massive war of conquest against Parthia. Trajan's motives have been much debated. Some see them as primarily economic – to control the trade routes through Mesopotamia; others stress the obsession with secure frontiers, which would be achieved by annexing Armenia and northern Mesopotamia; still others allege that Trajan was a mere glory-hunter, yet another Roman emperor with an 'Alexander complex'.[66] Naturally, he might also have been actuated multi-causally, by a combination of all these factors. There was, additionally, a punitive element, for Trajan's old enemy Decebalus of Dacia (see pp. 319–20) had tried to enlist Parthian support and been encouraged. The *casus belli* was, not surprisingly, Armenia. There the Parthian monarch Chrosroes had deposed the pro-Roman puppet ruler Asidares, son of the previous Parthian king Pacorus, and put in the pro-Parthian Parthamisiris, without any reference to Rome. Trajan at once hastened to Athens (AD 113) and made preparations for war. This alarmed Chrosroes, who knew Trajan was no bluffer, and he instructed his envoys to meet the emperor and conciliate him with talk and gifts. The ambassadors told Trajan that Parthia wanted peace, but that Parthamisiris had been installed because Asidares had proved incompetent and thus unsatisfactory to both Rome and Parthia. Trajan made no reply either verbally or in writing, but told the envoys flatly, 'Friendly relations are determined by deeds not words. When I reach Syria I shall take appropriate action.'[67] Cassius Dio regarded Trajan's failure to respond to peace-feelers as clear proof that the Armenian imbroglio was a mere fig-leaf for Trajan's lust for glory. The desire to emulate Alexander effortlessly melded with a policy of crude expansionism.[68]

Trajan travelled through Lycia and Syria and arrived in Antioch (January 114), where he began assembling and training his armies. The moment seemed propitious for a major war against Parthia, for the Parthians were once more engaged in one of their perennial civil wars, this time between Chrosroes and the pretender Vologases. To secure Armenia was Trajan's initial objective, so he first struck out for Satala, north of the Upper Euphrates in lesser Armenia. It took eight weeks for the Roman army to accomplish the long march of 475 miles through difficult country. Trajan then detached part of the force to cross the Euphrates beyond Melitene and capture Arsamosata, the fourth city of Armenia, which lay on the River Arsanias (Murat Su), an eastern tributary of the Euphrates. At this point many local lords and princelings came to do homage to Trajan at his 'durbah' there.[69] But the Parthian puppet Parthamasiris did not appear, instead compounding his error by writing to Trajan and calling himself 'king'. When Trajan did not reply, he wrote again, dropping the title of king but asking for the governor of Cappadocia to be sent to him; Trajan sent the governor's son instead. Concluding correctly that he would continue to be spurned unless he appeared in person, Parthamasiris met the emperor at Elegia, laid down his crown and publicly truckled. Trajan humiliated him by letting him have his say in front of the army, then publicly rebutting him by stating that he could not be a king since Armenia was in Parthian hands. Parthamisiris was then allowed to leave with a small escort of his own men and a larger body of Roman cavalry. On the road he was mysteriously killed – the obvious inference is that Trajan had him murdered as soon as he was safely away from the camp, so that the deed could not be pinned on him.[70]

With all Armenia at his feet, Trajan succumbed to the oldest temptation of all – what has been termed in the modern world 'mission creep'. Since the conquest of Armenia had been so easy, why not punch a hole in the rest of the Parthian empire?[71] Trajan wintered in Antioch, but the campaign of 115 was delayed as a result of the violent earthquake of January 115 in which large numbers perished. When hostilities recommenced, the Romans waged war on the Tigris, first chopping down trees and building collapsible boats and later building a pontoon bridge. They then scored a major victory at Adiabene and passed the site of Gaugamela, where Alexander the Great had won his great victory in 331 BC. Meanwhile Trajan's general Lusius Quietus captured Singara in Mesopotamia, on the southern side of the mountain ridge beyond the River Chaboras.[72] Leaving large numbers of troops on the Tigris, Trajan next turned down the Euphrates for an attack on the Parthian capital of Ctesiphon. Originally intending to link the Tigris with the Euphrates by a canal that would bring his boats across the narrow strip of land between the two rivers, he was advised that it would take too long and be too costly, so portaged his boats instead. The Parthians retreated, allowing him to enter Ctesiphon without resistance in January 116 – the first time a Roman army had ever reached the Parthian capital. Trajan then sailed down the Tigris to the Persian Gulf in a vast golden barge and announced that the conquered territory would form a new Roman province of Assyria.[73] Once at the Gulf, there clearly must have been a temptation to try and ape Alexander and aim for India. Trajan wisely realised that this was a chimerical target and rationalised his disappointment by telling his followers that he was too old. Anyway, he remarked, since he had started his career in Spain rather than Macedon, he had already travelled as far east as Alexander had done.[74]

Trajan returned to Babylon, but while he lolled in the city where Alexander had so mysteriously died, his Parthian triumph began to come apart at the seams. Suddenly it was reported that all the conquered territories had risen in revolt, and meanwhile there was a massive Jewish uprising, taking in Cyprus, Egypt and Cyrenaica. Trying for a twin-track approach, Trajan offered an armistice to the Parthians to settle the Armenia question and sent two armies against the rebels in Mesopotamia. One of these, under Maximus, was defeated, but the other, under Lusius Quietus, aided by Moorish cavalry, recovered Nisibis, took Edessa after a siege and gutted it, then sacked Seleucia near Ctesiphon. To save face, Trajan crowned a renegade son of Chrosroes, Parthamaspates, as King of Armenia, where he was the most obvious of Roman puppets.[75] Although he accepted the title *Parthicus* for his victories, Trajan sensibly concluded that Parthia was too difficult to subdue permanently, especially with a Jewish uprising in his rear. He began to retrace his steps to Italy, but died at Selinus in Cilicia on 9 August 117. Overall, Trajan's Parthian adventure had been a failure.[76] But the Romans had learned valuable lessons for the future. The legions had had to campaign in six-foot snow drifts in the winter and had learned to march in snow-shoes. Morale had remained high, with Trajan the hard driver marching on foot himself at the head of his men, fording rivers with them and even planting rumours of an imminent enemy attack to keep them up to scratch. The strategic failure of the campaign could be offset by a list of battles won and cities successfully besieged – Nisibis, Battuae, Edessa, Ctesiphon, Seleucia. And Rome had received homage from a host of client rulers beyond the Euphrates.[77] The many supporters and hagiographers of Trajan built up his flawed campaign by expert 'spin' as an exploit to rival Alexander's, and their propaganda was largely successful.[78]

Since Hadrian's 'peace at any price' stance was diametrically opposed to Trajan's forward policy, it was no surprise that Hadrian put Rome into reverse gear in the East. His appeasement made him the most popular emperor ever, in Parthian eyes. He conciliated King Chrosroes immediately after Trajan's death by deposing Parthamaspates, the renegade son whom Trajan had installed in Armenia, giving him the consolation prize of Osrhoene near Edessa. But he retained Chrosroes's daughter, whom Trajan had captured when he took Ctesiphon, as a bargaining counter at Rome. And he did not give up the new province of Arabia, which Trajan had added to the empire.[79] His summit conference with Chrosroes in 123 gave the Parthian king most of what he wanted. It was not that Hadrian lacked the military power to reconquer Mesopotamia, but on a cost-benefit basis he thought it pointless. There were other ways of keeping Parthia quiet. He retained the city-state of Mesene as an enclave independent of Ctesiphon and encouraged the endemic factionalism, which saw no fewer than three pretenders to the Parthian throne in 125–50.[80] Until Vologases IV ascended the throne in 148, it would be true to say that Rome dominated Parthia without the need for military action. Antoninus Pius was less friendly to Parthia and returned to the older thinking about the necessity for a Roman-controlled Armenia, partly for traditional reasons and partly because a new threat had arisen in northern Armenia from the Alans, the latest of the formidable steppe warriors. Some time in the early 140s Antoninus invested a new pro-Roman Armenian king (the sources do not make it clear whether his name was Sohaemus or Pacorus).[81] Antoninus is said to have stopped the Parthian king in his tracks by a mere letter when the Parthians appeared to be menacing Armenia, though papyrus evidence from Egypt shows that sterner, military measures were needed to make the Parthians back off. He also refused to return the royal throne Trajan had stolen from Ctesiphon, even though Hadrian had promised its restitution. Some have argued that of the two 'pacific' emperors, Antoninus was the more shrewd. His Jewish policy is also brought into this argument: while he lifted Hadrian's proscription on circumcision for Jews, he ordained that no Gentiles were to be circumcised, which prevented proselytising.[82] Antoninus did not trust the Parthians as Hadrian had done and, after 148, when Vologases IV came to the throne, his suspicion proved justified. It was Vologases he had principally in mind when he spoke on his death-bed of his anger with certain kings. His critics say that he should have done something about Vologases and not simply let things drift.[83]

Since Marcus Aurelius had never known a serious threat to the Roman empire in his entire forty years of life, and since all wars with Parthia hitherto had arisen from Roman imperialism or the lust for glory by individual Roman generals and proconsuls, one can only imagine the shock when Vologases IV launched a serious and unprovoked attack in 161: it was the biter bit with a vengeance. The assault should not have come as a complete surprise, since Vologases had been behaving aggressively from the beginning of his reign, and in 151 had conquered the Roman client state of Mesena in Lower Mesopotamia, which had been independent from Parthia since Trajan's conquests in 116–17.[84] Parthian coinage shows Vologases IV as a man with a long rectangular beard, or rather a tapered beard with a square-cut end. He wears a diademed tiara with hooks on the crest, a horn on one side and long curved earflaps.[85] In thirteen years he had reunited the two halves of the Parthian empire, previously split between his father and Vologases III. Some scholars identify him with King Volgash of Zoroastrian tradition, who began collecting the writings of the Persian prophet. Vologases thought, rightly or wrongly, that Antoninus Pius was pusillanimous and would do anything to avoid a war in the East; as so often in human affairs, restraint was construed as weakness. The accession of Marcus reinforced Vologases's conviction that the Romans were paper tigers.[86] To provide continuity during a change of emperor, Marcus retained the governors of Cappadocia and Syria at their posts, but Vologases read this as feebleness, slack administration and lack of interest in the area. He envisaged a campaign that would be something of a walkover.

Vologases began by invading Armenia, where he expelled its king and put in his own nomineee Pacorus. The governor of Upper Cappadocia, M. Sedatius Severianus, moved into Armenia with a legion to expel the intruder, but was trapped by the Parthian general Chrosroes at Elegeia, near the headwaters of the Euphrates. After a brief attempt at resistance, Severianus realised his position was hopeless and committed suicide.[87] His sad story provided a cautionary tale

for the Antonine age, for he was gulled by the chief religious charlatan of his time, the notorious Alexander of Abonoteichos. The Aimee
Semple McPherson of his era, Alexander specialised in soothsaying,
oracles and 'magic' of all kinds. The great comic writer and satirist
Lucian, an invaluable source for the age of Marcus Aurelius and an
expert in the scams and con-tricks of Alexander, tells us that the magus
had established a hold over elite Romans in Asia, beginning with the
proconsul of Asia, P. Mummius Sisenna Rutilianus, who married
Alexander's daughter. Severianus, a Gaul from the Poitiers area, appears
to have been a simple soul who became a devotee of Alexander's
hocus-pocus and had taken seriously the charlatan's promise that he
would win an easy victory against the Parthians. Lucian, who described
Severianus as 'that foolish Celt', predictably had fun at his (and
Alexander's) expense. Aiming for the heights of absurdity, Lucian had
Severianus starving himself to death, having first extracted a promise
from his centurion Afranius Silo that Silo would deliver a funeral
oration in the grand manner, as if he were an authentic Roman hero.[88]
Lucian did not need to expend his gifts of Swiftian indignation on
Severianus, who in fact committed suicide cleanly and rapidly. The
legion wiped out at Elegeia was probably the IX Hispana, originally
based near Nijmegen (modern Holland) and last heard of definitively
at York in the reign of Trajan. It is speculated that it had since been
switched to Cappadocia.[89]

Next the Parthians invaded Syria, defeated the Roman governor
there and put him to flight. This was the senior Roman military figure
in the East, L. Attitius Cornelianus, who had been at his post since
157 and was overdue for a transfer; the fact that Marcus had left him
there to ensure continuity was, ironically, one of the things that made
Vologases IV think the new emperor was a weakling.[90] The two
Parthian victories in Armenia and Syria meant that the situation on
the eastern front had reached crisis point, but Marcus found it difficult to respond immediately or rapidly, as imperial military resources
were already being stretched. There is evidence of major unrest in
Britain, with an attempt being made to reoccupy the Antonine Wall;
the new governor Sextus Calpurnius Agricola was sent to Britain with
express instructions to retrench behind a strengthened Hadrian's Wall.[91]
In Upper Germany there was trouble with the Chatti, so Marcus sent
a close friend Aufidius Victorinus (also fellow-pupil and son-in-law of

Fronto) to deal with it. But it was the senior military appointment
Marcus made in Syria that caused the most surprise. His choice fell
on Statius Priscus, a battle-hardened veteran, who began his career as
a cavalry officer and served with distinction in the Jewish rebellion
under Hadrian; he was even decorated by the emperor in person. He
then served as procurator in southern Gaul, before being made a
senator and commanding two legions in succession. Thereafter he
switched posts much as if he was playing musical chairs. A short spell
as governor of Dacia in 157–8 was followed by the consulship in 159.
He served a very brief term as governor of Moesia Superior in 160–1,
only to be moved suddenly to the governorship of Britain. He had
barely settled there before Marcus relocated him to the East; there
were also vague and unsubstantiated rumours that the legions in Britain
had urged him to declare himself emperor.[92] Maybe it was these
rumours, or maybe simply the sense of general crisis, that led Marcus
to switch two other notable ex-governors of western provinces to the
Parthian frontier: M. Iallius Bassus and C. Iulius Bassus, the latter the
recently retired governor of Lower Germany (152–5) and Britain
(155–8).[93]

Even so, sometime in the winter of 161–2 Marcus decided that either
he or Lucius Verus would have to go East to command in person.
Not surprisingly, Verus was chosen: Cassius Dio tells us this was
because 'he was physically robust and younger than Marcus, and better
suited to military activity'.[94] But in Marcus's mind he had made a
shrewd decision. Removing Verus to the East meant that all his sexual
excesses and debaucheries would be committed out of sight of the
Roman people, ensuring that the imperial principate did not lose caste
any further. It was also conceivable that Verus might grow up through
having to fight a war; that he would learn to accept responsibility and
take seriously his position as co-emperor; or that at least he would
learn *something*, if only the value of money, from his oriental travels.[95]
Needless to say, none of these pious hopes was fulfilled. But the Senate
readily agreed to the arrangement, and now there seemed method in
Marcus's apparent madness in appointing a joint ruler. It was never a
good idea for an emperor to be absent from Rome for too long, but
on the other hand some frontier crises, like this one, simply cried out
for an imperial presence. Antoninus Pius's blinkered approach to
Marcus's 'cadetship' (and Verus's, for that matter) had ensured that

neither had any military training or background or knew anything of 'abroad'. It has been pointed out that, of all the previous emperors, only Nero had never been out of Rome on his accession, and even such 'unready' princes as Caligula and Claudius had had foreign experience.[96] Antoninus's education of his heir apparent had in this respect been shockingly incompetent, and now events were finding him out.

7

Marcus Aurelius was always a man of supreme integrity, and there was nothing machiavellian about his sending Verus out East. The usual run of emperors might have taken this decision to discredit a co-ruler, to intrigue against him behind his back, or even in the hope that he might die on the battlefield. Marcus, on the contrary, gave Verus all the crack legions and all the best military equipment and materiel that money could buy. Legio I Minervia, based at Bonn in Lower Germany, began a five-month march to Syria. Legio V Macedonica left its base at Troesmis in Lower Moesia for the same destination, and headed there also was Legio II Adiutrix, whose headquarters were at Aquincum in Lower Pannonia.[1] Additionally, many tens of thousands of auxiliaries and *vexillationes* (mixed corps) were detached from northern garrisons to fight in the East. The northern frontier command probably suffered a loss of one-third its strength.[2] Marcus also provided his co-emperor with a top-notch general staff, not just Statius Priscus and Iallius Bassus, but also veterans like Cornelius Repentinus, though court gossip said that he was not that marvellous and had been promoted only through the good offices of Antoninus Pius's mistress Galeria Lysistrata.[3] Marcus also sent out some of his inner circle (*comites*) of consular standing, including the veteran M. Pontius Laelianus, who had seen distinguished service in Britain and Germany and had been governor of Pannonia Superior and Syria. Also making up the distinguished cast was one of the two prefects of the guard, T. Furius Victorinus.[4] It is noteworthy that only two of the eight

legions previously stationed in the East took part in the Parthian war
that Lucius Verus would unleash: Legio III Gallica of Syria and Legio
VI Ferrata of Syria Palestina. Some say this was because the Eastern
legions tended to be of inferior quality compared with those of the
West; or it may simply be that the initial losses to Vologases in
Cappadocia and Syria were greater than the Roman sources were
prepared to admit.[5]

Lucius Verus took his time about his preparations and did not leave
for the East until the summer of 162. He insisted on taking with him
his entire panoply of freedmen – Geminus, Agaclytus, Coedes, Eclectus
and, especially, Nicomedes, who was put in charge of the commissariat. The Misenum fleet was given the task of accompanying Verus
to Asia, and thereafter keeping the sea lanes clear and making sure
that all the young emperor's logistical requirements were met. When
Lucius left Rome with his huge retinue, Marcus accompanied his
colleague as far as Capua.[6] Lucius then made a leisurely progress
towards the East coast, hunting and carousing as he went. At Canusium
he fell seriously ill, to the point where his life was feared for and
Marcus went south to meet up with him. Showing great concern, he
stayed with Lucius until his recovery was assured and, immediately
on returning to Rome, had the Senate send him formal good wishes.[7]
Three days of fasting and some blood-letting had apparently done the
trick. Fronto saw a chance to be reconciled with his old pupil and
wrote a sympathetic letter to Lucius. In that patronising mother-hen
manner, in which Fronto was unrivalled, he wrote (either sycophantically or tongue-in cheek): 'As suits your outstanding character you
should be moderate in all your desires, which are bound to be keener
and more insistent than usual after this enforced abstinence.'[8] The
idea of a moderate or temperate Lucius Verus would have provided
a belly-laugh to anyone reading the letter. Some said that his illness
had been caused by over-indulgence of all kinds, but the likelihood
was that he had suffered a mini-stroke; it was a major stroke that
would eventually kill him.

But Verus had learned nothing from the episode and had forgotten
nothing of the art of debauchery. His leisurely and riotous journey
eastwards continued. When he reached Athens after a short voyage
on the Adriatic and a southward journey overland via Corinth, he was
greeted as a conquering hero; some scholars attribute this reception

to the close contacts of the Ceionius family with the Athenian aristocracy, who paid him the signal honour of inducting him into the
Eleusinian mysteries.[9] Since the ubiquitous Herodes Atticus had often
fallen foul of both Antoninus Pius and Marcus, it is not surprising
that Herodes was a prime mover in the initiation; it would have been
his way of thumbing his nose at Marcus.[10] Next Verus crossed the
Aegean Sea and made a lengthy stopover in Ephesus. Here too he was
lionised by the Greek-speaking elite. A prominent citizen named P.
Vedius Antoninus gave lavish games in his honour.[11] The halting and
reluctant imperial progress continued, along the coast and through all
the notorious fleshpots of Pamphylia and Cilicia. At last, a reluctant
Verus traipsed into Antioch, which would be his base for the next four
years.[12] By the time he reached Syria, Verus had gathered around him
a troupe of actors and musicians who enhanced his pleasure, but
scandalised the *bien pensants*. He acted as if he was about to build a
pleasure-garden rather than wage a war. Characteristically, his first
letters to Rome from Antioch concerned the progress of his beloved
racing faction, the Greens, in the races at the Circus Maximus.[13]

As Verus and his theatrical entourage fiddled while the eastern frontier blazed, the more serious-minded members of his general staff
assessed the prospects for the coming campaign. Parthia had long
fascinated the Romans: the references in Latin literature are abundant.[14] Pliny the Elder regarded Parthia as a barren waste, a land where
the locals went in for drinking rivers of alcohol on an empty stomach
and where the deserts were infested with venomous serpents – for
Pliny, snakes were always 'this accursed creature'.[15] Yet secure knowledge of Parthia is not easy to attain. As Parthian literature was oral,
there were few written records, and most of its history had (and has)
to be reconstructed from coinage. A non-Greek people, the Parthians
used Greek as their official state language and on most of their coins:
the most common denomination, the silver drachma, bore Greek
legends for 500 years. Unlike Rome, based on slavery, Parthian society
was basically feudal, relying on serfdom, as far as we can tell.[16] The
realm was not centralised; there were several different cultures in co-
existence, several different languages were spoken and each region had
its own mini-economic system, complete with its own coinage. This
made Parthia fluid, flexible and elastic: the Romans captured its capital
Ctesiphon three times in history, but this made little impact, as there

were other important centres. The Parthian economy was robust despite its patchwork nature. On the one hand, its ruling elite acted mainly as middlemen, taking profits from numerous customs posts and taxes on goods in transit, plus the control of important trade routes.[17] On the other hand, the well-managed agricultural systems of the many Hellenistic cities and the thriving riverine trade and agriculture in the Fertile Crescent gave Parthian rulers the surplus to support a large army. Parthian social structure was intimately linked with the state's military organisation, which in turn derived from ancient nomadic practices, hence the high value given in the culture to horse-riding, the hallmark of social rank. All this was well known to the Romans, even though they had never bothered to collect proper intelligence about their principal enemy in the East.[18]

Yet the fact that the 'empire' was a mere conglomeration of kingdoms, provinces and city-states was a weakness, as the King of Parthia had to respect local warlords. Internal strife and civil war were common, and very few Parthian monarchs survived their reigns without a challenge from a pretender. The long periods of peace with Rome were essentially years of strife and civil conflict within Parthia; cynics even said that Trajan won his victories in 113–17 only because the Parthian king was simultaneously battling a pretender.[19] One result of this internal weakness was that, unable to trust his nobles, the Parthian king could not afford to retain a standing army. Mustering a host in wartime was therefore a lengthy process. The reason Crassus penetrated so far into Parthia in 54–53 BC was that it took so long for the Parthians to marshal sufficient men to put into the field against him.[20] On the other hand, the Romans could no longer rely on covert support from the quasi-independent Greek city-states within the Parthian empire. The Greeks were shy, having been bitten twice. They rose for Crassus and again for Mark Antony, but on both occasions had been left high and dry. By the second century AD they had settled into a comfortable vassal relationship with the Parthian kings, rather like that of Alexander Nevsky and Novgorod under the Mongols in thirteenth-century Russia.[21] Above all, Parthian kings were weakened by baronial power, with warlordism rampant and the army recruited on a feudal basis from territorial magnates and their retainers. The highest social classes tended to provide the *cataphractarii* – the heavily armoured cavalry that acted as the Parthian army's elite squad, with

The death of Marcus Aurelius by Eugene Delacroix. In the 1840s Delacroix turned from the 'romantic' obsession with North Africa, which had consumed his twenties and thirties, towards a succession of classical subjects. What he particularly admired about Marcus was his lack of concern with socio-economic issues and his conviction that coming to terms with the harsh decrees of Fate was the true mark of a philosopher.

The triumph at the end of the German wars. Marcus is shown entering Rome in a four-horse chariot, being crowned by Nike, the goddess of Victory.

Commodus's self-identification with Hercules has usually been taken as the definitive sign of insanity in Marcus's son, but modern scholars argue there may have been method in his madness.

the classes below furnishing the swarms of mounted archers who had compassed Crassus's downfall. It was estimated that just 4,000 of the victorious Parthian army at Carrhae in 53 BC were nobles, with the remainder of the 50,000 being serfs or retainers.[22]

Yet another reason for Parthian weakness was that they had other frontiers to defend. Vologases IV's invasion of Armenia and Syria was an anomaly, since Parthian kings were in general far more concerned with their northern and north-eastern frontiers than with Armenia, Mesopotamia and the west. Rome came a distant fourth when Parthia drew up a list of its principal enemies: way ahead of the Romans were the Kushans, Sakas and Alans. There were really three realms, almost entirely independent from each other, in the 'empire' – the west, eastern Parthia and the Indo-Parthian domains of the extreme north-east – and they each faced formidable enemies.[23]

The Kushans were an Indo-European people, using the Greek alphabet, who crossed the Hindu Kush in the first century AD and created an empire that included land on both sides of it. Centred on Peshawar and Mathura, their domain reached east as far as the Ganges basin. Their empire was at its height in c. AD 105–250 and took in modern Tajikistan, Pakistan, Afghanistan and the Ganges valley in northern India.[24] Their most famous king was Kanishka (127–47), a contemporary of Hadrian and Antoninus Pius, who was a patron of Buddhism, but tolerated a syncretism of Greco-Zoroastrian-Buddhism. The Kushans were great traders and imported from both China and Rome (especially glassware); a Kushan ambassador was actually received by Antoninus Pius.[25] In return they exported fine woollen cloth, wool carpets, perfume, pepper, ginger and black salt. It was their trading prowess rather than their military ambitions that most upset the Parthians. It particularly irked them that, because of the Kushans' trade links with the Nabatean princes of Arabia, they themselves could not establish a commercial monopoly on Arabian trade by controlling the Tigris. But the Kushans were too powerful to alienate by out-and-out trade war. It was therefore a relief to Parthia when the Chinese general Pan Chao heavily defeated the Kushan king Kadphises near Khotan in AD 90. This was a consequence of yet another population shunt. The state of Ts'In in north-west China was in the first century AD the most powerful of the states in China and was then pushing westwards towards Turkestan.[26]

As if the Kushans were not enough, the Parthians also had to keep a watchful eye on the Sakas. In Sogdi and the Sind the last survivors of Alexander the Great's Indo-Greek states went down before a warrior people known as the Kangju, who were supposed to have possessed 120,000 warriors, 90,000 of them skilled archers.[27] The Kangju in turn succumbed to invaders from the steppe, a Scythian people known as the Sakas. Like their predecessors, the Sakas maintained a wary relationship with the more powerful Kushans on their border and, with this in mind, accepted the nominal suzerainty of the Parthians. Needless to say, from the time of the founding of their state in AD 78 they were frequently at war with their overlords. In their principality of Seistan (modern western Afghanistan), they expanded and were at their height under King Gondophanes. They later splintered again, into the two kingdoms of Sakastan and Turan.[28] The Sakas irritated their official masters by cosying up to the Kushans, cooperating with them to maintain trade relations through Carmania and Persia with the Arab states of Mesene and Charcene at the head of the Persian Gulf – exactly the situation that most angered the Parthians. Official state policy of Parthia was to encourage the passage of goods from China and the East over the old northern route used by the Medes and Assyrians (the Persians in the sixth century BC had diverted much of it onto the Royal Road to Lake Helmund via Susa).[29] The problem was that the southern kingdoms who were tributary to the Parthian empire were independent in commercial matters. The Parthians realised that to establish a true trade monopoly in their realms they would have to impose a centralised monarchy, and how was that possible, given the feudal state of Parthia? The two Lake Helmund routes could only have enjoyed a monopoly if Parthia had been prepared to make war on Petra and the Arabian states on the Gulf.[30] But this would have involved them not only in a war of pacification, but in a simultaneous war with the Sakas and Kushans; nor would the Romans have stood idly by if the Parthians had attempted to stifle the maritime routes to India.[31] So the Parthians had to grin and bear the existence of two powerful enemies in the north-east.

Yet in some ways their most pressing problem of all was with the nomadic Alans of the steppes. An Indo-Iranian nomadic people, one of a long line of steppe fighters that would culminate with the Huns and the Mongols, the Alans are thought to have been mentioned by

Herodotus, but receive their first definite mention in Latin literature in Seneca's *Thyestes*.[32] Tall, good-looking, blond and fierce-eyed, they occupied a heartland on both sides of the River Don in southern Russia and controlled the area between the Sea of Azov and the Caspian. A people reputed to live only for war, with a pronounced warrior culture, where women did all the hard work and old men were despised and ill-treated for not having died in battle, the Alans practised polygamy, but not slavery; instead they recruited prisoners into their clans and families.[33] When not on the warpath, they were pastoralists with huge herds and lived in wooden wagons drawn by draught oxen. Brilliant equestrians, they made formidable heavy cavalry. Frequently sallying out from their homelands and across the Iron Gates in search of plunder, they became a permanent and much-feared menace to both Armenia and the Parthian empire. Their prowess with spear and bow, as well as their astonishing horsemanship, was much commented on; as also were the weapons new to the Romans, such as the lasso and the *kontos* – a two-headed lance. The Parthians loathed and feared the Alans, not least because they fought in much the same way and could therefore beat them at their own game of charges by heavily armoured horsemen.[34]

Parthia and Rome each also played an elaborate game of trying to inveigle the Alans into attacking the other. Initially Parthia had sought an alliance with Rome to defeat the Alans, and in the decade of AD 70 the Parthian king approached the emperor Vespasian in this regard; Vespasian at first appeared keen to send his son Domitian out to the East on campaign, but nothing came of the idea.[35] But in the reign of Hadrian the Alans first appeared as a genuine menace to Roman inter-ests. Hadrian's eastern policy was as byzantine as one would expect from such a complex emperor. At first he appeared to be Parthia's friend and sent King Pharasmenes II presents and an honour guard of 500 men.[36] But he gradually came to suspect Pharasmenes of having incited the Alans to attack Georgia, which was a Roman client kingdom. Hadrian hit back by using the King of Georgia as his agent in an attempt to get the Alans to attack Parthia, but his diplomacy was unsuccessful, partly because of the Georgian king's duplicity, but mainly because Vologases III of Parthia bribed them to attack Armenia and Cappadocia, which they did with devastating effect.[37] By 135, his pacific policies notwithstanding, Hadrian decided that Roman credibility required a vigorous campaign against the Alans. Flavius Arrianus, governor of Cappadocia, led a major expedition against the horsemen of the plains. He enjoyed the benevolent neutrality of Parthia, since by this time Vologases III had his hands full with another of Parthia's perennial pretenders, a prince named Mithridates. Flavius Arrianus fought a skilful campaign in the year 136. Mindful of the mistakes made by Crassus and Mark Antony, he made a thorough study of the Alans' method of waging war, and noted their taste for the feigned flight. He used an infantry phalanx covered by missile shooters as the way to neutralise Alan tactics. With just one legion (XV Apollinaris) and some auxiliary regiments, mainly cavalry and mounted archers, he defeated the Alans in a number of skirmishes, overawed them with his steady determination and eventually cleared them from Armenia; he concluded by crossing the Caspian Gates and establishing a secure frontier. His campaign was one of the great unsung achievements of the Roman army, even though the resulting peace had to be consolidated with a hefty bribe to the Alans from the King of Parthia.[38]

The Alans were kept quiet in the ensuing decade by a defeat inflicted on them by the Parthian general Yodmangan (whom some identify with the son of Publius Agrippa, a Roman envoy sent to Georgia either by Trajan or Hadrian). Before the outcome with the Alans was clear, Hadrian had to appease a number of angry tribes on the frontier (including the Iazyges of Hungary, of whom we shall hear more). Cassius Dio tells us that Hadrian 'Introduced them to the Senate' and was empowered by it to return suitable replies, which he composed and read out to them.[39] Even Antoninus Pius, who had the devil's own luck in pursuing his particular brand of appeasement for twenty years, had to keep a wary eye on the Alans; there were periodic raids on the Greek cities of Asia Minor nearest to the Black and Caspian Seas.[40] Antoninus used the system of client kings to build buffers between the Roman empire and the Alans. In this regard he particularly courted the King of Georgia, who came to Rome in 141 with his wife and entourage. Antoninus lionised him, granted him increased territories, offered him an equestrian statue in the temple of Bellona, allowed him to sacrifice on the Capitol and then co-hosted with him a military spectacular (the modern equivalent would be a tattoo).[41] By the time of Marcus Aurelius, the Alans were no longer considered benighted barbarians, but significant enough to feature in the writings of Martial and other Roman luminaries. Moreover, the Roman army had learned valuable lessons from observing the way the Alans fought, which would help them enormously in the coming campaign in Parthia.[42]

If Parthia was seriously weakened by the struggle of king versus barons and the perennial motif of monarch versus pretender, to say nothing of serious incursions by Kushans, Sakas and Alans, it also held few of the cards in a sustained military struggle with Rome, for no other contemporary nation matched the Roman army in discipline, technique and efficiency. The Roman army was superbly trained, and its arms and equipment were superior to those of its enemies. Its commanders had perfected the use of cavalry as shock troops, and the skill of its engineers was legendary: whether the task was to build a bridge over the Danube or to break down the defences of 'impregnable' fortresses like Masada, they could always find a way.[43] At 500,000 strong, the army was a well-oiled machine. Its hierarchy was also a marvel of organisation, but class distinctions were important, for only men of senatorial rank could command a legion; members of the equestrian order were restricted to commanding the brigades of auxiliaries. The commander of a Roman legion was a legate, ranked as a senator and in his mid-thirties, who had already held a praetorship. Where there was only one legion in a province, the post of provincial governor and legionary commander was combined.[44] The legate served about three and a half years and had his family with him at his post. On military matters he relied heavily on the advice of the senior centurion (*primus pilus*), but his administrative deputy was an equestrian officer, the camp prefect (*praefectus castrorum*) chosen from ex-senior centurions. Technically outranking the camp prefect was the senatorial tribune, a young man of eighteen to nineteen; there were six tribunes in a legion, but the other five were knights. Before coming out to his army command, such a youth would have held one of the two minor magistracies in Rome known as the *vigintivirate*. The post of senatorial tribune was a military apprenticeship and was usually followed by the quaestorship. The senatorial tribune outranked the five equestrian tribunes in a legion, but everyone knew that these tribunes, men in their thirties, were the backbone of the army; though the same age as the legate, they had far more military experience.[45]

When it came to the hard business of actually fighting, no one doubted that the fifty-nine centurions in each legion were the hinge on which everything turned. Since each legion of roughly 5,000 men was divided into ten cohorts, the term centurion covered a large stretch of ground, embracing everyone from the senior centurion (*primus pilus*) to the *decimus hastatus posterior*, the most junior centurion in the tenth cohort. Unlike their superiors (the senatorial or equestrian officers, who served terms of three years or so), the centurions (like the men they commanded) were career soldiers who had signed on for twenty-five years' continuous service.[46] Their position conferred many privileges, among them the right to marry (this was denied the ordinary legionary) and a rate of pay sixteen times that of a ranker: whereas the ordinary soldier was paid twelve *aurei* (1,200 sesterces) a year, the centurion took home 200 *aurei* (20,000 sesterces). It has already been mentioned that in financial terms the Roman soldiers were the aristocracy of labour, and the non-legionary auxiliaries (on ten *aurei* a year) were not far behind them. Moreover, every emperor from time to time had to keep the army sweet by awarding generous cash-payments as largesse in addition to normal pay. Besides, every legionary retiring after twenty-five years' service received a cash bonus equal to thirteen years' salary.[47] The combination of twenty-five years' service with a large cash bonus was a cleverly calculated way of controlling the troops. Their traditional desire to buy Italian land had been a major cause of political instability during the late republic, but by the second century most veterans settled happily on retirement in the provinces where they had served most of their time. The long-service deal of twenty-five years (instead of the previous sixteen years) was introduced as a clever cost-cutting exercise, for many troops died in the last nine years of their service, so that the state did not have to pay out the generous pension, and the prospect of the mouth-watering terminal gratuity meant there were no serious recruitment problems.[48]

The presence of a powerful army in any society usually spells trouble, for the temptation for the military to intervene in politics is huge. One of the wonders of the Roman empire was the way that military coups were largely avoided during the first two centuries AD, the two notable exceptions being in 69 (the 'year of the four emperors') and 193, on the death of Commodus. The depoliticisation of the army had several causes, but one of the important aspects was the increasingly provincial origin of the armed forces. Under Augustus 68 per cent of the army was of Italian origin, but this reduced to 48 per cent by the year AD 50 and 22 per cent by the year 100.[49] When Marcus Aurelius came to the throne, only 2 per cent of the legionaries were of Italian origin. Demography provided the answer: 7,500 new recruits a year were needed for the legions, but, given ancient mortality rates, this would have equalled 17 per cent of all twenty-year-old males in Italy. If these soldiers then served abroad, it was obvious that Italy would rapidly become depopulated, hence the switch to foreign recruitment. The increasingly provincial origin of the army meant that Rome could uncouple military service from local loyalties, switching German legions to Syria, say. Long service on the frontier lessened interest in events at Rome, and meanwhile the link between citizenship and empowerment by military service had been severed. Moreover, there was no powerful officer class in Rome and no central army command.[50] In Rome itself the power vacuum was filled by the praetorian guard, which had its own ethos distinct from that of the legions; and the prefect of the guard was always of knightly rank and thus debarred from becoming emperor, and thus in turn less likely to be interested in a bid for power. For all these reasons Rome in the first two centuries AD never suffered from the disease of modern Latin America, where the military are politically ubiquitous. Yet this was only ever a *relative* consideration. No emperor could afford to ignore the army and its interests entirely, hence the frequent and munificent bounties.[51]

Even apart from the donatives, the costs of the Roman military establishment were astronomical. It cost 100 denarii to clothe a single centurion and thus 500,000 denarii to equip a normal-sized legion. With nine legions operating in peacetime, this meant an outlay of 4,500,000 denarii just to clothe them. In wartime this figure would be tripled at least. Food and drink were another massive item on the military budget, even if we accept that the Roman soldier, being smaller and older than the present-day front-liner, would need only 3,000 calories a day.[52] There were twenty legions in the field at the height of the Punic War, but by the end of the first century this would have counted as a small army. In Vespasian's reign there were twenty-nine legions (four in Britain, eight on the Rhine, seven on the Danube, eight in the East and one each in North Africa and Spain); even in the 'peaceful' reign of Antoninus Pius there were twenty-eight legions.[53]

The total figure of 500,000 for the Roman armed forces has been disputed, but lower estimates depend on counting only the legionaries and the auxiliaries. If to these we add the praetorian and other guards, the paramilitary police in Rome (some 10,000 strong) and the irregulars or *numeri* raised from tribes on the fringes of the empire (Palmyran archers, Balearic slingers, and so on, who retained their traditional methods of fighting and were used for strictly limited objectives), we edge close to half a million.[54] That figure is easily exceeded if we include also the marines and rowers of the fleets at Misenum, Ravenna, Alexandria and the Black Sea. In return for the massive costs incurred by the Roman state, Rome had the best-trained and most tightly disciplined force in the world, better equipped, protected and fed than any enemy, with better weaponry and armament, blessed with a superior organisation, which made more reserves available than any foe could hope to match. The tactic of the swift offensive was usually successful. Morale was high, and the aplomb and confidence of the legionaries was sky-high. Veterans claimed that they smiled when they saw the massed fire of a legion's artillerymen (*ballistae*) whizzing over their heads when they were drawn up in rank, knowing how demoralised their opponents must be when they found they could not close the range. A Roman commander could usually ask his men for the extra ounce in battle and get it.[55]

And so the Romans looked forward to the coming clash with Parthia with eager anticipation. The Parthians relied heavily on two tactics, used to devastating effect against the Romans at Carrhae: the charge by heavily armoured knights or *cataphractarii*, and a deluge of arrows raining down on an enemy fired by a throng of mounted archers.[56] The Parthians had become over-confident after the defeats of Crassus and Mark Antony and were overrated as military opponents as a result, but, certainly since the campaigns of Trajan, the Romans had the measure of them. Three counter-measures had been found effective: the use of slingers and other missile-firers as a primary weapon; the massed charge by heavy Roman cavalry; and the use of the square. At Carrhae the Romans had become disoriented and confused by the then-novel method of Parthian fighting, and had allowed themselves to become pincushions for a hail of Parthian arrows, prior to panicking when the Parthians unleashed their *cataphractarii*. But by Marcus's time Roman generals had learned that by judicious use of archers and slingers, the Parthian horse archers could be reduced to little more than irritants. Yet, except at very short range, missile-throwers could make little impact on the *cataphractarii*.[57] So the crucial thing in battle was to make sure the legionaries did not panic and could face the heavily mailed horsemen with confidence. The key was to create a huge square, with pikemen on the rim forming a hedge of steel; inside the square archers, slingers and cavalry would be readied for counter-attack. The square would also use pincer or blocking movements to obstruct certain avenues of attack and to furnish anchor points for the counter-offensive. Naturally such manoeuvres called for split-second timing, for otherwise the defenders might fragment dangerously, and here the discipline and training of the Romans paid off. By Marcus's time a direct charge of *cataphractarii* against a legionary square was almost certain to be repelled.[58]

The Romans would then face up to heavy cavalry in nine ranks. The first rank would hold its spear-like pikes at a forty-five-degree angle while the three ranks behind threw heavy spears, and the four ranks behind them hurled lighter throwing javelins; the ninth rank would contain archers. The ballistic trajectories were designed so that each of the three volleys would hit the charging cavalry at different points of their charge.[59] Meanwhile, if by chance the mounted archers had begun to cause demoralisation through their hail of arrows, contingency plans had been laid to deploy forces in a crescent formation or to order an advance on the double. Properly commanded and directed, the legions were invulnerable to charges by the *cataphractarii*. Yet Roman tactics depended heavily on the Parthian willingness to offer pitched battle and on suitable terrain. It was difficult to form a square on the march or on hilly terrain and the Parthians, after some bad maulings, became more cautious and concentrated on long-range attrition and impeding communications.[60] Julius Caesar had planned to wear the Parthians down before bringing them to battle, and in his era the strategy might have worked, but not in the age of Marcus Aurelius.[61] In fact the greatest obstacles to Roman success in Parthia were always geography, climate and disease rather than Parthian military prowess. It was hunger, disease and cold that had turned Mark Antony's retreat into a kind of forerunner of Napoleon withdrawing from Moscow. By foolishly venturing into Media, he had limited the availability of the Roman army's staple cereals.[62] It followed that, bearing in mind sickness rates, logistics, the need to protect supply lines and communications and to garrison captured strongholds, Lucius Verus would need to put massive armies into the field, creating the need in turn for massive logistical support. As Tacitus had long before pointed out, it was the scale of this task, not the quality of the Parthian army, that made a permanent Roman conquest of the old Persian empire a pipe-dream.[63]

Although the normal campaigning season in the East ran only from March to June, it was clearly imperative for the Romans to turn the tide in the year 163. After a year's preparation, spent building roads and bringing the legions up to full fighting pitch, Verus gave the nod to Statius Priscus to attempt phase one of the Parthian war: clearing the enemy out of Syria and reoccupying Armenia.[64] Priscus took with him the legions I Minervia and V Macedonica, with their respective legates M. Claudius Fronto and P. Martius Verus, on a twenty-day march through mountains, covering 300 miles. We cannot be certain of the route: the Romans probably crossed the Syrian frontier near Zeugma (modern Birecik, 37° N, 38° E) and then headed north-east, either to the head of Lake Urmia or via Lake Van; Latin inscriptions show detachments of the legions at Ecmiadzin, just south of Mouth Ararat.[65] The rigours of off-season campaigning in Armenia were well known to the Romans, but evidently Priscus had laid his plans carefully and intended to debouch from the mountains at just the right moment to take advantage of the supplies in the rich agricultural region around the Armenian capital of Artaxata.[66] Everything went according to plan, and Priscus crowned his achievement by storming and taking Artaxata itself, where he proceeded to evict Vologases's puppet Pacorus and install the pro-Roman Sohaemus (an Arsacid and a Roman senator). The storming of the Armenian capital was evidently a bloody and destructive affair, for the Romans rebuilt it some thirty miles closer to the frontier and renamed it Kainopolis, leaving behind a strong garrison of *vexillationes* attached to Legion XV Apollinaris.[67] Statius Priscus gained much kudos from the affair and added to his reputation. Unfortunately he also attracted sycophants posing as genuine historians. Lucian mentions one would-be Thucydides who credited Priscus with being able to kill twenty-seven of the enemy purely with the power of his war-cry.[68] The war provided the brilliantly satirical Lucian with some of his best material. He poked merciless fun both at the chroniclers' abysmal knowledge of geography and at their ludicrous exaggerations, of which the following is a good example: 'The Third Legion, the Celtic contingent and a small Moorish division have crossed the Indus.'[69] Lucian's withering scorn may even have frightened off chroniclers of genuine talent, who feared being the target of his humour, and this may partly account for the exiguous sources that remain for the campaign of 163.[70] Probably the most important event late that year was that Statius Priscus died suddenly. He was eventually succeeded as governor of Cappadocia by Martius Verus in 166, with Julius Severus acting as a stopgap appointee.[71]

The war in 163 was not confined to Armenia, for further south the Romans were fighting on a second front. The Parthians showed contemptuous defiance by deposing Mannus, the pro-Roman ruler of Osrhoene, a principality in north-west Mesopotamia with a capital at Edessa. The Romans responded by advancing on the Euphrates, with two legions, commanded by C. Avidius Cassius (in charge of III Gallica), together with II Adiutrix, stiffened by reinforcements from the Danube and commanded by Q. Antistius Adventus. Alongside them fought a large number of *vexillationes* commanded by P. Iulius Germinius Marcianus, another transferred Danube general.[72] These forces collided with the Parthians at Sura, on the Roman side of the river, suggesting that the Romans had still not completely cleared the enemy out of Syria proper. Lucian speaks of a hard-fought battle, which the Romans won; the star of the occasion seems to have been Avidius Cassius. Unfortunately, while Lucian scoffs at the casualty figures of 70,000, as reported by one of his despised would-be historians, he neglects to give us any figures himself. But we hear of horses without firm footing on icy ground, hands numbed with cold, and archers with bows made limp by incessant rain.[73] Cassius then proceeded to move forces down the Euphrates and occupied the towns of Dausara and Nicephorium (modern Rakka, 35° 50' N, 39° 5' E) on the Parthian bank (at the confluence of the Balikh and the Euphrates). The headwaters of the Euphrates were secured when Roman forces marching south from their victories in Armenia entered Osrhoene and occupied the town of Anthemusia, south-west of Edessa.[74] Elated by these successes, at the end of 163 Lucius Verus put out peace feelers to the Parthians, but Vologases, incredibly, still thought he would win the war and rejected the proposals contemptuously, to Verus's mortification; he later confessed to Fronto that he felt humiliated by the refusal of terms.[75]

Verus himself continued to be a source of concern to Marcus Aurelius in Rome. His troupe of players, jugglers, mime artists, musicians and assorted thespians interested Verus more than the war itself, and the oligarchs of Syria tittered behind their hands at his riotous behaviour. When the war finally ended, he took back with him to Italy such a multitude of actors that wags remarked 'that he seemed to have ended not the Parthian war but the Thespian one'.[76] Marcus received weekly reports from his cousin, the senator M. Annius Libo, whom he had sent out as Verus's 'minder': all were censorious in tone. In time Libo got above himself and forgot that he was dealing with a co-emperor. There was a stand-up row between the two men, in which Libo asserted that he had the greater authority as he was Marcus's plenipotentiary. Shortly afterwards Libo died suddenly; the inevitable rumour spread that Verus had had him poisoned. Undoubtedly he was irked that Marcus had sent out an agent to spy on him, and was alleged to have taken his revenge later by marrying off Libo's sister to his favourite freedman Agaclytus; this in turn was said to have so incensed Marcus that he refused to attend the wedding feast.[77] Perhaps more seriously, Verus seemed to have no interest in the war at all. He spent his winters at Laodicea on the River Orontes and most of his summers at the health and leisure resort of Daphne, a suburb of Antioch. He visited the front at the Euphrates just once in four years, and then only at the urgent insistence of his staff, who stressed the issue of his military credibility. Disingenuously he told Fronto that anxieties about the war brought him to despair and 'night and day made me utterly wretched'. To mitigate all this, it should perhaps be mentioned that Verus was by common consent a good delegator, who let talented generals have their head and did not interfere.[78]

Yet even without all this, there were headaches for Marcus. Soon word came in that Verus had conceived a mighty passion for a beautiful Ionian Greek woman from Smyrna called Panthea. Verus was so besotted by her that he humoured her every whim, even shaving off his beard at her request.[79] Verus's *coup de foudre* seems to have been well warranted. Even Lucian, with his customary Flaubertian ambivalence towards stunning women, admitted to being impressed by her and, underneath the prudential laying it on with a trowel, there is genuine admiration. He compared her to every conceivable classical model and spoke of her soft, bright-glancing eyes, her shapely wrists, delicately tapering fingers, superb, regular, gleaming teeth and her bewitching smile. 'I know now what men must have felt like when they saw the Gorgon's head. I have just experienced the same sensation, at the sight of a most lovely woman . . . It is a fitting crown to the happiness of our benevolent and gracious emperor that in this day such a woman should be born; should be his and her affections his.'[80] But to Marcus, who never really understood the power of sexuality, such a liaison was a threat to the stability of the empire. He decided to bring forward the already planned wedding between Verus and his own daughter Lucilla, who became of marriageable age on her fourteenth birthday (7 March 164). The moment was opportune, for the next phase of the war – the invasion of Parthia itself – was not scheduled to begin until early 165.[81] Marcus accompanied his daughter to the southern port of Brundisium (Brindisi) and at one point contemplated making the sea voyage with her, before deciding that the empire could not afford two absentee rulers. But Lucilla's seaborne progress to Ephesus was a grand affair. She was accompanied by the bridegroom's sister Ceionia Fabia and her uncle M. Vetulemus Civica Barbarus, step-brother of Aelius, the emperor who never was, and one of Marcus's outer circle of philosopher friends. Civica belonged to a circle associated with the Aristotelian philosopher Eudemus of Pergamum, who had influential pupils at the court of Marcus Aurelius.[82] Lucius Verus graciously met his bride at Ephesus, and the marriage was celebrated with due pomp. In Roman terms the marriage was a great success: Lucilla had the title Augusta and produced three children in quick succession. Whether Verus retained the dazzling Panthea as his mistress is not recorded.[83]

The Roman successes in the East were used to full advantage by the machiavellian Fronto, who had artfully written to Marcus at an early stage, prophesying ultimate success even in the dark days of 161–2. If we allow for the overblown rhetorical conventions of the time, the upbeat letter was something of a masterpiece, full of historical analogies purporting to show that reverses in war often led to victory and that the gods liked to send Rome major disasters before eventual triumph, to test its powers of endurance: there was the disaster against the Gauls in 390 BC, the humiliation by the Samnites at Caudine Forks in 321 BC, the debacle in Spain in 138 BC and the defeat of Albinus by Jugurtha in 109 BC, not to mention the heavy losses in Trajan's Dacian campaign and those in the Bar-Kochba revolt. The most obvious instance was of course Hannibal in the Punic Wars, but Fronto had a whole sheaf of examples with which to regale his emperor. 'Mars has spoken often to the Romans in this vein, in many wars . . . But always he has changed our troubles into successes and our terrors into triumphs . . . Who is so unversed in military annals as not to know that the Roman people have earned their empire as much by falling as by felling?' Fronto ranged far and wide with his examples, going back all the way to the tyrant Polycrates of Samos, who in Herodotus's account had all his good luck at the beginning of life and seemed Fortune's darling, only to take a sudden nosedive and end up crucified by the Persians.[84] When news of the victories in Armenia and Sura came in, Fronto was able to say, in effect, 'I told you so.'

Having gained Marcus's ear, Fronto then turned his attention to the co-emperor: as a good politician, he anticipated the possible conse- quences of a great triumph for Verus in the East. Relations between Verus and Fronto had reached a low point around 161–2, partly because of Fronto's 'old Roman' contempt for the actors of whom Verus was so fond. Moreover, to his horror Fronto found that he had gone out on a limb by vehemently attacking a man named Asclepiodotus in a speech and then discovering that he was in Verus's inner circle.[85] Fronto wrote a grovelling letter to Verus in Syria to patch things up, which the co-emperor replied to gracefully. No fool himself, he was already looking forward to the time when he would need an official chronic- ler of his campaigns, and Fronto seemed just right for the job. Verus encouraged Fronto to rebut the many canards that were circulating about his court in Rome. Fronto warmed to the task. Soon the man who had condemned spectacles and thespians was performing a 180-degree turn and sailing over his own intellectual tow-line. Verus's love of the theatre, Fronto said, showed that – like Trajan – he was 'inclusive' and anti-elitist, enjoying the same tastes as the people. As for his love of games and circuses, why, these were not just necessary for social stability, but benefited all classes, unlike the *annona* or free corn issue, which was a gift to the proletariat alone.[86] He also asserted that Verus's personal charisma lifted the morale of his troops, and here Fronto was on firmer ground, for inscriptions do indeed testify to Verus's popularity with the Roman 'squaddies'.[87]

The year 164 was spent in meticulous preparation for the invasion of Parthia. The Romans set a lot of store by cryptic support from their client or friendly states inside the Parthian empire or on its borders, and secret agents spent much of the year suborning important cities and states on the proposed line of march: Edessa (in Osrhoene), Adiabene, Dura-Europos, Hatra, Nisibis.[88] Rome had a strong hand in this area, for it had client kingdoms virtually in the heart of the Parthian empire, such as the King of Mesena (Charcene) in the extreme south of Mesopotamia, where Trajan had received a good welcome.[89] More important was the training of the army. The field commander was to be Avidius Cassius, who had made such an impression at the battle of Sura when commanding Legio III Gallica. Cassius was himself a Syrian senator; his father Heliodorus had not been, though he was one of Hadrian's top officials and had been Prefect of Egypt in his reign.[90] Avidius Cassius soon made his mark through soldierly ability, but more especially because he was a ferocious martinet. The Syrian legions had at the outset of the war been slack and undisciplined (though the extent of this is debated), but Cassius soon put the fear of the gods into them by his draconian practices. He winkled the scrimshankers among his legionaries out of the fleshpots of Danae, where they were accustomed to loll in hot baths; one of his first decrees was that there would be no more bathing except in rivers and streams. He made some early savage examples, beheading unruly troops or cutting off their hands for even minor infractions of discipline. He forbade his troops to carry anything with them on the march except lard, biscuits and vinegar; anyone caught disobeying the rules was instantly executed. A decree was promulgated that anyone found in Danae in uniform would be publicly flogged. Another of Cassius's innovations was a weekly kit inspection.[91] He addressed the men first and told them that if they did not shape up, they would be confined to their tents all winter under martial law – and the legionaries knew from bitter experience that their commander was no bluffer.

Lucius Verus meanwhile announced that, whereas his initial aim had been to restore the status quo ante Vologases's foolhardy invasion of Armenia and Syria, the fact that the Parthians had expelled the pro-Roman king Manus VIII of Edessa meant that henceforth it would be *guerre à outrance*. Sometime towards the very end of 164 or near the beginning of 165 the Roman armies got under way. Verus's strategy was that one army, under M. Claudius Fronto, would secure the north of Mesopotamia, helped by troops released from the Armenian front, and would then advance east beyond the Tigris to Adiabene and Atropatene in the heart of Parthia. The second army under Avidius Cassius would meanwhile advance south along the Euphrates.[92] Fronto achieved his tasks with ease. There seems to have been some kind of battle near Edessa (now Urfa in south-east Turkey), but the chroniclers spent most of their time gushing about how important a trade centre the city was and how good its water supply. Situated on a limestone ridge in the Taurus mountains of southern Anatolia (where the east–west highway from Zeugma met the north–south route to the Euphrates), Edessa was allegedly the perfect cosmopolitan city, where Greek, Semitic and Persian influences had melded to produce a unique culture that was neither 'Eastern' nor 'Western'. The taking of Edessa by the Romans brought its incorporation into the Roman empire a step nearer, though it was not formally annexed until the campaign by Septimius Severus in 194.[93] The Romans then pursued the Parthians eastwards and took Nisibis; the Parthian general Chrosroes is said to have escaped by swimming the River Tigris and hiding in a cave. Sources for this campaign are again meagre, but Lucian enjoyed himself, lampooning the would-be Herodotuses of the war. One source compared Lucius Verus to Achilles and the Parthian king to the demagogic barrack-room lawyer Thersites, while another spent hundreds of lines describing Verus's shield, though Verus was not even at the front.[94] A peculiar feature of the war was the way it generated what would now be called 'historical novels', including a then-famous one called *Babyloniaca* by Iamblichus.[95]

The second Roman army, under Avidius Cassius, achieved spectacular success. Against strong opposition Cassius crossed the Euphrates on a bridge of boats (it is uncertain where, and various candidates have been suggested: Zeugma, Sura, Nicephorium) and advanced on Dura-Europos where the Parthians awaited him. A ferocious battle ensued, in which the Parthians were utterly defeated. Once again casualties of 70,000 were mentioned – a recurring figure with which Lucian had predictable fun.[96] It is uncertain why the Parthians were so massively vanquished. It was said that Vologases's vassals had refused to turn out for him, and it may be that he received less-than-adequate support from the people of Dura-Europos, a wholly Macedonian city only loosely affiliated to the Parthian empire, where the only language spoken was Greek, in contrast to the Greek/Syriac bilingualism of Edessa, Hatra and Palmyra. Since the Parthians derived most of their revenue from tolls on trade routes, and Dura-Europos was a kind of oasis for goods from the Silk Road being taken from Media across the desert to Palmyra and southern Syria, perhaps the burghers of Dura-Europos were glad to welcome the Romans as conquerors.[97]

Towards the end of 165 Avidius Cassius launched the second phase of the campaign and advanced down the Euphrates to its near-junction with the Tigris. The Romans quickly mastered the art of amphibious warfare, for Mesopotamia was striated with canals – to prevent flooding from the Euphrates, which was engorged in spring with melting snow coming down from the north, and to link the Euphrates with the Tigris.[98] Where the two great rivers almost converged were located the twin cities of Ctesiphon and Seleucia. Ctesiphon was the Parthian capital and a prestige target, but Seleucia on the Tigris was a far more important objective. Ctesiphon, origi-nally a winter resort for the kings of Parthia on account of its salubrious climate, was by this date mainly used for billeting troops, and its signif-icance was purely symbolic: although the Romans destroyed it three times within a hundred years (in the campaigns of Trajan, Lucius Verus and Septimius Severus), its loss affected the loosely structured Parthian empire not at all.[99] Avidius Cassius put it to the torch, just as Trajan had done before him.

Seleucia was a very different matter. Eighteen miles south of modern Baghdad, and a showpiece of Hellenistic culture, it was widely consid-ered superior to Antioch and comparable only to Alexandria. Pliny the Elder reported that the plan of its walls resembled the shape of an eagle spreading its wings.[100] A huge city, with a population estim-ated at anywhere between 400,000 and 600,000, it was a key trading centre handling goods from central Asia, India, Persia and Africa and commanding the southern Silk Road running from Bactria and Ecbatana into Syria. From Seleucia the nearby Euphrates was navi-gable all the way to the Persian Gulf. Under the Parthians it retained some kind of Hellenistic city-state status, but evidently the Parthians did not entirely trust Seleucia's loyalty, for they had built up Ctesiphon to emulate it and then constructed an entirely new city of Vologesocerta as a trade rival, with the result that by the time of Cassius's assault, Seleucia was experiencing a relative decline in prosperity.[101] Perhaps this, rather than Avidius Cassius's menacing legions, explains why Seleucia opened its gates without a fight, having secured favourable terms of capitulation. But some time late in 165 Seleucia was brutally sacked and ravaged by rampaging legionaries. There was enormous loss of life (30,000 deaths by one calculation), and the Romans were said to have taken 40,000 prisoners.[102] Exactly what happened is unclear. The Romans, predictably enough, said that Seleucia had not kept the terms of surrender, so that fighting broke out. But 'failure to keep the terms of surrender' was the ancient Roman version of 'shot while trying to escape'. Some say that the disaster was a result of fighting between the Greek and Syrian factions in the city. There was a cultural division in Seleucia between the Syriac-speaking Asiatic people (Pliny the Elder calls them 'Arabs') and their Jewish allies on one side and the Greek-speaking majority on the other.[103] The famous *stasis*, or trans-class factional strife, had claimed many victims in the heyday of the Greek city-states, and it is not impossible that wholesale massacre was triggered by some low political intrigue. But the overwhelming likelihood is that Cassius's troops, bedazzled by the wealth of the city, simply ran amok and their officers were unable to control them. Avidius Cassius, who had made his reputation as a disciplinarian, was faced with a crisis of credibility and so wheeled out the old 'failure to keep the terms of surrender' dodge. The result was disaster in more senses than one, for some think that the plague that would overwhelm Rome in the following years was picked up by marauding legionaries in the temple of Apollo at Seleucia.[104]

The Parthians were now well beaten, and the Romans, emulating Trajan, extended their dominion right down to the Persian Gulf, though their hold over the areas south of Seleucia were precarious; they really held narrow strips of cultivated land rather than defended frontiers as such.[105] Verus and Avidius Cassius thought that, whereas imitating Alexander and trying to go all the way to India was several bridges too far, they ought to outdo Trajan with their conquests. This was the genesis of the obscure Roman expedition into Media proper in the summer of 166. Ancient Media roughly comprised the north-west of modern Iran, with some extensions into Azerbaijan. To the north were the Elburz mountains and beyond them the Caspian Sea, but the heartland of Media was the area around modern Teheran and Hamadan.[106] Media was important for two reasons: it was the agricultural core of the Parthian empire and it controlled the entire silk trade with China. Known for its profusion of sheep, goats, horses and clover, it possessed fertile plains that fed the realm. Its capital Ecbatana (modern Hamadan) was the terminus for the Silk Road that ran from China to Afghanistan and then due west from Herat to Ecbatana. Hamadan was thus the central node from which various subsidiary trade routes spiralled off to the south – to Syria via the Fertile Crescent, across the desert via Palmyra or south through Mesopotamia via Ctesiphon and Seleucia.[107]

To strike deep into Media was thus to sever Parthia's economic lifeline, and there was the added consideration that to sack Ecbatana, the traditional summer palace of the Parthian kings, would add to the tally of palaces in which Ctesiphon and Seleucia already featured. The incursion into Media was led by Avidius Cassius, commanding Legio III Gallica and VI Ferrata Palestina. Perhaps at some stage in the planning – and bearing in mind the 'imitation of Alexander' that always weighed so much with Roman glory-hunters – the fabled Caspian Gates featured as a target. In distinction to the modern location for the Caspian Gates (near Derbent in Dagestan in the extreme south-east of Russia), the ancient Gates were located near the south-eastern shore of the Caspian (where Alexander had pursued Bessus of Sogdiana in the 320s BC). Pliny the Elder described them as follows: '[mountains] pierced by a narrow pass eight miles long, scarcely broad enough for a single line of wagon traffic, the whole of it a work of engineering. It is overhung on either side by crags that look as though they have been exposed to the action of fire, the countryside over a range of twenty-eight miles being entirely waterless.'[108] There was a 'contradiction', however, between the imperatives of 'imitation of Alexander' and economic motives. It makes most sense to assume that Avidius Cassius departed from Seleucia and struck almost due east and then north towards the Caspian, possibly following a route that would take him through modern Quom and Teheran. On the other hand, if Ecbatana (Hamadan) was his aim, he would have had a shorter journey north-east. The stark truth is that we do not know which of these routes he took. We can be certain of two things. Because of the snow and ice that beset Media from December to March, he would not have left before the beginning of April, which left him just three months of good campaigning weather. And the results of the invasion were highly disappointing.[109] From the silence in the sources we may infer that Cassius ran into severe difficulties and retreated rapidly, but that this was immediately hushed up so as not to spoil Lucius Verus's triumphalism. It all reinforced the ancient Roman aristocratic wisdom that it was mindless to attempt the conquest of Parthia: even if you conquered the realm, you would then need a gigantic army to hang on to the annexed territory.[110]

A sober analysis of Lucius Verus's four-year Parthian campaign would conclude that it was in many respects a rerun of Trajan's exploits fifty years earlier. But judicious conclusions were not Verus's style: he wanted to be hailed as a unique warrior, even though he had seen nothing of the fighting. He showed no compunction in awarding himself the titles of *Armeniacus* in 164, *Parthicus* in 165 and, most barefacedly, *Medicus* in 166.[111] Marcus Aurelius always had his doubts about the value of these honorific titles and accepted them for himself only reluctantly, so as not to humiliate his colleague: to refuse them would be tantamount to calling Verus a liar. Whereas a salutation as conqueror of Armenia was no more than a statement of the plain truth, to claim to have conquered Parthia and Media was, for Marcus, to be economical with the truth. He made his feelings plain after the death of Verus by swiftly dropping the latter two titles.[112] But Verus could not get enough of flattery and fawning for the renown he had won through the talents of Statius Priscus and Avidius Cassius. He made a shrewd choice in appointing Fronto as his official campaign historian. He ordered Avidius Cassius and Martius Verus to make all their documentation available and made it quite clear to Fronto what he required of him. 'I am ready to fall in with any suggestions *as long as my exploits are set in a bright light by you* . . . One thing I don't wish to point out to you – the pupil to his master – but to offer for your consideration, that you should dwell at length on the causes and the early stages of the war, *and especially our ill success in my absence. Further I think it essential to make quite clear the great superiority of the Parthians before my arrival, that the magnitude of my achievements may be manifest.'*[113] This was very clever. Verus realised that he could not get away with claiming to have commanded the armies – everyone knew he barely stirred from Danae and Laodicea – but it would be hard to refute his thesis that he had prepared and animated an army in poor shape. The Verus–Fronto collaboration over the Parthian war was one of the most striking examples of 'spin' in the ancient world.

Fronto rose to the challenge magnificently, producing a masterpiece of sycophancy, an olio of exaggerations, half-truths and sometimes plain nonsense. The study of rhetoric had certainly taught the old man how to deploy both *suggestio falsi* and *suppressio veri*. The first thing to insinuate was that the Roman army in Syria had been in a lamentable state when Verus took over.

> The soldiers at Antioch were wont to spend their time clapping actors, and were more often found in the nearest café gardens than in their ranks. Horses were shaggy from neglect but every hair plucked from their riders; it was a rare sight to see a soldier with arm or leg hairy . . . Pontius Laelianus, a man of character and a disciplinarian of the old school, in some cases ripped up their cuirasses with his finger tips; he found horses saddled with cushions, and by his orders the little pommels on them were split open and the down plucked from their pillions as from geese. Few of the soldiers could vault upon their steeds, the rest scrambled up clumsily by dint of heel or knee or ham; not many could make their spears hurtle, most tossed them like toy lances without verve and vigour. Gambling was rife in camp; sleep was night-long or, if a watch was kept, it was over the wine cups . . . The most demoralised of all, however, were the Syrian soldiers: mutinous, disobedient, seldom with their units, straying in front of their prescribed posts, roving about like scouts, tipsy from noon one day to the next, unused even to carrying their arms and, as one man after another laid them aside from dislike of toil, they were soon like skirmishers or half-naked slingers. Apart from scandals of this kind, they had been so cowed by unsuccessful battles as to turn their backs at the first sight of the Parthians and to listen for the trumpet as the signal for flight.[114]

Although some of the Syrian units may not have been fighting fit, much of this is stock cliché and standard Roman propaganda of the

'West good, East bad' variety. It was an *a priori* staple of Roman ideology that Italy represented stoicism, asceticism, martial valour and civic *virtu* while the Near East represented corruption, luxury and decadence.[115] But Fronto soon moved beyond general stereotype to a personal paean to Verus. He claimed that the co-emperor marched on foot at the head of his troops, disdaining the burning sun and the choking dust, going bare-headed, visiting sick troops, enjoying an ascetic table with local wines, snatching fitful sleep. He went completely over the top in describing Verus as a veteran of battles, sieges and the storming of citadels, lavishing spoils on his men. Not mentioning the fact that Vologases's feudal vassals had let him down, Fronto spoke of the Parthians as doughty, well-nigh invincible opponents. Soon came the inevitable comparison with earlier emperors, especially Trajan. Where Trajan had set out for his Parthian war with the veterans of the Dacian campaign, Lucius Verus had had either to raise new men by a levy or use reserve legions; by every conceivable index, Verus's achievement in Parthia was superior to Trajan's. Fronto also took the opportunity to have a go at his old bête noire Hadrian, a man, he alleged, energetic in all the wrong ways and about all the wrong things; he was never energetic about training armies.[116] The extent of Fronto's humbug and two-facedness becomes clear when we find him writing to Avidius Cassius, praising him not just for his unremitting vigour on the march, his unerring instinct for the right moment to give battle and his strategic genius, but also for restoring discipline among the Syrian legions, in flat contradiction to the account in the official history, which gave all the credit to Verus.[117] But Verus, hardly surprisingly, was well pleased with his ex-teacher's fawning endeavours.

June 166 marked the definite end of Verus's Parthian wars. The Misenum fleet anchored off the mouth of the Orontes in late May, and a departure date was fixed for early July, giving the legions time to get back to the northern frontier before the winter snows.[118] Claudius Fronto and his fellow-field commanders were retained in the East for the time being, all as governors of provinces and holding absentee consulships in 166 and 167.[119] Marcus Aurelius vowed to watch the eastern frontier more closely in future, appointed Martius Verus to the governorship of Cappadocia and conferred on Avidius Cassius a special *imperium* in the East, making him a kind of viceroy.[120] The system of client kings was tightened. Mannus VII was placed on the throne of Edessa, which became a colony in all but name. Osrhoene became a vassal state again, while the free city of Carrhae was raised to the rank of colony. The only acquisition through conquest that the Romans held on to was Dura-Europos, though it is possible that garrisons were left at Nisibis in eastern Mesopotamia.[121] As for the wider effects of the war, it can be said that it certainly cost the loyal inhabitants of Asia Minor dear. The sophist Flavius Damianus, secretary of Ephesus council, provided food at his own expense for thirteen months for a constant coming and going of armies, and there were similar stories elsewhere, mitigated to an extent by the fact that the presence of large numbers of troops stimulated demand for the products of the Greek merchants of Anatolia.[122] There was heavy looting in the war zones: for example, the great statue of Apollo in Seleucia was taken back to Rome and placed in the temple of Apollo on the Palatine.[123] Most of all, though, Rome had demonstrated that it still had the resources to undertake major campaigns successfully and had definitively established its military superiority over the Parthians, though in a war so thinly chronicled there will always be sceptics about the extent of their success.[124] The devastating conquest of Parthia by Septimius Severus in the 190s was a kind of coda to Verus's wars, achieving much the same results, but with even greater slaughter.[125] By the dawn of the third century AD the Parthian empire was on the ropes. But, given that it was replaced by a far more powerful and fearsome Persian dynasty, which would virtually bring the Roman empire in the East to its knees, the law of unintended consequences was never seen more clearly than in Lucius Verus's 'glittering triumph'.

8

While Marcus was pleased to have a four-year break from the riotous escapades of his co-emperor – at least Lucius Verus was now doing his carousing on the other side of the Aegean – the normal stresses and strains of being an emperor continued. He often spoke of an immense workload relieved only by sleep. We owe the glimpses of Marcus the family man and private individual to the intermittent correspondence with Fronto but, as with all bores, Fronto too frequently turns the correspondence into a long discourse on *his* problems, *his* sadnesses, *his* illnesses – which in the case of a hypochondriac like him were, of course, legion. It is clear, too, that he never really reconciled himself to losing his star pupil to philosophy. His letters to others are full of contempt for philosophy. When ill, he lamented that there was no consolation to be had from the advice of sages: the stock tenet of Stoicism, that a wise man would still be happy even if shut up inside the bull of Phalaris, was demonstrably false, he averred.[1] With Marcus himself he had to tread more warily. The emperor summed up his distaste for rhetoric as follows: 'When I have said something rather brilliant, I feel gratified, and that is why I shun eloquence.' Fronto rebuked him for this, albeit indirectly and through a quotation from Plato: 'Perilous, young man, is that hasty avoidance of self-gratification, for the last cloak that wraps the follower after wisdom is the love of fame, and that is the last to be discarded.' But the epigrammatic mode was not really Fronto's style. He believed that if something was worth saying, it was worth saying in a hundred different permutations. He takes ten boring pages to say nothing more than is summed up in his pithy conclusion: 'Philosophy will tell you what to say, eloquence how to say it.'[2]

As always, Marcus was remarkably tolerant, perhaps too tolerant. But Fronto did leaven any criticism by excessive praise for his ex-pupil. Marcus was, he said, an outstanding emperor, and the irony was that although he had formally abandoned rhetoric, he now came across in his speeches as more eloquent than ever. 'I feel the same pleasure in seeing my teaching emerge as parents do when they see their own features in their children.'[3] Marcus, he remarked in another letter, was once the corn sprouting in the field, but is now the ripe and golden harvest. Most of this is the routine flattery of the courtier, but occasionally Fronto sounds a genuinely sincere note – the sincerity perhaps guaranteed by the circumstantial detail that surrounds it. He remembered Marcus's notable devotion to Antoninus Pius: how, when the old man was ill, Marcus gave up going to the baths in order to keep him company instead, and denied himself good food and fine wine just so that he could dine with the ailing emperor on the spartan fare of an invalid. He recalled how Marcus would even alter his natural pattern of sleep and waking – with Marcus an owl and Antoninus a lark – in order to fit in with the old man's timetable.[4] Fronto also talked good sense and gave sound advice when Marcus confided to him that he could not concenrate enough to read, except in snatches, because of his anxiety about the Parthian war. Fronto counselled him to follow the example of Julius Caesar, who in the darkest days of the Gallic Wars found time to compose a treatise called 'On Analogy'; since Marcus, he added, was every bit as intellectually gifted as Julius Caesar, he owed it to himself to emulate Caesar's sangfroid.[5] Fronto's pragmatic, down-to-earth advice was probably particularly valuable to Marcus, as he had a tendency to reverie and wandering away in the clouds. Fronto was forever hammering away at this theme that one should not be over-bookish: even great men had to relax. Trajan, for example, liked heavy drinking sessions and the company of actors; Hadrian was a trencherman who liked music; and even Antoninus Pius, the quintessence of foresight, continence, frugality, duty and personal righteousness, liked to go to the gym and wrestle, to go fishing and to laugh uproariously in the company of buffoons and nincompoops.

Get regular sleep, stop blurring the boundary between day and night, and everything else will follow, said Fronto.[6]

Most of what we know of the domestic Marcus Aurelius of this period comes from the letters he sent Fronto while he was vacationing at Alsium on the Etruscan coast, twenty-four miles from Rome. The majority of Marcus's work was done in the afternoon, after a midday siesta. He would begin writing, either practising a rhetorical exercise or doing some phrase-polishing, interspersed with readings from Cicero, Plautus, Ennius or Lucretius. In the early evening he liked to go for a walk along the shoreline or, if inland, somewhere off the beaten track, taking care to skirt the marshes. If the weather was dead calm, he might venture onto a ship and take pleasure from the rhythmic plash of the oars and the rasping, metronomic phrases of the *hortator* or 'exhorter'. When he got home he would go for a Turkish bath and then sit down to dinner: typical fare would be shellfish, capons, fruit, cakes and fine wines. An abiding concern was the health of his children for, as remarked before, all Roman infants lived on a knife-edge. His daughter Cornificia caught a bad fever at Alsium, and the parents suffered justifiable anxiety; fortunately on this occasion (162) all ended happily and Cornificia was reported running gaily round the bedroom.[7] Mostly in his letters Marcus refers to his daughters, but it was the twin sons who were (understandably) the main focus of interest for the worldly Fronto. Sometime in 163 Fronto actually met the twins and was torn between gushing over them to Marcus and trying to make homiletic points in the style of the professional orator. After saying that he could clearly see Marcus in the faces of the boys and even hear the emperor's voice in the 'tiny piping' of the infants, he went on: 'God be praised they have quite a healthy colour and strong lungs. One was holding a piece of white bread, the other a piece of black bread, quite in keeping with a philosopher's son.'[8]

In the first year of Marcus's reign his children had often stayed with his great-aunt Matidia, the great-niece of Trajan and sister-in-law of Hadrian. In 162 she died, involving Marcus in some tricky issues concerning her will. An immensely wealthy woman, the childless Matidia had been surrounded by parasites and hangers-on, who from time to time had managed to get themselves named as beneficiaries in codicils to the will. Matidia may have told these importunate gadflies that they were in her will to shut them up, but had taken the precaution of not sealing the codicils, which in Roman law would have made them certain heirs. As she lay near death, these unscrupulous fortune-hunters had sealed up the codicils, and she had died before the fraud was discovered. According to the strict letter of the law, the bequest would have to be honoured, yet under the will proper Marcus's wife Faustina was the heiress and her daughters legatees. If the disputed codicils were upheld, Matidia's family (Faustina and the children) would receive the 'paltry' sum of one million sesterces each in a lump sum, instead of a munificent annuity.[9] Moreover, the money paid out on the codicils would exceed three-quarters of the total legacy, and the *lex falcidia* would have to be invoked to make sure that the heiress (Faustina) received at least three-quarters of the estate. The punctilious Marcus Aurelius was in a quandary. He could disallow the codicils, accept them as valid or, at the limit, persuade Faustina not to inherit at all. He consulted the members of his inner circle. Fronto for one was outraged and appalled that Marcus would even consider allowing the tenets of his Stoic philosophy to prevail over due process; even to envisage honouring the phoney codicils seemed to him an imbecility. Was he really going to allow parasites and fraudsters to make off with their ill-gotten goods? And how could someone who was given a public funeral have her will and testament set aside? In the end Marcus ducked responsibility for the final decision by handing it over to Lucius Verus.[10] From the fact that we hear no more indignant explosions from Fronto we can reasonably infer that Verus disallowed the codicils.

Yet for most of the four years of Lucius Verus's absence Marcus could neither holiday at Alsium nor concern himself exclusively with the health of his children, for the wider problems of empire demanded his attention. At the most basic level every Roman emperor had to administer a far-flung empire. Rome was the headquarters of that empire, but no military reserve was cantoned there, or anywhere else in the empire, since no emperor wanted to concentrate in one place a large number of troops who could stage a military coup. In Rome the emperor's safety was guaranteed by three urban and nine praetorian cohorts, aided by seven cohorts of the *vigiles* or Night Watch.[11] The urban cohorts were the nearest thing in ancient Rome to a modern police force: they were the first line of defence in maintaining law and order, with the praetorians in reserve to deal with more serious outbreaks. The praetorians were officially the bodyguards for the

emperor and his family, but they also functioned as a militia, something akin to the National Guard in the contemporary United States,
in times of rioting.[12] The division of responsibilities between urban
cohorts and praetorians was complex, and complicated by class considerations: whereas the praetorian prefect was an equestrian, the urban
prefect was a senator. It was felt that, since senators were supposedly
the equals of the emperor, they could not serve as his bodyguards –
that is, as his subordinates; moreover a knight, in charge of the
praetorians, was less likely to aspire to the purple. By and large the
system worked, since the praetorian guard played no part in politics
save in the exceptional years of 68–9 and 193.[13] Clearly subordinate to
the urban prefect was the prefect of the Night Watch, an equestrian.
He recruited his *vigiles* paramilitaries from freedmen and the city proletariat.[14] All cohorts were 500-strong, but the praetorians served only
sixteen years, whereas both the urban cohorts and the Night Watch
signed on for twenty-five years. Service with the praetorians was
considered an attractive career option: they had higher pay than the
ordinary legions, higher status and served only in Italy. That was why
Italians still joined the praetorians long after they had ceased enrolling
in the legions.[15]

Marcus proceeded cautiously in his direction of the administration of Rome and Italy. He kept in office the two praetorian prefects
appointed by Antoninus Pius at the end of his reign – T. Furius
Victorinus, formerly Prefect of Egypt, and Sextus Cornelius Repentinus, both consuls in Antoninus's reign, even though the old emperor
had thereby broken the rule that only knights should lead the praetorians. Yet Marcus was dissatisfied with the old system whereby the
praetorian prefects were not professional military men, but merely
professional administrators, and sometimes over-promoted ones. He
gradually phased in a new 'precedent' (truly a case of the invention
of tradition) whereby praetorian prefects had to be men with actual
experience on the frontiers.[16] In the case of the administration of
Italy, Marcus partially returned to the thinking of Hadrian. In theory
the Senate had responsibility for governing Italy, but Italians resented
being ruled directly from Rome while they received no free corn.
Thinking it was unwieldy for Italy to be governed from Rome, Hadrian
controversially introduced four proconsuls, or *consulares*, to frame
laws for Italy. Many senators were deeply unhappy about this,

resenting an infringement of their old prerogatives, so the pliable Antoninus Pius abolished the system.[17] In 166 Marcus partially reintroduced it. Four new judges (*juridici*) of praetorian rank were appointed shortly after serving as praetors, but could only judge cases brought before them; they could not initiate investigations, as Hadrian's *consulares* had been able to. Thinking that tradition and the whims of the Senate should not outweigh the real needs of the Italian population, Marcus attempted what he thought was a judicious compromise.[18]

Outside Italy there was a complex system of formal imperial administration. Provinces were divided between those ruled directly by the emperor's nominees and those (theoretically) governed by the Senate. The idea was that imperial provinces were ones where there was danger, either from internal revolt or external enemies, and which therefore required the presence of legions.[19] The senatorial or proconsular provinces, on the other hand, were supposed to be peaceful and non-dangerous and (except for the case of Africa) no legions were stationed there. It was supposed to be a flexible system whereby provinces could be swapped if circumstances changed quickly and unexpectedly.[20] In the proconsular provinces the theory was that proconsuls, chosen annually by lot, represented the Senate; they were assisted in financial matters by a quaestor and in general administration by a legate chosen from their own kinfolk. In the time of Augustus they actually commanded armies, but already in Tiberius's reign this ceased to be the case. In military matters all governors acted under the emperor's orders, and the distinction between provinces was a polite fiction.[21] Thanks to his proconsular prerogatives, the emperor could intervene in senatorial provinces also, by appointing an imperial legate in place of the proconsul or by sending out a plenipotentiary mission. Usually, though, he simply told the departing proconsuls what he wanted and required.[22] Imperial provinces, properly so-called, were subdivided into three: consular, praetorian and equestrian, in descending order of importance. The consular and praetorian provinces were governed by senators, assisted in financial affairs by equestrian procurators and freedmen; the equestrian provinces, lowest of the heap, were assigned to knights. The history of the emperors is also the history of the decline of proconsular provinces. Whereas under Nero there had been ten of them, by the time of Marcus Aurelius there were just five.

Under Marcus too, for undeclared reasons, but obviously because he considered it a security risk, Bithynia became an imperial province and remained so, without any swapping or compensation to the Senate.[23]

We can easily reconstruct the administrative picture of the Roman empire under Marcus Aurelius. Sicily was a proconsular province, but two other large islands in the western Mediterranean, Corsica and Sardinia, were imperial equestrian domains. Spain was divided into three provinces, of which one (Baetica) was senatorial while the other two, Tarracona and Lusitania, were imperial (Tarracona of consular rank, Lusitania praetorian); there was one legion stationed in the Iberian peninsula.[24] Gaul contained one senatorial province (Narbonia) and three imperial praetorian provinces – Aquitania, Belgica and Lugdunum. The importance of Britain (Britannia) was underlined by its status as an imperial consular province with three legions.[25] North Africa was divided into three provinces, one of them consular (Numidia) and the other two imperial equestrian (Mauretania Tingitana and Mauretania Caesariana); one legion was thought sufficient to contain the hostile tribes of the Sahara.[26] Egypt was another imperial province, administered by a high-ranking knight, the Prefect of Egypt, with one legion at his disposal. Cyrenaica (including Crete) was a senatorial province, but Arabia, the newest province, was an imperial praetorian one, with one legion. The greatest concentration of legions was in Germany and the Danube area. Both Upper and Lower Germania were imperial consular provinces with two legions each, while the Alps, considered relatively secure, were divided into six imperial equestrian provinces: Norica, Raetia, the Po Alps, the Maritime Alps, the Alpes Cottiae and the Alpes Poenninae. Along the Danube there were eight imperial provinces: two of equestrian rank in Lower Dacia, two of praetorian rank (Upper Dacia and Lower Pannonia)[27] with a legion each, while four (Dalmatia, Upper Pannonia, Lower Moesia and Upper Moesia) were of consular rank. Upper Moesia contained two legions, Upper Pannonia three, while Dalmatia and Lower Moesia shared three legions. Cyprus, Greece and Macedonia were senatorial provinces, but Thrace was an imperial praetorian territory. Syria-Palestine (formerly Judaea) was a consular imperial province with two legions,[28] while directly facing Parthia were Syria, with three legions, and Cappadocia with two; naturally, in an area of great danger, they had the status of imperial consular provinces. Galatia and Cilicia were imperial praetorian domains, while in Anatolia there were five provinces, of which two were proconsular (Asia and Lycia-Pamphylia, Marcus having abstracted Lycia-Pamphylia). All of these provinces were tightly controlled from the centre by a raft of rescripts sent out by Marcus to the governors.[29]

Marcus Aurelius is generally considered to have run a more thorough, thoughtful, sensitive and more pro-Hellenic administration than Antoninus Pius. One sign of his ability was the way he increased the opportunities available to the equestrian class while not alienating or arousing the jealousy of senators. Men of non-senatorial status were found in a number of key positions, such as the Prefect of Egypt (the top equestrian post), the praetorian prefect (the second highest-ranking post for knights),[30] the two prefects for the grain supply and fire brigade in Rome, procurators of gladiators' barracks, public buildings and the water supply, administrators of inheritance and emancipation taxes, the state courier and transport systems, the prefect of vehicles, plus the posts as provincial procurators and other administrative posts in the provinces.[31] Although the Senate still in theory had responsibility for governing Italy, Marcus appointed as his judges equestrians who lived in Rome or its environs, though, as stated previously, these did not have the powers of Hadrian's powerful consular legates.[32] Another powerful equestrian post was the *a rationibus* (the central administrator of the emperor's finances), who had another senior equestrian procurator under him, the *procurator summarum rationum*.[33]

Grasping the need for better military appointments, Marcus replaced the *ab epistulis* (the official dealing with the emperor's official correspondence with governors, imperial agents, cities and foreign nations) whom he had inherited from Antoninus (one Caecilius Crescens Volusianus) with a man who had long experience of fighting the Moors in North Africa, T. Varius Clemens.[34] Other equestrian posts in the imperial bureaucracy were the *a libellis*, dealing with the numerous requests and petitions addressed to the emperor, the *a cognitionibus*, dealing with the ever-increasing number of judicial appeals to the emperor; the *a studiis*, controlling the imperial archive and library; the *a commentariis*, controlling the archives and records from other bureaux; and the *a memoria*, which provided the secretariat-general of the imperial Chancellery.[35] Moreover, equestrian procurators now received a salary that could be as high as 300,000 sesterces a year (a 50 per cent increase since Claudius's reign), and there even arose a knights' equivalent of the senatorial *cursus honorum*. Finally, and not insignificantly, Marcus promoted talented soldiers from this class, among them some of the famous names of the late second century: Pertinax, Septimius Severus, Vespronius Candidus, Ulpius Marcellus, Valerius Maximianus.[36] The rise of the equestrian class was largely a matter of simple demographics, because the old senatorial order was failing to reproduce itself and provide the state with sons and grandsons. Places were opening up in the Senate at the rate of about 200 per generation – enough to accommodate the sons of the equestrian procurators and more. In turn, each generation of equestrian officials recruited almost entirely from new families in the municipal aristocracies further and further from Rome. The result was that a Senate that was mainly Italian at the beginning of the Flavian dynasty was only half-Italian by the time of Marcus Aurelius.[37]

The undoubted rise of the equestrian class under Marcus was, however, only a relative phenomenon. Since large sums of money passed through the hands of public administrators, some safeguard against fraud and embezzlement had to be provided, and here Marcus cunningly appointed people of different social status to what was essentially the same post – what has been termed 'pseudo-collegiality'.[38] Hadrian had expelled all freedmen from key posts and replaced them with equestrian procurators, but he kept the freedmen on as deputies to benefit from their expertise. Moreover, it made sense to employ slaves and freedmen at this level, since they could absorb the sheer clerical burden – for all business between the emperor, his counsellors and the Senate had to be conducted in writing, even if all the parties were in Rome.[39] Hadrian had maintained a strict hierarchy, with equestrians as the administrative class of the civil service, and slaves and freedmen in executive and clerical grades, but Marcus improved the situation by virtually inventing a parallel or shadow administration; he aimed for continuity and stability by keeping freedmen at their parallel posts longer than the equestrians. Some say the parallel civil service operated by the emperor's slaves and freedmen was actually more important than that of the equestrians.[40] Furthermore, side by side with his promotion of equestrians, Marcus improved the status and prospects of senators. In his principate 160 senators held some sort of administrative post, so that nearly one-third of the Senate was engaged in official business.[41] When forced to take over provinces because of the needs of war, he was scrupulous in 'compensating' the Senate, and in this way senators became governors of Raetia and Noricum.[42] He also widened the composition of the 'sovereign body', so that most areas of the empire had at least one family in the Senate. Tyana in Cappadocia, the easternmost province of the empire, provided the first 'Far Eastern' senator in the shape of T. Claudius Gordianus. Fronto, meanwhile, as a powerful patron with the ear of the emperor, led a major breakthrough for African senators.[43] Marcus also increased the number of consuls from eight to ten per year.[44] And whereas Trajan had stipulated that every candidate for senatorial office must have transferred at least one-third of his fortune to Italy and have invested it in real estate there – to show a commitment to Rome and Italian supremacy – Marcus reduced the quota to a quarter.[45]

All this was pleasing to the Senate, which therefore regarded Marcus as a 'good' emperor. In senatorial terms, a good emperor was one who protected the social order by granting preference according to the traditional aristocratic criteria of birth and wealth, attributes that were thought to confer merit and excellence in themselves. Elite Romans disliked any sign of meritocracy or indeed equality in general.[46] They took grotesque inequality for granted as part of the natural order of the universe. On the rare occasions we find Romans actually arguing for inequality, they did so in a circular manner. Equality, they alleged, would destroy traditional rank and hierarchy, and therefore one could not have equality; they ignored the glaring *petitio principii* involved in such an argument. Marcus Aurelius was torn between his innate conservatism, which led him to side with the Senate, and the realisation that the problems of empire actually did require people with administrative gifts and talents. He usually made appointments to major offices by means of letters known as *codicilii*, and one extant example shows him nominating a man named Domitius Marsianus to a position as equestrian procurator in Gallia Narbonensis at a salary of 200,000 sesterces; Marcus added that what he needed was a man of good character, conscientiousness and experience.[47] This shows the emperor at a halfway point between tradition and meritocracy. Rather as in the time-honoured manner of the British Civil Service in modern times, specialist knowledge and technical abilities played little part in administrative appointments, and a man's general abilities and experience in a range of posts were regarded as the touchstone.[48]

Undoubtedly the Senate was as pleased with Marcus as it had been with the similarly obliging Antoninus Pius. Unprecedentedly, he was allowed to bring four different matters to the attention of the Senate at any one meeting.[49] He was scrupulous in getting the Senate's approval for erecting statues and always informed that august body of any treaty he had signed.[50] He was a regular attender at Senate meetings when in Rome and even travelled in from his holiday home at Campania for the purpose. He liked to take the pulse of oligarchic opinion or sometimes just liked to hear what people had to say. He attended as a private citizen even when he had no *relatio* to make, and was often present even on election days, something supposedly unprecedented for an emperor. Moreover, he always stayed for the whole session. And whenever he was absent from Rome on imperial business, he kept the Senate fully informed.[51] In return he expected to be kept informed of all senatorial business. Emperors could in any case attend the assembly as private persons, could vote or be called upon to vote. Also emperors had a de facto presidential veto. They could express disagreement with a Senate vote, if present, or, if presiding, could throw out the motion altogether.[52] But Marcus always liked to pay lip-service to the notion of the sovereignty of the Senate, and always went through the pretence of asking it for money, even though he could simply take it. Some say that in his exquisite politeness to the Senate, Marcus was just going through the motions, that in reality by this era emperors expected the Senate to rubber-stamp whatever they proposed. Certainly Marcus himself was not above employing an authoritarian tone, even using the future indicative tense ('this will be') when addressing the 'Conscript Fathers'.[53] Later in his reign, when he was absent from Rome, Marcus tended to send an *oratio* or communiqué to the Senate, which then simply ordered a senatorial command (*senatus consultum*) to cover all relevant points; this sometimes led to lawsuits because of the subsequent lack of clarity in law.[54] This was of course the logical outcome of a process begun by Hadrian, the first emperor whose addresses to the Senate were cited as statements of law by legal authorities. Indeed, by the end of Marcus's reign, the imperial *oratio* had virtually superseded the *senatus consultum*.[55]

Marcus's relationship with the Senate, in short, can be likened (*mutatis mutandis*) to that of a British prime minister with the monarch, rather than to that of a US president and the American Senate: a combination of unchallengeable power versus superficial deference, rather than genuine separation of powers. The emperor was chief political decision-maker, commander-in-chief of the army, high priest and tribune of the people. He controlled all foreign policy, made the decisions for peace or war, and claimed as his all military victories, even when he was nowhere near the battlefield. At the limit he could always pose as the champion of the people against the aristocratic selfishness of the Senate. The genius of Augustus had been to annex this tribunician power to the imperial throne so that the emperor could always claim to be 'above politics' and the genuine focus of the popular will. Augustus too had added the notion of *auctoritas* to the imperial portfolio, a kind of charismatic authority that gave his decisions the force of law and implied his divinity.[56] A Roman emperor was thus at once a republican magistrate, an absolute monarch and a future god: hence the famous anecdote that Vespasian, on his death-bed, remarked, 'I seem to be turning into a God.' But there was a certain everyday banality too attached to the imperial office. An emperor had to listen to requests and hear disputes. Under Marcus Aurelius, petitioners did not have to fear they would be put to death or asked to commit suicide (either explicitly or implicitly), as under the bad emperors. The consequence was a flood of petitions, with the Greek-speaking part of the empire leading the way; their cultural heritage gave them the confidence to petition emperors, even aggressively so.[57] The Greek-speaking empire was increasingly important under Marcus Aurelius. Indeed, some scholars see the 'Greek factor' as the key element in the many 'contradictions' involved in the transition from the classical world proper to that of late antiquity.[58]

Real power in Rome was concentrated in the person of the emperor, his personal cabinet and the imperial council, rather than the Senate. The outer circle of imperial advisers was formed by the so-called *amici* (literally 'friends')[59] – usually (but not exclusively) from the senatorial class – but the really important people were in the inner circle of *comites* (literally 'companions'). The technical distinction between the two groups was that the *amici* had the right to attend imperial audiences, but the *comites* were supposed to accompany the emperor everywhere. All *comites* were *amici*, but not all *amici* were *comites*.[60] Antoninus Pius had made the distinction explicit, taking a 'laid-back' attitude to *amici*, allowing them great personal latitude and never insisting that they be close at hand, while taking his *comites* with him on his rare journeys from Rome.[61] Marcus Aurelius was usually to be found at his residence on the Palatine when in Rome, where slaves and freedmen in sumptuary white could be seen in large numbers alongside the *amici*.[62] But for his journeys into the country he too took only the *comites*. Although the Palatine was the official symbol of imperial dignity, the popular saying expressed the truth of the matter: 'Rome is where the emperor is.'[63] As a conservative figure, Marcus did not dispense with the *comites* altogether, though he must have been tempted to do so. As the *Meditations* make clear, he had a low opinion of the calibre of his counsellors, and inferred from their moral and intellectual weakness that human beings in general were a bad lot.[64] This was why he was always explicit and meticulous in his laws and decrees: he feared that otherwise his subordinates might genuinely misunderstand his wishes or, more likely, 'fail to understand' on purpose. His thanks for this was to acquire a reputation for long-windedness and pedantry.[65]

In the early part of his reign it was Marcus Aurelius the judge that most impressed. Unlike a modern president or prime minister, an emperor had to spend much of his time in a judicial capacity; to deal with the huge inflow of cases he increased the number of court days to 230 a year. Nonetheless, one of his *orationes* laid down the general rule that no litigant could force the hearing of a case during the harvest or vintage, except that even this proviso could be overturned if pressing cause was shown, so that Marcus's courts were often found operating during these 'prohibited' seasons or on holidays.[66] But though keen to streamline the administration of justice, Marcus did not want cases truncated by bringing pressure on defendants to confess or by speeding things up unjustifiably; he once rebuked a praetor for trying to gallop through a trial too quickly.[67] He was against time-wasting or incurring unnecessary expense, such as making witnesses travel long distances and then not using them. He streamlined the law by appointing judges from whom there was no appeal. Much of his time on the bench was taken up with adjudicating on the numerous 'exemptions' and 'immunities' that made Roman law such a minefield.

One case concerning the legitimacy of the children of a man claiming an immunity showed the solomonic Marcus at work. The man had appealed to Junius Rusticus, prefect of the city, against a judgement of the consuls on the ground that one of them had made a technical error on a point of law. Marcus ruled that because the man was appealing against a decision by the consuls, it followed logically that he must accept the principle of jurisdiction by them, so that they would be left to decide the case.[68] If this seems narrowly legalistic, another judgement shows Marcus allowing compassion to trump the strict letter of the law. A woman appealed to him because she had married without realising that she was within the legally prohibited degrees of consanguinity. He replied, 'We are moved both by the length of time during which, in ignorance of law, you have been married to your uncle, and the fact that you were placed in matrimony by your grandmother and by the number of your children. So, as all these considerations come together, we confirm that the status of your children, who result from this marriage which was contracted forty years ago, shall be as if they had been conceived legitimately.'[69]

Marcus had a particular interest in family law and bequests and in the law governing slaves and freedmen. He was in no way dictatorial in these matters and took the opinion of his advisers seriously. A man wanted to bring an action to gain possession of the property of his grandfather's freedman. Marcus had been initially inclined to throw out the grandson's plea, as all precedent seemed to favour this course, but after a long discussion with his jurists and *amici*, he allowed himself to be persuaded that the intrinsic interests of justice overrode precedent.[70] A tricky case from 166 shows Marcus in typical form. A man drew up a will, had second thoughts and then erased the name of his heirs. The heirs then seem to have drawn up a codicil containing their names. Did either the initial erasure or the subsequent codicil invalidate the entire will? Marcus took the line that one disputed clause in a will should not be allowed to negate the rest of it, especially as other parts of the will manumitted slaves; the will was therefore declared valid.[71] As a general rule, Marcus sought to divine the wishes of the deceased testator and honour them. It sometimes happened that legacies in a last testament were prima facie invalid, either because the will had not been properly drawn up or because there were no legally entitled heirs – in which case the property of the deceased was usually

declared the property of the state. Marcus took the line that the real
wishes of the deceased, rather than legal technicalities concerning a
'true' will, should be the foremost consideration, and ruled accordingly
after hearing lawyers for both sides.[72]

Marcus was concerned to keep family estates intact and brought
in new laws to that effect. This was of a piece with his general concern
for the protection of minors. In theory the property of those executed
or exiled had to be confiscated, but Marcus did not believe in visiting
the sins of the fathers on the sons. It had become customary to allow
children of those executed or exiled to inherit half the patrimony
except in cases of treason, and this precedent was reinforced.[73] On
guardianship he brought in a number of new laws. One *oratio*
prescribed punishment for the plundering of the estates of minors by
trustees or guardians. Another permitted legates and proconsuls to
decide who should be guardians. Yet another laid down that only a
praetor could override the provisions of a will granting *alimenta*.[74]
Tutors were not allowed to marry their wards, or at any rate not to
contract the *matrimonium iustum*, the only form of marriage recognised in elite society.[75] Another *oratio* established that only freedmen
from the same area should be appointed as guardians to wards of
freedman status. Thus a free-born man assigned as tutor to a freedman
had a valid reason to decline.[76] A further *oratio* laid down that even if
a freedman enjoyed an exemption from the burden of tutoring, he
could still be appointed guardian of the children of his patron or
patroness.[77] If Dostoevsky is correct, and the true touchstone of
morality is one's concern for children, Marcus Aurelius certainly passed
the test with flying colours.

It is conventionally alleged that in his legal judgements Marcus
tended to take the side of slaves. The proposition is only partially true.
He was certainly in favour of manumission as a general principle and
removed barriers to allowing slaves to purchase their freedom.
Moreover, a slave sold with the promise of freedom had to be freed,
even if the requisite conditions were not fulfilled by vendor and buyer.
When clarifying the law on these points, he always tried to make sure
the processes of freeing a slave were not blocked by some legal tech-
nicality or cross-petition. He never wanted the power of money to be
able to trump anything that worked towards the betterment of his
fellow-man.[78] And one of his decrees set out to protect the interests

of slaves who, after investigation, were declared innocent of their master's murder and were then freed, or otherwise benefited from his will. Marcus laid down that any children born to them during the investigation were to be considered free-born, while they could also benefit from any of the profits or interest that had accrued to the legacies made in their favour, once they had been cleared of criminality.[79] On the other hand, he was a hardliner when it came to fugitive or runaway slaves or those suspected of homicide. On the murder of an owner, all slaves in a household were routinely tortured; by a *senatus consultum* of AD 57 this punishment could also be meted out to freedmen.[80] Marcus retained these draconian laws and was quite happy to let masters beat their slaves for disobedience or even hire out the task to professional whippers. Paid flagellators were something that dated from the Roman republic, and Juvenal famously indulged his hatred of women by instancing a lady owner who kept a *tortor* (professional whipper and slave-breaker) on an annual retainer.[81] So far from moderating any of this, Marcus strengthened the rights of slave-owners by decreeing that they had the right to enter the estates of anyone in the empire – country people, senators, even the emperor himself – in pursuit of fugitive slaves.[82] Severe penalties were set down for anyone who harboured runaway slaves, unless they relented and handed them over within twenty days. All governors, city magistrates and soldiers manning provincial guard posts had to assist in recovering such slaves.[83]

Marcus was very keen on absolute clarity concerning the status of all his subjects. He appointed a registrar of births and required *all* Romans, even those of bastard birth, to be registered. He employed detectives to investigate all suspect cases and to prevent fraudulent collusion between masters and slaves – either to declare that a slave birth was really a free birth or that a freedman was really born free.[84] Subject to provisos to be discussed later, it would be true to say that Marcus took the matter of Roman citizenship very seriously indeed and was determined to protect its envied status.[85] There is a very good example of this in the grant of citizenship that he and Lucius Verus made in 168–9 to Julianus Zegrensis, a headman of an ethnic group in the Atlas mountains in Mauretania Tinginata (modern Morocco). Granting this as a reward for loyalty and to persuade other clans of the Zeregenses to follow his example, Marcus nonetheless insisted that the headman send him the ages of his wife and children before the privilege of citizenship could be ratified.[86] Marcus was inundated with petitions asking for exemptions, immunities and grants of citizenship from all over the empire, but was careful never to establish precedents or insinuate any form of general regulation; he always preferred to work *ad hoc.*[87] He liked to grant Roman citizenship to people in outlying areas rather than found new Roman towns or *coloniae* to dominate the hinterland, and favoured granting citizenship en bloc to whole communities rather than individuals.[88]

Despite his philosophical predilections, Marcus was in many ways a political pragmatist and tried, as far as possible, to convert moral problems into legal issues to be settled by clear-cut laws. This accounts for the plethora of laws in his reign on every conceivable subject. He laid down strict time limits for legal appeals, based on a careful calculation of the courts' working days.[89] An *oratio* established the precise procedure when a governor consulted the emperor about a tricky case. Even if no appeal had been lodged against the governor's sentence, no penalty ordered by him could be carried out until the emperor had considered the case, replied and the reply was received and published by the governor. A sentence had effect only from the moment of its promulgation in Rome so that, for example, the will of a defendant who died while under sentence from a governor (but while it was not yet ratified by the emperor) would still be valid and not subject to confiscation.[90] Another thorny case, involving the liabilities of creditors and debtors when a loan had been made for house repairs, led to a general clarification of the situation between debtors and creditors.[91] Marcus spent a lot of time investigating Hadrian's ruling on treasure trove before concluding that his unfavourite predecessor was correct. Whereas originally treasure trove had worked on a 'finders keepers' basis,[92] Hadrian stipulated that you could keep the hoard only if you found it on your own property; if on another's, you had to share fifty-fifty with the state exchequer.[93] Lunatics of high status could not be found guilty of crime, but stringent safeguards were put in place to prevent anyone merely pretending to be mad.[94] If a citizen of good character died while he was under criminal investigation, but before anything could be proved, his status could never be questioned thereafter and all investigations pending at the time of his death had to lapse automatically.[95] Marcus took a very hard line with those who tried to defraud the tax system by claiming immunities and exemptions to which they were not entitled. If someone falsely claimed to be in the business of shipping corn or oil to Rome, when in reality he was neither ship owner or sea captain nor owned any property dealing in maritime trade, he would be automatically stripped of any other tax immunities that he enjoyed.[96] Finally, most signally trying to conflate sin and crime or morality with legality, Marcus made several misguided attempts to improve sexual morality – he considered that sexual promiscuity among the young had reached scandalous proportions – by abolishing mixed bathing in public baths.[97]

Marcus even extended the law into areas where previous emperors had hesitated to tread, for fear of the mob. His deep loathing of games and public spectacles must be emphasised: he considered them the preoccupation of lesser minds and the surest sign of the lowest common denominator. His distaste for games was an aesthetic one, not humanitarian or compassionate.[98] Though rarely seen at the theatre, Marcus as emperor was virtually obliged to be a regular attender at the Circus Maximus, where the crowds ululated their vociferous partisanship for Whites, Greens, Blues and Reds, at gladiatorial games and at animal shows – either ones where criminals were exposed to savage beasts or the even more bloodthirsty ones where dangerous animals were set upon each other.[99] At first Marcus tried to show his disdain and to assuage his boredom by reading or ostentatiously looking at something other than the events in the arena. But Fronto warned him that such *de haut en bas* behaviour appeared ungracious and risked alienating the volatile mob; they could see when he was reading and did not like it. And how could he pose as the father of his people if he made it so clear that he despised their precious pastimes? Marcus therefore began holding informal cabinet meetings at the games and dictating letters. The crowd could see him talking to his advisers, but assumed he was discussing events in the arena and instructing his scribes to take bets.[100]

He found other ways to make his displeasure felt. First, he insisted that strict class distinctions be maintained at public spectacles. As in the old days, there would be special rows of seats reserved for senators, knights and town councillors.[101] Next he introduced a *senatus consultum* that forbade masters of slaves to manumit any slaves among the performers belonging to himself or others; previously such manumission had occurred at the insistence or acclamation of the mob when it was delighted with actors, circus champions or gladia-tors.[102] On one occasion the mob bayed for the emancipation of a favourite animal trainer, whose man-eating lion had dispatched victims in a satisfactorily gory way; Marcus pointedly refused the request. He explained that he could not allow such manumission, as it interfered with the rights of property owners.[103] Finally he issued decrees enforcing a reduction in the cost of games. When this led to low prices being paid for gladiators, entrepreneurs looked around for other condemned men to fill the gap and so, indirectly, the hated sect of the Christians came to the fore. Critics say that Marcus's move to cut costs was ill thought out. If he really wanted less frequent games, he should have made the costs prohibitive, possibly by increasing taxes on the *lanistae*, the managers of the gladiatorial schools; incredibly (given his general posture), Marcus appears to have *abolished* such taxes.[104]

The thrust of Marcus's legal reforms was always towards the removal of cruel and unusual punishments, and his habit was to punish with lighter penalties than those allowed, or indeed recommended, by law.[105] Determined, like Antoninus Pius, that no senator should be put to death in his reign, he left the Senate to police its own and hear cases where the defendant was a senator in their own judicial councils – even in instances where he had full jurisdiction.[106] In the case of treason trials, he was forced to intervene. Marcus hated taking part in treason trials, even when he had initiated the proceedings under the *lex Julia maiestatis*, but had to put in an appearance at the conclusion of proceedings to prevent the death-penalty being meted out.[107] As part of his 'liberal' attitude to crime and punishment, he clamped down severely on payments made to informers and *delatores*, discouraging the growth of rewards and 'grasses' as the way to police Rome.[108] He studied legal theory assiduously and, at the beginning of his reign, was particularly influenced by the jurists Proculus and Q. Servidius Scaevola, whose methods involved rigorous attention to precedent.[109] But later in the 160s Marcus and Lucius Verus chose as their chief legal adviser Volusius Maecanius, formerly Marcus's law tutor, then equestrian Prefect of Egypt and finally (promoted to the Senate) consul and *éminence grise*. Volusius Maecanius nudged the co-emperors away from admiration of Proculus and even towards decisions that contradicted those they had taken earlier, when still in thrall to Proculus and Scaevola.[110] Above all, Marcus insisted on tolerance and a full avoidance of the tyranny of earlier emperors. He forbade his guards to drive away citizens who approached him with petitions.[111] He allowed mime writers and satirists, notably Marullus, to lampoon him with impunity, making something of a fetish of untrammelled free speech, even when it involved scurrilous comments on his own person.[112] He detested a certain politician named Vetrasinus, but allowed him to run for office even so.[113] He decreed that trapeze artists had to have a 'safety net' beneath them as they practised, in the form of thick, spongy mattresses.[114] But he liked to make it clear that, despite his tolerance and forbearance, he was no soft touch. When one of the defendants in a lawsuit protested vociferously against one of his judgements, on the ground that he had done no violence, Marcus replied, 'Do you think it is violence only when men are wounded?'[115]

The 200 imperial decrees, rescripts and *orationes* that have survived demonstrate that Marcus was an essentially conservative figure in law and administration, just as Antoninus Pius had been.[116] Although he assented intellectually to Fronto's strictures on the unpleasantness of the Roman upper class, he did not act upon the conviction, but rather shored up their position even more strongly. There had always been aristocratic resentment about freedmen who became too rich, powerful or 'uppity', and their aristocratic betters wanted to keep them in their place by legislation allowing them to be enslaved if they got above themselves.[117] Imperial freedmen were particularly resented for their influence, and especially for the favour shown them by emperors in the matter of anulling their slave past – by certifying that they had been born free. Marcus humoured the oligarchs in their prejudices and indulged their hatred. The most notorious example was when he backed the reactionary elements at Athens, expelling freedmen from the city council, preventing their descendants from holding office there and restricting membership of the Areopagus (the Athenian equivalent of the Roman Senate).[118] Marcus largely shared the aristrocratic phobia that any tinkering with the social pyramid meant defying the laws of nature itself, with the subsequent inevitable descent into a world of chaos.

In general Marcus always preferred reinforcing the old ways and the old laws to innovating – not surprisingly, since political conservatism was a logical concomitant of his beloved philosophy of Stoicism. This accounts for some of his almost antiquarian predilections, which he codified in law: for example, he revived the old fetial spear-throwing ceremony before Rome went to war and insisted that soldiers wear civilian dress when in Italy.[119] Some say that, while Marcus insisted on a rigid distinction *between* citizen and non-citizen, he was even keener on class distinctions *within* the citizen-body, as for instance the famous difference between *honestiores* and *humiliores* (see pp. 483–4). Marcus not only favoured acute socio-economic differences, but also wanted them to be made visible, in the form of differential clothing for the different strata of society. He was keen on differential nomenclature for the various social sectors: *clarissimus* for the senatorial order, *eminentissimus, perfectissimus, egregius* for knights, and so on. He wanted the barriers between social classes and subclasses maintained and their prestige upheld, and hated any move to merge traditional roles. He was adamant that knights had to be kept as praetorian prefects, and senators as commanders of the legions. He passed laws forbidding senators to marry or live with women who had a criminal record, and declared marriages between freedmen and ladies of senatorial rank illegal.[120] In all his legal judgements there is a clear tendency to take the side of the big battalions, the great landowners against the common man, senators against freedmen, oligarchs against 'new men'.[121] This was only partially mitigated by a grudging meritocracy whereby men of low birth but indisputable abilities – Pertinax and M. Bassaeus Rufus are the most obvious examples from his reign – were given their head.[122] A case could be made for saying that Marcus was much more meritocratic with the Asian provinces than with Italy or Greece. In this case he did not receive embassies from the provinces all on the same basis, but according to whether the petitioners were *worthy* to receive the favours they craved – citizenship, immunity, permanent or temporary relaxation of tribute, exemption from indirect taxation or direct financial support.[123]

As an administrator, Marcus was in general a great believer in the role of the state in the economy, and many of his measures smack of centralist dirigisme. His reign produced a deluge of legislation on the water supply, the correct distance between buildings, the architecture of public baths, graves and burial places and the proper conduct of religious rites. As with all emperors, his principate began with a flurry of new road-building and the erection of milestones to show that there was a new ruler in Rome, but this soon tailed off, and overall few new

roads or aqueducts were built, attention being focused on the maintenance of existing ones.[124] He was keen on maintaining streets and
highways in a good state and – because of traffic congestion – forbade
driving or riding in carriages within Rome's city limits.[125] Unlike, say,
Hadrian, he had no interest in magnificent new building programmes
or urban reform. The statue of Antoninus Pius in the Campus Martius,
the temple of Jupiter Heliopolitanus on the Janiculum and, later, his
own column were the only significant new buildings in Rome. One
severe recent judgement holds that he was 'too fussy a man to have a
wider vision; he seems to have been well-meaning but too concerned
with details'.[126] He did, however, exert himself on behalf of Spain, the
land of his fathers. The *Historia Augusta* reports: 'He made scrupulous
provision for the welfare of the provinces of Spain which, in defiance
of the law of Trajan, had been exhausted by levies from Italian settlers.'[127]

Another jolt to some of his modern admirers was his complete
disbelief in the efficient working of 'free markets'. He removed the
price of grain from the domain of market forces and carefully oversaw
its import, rightly concluding that bread (if not circuses) was *the* prerequisite for a peaceful Rome. The importance of the grain supply
can be seen from one simple fact: under Marcus Aurelius the *praefectus annonae* ranked third among all equestrian posts, inferior only
to the Prefect of Egypt and the praetorian prefect; he was also the
subject of many of Marcus's imperial rescripts, a pleasure that he
shared with the provincial governors. Meanwhile Marcus increased
the number of tax collectors, tightened up the collection of inheritance tax, overhauled the customs and excise system and began to
investigate more closely local government finance, a notorious seedbed
of corruption.[128] He insisted that the state have a say in all corners of
economic and financial life, whether in regulating trade, managing
the relations between business partners or in questions of mortgages
and contracts. If, to modern ears, this sounds too interventionist, it
must be conceded that in the early years of his reign Marcus enjoyed
almost unparalleled popularity, as attested by a wealth of epigraphic
evidence. The worst that his detractors found to say about him was
that he sometimes took books from the city libraries for his own use.[129]

Marcus's financial direction of the empire was less sure than his
administrative or legal touch, but here he was dealing with circumstances
largely beyond his control. It was widely alleged that Antoninus Pius

left the imperial finances in a healthy state, with 675 million denarii (2,600 million sesterces) deposited in the treasury.[130] This seems to be pure propaganda put about by his admirers, for Marcus's fiscal and monetary policies are inexplicable if he had inherited an economy on such a footing. Antoninus Pius had debased the coinage, and Marcus followed suit straight away on attaining the purple. His immediate deval-uation of the silver content of Roman coinage suggests both that he inherited an empty treasury and that he did not want this known. Since festivities and ceremonial expenses were high whenever a new emperor came to power, a depreciated currency was the stealthy way to deal with money shortages.[131] The real drain on the treasury was the army, for military pay consistently kept ahead of inflation in the second century, while soldiers expected (and received) ever-escalating levels of dona-tives. It has been estimated that half the money taxes (as opposed to grain taxes) of the provinces went on army pay and donatives.[132]

By the time of Septimius Severus at the beginning of the third century, ordinary military pay was 500 denarii a year per legionary. Praetorian guardsmen received three times the pay of a legionary, and a centurion *five* times the pay of a praetorian guardsman (a *primus pilus* was actually paid *twenty* times as much).[133] Each year about ninety-seven posts as centurion became available, of which about seventy were recruited from serving legionaries, ten were directly commis-sioned, and seventeen came from praetorians aiming to triple their pay. All the time larger discharge bonuses and higher per capita dona-tives were being paid. Given that under Marcus Aurelius there were twenty-eight legions, and there were sixty centurions in each legion, each year the bill for 1,680 centurions had to be met.[134] Donatives meanwhile were usually disbursed at the rate of five times the annual pay for a praetorian. These were paid on an emperor's accession, and as often thereafter as the ruler thought it necessary to keep the troops sweet. It is known that Marcus and Lucius Verus had to pay out dona-tives of 20,000 sesterces – the highest level since the civil wars of the late republic. Marcus had to distribute 240 million sesterces to the troops in Rome alone. If donatives were extended to the legionaries on a proportional basis of 30 per cent, as was customary, the total bill is likely to have cost at least another 1,000 million sesterces.[135] All this was at a time when, because the empire was no longer expanding, the revenue base was shrinking. This frightful situation was about to get worse when plague and German warfare hit Rome. For the time being Marcus tried hard to accommodate the drain on his resources without raising existing taxes or finding new forms of taxation.[136]

There was little enough to console him in his domestic life. In the winter of 165 he sustained further infant mortality, this time Aurelius Fulvius Antoninus, Commodus's twin, who died aged four. To assuage Faustina's grief, Marcus agreed that she should go to Asia Minor to be with her daughter Lucilla, who was pregnant again.[137] Presumably his Stoic creed was of some use to the emperor at this sad juncture, but his attention was soon distracted when the egregious Fronto 'hijacked' his sorrow by interposing a 'greater' one of his own. Fronto had just lost his wife Cratia, and hard on the heels of her death came the news of the loss of a three-year-old grandson. Although Fronto had never seen this boy, the dual tragedy seems temporarily to have unhinged him, and he poured out his grief in a most un-Roman effusion of naked emotion. What seems particularly to have upset him was that he had lost five children himself, but each had died before the next was born, so that in effect he lost an only child five times. Now his surviving child Victorinus had in turn lost his son; it was all too much, and Fronto railed bitterly against Providence and Destiny. 'Shall there, then, be no distinction of fortunes between the good and the bad?' Evil men, he pointed out, could rear children with impunity, while the good seemed to suffer all kinds of misfortunes. Maybe the only way to deal with all this is to reflect that death 'brings rest from toil and care and trouble and, freeing us from the wretched fetters of the body, transports us to those serene and delightful assemblies of souls where all joys are to be found'.[138] Fronto admits he would rather believe that than that Providence acts unfairly or, even worse, that there is no such thing in the first place. He clings to the consolation later summed up by Shakespeare:

> Fear no more the heat o' th' sun
> Nor the furious winter's rages:
> Thou thy worldly task hast done
> Home art gone and ta'en thy wages.[139]

Musing on the theme of 'only the good die young', he reflects that maybe to be taken earlier is to be especially beloved by the gods. But even if this were the case, it is not much comfort. It 'makes little difference to us who long for our lost ones, nor does the immortality of souls bring us the slightest consolation, seeing that in this life we are bereft our best-beloved ones. We miss the well-known gait, the voice, the features, the free air; we mourn over the pitiable face of the dead, the lips sealed, the eyes turned, the lure of life all fled. Be the immortality of the soul ever so well established, that will be a theme for the disputation of philosophers; it will never assuage the yearning of a parent.'[140] Fronto virtually broke down completely in this letter, but significantly it was addressed to Marcus. In the letter informing Lucius Verus of his loss, Fronto mentions his sadness only briefly, before moving on to his shameless and hagiographic history of the Parthian war, which he knew was what mainly interested Verus. Sure enough, Verus commiserated briefly and inadequately before turning to his abiding obsession: himself.[141] Marcus, however, who had over the years tried to distance himself from the old man's petty complaints and hypochondria, this time sensing real sorrow and real emotion, responded magnificently: 'I have just heard of your loss. Since I always suffer torment when a single joint of yours is aching, my master, what do you think I feel when it is your heart that is aching? I am so upset that I can only think of asking you to keep safe for me my sweetest of masters, in whom I have greater solace for this life than you can find sorrow from any source. I have not written this with my own hand, because this evening after my bath even my hand is trembling.'[142]

As 165 merged into 166, Fronto's grief lessened and he allowed himself to be distracted by news of Verus's return to Rome. Verus was both flattered by Fronto's eagerness to see him and delighted by the fawning tone of the old man's 'history' of the Parthian war. 'Why should I not picture to myself your joy, dearest master,' he wrote. 'Indeed I seem to myself to see you hugging me tightly and kissing me many times.'[143] When Verus arrived in Rome (in the late summer or early autumn of 166), he went out of his way to shower Fronto with favours, to the point where Verus's pet freedmen and other pampered members of his entourage exhibited open jealousy and resentment. Maybe Verus sensed that his old tutor was near death and so indulged him, or maybe the prospect of Verus's coming triumph made Fronto feel that he had fulfilled his life's work. Certainly it was strange that he died shortly after Verus's return.

His sudden demise casts a valedictory light on his last surviving letter, to Verus.

> This honour you reserved for me I regard as far outweighing everything. Many a time before this I have noted the special honour you have shown me by what you have done and said [was he contrasting Verus's 'loyalty' with Marcus's 'betrayal' in abandoning rhetoric for philosophy?]. I value most highly the many times you have supported me with your hands and lifted me up when I could scarcely walk through my infirmity. I value too your invariably cheerful and affable look when you speak to me and indeed your very readiness to talk to me and carry on the conversation as I choose . . . Therefore, whatever favours I have had to ask from my lord your brother [sc. Marcus], I have preferred to ask and obtain through you.[144]

Is this simply an old man being manipulative, or is it a definitive statement that Fronto always really preferred Verus? If so, and in the light of the differential treatment of Fronto by the two emperors, with Marcus always by far the more generous and altruistic, this would appear to be another manifestation of that old truth: no good deed goes unpunished.

It is probably natural for scholars to overestimate the influence and impact of Fronto, simply because we possess his correspondence with Marcus and not those of other men whom the emperor esteemed more highly. Fronto was, even by Roman standards, an oddity. From the tip-of-the-iceberg glimpses we get of the secret workings of his mind, it is fair to infer that his hypochondria also masked depression. Artemidorus tells a revealing story that Fronto prayed for a cure from arthritis and then dreamed that he was walking around the suburbs and discovered the secret of pain relief by being rubbed with bee glue.[145] Certainly his public influence was not wholly beneficial, as his championing of the cult of rhetoric led to some bizarre results. Apuleius, millionaire and famous author of *The Golden Ass*, was tried in Sabratha in North Africa in 158–9 on charges of magic and murder. His defence was a tour de force of 'eloquence' as Fronto would have understood it. In a lavish display of erudition, he managed to quote nearly everyone of importance in classical literature: Virgil, Sallust, Cicero, Homer, Euripides, Demosthenes, Catullus, Tibullus,

Propertius, Cato, Aristotle, Theophrastus, Solon, Ennius and many others.[146] This is much as if a man on trial for murder in a modern court were to defend himself by reference to, say, Dickens, Coleridge, Keats, Zola, Balzac, Tolstoy, Dostoevsky and Melville. Yet despite his excesses, Fronto did inculcate two important lessons while tending the mind of the young Marcus. The first was to cultivate a passion for the truth – not philosophical 'truth', but veracity, the opposite of lies. The other lesson that Fronto had dinned into him was how easy it was to become a tyrant. The good emperor was supposed to correct injustice; to consult and address both people and Senate; to govern the empire; to bring compulsion to bear on foreign rulers; to repress the faults of provincials; to quell sedition and terrify criminals; to praise good actions and always follow the path of virtue.[147] At the same time he was always to avoid the cruelties and excesses of a Tiberius, a Nero, a Caligula or a Domitian. Many of Marcus's 'notes to himself' in the *Meditations* were about the perils of tyranny in an emperor. He had a particular detestation for Nero, a man at the mercy of crazed impulses, like a wild beast, or, as Marcus memorably described him, 'A dark character: effeminate, harsh, savage, bestial, puerile, cowardly, false, foolish, mercenary, despotic'.[148]

The return of Verus to Rome brought down the curtain on the successful phase of Marcus's principate. Almost as though by pre-established harmony, little went right thereafter. Both men had relished the separation and Lucius, enjoying his role as virtually independent emperor of the East, was as reluctant to return as Marcus was to see him home again. It was widely remarked that when he returned, Lucius seemed far less deferential to his older colleague than in 161–2 and was, if anything, even lazier.[149] He made a point of bringing back his entire entourage of actors and musicians. Anticipating those noxious modern rock stars who obtain a twenty-four-hour licence for music and alcohol to the annoyance of their neighbours, Verus had a tavern built in the grounds of his villa, where he caroused, gambled and gourmandised all night until carried to bed, supine, next morning. As reported, the Syrians, who were glad to see the back of him and his theatricals, quipped that the end of the Parthian war was really the end of the Thespian war.[150] Marcus found it hard to rein in his anger and displeasure at his co-emperor's antics: Verus had, it seemed, learned nothing in the East and had forgotten nothing when it came to dissipation. He made a vain attempt to win his imperial partner over to his way of thinking, by having him as a house guest at his villa on the Clodian Way. Marcus showed willing by staying for fifteen days, but the would-be entente turned out to be a dialogue of the deaf. While Marcus worked away on affairs of state as if he were in his own home, Verus partied away unconcernedly.[151]

Cynics said that nothing had been achieved by the Parthian war, and that, but for the folly of Sedatius Severus, the same results could have been achieved by firm diplomacy, without such a great expenditure of blood and treasure. Yet Marcus decreed that a full triumph for the eastern victories be held on 12 October 166. He had little choice: to refuse these honours to Lucius Verus would have been an insult, causing a constitutional crisis and probably civil war. Marcus knew that Verus's grandiose titles of *Armeniacus, Parthicus Maximus* and *Medicus* were meaningless nonsense, but he went along with the charade so as not to offend Verus.[152] For the same reason he graciously consented to accept the titles himself, but, after the death of his co-emperor, made his true feelings clear by immediately dropping them and insisting that thereafter he bore only titles that he himself had won fairly and squarely. The October triumph, only one of thirteen such acts of mass self-congratulation in the entire period 31 BC–AD 235 and the first full triumph in fifty years,[153] was a lavish affair. In an evil hour Marcus – some say in 'compensation' for his despair at the unreformed and unreconstructed Lucius Verus – agreed to Verus's suggestion that the glory of the occasion would be enhanced if Commodus, now aged five, and his three-year-old brother Annius Verus were given the title Caesar.[154] They and Marcus's daughters rode through the cheering crowds in the triumphal procession, all in ceremonial robes. The Senate bestowed a 'civic crown' of oak leaves on the two emperors and both received the title *pater patriae* (father of the fatherland). The successful generals who had returned with Verus also received decorations. The trio of Furius Victorinus, Pontus Laelianus and Claudius Fronto received the ceremonial gifts of three crowns, four headless spears and four siege standards.[155]

Triumphs were immensely popular in Rome, as they inevitably meant that the emperor (or emperors) would distribute a *congiarium*. This was in fact the third such cash handout in just five years of Marcus's reign (the second had been distributed by Marcus himself in 165). An intoxicated Roman mob, euphoric with drink and civic pride, watched in awe as the procession wound along the traditional route, beginning outside the city gates, then passing the site of the modern Vatican, the Porta Triumphalis and the Via Triumphalis before crossing the Tiber.[156] Wagons groaning with the spoils of war were followed by cages containing chained prisoners destined for slavery. The chariots of the imperial families were followed by white oxen to be sacrificed to the gods. Senators, lictors, magistrates and generals walked on foot. It was considered too dangerous to allow large numbers of soldiers into the city of Rome, for that would provide a golden opportunity for an ambitious general to stage a lightning *coup d'état*. There is no reason to suppose that procedures in the 166 triumph were any different from previous ones, in which case a slave stood immediately behind the emperors, whispering amid all the acclamation, 'Remember, thou art mortal.' Then the parade took in the Circus Flaminius, the Forum and finally the Sacred Way, where the emperors dismounted from their four-horse chariots to place the victory laurels in the lap of the statue of Jupiter on the Capitol.[157] In addition to the *congiarium* and the spectacle of the triumph, the emperors then provided lavish games. One can imagine the differential response of the two emperors to this social necessity: Lucius Verus revelling in the blood and excitement, especially in the Circus Maximus; Marcus secretly disgusted and contemptuous, but stoically bowing to the inevitable. It may have been on this occasion that Marcus revealed himself as a 'spoilsport' by insisting that the gladiators fight with blunted weapons or buttoned foils. Chroniclers insist that he was compelled to sacrifice 100 lions to the gory instincts of the mob.[158]

The East was now definitively pacified, and it is possible that the Roman triumph of arms had more profound medium-term effects than is sometimes realised. One of the deep-seated motives for Roman wars against Parthia was economic, in particular the Parthian dominance of trade routes. The state policy of the Parthian empire was to encourage the passage of goods from Lake Helmund via Susa over the old northern route used by Assyrians, Medes and the Persian empire; it has already been remarked that such a policy could only ever be partially successful because of the trade links between the Kushans and Nabatean princes. The Roman campaigns of 163–5 tore further holes in this middleman fabric, and may have encouraged a growth in the silk trade between Rome and China. Most scholars agree that in the second century AD there was a flourishing east–west trade along what has come to be known as the Silk Road.[159] Of the Roman passion for Chinese silk there can be no doubt. The Senate vainly issued several edicts aimed at prohibiting the wearing of silk, on the grounds that its import led to the export of precious metals, especially gold; the fact that everything emanating from the 'Seres' (the Chinese) was thought to connote decadence was an additional consideration.[160] Seneca notably fulminated against the fashion for wearing silk: 'I see clothes of silk – if materials that do not hide the body nor even one's decency can be called clothes . . . Wretched flocks of maids labour so that the adulteress may be visible through her own dress, so that her husband has no more acquaintance than any outsider or foreigner with his wife's body.'[161]

Virtually any overland trade route between China and the Mediterranean had to pass through Parthia. The starting point for the silk trade was the capital of the Chinese empire at Loyang, whence caravans began along the inside of the Great Wall to An-Hsi before splitting into two great loops to bypass the grim Taklomaken desert. The two trails reunited at Kashgar, and from there the route wound round the Pamirs to Bactria. Goods headed for India and South-East Asia branched off south at Balkh and, at the upper Indus, this southern route bifurcated, with one branch following the river down to Barbarikon while the other headed east to Siagkot, Mathura, Ujain and Barygaza. There was also a shorter but more difficult itinerary that struck south from Kashgar through the Pamirs and reached Kashmir via Gilgit.[162] As far as the western route was concerned, Bactria was the nodal point, for here the route from China met the overland trails from the Mediterranean. The main west–east route began at Antioch, crossed the Syrian desert, took in Palmyra, Ctesiphon and Seleucia before heading east across the Zagros mountains to Echatana and Merv, where there was a fork, with one route threading through Bokhara and Ferghana to Mongolia and the other making for Bactria. Isidore of Charax, in his famous chronicle *Parthian Stations*, written in the first century AD, explained how the Parthian empire maintained forts and way-stations to protect this route.[163] The journey for the caravans began at Antioch and crossed the Euphrates at Zeugma (modern Birijik), making a straight line and avoiding the long bend in the river, before reaching it lower down near Neapolis and recrossing it to reach Seleucia on the Tigris. Thence the route ascended the hills of Media, crossed the Caspian Gates and followed the fertile valley eastward through modern Khorassan to the Herat river. Here the Parthians tried to force the route south to Lake Helmund and Kandahar in Afghanistan instead of following the obvious eastward path to Bactria and the Pamirs, which would mean paying tribute to the Kushans.[164]

A comparison of these routes with the campaigns of Lucius Verus's generals in 163–6 reveals at once the strategic importance of Ecbatana (modern Hamadan). Ecbatana lay at the junction of other trade routes, not just that from Antioch, but also the southerly trails across the desert to Dura-Europos and Palmyra, and the other main route into Mesopotamia via Seleucia or Ctesiphon and thence down the Tigris to the ports of the Persian Gulf. A network of sea routes linked the incense ports of southern Arabia and Somalia with the Persian Gulf and the Red Sea, whence a flourishing trade was carried on with Alexandria.[165] Parthia sat astride the meeting point of all the major overland trade routes to and from Asia, even though its control of them was never total or monolithic. It was an abiding aim of Roman, and later, Byzantine diplomacy to break this stranglehold.[166] In land-based terms the only option seemed to be to work round the north of Parthia by tracing a path from the Black Sea to the Caspian and thence down the River Oxus to Bactria (in those days the Oxus emptied into the Caspian rather than, as today, into the Aral Sea) or even to find a steppe route further north. In a later era the Byzantines tried to bypass the Persians (successors to the Parthians) both by a sea route via Abyssinia and a route north of the Caspian, though in Marcus Aurelius's time the latter scenario would have been regarded as far-fetched; geographical knowledge was so sketchy that many thought the Caspian and Aral Seas were one and the same or were joined by a canal, or even that the Caspian emptied into the Arctic Ocean.[167] The problems the Silk Road caused the West in the shape of a hostile Parthia (or later Persia) were formidable and abiding. They were finally solved only in the sixth century when Christian monks brought back to the emperor Justinian from China the secret of the silkworm's eggs. Although the loose and flabby nature of the Parthian empire meant that the Romans could never hope to conquer it permanently, it is clear that even the temporary paralysis of Parthia, following defeat by Rome, would have significant consequences in terms of west–east trade and contacts.

Before Marcus Aurelius's Parthian war, Rome had chosen to trade with China and the East by sea, cutting out Parthia altogether. By the time of Marcus's Parthian war the Romans had been trading with India for about 200 years. Two key events had made this possible. First was the discovery of the open sea route to India by the Greek navigator Hippalus, sometime before 31 BC. He observed the pattern of the south-west and north-east monsoons that blew across the Indian Ocean and, setting out from the Arabian coast, reached the mouth of the Indus in forty days. This meant that what was previously a three-year round trip by sea from Alexandria to India could now be accomplished in a single year without the need for Arab middlemen. Almost simultaneously, the Roman conquest of Egypt triggered an exponential growth in commerce between Roman Egypt and the East.[168] Greek mariners and merchants were in the forefront of this trade. Having built a fleet of large ships designed for safety rather than speed – capable both of conveying large cargoes and of weathering the elements – they ventured forth on the Indian Ocean in late July, returning with the north-east monsoon later in the year (usually December) with as many as 300 shipments. How lucrative this trade could be can be gauged from one simple set of statistics. Just one shipment contained 1,500 pounds of spice, 4,500 pounds of ivory and 600–700 pounds of silk.[169] Kaveripattam and Arikamedu emerged as the real meeting points of East and West, places for the exchange of Western goods and the treasures of the Ganges and modern Sri Lanka. The island of Ceylon was consequently well known to the Romans in Marcus's time.[170]

Few ships, however, risked the perilous passage round Cape Coromandel; instead they tended to dock at Muziris (Muchiri) and ship goods overland to other parts of India. As mariners grew more confident, they began sailing directly to Bombay and then to the Tamil-Dravidian kingdoms near the southern tip of the subcontinent.[171] Referring to the Westerners as *yavanas*, the Tamil princes began to compete for their favour. In the early days the Tamil kingdom of the Chola overshadowed the other Tamil states. Another mini-state, the Pandya kingdom, actually sent an embassy to the emperor Augustus with a gift of pearls; the envoy is said to have developed a taste for

Italian wine.[172] Summing up, we may say that the conquest of Egypt and the subsequent use of Alexandria as a key port for Eastern trade opened up both India and East Africa to the Roman global market.[173] Both routes made use of the monsoon. The African voyages proceeded down the Red Sea, through the Straits of Bab el Mandeb to the African coast of the Gulf of Aden and the Arabian Sea, and then proceeded to Rhapta, thought to be somewhere in the region of modern Dar-es-Salaam; both Roman and Parthian coins have been found in Zanzibar. The African route was 3,000 miles long, but was relatively risk-free and could be done in small boats. The snag was that the voyages were slow, so that entrepreneurs had to wait two years to see a return on their capital. The voyage to India and back took just twelve months, but was over open water and therefore potentially supremely perilous. The quicker return on investments had to be balanced against the risk of storms.[174]

The commerce between Rome and the East was overwhelmingly a trade in luxury items. From a number of sources it is clear that the balance of trade was against Rome and that it led to a controversial export of precious metals, since traders in India and beyond demanded payment in hard currency – the silver denarius was held to fit the bill.[175] The Romans exported Spanish oil, Italian wine, pottery, emeralds, wool, copper, asbestos and, especially, glassware – cut glass, coloured glasses and glass beads for necklaces.[176] From Africa they imported for the West ivory, tortoiseshell and cassia; from Arabia frankincense, myrrh and aloes; from India spices, pepper and drugs – shipping them either at the mouth of the Indus or, more usually, the estuary of the Ganges, a river well known to the Romans. The Ganges was reached either by the overland route that turned south at the Pamirs or via the seaborne route to Indonesia and then across the Bay of Bengal.[177] Other countries on the margins of the Roman empire got in on the act. Armenia, for example, exported to Rome quantities of azurite – a mineral dyed like malachite and costing (in the mid-first century AD) 300 sesterces a pound.[178] One of Rome's prized exports was red coral – there were such fisheries in Sicily, Sardinia, Corsica, the Balearic islands and off the coasts of modern Morocco, Algeria and Tunisia – as much a fetish in India as oriental pearls were in Rome. Another Roman ware in demand was a resin called liquid storax, which was much sought-after in China.[179] It must be stressed that trade with the East was always to satisfy the conspicuous consumption of the elites at either end of the world. Pliny the Elder relates that the emperor Caligula imported so many precious stones from the Orient that his wife Lollia Paulina went to a party wearing forty million sesterces worth of jewellery.[180] Marcus Aurelius seems to have tolerated the very un-Stoic trade in luxury items, although Indian iron and steel also appear as dutiable items in the customs records of his reign.

It is in the context of this general trade between Rome and the East, and the changes in it wrought by the 'unique conjuncture' of the victory over the Parthians, that one of the most sensational events of Marcus's reign has to be understood. In short, it was during his principate that the first direct links between the Roman and Chinese empires were achieved. Chinese sources relate that in the year 166 an 'embassy' from Marcus Aurelius arrived in the capital of Luoyang during the reign of emperor Huan of the Han dynasty.[181] To make sense of this we have to go back to the very first tenuous contacts between the Chinese and Roman worlds, which occurred, according to Strabo, around the beginning of the Han dynasty and about the time Rome was engaged in its do-or-die struggle with Hannibal for mastery of the western Mediterranean.[182] The fact that the Han dynasty and the Roman empire seemed thereafter to move on roughly convergent tracks has fascinated many comparative historians.[183] The Han emperors expanded westwards to the Pamirs not primarily for trade or out of intellectual curiosity, but in an attempt to solve China's perennial 'nomad problem'. Specifically the tribe that concerned them was the Xiongnu (whom some have identified with the Huns). There were many contacts between China and Parthia, established for the ultimate purpose of frontier security, such as the mission by Zhang Quian in 130–126 BC.[184] But the real breakthrough in China's 'opening to the West' came at the end of the first century AD, in the early years of the emperor Trajan. Commanding a huge army, the general Ban Chao crossed the Pamirs and inflicted several severe defeats on the Xiongnu, who were pushed back across central Asia as far as the Caspian. Ban Chao concluded an alliance with Parthia and installed garrisons a few days' march from Ctesiphon, to prevent the Xiongnu from returning eastwards. These garrisons were still in existence when Trajan invaded Parthia; for a while then, Chinese and Romans were within a few days' march of making direct contact. But the meeting never happened. Indeed, Ban Chao actually sent an envoy, Gan Ying, to Rome, but he got no further than Mesopotamia. The Parthians, in fear of direct contacts between Rome and China, bamboozled the Chinese envoy. Gan Ying was given the runaround by Parthian middlemen determined to maintain their position on the Silk Route. He was fed disinformation, told that the voyage across the Mediterranean was impossibly long, and effectively held under house arrest until he agreed to return to Ban Chao.[185]

In the immediate aftermath of the Roman victory over the Parthians in 165, Roman traders had a unique opportunity, for the land routes both north and south of the central Asian deserts had been made relatively safe by Chinese westward expansion. This was the context in which a group of merchants was able to make its way to the Chinese capital of Luoyang. The so-called 'embassy' did not consist of accredited envoys in any formal sense, and its members may not even have been Romans – most likely they were Greeks from Alexandria.[186] But they had the authority of the emperor to extend friendly greetings and build informal links with any great powers they encountered. When they arrived at Luoyang, the Han capital and one of the four great ancient cities of China, they were warmly welcomed by the emperor Huan, who would die two years later at the age of thirty-six after reigning for twenty-two years. Generally considered a disastrous ruler, he nonetheless presided over a Confucian state whose political and cultural influence extended over Korea, Japan, Mongolia and much of central Asia. It is recorded that the emissaries brought presents of ivory, rhino horn and tortoiseshell plus a treatise on astronomy – which did not impress the Chinese greatly, since all these goods were readily available in India. Nonetheless, there were preliminary talks on the possibility of buying silk directly from China overland and avoiding the middlemen charges of the Parthians.[187]

The Chinese sources state categorically that the strangers entered China at Jinnan on the Tonkin–Annam (Vietnam) border, and the fact that coins of Marcus Aurelius have been found in Indochina is sometimes thought to endorse this version.[188] Yet the circumstantial evidence is overwhelming that the travellers followed the overland route opened up by the defeat of Parthia. There are times when, to use the mathematical expression, circumstantial evidence approaches certainty as a limit, and this is one of them. It would indeed be the most extraordinary coincidence if, in the very year of a Parthian defeat that laid open the overland route, Roman traders should have arrived in China by a perilous seaborne route via the Bay of Bengal, Indonesia and Indochina, which none had ever attempted before. The account in Chinese sources was based on the obvious fact that most traders from India arrived by the Annam route, and so it was assumed that the newcomers must also have taken that route.[189] However, the overland route was no sooner opened than closed again. Military crisis in the West meant that the Roman garrisons in Parthia and its environs, such as the one at Palmyra, had to be withdrawn to the Danube frontier.[190] Ongoing direct trade between China and Rome remained as a 'might have been', although limited contacts did continue: the emperor Alexander Severus later sent an embassy to the Chinese emperor Taitsu of the kingdom of Wei. It remains an intriguing historical curiosity that the Roman emperor whose modes of thought had most in common with those of the Orient should have been the one to achieve this short-term breakthrough.

9

While majority opinion down the ages, pioneered by Julian the Apostate in his work on the Caesars, has agreed that as emperor Marcus was the 'best of the best' – the finest ruler in the Antonine golden age – what has won him immortality is his role as philosopher-king, and as the author of the *Meditations*, composed from about the mid-160s until his death. This is a curious work, which has been much misunderstood. It is not a diary like those of Pepys and Boswell, nor is it a commonplace book, and it was certainly never considered for publication, which is why its survival is a fascinating story in itself, albeit not relevant to a biography of Marcus. It is generally agreed that Marcus used his writings as a kind of meditative technique, that they were intended for his eyes only, and that he had no real ambitions as an author, though St Augustine claimed that at one time Marcus had intended to write a general history of the Greeks and the Romans.[1] The most obvious analogy for the *Meditations* are the spiritual exercises of Ignatius Loyola, founder of the Jesuit order in the sixteenth century, at once a method of self-discipline and self-address; there is also the Eastern notion of daily spiritual hard work in order to ascend to higher and higher levels of consciousness.

The book – if we may call it that – is a series of personal notes taken on a daily basis, which was a common practice in the ancient world, particularly as an aid to spiritual progress or self-improvement. It followed that even an emperor had to write such observations in his own hand, as they were too intimate to be dictated. One obvious clue that the *Meditations* were not a diary is that Marcus wrote in Greek, the formal language of philosophy, rather than his mother tongue Latin, which he would presumably have used in the case of a mere journal. For Marcus to write in Greek was rather like the way Frederick the Great of Prussia later wrote in French, and the scholar Ernest Renan thought that by favouring Greek over Latin (to say nothing of philosophy over literature) Marcus gave Greek a new lease of life, while sounding the death-knell for Latin.[2] This was an exaggeration, but Renan's point was presumably that by this time the previous bilingualism of the educated classes was becoming uncommon, with Greek and Latin cultures diverging and presaging the ultimate split of the Roman empire into Western and Byzantine halves. Marcus was not really a master of the Greek language, and some of his phraseology and construction is awkward and inelegant, relying on archaisms.[3] On the other hand his thought – though often confused – is lucid and never obscure; Philostratus, who saw some of Marcus's letters that have not survived, said they always conveyed precision and clarity.[4]

Nobody ever writes in a vacuum, and Marcus had the entire Stoic tradition to draw on. What, then, were the principal influences on his writings? It is interesting that he almost entirely ignores the work of Zeno, Chrysippus, Panaetius, Posidonius and Seneca – usually regarded as the founding fathers of Stoicism – and instead leans heavily on Socrates, Heraclitus, Diogenes and, above all, Epictetus. Socrates is much too famous to need any introduction, but two things about Marcus's attitude to him are noteworthy. In the first place, although he considered that the line of influence from Socrates, properly considered, ran through the Stoics rather than Plato – he was an early Stoic rather than an early Platonist – Marcus was in no sense averse or antagonistic to Plato himself, and so in the *Meditations* we find specific reference to Plato's famous works, the *Apology*, *Republic*, *Gorgias* and *Theaetetus*.[5] Indeed, some commentators have speculated that a good deal of Marcus's thought can be considered 'Platonism without Plato' – in the same way, perhaps, that Marx famously stated he was not a Marxist – and that there are signs of a kind of Neoplatonist withdrawal into the self.[6] Second, although Marcus admired Socrates as a true sage and one of the greatest humans of the ages, he thought he should be judged rigorously by proper philosophical standards, not accorded automatic deference or a spontaneous ovation as an unquestionable icon.⁷ Perhaps the real truth was that Marcus was a true eclectic, cherry-picking from both Socrates and Plato those aspects of their teachings that accorded with Stoicism. Well read and erudite, Marcus incorporated in the *Meditations* a diverse range of references and quotations, scavenging what he needed from all sources: Plato, Aristotle, the Cynics and the Epicureans.

A much more obvious influence on Marcus was the famous Presocratic philosopher Heraclitus, unquestionably a major figure in the history of thought since he, even more than Plato, influenced German thinkers such as Nietzsche, Spengler and Heidegger and the whole tradition of 'process' philosophy exemplified by those such as Hegel, A.N. Whitehead and Samuel Alexander.⁸ A notable misanthrope and advocate of war, Heraclitus had the same hostile and unbalanced view of Homer that George Bernard Shaw had of Shakespeare. He is famous for a number of aphorisms, since his work survives only in fragments, of which the most celebrated is: 'Everything is in a state of flux, forever changing . . . you cannot step into the same river twice' – a calculated rejoinder to the other famous Presocratic, Parmenides, who maintained that nothing ever changed. The imagery of the river and the trope of perennial change were constants in the *Meditations*, where Marcus additionally often refers to Heraclitus by name.⁹ Many of the apothegms in Marcus's work could almost be Heraclitus simply speaking, even when he is not being quoted directly, and the word-play used is also heavily redolent of the famous Presocratic.¹⁰ When he says that people in dreams act and speak while asleep, that is almost unadulterated Heraclitus.¹¹ Marcus cites Heraclitus on the relativity of human judgement, on the hidden nature of things, on the reciprocal process of change that absorbs an object's parts and then redistributes them.¹² The following are just a few sayings of the Heraclitean Marcus in action: 'Nothing is bad for things which are in the process of change, as nothing is good for things which exist in consequence of change'; 'A river of all events, a violent current: that is what Eternity is. No sooner has each thing appeared than it has already passed: another comes along, and it too will pass away'; 'Think often of how quickly beings and events pass and disappear; for substance is like a river in perpetual flux'.¹³ Hostile critics, however, said that Marcus was not really a great Heraclitus scholar and accepted the story that his hero both died of dropsy and tried to cure it by covering himself with dung – mere legends made up by his many enemies.[14]

While it is easy to see why Marcus appreciated and was influenced by both Socrates and Heraclitus, at first sight his liking for Diogenes of Sinope seems bizarre. Some critics have taken the line that Diogenes was yet another in the long line of charlatans by whom Marcus was bamboozled, and one can understand the distaste of those who have seen in him nothing more than 'an obnoxious ragpicker and offensive churl'. Diogenes (b. sometime between 412 and 399 BC, d. 323 BC) first swam into the public ken when he latched on to Antisthenes, a disciple of Socrates. Born on the shores of the Black Sea, Diogenes was the son of a forger and counterfeiter and by all accounts was a rebarbative figure, even when young. Antisthenes took an instant dislike to him and tried to drive him away by beating him with a stick, but Diogenes endured the beatings unflinchingly until Antisthenes agreed to take him as a pupil.[15] The next phase in Diogenes's evolution was when he decided to live like a dog. He and his followers became known as Cynics (from the Greek word for 'canine'). In this guise he rejected all conventions of dress and decency, ate sparingly, munched raw meat, walked barefoot in the snow, lived on alms, slept rough and made his home in a large burial pitcher – so that in legend he became 'the man who lived in a tub'. His behaviour was deliberately designed to shock and outrage. He masturbated in the marketplace, urinated on a man who insulted him, defecated in the amphitheatre and gave people the finger. He famously searched through the marketplace at Athens with a lantern in daylight, claiming to be looking for 'an honest man'.[16]

The stories about him were legion, and the most famous concerned the young Alexander the Great. Before he set out for his epic conquest of the Persian empire, Alexander one day came upon Diogenes basking in the sunlight and told him he would grant him any favour. 'In that case, stand out of my light,' was the sage's answer. Preaching the Stoic doctrine of the supremacy of 'virtue', he produced a number of vintage saws avidly quoted by his admirers. Asked which beast has the worst bite, he replied, 'Of the wild ones, the sycophant, and of the tame ones the flatterer'. When asked where one could find virtuous men in Greece, he riposted, 'Men nowhere, but boys, in Sparta'. Seeing temple officials arresting someone for stealing a bowl, he exclaimed, 'Big thieves are arresting a little one.' When captured by pirates and sold into slavery, and asked what skills he had, he answered, 'Does anyone want a master for himself?'[17] Incredibly, he found one. This, then, was the man whom Marcus regarded as the true heir of Socrates, far more so than Plato. Both he and Epictetus lionised a man who argued that virtue essentially meant that he should take while others worked and gave to him. Even Epictetus conceded that whereas Zeno's speciality was instruction and doctrine, Diogenes's was merely reproof.[18] But he thought that Diogenes's put-down of Alexander the Great was a piece of peerless wisdom.[19] Marcus, obsessed with the pointlessness of earthly fame and the superiority of philosophers to all other men, agreed: 'Alexander and Caesar and Pompey? Compared with Diogenes, Heraclitus and Socrates? No contest. The philosophers knew the what, the why and the how. Their minds were their own. And the three heroes? Nothing but anxiety and enslavement.'[20]

Yet unquestionably by far the greatest influence on Marcus was Epictetus. Born AD *c*. 60 in Phrygia (Pammukale in modern Turkey), Epictetus was brought to Rome as the slave of Epaphroditus, one of Nero's freedmen. Evidently a liberal by the standards of the age, Epaphroditus allowed Epictetus to attend the classes of the Stoic philosopher Musonius Rufus, who reportedly had the gift of looking into his students' souls and seeing all their faults.[21] Freed by his master, Epictetus then set up his own school in Rome, but was expelled as a result of Domitian's general purge of philosophers in 93–4. He relocated to Neapolis in Epirus, on the north-western coast of modern Greece, where he lived in poverty and died around or shortly after the turn of the century (AD 100). We owe the transmission of Epictetus's thoughts to Arrian, the man who fought the Alans under Antoninus Pius and who was thus a kind of Roman Xenophon (who fought the Persians *and* wrote about Socrates), a rare man interested in both thought and action. Additionally Marcus's tutor Rusticus passed on notes taken at Epictetus's classes. By the time of Marcus's reign Epictetus was regarded as *the* Stoic philosopher, admired by a wide circle of intellectuals including the great physician Galen.[22] Epictetus recommended the following routes to happiness and wisdom: talk as little as possible and, if you have to talk, don't talk about sport, food and drink or other trivia; don't blame or praise other people; avoid dinner parties and laugh and swear as little as possible. Don't make a big thing about sex and sexuality; avoid the theatre; be indifferent to who wins prizes; never mention your own achievements; if someone uses foul language, reprove him if possible and show your displeasure by silence, blushing and frowning.[23] A more priggish, inhuman, killjoy and generally repulsive doctrine would be hard to imagine, but it will be abundantly clear why the programme appealed to Marcus Aurelius.

Epictetus emphasised four key concepts: freedom, judgement, volition and integrity. Perhaps naturally, as a former slave, he emphasised freedom as it showed that, while the body could be enslaved, the mind never could be. Judgement meant both seeing the fallacy of 'representations' and distinguishing the things that are ours (for example, the power to say yes or no) from the things that are not ours and do not lie within our power. But Epictetus never dealt effectively with the objection that the things he classifies as 'not ours' are the things that actually drive and motivate people (desires, moods, passions, distractions, hopes, fears, ambitions, political opinions, the desire for comfort, and so on). What he means by volition is what one might call heroic strenuousness: as one Epictetus scholar has remarked, 'His intense preoccupation with volition, which will leave its mark on Marcus Aurelius, is quite distinctive.'[24] Integrity means the recognition that, although free, human beings have limited autonomy and that we have to make great efforts to achieve anything. 'What is it,' asks Epictetus, 'that every person pursues? To be in a good situation, to be happy, to do everything one wishes, not to be frustrated, not to be put under compulsion.'[25] Integrity also means gentleness and tolerance towards those who err: 'It is impossible to be free from error. What is possible is to be consistently on the alert with a view to not erring.'[26] Whereas for Chrysippus health, prosperity, the family – normal human aspirations – were correct choices in all normal circumstances, Epictetus was more radical. He wanted people to harden themselves against involvement in 'normal' desires so that they could 'bear and forbear', or sustain and abstain. It was imperative not to have emotional attachment to things one could not control: there was, for example, no point in a man admiring his wife's beauty if he was going to get angry the moment she was unfaithful. As Epictetus put it in his usual gnomic way, do not desire any dish that is not set before you.[27]

It has already been remarked that Stoicism was a doctrine that melded perfectly with the values, ideology and official myths of the

Roman elite and was never designed to appeal to the masses; sociologically, this was reflected in the fact that most of Epictetus's students
were destined for the higher reaches of the Roman civil service.[28]
Epictetus advocated political quietism on the grounds that the worst
the worst despot could do was essentially nothing – for thought
processes cannot be overcome by intimidation, and genuine 'thought
police' remain a fantasy of social control.[29] He suggested we should
wish for things to happen just the way they do happen, and it is here
that Stoicism once again lurches into absurdity. No one could wish
for a calamity or disaster of any kind and, even if one were masochistic
enough to do so, what currency could be given to 'wishing' for something that was going to happen anyway; apart from anything else, this
is a violation of linguistic usage, a semantic nonsense. Marcus's own
daft version of this doctrine is as follows: 'All that is in accord with
you, World, is in accord with me. Nothing which occurs at the right
time for you comes too soon or too late for me. All that your seasons
produce, Nature, is fruit for me. It is from you that all things come;
all things are within you, and all things move towards you.'[30] The political views of the Stoics were particularly absurd, for the only way an
inevitable order of things could coincide with a universal moral law
would be for everything that happens to be right – and Marcus certainly
endorsed this proposition.[31] A more interesting strand in Stoic political thinking is that which draws analogies between the emperor and
God and between the Roman empire and cosmology. A dutiful world
citizen, serving the 'Eternal City', should treat his life as if it were
service in God's army, for each person has been given the rank of
senator for life in the imperial city.[32] This conflation of Rome with the
'City of the World' – an attempt to link politics with cosmology –
eventually finds expression in an intellectual troika where Rome, as
the City of the World, becomes the realm of rational beings, something like what Kant meant by the 'kingdom of ends', and finds its
full expression in St Augustine's City of God.[33] For Epictetus, someone
whose views on the cosmos are intellectually fallacious is like a military
rebel vis-à-vis Roman government.[34]

However, Marcus Aurelius by no means assented to all of Epictetus's
propositions, particularly as his great forerunner's thought was very
confused, even on matters social and political. Some of his ideas were
potentially revolutionary and it would, after all, be surprising if the

pampered son of a wealthy Roman family saw the world through the same eyes as an ex-slave. Whereas Marcus, as we have seen, was generally concerned to reinforce the bonds linking masters and slaves, Epictetus took a much more jaundiced view of slavery. To someone who complained about his slave's laziness and insisted that his superior position gave him the right to do so, Epictetus replied, 'Can't you see where you're looking – to the pit, to the miserable laws made for corpses. You're not looking at the divine law.'[35] This certainly suggests that there was not, after all, much harmony between the laws of the Roman empire and the laws of the cosmos. Furthermore, Epictetus appeared to oppose capital punishment, one of the cornerstones of Roman rule. His argument was that brigands and adulterers were simply people who had been blinded by faulty 'representations' as to what differentiates the good from the bad; to execute them was therefore like executing the blind and the deaf.[36] He also suggested that the victims of crime were themselves to blame, by over-valuing their material possessions, by conspicuous consumption and flaunting their wealth, thus not only providing tempting targets for the have-nots, but being poor role-models as Romans.[37] Not all of this can have been palatable to Marcus, but Epictetus's saving grace, from the viewpoint of Roman rulers, was that he left everything at the level of abstract advocacy. Love of mankind was a purely theoretical notion for Epictetus. He did not even exhort his followers to put themselves out for the physical well-being of others, let alone engage in radical political activity. In the final analysis, a Stoic could always avoid commitment by citing his contempt for the external world. Nevertheless, some of Epictetus's more heterodox views on tolerance for wrongdoers probably did filter down into Marcus's thought.[38]

Epictetus was the real slave, but some commentators have suggested that in intellectual terms Marcus followed him too slavishly. This has sometimes been cited as 'proof' that environment and milieu play little part in the 'formation' of philosophers, since Epictetus and Marcus had very different life-experiences and lived in very different eras. It would be foolish to deny that Epictetus was a *massive* influence on the philosopher-emperor, but it would be equally foolish to overlook the many areas where the two Stoic theoreticians diverged considerably. Some of the differences between the two were obvious, deriving from the simple fact that Marcus was an emperor and Epictetus a professional teacher or academic, though, curiously, Marcus was much better read and more erudite, with Epictetus sometimes displaying signs of philistinism.[39] He taught that the philosopher should not simply be competent in matters of technical logic and philosophy, but be a genuinely wise man and play a full part in life. While Epictetus stressed the virtues of social life and communality, Marcus thought that loneliness and alienation were the inexorable lot of the thinker. As a philosopher and recluse, Marcus was closer to modern practitioners than was Epictetus. Epictetus always had the confidence of the professional lecturer, whereas Marcus was always more tentative and self-questioning.[40] Moreover, it was clearly always going to be more difficult for a reigning emperor to counterpoise as sharply the famous conflict between sage and tyrant.[41] Additionally, some have claimed that Epictetus's Stoicism links with modern psychoanalysis, and we have already seen that for Marcus such investigations were alien and pointless.[42]

Yet the differences were not merely those of temperament and social status; they extended to doctrine too. To begin with, Epictetus was very keen to delineate the areas where Stoicism differed from its closest rival, Epicureanism, but Marcus thought this unimportant.[43] He was more eclectic than Epictetus, more drawn to Platonism, more interested in the Cynics and Heraclitus; his psychology, in particular, was heavily influenced by Platonic dualism, stressing the mind/body division, rather than the monism of Stoicism.[44] On the strict doctrine of 'representations' he would not have been considered sound from Epictetus's point of view.[45] Epictetus was more interested in God and stressed the beauty, order and design of Providence much more;[46] Marcus was more interested in asceticism. Most strikingly, Marcus's cosmology was more complete than Epictetus's, for Marcus was obsessed with the immensity of the universe and of eternity, with man as an insignificant speck, in a way Epictetus never was.[47] Above all, Marcus was death-driven while Epictetus was life-directed. And anyone who thinks of the two as peas in a pod should ponder their very different attitude to the emotion of anger. As has been demonstrated, Marcus considered this a disastrous human manifestation, but Epictetus made praise of anger one of the key points where Stoicism differed from Aristotelianism and Epicureanism. They stressed the value to society and the individual of anger, especially in the form of moral indignation.[48] Roman aristocrats put a positive value on rage, and it was not considered an unspeakable atrocity when the emperor Hadrian blinded a servant in one eye during a temper tantrum.[49]

Stoicism may be considered to have had two main phases: the Greek and the Roman. The Roman thinkers – Epictetus, Musonius, Seneca and Marcus Aurelius – were far less interested in questions of abstract philosophy, logic and physics and eschewed theory in favour of a practical approach to ethics; Greek Stoicism was a theory of the universe, but Roman Stoicism was much more a guide to living. For this reason some commentators have alleged that the Romans salvaged what was valuable in the system and jettisoned the rest; others claim that the Roman 'late' Stoics departed too far from classical Stoicism to be considered part of the dispensation at all.[50] What is true is that Stoicism was like a pyramid, which reached an apex under Marcus Aurelius, but where each successive thinker added a layer of new ideas. Epictetus's original contribution was twofold: he emphasised the mind's capacity for autonomy to a degree without parallel in previous Stoic tradition;[51] and he introduced the idea of a triad of disciplines, of desire, action and assent, which was purely his innovation and did not exist previously in Stoic literature.[52] The discipline of desire teaches us what are the worthwhile objects of desire and which the futile objectives. The discipline of action teaches us what is in our power and what is not: the famous example of the archery contest shows that we should try to shoot well, as that is within our power, but not be disappointed if we don't hit the target, as the trajectory of the arrow depends on forces outside our control. The discipline of assent means making proper use of our 'impressions'. Epictetus thought that his triad of disciplines was the true meaning of the original Stoic trilogy of physics, logic and ethics: desire relates to physics, enabling us to locate ourselves within the immensity of the cosmos; action (or impulse) relates to logic, enabling us to take up our proper stance in society; and assent relates to ethics, enabling us to solve all psychological conflicts by recognising the logical necessity of universal reason.[53]

Marcus's originality as a cosmologist was to make his famous distinction between internal and external causes: external causes relate to a common and universal Nature and internal causes to one's own nature. This was an obvious attempt to escape the free-will/determinism dilemma: we are free, but Nature is determined.[54] Beyond this, he developed Epictetus's celebrated triad in his own idiosyncratic way. First, he went off at a tangent by looking at the classical Stoic doctrine that a human being is composed of three things: the body, the *pneuma* or breath of life, and the mind (*nous*), with only the third being under human control. Marcus thought that the triad needed refining, for the mind itself subdivided into an inferior computer-like part and a superior 'guiding principle' or governing self. Later he complicated matters still further with a *daimon* or 'god within', so that on this analysis the human being would have no fewer than *five* aspects.[55] Then he returned to Epictetus's triad and made it correlate with the four traditional virtues: prudence, justice, strength and temperance, collapsing the traditional four into Epictetus's three so that the discipline of action equalled justice, the discipline of assent equalled prudence and the discipline of desire equalled temperance with strength as an overarching principle.[56] Just as for St Paul, who identified a trio of faith, hope and charity (love) and said that the greatest of these was charity, so for Marcus the greatest of his triad was justice.[57] Yet it must be conceded that Marcus made something of a fetish of triads, which appear in all kinds of guises in his writings. First he speaks of three essential relationships: with one's body, with other people and with the divine.[58] Then he mentions three basic prohibitions: 'Not some way to sleep with her – but a way to stop wanting to'; 'Not some way to get rid of him, but a way to stop trying'; 'Not some way to save my child, but a way to lose your fear.'[59] Next comes the three basic things: substance, cause and purpose.[60] Finally Marcus mentions as an essential troika: one's own actions, external events and the pointlessness of the universe. In between he has also redefined his own essential trio, derived from Epictetus, as truth, justice and self-control.[61] It is difficult to avoid the conclusion that, like some other thinkers (Plato, Hegel, Freud, the American pragmatist philosopher C.S. Pierce), Marcus was besotted with the number three.

Another way to approach the complex and often self-contradictory collection of musings and jottings that constitute the *Meditations* is to identify three (that number again) distinct strands in the *oeuvre*: those that reflect and amplify orthodox Stoicism; those axioms and maxims that can stand by themselves detached from Stoic philosophy as superb distillations of common sense or examples of 'what oft was thought but ne'er so well expressed' – and it must be conceded that it is *this* Marcus Aurelius that has most attracted his self-help admirers in the twentieth and twenty-first centuries; and the original contributions of Marcus to thought, usually a by-product of his own deep pessimism. Of course it is always necessary to beware of anachronism: ancient Stoicism was not modern stoicism (with a small 's'), nor did 'following Nature' have anything to do with modern 'green' concerns about conservation and the environment.[62] And so, necessarily, many of the observations in the *Meditations* are concerned with the time-honoured Stoic issues: virtue is its own reward and is always to be chosen for its own sake and to be preferred to any combination of items with a non-moral nature; morality is the only good; we should spurn the things that humans usually long for, because these are 'indifferents'; asceticism alone makes for happiness; even if we are rich, healthy, brave or successful, we will be unhappy if we are unjust or intemperate; morality and happiness are indivisible, so that it is a fallacy that tyrants can have a happy life; happiness and virtue mean living according to Nature; and so on.[63] It should be said that Marcus nowhere solves any of the notorious self-contradictions that Stoicism throws up. For example, his discussion of freedom is badly flawed. He tacks at will between two very different conceptions: freedom of choice (the freedom to choose good and evil) and *real freedom* – the automatic choice of moral good or universal reason.[64] He uses a number of different terms, all of which seem to mean the same thing in his usage, though elsewhere he distinguishes between them: self, intellect (*nous*), inner *daimon* and guiding principle (*hegemonikon*). We are told that everything is in a state of flux, but the self, with its freedom, is somehow exempt from this. And when excoriating those who oversleep and are unconscious when they should be up betimes, making a contrast between the behaviour of the benighted masses and that of the sage, Marcus forgets that, since we all operate under universal Reason, even those who are asleep and unconscious contribute to the overall cosmic plan.[65]

It is notable that, while largely ignoring the physics and logic parts of the traditional Stoic triad, Marcus spends much more time on issues of cosmology than Epictetus does, though his treatment is well within the normal idiom of Stoicism. He is concerned to portray a universe of interconnectedness, where we see Providence operating in the motion of celestial bodies just as much as in the daily accidents of life. One obvious point of difference between Marcus and most modern thinkers is that he may be described as over-impressed by the vastness of the solar system, whereas the moderns, following Blake, are perhaps over-impressed by the grain of sand. He follows Heraclitus in an emphasis on constant change and metamorphosis, but adds no original insights to the notion; after all, the idea that everything is changing is one with which few people would disagree and was a cornerstone of the 'dialectics of Nature' in Marxism.[66] Another fundamental Stoic notion, all-pervasive in the *Meditations*, is *logos*[67] – a very slippery concept in the history of philosophy, as different thinkers have assigned it different nuances of meaning. The Stoics, first to introduce *logos*, gave it a pantheistic meaning and spoke of it as the rational principle in accordance with which the universe exists, the plan or model of the universe, the sense of order in the cosmos, that by which all things come into being and come to pass, and the source of human reason and intelligence.[68] In this sense it can be seen as similar to the *tao* of Lao-Tzu or the Brahman/Atman principle of the Upanishads. The Middle Platonists developed *logos* as a manifestation of God in the creation, the instrumentality by which a supreme being enters space and time. The Jewish thinker Philo, adapting Greek philosophy for use in Judaism, was obsessed with the idea, but in his hands the meaning became so protean that it embraced everything from an ideal world (as compared with the present perceptible world, a mere copy) to wisdom personified and thus the High Priest himself.[69] Most famously, in Christianity *logos* became 'the word made flesh', as in the celebrated formulation at the beginning of St John's Gospel. In this Neoplatonist version of Christianity, *logos* – the pre-human existence of Jesus Christ – was the 'word' in the sense that it was the only utterance of God, for without Christ as *logos* one might take a deistic view of a 'silent' God. Obviously the neat formula *logos* = the Christian God would cause any amount of difficulties once the doctrine of the Trinity was proclaimed. But a transmogrified form of *logos* can be traced through the history of philosophy, culminating in Hegel's Absolute Idea and the 'God' of process philosophers such as Whitehead and Alexander. The essential difference between the original *logos* of the Stoics and that of the Christians is that for Christianity it was an emanation or by-product of God, whereas in Stoicism *logos* and God are one and the same.

Another favourite cosmological principle of Marcus Aurelius was the notion of eternal recurrence, itself a Stoic 'standard'. The repetition of worlds, the Stoics thought, must be the case, as the universe is governed by the arrangement of its material particles and, as the number of such arrangements is finite, each one must repeat itself an infinite number of times in the course of history. This idea receives several formulations in the *Meditations*. 'Remember that everything has always been the same and keeps recurring, and it makes no difference whether you see the same things recur in a hundred years or two hundred or in an infinite period.' 'I am made up of substance and what animates it, and neither one can ever stop existing, any more than it began to. Every portion of me will be reassigned as another portion of the world, and that in turn transformed into another. Ad infinitum.' 'Remember to bear in mind that all of this has happened before. And it will happen again – the same plot from beginning to end, the identical staging.' 'Whatever happens has always happened, and always will, and is happening at this very moment.'[70] This was another very influential idea, which Lucretius had already appropriated from the Stoics and conflated with the notion of the wheel of Fortune.[71] Its most famous (and notorious) advocate in modern philosophy was Nietzsche, and it appears also in the thought of Schopenhauer and the revolutionary socialist Louis Auguste Blanqui, who wrote *L'Éternité par les astres*. An allied and derivate idea is that of recurring cycles of history, first promoted by Giambattista Vico in the eighteenth century, but reappearing later in transmogrified form in the work of Oswald Spengler, Arnold Toynbee and James Joyce.[72] The implict attack on linear time made by Marcus was perhaps most strikingly and startlingly expressed by the seventeenth-century mystic Sir Thomas Browne: 'And in this sense, I say, the world was before Creation, and at an end before it had a beginning; and thus I was dead before I was alive, though my grave be England, my dying place was Paradise, and Eve miscarried of me before she conceived of Cain.'[73]

Even more bizarre is Marcus's oft-repeated idea that we must live in the present and concentrate only on the present moment. 'Limit yourself to the present.' 'The present is the same for everyone; its loss is the same for everyone.' 'Forget everything else. Keep hold of this alone and remember it. Each of us lives only now, this brief instant.' 'If you've seen the present, then you've seen everything – as it's ever been since the beginning, as it will be forever.' 'Forget the future.' 'For me the present is constantly the matter on which rational and social virtue exercises itself.' 'Past and future have no power over you. Only the present – and that can be minimised.' And these are just some of Marcus's formulations.[74] His emphasis on the present engenders some of the very worst confusions and self-contradictions in the *Meditations*. It is important to be clear that Marcus is not just advocating Horace's *carpe diem* or enjoining us to live every day as if it were our last – though he also does that.[75] He very plainly preaches that the present is all there is. One can see why the Stoics taught this: not to worry about the future allegedly chokes off our worst fear of pain as well as worldly ambition, while it is also definitional of neurotics that they are locked in the past. We find the concentration on the present very clearly in the work of Seneca.[76] Marcus argued that such concentration allowed one's problems to be arranged in a series so that they did not all have to be dealt with at the same time.[77] But, taken seriously, the prescription to treat as real only the present instant would make life pointless, for not only would all striving, ambition and aspiration vanish, but so too would memory, nostalgia, sentimentality and all sense of what makes life valuable. Living in the present and thus preparing oneself all the time for the unexpected could easily lead to paralysis and depression. Taken seriously, 'presentism' would prevent all contingency planning – not a good recipe for a Roman emperor. A politician or soldier needs to be a chess-player, but this would be impossible if one was so ineluctably wedded to a doctrine of the present. Marcus himself is very confused on this issue, for at one time he tells us that the present instant is unreal and at another that it is all there is.[78] The famous advice that has caused so much controversy – 'When you kiss your child goodnight, whisper to yourself that you may be dead in the morning'[79] – supposedly a cornerstone of Stoical inuring oneself to pain, is an explicit projection into the future and contradicts the advice to concentrate on the present. Moreover, Marcus often looks back on his life and thanks the gods for what has happened to him:[80] how is this even possible if one's thoughts are entirely riveted on the present?

Yet the problems with Marcus's 'presentism' do not end there. His ideas on the present collide with other aspects of his overall doctrine, most notably that of holism, to say nothing of pantheism. Multiple philosophical puzzles are created by such a stance. If the present is all there is, what meaning can we attach to the idea of eternal recurrence, for by definition everything that has ever happened must be identical to what is happening now? If one insists that only the present instant is real, one falls into the fallacy of which Hume's scepticism was a deliberate *reductio ad absurdum*: far from not stepping into the same river twice à la Heraclitus, one would not be able to step into it once. Hume demonstrated that Descartes's famous *cogito ergo sum* makes no sense if there is no 'I' to do the thinking, and how could there be on a strict interpretation of the present instant? The most there could be would be a kind of solipsism of the moment.[81] To live in the present instant commits one also to the unreality of time, and in logic to the famous paradoxes of Zeno – the flight of the arrow, Achilles and the tortoise, and so on. To escape from this quagmire when talking about the present, the philosopher and psychologist William James famously popularised the idea of the 'specious present', defined by him as anything from a few seconds to (maximum) a minute.[82] The 'specious present' was conceived as an interval, not a durationless instant, and thus allowed an escape from the 'real present', which was durationless. In the 'specious present' there could be earlier and later parts, and thus no paradoxes about time. But the very notion of 'earlier' implies memory, and once you have admitted memory, there seems no good reason to entertain the fatuous prejudice about the past to which Marcus commits himself. The contrast between the philosophically vacuous idea of a durationless present and a 'specious present' that admits duration was heavily to influence the philosopher Henri Bergson (he went on to argue that duration implies vitalism as against mechanism) and the 'process' philosophers like Whitehead and Alexander, though it is true that some rearguard actions were fought in the twentieth century on behalf of the Stoic notion of the present instant.[83] However, a judicious conclusion would be that the Stoic notion of 'presentism' is a confused mess.

Another cosmological issue that exercised Marcus was whether the cosmos was to be considered a product of God's providence or a mere collection of atoms, as the Epicureans alleged. The rivalry between Stoics and Epicureans as philosophical schools was intense; Stoics tended to loathe Epicureans and make up libellous stories about them. The real 'mind' behind the Epicurean theory of atoms was Democritus, a Greek thinker of the fifth century BC and a superior theorist to the misanthropic Epicurus, who founded his school a century later. Epicurean ideas were popular in the Roman empire, having been transmitted in Latin form by the great poet Lucretius, who emphasised atoms, materialism and a loathing of religion. Democritus, the father of 'atom theory', was in many ways a modern thinker, a strict determinist who favoured mechanistic explanations and the search for causality rather than the 'final cause' or teleological explanations beloved by the Stoics.[84] Indeed, the great physician Galen, who supported the Stoics against the Epicureans, credited the latter with the celebrated distinction between primary and secondary sensations in sense-perception, which was to be made famous in the seventeenth century by John Locke.[85] Marcus frequently contrasted the 'correct' interpretation of the cosmos via Providence with the 'fallacious' Epicurean view that it was composed of atoms, while conceding that Epicureanism had its value. For example, it agreed with Stoicism in granting central importance to the present moment, which, according to Epicurus, the theoretician of pleasure, enabled us to grasp the incomparable value of the here and now and so diminish the intensity of pain; we should tell ourselves that we experience pain only in the present moment. Marcus has several arguments for preferring the idea of Providence to that of atoms, principally that atom theory makes men mere beasts – a point that Galen found particularly cogent.[86] Trying his hand at irony, Marcus addressed an imaginary Epicurean: 'What are you worried about? All you have to do is say your guiding principle. You are dead, you are destroyed. You have become a wild beast, you defecate, you mingle with the flocks and you graze.'[87] Another argument is that Epicureanism and atoms implies disjuncture and divergence, whereas Stoicism correctly stresses unity and holism.[88] Yet in the end, Marcus admitted that the atoms-versus-Providence conundrum was insoluble by empirical evidence and argued that it actually made no difference to ethical theory which view of the universe was entertained; we can still use reason to impose order on chaos. He himself believed in fusing Providence and determinism, as this enabled us to be happy with whatever happened, whereas unalloyed determinism bred a gloomy fatalism and resignation.[89]

Deeply involved in cosmology as Marcus was, his principal concern was always ethics, and here he tended to follow the Epictetus line

Under the Roman Republic gladiators were always slaves, but in the Roman empire free men and even aristocrats took part in the 'sport'. The ultimate absurdity was reached when Commodus, emperor and Marcus's son, himself fought in the arena.

Wild beast shows were a Roman fetish. The trinity of animal fights, gladiatorial combat and chariot-racing was both the means by which the Roman elite kept the masses quiet and a kind of 'compensation' for the general loss of political rights under the Empire.

Mystery cults had always existed in Rome, but the late second century A.D. saw an exponential rise in interest in their popularity. Marcus himself was inducted into the Eleusinian mysteries – the most esoteric of all cults – at Athens in the autumn of 176

Romans were notorious gourmandisers, and members of the elite tried to outdo each other in the sumptuousness of their banquets and the originality of their cuisine. Both Antoninus Apius and Marcus Aurelius, however, ate sparingly

Herodes was the Ancient World's equivalent of a billionaire but, although he financed some worthwhile projects, he was a thorn in Marcus's side, being litigious, intemperate, quarrelsome and physically violent – it is a moral certainty that he killed his own wife.

Galen, the greatest physician and surgeon of the ancient world, also Marcus's personal doctor, was a genuine polymath but also a tiresome show-off and know-all, hugely self-loving and self-regarding.

The portrait of Marcus as a young man is compatible with our knowledge of him at this stage as over-serious, priggish and humourless.

Marcus receiving the symbol of imperial power. In Roman legal theory the emperor's power was a combination of the original legal prerogatives of magistrates (*potestas*), purely military power (*imperium*) and the *auctoritas* (legitimacy) which the Senate had enjoyed under the Republic.

Scholars dispute about whether the Roman Empire was a 'market economy', but Marcus himself was no believer in the automatic benevolence of the market. He favoured state intervention at all levels of economic and financial life, as here in a decree of 177 A.D, limiting city boundaries to stop disputes over taxation.

M·AURELIO   FAUSTINA   ROMA

The idealised royal family. To quote a latter example, 'there were three of us in this marriage', but the other woman was Rome itself.

Faustina did all that was expected of a Roman wife by bearing fifteen children, but the chroniclers of the *Historia Augusta* and Cassius Dio concur in finding her a promiscuous adulteress. This is one issue of Antonine scholarship that no modern Gibbon has been able to solve satisfactorily.

The bronze equestrian statue of Marcus in the Capitoline Museum in Rome is thought to have survived only because Christians in the Middle Ages mistakenly thought the rider was the emperor Constantine – the first Christian emperor and therefore their hero.

Aurelian relief from the Arch of Constantine in Rome. Marcus Aurelius in a toga is seated on the *sella curulis* (the curule chair on which all senior Roman magistrates traditionally sat) dispensing *liberalitas* (generosity) or welfare to the people. The emperor had the ultimate responsibility for providing for all the needs of the Roman people and for the building of roads, bridges, aqueducts and amphitheatres.

Marcus as high priest. One of the key roles of the Roman emperor was as head of the state religion. Devotion to the traditional gods and ancient Roman customs was part of the definition of being an emperor. Marcus eagerly embraced this role, as it both symbolised his hatred of change and enabled him to indulge his fondness for animal sacrifice.

scrupulously. As we have seen, probably *the* fundamental Stoic proposition is that we are led into moral error by our 'representations',
which inveigle us into bothering about things that have no moral value
and thus provide us with a skewed perspective on the world. Epictetus
considered that we over-value the external world. We receive impressions from it, which the mind processes in such a way that 'indifferents'
come to seem valuable. We think that a gold ring is desirable or our
child's illness is a bad thing, but the correct judgement is that a gold
ring is unimportant and that my child's illness does not harm me.
Wisdom consists in not thinking that events in the external world are
good or bad, and still less to want them or fear them, but just to
accept them. When non-moral things bother us, it is because we have
forgotten the basic precepts of Stoicism. Epictetus expressed this as
follows: 'Just as Socrates used to say, we should not live an unexamined life, so we should not accept an unexamined impression but
should say, "Wait a minute, impression, let us see who you are and
where you are coming from. Do you have your guarantee from Nature,
which every impression that is to be accepted should have?"'⁹⁰ In social
life, instead of saying, 'I don't like so-called leisure activities and prefer
solitude', you should use the situation in the right way. Talk to yourself, train your representations, work at your preconceptions. If you
fall in with a crowd, whether at the games, a festival or during a
holiday, try to celebrate with the people.⁹¹ Marcus glosses all this as
follows: 'Your mind will be just like the repetition of your impressions, for the soul is coloured by its impressions.'⁹² Epictetus went on
to say that 'representations' are the cause of everyone's unhappiness:

One person thinks he is sick; he's not, but he is not applying the proper
preconceptions. Another thinks that he is a pauper, another that he
has a harsh mother and father, and another that Caesar is not gracious
to him. All this is one thing only – ignorance of how to apply preconceptions. For we all have preconceptions of badness, what is harmful,
what is to be avoided and banished in every way . . . A person says he
is not Caesar's friend but he has gone off the right track and missed
the right application. He is ailing, he is seeking what has nothing to
do with the matter in hand. Because if he succeeds in being Caesar's
friend, he has no less failed in his quest. For what is it that every person
is seeking? To be serene, to be happy, to do everything he wants, not

to be impeded or constrained. So when someone becomes Caesar's friend, has he ceased to be impeded or constrained? Is he serene and flourishing?[93]

Whereas Marcus liked to illustrate his quasi-oracular pronouncements with examples drawn from the history of the Greeks and Romans, Epictetus was fond of drawing his from classical mythology. His highly eccentric take on the Trojan War was as follows: 'The *Iliad* is nothing but an impression and the use of impressions. Paris had an impression of abducting the wife of Menelaus, and Helen had an impression of following him. If Menelaus had had the impression that it was an advantage to be robbed of such a wife, what would have happened? We would have lost not only the *Iliad* but the *Odyssey* as well.'[94] The common-sense view would be to say that the Trojan War was just a myth, but Epictetus takes it seriously, only to dismiss it as unreal on quite other grounds. His cavalier way with Greek mythology is evident elsewhere. Once, when he was lecturing on the general theme that it was impossible for happiness and things not present to coincide, he claimed that happiness was incompatible with even the possibility of misery or disappointment. Someone in the audience mentioned the scene where Odysseus sits on a rock and weeps for Penelope, whereat Epictetus airily replied that one could not take Homer seriously[95] – even though he himself had taken him seriously enough to make the Trojan War an object lesson in impressions!

Similar considerations apply to Epictetus's famous treatment of the story of Medea, the princess who helped Jason win the Golden Fleece, married him, but was later abandoned by him. Medea was one of the Stoics' favourite paradigms for a noble nature gone wrong, for in the play by Euripides she murders her own children.[96] Epictetus argued that it was impossible for someone to think that something is in his interests and not choose it, but the thinking often masked a trap set by 'representations'. Medea thought that gratifying her anger and taking revenge on her husband was more in her interest than saving her children: this was not the case, but she *thought* it was. She would not have thought saving her children was the most important thing and still have acted as she did.[97] Once again we see Epictetus taking a cavalier line with mythology. Medea was a familiar figure in Greek mythology, but the idea that she killed her children was an original invention of Euripides. The traditional story was that the Corinthians stoned her children to death because she had poisoned their princess, the rival for Jason's affections who had displaced her. Later Corinthians, tired of this slur on their city, are said to have bribed Euripides with fifteen talents of silver to make Medea the murderess of her own children.[98] This of course is the version that has stuck and that over the centuries has attracted dramatists and poets of the calibre of Chaucer, Corneille, William Morris and Jean Anouilh. But a cynic might say that Epictetus had been seduced by his own false 'representation' of the Medea story. The moral surely is that you cannot base ontological arguments on a foundation of classical mythology, as Epictetus did. Marcus at least escaped the worst excesses of 'the master'.

Alongside outré excursions such as the above, Marcus's examples of misleading 'representations' are positively prosaic. He sticks very closely to the orthodoxy that most ethical problems come from fallacious judgements, that the true reality is mental, and that the external world is nugatory. It is not external things that are the problem, but how you interpret and assess them; nothing hurts unless I myself am prepared to interpret it as harmful.[99] Typical is this: 'To erase false perceptions, tell yourself: I have it in me to keep my soul from evil, lust and all confusion. To see things as they are and treat them as they deserve.' 'If you are grieving about some external thing, then it is not the thing that is troubling you, but your judgement about that thing.'[100] There is a whiff of triumphalism in some of the remarks: 'This day I have escaped all trouble or rather have cast out all trouble; for the trouble did not lie outside me but within me in my own conceptions.'[101] Occasionally Marcus indulges his distaste for corporeality by telling us that the problem of 'representations' occurs when the body leads the mind astray: 'Let the part of you that makes that judgement keep quiet even if the body it's attached to is stabbed or burned, or stinking with pus, or consumed by cancer.'[102] Yet it cannot be denied that sometimes Marcus's formulations are obscure or puzzling. He tells us, for instance, that external things cannot touch the soul; they cannot produce our judgements; they are outside of us; by themselves they know nothing and by themselves they affirm nothing.[103] In the light of the general theory of representations, this is at the very least enigmatic. It is possible that the apparent self-contradiction is the result of Stoic ambiguity in the use of the word 'soul', or at least in Marcus's personal use of it. We have seen how he further subdivides the soul into the reality made of air (*pneuma*) – which animates our body and receives impressions from external objects – and the superior or guiding part of the soul that the Stoics called *hegemonikon*. The apparently contradictory remarks might then be held to apply only to the *hegemonikon*, which would then presumably be thought of as invulnerable to 'representations'.

Yet ultimately, like so many other aspects of Stoic doctrine, the theory of representations ties itself in knots. The Stoics could never give a consistent answer to whether notions like good and evil related to our mental processes or to events and objects in the external world. According to the notion of freedom that the Stoics plug so assiduously, it must be our own fault, not that of the representations, if we misinterpret them. Yet in places Epictetus states that it is the *representations* themselves that are good or bad.[104] He also tells us over and over again, and Marcus concurs with the same level of iteration, that we must cross-examine our representations and keep running through them to make sure we get the right one. But, if they are all superficially attractive, how could one possibly know which was the right one? Stoics tried to get round the issue of competing goods by saying that, *a priori*, internal conflicts and inconsistencies are signs of unhappiness, so that only unhappiness (false representations) could ever lead to internal conflict. On the other hand, they contend that we are conflicted by the first impressions and preconceptions that make-up our 'representations'. Stoicism, in short, attempts to produce a system whereby, by sleight of hand, the self-contradictions imbricated in its own theory could not arise in a happy person.[105] This is sidestepping the issue, not resolving it, and in its barefaced *ad hoc* nature reminds one of that famous *petitio principii* in Marxism: 'false consciousness'. Epictetus tried unsuccessfully to solve the entire 'representations' imbroglio by saying that we should measure our impressions and accept or reject them according to whether they match (or fail to match) our desire for happiness. But since the only way we can conceive of happiness is through our representations, we are once again involved in circularity. Marcus exhorts us to consider 'what precisely is it that is generating your representation, and to disclose it by analysing its cause, material reference and necessary duration'.[106] But this implies we can get behind our representations to discern a prior form of knowledge. If we could, the question arises: what would be the epistemological basis of this deeper process? And, even more tellingly, if we could, why would we need the theory of 'representations' in the first place? It is unfortunate for Marcus that he fails to spot this deficiency and only occasionally addresses himself to the concerns of modern philosophy, in terms of the relation of perception to the external world.[107]

IO

For long stretches of the *Meditations* Marcus keeps very close to Stoic orthodoxy, even making a nod to Chrysippus and the founding fathers by agreeing that the world will be consumed by fire.[1] Yet it is the aphoristic Marcus, dispensing saws, adages and apothegms that can be appreciated by people without any knowledge of or interest in Stoicism, that has ensured his popularity down the ages. Some of these maxims are both pithy and striking. 'All you have to remember is three things: when it comes to matter, you're just a tiny part of it; when it comes to time, your share is a tiny and fleeting moment; and when it comes to Fate, your role in it is tiny.'[2] 'It is crazy to want what is impossible, and impossible for the wicked not to do so.'[3] 'Does the sun try to do the rain's work? Or Asclepius Demeter's? And what about each of the stars – so different yet working in common?'[4] 'Ambition means linking your well-being to what other people say or do; self-indulgence means linking it to the things that happen to you alone; but sanity means linking it to your own actions.'[5] 'Honey tastes bitter to a man with jaundice. People with rabies are terrified of water. And a child's idea of beauty is a ball. Why does that upset you? Do you think falsehood is less powerful than bile or a rabid dog?'[6] 'Never assume something's impossible because you find it hard. You should recognise that, if it's humanly possible, you can do it too.'[7] 'This is what you deserve. You could be good today. But instead you chose tomorrow.'[8] 'Never let go of philosophy, no matter what happens. And don't waste time bandying words with philistines and crackpots.'[9]

'Stupidity is expecting figs in winter, or children in old age.'[10] 'The student should be a boxer, not a fencer; the fencer's weapon is picked up and put down again; but the boxer's weapon is part of him – all he has to do is clench his fist.'[11] 'Practise even what seems impossible. The left hand is useless at almost everything, for lack of practice. But it guides the reins better than the right. From practice.'[12] It is this kind of epigrammatic richness that has always made Marcus Aurelius a favourite with devotees of 'self-help' and why, except for the purist, his reflections are usually preferred to the more enigmatic and esoteric ones of Epictetus.

Yet the essential Marcus lies neither in his role as a purveyor of Stoic orthodoxy nor as a dispenser of popular axioms and folk-remedies, but in those areas where his thought is at its most idiosyncratic: in the discussion of religion; in his treatment of evil; and in his reflections on death. His attitude to religion and the gods is problematical not just because he exhibits the usual Stoic confusion between theism and pantheism, but because of his official (and apparently sincere) devotion to the traditional polytheistic religion of the Olympians, the state religion to which he was committed as chief priest or *pontifex maximus*. Until the coming of the Roman empire, the post had usually been held by a member of one of the prominent families; Julius Caesar, for instance, was appointed in 63 BC and kept the office until his death. In republican times it was not a full-time job, and the holder could also hold a secular magistracy or serve in the military.[13] From the time of Augustus it became customary for the emperor to be *pontifex maximus*; he would usually have a vice-master to carry out his duties when he was absent from Rome.[14] The prestige of the post came from the administration of the divine law (*ius divinum*), making the chief priest the principal conduit to the gods. Among his functions were consecrating temples and altars, carrying out expiatory ceremonies to ward off or palliate pestilence, plague, famine, flood, lightning strikes, and so on; the regulation of the calendar; the administration of the law relating to burials; superintending marriages; administering the law relating to adoptions and wills; and custodianship of state archives and official records and minutes of decisions taken by the magistracies.[15] Marcus inherited this mantle as senior partner in the empire in 161, but a secret unbeliever would presumably have used the opportunity to slough off this part of the emperor's job onto Lucius Verus;

quite the reverse happened, for Marcus employed as his *pontifex minor* a certain M. Livius, whose task was to oversee all cults in Rome, both indigenous ones and foreign imports, whether Greek or Asian. It seems clear that Marcus wanted Verus as far away from the state religion as possible.[16]

Most educated Romans and most emperors did not really believe in the Olympian gods (or, indeed, any gods). It was almost a badge of honour for the senatorial class to be sceptics, as though this was a mark of their status, and belief in the gods something for the mob at the arena and the Circus.[17] Cicero was a convinced atheist, but thought religion and belief in the Olympians played a vital part in promoting social stability. Long before William James, the Romans had invented the pragmatic argument for religion. But Marcus Aurelius presents a conundrum, for there are clear signs in him of a belief in traditional religion. Naturally a sophisticated reading of the use of Olympian polytheism by successive emperors can easily construe it as an allegory for deism or pantheism,[18] but this is difficult to do in Marcus's case, not only because he mentions the deities of Greek and Roman mythology so often – Clotho, the Muses, Zeus, Asclepius, not to mention a fertility goddess[19] – but because his coinage foregrounds the traditional deities like Minerva, Mars and Jupiter instead of emphasising the glorious and legendary early figures of Roman history, as Antoninus Pius did on his coins.[20] The other well-known aspect of Marcus's traditional worship was his fondness for sacrifice, an attribute shared with a later 'intellectual' emperor, Julian the Apostate. This propensity was burlesqued in a ditty of the times: 'the white cattle to Marcus, greeting. If you conquer on the frontier, there is an end of us'.[21] At the very least there is a tension between Marcus Aurelius's cult practice as high priest and his philosophical beliefs as a Stoic. Critics have read this in different ways. One describes him as 'a Stoic philosopher of the superstitious rather than the rational type'.[22] Renan thought him a great intellect who could not quite surmount and abjure the supernatural.[23] Perhaps the most convincing explanation for Marcus's apparent eccentricity in the matter of the Olympians is that he was using the state religion to promote very heavily the notion of the divine right of emperors – an idea he had taken over from Antoninus Pius.[24]

That Marcus was more superstitious than most emperors and

peculiarly susceptible to a belief in the paranormal emerges from his belief in using all means to placate possibly angry gods (hence the plethora of animal sacrifices) and his sympathetic interest in Eastern mystery religions and especially his tolerance for notorious charlatans such as Alexander of Abonoteichos. The late second century was a golden age for astrology, magicians, maguses and so-called 'holy men' (like Apollonius of Tyana and Julian the Theurgist), and Marcus seems to have been vulnerable to them.[25] His gullibility concerning Alexander of Abonoteichos was notorious. Introduced to Marcus by Rutilianus, this master of knavery and duplicity (c. AD 105–75) made an impression on the emperor, being physically a very fine specimen, fair-haired, bearded, white-skinned with piercing blue eyes and a euphonious voice (though he wore a toupee to conceal his baldness).[26] A catamite from his early youth, Alexander learned a farrago of magic tricks from an Eastern magus – he seems to have been the original sorcerer's apprentice. When the magus died, he teamed up with a Byzantine dancer named Coconnas and together they practised confidence trickery on a lavish scale. Realising that the key to all religions and belief systems is the human wish to enhance hopes and allay fears, they played on the equally pressing human desire to know the future – through oracles or any other method. Alexander set up his stall at Abonoteichos, but, as with Hadrian and Antinous, his lover died suddenly – bitten by a snake, it was said. Feigning temporary madness, Alexander claimed to be a prophet of Asclepius and performed conjuring tricks with a tame snake, dressed for the part in a purple and white robe, his hair flowing in long, matted locks and with a sickle in his hand. He then graduated to grosser methods of hocus-pocus, using trained animals and the hollowed-out statues of gods in which he concealed his accomplices.[27]

He founded an oracle that charged extortionate sums for making 'true predictions' and made a fortune from it. He even hooked up a primitive form of autophone, with long tubes and wind pipes interconnecting, so that the 'god' would appear to answer people's questions.[28] He made another pile of money by pretending that he had a febrifuge that could protect people against all known diseases. His favourite scam was getting people to ask the gods questions in papers sealed with wax. The papers would be returned with the seals apparently unbroken and convincing answers relayed to the petitioners, but in fact Alexander had perfected an ingenious method for burning through the wax, reading the letters and then resealing them.[29] He was a master of the usual bogus 'cold reading' responses, and one of his favourite dodges was to recommend sham 'remedies' and prescriptions, naturally charging a fee for each 'consultation'. While indulged by the Stoics, Alexander was detested by both the Epicureans and the Christians, who saw right through him; he returned their hatred manyfold and indulged in vicious propaganda warfare against both groups.[30] He was yet another in the long line of homosexualists who denounce 'the vice' while practising it themselves. How he escaped exposure as a charlatan is a nice question, but local magistrates hesitated to prosecute leaders of sects, partly because the entire sect then demanded to be lodged and fed at public expense because it was denied the 'sustenance' of its leaders.[31] In Alexander's case there was the additional factor that he had powerful friends like Rutilianus. He successfully petitioned Marcus to have his native city renamed Ionopolis and even gained from the emperor the extraordinary privilege of being allowed to mint his own coinage.[32] Moreover, later on military campaign Marcus took his advice, with embarrassing results (see pp. 353–4). Marcus's partiality for such an obvious impostor is one of the things that have led some of his modern critics to doubt the calibre of his mind.

It is tempting to see Marcus's different oscillations – between pantheism, the official doctrine of the Stoics and the Olympian polytheism he had the civic duty to propagate, and between superstition and scepticism – as the product of a self-induced confusion. Yet it is clear that at least some of these confusions and self-contradictions were already there in the work of Epictetus, who was also capable of moving, without prior notice, between three entirely different notions of God: the polytheistic Olympian creed, God as *logos* or Nature and God as the 'god within' – not so much a case of 'double-talk', but more like triple-talk. Some apologists for Epictetus claim that his references to 'Zeus' are simply his demotic way of addressing a crowd and that 'Zeus' always means *logos* or universal reason. Yet some of his statements are simply impossible to interpret that way and pay more than just lip-service to polytheism: 'Let your desires and your aversions become attached to Zeus, and to the other gods, give them to them, let them govern them, and let this desire and this aversion be ranged in accordance with them.'[33] As against a deistic stance, Epictetus often pictures God as an Olympic coach, one it would make sense to pray to.[34] Some of his remarks would fit very well in a 'God made me' Christian catechism. 'This body made of mud: how could God have created it free of impediments? He therefore submitted it to the revolution of the universe, as he did with my possessions, my furniture, my house, my children, and my wife. Why, then, should I fight against God? Why should I wish for things that ought not to be wished for?'[35] Epictetus further argues that we should not blame God for taking anything away from us, as he gave us everything in the first place; by the same token, we should not pray to the gods for favours, but sing songs of praise for the benefits they have already given us.[36] And he recommends that the good, moral man should depart this life with the following words on his lips for the Maker: 'I leave full of gratefulness to you, for you have judged me worthy of celebrating the festival with you, of contemplating your works, and of following together with you the way in which you govern the world.'[37]

Yet Epictetus consistently muddies the waters. Not only is he confused as between 'the gods' of official religion and God as reason or *logos*, but, having categorically stated that God is transcendent, 'out there', he then changes tack and speaks of an immanent deity, the 'god within'. 'You are carrying God around, you poor thing, and you don't know it. Do you think I am talking about an external God made of gold or silver? You are carrying him around inside yourself, and you fail to realise that you defile him with unclean thoughts and foul actions.'[38] As if the contrast between an immanent and transcendent God did not make the picture cloudy enough, Epictetus also gives us occasional measures of full-throated pantheism: 'What else am I, a lame old man, capable of except singing hymns to God? If I were a nightingale, I would do the nightingale's thing and if I were a swan, a swan's. Well, I am a rational creature; so I must sing hymns to God. This is my task: I do it and I will not abandon this position as long as it is granted to me, and I urge you to sing this same song.'[39] To this already turgid brew Epictetus adds further ingredients, turning the soup into a dark, turbid pool. He links the argument about how we should conceive and interpet God (literally, symbolically, allegoric-ally or pantheistically) with the quite separate Stoic confusions about an individual and a general Providence, and whether said Providence is something especially designed for the sage, from which lesser beings are excluded, but may also benefit indirectly.[40] With his lack of interest in cosmology, Epictetus failed to spot the contradiction between gods or God being uninterested in 'unimportant' men and the fact that Providence or Destiny has designed them as such since the beginning of the world; sadly, Marcus also fell into the selfsame trap.[41]

In general Marcus incorporates all Epictetus's confusions about God and adds further elements of his own. His treatment of the divine faculty within us, or *daimon*, is particularly obscure. Why does he tack between a number of different terms, all of which seem to mean the same: self, intellect (*nous*), guiding principle (*hegemonikon*) and inner *daimon*? Is the *daimon* merely a synonym for reason? Is it simply the godlike portion within each person (the god within) or should it be understood more like the Christian idea of a guardian angel? In other words, should it be conceived as an immanent or transcendent entity? Sometimes he seems to imply that the correct meaning must be something like 'guardian angel', for otherwise what would be the point of sacrifices, oaths and prayers?[42] Part of the problem is that Marcus has added an extra layer to the basic Stoic mind/body dualism, by introducing a third element and producing a troika of body, *pneuma* and intelligence or even, as we have seen (see p. 214), by replacing a Stoic trio with a quincunx, but without saying what the basis of his reasoning is. Another difficulty is the semantic point of not knowing when we are comparing like with like, for Marcus identifies the 'command post' of the self with reason (*nous*), whereas orthodox Stoicism located it in the soul (*psyche*). Let us leave on one side the awkward 'sore thumb' of a self that is supposedly one, yet divided. Even if we could clear away all the thorny linguistic issues, there is no getting round the fact that, in discussing *daimon* (as well as in discussing God in general, though we cannot be sure that they are synonymous terms), Marcus confusingly oscillates between an immanent meaning[43] and a transcendent one.[44]

In discussing God, Marcus moves some way from the position of his supposed teacher, Epictetus, and this may be, as has been suggested, simply a difference in their life-experience, their temperament and, most obviously, their social status.[45] Certainly, in contrast to Epictetus, Marcus rarely refers to God in the singular, preferring to talk of Nature or the Whole, which clearly allows us to see the gap between Epictetus the theist and Marcus the pantheist.[46] On the other hand, strict pantheism would imply that the divine order would be concerned only with the design and running of the cosmos, not with individual humans or even humanity at all, so that sacrifices, prayers and oaths would make no sense. Marcus never decides categorically between the idea of gods that we can appeal to and the pantheistic notion of an impersonal deity woven into the very fabric of the universe, and oscillates wildly between the two mutually exclusive conceptions.[47] To complicate matters still further, Marcus is adamant that the gods help us via our dreams and through oracles and omens and aid us to get the things we need.[48] We may differentiate Marcus from Epictetus by saying that the emperor tacks mainly between 'the gods' as the proper name for reason or Nature and a superstitious regard for the Olympians, while Epictetus almost always refers simply to 'God'. On the other hand, Epictetus's deity is largely theistic and personalist, whereas Marcus's is largely abstract and pantheistic.[49] Epictetus's God also seems more limited in power than Marcus's.[50] We are told that God is more powerful than any individual human, but not necessarily superior in virtue or happiness, though what any of this could mean if we conceive God pantheistically is a moot question.[51] For Marcus, but not for Epictetus, there is a further problem, aside from the riddles concerning polytheism, monotheism, deism and pantheism and the immanent/transcendent issue. Given his Gnostic distaste for the body and the physical world, how could he logically accept the Stoic argument for God's existence from design? Marcus's tendency towards nihilism is frequently in conflict with his official belief that everything in the world is the product of divine reason. On the one hand, he tells us that without the existence of God and Providence, life would be meaningless; on the other, he often tells us that it *is* meaningless.

Marcus Aurelius is a notably inconsistent thinker, and the coils he wraps himself in when discussing God raise the inconsistency to new heights. On the one hand, he is concerned to defend belief in the Olympians and rounds on sceptics who will not even pronounce the name of Zeus; if we are not prepared to say his name, we should not be praying in the first place.[52] And he is concerned to stress the immortality of the gods, by which he must mean the Olympians, for by definition a pantheistic God could never die.[53] On the other hand, he never attached himself to a named god in the way Galen and Aelius Aristides did with Asclepius, or Apuleius did with Isis. In Book Twelve of the *Meditations* he even manages to insinuate a transcendent God, only to contradict it with an immanent 'god within' a few paragraphs later.[54] It may be, as has been suggested, that Marcus was as uneasy talking about God and religion as he was about sex.[55] Tied down and circumscribed by, on the one hand, the traditional Roman religion of which he was high priest and, on the other, Stoicism with its insistence on the 'god within', Marcus only occasionally allowed himself to cut loose with the full-blooded pantheism that probably represents his true attitude. When he does so, he is at once at his most original and his most modern; there is nothing like it elsewhere in the Stoic literature. Some critics have compared his treatment of the *daimon* to passages in Shakespeare and Tennyson.[56] Most strikingly mystical is the address to his soul at the beginning of Book Ten of the *Meditations*, which has been compared to a Hebrew psalm and to Thomas à Kempis. The nearest equivalent of the enthusiastic passages in which Marcus rhapsodises about the divine universe must be sought in the Nature poetry of the early nineteenth-century English Romantic poets: Shelley's 'Adonais' and Wordsworth's 'Tintern Abbey' have been cited in this regard.[57]

The nature of evil is another subject where Marcus evinces an independent turn of mind. The path to his thinking is winding and devious, so that we must first consider his notion of goodness. We begin with the familiar Stoic notion that the only good is moral good (and hence the only evil moral evil), and that neither pleasure nor pain is an evil.[58] For Marcus, the true philosopher concentrates on the positive quality of goodness, not its negative opposite. Doing good not only benefits others, but also benefits the benefactor.[59] This is in accordance with the Stoic doctrine that doing good to others is the same as doing good to ourselves – though critics allege that this fatally blurs the distinction between selfishness and altruism, thus giving fortune's hostages to those who claim that altruism is anyway merely a disguised form of selfishness. There is also the 'holistic' argument that by doing good to a part we are thereby doing good to the whole. Love is the logical corollary of the union of all things on the Earth, so that the closer you get to wisdom and God, the more you should love your neighbour.[60] Marcus distinguishes three types of benefactor: the Stoic who is conscious that he does good for the sake of another; the non-Stoic who considers his beneficiary to be in his debt – the ultimate sin for the Stoic; and the so-called benefactor who is unaware of what he has done.[61] For Marcus, altruism is merely the perception that our own self-interest lies in doing good to others. We owe a duty to our family, for example, no matter how atrociously our parents or siblings behave. The beginnings of morality are in our family relations, but this should be extended outwards to our neighbours, to fellow-Romans and ultimately to the entire world. Marcus thought that personal goodness was palpable, that you could sense it and almost smell it in the virtuous.[62] Goodness, not anger or power, is real strength. The man who concentrates on goodness is a kind of priest of the cosmos, a servant of the gods, using the element within himself that transcends pain, pleasure, passion and evil, devoted to justice and welcoming in his heart whatever happens as the best thing that could happen. In so doing we are manifesting the strength of reason and the power of the god within us.[63]

Marcus stressed that we should even be benevolent to the unjust and to liars, because such people retain their rational nature and therefore unconsciously desire good.[64] Here he followed closely in the footsteps of Epictetus, who taught gentleness and tolerance even to those who think and act erroneously; if you can't get such people to reform or change their minds, simply reflect that that was why benevolence was given to you, and that the gods are merciful to the hard-hearted and refractory.[65] You cannot go too far wrong if you always direct your actions towards some goal that serves humanity, which means that altriusm is a core value. Another is seriousness, single-mindedness and the ability to focus. Marcus exhorts us to stop being puppets pulled by the strings of selfish desires and to stop spinning around like a top.[66] No wise man can be a dilettante, he argues. Believing strongly in professional expertise and a strict division of labour, he considered that the ultimate horror was the man who flitted from thing to thing, one year being an athlete, the next a gladiator, the next an orator and finally a so-called philosopher.[67] To act morally brings joy, which is a key motif in Marcus's writings, and denotes the emotion we feel when we are truly fulfilling the function for which we were put on the Earth, and when we consent to the reality of Providence, pantheism and the 'city of the world'.[68] Here we see that virtue is truly its own reward, for joy is not the *end* of moral action, as the Epicureans thought. The sage does not choose virtue because it causes pleasure, but it is a fact that, if chosen, virtue does cause pleasure. It is a curiosity that under Stoicism the individual is exhorted to sacrifice himself for the good of the cosmos, just as the revolutionaries of the nineteenth century were urged by Marx to sacrifice themselves for the good of future generations. The liberal theory of self-assigned self-interest would say that both of these propositions are nonsense.

There is a self-contradiction right at the heart of the Stoics' version of goodness or virtue, which is compounded when we come to discuss their conception of evil. We are constantly told that the only good is moral good and that what defines moral good is that it should conform with the law of reason and be located within the domain of humanity; everything else is 'indifferent': life, health, pleasure, beauty, strength, renown, noble birth – as well as their opposites (death, sickness, pain, ugliness, weakness, poverty, obscurity, humble birth).[69] All these things are 'indifferent' as they are governed by Destiny and do not depend on us; they cannot generate happiness or unhappiness since these relate to moral categories.[70] The implication of Stoicism is the novel idea that we should limit ourselves to internal objectives, where success can be guaranteed. This does not sound much like happiness and, if it were, would anyone want it? On the other hand, we are told that morality depends on our relations to others and informs the world of politics. As later thinkers might have put it, economics begins the moment Robinson Crusoe sets foot on his island, but politics and morality can only arise with the arrival of Friday. In accordance with this doctrine we are enjoined not to mourn children and loved ones. With so many 'indifferents' at play, how can human beings ever solve the conundrum of how to live well – which Socrates taught was the key ethical question? The Stoic answers that we know naturally by reason. It is natural for us to love our children, to get married, to love our country, to live in cities, to form assemblies and Senates and so on. But in that case, reason directs us to cherish things that have already been described in the main Stoic doctrine as 'indifferents'; it seems they are no longer simply in the realm of Destiny and the external world, but in the universe of morality after all. In Marcus's case, additionally, the emphasis on altruism and love of humanity sits uneasily with other passages in the *Meditations* that are quasi-solipsistic, despairing and misanthropic.[71]

As has been remarked, the problems concerning goodness, virtue and morality are simply enhanced when the Stoics turn to deal with the problem of evil. The early Stoics tended to deny the reality of evil, and we find the same doctrine in Epictetus. Yet Epictetus trips himself up when discussing the merits of the Cynics and his beloved Diogenes. While conceding that some people posed as Cynics just so as to be able to live on alms, avoid hard work and revile the rich and powerful, he maintained that the true Cynic renounces possessions and family to devote himself entirely to God's work, or the moral improvement of his fellow-men. The way of life of the Cynics was not the best way, and still less was it the way of the sage, but it was one forced on us by the wickedness of the world: Cynics are foot soldiers in the war against evil where Stoics are the officer class.[72] Yet since Epictetus has previously told us that evil is an illusion, it is difficult to see exactly what such a war would be waged against. Marcus too falls into this trap. Having accepted that evil is an illusion, he also says that problems arise because people do not know the difference between good and evil.[73] In an attempt at once to claim that evil was an illusion and that evil men did exist, the Stoics, not surprisingly (one is tempted to say predictably), fell back on their catch-all explanation: the fallacy of representations. Marcus tells us that evil arises from false representations and false judgements arising from ignorance; this is one reason why we should be charitable to the wrong-headed.[74] Epictetus provides a striking example of 'false representations'. He says that although a person in a temple, in the presence of images of God, would not indulge in impure thoughts or actions, he would be quite happy to indulge in all kinds of blasphemy once outside the temple, even though, carrying God within him, he is still in reality in the holy of holies.[75] An extension of this idea of misperception or 'false representations' harks back to Platonist thinking, where Plato maintained that no one is voluntarily evil; even egregiously wicked men, parricides, tyrants, despots and mass murderers believed that when they committed evil actions they were really working for the greater good.[76] There is much to be said for this notion, for it is obvious that the great monsters of the twentieth century – Hitler, Stalin, Franco, Mao – committed their unspeakable acts for what, in their minds, were noble ends. Marcus endorses this view, but adds that it is just one more reason why we should be kind, noble and forgiving.[77]

Yet because Marcus's thought is more complex and nuanced than Epictetus's, we find many more possible definitions and musings about evil in the *Meditations*. One idea is that God permits evil in order to allow us to appreciate beauty: many ugly and ungraceful entities are placed in the universe by Providence to enhance our aesthetic sense; the catch is that only the sage can appreciate this beauty.[78] So dirt, mud, poison, earthquakes and storms come from the same source as roses, seascapes and the wonders of spring. Marcus is pulled in several different directions by the fissiparous elements in his thought, especially the conflict between Stoic orthodoxy and his Gnostic attitude to matter and the physical world. Strictly speaking, notions of good and evil should arise only in the use of reason by a sentient human, but Marcus was clearly unhappy with this attitude to matter. He uses two techniques to try to reconcile his thoughts. One is that beauty and morality – and hence evil – inhabit separate spheres, which are separated by a hierarchy of perspectives. Objects in the external world are both beautiful and worthless; beautiful because they exist, and worthless because they cannot access the realm of freedom and morality. Beautiful things are impermanent and vanish into the flux: 'Who would attach any value to any of the things which simply flow past us?'[79] Another is that beauty is a kind of halfway house between the 'illusion' of evil and the reality of virtue. 'The lion's jaws, the poisonous substances, and every harmful thing – from thorns to mud – are by-products of the beautiful.'[80]

Although Marcus sometimes pays lip-service to the Stoic view that good and evil arise only from the use of reason and from misperceptions and 'false representations', a strong element in his thinking, in flat contradiction to this (and here we can see the Gnostic element in his thinking), is that evil is a 'partial' phenomenon, something that exists in Nature, but not in the realm of reason. Evil is a secondary phenomenon that can sometimes be a spin-off from the primary quality of good; good is in the realm of nature, but evil is in the domain of physics. In terms of cosmology, evil is unimportant: 'The existence of evil does not harm the world. And an individual act of evil does not harm the victim. Only one person is harmed by it – and he can stop being harmed as soon as he decides to.'[81] Evil exists in the realm of 'indifferents' – a trivial realm of which the gods take no notice, for they are concerned only with great issues and not minor ones. Cicero expressed this as follows: 'If drought or hail do harm to a landowner, that is no business of Jupiter's.'[82] An allied view is that because God does not operate in the world of matter, if we look only at the world of matter we will see reality askew. The truth about the universe is holistic, and it is only with a tunnel-vision one-dimensional view of matter – seeing the part, but not the whole – that we come to think of evil as a universal principle and something to be taken seriously. What we experience is only an infinitesimal part of the universe, so how could we possibly grasp the entire workings of Destiny?[83] Yet it cannot be stated too often that this emphasis on cosmology, with evil in an unimportant role in the external world, is frequently rebutted by Marcus himself elsewhere in the *Meditations*. 'You take things you can't control and define them as "good" or "bad". And so of course when the "bad" things happen or the "good" ones don't, you blame the gods and feel hatred for the people responsible – or those you decide to make responsible. Much of our bad behaviour stems from trying to apply those criteria. If we limited "good" and "bad" to our own actions, we'd have no call to challenge God, or to treat other people as enemies.'[84] It is the latter view that has been most influential in the history of philosophy. The seventeenth-century rationalist Spinoza famously announced that it was pointless to seek explanations for good and evil in Nature, since the category of the physical universe was purely natural, whereas the category of good and evil was ethical – something quite different.

It is easy, and perhaps even facile, to point up the numerous contradictions in Marcus's thought, most of them caused by the Nessus's shirt of Stoicism that he chose to wear. Far more interesting from the standpoint of ethical theory are the many instances where his thinking seems a forerunner or adumbration of the theories of the early Church Fathers and, beyond them, the medieval schoolmen. The three most salient issues are: evil as a prerequisite for freedom; evil as a manifestation of God's ulterior purpose, which we cannot discern; and evil as pure negativity, the mere absence of good. The alleged connection between freedom and evil pervades both Epictetus and Marcus's work, but was perhaps summed up most succinctly by a later thinker, John Stuart Mill. The evil in the universe is caused by man's wickedness. Man is free, which means free to do evil as well as good. Even an omnipotent being could not make man free and yet not free to do evil. Evil is thus an inevitable concomitant of man's freedom.[85] Marcus takes over Epictetus's frequent observations on freedom, which contrast it with cowardice, liken it to manumission from slavery and to being an athlete in an open, unfixed contest (and with God as a kind of Olympic coach).[86] Epictetus adds the further point that freedom must be considered holistically: you should bathe as someone who keeps his word and eat as a man of integrity.[87] Concentration on freedom also leads Marcus to a holistic, Platonic and inegalitarian conception of justice.[88] The basic point is clear: without the ability to commit evil, man is not free, but a mere automaton. Yet this does not explain why God did not create humans with freedom, yet unable to commit evil, just as they are created with reason, but unable to fly. To make it definitional of humans that they should be capable of evil begs every conceivable question. And no amount of talk about divine justice or cosmic perfection in the long term could ever annul the suffering in this world. As Dostoevsky pointed out in *The Brothers Karamazov*, in the case of a brutal army officer who had a child torn apart by dogs, what conceivable cosmic outcome could ever undo such appalling evil?[89]

The second proto-Christian argument that Marcus uses is that evil must have a purpose that we, as mere humans, cannot discern. To use one of his favourite sayings: 'If I and my two children cannot move the gods, the gods must have their reasons.'[90] For Marcus, there is no point in railing and querying why unpleasant things exist, even the minor annoyances like bitter cucumber or brambles in the path: 'Anyone who understands the world will laugh at you, just as a carpenter would if you seemed shocked at finding sawdust in his workshop, or a shoemaker at scraps of leather left over from work.'[91] You can be sure, he says, that the gods 'would have arranged things differently if that had been appropriate. If it were the right thing to do, they could have done it, and if it were natural, Nature would have done it.'[92] But all such talk requires a leap of faith, a belief in the beneficent workings of Providence, which cannot be based on reason alone. Reason is supposed to work forward from the unknown to the known, not from the known to the unknown. As with all quasi-theological systems, Stoicism constantly assumes that which has to be proved. Marcus's thought is teleological, it looks forward to an ultimate and eventual explanation of evil that is not within the power of humans to elucidate. Despite his many exhortations to live in the present, Marcus often projects forward to a mystical future, an 'end of times' scenario where evil will be harmonised with good under divine direction. This links with another of his mystical tropes: that the philosopher can cut himself off temporarily from the whole, but in the end return to it.[93] Both ideas strongly point forward to the theology of Origen, greatest of the Church Fathers, who in his doctrine of *apocatastasis* (later condemned as a heresy) hypothesised that at the end of time Satan and all the demons would be reconciled with the Almighty.

Despite Marcus's occasional forays into evil in Nature, he usually shared the general Stoic view that evil is a human aberration, for which God is not responsible. Yet if we concentrate on evil in Nature, all the talk about freedom and human reason becomes irrelevant and we have to face the ultimate question, first posed by Epicurus, but echoed by every theologian since. 'Is God willing to prevent evil, but not able? Then he is not omnipotent. Is he able, but not willing? Then he is malevolent. Is he both able and willing? Then whence evil?'[94] Or as Man Friday said when Robinson Crusoe told him about the Christian God and Satan: 'Why God him not kill debil?' All the Stoic talk about moral evil does nothing to answer the questions posed by natural evil. William Blake wondered if he who made the lamb made the tiger. Or, as William James memorably put it:

Crocodiles and rattlesnakes and pythons are at this moment vessels of life as real as we are; their loathsome existence fills every minute of every day that drags its length along, and whenever they or other wild beasts clutch their living prey, the deadly horror which an agitated melancholic feels is literally the right reaction on the situation. It may indeed be that no religious reconciliation with the totality of things is possible. Some evils, indeed, are ministerial to higher forms of good but it may be that there are forms of evil so extreme as to enter into no good system whatsoever, and that in respect of such evil, dumb submission or neglect to notice is the only practical recourse.[95]

There are, of course, those eccentrics who claim to see nothing evil in sharks, crocodiles, black mambas or king cobras, and who berate Sir Thomas Malory for having Sir Percival take the side of a lion fighting a serpent because it was a more 'natural' animal.[96] They seek comfort in the words of Sir Thomas Browne: 'I cannot tell by what logic we call a toad, a bear or an elephant ugly.'[97] Here, of course, Browne had loaded the dice, for most people simply would not call a bear or elephant ugly, but the general point is clear: humans construct a hierarchy of desirability in the wild beasts, and bottom of the heap are the animals dangerous to man.

Even if we were to allow the extreme critics their day and exclude snakes, crocodiles, sharks *et hoc genus omne* from the category of evil, how – on a theory of divine benevolence – do we explain earthquakes, volcanic eruptions, tsunamis, 100-foot oceanic waves, to say nothing of the plethora of diseases, both the specifically human ones and those spread by mosquitoes, locusts, rats, and so on? The Stoics always provided the most facile and unconvincing answers to such questions. The existence of rats teaches us not to leave garbage around; the existence of mosquitoes teaches us to bear loss of sleep with courage; winds cause typhoons and hurricanes, but if there was no wind, nothing would sweep the 'miasmata' away; a few shipwrecks are the price we pay for not being exterminated by disease.[98] The nineteenth-century Romantics and proponents of the modern, pessimistic version of 'stoicism' have no problem with this for, to use Nietzsche's words, God is dead and the universe is meaningless. To use the formulation of Alfred de Vigny:

> Toil vigorously at the long and heavy task
> In the path where chance chose to call you.
> Then, done, suffer, as I do and die without a word.[99]

This 'solution' is not available to Marcus, as Nature and Providence are supposed to guarantee our happiness. Stoicism shared with all other ancient philosophies the idea that life must have some purpose, and this explains the ubiquity of *logos* in the *Meditations*; it was only after the Romantic movement that people could conceive of unhappy endings and conclude that everything was meaningless – 'merely the hurrying of material, endlessly, meaninglessly', as A.N. Whitehead put it.[100]

Marcus also on several occasions suggests that evil is unreal and is a mere absence of good, anticipating the Christian notion of *privatio boni*, suggested by St Augustine and later taken up by Thomas Aquinas.[101] This is Panglossian philosophy at its worst and seems a mere semantic parlour-game. Any set of antonyms – war and peace, lust and chastity, beauty and ugliness – can be juxtaposed, with one assigned the primary place as a 'real', positive feature and the other being classified as 'unreal' or negative. One might just as well say that 'good' is a secondary quality, being the mere absence of evil. As has been remarked, the sick man usually does not suffer from an absence of something but its *presence*, in the form of a deadly virus.[102] The psychologist C.G. Jung once scathingly remarked that on the *privato boni* principle, Auschwitz and the other death-camps would have to be characterised as a mere absence of good. In any case, an entire school of modern philosophy, associated with Martin Heidegger, has asserted that 'nothingness' (*le néant* in the writings of J.-P. Sartre) is not a mere absence, but a positive force.[103] The idea that unpleasant or evil things are somehow 'accidental' or 'secondary' manifestations of some overarching principle of Goodness is of course a very convenient doctrine, nonsensical, but highly influential. Modern critics claim that attempts to explain evil either fall into the error of Providentialism, denying the reality of evil, or opt for the Christian tactic of trying to differentiate good and evil too sharply, decanting all evil into notions like Satan and Hell.[104] That kind of dualism, sometimes hinted at by Seneca, would be impossible for Marcus Aurelius, wedded as he is to holistic notions. Yet for all the failings and inadequacies of his conception of evil, he must be credited with at least intermittently trying to deal seriously with the notion; by contrast, the effusions of Epictetus on the subject are pat, formulaic and totally unconvincing.

The third area where Marcus blazes an independent trail, in places diverging very much from orthodox Stoicism, is in his treatment of death. Some critics have accused him of a kind of thanatophilia or, at any rate, of being death-driven and death-obsessed. He is certainly at the opposite end of the scale from a thinker like Marx, whose work is characterised by a total incuriosity about corporeal existence and, especially, death.[105] Marcus, by contrast, has almost no interest in social and economic matters or the deep currents of socio-economic causation; the masses do not feature, and the individual is usually conceived as being at the very least a trainee sage. But death is his central concern, and the subject is referred to more than any other in the *Meditations*. For much of the time Marcus cleaves to the Stoic line, stressing in particular that death is simply a specific form of change; since everything else changes, why not human life?[106] It is also part of Destiny, part of a pattern prepared from eternity. 'Every event that comes your way has been linked to you by Destiny, and has been woven together with you, starting from the whole, since the beginning.' 'Whatever happens to you was prepared for you in advance from all eternity, and the network of causes has woven together your substance and the occurrence of this event for all time.'[107] Marcus also links it to his motif of the present instant. From the perspective of death, each instant has an infinite value and, besides, there is something unreal about death – for if we are dreading it, by definition we are still alive and death is absent; or, if death has come, we are no longer conscious anyway.[108] Some people dread death as they fear they will be robbed of a normal span of life, but, as Marcus often remarks, observing life for forty years is as good as a thousand-year existence, for after forty you would never see anything new.[109] 'If it ends when it's supposed to, it's none the worse for that. And the person who comes to the end of the line has no cause for complaint.' 'Human lives are brief and trivial. Yesterday a dollop of semen; tomorrow embalming fluid and ashes.'[110]

Besides, by departing this vale of tears we are not missing much. We are half-dead anyway, by being anchored to the body, which is in essence a corpse. 'As if you were dying right now, despise your flesh. A mess of blood, pieces of bone, a woven tangle of nerves, veins, arteries.'[111] And, with any luck, we will miss all the horrors of old age.[112] Marcus frequently reminds himself that he is, by the standards of the age, already an old man when in his late forties and fifties; he does not like the condition, but does his best to come to terms with it, sharing neither Cicero's unbridled optimism nor Juvenal's extreme pessimism and disgust.[113] There's no special advantage about dying old. 'A trite but effective tactic against the fear of death: think of the list of people who had to be pried away from life. What did they gain by dying old? In the end they all sleep six feet under – Caedicianus, Fabius, Julian, Lepidus, and all the rest. They buried their contemporaries, but were buried in turn.'[114] Moreover, what you are leaving behind on expiring is not much: most human beings are despicable so there's no great wrench about departing and a lot of the so-called intimates and nearest and dearest want you out of the way anyhow: '"what a relief to be rid of that old pedant," they will say. "Even when he said nothing, you could feel him judging you." And that's just the good people talking about you.'[115] Marcus's great contemporary Lucian felt very similarly. 'They talk about being as happy as a king – but when you come to look at a king's life, you find that, quite apart from its insecurity and the so-called fickleness of fortune, it has far more pain than pleasure in it, if only because of the fear, anxiety, hatred, intrigue, resentment and insincerity that always surrounds a throne – to say nothing of all the sorrows, accidents and diseases which kings share with the rest of humanity.'[116] At a more philosophical level, Marcus frequently states that death is to be understood holistically, closing a process that is subordinate to the Whole; by the decay and passing away of its parts, the universe renews its youth. Once again we can see Marcus as a kind of forerunner of the Church Fathers, for an almost identical argument was used by St Augustine.[117]

Marcus evinces particular contempt for those who try to cling to life and go into denial about death. To fear death is like the child who was frightened of a mask he himself has made.[118] We should leave life with the same happy indifference with which we take leave of a banquet if a boorish guest arrives or the drink runs out. There is nothing objectively fearful about death; it is only our representations, false perceptions and value-judgements that make it appear so. Death cannot be evil, for otherwise the gods would have not permitted it; like honour and dishonour, wealth and poverty, pain and pleasure, it is just another of the 'indifferents', albeit more dramatic than most.[119] If the gods exist, the afterlife will be good. If they don't, or if the Epicureans are right in their deistic views and the gods have no interest in humans, why would you want to live in such a world, adrift rudderless on an ocean of godless nothingness, with no Providence to steer by? Besides, if you could sit in the seat of the gods, above the clouds, you would see how insignificant human life is.[120] Of the literally dozens of variations Marcus weaves on the 'welcome death as human life is meaningless' theme, let us select just three. 'Suppose that a God announced that you were going to die tomorrow "or the day after". Unless you were a complete coward, you wouldn't kick up a fuss about which day it was – what difference could it make? Now recognise that the difference between years from now and tomorrow is just

as small.'[121] 'Don't look down on death, but welcome it. It too is one
of the things required by nature. Like youth and old age. Like growth
and maturity. Like a new set of teeth, a beard, the first grey hair. Like
sex and pregnancy and childbirth . . . So this is how a thoughtful person
should await death: not with indifference, not with impatience, not
with disdain, but simply viewing it as one of the things that happen
to us. Remember how you anticipated the child's emergence from its
mother's womb? That's how you should await the hour when your
soul will emerge from its compartment.'[122] 'When we cease from
activity, or follow a thought through to its conclusion, it's a kind of
death. And it doesn't harm us. Think about your life: childhood,
boyhood, youth, old age. Every transformation was a kind of dying.
Was it so terrible? Think about life with your grandfather, your mother,
your adopted father. Realise how many other deaths and transform-
ations and endings there have been and ask yourself: was that so
terrible? Then neither will the end of your life, its ending and transformation, be terrible.'[123]

In all these formulations Marcus writes and thinks as a true Stoic.
He even links death to pantheism, and toys with the idea that one
might be reborn as a tree; at the very least we will fall into the Earth's
lap like a ripe olive.[124] Yet the sheer number of references to death
and the constant self-examination on this theme prompt the suspicion
that Marcus is protesting too much, that there is something about the
notion of extinction that troubles him deeply; it is no mere hyperbole
that has led one critic to speak of the emperor's 'metaphysical horror'.[125]
Without question, death obsessed Marcus far more than it ever did
Epictetus, who tended to take the idea of mortality in his stride and
was unconcerned about the traditional Platonic questions about where
the soul went. When Epictetus asserted that the end of life was simply
the last in a series of bugbears, he sounded convincing.[126] He considered that an unwillingness to die was mere selfishness, as human
immortality would clog up and overpopulate the Earth.[127] His attitude
to the Grim Reaper was always humorous, even jocular, whereas
Marcus was grave, po-faced and deadly serious. Where Epictetus was
content to take human life and death as he found them, and to use
the human condition to investigate ethical theory, Marcus, – fascinated
as he was with the vastness of the universe and with cosmological
issues – worried away about his relationship with the immensity of

eternity. His attitude was that of Lampedusa's Prince: 'O fixed star, when will you find me an appointment less ephemeral, in your region of perennial certitude.'[128] Where Epictetus is often a pre-echo of Spinoza, Marcus, in his attempt to make sense of cosmology *and* human morality, foreshadows Kant. There is the sensible world of perception, which depresses us with the numbers of stars in the heavens and the immensity of the universe; alongside this, humans may appear an insignificant speck. But there is also the intelligible world of reason, which reasserts the importance of human beings, stressing that moral laws – the Categorical and Hypothetical Imperatives in Kant's system – are just as impressive as the power, brilliance and profusion of the stars.[129]

Just as the pessimistic Marcus often takes over from the Stoic apologist in his broodings on human nature, so in his thoughts on death he seems unable to derive ultimate comfort from the dogmatic certainties of Stoicism. He returns again and again to the question of meaning, particularly in relation to the lives of the great and famous. At one point there is a catalogue of Roman heroes, including Camillus, Scipio, Cato, Augustus, Hadrian and Antoninus Pius – all very different, but all alike in that they no longer walk the Earth.[130] Augustus, Vespasian, Trajan and Hadrian were all supposedly 'great emperors in their time but are now no more'.[131] Marcus lists the famous conquerors and statesmen who are now dead: Philip of Macedon, Alexander the Great, Pompey, Julius Caesar. He always evinces particular contempt for Alexander the Great, perhaps to boost the claims of his hero Diogenes, and points out that both Alexander and his mule-driver alike were victims of mortality. At one point he jeeringly contrasts the conquerors Pompey, Caesar and Alexander with the far superior philosophers and thinkers of the Greek world – Heraclitus, Pythagoras, Socrates and Archimedes – but then remembers the canons of mortality and concedes that all alike have vanished into the maw of oblivion.[132] To lust after posthumous fame is mindless, because the people who do remember you die off in turn, and soon your name is known only to academic specialists and antiquarians. Besides, what is the point of trying to impress posterity; these are people we are never going to meet.[133] And what will their opinion be worth? The generations to come will also largely consist of fools, knaves and morons, so who would want their plaudits? No one understands death, and the only consistent wisdom is that no one gets out of here alive.

'Always remember how many doctors have died after furrowing their brows over myriad death-beds. Or how many astrologers after pompous predictions about the death of others. Or how many philosophers, after endless treatises on extinction and immortality. Or how many warriors, after inflicting thousands of casualties themselves. Or how many tyrants after systematic abuse of their power over life and death, as if they were immortal.'[134]

Given that human life is insignificant when viewed against the background of the universe, this alone should alert us to the pointlessness of ambition, the quest for fame and the lust for glory. Although he did not use the exact words, Marcus inculcated the message conveyed by two well-known axioms: 'Vanity of vanities, all is vanity' and 'All this too will pass away'.[135] This takes him to the depths of pessimism, as when he describes human life as 'The pointless bustling of processions, mere opera arias, herds of sheep and cattle, military exercises, a bone flung to pet dogs, a little food in the fish-tank; the miserable servitude of ants, the scampering of mice, puppets jerked on strings.'[136] We are all standing stalks of grain, which are grown and then cut down by the harvester.[137] The generations of men are simply leaves that the wind blows to the earth. 'Your children too are leaves, and it is mere leaves that applaud you or eulogise you, or who call down curses on you, sneering and mocking from a safe distance. Fame is simply a reputation handed down by other leaves, all destined to be blown away by the wind.'[138] Reflection on death led Marcus to a profound melancholy, which at times verged on nihilism. His more upbeat defenders claim that he is not unduly pessimistic, merely trying to get us to see how things are. Yet an obsession with how things really are, with brute contingency and mortality emphasised, does in the end lead to the pointlessness that Marcus so often describes. It is a gloomy form of materialism, eked out with some unconvincing flapdoodle about Providence, which provides no place for spirituality or creativity. The official Panglossianism of the Stoic doctrine finally unravels when Marcus ponders human mortality, showing his deep convictions triumphing over the philosophy of which he is officially an advocate.[139] If Marcus's death-fixated pessimism were taken seriously, it is difficult to understand how a Mozart or a Shakespeare could arise. Marcus suffers as much as Marx from tunnel vision, but with both looking from different ends of the tunnel.[140]

It is not surprising, then, that Marcus finds the Stoic doctrine on suicide a comfortable crutch. It will be recalled that the Stoics in general approved of suicide in the following circumstances: if the fatherland or your friends require you to do it; if a tyrant forces you to act dishonourably; if, afflicted by an incurable disease, the body is letting the soul down; if you are destitute or indigent; or if you go mad.[141] But those who considered themselves disciples of Socrates faced the difficulty that he opposed it, as in Plato's *Phaedo*. This particularly bothered Epictetus, whose remarks on self-slaughter are more than usually ambivalent: while allowing it in principle, he wanted to follow Socrates in permitting it only in exceptional circumstances.[142] Interestingly, Marcus was much more forthright in accepting *felo da se*: this may be because temperamentally he was more pessimistic than Epictetus and could see less point in life; or it may be because, as an emperor, as opposed to an abstract advocate like Epictetus, he actually faced the daily reality of having to refrain from 'inviting' his political enemies to open their veins. He makes it clear that all the great Roman heroes who took their own lives to escape tyranny – Marcus Brutus, Cato the Younger, Petronius and even Seneca (for whom he normally had little time) – acted rightly. Suicide was always justified as an escape route from insuperable moral evil, whether imposed from within or without; it is better to depart this life than live in evil.[143] Marcus also thinks that as one's mental faculties decay with old age, one may no longer be able to see clearly where duty lies; in these circumstances also the hot bath and the dagger beckon. He partly turns the tables on the ambivalent Epictetus here by quoting him, to the effect that one should leave a room if it it becomes full of smoke.[144] Yet above all suicide should always be a *moral* act. The life of liberty is the only true life, and when a good life is made impossible by the action of others, suicide becomes almost a moral duty; one should not lament if the impediment that thwarts moral activity is not one's fault.[145] It is always better to shuffle off the mortal coil than to live in evil; if you cannot escape from vice, departing this life means that you have at least performed one good act. 'What prevents you from being good and simple? Just resolve to live no longer if you are not. Reason does not demand that you should live if you lack these qualities.'[146]

It has often been alleged that people adhere to religion chiefly in the hope of achieving immortality, that the real function of religion is to allay fears and enhance hopes. Did the secular religion of Stoicism offer any such comfort to Marcus? Here we see again the gap that separates him from Epictetus, for the Greek philosopher has no interest in whether the soul survives, whereas for Marcus the subject is of consuming interest.[147] Most of the time he remains agnostic and remarks somewhat lamely that survival after death depends entirely on whether the gods think it necessary for cosmic order.[148] Seneca is certainly more optimistic and sanguine about the chances of posthumous survival than Marcus, though in no way more absorbed with the topic.[149] One Stoic idea was that only the true sage would be guaranteed personal survival, but then they faced the difficulty that probably no such person had ever existed; Marcus expressly and categorically denied that he could be considered a sage in the full Stoic meaning of the term. He also rebuked those who say that if the gods (or God) are both omnipotent and benevolent, they should have set it up so that the truly good people – those whose piety and good works brought them closest to the divine – survive to continue their benefactions.[150] These critics are in effect adumbrating a proto-Christian distinction between the blessed and the damned. Here Marcus gives the same answer as to the question of evil: 'If that's really true, you can be sure they would have arranged things differently, if that had been appropriate. If it were the right thing to do, they could have done it, and if it were natural, Nature would have demanded it. So from the fact that they didn't – if that's the case – we can conclude that it was inappropriate.'[151] It seems abundantly clear that personal survival is ruled out on the grounds of pantheism, if nothing else, and Marcus hints broadly that this is the case.[152] In the same passage he suggests that concern with survival in any case collided with the maxim that one should concentrate on the present; by definition such an approach ruled out anxiety about the future. Although it is fairly clear that Marcus did not believe in personal survival, he suggested that one should approach the issue in the spirit of a Pascalian *pari*: 'You boarded the ship, you set sail, you made the passage. Now it's time to disembark. If it's for another life, well, it's pretty clear there must be gods on the other side too. If to nothingness, just think, you no longer have to put up with pain and pleasure, or go on dancing attendance on this shattered hulk of a body – so much inferior to that which serves it.'[153]

Nowhere is Marcus's courage more evident than in his constant strivings to curb his natural pessimism and submit his gloomier forebodings to the judgement of Stoicism, rather in the way that the most courageous Christians are those who wage a lifelong struggle with doubt. His natural repugnance towards the physical world and his musings on death as a process of decay that compounds the existing filth and entropy make it hard for him to take Epictetus's laid-back stance and to convince himself that these 'inferior' manifestations are mere 'epiphenomena' that can be traced back to universal reason. Since he despairs of attaining either Plato's Republic or even real moral values, death is to be welcomed, though this posture is hardly orthodox Stoicism. The brave face he puts on is all the more to be applauded (except by cynics in the modern sense, who would see it as stupidity). 'Don't look down on death,' he exhorts himself, 'Say to death "Come quickly" before I start to forget myself.'[154] And again: 'Remember all the fine things you have seen; all the pleasures and sufferings you have overcome; all the motives for glory which you have despised; all the ingrates to whom you have been benevolent.'[155] There is a terrible poignancy about his valedictory message, placed right at the end of the very last book of the *Meditations*, where he imagines God as an impresario bringing down the curtain on an actor. 'But I've only performed three of the acts,' the actor protests. 'Yes,' says Marcus. 'This will be a drama in three acts, the length fixed by the power that directed your creation, and now directs your dissolution. Neither was yours to determine. So make your exit with grace – the same grace shown to you.'[156]

Marcus's original thoughts on the nature of God, evil and death show clearly that he is no mere parroting follower of Epictetus. Similarly he evinced originality in yet a fourth sphere, which Epictetus had adumbrated and expressed in inchoate form. The Greek sage asserted that a dutiful citizen of Rome should evolve beyond mere patriotism and treat his life as serving in God's army, since each person vis-à-vis God has been given the rank of senator for life in the imperial city; he added that anyone whose judgements on the world are fallacious stands in the same position as a military rebel to legitimate government.[157] Marcus took these sketchy thoughts and elaborated a more 'holistic' vision, incorporating politics, philosophy and cosmology, thus imposing his own trilogy in place of the traditional

Stoic triad of physics, logic and ethics. An important theme that appears in the *Meditations* for the first time in Book Five is the opposition between the court where he is obliged to live as an emperor and the life of philosophy to which he would like to devote himself entirely; Marcus proclaims himself as a dual man, at once the emperor and the man whose city is the City of the World. He 'solves' this disjuncture by a dialectical display of 'holism' that would have delighted Hegel.[158] He argues that Rome is the microcosm of the City, which in turn in the microcosm of the Universe, which means that, in principle, there should be no 'contradiction' between sage and emperor and that a philosopher-king is feasible. He adds that holism is one more reason for preferring an interpretation of the cosmos via Providence to the atomic vision of the Epicureans, since atoms imply disjuncture whereas Stoicism underlines unity and interpenetration.[159] Marcus is aware that when he speaks of the Eternal City, this could be read simply as a metaphor for Rome, but stresses that he is aiming at something more – something remarkably similar to St Augustine's City of God, itself an ur-version of Kant's Kingdom of Ends: 'mankind is a citizen of the highest city, of which other cities are like mere households'.[160] So: patriotism leads to love of our neighbour, which is like the marriage of Earth and Heaven, for the Earth loves rain, which comes from Heaven; and so what is good for Rome will ultimately be good for the cosmos. Holism stresses the fundamental unity of all things, a unity of which the sun, substance and the soul are three different manifestations; similarly universal Nature has made rational beings for the sake of one another, so that ethical perfection is possible. Yet it typifies the tension between the Panglossian element in Stoicism, of which Marcus was officially a practitioner, and his own pessimism that he ultimately declared the unitary project of Plato's Republic (or his own holism) to be an impossible dream – one more reason to welcome death.[161]

Yet it is not Marcus's original contribution to Stoicism of which he was, ironically to be the last major exponent that has won him the accolade of the ages, so that the *Meditations* always appears in any list of 'One Hundred Great Books'. John Stuart Mill thought the twelve books of reflections were the equal of the Sermon on the Mount, while Renan called them 'the most human of all books'. It is the pantheistic mysticism of Marcus that has had most resonance. One passage thought especially beautiful is the following: 'I say to the world: your harmony is mine. Whatever time you choose is the right time, neither too late nor too early. I say to Nature: Whatever the change of your seasons brings me is like the fall of ripe fruit. All things are born from you, exist in you and return to you.'[162] This has been compared to Thomas à Kempis's 'I am in Thy hand, spin me forward or spin me back.'[163] Still others point to passages on the sun that would have appealed to the later sun-worshipping emperor Julian the Apostate.[164] There are also those who construe certain obscure passages in Marcus's writings as evidence that he believed in spirits that walk the Earth – a common belief in the seventeenth century.[165] But the most fruitful source of analogies has been Eastern philosophy: the Bhagavad Gita, the Upanishads, Buddhism's Dhammapada and Lao-Tzu's Tao Te Ching, with their emphasis on meditation, the soul, detachment and renunciation.[166]

Marcus's critics say that he was a second-rate philosopher and a second-rate emperor and that, instead of trying to be a philosopher-king, he should either have abdicated to become a professional teacher of Stoicism or junked the philosophy and spent more time on imperial affairs. Many consider that he had a poor understanding of human nature, and that this was confounded by the 'impossibilism' of Stoicism; some conclude it would have been far better if he had never studied philosophy.[167] Moreover, the self-sufficiency taught by Stoicism did not encourage either wide administrative experience or exposure to a wide range of human beings.[168] Others say that he lacked the imagination to be a great ruler of Rome. His neglect of social and economic issues, and his seeming ignorance of social structure and socio-economic dimensions – given that his entire interest was focused on individual human psychology and motivation – put many of Rome's deep-lying problems beyond his ken.[169] Some go beyond this to say that Marcus has been over-rated as a writer. Where Pierre Hadot and others saw him as a poetic master, taking basic themes by Epictetus and providing them with a set of brilliant variations, rather like Brahms with Haydn or Vaughan Williams with Thomas Tallis, always using fresh imagery and never degenerating into stock metaphor or cliché,[170] the anti-Marcus faction has seen it very differently. Cynics in the modern sense claim that Marcus rams home the message about eternal repetition with an eternal repetition of his own; that he exhibits the worst fault of Dickens, whereby nothing can be left understated or allowed to speak for itself, but must be hammered home ad nauseam, often in the selfsame phrases. For such people, it is not just in content that the *Meditations* often resemble Indian philosophy; the notion of the mantra is here as well. Above all, it is said, Marcus is sometimes that worst of didactic creatures: the utter bore.[171]

The response to Marcus's thought and writing is bound to reflect the temperament of the reader; there is no point in disputing about taste, as the ancients said.[172] His greatness as a human being, though, is incontestable, and it comes down to two main propositions. Marcus had the very highest standards of integrity and responsibility; perhaps no man in history ever had a more elevated sense of duty. But as a Stoic emperor, he faced the problem that on the one hand he had to love mankind, but on the other he despised what they wanted and hated what they loved. He had to seek the happiness of his subjects in 'indifferents' – and he accepted that this was his duty – but recoiled from the mob's worship of things that had no value for him.[173] He tried to comfort himself with the thought that the gods also seemed lenient towards the human desire for 'indifferents,' as when they helped them through dreams and oracles.[174] Yet to encourage what one is convinced is 'false consciousness' is a hard furrow to plough; only the very greatest human geniuses can manage this. To put the false values of others before one's own, out of a sense of duty, is something very few individuals in history have ever compassed. The other obvious sign of Marcus's greatness was that he himself was a standing refutation of the famous dictum of Lord Acton: 'power tends to corrupt and absolute power corrupts absolutely.' Marcus had absolute power, but never used it for selfish, evil, despotic or corrupt purposes.[175] Unlike those who contrast the will of the people with their 'real will' or the 'General Will', Marcus never imposed his own world view on those who hankered after trivial pleasures like chariot races or gladiatorial contests, as so many authoritarian personalities (in modern history from Cromwell to Stalin) have done, even though he was convinced he knew what was best for his people.[176] Marcus had a duty both to the Roman people and to his beloved Stoics, but he fully lived out the meaning of whatever was best in that doctrine, while suppressing his own pessimistic doubts and never playing the dreaded role of the professor in politics.[177] The greatness of the *Meditations* is that they show us all his internal conflicts going on simultaneously.

II

The reign of Marcus Aurelius has often been seen as a watershed, and nowhere is this truer than in the realm of religion. In retrospect one can see his reign as one where Christianity began to triumph; to amend a famous phrase, it was not so much the beginning of the end for paganism, as the end of the beginning for those who worshipped a dead carpenter, as the new creed's enemies so contemptuously put it. Before AD 180 the dominant tradition in culture and religion was Greek; thereafter the Judaeo-Christian ethos gradually asserted its hegemony. Superficially, Christianity shared many points of similarity with Stoicism, for both belief systems taught that one should love one's neighbour, though the new religion founded this belief on a law of love, whereas for the Stoics charity was the logical corollary of the union of all things on Earth; the closer you got to wisdom and to God, the more you loved your neighbour.[1] The comparison of the moral struggle to the heat and dust that the athlete must endure in the arena, a common motif of Marcus and the Stoics, is found also in St Paul and Timothy and was, truth to tell, almost a cliché by the second century.[2] The Christians were in their own way as obsessed with death as Marcus: Jesus himself worried about death, while St Paul tells us that 'the wages of sin is death' and that 'the last enemy to be destroyed is death'.[3] One of the 'selling points' of Christianity was its promise of eternal life, and for many Christians death was an evil that could be overcome only by the Resurrection; the gulf that separates the sensibility of St Paul from that of Socrates, in, say, the

Phaedo, is a veritable crevasse and we should never construe Epictetus as a kind of parallel doctrine to the New Testament.[4]

This alerts us to the incontestable fact that the superficial similarities between men like Epictetus and Marcus Aurelius on the one hand and the Christian apologists Justin and Tertullian on the other conceal enormous differences. While it is true that the Christian apologists liked to defend themselves in terms taken from Greek philosophy and the Second Sophistic – indeed, Tertullian himself was once a Stoic – on all important points of doctrine the two creeds were poles apart. Stoicism had no time for a transcendent deity, was tougher and harsher (Nietzsche would never have described it as a religion for cowards) and would have found almost viscerally offensive the notions of the incarnation and of human imperfectibility and sin. Christianity, by contrast, rejected the immanent notion of God (except for some puzzling passages in St Paul), elevated faith over reason and spurned the Stoics' belief in mechanism, determinism, materialism and anti-individualism. Psychologically, Christians had the upper hand, as theirs was a belief more geared to fallible human nature: they linked cosmic love with the person of Jesus, giving the idea a stronger emotional appeal, and, like the devotees of Isis, introduced the concept of miracles to go alongside the notion of design and providential order that they shared with the Stoics.[5]

The history of early Christianity is a minefield for the historian. Alongside the perennial debate about the reliability of the Gospels as historical sources, there is a school of extreme scepticism that asserts that nothing whatever can be known about the Christians before the reign of Marcus Aurelius, and that the well-known sources in pagan writings are all later Christian forgeries or interpolations. Most sensational is the claim that there was no historical Jesus, that the assertion for his historicity was made only in the second century by revisionists who abandoned the earlier belief in a purely mythical figure.[6] However, scepticism about the classical pagan sources seems misplaced, since most of the alleged interpolations would serve no real purpose. The orthodox view, which we have no reason to dissent from, states that Christianity became a world religion in embryo when St Paul, sometime in the early 50s AD (but some say 49), won the battle to take the teachings (of what was then a Jewish sect) to the uncircumcised Gentiles.[7] Always a religion with a strong urban profile,

Christianity must have spread like a forest wildfire, for some ten years later it was sufficiently established in Rome to make it a target for imperial persecution. On 19 July 64 a Great Fire started in Rome and raged for six days, destroying much of the old city. It has always been thought that the emperor Nero played the arsonist, wanting to build a new Rome, and then scapegoated the Christians. As the historian Tacitus reported: 'Nero fastened the guilt . . . on a group hated for their abominations, called Christians by the populace. Christus, from whom the name had its origin, suffered the extreme penalty during the reign of Tiberius at the hands of . . . Pontius Pilate, and a most detestable superstition, checked for the moment, began to break out again not only in Judaea, the first source of the evil, but even in Rome.'[8] Tacitus tells us that the Christians were massacred in large numbers, either being burned alive on sacrificial pyres or exposed to wild beasts and packs of savage dogs in the arena.

The Great Fire of Rome, which undoubtedly took place, has been encrusted with powerful anti-Nero propaganda down the centuries, so that it is hard to get at the truth. One is tempted to think that arch-scepticism might have attended this event, just as much as early Christianity, but for a throwaway remark by Pliny the Elder.[9] Suetonius and Cassius Dio started the rumour that Nero gloatingly played a stringed instrument while Rome went up in flames, but even Tacitus – no friend to Nero – concedes that the emperor was at his country retreat at Anzio.[10] Until recently the combined weight of Tacitus, Suetonius and Dio has been enough to convince most historians that Nero really was the villain of the piece. Recent pyrotechnical and meteorological experiments, as well as archaeological data, open up the possibility that the conflagration was just as much an accident as the infernos in the reign of Vespasian and Titus. The most spectac-ular piece of revisionism is to the effect that Nero was right after all: the Christians really were the incendiarists. The theory is that a millenarian Christian sect, anticipating the imminent Second Coming, was over-impressed by a prophecy that Rome would fall on the day the dog-star Sirius rose in the sky; and since it rose on 19 July 64, they chose that day to usher in the kingdom of God by fire.[11] There are, then, at least four main hypotheses in the field: that Nero sent his men to burn down Rome secretly, instructing them to pretend to be drunkards who started fires accidentally; that he really did behave as in the traditional accounts and openly gutted the city; that the entire conflagration was an accident, and that in firestorm conditions the stone buildings of the aristocrats would not have afforded much more protection than the wooden hovels of the poor; and that the Christians were the true arsonists.[12] Of course, a mixed verdict is still possible: it is plausible that Nero got his henchmen to start the blaze, but that the Christians then joined in with gusto, thinking that the Second Coming was at hand.

Apart from a few enigmatic references in Josephus and the *Babylonian Talmud*,[13] the Christians then fade from pagan history until the reign of Trajan, although there were executions of individual members of the sect in the reign of Domitian. It would be incorrect to refer to 'persecution', since no general pogrom was instituted; what happened was that the emperor targeted a number of influential Christians whom he personally disliked.[14] Matters become clearer in the reign of Trajan, though even here the sceptics tend to deny the authenticity of key documents. Pliny the Younger, appointed in 110 at the age of forty-eight as governor of the troubled province of Bithynia and Pontus (in present-day modern Turkey), found himself deluged with complaints from the local Greek population and wrote to Trajan for guidance, explaining the actions he had already taken. Pleading ignorance of the general rules for punishing Christians, Pliny reported that he had instituted a rough rule-of-thumb. He asked the accused individuals if they were Christians, giving them a chance to recant and warning them that capital punishment lay ahead; if they persisted in their 'contumacity' and continued to assert that they were Christians, he ordered them led away to execution. In the case of Christians who were also Roman citizens, he ordered them gazetted for trial in Rome. Those who denied being Christians, whether through wrongful accusation or fear of the consequences, were given a simple test: they were asked to invoke the Olympian gods and make a sacrifice of wine and incense before a statue of Trajan; finally they were asked to revile the name of Christ. Some of the accused claimed that they had once been Christians, but were no longer believers. They reported that the 'unspeakable acts' of which they stood accused amounted to no more than meeting regularly before dawn on a fixed day to chant verses to Christ as if to a god, and to pledge themselves to avoid theft, robbery, adultery and the repudiation of honest debt.

Pliny ended his letter by asking for further guidance on how to proceed with this 'wretched cult'.[15]

Unwittingly, perhaps, Pliny had escalated Pagan–Christian conflict and set a dangerous precedent. The idea of making those accused of Christianity sacrifice to the Roman gods was something seemingly plucked from the air and their refusal was made the core offence. This meant that the penalty for Christianity was almost always death and was inflicted for the name alone. Neither the status of the accused in the Christian community nor any specific action committed by Christians was deemed relevant. Trajan either did not think the issue through or was bored with it, since he did not construe the new creed as a threat to the empire. He therefore endorsed and rubber-stamped Pliny's actions in the case of those hauled before him, but stressed that Christians were not to be sought out and persecuted.[16] But there were at least two major illogicalities in his judgement. If Christians were accused of specific crimes, the mere fact of their apostasy, which in itself should not have justified exemption for past criminal behaviour, was enough to see them freed. On the other hand, mere abstract advocacy or private belief was being punished by death, simply because Christians would not abjure the name of Christ and were thus deemed 'contumacious'. Even more spectacular was the second illogicality, as Tertullian pointed out. On the one hand, Christians were to be punished, implying guilt; on the other, they were not to be sought out, implying innocence.[17]

Pliny's correspondence with Trajan engenders all kinds of scholarly problems, quite apart from the issues already mentioned. It seems odd that he should plead ignorance of the correct procedures to be taken against Christians, and yet go on to say that he had had the recalcitrant ones executed. Even more problematical is that no one can be sure of the legal basis on which he did so. There is no surviving law, rescript or *senatus consultum* that formally declares Christianity to be a criminal offence, but Pliny's confident application of the death-penalty means that the religion must have been an illegal one.[18] The usual view is that the Christians were dealt with under general enabling criminal acts, such as the *cognitio extra ordinem*. This meant proper trials under Roman law, not police measures, though it is as well to be clear that the rule of law as we understand it did not exist in Roman society.[19] The crime of the Christians, in Roman eyes, has been variously interpreted. Some say that they were punished for specific *flagitia* or crimes, including incest and cannibalism; others that the refusal to sacrifice to the Roman gods was the problem. The religion's status as a so-called secret society has been mentioned as a key factor, as also its defiant stance as an illegal superstition. Still others claim that the Christians were punished for contempt of court or a more general defiance of Roman authority. Finding all these reasons for the illegality of the new creed unconvincing, a minority of scholars has claimed that there must already have been an overarching, specifically anti-Christian enabling act and have speculated that this would probably have dated from Nero's persecutions.[20]

Romans notoriously feared political clubs, cabals, any kind of secret society or esoteric group (*hetaira*) that could serve as a focus for opposition to the regime, which is why Trajan – at first sight oddly – turned down what looks like an innocent request from Pliny as governor of Pontus and Bithynia to form a fire brigade there.[21] Yet as a reason for hostility to the Christians, this alleged factor fails to convince. Pliny, who dealt with both pressure groups (*collegia*) and the Christians, never connected the two; moreover, the Christian apologist Tertullian expressly rejected the idea that this was the root cause of Roman persecution.[22] Indeed, Tertullian tried to turn this argument on its head by pushing the point that Christianity was not essentially different from other associations with an everyday familiarity in the Roman world: burial societies, cults of Mithras, temples of Isis, and so on.[23] We are on firmer ground in stressing the concept of *superstitio*: any religious belief that was alien or strange to the Romans. Before Christianity became a major issue, Tacitus had identified Judaism as the salient example of 'superstition' with which Rome had to contend, but Suetonius quickly added the new creed to the list.[24] Christianity seemed to strike at the very core of both pagan belief and Romanness itself, whether one looked at its contempt for the Olympian gods and for oracles or at its disdain for martial honour and renown. The Romans believed that social control and authority rested ultimately on religion – hence Pliny the Younger's campaign to encourage greater attendance at the pagan temples in Bithynia. For the Roman elite, regardless of the reality of their private beliefs (which may not have been quite as sceptical as has sometimes been thought, as we have seen in the case of Marcus),[25] denial of the traditional gods opened up the possibility of a chaos world and the dissolution of all norms, values and bonds, and hence the disappearance of all forms of social cement and control except force. Hence the fear of 'superstition'.[26] The issue of contumacy is also controversial. Some say that *contumacia* – disobedience, defiance of authority or contempt of court – is not the issue, but rather *obstinatio* – the pig-headed obstinacy of the Christians to make any concessions in their dogmatic beliefs and their refusal to bend to the prevailing wind.[27]

Yet if the alleged legal basis for Roman persecution of the Christians is sketchy or unclear, there can be no doubt about the general *reasons* why the Romans loathed and detested them. As the bonds of official religion loosened in the late second century, and men and women turned increasingly to magic, astrology and the mystery cults, so a backlash from Roman officialdom manifested itself, stressing the dangers of abandoning the Olympian deities. As long ago as Augustus's reign, his adviser Maecenas had said that new gods should always be resisted as they both offended the real (that is, Olympian) gods and seduced men and women into the alien habits of conspiracy, faction and secret society.[28] The Romans hated the new in any form, and in matters of religion they were particularly conservative, suspicious of innovation and mistrustful of all new religious ideas and practices.[29] Many considered that even pagan private cults weakened social cohesion and made people more selfish.[30] That is why the Roman authorities made it a point of policy that religion should permeate all levels of social life, and why even a drinking party had to be 'legiti-mated' by reference to Bacchus. It was not surprising, then, that a group that refused to have anything to do with the old gods was regarded as misanthropic and 'atheistic'.[31] The oriental religions did not deny the existence of other gods, even when they used formulae like 'There is but one God, Mithras.' What they meant was that Mithras was the most important deity and had assimilated the others; Christianity, by contrast, *literally* meant there were no others. This was perhaps the most important reason why the Romans perceived the Christians as a unique problem, uniquely contumacious and dangerous, and why the mere name of the religion was enough to consign its practitioner to the executioner's block.[32]

It is abundantly clear that the Christians were always regarded as a special problem, requiring special measures and special punishments;

they were not to be classed alongside Jews, Druids or Bacchantes. Why, it may be asked, was such favour shown to the Jews, who had in common with Christianity the embrace of an alien world view? Roman tolerance in this area is odd, for two reasons. In the first place, many Romans felt that the Jews promoted the dreaded and detestable notion of *superstitio*, and were indeed prime movers in this regard.[33] Second, there had already been, by the time of Antoninus Pius, two massive Jewish revolts, which had cost huge amounts of Roman blood and treasure to suppress. By contrast, there had never been a Christian rising, nor even so much as a Christian riot. By all laws of logic the Romans should have regarded the Jews, not the Christians, as Public Enemy Number One. Doubtless aware that they were on thin ice, the Jews often tried to distract Roman attention by foregrounding the Christian threat and instigating persecutions against them.[34] The Jews in any case hated the Christians as renegades who had appropriated the scripture and traditions of Judaism. Their smokescreen tactics seem to have been very successful, for many Romans confused the Christians with extremist Jewish sects like the Zealots or *sicarii* (dagger men). The empress Poppaea protected the Jews in Nero's reign and encouraged him to scapegoat the Christians instead.[35] Yet the emperor and his officials always sharply differentiated Jews from Christians, and many emperors expressly endorsed the right of Jews to observe their ancient religious customs.[36] Although Jews would not sacrifice to the emperor, they were prepared to sacrifice to their god *for* the emperor.[37] Moreover, they successfully plugged the line that their monotheism had a thousand years of history behind it, in which time it had never threatened state power (amazingly, they seemed to have convinced successive emperors that their two massive revolts had not been 'against Caesar'), so that they should be allowed to be the empire's 'licensed atheists': as Edward Gibbon put it, 'The Jews were a people who followed, the Christians a sect which detested, the religion of their fathers.'[38]

When the gap between traditional religion and the new Eastern cults opened up, Christianity's strength was that it both absorbed and transcended this trend, being in many ways a perfect emergent synthesis. But it was precisely this quality of overarching synthesis that drew Roman fire at so many levels simultaneously. In earlier eras *superstitio* had been a serious offence, not just because it encouraged the dread of the supernatural, credulous wonder and anxious credulity, but also because it opened the door to alien creeds. Even secret atheists like Cicero and Plutarch cynically thought that belief in the official religion was necessary for the masses, to promote social solidarity and ward off envy and discontent; they were in effect early believers in the 'opium of the masses'.[39] The hatred of Christian *superstitio*, however, had an extra edge. It was alleged to encourage groundless fear of the gods and to make people tremble with fear at the very thought of immortal deities. What was feared and hated could be rebelled against, for it was that precise emotion that Spartacus had harnessed in the great slave revolt of 73–71 BC. Since Christianity was allegedly a religion of slaves, it was thought to accentuate tensions between slaves and masters, as well as depressing the populace with gloomy thoughts about sorcery and the power of the supernatural; in all these ways, therefore, it was a threat to the social order.[40] For the Roman, Christianity was intolerable at every level: Christians refused to acknowledge other gods; they declined to sacrifice to the gods or the emperor; they worshipped a man who had been crucified as a political criminal; they refused to swear an oath by the emperor's name; they evinced bitter hatred of Rome, gloatingly prophesied the end of the world and gleefully looked forward to the destruction of the Eternal City in a holocaust.[41] The Roman public hated the exclusiveness, monotheism, truculence and arrogance of the Christians, which seemed to them to elicit the anger of the gods. There could never be any special pleading for a new dispensation, as there was for the Jews, with bogus claims that Christianity was a mere sect. It was avowedly and unapologetically a world religion, with all that implied. As has been well said, 'It is one of the unrecognised effects of Paul's later career that it caused Christians to be persecuted by Romans.'[42]

Naturally the ordinary Roman had other, baser motives for hostility to the Christians. There was the natural desire to dispossess them, to seize their goods or get them dismissed from jobs. Above all, they needed a scapegoat, and Nero had already demonstrated how easy it was to frame Christians. Scapegoating has been described as the process of singling out an arbitrarily selected 'other' whose destruction serves to concentrate minds, decant conflict in society into a single focus and thus re-establish social solidarity.[43] In the case of Roman society,

Christians were scapegoated for two main reasons: either to appease the mob angered by quite other causes; or to blame natural phenomena like droughts, plagues and famines on a sect that had allegedly angered the gods; 'there is no rain because of the Christians' was a common lament in drought-stricken areas.[44] Tertullian summed up well the mindset whereby the Christians were routinely blamed for everything: 'If the Tiber overflows, or the Nile doesn't, if there is a drought or an earthquake, a famine or a pestilence, at once the cry goes up: "Christians to the lions!"'[45] The visceral and mindless hatred provoked by the Christians cannot be exaggerated. One study of anti-Christian propaganda in the second century uncovers these descriptions of followers of Christ: 'scum', 'nothing but dung', 'lower-class, vulgar, ignorant', 'perpetrators of hypocrisy', 'gullible believers', 'babbling fools', 'charlatans', 'people who detest each other and fling abuse at each other', 'no better than dog or goat worshippers at their worst', 'people who go out of their way to insult the emperor'. As for Jesus himself, he was described as 'arrogant', 'an evil-doer', 'a sorcerer', 'a conspirator', 'a consorter with low-lives', 'a coward and a liar', 'an author of rebellion and insurrection'.[46] It is well known that to prepare the climate for persecution, pogrom or worse, one must first convince the masses that those being persecuted are vermin and not really human.

One of the things that worried thinking Romans was that the new religion provided a complete ideology with which rebels and dissidents could challenge the status quo: many risings in Rome's past had failed because of a sense of hopelessness among the rebels that things could ever really be otherwise. This was just one of many aspects of Christianity that made it superior to its rivals in the struggle for cultural hegemony in the second and third centuries. Although belief in astrology and magic was widespread and growing as the appeal of the Olympian deities faded, all such sects and religions were fundamentally pessimistic and death-obsessed.[47] The mystery cults, which particularly appealed to the elite, were backward-looking and stressed conservatism and conformity; unlike Christianity, they did not look forward to a messianic age in which the world would be transformed. The cult of Cybele was strong in the cities and among the upper classes, while that of Isis (originally regarded with suspicion by the authorities) appealed to freedmen and slaves; it had been free of persecution since the time of Tiberius.[48] Roman soldiers, who because of their pay and income did not slot easily into any formal class system, had their own religion, Mithraism, the easiest of the mystery religions to syncretise with the traditional Roman gods, less concerned with death than the Isis and Cybele cults – a genuine soldier's religion, but suffering from the ultimately fatal flaw that it excluded women. Christianity soon found ways to take the sting out of all three rivals. By the time of Marcus Aurelius's death, it was making considerable inroads into the ranks of the free soldiery.[49] Slaves and freedmen were deserting Isis to embrace Christ. It has even been speculated that in Apuleius's famous work *The Golden Ass*, written during Marcus's reign, the hero is converted to Isis as a propaganda ploy to assert the claims of the goddess against the increasing influence of Christianity.[50] Finally, in the third century Christianity would achieve its greatest ideological coup by transmogrifying the cult of Cybele, the Great Mother, into the worship of the Virgin Mary.

Christianity's promise of salvation and an afterlife made a particular appeal to two key groups: women and the have-nots. Even before Mariolatry became established as a pillar of the Church, women played a role in the Christian Church that went far beyond anything they could aspire to in any of the rival religions. The Gospel of Luke mentions several important female followers of Jesus, including Joanna, the wife of King Herod's steward, Susanna, Mary Magdalene and Salome, the mother of the two Zebedees. The Acts of the Apostles mentions the crucial back-up role played by women such as Tabitha (Dorcas), Lydia, Phoebe, Priscilla, Claudia and a Mary who is said to have done so much for St Paul. On their missionary travels Paul and Barnabas were accompanied by women who played the part of apostolic auxiliaries.[51] It seems that the domestic arena was a vital transmission belt for the spread of Christianity from the lower to the upper classes. Slaves told their aristocratic mistresses about the new doctrine, and it is significant that so many early Christians were aristocratic women – something that further enraged the mob, who relished the quasi-sadistic sexual thrill of seeing high-born ladies tortured and killed in the arena.[52] The importance of the conversion of oligarchic women can hardly be exaggerated. While a Roman matron usually had minimal influence on her husband, it was a different matter with their sons; women could inculcate Christianity in the nursery and thus produce believers in the next generation. It has been well said that the triumph of Christianity was also the greatest triumph of feminism in history.[53] The doctrine of love was clearly attractive, as was the contempt and disparagement of machismo and the martial ethos. Christian teaching was particularly critical of the notion of *philotimia* or love of honour, which it construed as mere vainglory. Women were drawn to the superior morality of the new creed: an early Church council in Spain decided that if any woman put her maidservant to death, she would be denied communion for years until she had purged her sin.[54] Also attractive to women was the Christian attitude to sexuality, which offered a relief from the rampant priapism of Roman society, amply evident from Artemidorus's dream studies.[55] The new Church emphasised that sex was primarily for procreation and frowned on fornication, adultery and all forms of sexual permissiveness. Although Christian leaders grudgingly accepted marriage, there was an increasing idealisation of virginity.[56] Sadly, the cult of virginity became the launch pad for an increasingly virulent misogyny among the early Church Fathers – an attitude that was already there in embryo in the teaching of St Paul.[57] It is one of history's great ironies that women, who enabled the early Christian Church to survive, were subsequently downgraded as second-class citizens. Real women tended to be regarded as actual or potential whores, while the feminine principle was hypostasised and decanted into the ideal personage of the Virgin Mary.[58]

It was a common slur in Roman propaganda that Christianity appealed to the stupid and moronic. 'For hysterical women, children and idiots' was the mantra of the vehement anti-Christian Celsus, who added the refinement that the doctrine was perfectly designed to appeal to females with just enough education and culture to be attracted to it, yet not enough to be able to see through it; thus did he anticipate Alexander Pope's diatribe on 'a little learning' by 1,500 years.[59] The 'religion of slaves' tag has encouraged the idea that early Christianity was entirely a religion of the have-nots, attracted by the Gospel message that the first shall be last and the last first in the kingdom of heaven. Undoubtedly it had an appeal for slaves, working men and the so-called *canaille* that no other creed could match, but there were converts in all the social strata, and it is probably more accurate to see the lure of Christianity in the realm of 'relative deprivation' than among the outright poor and needy; in other words, it attracted those disgusted by the conspicuous consumption of the rich and powerful, their venality and corruption, cruelty and harshness – the very people likely to be alienated as class divisions became more rigid towards the end of the second century and social mobility appreciably lessened.[60] As for slaves, the Christians were not against the idea in principle and tended to keep slaves in their station; theirs was certainly not a doctrine of liberation from quotidian bondage.[61] That Christianity had a powerful proletarian profile and was persecuted has led some historians to draw analogies with those modern communist parties in a tiny minority in Western societies; the idea was particularly popular with the early Marxists.[62] Leftist theologians too have been fascinated that the early Christians practised a form of primitive communism; the idea is that socialism must be 'right' since that is what the disciples turned to immediately after receiving the grace of the Holy Spirit. Certainly one can see vague parallels with Christianity under Marcus Aurelius and communists in the United States in the 1950s (with the obvious difference that no one was executed in the latter case for the mere name). And there are other interesting similarities. Both creeds believed in the Second Coming, the Christians literally, the communists figuratively – their *parousia* would be the communist society achieved after the interim of the dictatorship of the proletariat, when absolute equality and nil division of labour would hold sway. Yet revolutionary as communism was in the twentieth century, it could hardly match early Christianity for originality. Marxism was firmly and clearly rooted in the ideas of the Enlightenment, whereas Christianity seemed to come from nowhere, with no precedents or counterparts in pre-existing religion or philosophy.[63]

After Trajan, Christians continued to be harassed intermittently for the mere name. All that was required to sustain a charge of Christianity was an informer (*delator*) and a sympathetic governor who would demand admission of the name and recantation; those refusing in open court would be executed, either by beheading if the accused was of superior social class, or by being crucified or exposed to the wild beasts in the case of an artisan or proletarian.[64] Pliny's entirely adventitious system of 'proof' – sacrificing to the pagan gods – became the gold standard by which successive provincial governors operated.

Naturally the system was abused in more ways than one. Not all Christians relished a martyr's death, and some got round the necessity of sacrificing to Jupiter or the emperor by sending their slaves to do it for them (and presumably risking the obvious danger of blackmail). Others simply fled the territory, became outlaws or went to live in the desert. But most simply bribed their way out, suborning court officials, the informer or even the governor himself, much to Tertullian's disgust.[65] Bringing trumped-up charges was an obvious racket, and the scapegoating of Christians for matters with which they had not the slightest connection was routine; Apuleius was brought to trial in Sabratha in North Africa in 158–9 and immediately entered the defence that his accusers were Christians.[66] The emperor Hadrian became severely irritated with this knee-jerk ploy by malefactors. He issued a rescript stressing that all accusations against Christians must be watertight. If it was proved that they had performed criminal or unlawful acts, well and good; but he was not prepared to entertain mere clamour, outcry or hearsay, and woe betide the informer who was found to have brought a gratuitous and slanderous accusation; in that case the full force of the law would be visited on the person bearing false witness. Hadrian was thus a net protector of the Christians, since he not only protected them against slander and wrongful arrest (insisting that the law, not the mob, must decide the issue), but also demanded that there must be cast-iron proof, even when someone accused a Christian of the name. Thereafter a governor would not normally take action until the *delator* was prepared to prosecute personally and thus run the risk of malicious prosecution.[67]

Antoninus Pius had little to do with the Christians, apart from considering the question of the responsibility of this new sect for the plethora of natural disasters that hit the empire during his reign.[68] By the time Marcus Aurelius came to the throne, the battle-lines between the ideologies of paganism and Christianity were drawn up so tightly that no compromise seemed possible. We shall consider first the ferocity of the pagan propaganda onslaught and then the Christian reply. The most noteworthy anti-Christian ideologists were, in descending order of hostility, Celsus, Porphyry and Galen. Celsus wrote his diatribe *The True Word* sometime between 170 and 180, so that his arguments would have been very well known to Marcus. He starts with the proposition that tradition is sovereign, that old-time religions

are always superior and that the very oddness and newness of
Christianity represent a strike against it. The new creed is a break with
all the antique cultural and religious traditions of the human race,
stretching back to the Golden Age. Celsus makes it clear he is 'rela-
tivistic' in the sense that he recognises that all cannot worship the
Olympians, that each nation and culture has its own peculiar ancient
laws; all this is fine as long as we are still in the area of the traditional,
which means polytheism.[69] It is true that the Jews introduced
monotheism with Moses, but theirs is still an ancient belief, hallowed
by custom and habit. Celsus has no time for the Jews – 'runaway slaves
who have never done anything worth mentioning' – but at least Judaism
is legitimated by antiquity. The Christians claim that they are the
proper realisation of Judaism while rejecting core Jewish customs and
laws on circumcision, diet, festivals and keeping the Sabbath.[70] They
cannot have it both ways: either they are a new sect with no relation
to Judaism, or they are a cousin of the Jewish faith, in which case they
are not entitled to take a pick-and-mix approach to its doctrines. Even
some Christians acknowledged that this was a telling point.[71] Judaism
was a nationalistic sect, with no claims to universifiability, but
Christianity claimed to be a world religion; it was thus both implicitly and explicitly a threat to the Roman empire and to social stability
in general: implicitly because of its dogmas, and explicitly because it
proselytised. Judaism was compatible with paganism since both
practised sacrifice; Christianity emphatically was not.[72]

The issue of the Jews aside, for Celsus it was an axiom that only
the old, the ancient and the antique could ever inform true religion.
Himself a Platonist, he argued that anything good in Christian doctrine,
such as turning the other cheek, was already in Plato, who had been
shamelessly pillaged by half-wits with no understanding of Plato and
Aristotle.[73] The old is the venerable and the venerable is the true is a
quasi-syllogism that is often found in Latin literature. Cicero argued
that in ancient times people were closer to the gods – one reason why
the republic would always be superior to the empire. Plato too argued
that 'the ancients are better than we for they dwelt nearer to the
Gods'.[74] There is an ancient *logos* that all civilised nations – Egyptians,
Assyrians, Persians, Indians – agree on.[75] Some Christians who felt
uncomfortable about their religion's originality liked to answer Celsus
with the Judaic card, arguing that Moses was older than Plato.[76] Celsus

would have none of this and claimed that the new creed severed the bond between religion and nation, creating a counter-culture that threatened social stability: once you start questioning the established gods, you can proceed to question other 'fixed' things about the status quo. Christianity in effect aimed to 'privatise' religion (just as Catholics in the sixteenth century saw the Reformation as a privatising of Christianity). For Celsus, once you overthrow traditional teaching you must needs embrace the chaos principle. There would be 'nothing to prevent the emperor from being abandoned, alone and deserted, while all the good things of the earth came into the possession of lawless and savage barbarians'.[77]

Having, as it were, demonstrated to his own satisfaction the *a priori* absurdity of Christianity, Celsus then attacked the personality of the Christians themselves, condemning them as morons, purveying a lowest-common-denominator creed that appealed to slaves and the lower classes, while thumbing its nose at Rome by refusing public office and military service.[78] He appealed to a deep Roman snobbery by asking rhetorically how the thoughts of cobblers and weavers could be put in the same class as the ideas of learned philosophers. This aligned with the deprecating comments of Epictetus, who said that Christians could face death fearlessly because they emphasised the irrational over reason and were childishly ignorant.[79] Christians were both natural rebels (not surprisingly, since their leader was executed as a political criminal) and a natural prey to charlatanry, to say nothing of their consorting with demons and practising black magic, which made them no better than the begging priests of Cybele, the bone-headed followers of Mithras, the Bacchantes or the purveyors of Egyptian superstitions.[80] Their adherents, workers in wool and leather, fullers and tanners and the like, made a point of getting contracts to work in private houses and then corrupting the young of the absent aristocrats while they were there.[81] Celsus made the same criticism of Christians as the middle classes made of hippies in the twentieth century: they were people who wanted all the advantages and privileges of civilisation, but none of the burdens and duties.[82] Their doctrine of salvation carried the detestable consequence that the thief, the robber, the burglar, the poisoner and the blasphemer would all be saved along with the virtuous. The stupidity of Christians was evident from a number of pointers, quite apart from their verifiable lack of higher education. They claimed that their superior intellect made them contemptuous of idolatry, but such a claim simply demonstrated their abysmal ignorance; the merest child in Rome knew that idols were symbols, not the gods themselves; the Christians were too stupid to be able to differentiate the naturalistic and symbolic worlds.[83] Their 'atheism' consisted in setting up a 'church' that diverted allegiances that should properly be the state's, and in worshipping a man (Jesus) instead of a god, thus building up a mere man at the expense of the gods.[84] Despite the contrary proposition maintained by the Christian evangelists,[85] one could not differentiate the realm of God from that of Caesar for that meant serving two masters – a house divided against itself must fall – quite apart from the absurdity of worshipping both God *and* his servant. Not only were Christians building up a man (Jesus) at the expense of God, but since he was dead, they were committing the ultimate blasphemy of worshipping a corpse.[86]

Thence Celsus proceeds to a dithyrambic attack on the personality of Jesus – and it is interesting that at no point in his catalogue of crimes does Celsus suggest that Jesus was anything other than an historical personality. He sought to explain him mainly by an extrapolation from the notorious personality of Alexander of Abonoteichos. Interestingly, Celsus does not deny that Jesus performed miracles, but he wants to know: by what power? The answer is predictable: Jesus was a master magician and illusionist, trained in Egypt in the black arts.[87] This novel slant on the flight into Egypt gives Celsus the chance to launch a major attack on Jesus's mother Mary. It is plain, says Celsus, that the story of the Virgin Birth is nonsense; what actually happened was that Mary was a poor spinner who committed adultery with a soldier called Panthera and was then kicked out by her carpenter husband.[88] When she gave birth to her illegitimate son, he went to Egypt and learned magic and prestidigitation. This is the basis for all the exorcisms and miracles related in the Gospels, especially that of Mark.[89] But other people can do similar tricks, so what exactly entitles Jesus to claim the accolade of Son of God?[90] The whole story of Jesus thereafter is a mishmash of different traditions. Jesus was essentially an intellectual scavenger who got the best of his eclectic ideas from Plato and the Greeks. However you look at it, the Christian version of Jesus makes no sense. God seems to have given two contradictory sets of laws, one to Moses and the other to Jesus. Which is right? If Jesus is right, then God must be an incompetent bungler, for what could he have been thinking of when he handed Moses the tablets on Mount Sinai some thousand years earlier? It is no use saying that he might have changed his mind; we are supposedly talking about an omniscient being.[91] Meanwhile Jesus is supposed to be the true heir of the Judaic tradition, yet the Jews do not accept him as a Messiah.[92] The worship of Jesus not only works against the supposed monotheism of Christianity, but is in every sense an unworthy devotion, as Jesus did nothing that made him worthy of worship as a divine being: Jonah and Daniel had better claims as objects of worship.[93] Celsus's best point here is the one about monotheism; this worried his great critic Origen, who replied that it was obvious that Jesus was subordinate to God.[94] Origen of course wrote before the famous council of Nicaea in 325, which announced the dogma of the Trinity and condemned Origen's views as heresy. That Celsus had touched a raw theological nerve here is clear from the famous disputes at the Council of Nicaea about *homoousia* and *homoiousia*.[95]

Finally Celsus prepares for his tour de force: a no-holds-barred attack on the Christian doctrines of creation, original sin, redemption and the Incarnation, as well as the Crucifixion and Resurrection, all of which he sees as obvious anthropomorphic nonsense. Most of his remarks about the Crucifixion rise no higher than knockabout farce; for him, it is simply against the law of nature that someone both poor (a carpenter) and a victim of crucifixion (the type of death-penalty reserved by the Romans for the 'lowest of the low') could be divine. A typical passage showing Celsus in action uses ridicule and irony to pour scorn on the Crucifixion, suggesting that the whole idea of death on a wooden cross arose in the first place only because Jesus was a worker in wood. 'So that if he had happened to be thrown off a cliff, or pushed into a pit, or suffocated by strangling, or if he had been a cobbler or stonemason or blacksmith, there would have been a cliff of life above the heavens, or a pit of resurrection, or a rope of immortality, or a blessed stone, or an iron of love, or a holy hide of leather. Would not an old woman who sings a song to lull a little child to sleep have been ashamed to whisper such tales as these.'[96] The Resurrection story is a staple of all myths, yet the Christians have the audacity to expect us to believe that on this one occasion it actually happened. But why is it a narrative at any higher level of reliability than the stories about the Greeks and the Trojans, Oedipus and Iocasta and all the other myths? The chief witness turns out to have been a hysterical female (Mary Magdalene), 'half crazy from fear and grief, and possibly one other of the same band of charlatans who dreamed it all up or saw what they wanted to see – or more likely simply wanted to astonish their friends in the tavern with a good tale'.[97] Besides, the story is a philosophical impossibility. The Christians like to parrot that with God all things are possible, but even God cannot subvert reason and Nature and, if he were able to do so, would in any case not be a suitable object of veneration.[98] If God was not bound by the laws of nature, he would not really be God, but a demon or demiurge, since the entire universe would be governed by principles of chaos.[99]

But Celsus saves his supreme Platonic contempt for the doctrine of the Incarnation. What was the point of this? The Christians say that God needed to know what was going on among humans. But if he was omniscient, why did he not know? The Incarnation for the purposes of redemption is likewise gobbledegook. If an omnipotent God wanted to achieve the moral reformation of humanity, why did he not do so by a simple exercise of willpower?[100] As for redemption, what about all the innumerable people who lived before he was incarnated? Don't they count, or did God simply not care before the Christian era?[101] Whichever answer we give, it will not satisfy Christian doctrine. Maybe God is not omnipotent, omniscient or benevolent, or maybe he possesses at most two out of the three attributes? Whatever the case, he emerges as the kind of arbitrary and capricious deity that only morons could believe in.[102] And how exactly can an immortal being – by definition immutable and eternal – enter space and time, and undergo change and alteration to live as a human being? Yet Celsus's most powerful argument derives from his own Platonism. The Platonic system involves progression from perception through mathematics to a realm of perfection, from particulars to universals, from substances to Forms, from matter and the physical world to the spiritual and the world of Ideas, from imperfection to perfection. The doctrine of the Incarnation, by contrast, is literally preposterous, since it envisages a descent from perfection to imperfection, a breach of the Law of Nature as fundamental as postulating that Time could flow backwards.[103] To descend from a realm of perfection to one of quotidian imperfection flies in the face of all known philosophy, not just Platonism, but Buddhism and the wisdom of the East, which similarly stresses the ascent to higher and higher levels of Being. It would be an especially impossible progression for an immortal entity.[104]

Similar Neoplatonist contempt for Christianity was voiced by the third-century thinker Porphyry in the course of ploughing his own furrow, which was essentially to move Neoplatonism away from the abstract form in which it was couched by his teacher and mentor Plotinus – in which guise it attracted many Christians – to a more mystical, supernaturalist species of metamathematics essentially going back to Pythagoras.[105] For such a man, Christianity was a particularly deadly enemy, and he added to the arsenal of anti-Galilean propaganda so loathingly assembled by Celsus. Like Celsus, Porphyry spent a lot of time jeering at the career and perceived failure of Jesus himself. He shares Celsus's disgust with the idea of making a convicted criminal a god – in itself proof that the Christians are traitors and a fifth column in the empire's midst.[106] He adds to Celsus's slanders against Mary the Mother of God by claiming that Jesus was the son of an insignificant woman named Miriam who was raped and impregnated by a Roman soldier, whom he too identifies as one Panthera; Jesus's illegitimacy, he claims, is obvious even from the work of Mark the Evangelist.[107] Yet Porphyry's main target is not Jesus himself. He dissents from the Celsus view that Jesus was a magus, wizard or sorcerer; he really was a great, good and wise man, though naturally not God. It is St Paul, the evangelists and especially St John who are Porphyry's main targets, as these are the people who tried to incorporate Neoplatonic ideas as an adjunct to Christianity.[108] Jesus, he says, was no fanatic since he accepted the syncretism of the Roman and Jewish religions with local gods, saw some virtue in the Roman view of religion as a *social* activity and generally took a 'laid-back' attitude to the Romans.[109] He even showed himself very human, both in his despair in the Garden of Gethsemane and in his meekness towards his accusers. The real problem is not Jesus, but the zealotry of his followers.

If Porphyry is just as contemptuous as Celsus, while more detached and less emotional,[110] the third important critic of Christianity, the great physician Galen, is more nuanced. Having studied Philo and Josephus and been influenced by a Hellenised Jew while in Rome, Galen was more sophisticated, broad-minded and insightful than the other pagan critics. He does not have the obsession with the personality of Jesus shared by the other two, or their detestation of the content of the religion and its form of worship, but is more concerned with logical and moral issues. There is, he says, no *a priori* reason to regard Christianity as a 'detestable superstition'; the problem for him is that the creed does not meet his high standards of scientific and logical explanation, because its adherents are blinkered by 'faith'; for this reason it is a waste of time to try to argue with a Christian – they always know the answer they are going to arrive at before they start 'debating'.[111] Where the Christians claimed that whatever is good in paganism is an adumbration of the truth of Christianity, Galen is emphatic that whatever is good in Christianity is already there in paganism. Christians work from an infantile misunderstanding of the nature of the deity. As a faithful follower of Plotinus, Galen believed in the Neoplatonist trinity (not to be confused with the much later and very different Christian dogma of the Trinity) of the One (roughly God), Nous (Spirit or Demiurge) and Soul. Galen praises the wisdom and power of the Demiurge and (in a sly hit at his patron Marcus Aurelius) says that real piety means praising Nous or Spirit for his work in creating the universe, not sacrificing hecatombs of oxen.[112] For Galen, as for Plotinus, the universe is a complete work of art, and the demiurge is responsible for beauty and for art in the cultural sense (the statues of Phidias, for example), just as much as for ugly things; it was the fallacy of the Gnostics to make the demiurge responsible only for matter and evil.[113]

Even granting Judaism and its offshoot Christianity every latitude, it is impossible not to fault their simple-minded Mosaic cosmogony (the biblical story of the creation) on the basis of Aristotle's Four Causes.[114] The long and the short of it is that Plato, Aristotle and Plotinus are immensely superior intellectually to anything produced by Judaism or its bastard offspring Christianity. The idea that God could create out of nothing was a doctrine that particularly irked Galen for its naivety. This was unscientific and ignorant, and the only home for progress in human knowledge lay with science and logic: 'Could we live a life three times as long as our present one, even then we would not know everything accurately, so obscure are the facts.'[115] The idea that 'faith' could reveal the truth was stunningly obtuse, no more advanced than the mentality of a child believing in fairy tales. The critics loathed the Christian mantra 'with God all things are possible'[116] – regarded as already a hoary old cliché in the second century. The impossible is a logical category – you cannot have a round square – and the impossible remains so in spite of God's alleged omnipotence. The Christians cling to the idea of a God who can reverse the laws he has imposed on his own creation, since this is the only way they can smuggle in the absurd doctrine of the Resurrection, which certainly deserves all the abuse it has received: 'What sort of human soul would still crave for a rotten body?'[117] Nonetheless, Galen does not find Christianity totally negligible, as Celsus does. Three things impress him: the Christian contempt for death, their concern for the broad mass of humanity, as against the elitism of the Stoics, and their morality, especially in the sexual sphere. Galen did not share Celsus's contempt for the unwise, foolish and wretched of the Earth, pointing out that all the main currents in Greek philosophy emphasised the importance of the moral education of the average man. Aristotle's *Nicomachean Ethics* had made this the central concern, while even Plato, sometimes regarded as the ideal-type of elitism, moved away from concern with the Brahmin-style class of Guardians in the *Republic* to the concerns of the common man in *The Laws*.[118] Christianity was to be admired for taking a similar line. Moreover, Christians were to be commended for having so successfully invented tales of an afterlife which, together with a belief in miracles, raised their moral standards to a higher level: 'For their contempt of death and of its sequel is obvious to us every day, and likewise their restraint in cohabitation. For they include not only men but also women who refrain from cohabiting all their lives; and they also number individuals who in self-discipline and self-control in matters of food and drink and in their keen pursuit of justice have attained a pitch not inferior to that of general philosophers.'[119] Galen praised the Christians for possessing the three cardinal virtues of valour, temperance and justice – which meant they had attained moral virtue – but their weakness was that they had not achieved self-realisation based on philosophical knowledge.

Most pagan propaganda, however, was not at the level of Galen, Porphyry or even Celsus, who all started from a Neoplatonic standpoint. The two great writers of the reign of Marcus Aurelius, Lucian and Apuleius, contented themselves largely with knockabout farce and easy one-liners of the sort that would appeal to the groundlings. In Apuleius's *Golden Ass* the baker's wife appears at a signal disadvantage largely because she has converted to Christianity: 'She scorned and spurned the gods of heaven, and in place of the true religion she professed some fantastic, blasphemous creed of a God whom she named The One and Only God. But she used her deluded and ridiculous observances chiefly to deceive the onlooker and to bamboozle her wretched husband; for she spent the morning in boozing and lent out her body in perpetual prostitution.'[120] Lucian's *Peregrinus* is the biography of a Cynic philosopher who for a time in his early life embraced Christianity. In reality a charlatan whose concern was not with truth, but with applause, renown, money and the pursuit of loose women, Peregrinus Proteus – phoney evangelist and 'shyster', an obvious forerunner of Sinclair Lewis's Elmer Gantry – was taken up by the Christians as a wise teacher, a true prophet who could interpret Christ to them. When he was imprisoned in Asia for Christianity, his Christian followers brought him food, bribed the guards to let them enter his cell and confer with them, and even held sacred meals and services with him inside the jail. All over Asia Minor Christians put themselves out to protect and cherish him; meanwhile he persuaded them to give him large sums of money for his legal defence. 'The poor wretches have convinced themselves,' writes Lucian:

> first and foremost that they are going to be immortal and live for all time, in consequence of which they despise death and even willingly embrace it – most of them at least. Furthermore their first lawgiver (Christ) persuaded them that they are all brothers of one another after they have transgressed once ... Therefore they despise all things indiscriminately and consider them private property, receiving such doctrines traditionally without any definite evidence, so if any conman or trickster, able to profit by this, comes among them, he quickly acquires sudden wealth by imposing upon these simple folk.[121]

Peregrinus was released by the governor of Syria and promptly abandoned Christianity, decamping with a sack of money. Lucian's point was that charlatans can be imposed on by other charlatans: 'great fleas have little fleas upon their backs to bite 'em, and little fleas have lesser fleas and so ad infinitum'.[122]

12

The Christian counterblast was powerful, though it is doubtful whether it did much to convince hostile critics. The two most influential ideologists of the new creed were the early Church Fathers Justin Martyr and Tertullian, two men in other respects as unlike as could be.

Born in Palestine in the year 100, Justin was something of a fanatic who invented large slabs of the Christian tradition on his own and was convinced that the Second Coming or *parousia* was imminent. Using Genesis (6.2) as his inspiration, he moved theology away from Jewish monotheism towards something like the later Manichaean view of the world as divided into principles of good and evil – an idea already adumbrated by the Gnostics. Justin forged the legend that the prince of darkness, Satan, and his demons had originally been good angels, and the primordial name of the Evil One was the archangel Lucifer, the bringer of light. In later versions of the story of the celestial fall (as in Milton), Lucifer was cast out of heaven for disobedience or rebellion. Justin's version, however, was that Satan and his followers had been deposed for having sexual relations with the daughters of men; Justin called them *angeli fornicatores*.[1] The Miltonic version of rebellion was invented later to get round the obvious difficulty that, if Justin's account was correct, Satan as a prince of darkness could not then have been present in the Garden of Eden to tempt Eve – for at that time there were no other 'daughters of men'. Justin's dualism raised obvious difficulties for the notion of a benevolent and omnipotent God, and it is surprising that Christianity took it up with such alacrity. Even odder was that Justin posed as a man who would unite the Greek and Hebrew traditions, yet in traditional Greco-Roman thought there had never been any necessary association of ideas between demons and the concept of evil.[2] But Justin argued that if God produces only good, the evil in the world must come from demons. Moreover Justin, less dishonest than later theologians, accepted duality at many different levels (there is almost something 'dialectical' in the way he suggests that damnation and salvation come by the same route, which is why Mary is the apotheosis of Eve)[3] and accepted that Christ as the *logos* was a quite different person from the smiting Yahweh of the Old Testament who appeared to Moses and the prophets. Sadly, he was very confused on this point and seems to have thought that the *logos* was a kind of 'son' (whatever that might mean) of the deity, who was 'begotten' shortly before the creation of the universe.[4] The explanation may well be that Justin, anticipating the later doctrine of the Trinity, tried to have it both ways: the *logos* was a unity with God the Father while being a distinct personality. In this sense the later heresy of Arianism was much more lucid. Justin's thought was always a muddled mishmash, with elements drawn from Middle Platonism, Stoicism and the Judaism of Philo. It has been well said that Justin was 'a poor writer, a confused thinker and no philosopher'.[5]

Nonetheless, he was no slouch as a propagandist. He famously addressed his *First Apology* to the emperor Antoninus Pius in the early 150s. He appealed to the emperor and his advisers as men of learning, and argued that Christians should not be condemned for the name alone. He reminded the imperial court of the precedents of Trajan and the letter sent to Silvanus Gravianus, insisting on proper proof when charges were brought against followers of the Galilean saviour. Christians, he argues, should not be victimised, since they are loyal, law-abiding payers of tribute and taxes; they pose the least threat of any minority to Roman rule since their kingdom is not of this world.[6] But Justin saves his best efforts for his argument that Christ is divine and his coming the fulfilment both of possibilities latent in Greek philosophy and of ancient prophecies in Judaism. Justin draws heavily on Platonism to buttress his arguments, and argues that it was the study of Greek philosophy that led him to Christianity and made him the most important Hellenist in the development of the religion since St Paul.[7] Yet much of first *First Apology* is given over to the thesis that Christianity is not something totally new and original, but simply a development of Judaism. The idea of the Messiah, the Virgin Birth, Bethlehem as Jesus's place of birth, the destruction of Jerusalem (which had occurred in AD 70) and the acceptance of the new creed by the Gentiles can also be found in the Old Testament prophets.[8] Christians expect personal immortality, divine reward and the final destruction of evil, but what of it? Where is the harm for the Roman state in these aspirations? As for the standard accusations of cannibalism, incest and atheism brought against the Christians, these are mere nonsense, based on a misunderstanding of the Eucharist and the kiss of peace, or disingenuously attributed to Christianity when they were in fact aspects of other, much more esoteric cults; baptism and the Eucharist themselves were simply harmless reminders of Christ.[9] The Christians were accused of 'atheism' because they did not believe in the Olympian deities, but on that basis most of Rome must be atheist; Jupiter and his myrmidons were denied by philosophers, laughed at by satirists and largely ignored by the common man. Why should Christians alone have to bear the charge of atheism? Was it not simply a bogus excuse used to whip up the mob against them as scapegoats? Of course there might be a few bad apples among the Christians, just as there are charlatans and impostors in every philosophical school, but Justin is confident that no true Christian could ever be found guilty of a genuine crime, beyond the absurd 'criminality' of professing the name.[10]

Not content with his audacious identification of Christ with the Neoplatonist secondary deity, the Demiurge or Nous – which would make him a suspect figure when Christianity was systematised after the Council of Nicaea in 325 – Justin tried to appropriate Greek philosophy entirely by claiming that Socrates himself was in fact a Christian *avant la lettre*.[11] Above all, Justin based his case for the new creed on its superior morality. He cited the Sermon on the Mount, the Christian belief that human life is sacred, their famous concern for and love of children, their pacifism, turn-the-other-cheek compassion, philanthropy and lack of hatred even when persecuted to emphasise the role of the Law of Love as the apogee of morality, entailing truth, purity, generosity, humility, courage, patience, universal love and absence of racial prejudice. Their high standards in sexual morality were exemplary, and maybe this was what so angered their pagan critics.[12]

> Those who once rejoiced in fornication now delight in continence alone; those who made use of magic arts have dedicated themselves to the good and unbegotten God; we who once took most pleasure in the means of increasing our wealth and property now bring what we have into a common fund and share with everyone in need: we who have hated and killed one another and would not associate with men of different tribes because of their different customs now, after the manifestation of Christ, live together and pray for our enemies and try to persuade those who unjustly hate us, so that they, living according to the fair commands of Christ, may share with us the hope of receiving the same things from God the master of us all.[13]

For this reason Christianity has a power that no religion, ideology or belief system has ever had before. No one trusted Socrates enough to die for his doctrine, but Christ is believed by philosophers and scholars as well as artisans and illiterates – all despising glory, fear and death.[14]

The other great early ideologist and propagandist for Christianity was Tertullian (c. 155–230), a personality quite unlike Justin. Although he shared some points of emphasis with him, Tertullian was utterly different in tone and approach. To begin with, he was a Roman African, who was born in Carthage, lived most of his life there and died there.[15] By all accounts an impulsive and neurotic man, Tertullian began life as a pagan, converted to Christianity sometime in 197–8 and later switched to the heretical sect of Montanism, before finally apostasising even from the Montanists. A pathological controversialist, Tertullian was more intolerant than Justin and even seemed to enjoy trailing his coat and deliberately giving offence to his pagan enemies. Unlike Justin, he despised Greek philosophy – 'What has Athens to do with Jerusalem?' was one of his famous apothegms – and it is not surprising to find him enlisting in the extremist cult of the Montanists, who believed in asceticism, the importance of prophecy and omens and the denial of the apostolic succession, and in fasting and the supreme importance of the Holy Spirit; it has been said that if Justin overemphasised the Second person of the Trinity, the late Tertullian overemphasised the Third. They were also chiliastic – they believed that Christ would literally reign on Earth for 1,000 years after the Second Coming before ascending into heaven.[16] It was in his Montanist period that Tertullian became notorious for his misogyny, describing women as the accursed and fallen daughters of Eve, the original temptress, and speaking of the vagina as the 'devil's door' or 'the gate to hell'.[17] He was a talented propagandist who could turn a neat phrase. 'In the blood of the martyrs lies the seed of the Church' was one of his axioms,[18] and he was responsible also for the argument that the Resurrection was certain precisely because it was a naturalistic impossibility.[19] He invented purely off the cuff many of the ideas that later became Church dogma, such as that priests should avoid the theatre as the special haunt of the devil.[20] He concurred with Justin, in the teeth of all historical evidence, that Jesus was not crucified on a T-shaped cross, but on a *crux immisa*, where part of the vertical pole extends above the horizontal beam to form the now-familiar sight of the Christian Cross.[21] He also agreed with Justin, and with all other early Church Fathers, that Jesus was physically ugly – so ugly in fact, says Tertullian, that that was why the Roman soldiers spat on him.[22] Tertullian, in short, was a prolific author whose output can be searched profitably for many bizarre and fascinating aspects of early Christianity and its subsects.

Widely, though not deeply, read, he knew how to scour Greek and Latin literature, as well as Judaism, for telling propaganda points. His *Apologeticum* is very different from Justin's two *Apologies*, in that he does not simply make a calm defence of Christianity, but combines the defence with a vociferous attack on paganism, often going for the jugular in a particularly intemperate way, describing all pagan deities as demons.[23] His display of erudition and rhetorical fireworks is shallow as intellectual argumentation, but very impressive as propaganda. While recapitulating all Justin's theses, particularly those relating to the purity and moral excellence of the Christians,[24] he has many original arguments to deploy. He accuses the Roman authorities of being in denial about the miracles wrought by Jesus, even though they knew the truth about the trial under Pontius Pilate and its background: 'you have it in your archives', he asserts challengingly.[25] He is not content merely to deny the charges of incest, cannibalism and child sacrifice (calmly pointing out the misunderstandings that have arisen), as Justin did, but takes the fight to the enemy, claiming that these are barbarities practised exclusively by pagans, which is precisely why they find the accusations so plausible; after all, it was Artemidorus in his interpretation of dreams who claimed that eating human flesh was the most auspicious dream one could have.[26] Tertullian declares that the Romans practise child sacrifice, albeit in private. This sounds like a feeble *tu quoque* playground taunt, but many other good authorities, including even Porphyry himself, could be found to support him on this point.[27] He then hits two targets with one arrow by expostulating against the Roman charge that the Christians are disloyal. On the contrary, no Christian can be found to have been involved in any of the rebellions, revolts, riots, political murders and assassinations that have blemished the history of the Roman empire.[28] The absurdity is that the Jews were responsible for two of the most ferocious rebellions in Roman history, lasting about a decade when put together and costing Rome masses of blood and treasure, yet they are treated as a pampered minority while the pacifist Christians are persecuted. You will never find Jews constantly praying for the empire, the Senate and the person of the emperor, as the Christians do.[29]

Tertullian also plugged one of Christianity's undoubted strong suits: miracles. Certainly the new faith made an appeal to those who welcomed direct divine intervention and hoped fervently for the survival of the soul. It has been observed that there was something of a drift towards a general belief in the afterlife in the late second century after the notable pessimism of the first century, which may be one of the reasons why the Roman religion itself switched from cremation to burial around the time of Nero – after all, burial fits better with hopes of survival and resurrection.[30] Finally, Tertullian confronts the economic argument against Christianity, that the asceticism of the 'Galileans' made them poor consumers and low spenders. He points out how much money they spend on food and flowers, albeit not on incense or garlands for idols – a subject for which he has a positive mania.[31] While it is true that temple revenues take a loss from Christianity, this is more than compensated for by the fact that Christians *never* evade taxation – a positive fetish among pagan Romans – and give generously to charity and to support the needy.[32] It is true that all the following make no money from the Christians – panders, pimps, poisoners, assassins, magicians, soothsayers, wizards, astrologers – but so what? Is that supposed to be a bad thing?[33] The main source of shrinkage of revenue to the state from Christians is the mindless insistence by the state of executing them for the mere name, thus making sure the pool of consumers grows smaller.[34]

Tertullian was not above making veiled threats to his Roman over-lords – hardly the kind of thing to conciliate hostile emperors and Senates. If the Christians were vindictive, they would retaliate for this treatment by withdrawing their protection of the empire – since it is only through their prayers that the world is safeguarded from Satan and his demons.[35] Passive resistance or secession by Christians, given how many of them now serve in the army, would soon bring the empire to its knees. 'We could take up the fight against you without arms and without commotion . . . With our numbers, the loss of so many citizens in the far corners of the earth would be enough to undermine your empire, our mere defection would hit you hard. Imagine the horror you would feel at finding yourselves thus deserted, in the uncanny stillness and torpor of a dying world. You would look in vain for your subjects – the enemy at your gates would be more multitudinous than the population of your empire.'[36] Tertullian was being slightly disingenuous in stressing the services of Christianity to the empire, for it was he as a hardliner who, more than any other, argued that Christians should refuse military service.[37] His defence of Christianity also had a somewhat hollow ring after his conversion to Montanism, for it was the Montanists themselves who revived and popularised some of the most notorious pagan charges against the Christians, such as holding orgies during the love-feast or *agape*.[38]

The sound and fury of ideological battle gave way in the reign of Marcus Aurelius to active persecution. The first signs of a new, tougher Roman attitude to the Christians, and a disregard of the precedents set by Trajan and Hadrian, came in the latter years of Antoninus Pius's principate. A dissolute pagan, whose wife had converted to Christianity and tried to divorce him, turned his wrath on his wife's Christian instructor Ptolemaeus. On being hauled into court, Ptolemaeus was asked the standard question, 'Are you a Christian?' – and at once admitted it.[39] He was then arraigned before Q. Lollius Urbicus, a senior magistrate who had made his name under Hadrian. At first Urbicus tried to make light of the case and imprisoned Ptolemaeus, but his vengeful accuser was not satisfied. Urbicus was forced to try him again and, when Ptolemaeus persisted in his 'contumacious' assertion that he was a Christian, Urbicus ordered him executed. Lucius, another Christian who was in the courtroom, protested at the rank injustice of being condemned to death for the mere name, when no proof of any crime had been adduced. Clearly nettled, Urbicus said to Lucius, 'I think you too are one of them.' Lucius confessed that he was and was immediately gazetted for execution alongside Ptolemaeus.[40] This was a clear break with the guidelines laid down by Trajan and Hadrian. The implicit doctrine now seemed to be that the mere fact of Christianity logically entailed that the believer 'must have' committed other crimes – a new and sinister development. As Macaulay famously stated: 'There never was a religious persecution in which some odious crime was not, justly or unjustly, said to be obviously deducible from the doctrines of the persecuted.'[41]

A much more draconian attitude to Christianity is immediately evident from the very earliest years of the reign of Marcus Aurelius. In Pergamum (in modern Turkey) three further martyrs fell foul of the tightening up on the requirement to sacrifice to the Roman gods. A man named Carpus compounded his offence not just by refusing to sacrifice when ordered by the proconsul, but by calling the Roman gods demons.[42] At this the proconsul became angry and said, 'Sacrifice to the gods and don't play the fool.' Carpus replied that the living should not sacrifice to the dead. The proconsul pounced and asked him for a categorical statement that he thought the Roman gods were dead; Carpus replied that the Olympian statues were simply man-made artefacts and had nothing to do with the true God. The proconsul pronounced this blasphemy, but gave the accused one final chance to recant and sacrifice. When Carpus refused, he was hung up on a meathook and 'scraped' (the meaning is uncertain: it could refer to multiple stab wounds or flaying). After screaming for a long time, 'I am a Christian', he grew exhausted and lost consciousness with the pain.[43] The proconsul then turned to a second man accused of the same offence and asked if he was of senatorial class; this man, Papylus, replied that he was a Roman citizen. When the proconsul asked him if he had any children, Papylus replied that he had many, but this caused an uproar in the courtroom, with one of the crowd calling out that 'children' meant other Christians. When the point was pressed, Papylus said, 'I have children in the lord in every province and city.' Tired of this charade, the proconsul insisted that he sacrifice to the Roman gods. When Papylus refused, he received the same treatment as Carpus, but this time we are given the added detail that three sets of torturers went to work on him. It is said that Papylus uttered not a sound during the ordeal, whereupon the frustrated proconsul ordered him and Carpus burned alive.[44] They were nailed to a stake that was raised aloft and there the flames consumed them. A woman named Agathonice was also arraigned, refused to sacrifice and was likewise burned alive.[45] Hideous torture like this had not been visited on Christians since the time of Nero. It was with justice as well as bitterness that Tertullian accused the Romans: 'Others, who plead not guilty, you torture to make them confess; the Christians alone to make them deny.'[46]

In the year 165 it was the turn of a very big fish indeed to face Roman justice: none other than Justin himself, who acquired the title 'Martyr' as a result of his ordeal. A cynic philosopher named Crescens had come off second best after a number of dialectical maulings by Justin. Apparently with an unstoical terror of death himself, he intrigued to have Justin face the executioner's axe. Since the mere name of Christianity was enough to warrant death, Crescens's task was easy, and Justin seems to have made the mistake of thinking that when summoned before the prefect to answer charges, he was involved in just another philosophical debate; that would explain, at any rate, his rather pointless exclamation that Crescens knew nothing about philosophy and that he, Justin, would be happy to demonstrate this in the presence of the emperor himself.[47] Crescens had apparently taunted that if Christians welcomed death and martyrdom, they should kill themselves. Justin reported that the two things were not the same, and that mass suicide by Christians would mean that the word of God could not be spread. Crescens further jibed that if God was on the side of the Christians, he would presumably protect and rescue them, but Justin replied that since God permitted free will, and thus evil and demons, he had also allowed evil men like Crescens to rise up.[48] There was in any case a very clear difference between Roman suicide of the kind advocated by the Stoics and Christian martyrdom. The former was private, concerned with individual problems and solutions; the latter was a public act of witness, intended to give heart to the less intrepid Christian brethren and to make a demonstration of faith before unbelievers.[49]

The truly interesting thing about Justin's case was that the investigating prefect was none other than the Q. Junius Rusticus who had influenced Marcus Aurelius to abandon rhetoric for philosophy; during the years 163-8 he was urban prefect at Rome.[50] We cannot be certain that the Christian account of Justin's examination by Rusticus is anything like a verbatim transcript – it seems too tendentious for that – but it is clearly generically correct, providing a summation of the usual questions and answers at such sessions:

RUSTICUS: What kind of life do you lead?

JUSTIN: Blameless and uncondemned by all men.

RUSTICUS: What doctrines do you practise?

JUSTIN: I have tried to learn all doctrines, but I have committed myself to the true doctrines of the Christians, even if they do not please those with false beliefs.

RUSTICUS: Those, then, are the doctrines that please you?

JUSTIN: Yes, since I follow them with belief.

RUSTICUS: What sort of belief?

JUSTIN: Our worship of the God of the Christians who alone, we think, was the maker of all the universe from the beginning, and the Son of God Jesus Christ, who was also foretold by the prophets, that he would come down to mankind as a herald of salvation and a teacher of good knowledge. But I think my words are insignificant in comparison with his divinity, acknowledging the power of prophecy, in that it was proclaimed about him who, as I said just now, is Son of God. For you know that in the past the prophets foretold his presence among men.

RUSTICUS: Where do you meet?

JUSTIN: Wherever each prefers or is able. Besides, do you think we can all meet in the same place?

RUSTICUS: Tell me where you meet – or in what place?

JUSTIN: I have been living above the Baths of Myrtinus all the time I have been in Rome (and this is my second visit). I know no other meeting-place but there; and if anyone wanted to come to me, I shared the words of truth with him.

RUSTICUS: So you are a Christian?

JUSTIN: Yes, I am a Christian.

Rusticus adjourned proceedings to question a number of witnesses, then returned to press Justin further:

RUSTICUS: If you are scourged and beheaded, do you believe that you will ascend to heaven?

JUSTIN: I hope for it if I am steadfast in my witness. But I know that for those who live the good life there awaits the divine gift even to the consummation.

RUSTICUS: So you guess this, that you will ascend.

JUSTIN: I do not guess. I am completely convinced.

RUSTICUS: If you do not obey, you will be punished.

JUSTIN: We are confident that if we are punished we shall be saved.

RUSTICUS: Those unwilling to sacrifice to the gods are to be scourged and then executed in accordance with the laws.

Justin and his five Chrisitan companions were then scourged with whips and beheaded.[51]

Sometime in the next two years (166–7) the Romans notched up another major scalp, in the form of Polycarp (later St Polycarp) of Smyrna.[52] Polycarp, whose most famous pupil was the patristic master Irenaeus, was eighty-six years old when he died. He was supposed when young to have met people who had known Jesus, including John the Evangelist – though he would have been even older than his four score and six years for this to be convincing. It seems that Polycarp fell foul of the local Jewish community, which denounced him. He was arrested by a police captain named Herod, who asked him to sacrifice to the gods, adding that it was a small thing indeed to do rather than lose one's life. At first Polycarp did not answer, then he stated boldly that he had no intention of doing what was asked of him. He was hauled before the provincial governor, who tried to break his will by threatening Polycarp with death in the jaws of wild beasts. This was clearly a bluff since, after the usual question-and-answer session, Polycarp was taken out and burned at the stake; it was said that his Jewish enemies proved zealous in collecting firewood for the pyre.[53] Another version of the martyrdom has it that he was incinerated as part of a great pagan festival, also featuring animal hunts and gladiatorial duels.[54] The Christian legend says that Polycarp was so pure that his body would not burn, whereupon the Romans ordered a *confector* to plunge a dagger into his body; such a quantity of blood then flowed out that it extinguished the flames.[55] Whether the proconsul who condemned him was L. Statius Quadratus (consul in 142) or some other official, this was not the sort of execution that could have taken place without the knowledge of the emperor.

Persecution of the Christians increased in quantity and scope during Marcus Aurelius's reign. The most terrible events were those at Lyons in the year 177, where mob violence and xenophobia erupted in a veritable pogrom. At the tacit prompting of the authorities, large numbers of Christians were rounded up by vigilante groups and then herded into the town forum, where they remained under the uneasy protection of the local magistrates and police until the provincial governor arrived; this was of course contrary to Trajan's standing order that Christians were not to be sought out.[56] An open hearing, similar in many respects to that of Jesus himself before Pilate, ensued, with the governor trying to dispense Roman justice to the background of a howling mob. The impact of the plague, the casualty lists from the long war in Germany and the fact that many of the accused were immigrants from Asia Minor meant that feelings were running very high against the Christians, who were thought to have angered the gods.[57] When a local bigwig, Vettius Egapathus, tried to intervene on behalf of the accused, the mob began baying for his blood also. The governor then asked Egapathus if he was a Christian; when he replied that he was, he too was arrested. In a clear breach of the guidelines laid down by Trajan and Hadrian, the governor then accepted hearsay evidence from pagan slaves who had been bribed or browbeaten to give evidence against their masters. The main charges were cannibalism ('Thyestian feasts'), incest and 'Oedipal marriages'.[58] The recital of the 'evidence' against the Christians whipped up the mob to a fresh diapason of rage and fury; they demanded that the governor hand them over for an initial bout of rough justice before he proceeded to execution. The accused were then tortured and beaten; Pothinus, a ninety-year-old bishop, died from the effects of the beating without ever facing the final ordeal.[59]

The maimed and bloodied Christians were then led into the arena to be sacrificed according to the ancient and bestial Gaulish ritual of *trinqui*, about whose gory details the sources are mercifully silent.

Maturus and Sanctus, two of the accused, had to endure a whole day of ever-escalating refinements of viciousness before being burned at the stake. A woman named Blandina was then hung on a stake and a variety of wild beasts released in the hope they would devour her; unaccountably, the animals showed no interest in her, so the disconsolate Romans took her down from the stake and returned her to prison while they pondered a certain way to make an end of her.[60] The day's barbarity seems merely to have whetted the crowd's appetite for more, but, instead of cowing the remaining Christians, it appears to have encouraged and reanimated them, so that even more of them came forward to confess the name of the religion and thus join the ranks of the condemned. This time the governor was determined that wild beasts would be used against the contumacious 'atheists'. Whether he was a weak man himself and at the mercy of the mob, or merely a psychopath in an administrative role, he decided that all Christians would be sacrificed in the arena, including men like Attalus, who was also a Roman citizen. All precedent and all imperial prescripts made it quite clear that a Roman citizen had to be beheaded when sentenced to capital punishment – the fate St Paul had suffered under Nero – but the governor ignored this: Attalus joined his co-religionists in the arena.[61] A fifteen-year-old boy, Ponticus, was among those torn apart by wild dogs. For Blandina a special refinement was prepared. Having failed to get the fanged predators to act against her, the Romans introduced a bull, which duly tossed her, gored her and then trampled her to death.[62] The governor made a point of denying the victims Christian burial. Knowing the importance the sect placed on burial, he threw the bodies to the dogs and then, after six days, had them burned and the ashes thrown into the Rhône. The elated persecutors were heard to gloat that it would be interesting to see how the Christian god would be able to resurrect piles of ashes into risen bodies; now get out of that, was the burden of their quasi-sadistic glee.[63]

The final major persecution of Marcus Aurelius's reign took place in North Africa. In July 180 twelve Christians, always thereafter known as the Scillitan martyrs, appeared before the proconsul Vigellius Saturninus, charged with the name of the detested religion. Saturninus did not submit the twelve to hideous tortures, as at Lyons, and they were simply beheaded after going through the usual procedures.[64] He appears to have been Pilate-like in quite another sense from the governor at Lyons, not under pressure from a mob, but trying to give the accused every chance to escape death. The exchanges between judge and accused have none of the ferocity and animus of the Lyons case. Speratus, who seems to have been the chief spokesman of the Christians, began by stating that he could not understand why he and his co-defenders were in the dock, since they had done no wrong, had never turned their hands to wickedness and had never cursed anyone, but rather returned thanks when abused; moreover they were totally loyal to the emperor. Saturninus replied as if at a philosophical symposium: 'We too are religious, and our religion is simple, and we swear by the Genius of our lord the emperor, and we pray for his welfare, as you also ought to do.'[65] This was of course one of the long-running grievances against the Christians: they did not worship the gods and they did not sacrifice to the emperor; this was much more important in most Roman eyes than far-fetched tales of orgies, cannibalism and incest. Speratus then replied: 'If you will give me a quiet hearing, I will tell you the mystery of simplicity . . . I do not recognise the empire of this world, but rather I serve that God who no man sees or can see with these eyes. I have committed no theft; but if I buy anything, I pay the tax, because I recognise my lord, the king of kings and the emperor of all peoples . . . it is evil to advocate murder or the bearing of false witness.'[66]

Saturninus became irritated and said he would not listen if Speratus spoke evil of what the Romans held sacred, and requested that he swear by the Genius of the lord emperor. He then turned to the others, exhorting them not to be led astray by Speratus's bad example. Speratus interjected, saying that no evil had been spoken; the only belief was that it was not right to commit murder or to bear false witness. Saturninus continued to try to appeal to the others over Speratus's head, but they all cried out as one that they were Christians. Saturninus said their conduct was madness and asked if they wanted time to think it over. Speratus, displaying that obstinacy and 'contumacy' that the Romans so detested, said there was nothing to think over when their cause was so just.[67] Trying to lower the temperature, the proconsul asked what was in his satchel; Speratus replied that it was the Epistles of the Apostle Paul. There is perhaps a hint that Saturninus was moved by the fearless sincerity of the accused, as he suddenly proposed an adjournment of thirty days as a 'cooling-off' period. But the accused all clamoured as one that they were Christians, as if inviting martyrdom. Seeing that further argument was useless, Saturninus pronounced the sentence of execution by beheading.[68]

There are several points of great interest in the case of the Scillitan martyrs. One is that the Christians made it clear that they never blamed the emperor personally for persecution; they saw this ultimately as the perversion of the Roman system by wicked demons.[69] Second, the psychology of martyrdom was essentially the same in the case of the second-century Christians as in that of fanatical Muslims today: as Tertullian put it, 'Your blood is the key to Paradise.'[70] Third, the sheer uncompromising nature of the Christian martyrs (some have speculated that having a crucified founder made compromise diffi-cult) made it impossible for governors, proconsuls, procurators and others to order lesser penalties, such as hard labour.[71] Fourth, the Romans made a bad tactical error in setting so much store by sacrifice to the Roman gods. If, as Marcus Aurelius in his more sophisticated guise maintained, the gods were pure spirit and reason, then what they required was purity of mind and 'spiritual sacrifice' rather than burned offerings; for this reason it was not just Christians who refused to sacrifice on principle.[72]

There is no question but that the persecutions under Marcus Aurelius hit the Christian communities very hard; with reason Marcus's reign has been dubbed 'the years of crisis'.[73] After all, there were only about 50,000 Christians (as against four to five million Jews) in the Roman empire at the death of Trajan and even if, as seems plausible, given the growth of the new creed above all in the cities (starting with Antioch), this figure can be doubled by the time of Marcus Aurelius, it would have gone hard with the Galileans if this level of persecution had continued to be official state policy after 180.[74] The pogroms and martyrdoms of Marcus's reign convinced many Christians that the end of the world was at hand, while others were simply scared off. This is why, from about 180 to 220, one can detect a growth in the strength of both Gnosticism and Montanism. Gnostics were not persecuted because they agreed to take part in pagan religious ceremonies.[75] They held the convenient doctrine that knowledge, not baptism, was the key to salvation and therefore that the ascetic or monk was equal in the sight of God to the martyr. One can see the Gnostic influence in later Church Fathers like Clement, who argued that verbal confession to Christianity – virtually *the* classical hallmark of the martyrs – was not an overriding duty. Apostasy, according to Clement, was both irrelevant and impossible, because a true believer could never truly deny Christ, whatever he said with his tongue; this is why, when a later persecution hit Alexandria, Clement did not stay to bandy words with the authorities.[76] Gnosticism in the early third century evinced extremes of both cynicism (in the modern sense) and extreme otherworldliness. One of their number, Basilides – the man later so reverenced by C.G. Jung – had already produced the radical view that God was 'non-existent' – being superior to any existent being. Basilides thus engineered a philosophical *reductio ad absurdum*: taking the famous argument in the second half of Plato's *Parmenides* to the extreme, and providing a standing refutation of the ontological argument for the existence of God so beloved of medieval schoolmen.[77] It was against the background of uncertainty and persecution that Montanism too enjoyed its finest hour.[78] Gaining its greatest success in North Africa, it engineered the first serious schism in the Christian Church. Orthodox believers accused the Montanists of gluttony, avarice, gambling, the exploitation of widows and orphans, robbery, usury, dyeing the hair, painting the eyes, avoiding martyrdom and even the ritual murder of infants.[79] And so, in a curious way, the original ideological battle between Christians and pagans was internalised as an orthodoxy–Montanist conflict.

How severe was the persecution of the Christians under Marcus Aurelius? Were such actions centrally directed by the emperor? What were the reasons for this period of exceptional severity towards the new creed? Nothing is more controversial or so warmly contested by professional historians. It is best to begin with the incontestable proposition that the persecutions during this reign were a fairly sustained affair. We have already examined the *causes célèbres*, but Eusebius, the Church historian, tells us that in addition to these, there were pogroms at the beginning of Marcus's reign.[80] Lest this should be thought mere Christian propaganda, it is as well to bear in mind that other sources tell us that even during the Parthian war of 161–6 there were major persecutions of the Christians.[81] Further circumstantial evidence of severe trouble comes from the number of Christian 'Apologies' addressed to the emperor in this reign. Although Eusebius states that the first such addresses to the emperor occurred in the reign of

Hadrian, it is likely that the earliest known (those of Quadratus and Aristides) were presented to Antoninus Pius some time before 147. But Marcus's principate brought a positive deluge of such petitions. As has been well said, 'the concentration of Apologies to the emperor is entirely unique in the second century'.[82] In addition to the famous *Apology* by Justin Martyr, addresses to Marcus Aurelius were made by a number of Christian notables, including Bishop Apollinaris of Hierapolis (contents unknown),[83] Melito, Bishop of Sardis, and the famous Church Father Athenagoras. The Christian apologists had two main aims: to get the emperor's protection, taking in good faith the theory that he truly was available to all his subjects; and to reach out to a wider reading public and so convince them of the merits of Christianity and dissuade them from stirring up enmities or taking part in round-ups and purges.

Melito, whose address may be dated any time from 170 to 177 (but definitely in the reign of Marcus), queried whether the new edicts compelling worship of statues of the Roman gods were a personal edict of the emperor, reminding Marcus respectfully of the tolerant precedents set by Hadrian and Antoninus Pius. He pointed out that the birth of the Roman empire under Augustus and the birth of the founder of the Christian faith were virtually simultaneous events and argued that this was no mere coincidence. Such 'synchronicity' also explained why Christianity was an organic aspect of the empire and integral to its development; again it was not just accident that the only emperors to persecute Christians hitherto were the notoriously 'bad' emperors, Nero and Domitian.[84] Even more vigorous and forthright was the *Apology* of Athenagoras, which was of particular significance. Whereas there is no evidence that Marcus ever replied to the Apologies of Justin, Apollinaris or Melito, or even that he read them, in the case of Athenagoras he was bearded in his den, for the apologist delivered a speech in person to him at Athens in 176. It is not without significance, too, that this was the last Apology delivered to an emperor.[85] Having stressed that he was previously an anti-Christian like the Apostle Paul, Athenagoras defended his religion against the absurd charges of cannibalism, incest and atheism, arguing that Christianity, properly understood, was a superior form of worship of the gods to whom the pagans prayed; monotheism made more sense than Olympian polytheism. It was not that Christians did not honour the emperor –

they did, most sincerely – but they refused on principle to venerate images of the pagan gods or to sacrifice to them. The motives of the new creed's accusers were always worldly and suspect, he claimed; Christians were the victims of intrigues by the Jews, witch-hunts by the rabble, the malevolence of local magistrates and even – such was human nature – a simple detestation of goodness; and what seemed particularly to irk the *delatores* was the superior Christian morality.[86] It was not just that the story of Jesus Christ contained nothing even remotely so scandalous as the stories of Zeus's (Jupiter's) incest with Rhea and his daughter Chore, but also that the Christians had a manifestly superior attitude to sexuality: they were not promiscuous, did not believe in sex outside marriage – and inside it only for the purpose of procreation – abortion or even remarriage, which in their view was still 'adultery'. Christian meetings were presided over by venerable elders chosen for their probity, not wealth. They raised large sums of money by voluntary contributions, which went on supporting the needy, widows, orphans, the aged, shipwrecked travellers and also those co-religionists who were in jail, exiled to islands or condemned to the mines. Christians shared everything except their wives; their common meal, or *agape*, simply meant love in Greek, and was the exact opposite of an orgy: after the meal scriptures were read, contributions were invited from the floor, and then all dispersed quietly after prayers.[87]

The plethora of Apologies alone shows clearly that this was an era of 'the Church in danger'. The usual verdict of historians has been that before about 250 it is idle to look to the emperor as a factor in persecution of the Christians; that before the great Decian persecutions, emperors played no part in the fate of early martyrs, which was usually the reaction of hard-pressed local magistrates to the bloodthirsty howling of a baying, scapegoating mob.[88] Yet there is something deeply unsatisfactory about such an intepretation, which is *a priori* methodologically unsound, as it depends on an either/or antinomy – either local magistrates or the emperor as fount and origin of persecution – as if an either/or proposition in logic was being advanced, complete with a law of excluded middle. If we take the line that Marcus Aurelius had no interest or involvement in the persecution of Christians, does it not seem passing strange, and a mighty coincidence, that so many 'local initiatives' should have manifested themselves in his reign, never having been seen before and never to be experienced again? Again, local initiatives are understandable, but would they really have arisen almost simultaneously in Rome, Gaul, Asia and Africa, to name only those cases involving the most celebrated martyrs? The most obvious contrast is between the fate of the Christians under Marcus and under his successor Commodus. Eusebius is explicit about Commodus's more favourable attitude: 'During his reign our affairs took an easier turn and, by the grace of God, the churches throughout the world were lapped in peace . . . already large numbers even of people at Rome, of the wealthy and the wellborn, were drawing towards salvation with their household and kindred.'[89]

Let us grant the 'Marcus not a persecutor' factions all their obviously incontestable points. It is extremely unlikely that Marcus was so enraged by the Christian refusal to sacrifice that he took it as a personal insult, bent as he was on promoting the cult of emperor worship, even though both he and Antoninus had pushed the imperial cult and the divine right of Caesars harder than previous emperors.[90] There cannot have been a general no-holds-barred persecution of Christians, for this would have been a central event of the reign, from which the new religion would have been unlikely to survive. Imperial rescripts and other commands did not absolutely bind provincial governors who could plead the necessity to placate the mob as a motive to overrule the emperor's general guidance. There was always some tension between the general standing orders of an emperor and the demands of provincial security.[91] If large-scale riots got out of hand, the emperor would have to use scarce troops to put them down and, in a reign marked by constant warfare, when the resources of the army were stretched to the limit, this might not even have been feasible. This was apart from the consideration that the Roman state usually believed in giving in (even to unreasonable demands by the mob) rather than face social unrest; the ghost of Spartacus was never far away from the surface in Roman history. Tertullian, for one, believed the mob was always the major culprit, with the crowd as the hawks to the governor's dove, so to speak.[92] Moreover, proconsuls were allowed to issue edicts on taking up governorships and a certain latitude was permitted. A governor might declare that for the first time he was going to 'target the 'crime' of Christianity.[93] This would encourage the informers, who would know both that the new governor was keen to convict Christians and that he would not round on them (the *delatores*) as bearers of false witness. On the other hand, it seems unlikely that so many anti-Christian officials would spring up spontaneously in the four corners of the empire during a single reign. If 'hawks' were deliberately appointed by the emperor, on the other hand, that would dispose of the 'Marcus Aurelius not guilty' argument. So, a *priori* one cannot say that an emperor was necessarily behind persecution or martyrdom. But this argument cannot be pushed too far. The Lyons outrage, where the mob clearly was the major factor, cannot be taken as a typical example of the fate of persecuted Christians. In other instances, 'security' was cited where there was no mob violence, but 'security' made no sense, given the small numbers of Christians and their pacific nature. It must have been their *example* that was most feared, which would surely take us back to the possibility of a secret campaign by the emperor.[94] And if governors habitually disregarded Rome when it came to the Christians, what was the point of Antoninus Pius's 'pastoral letters' to cities in Greece and Asia to forbid victimisation of Christians after the earthquake of 160–1?[95]

Mere common sense and logic tell us that Marcus Aurelius cannot have been an innocent bystander at the anti-Christian events of his reign. If all the persecutions were purely local initiatives, without any direction from Rome, one would give a lot to see actuarial figures on the probability of so many local initiatives taking place all over the empire in a single reign, when they had never happened before and would never happen again. The idea that Marcus knew nothing of what was going on defies credibility. The prosecutor of Justin Martyr, the prefect Rusticus, was an old friend and mentor. As for Lyons, the governor there went so far beyond normal practice that he must have had some tacit encouragement from Rome. He condemned Attalus to the beasts when Marcus had only just sent out official instructions that Christians who were Roman citizens should be beheaded. The governor pleaded the necessity of appeasing the mob and was not reprimanded by Marcus Aurelius.[96] As the eminent historian Albino Garzetti has remarked: 'The horrible events at Lyons in 177 . . . certainly did not occur without the knowledge of the princeps.'[97] Moreover, historians have often made the absurd 'impossibilist' demand that we should have documentary evidence in Marcus's own hand of an order

for active persecution; no similar demand for 100 per cent documentation is made in other areas of the historiography of the empire, and
it would be risible anyway, given how little of the imperial archives
has survived. We should remember also, as a cautionary tale, that,
although no one doubts Hitler ordered the Final Solution and the
Holocaust, no one has ever been able to find a document in his hand
so ordering it. Rulers who commit atrocities, even those they consider
justifiable for reasons of state, rarely leave written evidence of their
deeds for posterity to find.

The other drawback of historians investigating the persecutions
under Marcus Aurelius is that they have failed to make anything of
one very obvious correlation: on the one hand, Christians suffered
more grievously under him than under any emperor between Domitian
and Decius, but on the other hand he was the only philosopher-
emperor in these years. Might the two things be connected? There is
much both in Marcus's own writings and in those of the Christian
apologists that suggests two camps with irreconcilable differences, an
immovable object against an irresistible force, creating tensions that
would not have arisen with a more worldly prince. It is usually assumed
that the Christians were either numerically or ideologically too insignificant at this juncture for Marcus to have any interest in them; it is
considered inconceivable that he could have studied their doctrines.[98]
But how do we know this? If we posit that Marcus was intellectually
curious, and we know that he was, and further that he was an intelligent man, it is eminently feasible that he could both have read
Christian writings and been alarmed by what he found there. There
would be much to anger him, even in the work of the apologists we
know he was aware of, such as Athenagoras. A quick checklist reveals
many red rags for this particular bull. Justin's description of pagan
gods as demons would have been apoplexy-inducing; according to
Justin, demons were responsible for what a later age would call 'false
consciousness'. Christianity was never a 'live-and-let-live religion': all
rivals, whether the offical Roman religion, Mithraism, or devotion to
Isis, were without exception the work of Satan.[99] Justin in particular
was an infuriatingly arrogant thinker: he had the audacity to suggest
that Plato filched the notion of *logos* from Moses; and he equated the
death of Socrates with the martyrdom of Christians, co-opting all
great non-Christian heroes as being essentially fellow-soldiers in the

fight against benighted superstition.[100] Tertullian was not much better when it came to deliberate provocation. He was particularly annoyed that philosophers were allowed to attack pagan religions, but the Christians were not: 'They openly demolish your gods and also attack your superstitions, and you applaud them for it.'[101] Marcus would doubtless have replied that this was missing the point: the philosophers would have been perfectly willing to perform cult acts and make obeisance to the official religion; only the arrogance of the Christians prevented them from doing so.

It is impossible to imagine that Marcus placed much credence on the stories of cannibalism, orgies, incest and black magic, though the Christians did play into the hands of their enemies by boasting that they could exorcise demons. The Romans replied that demons will only obey you if you consort with them or are in league with them; moreover, could it just be accident that the rise of Christian exorcists coincided with an outbreak of the plague, which Romans could not explain naturalistically? Pagans and Galileans tended to get bogged down in fruitless to-and-fro arguments on the subject of demonology. Tertullian, always provocative, might have given particular offence to the emperor by jibing at the cult of Asclepius to which Marcus, his physician Galen, Aelius Aristides and many other notables were devoted; he declared that if someone believed himself possessed by Asclepius, he should let a Christian speak to the being within him, 'Asclepius' would then confess that he was a demon.[102] As for the appeal to women, slaves and the dispossessed, the semi-socialism and the charitable works, none of this in itself would have worried Marcus. But he would have seen hidden dangers in the ethos of Christianity, not just its tendency to pacifism and its gospel of love, but in its very anti-social withdrawal from reality. Otherworldliness should have implied no challenge to the Roman state, but Marcus was probably intelligent enough to see that the very act of withdrawal was *itself* a challenge. The flight from reality was even worse in the case of people who, consciously or unconsciously, acted as fifth columnists, encouragers of social unrest and net encouragers of slave revolts like those of Spartacus. An allied problem was the notion of a universal church – something alien to the pagan cults. One city's temple of Isis or Bacchus had no more connection with another's than one village bakery with another; there was no central 'church' of paganism, with doctrines, dogmas and catechisms. Stoicism, for example, was merely a universal *prescription*, not a political or religious movement that proselytised; this made Christian attacks on Stoic doctrine all the harder to stomach.[103] Christianity had the added advantage that it offered salvation to all, whereas Stoicism was an elitist creed, offering its soteriology only to those who could perfect the life of reason. Above all, Christianity was a perversion of normality, a social cancer. Marcus loved bees and often likened society to a beehive – 'what injures the hive injures the bee'; in terms of that analogy, Christians were predator wasps, vermin at any rate; Celsus had compared them to a flight of bats, a swarm of ants or a council of frogs in a marsh.[104]

Most of all, Marcus may have feared that Christians were winning the ideological battle against their pagan rivals, and that as a 'hegemonic' creed it was displacing both Stoicism and the official Roman religion. Here we must bear in mind Marcus's odd and unusual devotion to the Olympic deities and correlate it with the oft-confirmed tenet that those instigating persecutions against the early Christians were often motivated by a special devotion to the traditional gods of the state.[105] Every single aspect of Christianity would have seemed threatening to a devout defender of the old ways. It was not just that Christians appeared more ruthless and dauntless, braver and more moral than their rivals. Their real strength was they had everything that official religion and the pagan cults had, and more: a dependence on revealed texts, a stress on the importance of theology, an insistence on moral purity and, above all, the conviction that the soul survived death and they would achieve salvation.[106] The increasing trend towards monotheism, clearly observable towards the end of the second century, also played into their hands. The intellectual weakness of paganism, on the other hand, was that it was founded on 'ancestral custom' and did not rest on authoritative texts, interpreted by a professional priesthood.[107] This was particularly a problem with worship of the Olympians, where there was too much reliance on mythology interpreted by artists and poets; by contrast, even the Eastern cults scored heavily, since hermetic writings and Chaldean oracles appealed to intellectuals. Monotheism was more easily melded with the Eastern cults, since the 'theological sociology' of monotheism was that lesser gods sank to the level of demons. Sacrifice – inexplicable to a philosophical God like that envisaged in Stoicism – made sense in the Eastern religions, as it was directed to these 'demonic', lesser intermediaries.[108] Marcus could have salved his love of sacrifice and squared it with the Stoic God, but only by abandoning the Olympians.[109] There were ludicrous inconsistencies in the state religion, even for believers; the maddening thing about Christianity was that, once the initial leap of faith was taken, it was intellectually coherent thereafter. As one scholar has put it, paganism was 'a very spongy, shapeless, easily penetrated structure', vulnerable to attack from 'a sharply focused and intransigent creed'.[110]

If the motives for Marcus's hostility to Christianity must perforce remain speculative, his direct attitudes can be inferred from four separate pieces of evidence. In the first place, it is clear that sometime during the years 161–8 he issued a decree making worship of the Olympian gods inescapable. Although Justin says that this decree was aimed expressly at the Christians, this is unlikely. It is more likely to have been a gesture of despair as Rome reeled under a succession of blows: the flooding of the Tiber, the Parthian war, the outbreak of plague and the German invasion.[111] Nevertheless, the emperor cannot have been unaware that this decree would hit the Christians harder than anyone else, and perhaps it evinces his particular anger that, at a moment of supreme peril, he had fifth columnists, as he saw it, sabotaging the empire from within. Another interesting piece of evidence is the law ordaining banishment to an island for anyone who tried to fill the minds of simple people with terror of the gods; once again, Christians seem to have been the main target, and Tertullian tells us explictly that some of the faithful were languishing in exile on islands.[112] This law, incidentally, is further evidence of Marcus's confused state of mind on issues of religion: not only was he himself prepared to propitiate angry gods, whereas the logic of this law implied that the gods did not get angry; even worse, if the gods really were angry, the 'benighted' people who had been 'led astray' did right to be afraid of them. The third piece of legislation is in some ways the most interesting. A *senatus consultum* – which may even be the one referred to by Bishop Melito in his Apology – allowed provinces of the empire to obtain gladiators at lower than market prices by purchasing condemned criminals. This was because there was a shortage of gladiators, and this threatened the social opiate of 'bread and circuses'. Some historians think that this law was the trigger for the mass persecutions at Lyons in 177, but there are two obvious snags with this theory: first, we have no means of knowing if the *senatus consultum* immediately preceded the events at Lyons and can therefore be confidently cited as their cause; second, it seems odd that, if pagans were rounding up Christians to turn them into cheap gladiators, they should have exposed so many of them to the beasts.[113]

The final piece of evidence for Marcus's attitude to the Christians comes from his own *Meditations*, where he contrasts the heroic doctrine of suicide by the Stoics with Christian martyrdom: 'How resolute is the soul! Ready to be released from the body at any moment, whether to be extinguished, to be scattered or persist. But this readiness has to be the result of its own decision, not a mindless reflex, like the Christians; it should happen after reflection, with dignity and in such a way as to convince others, without any histrionics.'[114] Although the authenticity of these words has been challenged (it is alleged that 'like the Christians' is a later interpolation), it seems clear that this is an authentic reflection on the Galilean sect.[115] Other passages in the *Meditations* have also, far less convincingly, been ransacked to find further alleged references to the Christians.[116] The various fragments of evidence allow us to draw a tentative conclusion. It seems likely that Marcus issued his provincial governors, proconsuls and procurators with orders that stopped short of general persecution of the Christians, but insisted that they visit the full vigour of the law on a treasonable sect. For this reason the old proscription on hunting them down was waived, as were the old prerogatives allowed to Christians who were also Roman citizens. Marcus in effect rescinded the directives of Trajan and Hadrian by allowing hearsay evidence from slaves and other malcontents. The Christians, it seemed to him, started by provoking the gods with their atheism, then compounded this by refusing to sacrifice to them, and finally by exulting in Roman miseries caused by the gods' anger because they thought this brought the end of the world closer. The continuity of the persecutions may be explained by the non-stop deluge of disasters that hit the empire: first the Parthian war, then the Antonine plague, and finally the titanic struggle with Germany (see pp. 325–69). Some scholars like to differentiate between early and late phases of the persecution, with local issues, such as the alleged gladiator factor, uppermost in the second stage during the 170s.[117] But it seems more likely that an empire-wide continuous policy of repression was all but guaranteed by the seismic rebellion of Avidius Cassius in 175 (see pp. 368–82).[118] If in these years the Church was in danger, the empire was even more so, and the first signs of possible catastrophe now appeared on the frontiers of the Danube.

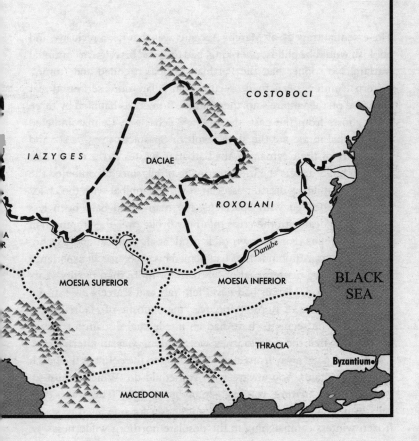

Provincial boundaries

Frontier

N

0   Miles   150

0   Kms   250

COTINI

COSTOBOCI

IAZYGES

DACIAE

ROXOLANI

Danube

MOESIA SUPERIOR

MOESIA INFERIOR

BLACK
SEA

THRACIA

Byzantium•

MACEDONIA

13

The essential tragedy of Marcus Aurelius was that he, a reclusive and bookish would-be philosopher-king, had to spend his reign in continual warfare. No sooner had the Parthian campaign ended and Rome's eastern frontiers been made secure than a far more serious threat appeared on the empire's northern limits. Rome was haunted by three main ghosts from the past: the military debacle at Cannae inflicted by Hannibal in 216 BC; the slave revolt of Spartacus in 73–71 BC; and the spectre of the Germans in the barbarian wastes to the north. The German bugbear was the most terrifying of all, since it combined the element of military disaster associated with Hannibal with the chaos principle associated with Spartacus. No man could have been less equipped to deal with the crisis that now broke over the empire than Marcus Aurelius. For his own odd, prudential, political and psychological reasons, Antoninus Pius had denied his successor all experience both of military matters and of 'abroad' for more than twenty years of his adulthood. Marcus had never left Italy and scarcely ever stirred from the environs of Rome. Moreover, the opposite of Hadrian in so many ways, he seems to have had an intellectual disdain for travel. He thought that the only journey worth taking was an internal one. 'People try to get away from it all – travelling to the country, the beach or the mountains. You always wish you could do. Which is absurd: you can do so anytime you like: simply go within.'¹ This was a typically Roman attitude, but not a good mindset for one fated to spend frozen winters campaigning in the desolate northern wilderness.

Marcus was thus triply handicapped when the threat from Germany manifested itself in the late 160s, quite apart from the lack of training and experience that Antoninus had unpardonably left as his bequest to his heir and adopted son. Not only did he regard warfare as a contemptible activity, as did his great influence Epictetus, who suffered from the delusion that most wars (he instanced the Trojan, Persian and Peloponnesian wars as well as Trajan's Dacian campaign) broke out by accident.[2] As a Stoic, Marcus also considered defending the empire an 'indifferent' moral end; and as a 'little Roman' he shared Horace's famous scepticism about travelling to foreign lands.[3] He had to take what comfort he could from the gung-ho enthusiasm for war inculcated by another admired figure, Heraclitus, who said, 'War is the father of all and the king of all . . . We should realise that war is common to all and strife is justice, and that all things must come into being and pass away through strife.'[4]

Roman encounters with hostile and dangerous German tribes went back 300 years, and the massive armed clashes at the end of the second century AD were considered the most serious crisis the Roman republic had faced since Hannibal and the Punic Wars. Large numbers – maybe 250,000 in all – of the Cimbri tribe, based in Jutland and southern Scandinavia, began migrating south in the years 120–115 BC; the reason is uncertain, with some historians opting for floods of biblical dimensions and others for a more generalised climate change.[5] Moving into Gaul, the Cimbri heavily defeated the Romans at Boreia in 112 and, in the years 109–107, won three more battles against the legions. The seemingly unstoppable German tide reached its apogee at Arausio in 105, when the Cimbri defeated a Roman army 80,000 strong, because the two consuls (G. Mallius Maximus and Q. Serrilius Caepo) refused to cooperate. Some military experts claim that casualties at this battle amounted to more than 80,000 and that Arausio notched up the fourth-highest casualty rate in all one-day battles in recorded history before the twentieth century. With Rome at their mercy, the Cimbri and their allies did not go for the jugular. Instead, the Cimbri proper diverted into a protracted raid on Spain, while the Teutones marked time in Gaul. The German crisis, which shook Rome to its foundations, gave Gaius Marius his great opportunity.[6] Learning that in the year 102 the Cimbri and Teutones intended to unite for an invasion of Italy by two different routes (along the Mediterranean coast and through the

Brenner Pass), Marius marched against the Teutones while his consular colleague Q. Lutatius Catullus was given the task of halting the Cimbri in the Brenner. Marius annihilated the Teutones at Aquae Sextae, but Catulus botched his part of the operation. Marius was forced to march against the Cimbri in Cisalpine Gaul. There, the following year (101) he engaged them at Vercellae (seventy miles north-west of Milan) and annihilated them in a victory so crushing that the ancient sources (never to be trusted in estimating numbers) speak of 140,000 casualties. The completeness of the Roman victory can be gauged from one significant pointer. The German women killed their children and then slaughtered themselves to avoid slavery, so that a war that began with mass migration ended with mass suicide.[7]

Nevertheless, the memory of the Teutones and Cimbri was never far from the surface in the Roman collective unconscious and was played on forty or so years later by that self-publicist Julius Caesar, a past master of propaganda and the black arts of spin. Historians dispute whether Caesar, in his famous conquest of Gaul in the years 59–49 BC deliberately picked a fight with the German 'king' Ariovistus or whether he genuinely perceived German migration into Gaul as the prelude to another Teutonic tide washing into Italy. It is clear that he was determined to be *the* power in Gaul and that Ariovistus resented this and considered that Caesar had infringed on his sphere of influence. Inconclusive peace parleys petered out and then, in 58, battle was joined, with Caesar provoking the enemy to attack deliberately, having learned that German soothsayers had prophesied to Ariovistus that he could triumph only if he waited for the full moon.[8] In the ensuing battle Caesar decisively defeated the enemy and massacred his routed foe in large numbers. Four years later there was a further defeat and rout of German migrants.[9] Well aware of the role of Germans as bogeymen in Rome, in his *Commentaries on the Gallic War*, Caesar played the 'Cimbri and Teutones' card no fewer than five times. As with much of his classic work on the war in Gaul, Caesar was forever insinuating self-serving propaganda into his brilliant storytelling, in effect telling his fellow-Romans that he was saving them from the nightmare of the northern barbarians and skating over the objection that, when appointed to his command, he was not supposed to be operating so provocatively close to the Rhine.[10] The value of Caesar's writings for the historian of early Germany is the mention of a number of tribes operating with Ariovistus, who was leader of the Suebi: these include Harudes, Triboces, Vangiones, Nemetes, Sedussii and the people who would later be Marcus Aurelius's bane, the Marcomanni.[11]

The German frontier remained relatively quiet for another forty years until the first Roman emperor, Augustus, decided on a policy of expansion across the Rhine. The reasons are obscure: it may have been simple glory-hunting by Augustus or, more seriously, he might genuinely have been concerned about secure frontiers. Some say that a salient motive was to protect the north–south amber route with its terminus on the Danube, at modern Vienna.[12] In the year 15 BC Augustus sent his stepsons Tiberius and Drusus on a successful campaign against German tribes living near the Alps. In the year 11 Drusus waged an equally successful war as far east as the River Weser, and two years later moved against the peoples east of the lower Rhine: the Chatti, Suebi and Cherusci; this campaign, however, was less decisive. After Drusus's death, Tiberius took over command of all Roman legions in Germany, and by AD 6 it was generally considered that the German tribes were either conquered or pacified. Then two events changed everything. The Marcomanni, now based in Bohemia, emerged as the principal power in Germany. Their leader, Maroboduus, who had been educated in Rome and trained with the legions, in effect set up the first German 'state' – a federation of tribes stretching from the Baltic to the Danube.[13] But the Romans viewed this Marcomannic federation as a threat to their Danube bases at Noricum and Pannonia and prepared a campaign of conquest to stifle this German state at birth. Tiberius was switched from the Rhine to the Danube to oversee operations in AD 7, the command on the Rhine was given to P. Vinctilius Varus.[14] The assumption was that the Romans had nothing to fear on the Rhine since the most powerful tribe there, the Cherusci, were pro-Roman. To a point that was true. Segestes, their peacetime leader, was pro-Roman. The Romans had perfected 'divide and rule' tactics when dealing with the German tribes. They liked to support one faction against another in the internal tribal power struggles, usually trying to detach the nobility from the common people so as to create a loyal native elite.[15] But the Cherusci war chief, Arminius, who had been elected to that position in AD 6 at the age of twenty-six, had ambitions to rival those of Maroboduus. While not yet openly declaring

himself Rome's enemy – he too had served with distinction in the
legions – he began surreptitiously to build up his own alliance of
hawkish Cherusci and disaffected warriors from other tribes.[16]

The Cherusci lived on either side of the middle Weser as far as the
Elbe. In September of the year AD 9 Varus, commanding three legions
(17th, 18th and 19th) plus auxiliaries (20,000 men in all), was advancing
through the forests that lay between the Ems and Weser rivers. Here
Arminius and his men trapped Varus in a brilliantly laid ambush in
the Teutoburg forest (near modern Osnabrück). When Varus saw that
all was lost, he committed suicide. The 20,000 Romans were slaughtered to a man, either in the battle itself or by being sacrificed
afterwards in gruesome rituals to the Germans' gods.[17] When told of
the disaster, Augustus was inconsolable and was said to wander round
his palace crying out to no one in particular, 'Varus, give me back
my legions!'[18] Tiberius had to abandon his project to conquer the
Marcomanni. This was the moment when, if Maroboduus and
his Marcomanni had made common cause with Arminius and the
Cherusci, the entire Roman client system beyond the Alps would
have collapsed and Rome itself would have been in deadly danger from
the combined forces. As it was, only the presence of the Roman
fleet kept coastal tribes like the Frisians loyal. Arminius even sent
Maroboduus Varus's head as a supposed incentive to join him.[19]
But Maroboduus and Arminius hated each other, and neither was
willing to concede eminence to the other. The upshot was war between
the Cherusci and Marcomanni, which gave Rome the breathing space
in which to recover. Arminius gradually lost his commanding position, being opposed by Segestes and the pro-Roman party at home
and by Maroboduus abroad.

In AD 13, the year before his death, Augustus sent Drusus's son
Germanicus to command eight legions on the Rhine and retrieve the
situation in Germany. For two years he and Arminius fought a series
of inconclusive battles. Finally in AD 16 Germanicus won a face-saving,
though not decisive, battle against Arminius, with the help of pro-
Roman members of the Cherusci allied to Segestes.[20] Tiberius, who
wished to reverse Augustus's forward policy in Germany, then considered that revenge had been taken and honour satisfied; he ordered
general withdrawal and retrenchment. At the same time Segestes, who
had been held prisoner by Arminius since the Teutoburg disaster,

escaped to the Rhine, where he was retained by the Romans as a 'pretender' to leadership of the Cherusci; it is said that he had to endure the humiliation of watching some of his closest kin being paraded in triumph after Germanicus's victory in 16.[21] Maroboduus, after a protracted war with Arminius, also fled to the Romans and was kept by them in honourable retirement at Ravenna, again as a pretender to the kingship of the Marcomanni.[22] With all his enemies dispersed, Arminius's hour seemed to have struck. But he developed megalomania and aspired to be recognised as king of the Cherusci, even laying plans to replace the clan system with a quasi-feudal hierarchy of personal retainers, thus alienating the very 'proletarian' tribesmen whose help he had previously successfully called on against Segestes. In the year 21 Arminius was killed by his own people.[23] Soon afterwards the Cherusci fell apart as a significant factor in German politics, racked by civil war.

Under Claudius and Nero the Roman presence in Germany tended to cluster around the Taunus–Wetteran salient and the Black Forest–Neckar river area (near the source of the Danube). Tribes who accepted the status of Roman clients in Nero's reign included the Cherusci, the Vannian kings of the Suebi on the middle Danube and the Quadi and Marcomanni in Bohemia and Slovakia. The Romans built forts round the Taunus salient, on the Neckar and around the headwaters of the Rhine.[24] The Rhine was ceasing to be a problem area as the power of the Cherusci declined. There was a bloody conflict between the Cherusci and Chatti (who lived to the south-west, around the upper Weser and the Diemel), which began in 85 and dragged on for years. At the end of it the Cherusci, erstwhile destroyers of Rome, had been fatally weakened and were henceforth of negligible importance.[25] But, as if in compensation, a new threat arose on the Danube. The Sarmatian tribes (principally the Iazyges and the Roxolani), migrating west in large numbers from the steppes north of the Black Sea and debouching onto the Hungarian and Wallachian plain, threatened to overwhelm the Danube frontier. Before his death Nero was said to be planning an ambitious expedition into the Caucasus, aimed at eliminating the Sarmatians and the Alans once and for all. To this end he raised a new legion of Italian recruits, all at least six feet tall, which he called 'Alexander's phalanx'.[26] Whether this was a serious response to a perceived threat, a piece of Neronian glory-hunting or a simple piece of kite-flying cannot be determined, for Nero himself was toppled in the year 68. In the confused maelstrom of the 'year of the four emperors' that followed, the Iazyges shrewdly backed Vespasian, the eventual winner, but the Roxolani made three separate raids against the empire, heedless of who would win the contest for the purple.[27] Nevertheless it would be true to say that in the reign of Vespasian, who enjoyed the backing of most Germans and most major players along the Danube, the perennial Roman anxiety about the German menace abated.

Matters took a more serious turn under Domitian. While the Cherusci were fading away in the west, the Sarmatians allied themselves with the Dacians of Transylvania. Domitian found himself campaigning against Dacians, Sarmatians and the Suebi and devoting much of his military resources to the Danube. When he called on the Quadi and Marcomanni to supply troops for these operations, as they had to Vespasian, they refused, alleging that he was a treaty-breaker and had not honoured his commitments.[28] The enraged Domitian struck back and eventually found himself at war with the Quadi and Marcomanni as well. The fact that he had been spectacularly inept at Danubian diplomacy did not stop him from elaborating the most grandiose and quixotic plans for encircling the Quadi, Marcomanni and Iazyges in a grand-slam strategy.[29] The truth, however, was that Domitian's campaigns were singularly unsuccessful. He was defeated by a coalition of Dacians, the Quadi and the Marcomanni, while the Sarmatians wiped out an entire legion. A victory he gained in a minor skirmish was a face-saver portrayed at Rome as a great triumph, but the reality was that Domitian had to pay the Dacian king Decebalus tribute to bring the war to an end.[30]

By the end of the first century AD two significant changes were visible on the German frontier: the switch of Roman resources from the Rhine to the Danube; and the increasing Romanisation of Germania, the name given to all the lands north of Switzerland to the North Sea and the Baltic and as far east as the Vistula. Augustus had stationed eight legions on the Rhine for action against the tribes between the Weser and the Elbe as part of his over-ambitious plan to extend the frontier to the Elbe – something that proved beyond Rome's capacity. The Army of Upper Germany was based at Mainz (four legions) and the Army of Lower Germany at Cologne (another four legions).[31] Indeed, in the period 13 BC–AD 70 it has been estimated that fourteen legions were stationed between the Alps and the Dutch coast.[32] One hundred years later there was just one legion there, and nine on the Danube; by the time Marcus Aurelius became emperor, the number of Danube legions had increased to twelve. The switch from Rhine to Danube was partly the result of Vespasian's principate and partly sheer strategic necessity. Since the Rhine legions had opposed Vespasian and backed his rival Vitellius, the emperor downgraded their importance, decreased their number and even sent them on suicide missions.[33] The virtual euthanasia of the Rhine legions was aided by the one campaign that Domitian actually succeeded in: his war of 83–5 against the Chatti around Mainz, which finished them off as a major factor on the Rhine; what strength the Chatti had left they wasted in a war with another busted Germanic flush, the once-mighty Cherusci.[34] The success of that war meant that the old military zones of Upper and Lower Germany could thenceforth be converted into two new provinces. This was the development that led Tacitus to his premature announcement that the German wars were now at an end. A *limes* or frontier was built – ultimately a kind of Hadrian's Wall – between the Rhine north of Coblenz and the Danube valley near Regensburg. The frontier line was a narrow path planted with a barricade along which, at intervals, were forts.[35]

But it was not just Vespasian's personal predilections that led to the switch from the Rhine to the Danube. Once the Sarmatians allied with the Dacians, the Romans responded by building a cordon of bases on the right bank of the Danube, all the way from Germany to the Black Sea. In the provinces of Raetia, Noricum and Pannonia the legions moved right up to the river bank and constructed bridgehead forts on the far side; later this system was extended to the lower Danube, with Poetevio (Pettau), Brigetio and Carnuntum as key fortresses. The defence of the Danube was more difficult than that of the Rhine, because of the abrupt angle the river makes as it turns south. Roman fleets put out onto the Danube and attempts were made to overcome the whirlpools and cataracts of the Danube Gorges and the Iron Gates, those notorious barriers to riverine navigation. Complete mastery of the Danube was not achieved until around the year 100, when Trajan's engineers hacked out a road along the rock face of the lower (Kazan) gorge and, the following year, cut a three-mile canal to bypass the rapids of the Iron Gates below the exit from the gorges.[36] These vast public works were undertaken in part because of the profits from mining, especially iron in Noricum, silver and lead in Dalmatia and Pannonia and copper, lead and silver in Moesia.[37] The Roman effort to contain Germany's warlike tribes was titanic. Some historians say that the number of Roman troops on the Rhine and Danube plus their auxiliaries amounted to some 200,000 men. It is possible that Rome at this juncture overrated the menace from the barbarians. Experts reckon the total population of Germany at this time was only about two million at the maximum, although Arminius was said to have assembled an army of 75,000 for his Teutoburg forest exploit. The Marcomanni – later to be Marcus Aurelius's most steadfast foe – may only have numbered about 100,000 in all.[38]

Meanwhile the German tribes were becoming steadily Romanised. German society in the first century BC was primitive and clan-based, with the emphasis on communal ownership; the gap between rich and poor was not large. Primarily pastoralists, the Germans enjoyed a climate and corresponding vegetation that made it unnecessary for them to be nomads.[39] Highly dependent on cattle, they ate little grain and made limited use of iron; they tended to live in open-plan villages, particularly detesting the kind of overcrowding that was routine in Rome.[40] Clans would occasionally combine into larger units that the Romans identified as tribes (*pagi*), but the only real federations were in wartime. Relying on serfdom rather than slavery, the Germans tended to use females only as slaves; males they either killed or traded to the Roman empire as slaves.[41] Feuds were widespread, but were usually settled by reparations in the form of sheep and cattle. Routinely cruel, the Germans practised various refinements of capital punishment, quite apart from the human sacrifice of those captured in war. Traitors and deserters merited hanging from trees, but cowards and criminals were plunged into marshes with weighted hurdles on their heads to endure a slow drowning.[42] Largely an illiterate society, Germania was nonetheless distinguished by respect for women (whose intuitive and prophetic powers they prized) and strict sexual morality. Husbands provided dowries for wives and practised monogamy, with adultery being regarded as a great crime and punished accordingly. As Tacitus put it, there was 'no arena with its seductions, no dinner table with their provocations to corrupt them'.[43] Yet German society was no utopia and suffered from several drawbacks. One was the warrior ethos itself. Although Tacitus claimed that the landscape had produced a physically huge and savage people, which made the Germans particularly dangerous – 'neither Samnite nor Carthaginian, neither Spain nor Gaul, nor even the Parthians have taught us more lessons'[44] – outside warfare there was no focus for their energies and ambitions. In peacetime there was no proper civil or political society, no cities, proper houses, cultural pursuits or even very much agriculture. The men were notoriously lazy, doing nothing but eat, drink, pick fights and take offence. They had no awareness of chronology or notions of time-keeping, which merely compounded the general idleness. Consequently much of the ferocity manifested in war went into their two great weaknesses: drunkenness and gambling.[45]

All this began to change as the Roman impact on Germania became more pronounced after 50 BC. The influx of wealth from trade with Rome and from money subsidies paid by the Romans to keep the tribes quiet made certain individuals wealthy and gradually displaced communalism with private property. Trade burgeoned as Roman merchants penetrated into Germany and even took up permanent abode among the tribes.[46] The demand for Roman goods grew, imports increased, the wealth owned by individuals burgeoned and the economy became monetised, by trade, by wages paid to those Germans who served with the legions and by the subsidies paid to the chiefs. Trade in cattle and slaves with the Romans was important, but the dynamic new element was commerce in amber. Since the only source of high-grade amber was the southern shores of the Baltic, and it was in high demand at Rome, areas engaged in this long-distance trade, such as Pannonia, especially benefited.[47] Salt, fur and hides were also exported from Germany, while imports included Roman ceramics, especially the finest red tableware or *terra sigillata* and the best Roman vintages, which were greedily devoured by wine-crazy Germans. As the demand for Roman goods increased throughout the first century AD, more and more Roman traders and money-lenders were found on German territory. Meanwhile German society itself became markedly more stratified, with something of a crevasse opening up between the wealthy nobles and the masses. By the end of the century the old clan system had virtually disappeared, displaced by a quasi-feudal grouping of rich aristocrats with their personal retainers.[48]

The new class-bound society was the entering wedge the Romans used to control Germany. Their policy was to tie the new aristocrats to them with money and trading favours, while dealing harshly with the have-nots.[49] They liked to take hostages from the sons of the tribal leaders and then educate them in Rome, teaching them to despise their roots, then sending them back to subvert any anti-Roman trends among the tribesmen. The key to Maroboduus was that he had had such an experience at Rome, where he was lionised by Augustus.[50] Roman strategy was to set up 'kings' to rule the tribes who would be pro-Roman stooges, preventing the possible anti-Roman policies that might arise if decisions were made in a full assembly of all the people, as used to be the case. These kings were given money to buy off the opposition and to spend on conspicuous consumption that denoted their new 'royal' status; they thus became creatures of Rome, in some cases more sympathetic to the interests of the Roman state than to those of their own people. For them the advantage was not just undreamed-of wealth, but the instrumentality to impose their will on the tribesmen as they had never been able to before.[51] To cow the opposition expected from the masses, the Romans would threaten at the limit to invade and lay waste the tribal lands, though they rarely had to intervene; their client kings usually performed effectively.[52] Even if a pro-Roman ruler actually was expelled by the masses because of unpopular pro-Roman policies, as happened eventually to Maroboduus, the Romans still had a card to play: they would keep the expelled puppet as a 'king over the water', ready to lead dissident factions against the new rulers if they did not come to terms with Rome; hence Maroboduus's comfortable eighteen-year sojourn at Ravenna.[53] The final weapon the Romans had was to refuse to ratify any new ruler they did not approve of, which meant the end of trading privileges and money subsidies and the threat of invasion. The Romans perfected 'divide and rule' in Germany, both by setting the different tribes at each other's throats *and* by generating strife and class conflict within the tribes, setting feudal retinues and private property against the masses, who were dedicated to clans and communalism.[54] The trick was to keep powerful tribes like the Marcomanni in a state of permanent chaos and near civil war, while at the same time ensuring that the Roman protégés never became powerful enough to bite the hand that fed them.[55] It is no exaggeration to say that the combination of increased wealth, private property and the aristocratic–plebeian split engineered by Rome bade fair to tear Germania apart.[56]

These 'divide and rule' tactics could doubtless have been continued almost indefinitely, but at the end of the century the situation on the Danube was transformed by the Roman annexation of Dacia (roughly modern Romania). This was the work of the alcoholic, homosexual emperor Trajan, a Spanish Roman born at Italica near Seville in 53. Trajan had been adopted by Nerva in 97 as co-ruler, possessed tribunician power and held the title *imperator*, so the transition of power was the smoothest possible. He was on the German frontier when news of Nerva's death came in, but decided against a new war of conquest in Germany as he needed time to establish good relations with the Senate.[57] Yet he was already revolving in his mind a scheme to chastise King Decebalus of Dacia, who had meddled extensively in the Danube provinces of Pannonia and Moesia and had humiliated Domitian in the latter's ill-advised campaign. Having secured the endorsement of the Senate for his plans, Trajan assembled the greatest Roman army ever seen – no fewer than thirty legions – and took the field against Decebalus in 101. The campaign was noteworthy for Roman discipline, ingenuity and engineering feats. The master engineer Apollodorus of Damascus built a roadway through the Iron Gates by cantilevering it from the sheer face of the rock, so that the Romans appeared to walk on water; then he constructed a great bridge with sixty stone piers to span the Danube. Then Trajan struck hard into the heart of Dacia. Rolled over in a lightning campaign, Decebalus surrendered, prostrated himself before the emperor, swore obedience and accepted the status of a client king.[58]

But as soon as Trajan returned to Rome, Decebalus began to backslide and raid across the Danube; he also got involved with hostilities with the Iazyges. Trajan concluded that he had made a mistake in making the treacherous Decebalus a mere client; his advisers whispered that the Dacian ruler was still too powerful and would have to be extirpated. While historians can see the rationale for the first Dacian campaign, the second has engendered diverse opinions. Some see Trajan as an unregenerate war-monger, simply looking for an excuse to settle accounts with Decebalus once and for all. Others stress the economic motive, pointing to the great wealth of Dacia's gold mines; it has even been suggested that only the Dacian gold mines saved Rome under Trajan from financial disaster.[59] Whatever the true motivation, the second Dacian campaign of 106 was waged as a war of extermination. Even by Roman standards it was nasty, brutal, murderous and barbarous, with atrocity and war crime rampant, and no quarter asked or given. Dacia could not withstand the might of eleven Roman legions and soon Decebalus was on the run. Finally cornered, he chose to commit suicide. Having been pardoned once, he had no desire to face the wrath of Trajan, knowing that this time he would be paraded in triumph in Rome before execution. Still, he had given a good account of himself and Rome had been pushed to the limit.[60] Trajan proceeded to annex Dacia as a new Roman province – the first on the far side of the Danube. Most of the original inhabitants were either killed or enslaved, with a residue resettled elsewhere in the empire. Back in Rome, the emperor enjoyed a triumph that lasted 123 days, with lavish provision of gladiator shows, chariot races and animal spectacles in the arena. Massive wealth from the gold mines began to flow into Rome, financing a huge public building programme. Apollodorus designed a sculpted column 100 feet high, with twenty-three spiral bands filled with 2,500 figures – a complete picture of the Dacian war.[61] The ancient writers claimed, with typical hyperbole, that Trajan took 500,000 slaves as a result of the Dacian campaign. Certainly there was a glut in the early second-century slave market, but a more likely explanation is the more realistically grounded figure of 97,000 slaves that accrued to Rome after the Jewish Bar-Kochba revolt.[62]

Yet in all this triumphalism it was forgotten that Rome had drastically altered the fragile dynamic on the Danube frontier. To begin with, the empire now shared a frontier with the troublesome and unreliable Sarmatians, who were officially clients. Rome also had to deal now with a German frontier that ran all the way from the Rhine to the Black Sea. Sometimes, when reading the annals for the years 100–60, it is hard to remember that Rome had any other preoccupation than the German frontier, and it requires an effort of imagination to call to mind major incidents elsewhere, like the Parthian wars and the Bar-Kochba rebellion. A tough nut to conquer, Dacia proved particularly troublesome to administer and at the beginning of Hadrian's reign had been divided into three military commands: the heartland,

Dacia Superior, under a praetorian legate; Dacia Inferior in the south-east facing the Wallachian plain, under an imperial procurator; and Dacia Porolissensis in the north-west, facing the northern part of the Hungarian plain and also under an imperial procurator.[63] Both Dacia and the other Danube provinces were packed with Roman legions and allied auxiliary forces, particularly dedicated to blocking all passes into Transylvania from the Carpathians. The province of Pannonia alone contained four legions, three in Pannonia Superior facing the German tribes north of the Middle Danube and another one monitoring the Sarmatians in the East.[64] These four legions, based at Vindobona (Vienna), Carnuntum (Deutsch Altenburg), Brigetio (Szony) and Aquincum (Budapest), dominated the entire middle Danube with a kind of chain of steel.[65] The province of Moesia, a hugely important centre of Rome's mining wealth, between the middle and lower Danube, was divided into Moesia Superior and Moesia Inferior and was typical of the entire theatre. Between the legionary garrisons all river crossing-places and fords were under surveillance by auxiliary units, using watchtowers; along the entire Danube was a series of observation posts and signalling points.[66] Above the Danube gorge the legions of Moesia Superior deployed towards the west at Singidunum (modern Belgrade) and Viminacium (Kostillac) facing the Hungarian plain. The other Roman innovation was a determined effort to settle colonies of retired veterans, particularly in Pannonia; it is claimed that sixty-six new townships were created along the Danube during Hadrian's twenty-year principate.[67]

Although there were a few rumblings from the most warlike German tribes, the Quadi and the Marcomanni in Bohemia and Slovakia, in the reign of Hadrian the German frontier properly so-called held up well. The power of the German kings was no longer their old status as sacred rulers, but simply their status as Roman clients, which gave them military power, cash subsidies and the promise of armed intervention if the anti-Roman opposition grew too strong.[68] The primary duty of the legions of Pannonia Superior and Noricum was to watch and monitor the Quadi and the Marcomanni, and this they did effectively. Roman control of the Sarmatians was far less effective, even though the Iazyges on the Hungarian plain were hemmed in on three sides by the armies of Pannonia Inferior, Moesia Superior, Dacia Superior and Dacia Porolissensis; the Roxolani on the Wallachian plain were under similar surveillance from Dacia Inferior and Moesia Superior.[69] Both the Sarmatian tribes chafed at the strictly controlled economic intercourse they were allowed with Rome and could not curb their ancient raiding instincts. Hadrian had to go in person to Moesia to deal with the threat from the Iazyges and Roxolani, in effect submitting to blackmail when the king of the Roxolani claimed his subsidy had been cut; Hadrian simply gave him another bite at the cherry without examining the books too closely.[70] The Sarmatians had a worse reputation than the Germans, being regarded as inherently unfaithful and treacherous. There was much resentment at the costs of keeping them quiet, especially when the Roman tactic of supporting pretenders in the wings seemed to backfire. One Sarmatian ruler moved his entire household to luxurious exile at Roman expense on an island off Pola in Istria; it was whispered that he had deliberately engineered a situation where his people rejected him so that he could live a life of sybaritic idleness and send the bills to the empire.[71] More serious critics contend that Hadrian's Danube policy was self-defeating and contained the seeds of ultimate destruction. Hadrian tried to integrate the provinces instead of leaving them as secondary appanages to Rome, but this tended to increase the gap, and hence the friction, between those within the magic circle of empire and the 'barbarians' outside. It was not possible for Hadrian to align military frontiers effectively with provincial governments as long as there was a significant Roman presence, in the shape of financiers and merchants, on the other side of the *limes*. Paradoxically, Hadrian's attempts to limit the empire and rationalise the frontiers may have created a time-bomb on the Danube.[72]

Superficially, the reign of Antoninus Pius was an era of peace on the Danube frontier, as elsewhere. Archaeological finds reveal a huge and thriving trade across the Danube, and this picture is confirmed by coin evidence.[73] We learn that Antoninus 'intervened' to settle a friendly pro-Roman king among the Quadi. Auxiliary forces in Pannonia, Noricum and Dacia were strengthened, new roads built and stone forts constructed.[74] From his dominant position on Antoninus's council, Marcus Aurelius would have been well versed in the nuances of Danube policy. Yet, as elsewhere in the empire, the superficial peace and tranquillity masked deep-seated problems, many of which would burst into the open when Marcus was emperor. We know that there was trouble with both Dacians and Germans in the early years of Antoninus's reign, if only because Aelius Aristides referred to them in his famous triumphalist speech of the mid-140s.[75] But those who say that all the problems on the German frontier were the product of the opening years of Antoninus's principate have to explain the 'curious incident' of the little-known campaign in Dacia Superior waged by M. Statius Priscus in 156–8.[76] There are some other pointers to Danubian instability. Under Antoninus the frontier was advanced in the Odenwald–Neckar section of Upper Germany and Raetia, leading some historians to think that the empire was expecting major trouble with the German tribes even before Marcus came to the the throne.[77] Others say that the 'kings' with whom Antoninus was angry on his death-bed included not just Vologases of Parthia, but German rulers as well.[78] Yet another straw in the wind comes from Antoninus's policy in Britain. There the dithering and uncertainty about whether to hold the line at Hadrian's Wall or further north, at the Antonine Wall (roughly linking modern Glasgow and Edinburgh) did not reflect the situation on the ground in Britannia, but nervousness about the future course of events in Germany.[79]

Despite his pious obeisance to Antoninus, Marcus Aurelius knew that his predecessor had severely neglected the deep problems of the empire and particularly the northern frontier. The Marcomanni and Quadi were pressing for admission into the Roman empire, or at least into a free-trading 'common market' of associated nations in which they would confront no tariff walls. This was a concession Marcus would not permit, not least because it would have provoked dissension among the Danube legions, which had their own perks and scams to protect; we should never forget the perennial problem of corruption in Roman society, which was why, after all, Marcus abandoned the idea of tax-farming in the Danube provinces and handed the task over to the equestrian procurators.[80] It says much for Marcus's diplomatic skill that he managed to stall and deflect major trouble on the northern frontier while he brought the Parthian conflict to a successful end.[81] There was no real sign of trouble in Germany in the years 161–5, for we can observe a regular discharge of veteran auxiliaries in these years, as well as legionaries being transferred away from the frontier. It is true that the Chatti launched a raid along the Rhine frontier in 162, but this was dealt with swiftly by Victorinus, governor of

Upper Germany, whose subsequent three years as governor there were very quiet.[82] The flurry of new road-building in the Danube provinces need not mean that Marcus expected major trouble there, since the accession of a new emperor was often celebrated with highway construction and the erection of milestones. But the infrastructure of the Roman Danube was certainly improved in this way, with roads being built from Aquincum to Brigetio and Sirmium and from Sirmium to Taurumum.[83] The extravagant festivities held on Lucius Verus's return from Parthia also argue against the perception of an imminent threat on the German frontier.

On the other hand, there is much evidence that Marcus divined a long-term threat to the empire on the Danube frontier and was taking unostentatious steps to deal with it. The unification of Dacia province, previously a tripartite administrative unit, was one straw in the wind. Marcus appreciated the opulence of Dacia – it boasted great wealth in timber, cereals, agriculture, salt, fruit, wheat, wine, cattle, sheep, horses, even bees and honey, to say nothing of the prodigious mines of iron, gold and silver, which had allowed Trajan to bring back 165 tons of gold and 330 tons of silver after his conquest.[84] What concerned Marcus was the extreme factionalism and tribal splintering in the province. Dacia, a polyglot mixture of Germans, Thracians and Sarmatians, was a veritable tribal United Nations, with many distinctive groupings: the Apuli in central Transylvania, the Buridanenses in northern Moldavia, the Costoboci in the north-east of Moldavia and spreading out into the Ukraine, the Carpi east of the Carpathians, the Calipizi between the Dnester and Brg rivers, the Crobobosi in Dobruja, the Suci near the mouth of the River Oct, and the Tyragetae around the mouth of the River Dnester, to say nothing of the migrants who made Dacia their temporary home: the Sarmatians, Alani, Roxolani and Bastarnae.[85] Hadrian's division of Dacia into three provinces seemed to compound the problems rather than solve them. Marcus therefore united the three and formed a military 'super-command' of two legions to oversee the new province.[86] The first governor of the new united Dacia was Sextus Calpurnius Agricola, summoned from Britain, where Marcus had sent him at the beginning of the reign to quell disturbances.[87] It is interesting that Marcus, usually criticised for his supine conservative instincts, in this instance reacted dynamically and showed that he had the ability to improvise where necessary.

More serious evidence that Marcus was departing from the 'let sleeping dogs lie' policy of his predecessor comes in the remarkable fact of his raising two new legions. These were II and III Italica, notable not just as the first new legions raised since Trajan's time, but because they were recruited from Italians and by this date there were virtually no Italians in the existing legions.[88] II Italica was sent to Raetia in 165 and III Italica to Regensburg, making ten legions in all on the Danube frontier, with six of them on the upper Danube between Regensburg and Aquincum, just below the 'bend' in the river. Moreover, out of 440 auxiliary regiments deployed throughout the Roman empire, half were now stationed in the Danube provinces.[89] The official reason for the creation of the new legions was to replace the missing IX Hispania (which had perhaps been destroyed in the Parthian war) and the XII Deitorarius, thought to have been annihilated in the Bar-Kochba revolt in Palestine. But all historical precedent – and Marcus Aurelius was certainly a creature of precedent – suggested that Roman emperors raised new legions only when they intended to go on the warpath.[90] So what was Marcus's intention with his two new legions? A pre-emptive strike into Germany worked against the Roman notion of just warfare. It is therefore likely that Marcus originally intended a war of annexation and conquest against the Marcomanni. To annex willing German tribes would have been a simple matter, but the problem was that the Marcomanni were not willing to submit to annexation; they wanted incorporation into the Roman empire on their own 'most favoured nation' terms. Marcus, it seems, had lost patience with them and privately acknowledged that his 'divide and rule' policies with them and the other German tribes had not worked.[91] Two other possibilities have been suggested. One is that the conspiracy among the Germans which later came to light had been uncovered at an early date by Marcus, and he was therefore preparing for the inevitable war. The other is that Marcus feared the army was too powerful and interfered with his joint rule with the Senate; he accordingly intended to displace its energies in external warfare.[92] Whatever the truth behind his motivations, his aggressive intentions seem clear. This explains the oddity whereby two legates were withdrawn from the war in Parthia while it was still in full swing. M. Claudius Fronto, commander of I Minervia and governor of Syria, and C. Iulius Verus (the driving force in the actual recruitment process) were both recalled from the East in time for the raising of II and III Italica.[93]

An examination of all the evidence suggests that Marcus had been planning an expansionist campaign against Germany from the earliest days of his reign and may have been recruiting for his new legions as early as 161.[94] That he had not proceeded with his plans is obviously explicable by the conflicting demands of the unexpected war with Parthia, but other factors were involved. In the first place, despite assertions that Antoninus Pius had left the economy in a healthy state, repeated by many ancient historians,[95] certain plain facts make it likely that Marcus's financial situation was parlous. His immediate devaluation of the silver content of the coinage suggests that money was tight. Not wishing this to be generally known, Marcus depreciated the currency to pay for festivities and ceremonial expenses.[96] Some say that the reason Marcus was unsure about the loyalty of the army was that, the *Historia Augusta* notwithstanding,[97] he did not pay a donative of 5,000 denarii per soldier as this was beyond his resources, being five times greater than any previous donative. On the other hand, one could argue that the apparent discrepancy between the bulging treasury bequeathed by Antoninus and the apparent economic austerity just a couple of years later could be explained if Marcus really did award a donative at that level. Unfortunately, the links between public finances and war expenses on the one hand and the *annona* issue and level of booty uplifted from Parthia on the other are far from clear.[98] If financial uncertainty as much as the war in Parthia delayed a planned Roman war in Germany, they were not the only issues. There is strong evidence of a famine early in Marcus's reign, and we can probably date it to 162–5.[99] Rome was just recovering from the effects of dearth when it was hit by plague, as the returning veterans brought the disease back from the East. Yet it seems clear that Marcus thought he had all the time in the world to prepare his campaign against the Marcomanni. He certainly did not anticipate a pre-emptive move by the Germans, at any rate if we can infer from the 'laid-back' attitude evinced by his continuing attendance at philosophical lectures.[100] Unfortunately for Rome, the Marcomanni made their move first.[101]

Sometime in the winter of 166–7 6,000 Langobardi and Obii tribesmen launched a surprise attack on Pannonia.[102] The curiosity of this was that these tribes had no common frontier with the

Roman empire, and could only have reached the Danube with the collusion of the Quadi. The pretext for the attack was the self-evident absurdity that Rome had not paid them the agreed subsidies – a nonsensical argument since Rome had not only *never* paid them subsidies, but had never even had the most fleeting contact with them.[103] The attack was easily swatted aside by a makeshift Roman force, principally cavalry commanded by Macrinius Avitus Catonius Vindex, who also drew on infantry stationed at Arrabona in Upper Pannonia; it may have been no more than a large-scale skirmish, with at most 2,000 men engaged on either side.[104] Almost simultaneously the Chatti probed into Raetia, where they were dealt with firmly by Aufidius Victorinus, though once again it was an affair of skirmishes rather than pitched battles.[105] Thus convincingly put in their place, these minor German tribes sent a deputation that represented eleven of their clans and which was received by M. Iulius Bassus, governor of Upper Pannonia. The significant aspect of this conference was that the German delegation was led by Balomar, King of the Marcomanni. The Romans bound Balomar over to guarantee the behaviour of the minor tribes, and all seemed satisfactorily settled by 5 May 167, when the records show a routine discharge of veteran auxiliaries in Lower Pannonia, suggesting that the temperature had cooled considerably.[106] But this proved to be a false dawn. On 29 May the Dacian gold mines at Rosia Montana ceased working and the careful system of logging and archiving was abandoned.[107] What was the explanation?

Suddenly the duplicity of Balomar was palpable. A huge force of Quadi and Marcomanni burst like a tsunami on the Roman empire. It immediately became clear that the Marcomanni had been the hidden hand behind both the initial probing raids and the farcical peace talks. After seizing the Dacian gold mines, the German host overran Raetia, Noricum, Moesia and Pannonia before crossing the Alps and devastating the amber route.[108] The amber trail can in some ways be likened to the Silk Road in the East, as we can see if we reverse its normal direction. Starting from Aquileia in northern Italy, it ran to Carnuntum and Vindobona on the Danube and thence northwards to the upper valley of the Oder, and from there to the Baltic shore of Poland, with sidetracks diverting off the main route towards the Black Sea, Denmark, Sweden and the Baltic islands.[109] The huge German army did not stray far from the beaten track, but relentlessly followed the route down to its terminus at Aquileia, burning, looting and raping as they went; 20,000 Roman citizens are said to have perished during this large-scale raid, though the alleged figure of 100,000 captives taken back to slavery probably does no more than indicate the usual hyperbole of ancient sources with figures and statistics.[110] Numismatic evidence suggests that Carnuntum, Brigetio and Poetovio were not taken, though Opitergium probably was and maybe Emona and Celeia as well (though the unwalled city of Virunum, lying off the main route, survived undamaged).

The Quadi and Marcomanni sat down outside Aquileia, uncertain what to do next, as they lacked the siegecraft skills necessary to take a city of 100,000 inhabitants. Clearly the wealth of Aquileia was the magnet that drew them. Originally founded to check the advance of another northern people, the Gauls, in 181–80 BC, Aquileia had grown rich from the amber trade and the discovery of gold fields along the route, notably that near modern Klagenfurt.[111] While the Germans pondered their next move, they were given a decisive check by one of Marcus's new rising stars, Claudius Pompeius, who first made his name in this campaign. We do not have the details of his successful repulse of the raiders, but evidently they lost heart and nerve and retreated back over the Alps in short order. The Germans calculated, correctly, that as winter approached, their supply lines would become dangerously exposed; the route back to the Danube was long, arduous and precarious.[112] Nevertheless, the damage done to Roman prestige was immense. Objectively, the output of the Roman mint fell 75 per cent below normal production levels (75 per cent fewer denarii issued) as a result of the German seizure of the Dacian gold mines – a catastrophic decline not explicable in terms of the outbreak of plague, since the output levels returned to normal the next year.[113] Perhaps even more importantly, the Quadi and Marcomanni had delivered Rome a devastating psychological blow, calling forth the demons in Rome's collective unconscious and reminding them only too forcibly of the Cimbri and Teutones. There was no greater monster in the Roman id than the thought of German tribes on the loose in Italy.[114]

What lay behind this sudden extreme turbulence on the German frontier? Why did Marcus Aurelius face a German crisis that no previous emperor had had to confront? The normal explanation is that some unusual factor operating in northern Germany – possibly climate change or over-population and subsequent land-hunger – triggered a process whereby 'Goths' migrated from their homelands and impacted on the Langobardi, who in turn shunted the Quadi and Marcomanni across the Danube.[115] On this view, the Marcomannic wars were merely the first act in a long-running drama (the migration of the Goths) that would take two and a half centuries to unfold. The obvious analogy is with the old explanation of the *mfecane* in southern Africa in the early nineteenth century, whereby the rise of the Zulu nation under Chaka was said to have engendered a 'crushing' when the expanding Zulus pressed on neighbouring tribes who in turn migrated elsewhere, causing a general shunting dislocation and massive loss of life. But just as historians like Julian Cobbing have arisen to doubt this explanation for *mfecane*, preferring to concentrate on the impact of the slave trade, so in the case of second-century frontier studies many scholars have found the 'Goths' thesis implausible.[116] The most persuasive studies of 'northern barbarians' show the Goths migrating from Scandinavia via Poland and the Dnieper early in the third century and not reaching even as far as the Sarmatians and the Alans in the Crimea until *c*. AD 250; indeed, some authorities roundly condemn the term 'Goths' in connection with Marcus Aurelius's wars as absurdly anachronistic.[117] Moreover, archaeological studies show areas of acute economic privation in northern and central Germany, but no mass migration of peoples as required by the 'Goths' thesis or even changes of agricultural methods or a switch of trade routes. Hoping to save something from the apparent wreckage of the 'Goth-*mfecane*' thesis, its proponents have sometimes switched tack and brought in the Alans as the original dynamic factor, providing the first push in the shunt.[118] It is true that the Alans were a persistent menace on the frontier at this time, but there is not a shred of evidence to suggest that their socio-economic position altered significantly *c*. 160–80. The more one examines it, the less plausible the over-population/migration hypothesis seems.

Far more convincing is the notion of a massive conspiracy among the German tribes – the explanation that the ancient authorities themselves provided.[119] This would explain so much that seems obscure: the transit of the Langobardi and Obii through the territory of the Quadi to launch the raids of 166–7, for example. This probe, the actions of the Chatti on the Rhine, the abortive peace conference and finally the mass German descent on Aquileia, would all make sense as part of a grand plan, testing Roman defences and resolve, alternating soft with very hard approaches.[120] There is further circumstantial evidence from the amount of Roman armour and swords found in warrior graves as far north as Denmark and Schleswig-Holstein, suggesting that tribes not even mentioned in the sources took part in the war on Rome.[121] Whether Balomar, King of the Marcomanni, one of his counsellors or even the King of the Quadi was the mastermind is uncertain – the sources do not mention *one* great enemy of Rome, which is in part what has encouraged the rise of the migration thesis. What is certain is that Marcus Aurelius now faced a war with a massive German confederation along a front extending from the source of the Danube in the Black Forest to its estuary in the Black Sea. The dream of Arminius would finally come to pass, and this time the unknown mastermind would find his Maroboduus among willing German allies. The Germans along the Rhine and Weser – the Chatti, Chauci, Hermunduri – played a minor part in the conspiracy, limiting themselves to raids and avoiding pitched battles, though the Chauci did resort to their old trick of corsair raids on Gallia Belgica.[122] The core and cutting edge of the German alliance was the coalition of the Quadi and the Marcomanni along the Danube front, but other tribes involved in the anti-Roman bloc were the Naristae, Suebi, Buri, Victuali, Cotini, Osi, Bessi, Cobotes, Bastarnae, Peucini and Costoboci, of which the Naristae were the most important.[123] Originally the Quadi and Marcomanni lived in Moravia, Slovakia and Bohemia, with the Naristae and Buri as neighbours and the Celtic Cotini and Osi – the so-called 'Elbe Germans' – on the eastern fringes.[124] The power of the Marcomanni had long been recognised by Rome, and Tacitus paid tribute to them, but with an important rider: 'The fame and the strength of the Marcomanni are outstanding . . . nor are the Naristae and Quadi inferior to them; these tribes are, so to speak, the brow of Germany, so far as Germany is wreathed by the Danube.'[125] From a Roman point of view, the appearance of the Quadi in the field against them was particularly disappointing, since this tribe – clients since the time of Augustus – had always been earmarked for special treatment and it had long been hoped that they had permanently turned their spears into ploughshares.[126] However, there had been straws in the wind and relations became prickly around the time of Hadrian's principate. The Romans always identified the Quadi as key players in Germany and, when Antoninus Pius appointed a new king over them, the event was thought sufficiently important to warrant a new issue of coinage, which ran from 140 to 144.[127]

Three separate but interlinking factors seem to have actuated the Marcomanni and Quadi to form the great anti-Roman coalition that convulsed the Danube frontier in the late 160s. A major help in the formation of a credible German federation was the melding of tribes into larger and larger units of 'supertribes' with the minnows as their vassals, in place of the old rough-and-ready chaotic independence of all from all – a trend particularly noticeable by the time Marcus Aurelius became emperor. So, for instance, the Cotini and Osi paid tribute to the Quadi, and the Buri to the Marcomanni.[128] In previous times, Roman commanders and administrators had headed off any tendencies towards supertribalism by supporting the lesser tribes against the encroachment of the greater ones, but the departure of so many Roman personnel for the eastern front and the war with Parthia in 161–6 had created a unique window of opportunity for the big German battalions. Yet the power vacuum created by the Parthian war was not the only problem. Basically there was a 'contradiction' in the Roman system of clientage on the Danube that could never be resolved. The paradox was that to get a fixed system of clients, the kings or chiefs had to exercise tighter control and thus become more powerful, but this increased power in turn alarmed the Romans.[129] The most powerful tribes were also those furthest advanced along the transition from the old clan system to the new quasi-feudal dispensation of great wealth and extreme socio-economic inequality. This can be very clearly correlated with proximity to the Roman frontier on the Danube. Whereas the northern Germans lived in primitive conditions like Yahoos or Morlocks, the Marcomanni by the time of Marcus Aurelius lived in stone houses.[130] By contrast the Teutonic tribes of the Baltic shores (the Aestrii, Sitones, Fenni, and so on) still practised agriculture rather than commerce, had no houses but slept on the ground, and in some cases employed 'primitive' social systems like matriarchy.[131] The correct model for the Marcomannic wars is not 'civilisation against barbarism', but a clash of convergent wealth systems, with the Quadi and Marcomanni seeking to put themselves on a level with the Romans and increase the distance in wealth between themselves and their benighted Baltic kinsmen. To put it in sociological terms, the model for the 'revolution' on the Danube under Marcus Aurelius was Tocquevillean rather than Marxian. To put it in Gibbon's terms, proximity to the Romans on the Danube had corrupted the 'noble savages'.

Why, then, were these economic aspirations of the Quadi and Marcomanni resolvable only by war, rather than by cooperation with Rome? It is necessary first of all to appreciate the spectacle of undreamed-of riches, which the Roman empire appeared to present to the German tribes. Unfortunately for themselves, the Romans had given the impression that the empire was awash with riches and easy pickings, groaning with gold and silver, but that these glittering prizes were available only to those within the tariff walls of the empire. By the time of Marcus Aurelius the Germans were bedazzled by the sumptuousness of the Roman way of life, by its ornate tableware, gaudy ornamentation and what seemed like a plethora of gold. To get inside this economic cordon and enjoy such riches was the abiding goal of the most advanced tribes, like the Marcomanni and Quadi.[132] The 'barbarians' were becoming steadily Romanised: many Roman traders and even soldiers lived among them, the legions had all kinds of scams that benefited them and their hosts, and the Germans were especially impressed by the medical facilities available to the Roman armies.[133] There was a vigorous trade between the legions and the Germans, for Rome always made sure that its officers and its military were well and regularly paid. The problem was that, outside the imperial free-trading system, taxes on commerce were high; by analogy with import taxes on the eastern frontiers of the empire, it is likely that the tax on the Danube was 25 per cent.[134] The Quadi and the Marcomanni wanted to maintain their political independence while enjoying all the economic advantages of the Roman empire; for obvious reasons, emperors found this a non-negotiable demand.[135] It was possible for small tribes to double-cross each other and even agree to break up as a unit and relocate inside the empire, provided they could attain the supposed El Dorado.[136] This was not an option for the Quadi and Marcomanni. They wanted the economic benefits of empire or, at the very least, most-favoured-nation status. Marcus consistently refused the demands of the Quadi and the Marcomanni; he would agree only to incorporation in the empire as ordinary subjects without tribal affiliations, and even that offer was pitched some time in the future. Because of the Parthian war, the Romans did not have the manpower to process mass immigration into the empire.[137] Besides, Marcus made the calculation that the Quadi and Marcomanni were inherently unreliable. The probable result of granting them incorporation or most-favoured-nation status would be that they became a drain on imperial resources, a mere incubus – and a blackmailing one at that.[138]

The Quadi and Marcomanni reacted with indignation to the Roman refusal. They were always subject to market cycles and sudden shifts in the terms of trade, leaving the Bohemia–Italy trade nexus vulnerable. For this reason they envied the Rhine tribes, located in areas where the Romans coveted not just the products of agriculture, pasture and the forest, but the lead, zinc, coal, copper and stone available from the mines and quarries.[139] And it was not just their economic interests that put them on a collision course with Rome. The Marcomanni aspired to be the rulers of Germany, with the lesser tribes as their satellites. Yet the Romans opposed supertribalism; their interest was in maintaining small tribal entities, which they could dispense with at any time it was inexpedient, and their main interest in the Marcomanni was as mercenaries.[140] Unfortunately, Hadrian's policy of aligning military frontiers with areas administered by provincial governments generated unintended consequences. With Roman agents and merchants roaming at will among the Danube tribes and often 'going native', a kind of symbiosis soon developed between Romans posted to the frontier and the tribes. By working for wages in Roman camps and trading directly in Roman markets, the Germans got a taste of the good life and they relished it. Paradoxically, the very attempt to limit empire may have precipitated conflict with the 'barbarians' outside. Contact with Roman technology, diet and lifestyles gave the Teutons confidence; as always, familiarity bred contempt. The Germans increasingly saw little to fear in Roman military technology and much to envy in their way of life.[141] Certainly the Marcomanni were not inclined to be shut out from the imagined economic Eden without a fight. Their attitude was 'If you can't join them, beat them'. Somehow, by diplomatic stages lost in the mists of time, they persuaded the other German tribes that the Roman empire was a paper tiger, militarily vulnerable and easily conquerable. That the war was a long-odds gamble was clear from the inherent factionalism and political instability of Germany. Could such an unwieldy coalition hold firm against Roman counter-attack? Perhaps the unknown political genius who devised the alliance had such a high sense of injustice that he took the line of 'Let the heavens fall, provided justice be done'.

The Marcomannic wars suggest once again that there is nothing new under the sun. The feeling of being economically strangled, of being denied autarky and a place in the sun, followed by disingenuous negotiations and a surprise attack on a great power with far more considerable resources seems an eerie pre-echo of the history of Japan in 1940–1. But from Marcus's point of view, the 'Pearl Harbor' of Aquileia seemed to place the Roman empire in deadly danger and to pitch the Roman state into its worst crisis since Hannibal invaded Italy 400 years earlier. Contemporaries were alive to the obvious analogies with the Second Punic War.[142] The raiders came from beyond the Alps; they had surprised Rome by winning a stunning victory; and their success seemed to suggest that the gods were angry. Marcus had already decided to hold a *lectisternium* to avert the omens presaged by the plague that was currently devastating Italy; now he decided to have an enhanced ceremony to win the gods over for his campaign against the Germans. The *lectisternium* – a propitiatory ceremony performed at times of great calamity and offered to the gods, represented by their busts and statues or other symbols – was another link with the Punic Wars, for after the defeat by Hannibal at Lake Trasimene in 217 BC the Romans had offered the placatory sacred meal to six pairs of gods (Jupiter/Juno, Neptune/Minerva, Mars/Venus, Apollo/Diana, Vulcan/Vesta, Mercury/Ceres) in ceremonies lasting three days.[143] Marcus in effect doubled up on this procedure, since he had the evil both of the plague and the Germans to ward off. Evincing at once his deeply superstitious nature and his religious eclecticism, he carried out further ceremonies, not just those directed to the Olympians, but aimed at enlisting the possible help of other gods: Isis, Magna Mater, Mithras, and so on (but not, of course, Jesus Christ). He carried out all the non-Roman rites, summoned priests of every stripe and denomination, and purified the city by every known technique. He even employed Chaldean necromancers and assorted maguses and magicians.[144] At the back of his mind was the thought that the plague, and possibly the German invasion also, was divine punishment for the blasphemy committed when legionaries removed the cult statue of

Apollo Comaeus during the sack of Seleucia in the Parthian war.[145] As a further prop for Roman morale he distributed the fourth *congiarium* of his reign. He had no doubt that, whatever military preparations he himself had made on the Danube, he was now engaged in a just war, for the Germans had struck first.[146] But there was more. In Marcus's mind he was involved in the most serious fight for survival that any emperor had ever had to deal with. Defeat could mean the end of Rome, the empire and all that was connoted by Roman civilisation.

14

From the time the Marcomanni made their sensational march on Aquileia in 167 until the departure of Marcus for the same city nearly a year later, a sense of gloomy foreboding suffused the city of Rome. All were aware that Rome faced a grave crisis, and the emperor had to tack between stressing the urgency of the situation and not affecting the morale of Romans by anything that smacked of panic. He began by raising money to pay for new troops. Leading by example, he conducted a two-month sale of imperial effects and possessions, putting under the hammer not just sumptuous furniture from the imperial apartments, gold goblets, silver flagons, crystals and chandeliers, but also his wife's silken, gold-embroidered robes and her jewels.[1] Clearly the auction of imperial property was more a propaganda move than a serious fund-raising effort, but it did the trick in terms of public relations, especially when Marcus suspended all debts to the imperial treasury. To an extent he was lucky. The Germans seemed to have surprised even themselves by the success of their first raid, which left them uncertain what to do next. Had they continued to stay on Italian soil, Marcus could not have allowed himself the luxury of so much time in the bosom of his family. While they withdrew across the Alps to ponder their next step, Marcus was left with a vital breathing space in which to plan the counter-strike. Massive numbers of new troops were raised, partly to relieve the fall in numbers caused by the plague, partly as one strand of an obvious grand strategy of counter-attack.[2] There was an unusually large intake in the legions, and additionally

Marcus was assembling new, special units, for which he recruited from slaves (as in the Punic Wars), gladiators and members of city police forces (especially in the Greek cities of the eastern empire); he even paid a substantial bounty to members of bandit groups, whether real or so-called, to abandon their precarious life of brigandage and serve with Rome instead.[3] Altogether, the equivalent of about six modern divisions were recruited by these extraordinary methods. Additionally, Marcus withdrew troops from Britain to shore up the defences of Italy.[4]

Meanwhile Marcus kept the volatile Roman population quiet with a series of lavish games and spectacles, including one where 100 lions were exhibited, only to be shot to death by archers.[5] Such diversions were more necessary than ever, for this was the most devastating period of what came to be known as the Antonine plague; its impact was so great that most of the praetorian guard, together with its commander, Marcus's trusted colleague Furius Victorinus, perished in these years. Once again Marcus showed a sure touch for public relations, ordaining that all funerals for plague victims were paid for by the state.[6] But perhaps his most urgent task was to try to protect Italy against a repeat invasion by the Quadi and Marcomanni. To this end, most of the year 168 was spent constructing elaborate defensive fortifications at the Italian end of the alpine passes – the so-called *praetentura Italiae et Alpium*.[7] This task was entrusted to another member of Marcus's inner circle: the ex-consul Q. Antistius Adventus Postumus Aquilius, commanding two legions, possibly the two new Italian ones that now functioned as a mobile reserve. Adventus was one of a tiny select group, including Martius Verus in Cappadocia and Avidius Cassius in Syria, who had special consular commands that cut across the usual boundaries and time limits; both Verus and Cassius, for example, served nine-year stints as provincial governors.[8] The defences of the *praetentura* were powerful and prohibitive in the case of the classic alpine passes – the St Gothard, St Bernard, Simplon and Splugen – but did not provide a watertight barrier against northern tribes wishing to penetrate south, as the Julian Alps were not effectively sealed. In Roman times the *Alpes Iuliae* were far more extensive than today's mountains with the same name. They extended from the Velebit range on the northern Dalmatian coast through the Cicarija and Brkini ranges north of Istria, the rugged plateau of Trnovski Gozd

(Birnbaumer Wald) to the higher peaks at the eastern end of the main alpine chain, taking in the Steiner Alps, the Carnic Alps, the modern Julian Alps and the Karawanken range.[9] Clearly no system of defences could make the Mediterranean hermetically sealed against invaders from beyond the Alps, as the events of 170 were to show. What the *praetentura* did do was ensure that such a threat was unlikely to recur from the Marcomanni and Quadi.

Another early sign that Marcus was an effective commander in war was his shrewd and careful personnel selection. The *comites* he chose as his effective cabinet during these crucial early stages of the Marcomannic conflict included Claudius Fronto (Lucius Verus's former legate in Parthia), M. Valerius Maximianus, Pontius Laelianus, Vitrasius Pollio, Aufidius Victorinus and M. Nonius Macrinus, former governor of both Pannonian provinces. Aufidius Victorinus was the emperor's strong right arm in Dacia and Claudius Fronto in Upper Moesia. Fronto, originally a close adviser in Rome, was swiftly appointed to Upper Moesia, now a praetorian province, when the crisis broke and soon assumed part of the command in Dacia as well (Dacia Apulensis).[10] Scholars suggest that the latter development was a sure sign that the contagion of war had already spread to the mouth of the Danube and that the Iazyges were involved.[11] Both Fronto and M. Valerius Maximianus were to be heavily involved in the war against the Germans, but it is hard to track their precise movements during the campaign.[12] Actions more easy to identify are those of the two rising stars who had made their name in 167 when first contacts with the enemy were established. Claudius Pompeianus was the man who had defeated the Germans in the initial skirmish; hitherto unknown, he seems to have come from nowhere to ascend to the right hand of Marcus Aurelius in little more than two years. M. Julius Bassus, governor of Upper Pannonia, was the man who had held the abortive and disingenuous peace talks with the eleven tribes led by Balomar, King of the Marcomanni. War, as always, opens up vast opportunities for ambitious men, who would have languished in obscurity in peacetime; both Bassus and Pompeianus were in this instance major beneficiaries of this universal trend. Indeed, Pompeianus comes across as a Napoleon *manqué*. From an obscure family, he got his chance in war, climbed the greasy pole and ended by being offered the imperial throne twice, after the deaths of Commodus and Pertinax.[13]

Amid the flurry of military preparations in 168 we suddenly get a clear glimpse of Marcus himself. On 6 January he made an obvious gesture of amity to the praetorian guard on whom he relied so heavily in a speech whose words are preserved: 'In order that our veterans may more easily find fathers-in-law we shall tempt them also with a new privilege, namely that a grandfather whose grandchildren have been born to a veteran of the Praetorian Guard shall enjoy the same advantages in their name as he would enjoy if he had the grandchildren from his own son.'[14] By the spring of 168 Marcus was happy enough with his fund-raising and military preparations that he thought the time had come to make a morale-boosting visit to Aquileia; he also intended to 'show the flag' briefly on the other side of the Alps, to cow the Germans with the warning of the wrath to come. But he was unwilling either to leave his co-emperor Verus behind in Rome or to send him on ahead to the Danube, knowing his unreliability.[15] He put it to the Senate, and easily carried his way, that both emperors were needed initially at Aquileia. Cynics said the imperial pair were only too willing to shake off the dust of Rome, as plague was more virulent in the densely packed capital than in the countryside. The two emperors set off with the praetorians, accompanied by Furius Victorinus, in April. Aged forty-seven and already an old man by Roman standards, Marcus for the first time in his life travelled beyond the immediate environs of Rome and southern Italy. Aquileia was delighted with its distinguished visitors, and Marcus made the city his base, sending out detailed instructions for the building of more forts along the frontier.[16] As expected, Verus proved a problem. Interested in nothing but hunting, he received with elation the news of an interim truce signed with the Germans on the Danube and suggested to Marcus that he should return to Rome, as matters were settled on the frontier.[17] But Marcus insisted that Verus accompany him to the Danube in a brief show of strength; he did not trust the Germans and thought the temporary armistice worthless – something that would hold only while it was convenient for the Marcomanni. Verus then thought of another excuse, namely that the recent death from plague of Furius Victorinus and numbers of the proletarians meant that they no longer had the strength to go to the Danube.[18] Nevertheless, Marcus prevailed, although the trip to the Danube was the briefest possible.[19] Marcus now intended to winter at Aquileia prior to a campaign in 169, but this time Verus was adamant that he had to return to Rome. Reluctantly Marcus agreed to accompany him; it was a fixed idea with him that he could not let Verus out of his sight.

It seems that Verus's health was already giving cause for concern before he left for Rome, but at Altinum on the return journey he was mortally felled by the same kind of apoplectic stroke that had nearly done for him seven years earlier on the way to Parthia. He collapsed while riding in a coach with his brother and lingered for three days before dying.[20] It was January 169. Inevitably, in a cultural milieu where it was thought impossible for any great man to die suddenly of natural causes and where all coincidences and acts of contingency were construed as conspiracy, poisoning was suspected. There were many theories, each rivalling the last one in absurdity.[21] The most straightforward was that Marcus himself had had Verus poisoned, though there was no agreement on the means or instrumentality. That hardy perennial of ancient conspiracy theories – the knife used to cut up meat that was poisoned on one side only – duly made its appearance, though some said Marcus had employed a physician named Posiddipus to overbleed his fellow emperor, since bloodletting was then considered a panacea.[22] A more outré theory was that Marcus's wife Faustina had been Verus's lover – technically an act of incest, since her daughter Lucilla was his wife; somehow Faustina blurted this out to her daughter, whereat one or other of the two women (or possibly the two in collusion) poisoned Verus with oysters to prevent this scandal from ever coming out.[23] The incest theory actually subdivides, with some making Faustina the secret killer and others Lucilla. Another version was that Verus betrayed the incest to Lucilla during pillow talk, and that when Faustina learned this she took her revenge swiftly, fearing that now the secret was out, Verus would try to do away with her. Yet a further variant is that Lucilla was the assassin, motivated by jealousy of Verus's sister Fabia Ceionia, to whom she thought Verus was too close.[24] Even more far-fetched – and explicitly rejected by most classical authors – was the idea that Verus had been hatching a plot to assassinate Marcus, together with Herodes Atticus (who certainly had no particular fondness for Marcus) and other grandees, but that Marcus discovered the plot and staged a pre-emptive coup of his own by having Verus assassinated.[25] The final entry in this ledger of implausible conspiracy theories is that Verus and Fabia were secret incestuous lovers who planned to assassinate Marcus; the plot was then betrayed to Marcus by the freedman Agaclytus, who got his retaliation in first.[26]

All one can say after this welter of implausibilities is that, although we do not have the historical evidence definitely to rule out the many canards, none of them makes sense in a context where Verus was known to suffer from poor health, had nearly died once before and came from a notoriously short-lived family. It is not enough to posit that Marcus was relieved by his colleague's death; he would have been less than human not to be overjoyed at being rid of someone who was increasingly a burden and who had never really grown into the role of co-emperor, preferring instead to be the eternal youth, hunting and carousing. Certainly Marcus felt that he could now administer the empire more efficiently, without an annoying veto from an ignoramus.[27] Yet in some strange way, hard to pin down, the death of Verus created a bad impression at Rome. Avidius Cassius, for one, suspected foul play, and his conviction was later to have momentous consequences.[28] Certain senators found some of Marcus's less-than-laudatory remarks when back in Rome deeply critical of the departed Verus. It was true that Marcus took the opportunity to divest himself of some of the ludicrous titles that Verus had insisted on sharing with him after the Parthian war – *Medicus* most obviously. And, now that he was relieved of the burden of his hot-headed and outspoken 'brother', he allowed it to be known that the entire story current hitherto about the victory in Parthia was one of Verus's fabrication; in reality, he, Marcus, had devised the grand strategy that brought Vologases to his knees.[29] On the other hand, Marcus directed a lavish funeral in Rome, deified his late co-ruler as Divus Verus Parthicus Maximus, and made generous financial provision for his relicts and extended family.[30] It was not Verus's kin who suffered from his death, but his wife and his freedmen. Marcus had never been happy with the influence wielded by Geminus, Agaclytus and Coedes (the Catesby, Ratcliffe and Lovell to Verus's Richard III), or by that of the 'lesser' freedmen Eclectus, Apolaustus and Pergamus and, in a notable clean sweep, purged them all except Eclectus (ironically the man who would later kill his son Commodus).[31] Then, to her fury, he married off Verus's widow Lucilla to the rising star Claudius Pompeianus. This infuriated both Lucilla and her mother, who despised Pompeianus as being both too old and an Antiochine of low birth. Outrage was added to insult when Marcus announced the new marriage before the formal period of mourning for Verus was over.[32] That Marcus married his own daughter to Pompeianus shows that he had no very high opinion of his latest favourite. In his mind he was merely following his consistent policy of marrying off his daughters to nonentities who would never challenge him or his beloved Commodus.[33]

Marcus had originally intended his stay in Rome to be short, for he planned a trans-Danube campaign for spring 169. Yet the impact of the plague was so severe that in the end he had to postpone his plans and eventually abandon all hope of closing with the Germans that year. It was typical of the otherworldly Marcus that, while enduring what seemed to most Romans the wrath of the gods, he could convince himself that the daily scenes of death and dying around him were essentially nothing and that moral evil was worse than the pangs of expiring in agony. He suggests that we should avoid evil like the plague 'because it *is* a plague – a mental cancer – worse than anything caused by polluted air or a disease-racked climate. Diseases like the plague can only threaten your life; this one attacks your very humanity.'[34] Yet while he dilated on the 'unreality' of the physical world, he continued to tighten up training and discipline among the Danube legions, ready for the eventual invasion of Germany. He planned to make his incursion with his newly raised forces and some of the veteran legions, with a reserve formed by the two legions of Upper Moesia (IV Flavia and VII Claudia) plus the Dacian legion (XIII Gemina) based at Apulum.[35] Doubtless the Germans had their own secret agents who followed the preparations in Rome, for sometime that year they made a surprise offer to return large numbers of deserters and captives from the 167 raid on Aquileia.[36] Marcus read this as a delaying tactic and initially ignored it. He kept the Roman people amused and distracted with more public spectacles, but never had the common touch and could not be the darling of the mob. His simple wisdom in taking gladiators to fight at the front was interpreted by the common people as an attempt to cut down on one of their favourite amusements; it was said that he intended to take all who fought in the arena and turn them into desiccated philosophers.[37] In the ranks it was whispered that his study of Stoicism made him a harsh and unsympathetic disciplinarian.[38] Marcus himself had no illusions about his personal popularity, especially after a rumour circulated that the day before he departed for the wars he had lectured on philosophy to an audience of enthusiasts.[39] Another similar canard was that he had asked to have his own book called *Precepts of Philosophy* published after he had left, just in case anything happened to him.[40] With great shrewdness he put the following words into the mouth of an imagined Thersites in the mob: 'At last we can breathe freely again, without our master! To be sure, he was never harsh with any of us; but I always felt that he had a silent contempt for us.'[41]

Sometime in late September or early October Marcus finally departed for the front, having completed his preparations; he gave out that he would be away for about a year.[42] It was too late for campaigning in 169, but it was hoped that spring 170 would finally bring the long-hoped-for Roman offensive. He based himself in Pannonia, where he spent the winter of 169–70 and opened negotiations with the Germans, seeking to detach flaky and unreliable tribes from the barbarian alliance. One of the first targets for his diplomacy was the Quadi, who offered to return 13,000 captives and deserters if they could have a secure peace.[43] Marcus did eventually manage to secure a temporary peace with the Quadi, which kept them out of the war for a while; it was agreed that the Marcomanni and their allies the Sarmatians would be denied the territory of the Quadi, and that the Quadi would return the 13,000 prisoners and deserters. But Marcus was not confident that this arrangement would hold, and his scepticism was increased when the Quadi returned only the sick, useless and aged among their captives.[44] Senior *comites* like Pompeius Sosius Priscus were with him, and to Pannonia too went the new favourite (and now son-in-law) Claudius Pompeianus, whose marriage to Lucilla had not pleased Roman public opinion either, since he was twice her age. So far 169 had been a quiet, yet not particularly successful year, combining as it did the unpopular marriage, the passing of Verus and the melancholy circumstances of the death of his son Annius Verus from a brain tumour. Marcus's apparent partiality for his new low-born son-in-law revealed the meritocratic streak that sometimes surfaced in him along-side the innate conservatism, but Pompeianus was far from the only personality to enjoy a meteoric rise in the late 160s because of the German war. The German frontier proved to be a nursery for future emperors.

Among the breed was Publius Helvius Pertinax, another 'new man', destined to be a short-lived ruler during the 'year of the five emperors' in 193.[45] A study of his career shows clearly the obstacles to success to anyone not born into the senatorial class, the 'natural' elite. Born in 126 at Alba Pompeiana in Liguria, north-western Italy, Pertinax was the son of a freedman – a fact always held against him by his snobbish critics. His father Helvius Successus was determined to give him a good education, so he was sent to Rome to study with the illustrious grammarian Sulpicius Apollinaris of Carthage. In Rome young Pertinax was taken under the protection of Helvius Successus's patron, senator Lollianus Avitus, on whose estates Helvius's family lived. Once 'graduated', Pertinax worked as a teacher for ten years, but, tired of low pay, he then joined the army and tried to secure one of the coveted posts as centurion. In this ambition he failed – the sources do not tell us why, and maybe it was simply because Lollianus Avitus did not lobby hard enough.[46] The best Pertinax could manage was a post as prefect of a cohort of Gauls serving in Syria, but commanding a 500-strong infantry battalion of non-citizen soldiers, with no tenure or future security, was hardly going to be a stepping stone to fame and fortune. It was now that Pertinax hitched his wagon to a much more powerful star – none other than Claudius Pompeianus. Despite falling foul of Attilius Cornelianus, Pertinax made steady progress during the Parthian war by means of hard work and innate talent.[47] He was then promoted to the Second Militia and sent to Britain, where he became one of five equestrian tribunes with Legio VI Victrix at Eboracum (York).[48] Given command of another unit, the First Tungrians, at Housestead in the middle of Hadrian's Wall, he caught the eye of his commander Calpurnius Agricola, who secured him another promotion, to lead a cavalry regiment as *praefectus alae* (Third Militia) in Moesia. With Claudius Pompeianus already on the Danube as governor of Lower Pannonia, Pertinax could hope for further advancement, but openings at the next rank (as equestrian officer in the Fourth Militia) were rare. Thinking laterally, he used the patronage of Pompeianus to obtain the post of procurator of the *alimenta* system for the Via Aemilia region of northern Italy. This was the lowest rung of the procuratorial ladder, with a salary of 60,000 sesterces a year, but became a key position when Marcus and Lucius Verus made their headquarters at Aquileia in 168. Impressed by Pertinax's administrative ability, Marcus promoted him to command the Danube fleet, at a salary of 100,000 sesterces a year. This was a top posting, for Marcus had detached ships from the fleets operating from Misenum, Ravenna and Britain to ensure that he had command of the Danube itself.[49] Less than a year later Pertinax had doubled his income and risen still higher: to a position as special procurator for Dacia on 200,000 sesterces a year. He was right in the war zone, and well placed to impress the emperor further with his almost unique combination of administrative and military experience.[50]

A very different personality and in a totally different sphere – who, nonetheless, like Pertinax, rose to Marcus's favour on talent rather than aristocratic connections – was the physician Galen, destined to become Marcus's personal doctor and the most famous scientist of the second century. Born in Pergamum in 129, he was brought up in comfort by his father, a wealthy architect with creative pretensions, who wrote verse and took his young son to philosophical lectures. A priggish schoolboy, disliked by his peers, Galen showed his intellectual distinction early, to the point where he was said to have refuted one of his philosophy teachers while in his early teens.[51] Encouraged by this, Galen's father Nikon intended him to be a professional philosopher, but events supervened. Galen very soon became a devotee of the god Asclepius, whose magnificent suburban shrine was near Pergamum. There he became acquainted with Aelius Aristides, the orator who had extolled the empire to Antoninus Pius in 144. Many people found the valetudinarian Aelius tiresome, but the young Galen was impressed by what he saw as a lifetime's valiant struggle against illness; from this he proceeded to a general belief in the supremacy of mind over matter.[52] Galen's fanatical commitment to Asclepius eventually led him to believe that he had a hotline to the god; Asclepius began appearing to him in dreams, speaking to him and even recommending drugs and cures. Whether by a process of collective hysteria or by some other mechanism, Nikon also started dreaming of Asclepius, and as a result of one such experience he decided to direct his talented son towards medicine (this was in the winter of 146–7).[53] Galen then studied initially at Pergamum and later at Smyrna under a tutor named Pelops. He next sought out the noted physician Numisianus in Corinth, but, finding him lately departed for Alexandria, followed him there. Under his tutelage at Alexandria, Galen came to regard Hippocrates as the alpha and omega of medicine and to stress the importance of theory. His mastery of theory soon brought out an arrogant streak, which made him despise all doctors who were not saturated in the lore of Hippocrates and made all their diagnoses purely from books of cases.[54] As a physician Galen first made his name by finding a cure for the Syrian sophist Pausanias, who had lost all feeling and function in two fingers after falling backwards out of a chariot.

Yet Galen was not just a skilled physician. He had a vast knowledge of mathematics and astronomy also. Renaissance man *avant la lettre*, he was a polymath with interests ranging from Aristotelian logic to the plays of Aristophanes.[55] A shrewd 'horses for courses' devotee of arcane knowledge, he used his time in Alexandria well, prowling among the shipping in the dockyards, learning from mariners how to navigate by the stars and mastering the minutiae of seaborne trade, with special reference to the cargoes of drugs and minerals transported around the Mediterranean.[56] Only at twenty-eight did he consider his education complete. Returning to Pergamum, he set up in practice, massively assisted by his father's money. It was typical of Galen to claim personal credit for anything, including slices of almost supernatural luck; it followed that he denied that his family money had anything to do with his success, even though on Nikon's death in 150 he inherited vast estates and a huge income, which allowed him to endow a medical library. Not having to practise for a living, he liked to boast that he never charged a fee – though he did not turn down lavish gifts bestowed on him by grateful clients. His first official post was as physician to the gladiators owned by the high priest of Asia; his wealth and status effectively enabled him to start at the top. He developed a method of treating thigh wounds and within four years reduced the deaths from wounds in the arena from sixty a year to just two. Combative, intellectually audacious, resembling Hadrian in his self-assigned 'know-all' status, Galen made a serious study of all philosophical systems, being particularly drawn to Platonism, but also extremely well versed in Stoicism.[57] But his arrogant assumption of effortless superiority made him many enemies, who alleged that he was a mere glory-hunter who subordinated science to his own pride, ambition and self-love; modern scholars on the whole tend to endorse this judgement.[58] Certainly bombastic, boastful and humourless as he was, Galen was not an attractive man.

It seems likely that his skills deserted him when it came to politics, for he backed the wrong political party in Pergamum during the acute 'stasis' or strife that affected the community, and in 162 departed for the bright lights of Rome. Disingenuously, Galen pretends in the autobiographical fragments of his extensive writings that he arrived in Rome as a poor, friendless immigrant, battling against a hostile world, with only his genius to declare. In fact his old philosophy tutor Eudemus, now in Rome, had access to the very highest circles and made straight the ways for his protégé.[59] Moreover, one of his very first clients was Flavius Boethius, an oligarch of consular rank in the emperor's inner circle. When Galen cured Boethius's wife where all previous physicians had failed, Boethius introduced him to court circles. Very soon Galen was giving anatomy demonstrations to the inner circle of Marcus Aurelius's most trusted senators. Correctly reading the runes when the troops arrived back from Parthia bringing the deadly plague, Galen departed for healthier climes in 166.[60] Yet it was typical of him not to admit the truth, but to claim that the envy of small-minded rivals and their detestation of his medical brilliance meant that he had to give up his anatomy demonstrations and eventually leave Rome altogether. From 166 to 168 the historical trail on Galen goes cold, but then in 168 he was ordered to join Marcus Aurelius and Lucius Verus at Aquileia.[61] At this time he was far from being the top physician on the imperial staff and was left behind in Aquileia (not deemed to be one of the truly essential personnel) when Marcus set off back for Rome with Verus in January 169. He seems to have spent much of his time fulminating against the incompetence of the other doctors whom Marcus had around him.[62] But Galen had clearly made his mark, perhaps from discussing Stoic doctrines with the emperor and perhaps from so perfectly endorsing Marcus's strictures about rage. Galen had had two notable encounters with the deadly sin of anger. His mother was a shrew who ranted and raved at her slaves and even bit one of her servants. His father had taken him on one side and stressed that he should never emulate his mother; a slave should never be beaten in hot blood, but only after due thought and consideration.[63] Later Galen had an irascible Cretan friend who was travelling with him once from Rome to Athens. Just after they landed at Corinth the friend lost his temper with two of his slaves and set about them with a scabbarded sword, beating them over the head.

The sword burst its scabbard and the naked blade seriously injured the two unfortunates. As soon as he saw the blood, the Cretan bolted, for he knew the rules on killing slaves.[64] Under Roman law this counted as murder, unless the killing occurred during reasonable punishment administered in cold blood. One imagines Marcus taking quiet satisfaction from the moral of these narratives.

At all events, Marcus had not forgotten Galen, and in the summer of 169 ordered him to Rome prior to being posted to the Danube frontier. This was not at all what Galen had in mind. Always the survivor, he wrote bare-facedly to Marcus to inform him that Asclepius had appeared to him in a dream and told him in no circumstances to travel to Germany.[65] Amazingly, Marcus let him get away with this piece of flimflammery; or was he even more superstitious than we can imagine and placed some credence in this 'manifestation' of Asclepius? At all events, Marcus changed his instructions: Galen was now to come to Rome and be Commodus's personal doctor.[66] Awarded this sinecure, Galen had plenty of time to read, write and pursue his polymathic inclinations. He branched out into dream interpretation, claiming to be able to diagnose diseases with its aid.[67] Later he tended the emperor himself, supervising the daily doses of theriac and winning from Marcus the accolade 'first among physicians and unique among philosophers'.[68] Galen continued to treat Commodus until Marcus's infamous son died in 192, and later acted as physician to the emperor Septimius Severus, before dying in extreme old age, probably in 216–17.[69] He had outstanding achievements in anatomy and pharmacology to his credit and rivalled Pliny the Elder as an omnivore, polymath and restless workaholic.[70] But he had many signal intellectual weaknesses, principally prolixity, windbaggery and lack of lucidity. In debate, truth came a poor second to the intellectual demolition of his opponent, and Galen would use all the low tricks of the intellectual charlatan, disingenuously employing the arguments of one philsophical sect, which he had elsewhere repudiated, to knock down the tenets of another.[71] He had some of Marcus's gullibility when it came to mountebanks and impostors, taking advice from well-known shady hucksters such as Simmias the thaumaturge, a crooked schoolmaster called Philogenus, and a ship's doctor of the quack variety named Axius.[72] Yet for all his faults, Galen raised the intellectual tone of Marcus's court and is an invaluable source for the reign. Without his voluminous writings, our knowledge of these years would be considerably poorer.

While adventurers, opportunists and men generally on the make used the 'window' of the German war to climb the greasy pole, in his lonely eyrie on the Danube Marcus had to work out how best to crush the Marcomanni and what tactics and strategy to use. The size of the army he assembled for the campaign was huge, at least 100,000 strong and it may have numbered 140,000 (twelve legions of 60,000 men, plus one-third of all auxiliaries in the empire, or another 80,000 troops). We can trace the numerous *vexillationes* that he summoned from the legions III Augusta, III Cyrenaica, X Fretensis, XV Apollinaris and XII Fulminata (all in addition to the twelve legions stationed on the Danube), and also thirty-four cavalry wings and ninety-six cohorts of *numeri* and other irregulars. Altogether Marcus commanded the largest army ever assembled on the frontier of the Roman empire. Such high numbers have sometimes been queried, but are not seriously out of line when one considers that Caesar assembled 90,000 troops in 45–44 BC for the proposed conquest of Parthia, and Trajan headed 100,000 for each of his Dacian wars, while at Lyons in 197 when Septimius Severus fought Albinus there were 150,000 men on the field of battle.[73] A curiosity of the Marcomannic wars was that this was almost the last appearance of the classic Roman legionary equipped with segmented armour (*lorica segmentata*) and curved rectangular shields. Early in the third century when there was a mass grant of Roman citizenship to aliens, the legions lost both their clear social status and their clearly differentiated appearance, with oval shields replacing the rectangular *scutum* and the *segmentata* falling into disfavour.[74] Problems of transport, supply, communications, logistics and commissariat for such an army and its horses were colossal, though no detailed facts and figures are available for this aspect of the Marcomannic wars.[75] Compounding Marcus's problems were the absence of good roads on the other side of the Danube, the damp climate, the inhospitable terrain of bristling forests, vast mountains, dank moors and swamps, the vulnerability of Roman supply lines to guerrilla attack and the normal lack of a local food supply, which meant that the Romans would have to take all their victuals with them.[76]

Facing them were maybe 70,000 Marcomanni and their German

allies, plus the countless numbers of Sarmatians operating on the Hungarian plain.[77] Surprise has sometimes been expressed that the Marcomanni, who cannot have numbered much more than 100,000 all told, should have been able to field such large numbers of warriors, but two factors are relevant. Many women fought alongside their men, and female warriors were found in full armour (albeit of a very basic kind) in the aftermath of a battle. Moreover, many tribes, like the Astingi on the lower Danube, operated as a mobile army with entire families on the march, enabling old men and young boys to take part in the fighting.[78] The Romans certainly respected the Germans as adversaries. Tacitus argued that a harsh landscape and climate had, by challenge and response, produced a savage people, physically huge with a natural penchant for battle, impressive with their 'fierce blue eyes, red hair, tall frames'.[79] Although Marcus undoubtedly shared the general Roman view that all barbarians deserved to be killed or enslaved, especially if they resisted the will of Rome, it is likely that he perceived them with some ambivalence, as at once 'noble savages' and as precursors of a chaos world. On the one hand, they were naturally evil, treacherous, destructive, anarchic and benighted; on the other, they exhibited the old-style virtues of Cato and the Roman republic and had avoided the corruption and decadence of the empire. Marriage was strictly observed, with adultery and seduction frowned upon, infanticide regarded as evil; mothers suckled their own children, there was no ostentation at funerals, no usury, and freedmen were not allowed to rise high.[80] In military terms Marcus was confident of success. He planned to encircle the enemy using a subtle mixture of the legions and the Danube fleet and he did not fear defeat. Formidable as they were as individual warriors, the Germans could hope to beat the Romans only if they massively outnumbered them, encountered them on terrain exceptionally favourable to themselves or were faced by incompetents such as Varus in the Teutoburg forest. The only dispiriting thing about the coming war was that there were no fixed assets to attack and destroy – even Parthia had a supply of those – since the Germans did not live in towns.[81]

On the whole Marcus's sanguine estimates were warranted. The Germans were afflicted by a number of severe military weaknesses. They were hopeless at siegecraft and had no idea what to do once they had surrounded a city or fortress.[82] Their primitive technology and lack of iron meant they possessed few swords (though this defect was often remedied by collecting the weapons of Romans slain on the battlefield) and relied heavily on long spears as their principal weapon. Their armour was inferior and sometimes non-existent, and their archers few. Sometimes in desperation they were reduced to throwing stones at the enemy; even the cavalry did this. German horsemen were usually better than the infantry, but again few in number because few tribesmen, even among the more affluent Marcomanni, could afford to keep a horse.[83] The natural Teutonic mode of warfare was the massed charge by infantry in a pitched battle; their cavalry often dismounted once battle was joined and fought on foot, keeping the horses ready in case they needed to flee. The Germans depended on a swift, wild rush in a wedge-shaped formation, with the nobler and better-equipped warriors in the front rank, hoping to break up the Roman line with the impetus of the first charge.[84] Unlike the Parthians, who relied on cavalry and sought to attack the Romans at their weakest point, for the Germans it was a matter of pride to attack the legions at their strongest, when they were drawn up and ready for pitched battle.[85] Partly this was a macho code whereby warfare was the only true avocation for a man, where noble youths hired themselves out as mercenaries when their own tribe was at peace, where even some sort of vague equivalent of Japan's later *ronin* or lordless samurai could be discerned.[86] Partly it was because there was no organised military hierarchy: every tribe fought under its chief, who led by example and did not coordinate with leaders of the other clans. It stood to reason that a series of disconnected and sporadic assaults on the enemy's line by various heterogeneous kinship groups and retinues was never going to prevail against the discipline of the Roman army.[87] As one expert on the 'barbarians' has noted, '[It was] little, if at all, more effective than the Achaean warriors of Homer would have been . . . It was useless to fight the imperial armies with the tactics and equipment of Achilles and Agamemnon.'[88]

Given the propensity of the German tribes to engage the Romans in a frontal assault, to be clumsy forces incapable of subtle manoeuvre and to go for a once-and-for-all solution, they were dangerous only when united under a single charismatic leader, yet not even the prestige of an Arminius or a Maroboduus had been able to effect that. Could the Marcomanni do any better? Apart from the superior armour, weaponry, discipline and training of the Roman legionaries – German warriors would never do anything so 'banausic' as train for a battle – logistics, ideology and culture all worked against the barbarian tribes. Logistics made it difficult for them to fight a protracted campaign, and only the Chatti had anything like a standing army; significantly they were unique in that they came equipped for a full campaign when they went to war and did not just carry enough food to fight a single battle.[89] Mostly the Germans dispersed after a battle, whether beaten or victorious. German culture and ideology were also counter-productive. They spent precious time carrying off their dead and wounded – a point of honour to them – and even after a victory liked to loot rather than pursue a stricken enemy.[90] Guerrilla warfare, too, was ruled out, not just by lack of resources and logistics, but by a dogmatic and blinkered warrior ethos. Slow and ponderous, the tribes took time to assemble their armies, which was why the Romans so often encountered them on their *return* from a raid outside Germany.[91] Even the dark and gloomy forests, which the Romans feared so much and which were thought to be harbingers of evil, were never used as a secret weapon by the Germans. This was partly because they liked to live in depopulated desert areas with clear visibility around, so that they could not be suddenly raided.[92] And it was partly because their long spears were unwieldy in the forest; if a mass of warriors was crowded together among trees, it followed that they could not emerge from cover to retrieve a lance or other weapon and could not therefore exploit any advantage they had over the Romans in fleetness of foot. It was only when the barbarians began to master the bow and arrow in the third century that they started to exploit the natural advantage of the forest.[93] Eschewing the forest, they liked to fight on the flat plain, trying to catch the Romans in open country surrounded by woods and marshes; using these as cover, they would then launch incessant, short, sharp attacks. Yet even then they usually ended up hurling torches and jars of liquid in frustration at some disciplined Roman *testudo*.[94]

Yet over the three centuries since the encounter with Marius, the Germans did gradually learn things from the Romans, even if it took them an unconscionable time. In the early days one of their military weaknesses had been that they did not keep back a reserve, pinning everything on the first frenzied charge; this, after all, was why most of their early successes were gained by ambuscade. The only notion of strategy the Germans had was to guess the likely route of a Roman retreat and set multiple ambushes along the line of the supposed itinerary.[95] The lack of a reserve was in part the result of an individualistic culture in which there was no notion of the common or greater good; rationality for the tribesman meant acting purely for oneself or one's family.[96] Gradually the Germans learned bitter lessons from the Romans and came to appreciate the virtues of patience, discipline and keeping a reserve.[97] The greater the social change towards inequality and a full-time warrior class and the more contact there was with the Romans, the more formidable the Germans became in terms of weaponry, discipline, tactics and strategy. It was Marcus's misfortune to encounter the Marcomanni when they were at the peak of their military efficiency.[98] The greater the economic surplus a tribe engendered by trade and mercenary service, the more it could afford to employ what were in effect full-time troops. That a successful pan-Germanic conspiracy – never before achieved by anyone, not even Marboduus or Arminius – should have emerged at almost precisely the same moment the Marcomanni were on the crest of an economic wave may be interpreted as the work of an unknown political genius. But it looks like the kind of historical determinism that, when it impacts on an unfortunate victim, can seem to exhibit all the symptoms of supernatural ill-luck. It is perhaps no wonder that Marcus sacrificed to every god imaginable.

That the new German alliance was more formidable in fighting skills than anything the Romans had previously encountered north of the frontier quickly became apparent in the first year of continuous warfare in 170. At the same time the extent of the German conspiracy became clear when Marcus found himself fighting on four different fronts: in Pannonia, Dacia, the lower Danube and the upper Rhine. Details of his own campaign in Pannonia are sketchy, but it is clear that when the Romans crossed the Danube to attack the Marcomanni, they sustained a major defeat in this sector with losses of 20,000 reported; among the dead was Macrinius Vindex.[99] Roman sources hushed up the defeat, but, if Lucian can be believed, this campaign had got off to an inauspicious, not to say risible, start. The charlatan Alexander of Abonoteichos, whose 'oracles' were still listened to by Marcus, had foretold a victory in 167, but when the disaster of Aquileia unfolded, he blithely stated the 'god' had not told him whether the Romans or the Germans would win it. This does not seem to have dented his credibility, for his next trick was to inform Marcus that he would win the campaign in 170 if he threw two lions into the Danube.[100] This was done and the lions swam across the river to the far shore, where they were immediatedly clubbed to death by the Marcomanni, who took them for a new breed of dog or wolf. Most authorities accept as authentic this tale, which does not redound to Marcus's credit, but some mitigate the emperor's folly by saying that he obeyed Alexander's oracle not because he believed it, but because he was under pressure from his superstitious troops.[101] Quite where the devastating Roman defeat took place is unclear: some say that Marcus himself was not involved, that his forces were pinned down by the Marcomanni in Upper Pannonia and that the German victory occurred further down the Danube.[102] Whatever took place on the battlefield, two factors seem to have aided the Marcomanni materially. In the first place, the Quadi acted as benevolent neutrals towards their fellow-Germans. While not formally abrogating their treaty with Marcus by openly appearing in the field against him, they provided sanctuary for the Marcomanni, confusing Roman commanders, much as Cambodia was later to confuse US generals in the Vietnam war. Marcus contained his anger and vowed to deal with the Quadi at a later date; his precarious peace with them held until the winter of 172–3.[103] Second and more significantly, the Marcomanni produced their trump card: the Sarmatians. The Iazyges, the most warlike branch of the Sarmatians and now occupying the Hungarian plain, suddenly appeared at the side of the Marcomanni, making it clear that Marcus had not just a pan-German conspiracy on his hands, but an alliance between the Teutons and these formidable raiders of the steppes.[104]

The Iazyges were also involved in serious turmoil in Dacia in 170. In the winter of 169–70 Marcus seemed to have bought off a Sarmatian chief named Tarbus, who threatened to raze Dacia in flames unless he was given a huge bribe; this was perhaps an early version of the 'shakedown' procedures later used by Attila the Hun. Marcus paid him off, but Tarbus did not keep his side of the bargain and sent his men to assist an internal revolt in the province. In the fierce fighting that followed, Claudius Fronto was killed, the second notable Roman to become a war casualty that year.[105] But serious alarm was caused by the third major offensive in 170. In alliance with the Roxolani, the Iazyges' Sarmatian cousins, the Costoboci tribe made a great trek from Poland south-west across the Carpathians to the lower Danube and Thrace. Thence they raided throughout the Balkans all the way to Greece, rampaging along a corridor 650 miles long, with plenty of leisurely plundering stops along the way; their vanguard got as far as Elateia in Boeotia and Eleusis in Attica.[106] Not surprisingly this foray, which occupied most of the year 170, created a sensation almost as great as the raid on Aquileia three years before. The Costoboci met no opposition until Greece, but there they were defeated and thrown back by *vexillationes* under Vehilius Gratus, who did such a good job that Marcus promoted him and at once transferred him to Spain to deal with Moorish raiders there.[107] By early 171 the emergency in Greece was over, though there were still Costoboci stragglers in Epirus and Macedonia that year, some of whom had joined bands of brigands and others of whom made common cause with Roman deserters to form fresh bandit units. Roughly speaking, it seems that by the end of 170 the Romans had managed to regroup, restore their Danube communications and stabilise their position on the river frontier; above all, they had managed to hold the line of the *praetentura*.[108]

The fourth front, the Rhine, was the least troublesome. Here another probe, presumably by the Chatti, was repelled by Didius Julianus, previously proconsular legate in Africa and now commanding Legio XXII Primigenia in Upper Germany.[109] But Marcus evidently considered the threat on the Rhine serious, for he dispatched his favourite and son-in-law, Claudius Pompeianus, to deal with it. Pompeianus used the opportunity to turn the tables on his political enemies. It seems that when Claudius Fronto was killed fighting the Iazyges, the anti-Pompeianus faction (not daring to confront him openly) attacked his protégé Pertinax instead and poured poison into Marcus's ear to the effect that Pertinax was really to blame for Fronto's death. Perhaps temporarily disorientated and discomfited by a series of defeats, Marcus listened to the calumny and dismissed Pertinax.[110] Pompeianus immediately hit back by making Pertinax his field commander on the Rhine. When Pertinax won a decisive victory there, Pompeianus persuaded Marcus that his treatment of Pertinax had been a mistake. In a possible overreaction once he realised he had been hoodwinked, Marcus recalled Pertinax and put him in command of the Danube *vexillationes*. When his continued good showing in that post convinced Marcus that Pompeianus's opinion had been correct, he made Pertinax a senator and also a praetorian so that he could command a legion.[111] By the year 171 Pertinax had reached the top of the tree, commander of I Adiutrix in Raetia and Noricum. He in turn was then able to help *his* protégé Valerius Maximianus, a man whose career always seemed to run in tandem with that of Pertinax. Maximianus was given responsibility for escorting the supply caravans down the Danube to the armies in Pannonia. Thereafter he commanded detachments of the fleet. As Pertinax rose higher and higher, so did he. He was prefect of the cavalry detachments *ala I Hispanorum Aravacorum* in Upper Pannonia and later prefect of the *ala Contariorum* at Arrabona on the Danube (east of Brigetio).[112] Like Pertinax, he eventually became one of Marcus's most trusted commanders. From the acorn when Marcus adopted a nonentity as son-in-law, and thus engendered the nexus Marcus-Pompeianus–Pertinax-Maximianus, the oak of two great military careers grew up.

All in all, 170 had not been a good year for the warrior Marcus and, although the Romans had not been routed or driven from the Danube, they had taken heavy losses. Unquestionably the German alliance won that year's contest on points. In Rome the faint-hearted clamoured for Marcus to make a makeshift peace – any peace – and to cut his losses. But he was determined to stick it out, confident that in a long war of attrition, Roman discipline, stamina, resources and moral fibre would in the end tell.[113] There are few direct references to the war in Marcus's own *Meditations*, but one passage can perhaps be read as expressing his ambivalence about the 'indifferent' task he was engaged in, his contempt for the barbarians and perhaps a growing realisation that, in the long term, his most dangerous enemy was the Iazyges: 'A spider is proud when it catches a fly, a man when he snares a hare, another when he nets a fish, another wild boars, another bears, another Sarmatians. If you test their principles, aren't they all brigands?'[114] Marcus certainly needed all his Stoic detachment at this juncture. The war was going badly and the desertion rate was growing alarmingly, contributing in turn to the increasing problem of banditry in the empire.[115] Further evidence of Roman setbacks in this year comes from the coinage. The high output suggests the increasing amounts of money having to be paid for troops and the replacements for heavy casualties. Another sign that the treasury was having to withstand rude shocks comes from the progressive debasement of the silver content of coins that were being minted – a process that would continue until 173.[116] Naturally, as in all wars, there were winners and losers. The war generated huge profits and fortunes for some Romans, as there were new roads to be built and old ones repaired, new ships to be launched and arms and armour to be manufactured, to say nothing of the horses, mules and draught animals to be supplied, the clothing, shoes and other artefacts to be sold, and the contracts for supplying food and materiel to the army, which lucky agents could win. Since all requisitioning took place on the Danube frontier, Rome and Italy were largely saved the impact of the war, except for the loss of family members in the army. Marcus took comfort from the lessons he had learned from a year of disappointment and concentrated the legions II and III Italica between Noricum and Raetia, the sector where the Germans seemed to have won their surprise victory.[117]

The year 171 saw Marcus vindicated in his determination to play the long game. Carefully and systematically he played the game of 'divide and rule', sowing dissension among the Germans, setting tribe against tribe, encouraging personal rivalries within tribes and above all hammering home the lesson that the Germans were engaged in a struggle they could never win. The solid German coalition had already cracked when the Quadi signed a peace treaty with Rome in 169–70, even if they were perfidious in keeping its terms. Their unilateralism underlined the moral that, at the limit, the tribes would always put self-interest ahead of anti-Roman hatred or pan-Germanic solidarity. Testing to see how many advantages they could derive from their officially neutral status, the Quadi once again raised the issue of incorporation into the Roman free-trade area or being granted most-favoured-nation status. Once again Marcus brusquely turned them down.[118] The Quadi bided their time, waiting to see the outcome of his expected offensive against the Marcomanni, but Marcus was in no hurry to engage them. He could not risk another defeat, so he concentrated on building up his forces, always waiting for a mistake by the foe that would allow him to strike. In the meantime 'divide and rule' paid dividends. By the end of 171 the Costoboci, who had convulsed Greece and the Balkans the year before, were no longer a serious factor. Skilfully exploiting inter-tribal rivalries, Cornelius

Clemens, governor of Dacia, managed to divert a migration by the Vandal tribes of the Asdingi and Lacringi into the territory of the Costoboci, and then tempted the Costoboci to attack the interlopers by promising Roman aid and subsidies. The Asdingi were at first successful, whereupon Clemens proved the arch-Machiavellian by gulling the Lacringi into attacking their 'brothers', who had become too powerful. He then encouraged the vanquished Costoboci to rise up and deal with the Lacringi. When the Costoboci won this engineered 'civil war', Marcus encouraged them to become loyal Roman allies by generous gifts of land and money. Thoroughly made over by the combination of stick and carrot, they proved loyal allies in the struggle against the Marcomanni.[119] But the Roman ploy did not always work. Marcus's *ab epistulis Latinis*, Tarruttienus Paternus, was given the mission to persuade the Cotini, a tribe that lived in the rear of the Marcomanni, to launch a sneak attack from behind. But the outraged Cotini beat up the envoy and threw him out, telling him he was lucky to escape with his life.[120]

Overall, though, the 'divide and rule' tactics worked. More and more tribes put out feelers to Marcus, hoping to steal a march on the other Germans by getting special and exceptional terms. Even within the tribes that remained hostile there was dissension, with individual clans breaking rank and surrendering to the Romans. Sometimes embassies were sent directly by councils of the whole people, bypassing the tribal leaders.[121] Gradually Roman successes grew and, with them, increasing confidence. The new military star Pertinax cleared every last German out of Raetia and Noricum, even though his enemies in Rome continued the snobbish whispering campaign against him, bruiting about his 'low birth'.[122] Another great coup achieved by the Romans in 171 was by Pertinax's friend and colleague, Valerius Maximianus, who effectively ended the participation of the Naristae in the war when he slew their chief Valao in single combat – an exploit that seemed to recall the glory days of the Roman republic.[123] Having whittled away most significant Marcomanni allies, Marcus crowned the achievements of that year right at the end of the campaigning season when he caught the enemy as they crossed the Danube from Upper Pannonia into Bohemia, laden with booty. A complete Roman victory was the result.[124] It was Marcus's first battle, probably his first close-up taste of heavy fighting, and he was completely successful. It was also the last time the Marcomanni were able to cross the Danube in pursuit of plunder. That the defeat was heavy can be seen from one significant detail. Marcomannic embassies usually consisted of one representative from each of the ten clans in the tribe, plus the war chief. This time the Marcomanni sent two leaders with shared powers and two warriors from the rank and file.[125] Defeated in war and deserted by most of their allies, the Marcomanni grudgingly agreed a truce. As Marcus wintered for 171-2 in Carnuntum he was able to congratulate himself on a careful strategy efficiently carried out.[126] The year 171 had been as satisfactory as 170 had been disastrous. Roman spirits were buoyed, and the new mood of optimism found expression in the first issue of triumphalist coinage. Marcus was acclaimed on these coins as *Imperator VI*; other issues bore the legend *Victoria Germanica*.[127] It was a fitting commemoration of the ten years he had served as emperor.

The year 172 saw further Roman triumphs. This was the year when Marcus finally felt ready to take the war to the enemy and, in a major offensive, he invaded the territory of the Marcomanni. Coinage shows him crossing the Danube by bridge, accompanied by troopships on the river, and Cassius Dio confirms the details.[128] A brilliant campaign, with at least one further major defeat for the Marcomanni followed, with the Romans penetrating Moravia and western Slovakia above the Danube bend. Thoroughly worsted, the Marcomanni agreed peace terms that included the giving of hostages, the surrender of all Roman prisoners and deserters, a restriction on their right to assembly, a punitive ban on all trade with the Roman empire, and a ten-mile demilitarised zone on the northern bank of the Danube.[129] This may have been the occasion when the legionaries demanded a donative for their victories, but Marcus refused, saying that the money would have to be squeezed from the blood of the troops' relatives and families.[130] This was a dangerous thing for him to do, given the heavy fighting, uncertain morale and high desertion rate among his troops, but it shows signs of an unexpected toughness. It certainly contrasts with the liberality of the four donatives granted in 162, 164, 165 and 167, but Marcus probably granted these mainly to placate Lucius Verus, who liked to pose as the soldiers' friend. As sole emperor, Marcus took a much harder line with the army than as co-emperor.[131] His one, dubious concession to the soldiers was to bring his son Commodus to the front and present him to them. On 15 October he gave his son the title 'Germanicus'.[132] It seems, however, that the legionaries genuinely were mollified by Commodus's presence. Always personally courageous, he impressed the fighting men and became a kind of popular mascot.[133]

That year was not an entirely unalloyed triumph, for on the Rhine, Didius Julianus had to fight off yet another incursion, this time by the Chauci who, based on the Elbe, mounted a seaborne attack on Gallia Belgica down the North Sea coast. Hastily raised auxiliaries saw off the invaders without too much difficulty.[134] With the Marcomanni humbled and the Quadi still maintaining their sullen, grudging and uneasy peace, Marcus's next target was the increasingly dangerous Iazyges. These warlike nomads on the Hungarian plain vexed and tasked him far more than the Germans proper: he declared that since the Iazyges were inherently untrustworthy, he intended to exterminate them utterly.[135] Eyebrows may be raised at this declaration of genocide from a philosopher-king, but Marcus was always a Roman first, last and foremost, and such attitudes were common currency with the 'master-race', who evinced a particular antipathy towards foes that stretched them to the military limit; a similar view was in evidence towards the Jews during the Bar-Kochba revolt.[136] Without entirely abandoning his headquarters at Sirmium, Marcus set up command bases at Vindobona and Brigetio also; he was not always at the front, and sometimes in the years 172–5 could be found in Aquileia. But it made sense to shift his base into Lower Pannonia so as to cross the frontier onto the Hungarian plain below the bend in the Danube.[137] It took until the new year of 173 before Marcus was fully ready to chastise the Iazyges, but, once again, his enemies may have beaten him to the punch, for we hear of a great land battle on Pannonian soil in which the Romans scored a signal victory.[138] The coin issues for 173 show the switch from German to Sarmatian concerns, for the religious motifs of Jupiter and Mars embossed on them move from the theme of 'Germania Subacta' and 'Victoria Germanica' to Sarmatian themes. The legend 'Securitas', showing Marcus raising up a turreted Italy, appears on sesterces issued at the end of 173.[139]

It was probably the defeat of the Iazyges, following hard on the humiliation of the Marcomanni, that finally snapped the nerves of the Quadi. They watched appalled as Marcus successfully broke up the grand coalition, setting German against German, easily swatting aside the military might of the Marcomanni. Now the Romans were prospering in their campaign against the Sarmatians. It must have seemed that an alliance with the Iazyges was their last chance and only hope. The war party among the Quadi began by expelling the pro-Roman 'king' Furtius, whom Marcus had imposed, and installing the pro-Sarmatian Ariogaesus.[140] This was a clear abrogation of the treaty with Rome and a declaration of war in all but name. An enraged Marcus broke his own strictures about anger and put a price on Ariogaesus's head: it was to be 1,000 *aurei* if the usurper was brought in alive, and 500 if his head was produced. Moreover, Marcus announced that the Quadi had joined the Iazyges as a tribe marked down for extermination and genocide.[141] The Quadi sent their levies to join the Iazyges on a further raid into Pannonia, but sheer numbers and the euphoria of the alliance must have made the new allies incautious. Winter seems to have come early in 173, and the Danube was frozen when the Iazyges and Quadi headed back across the border into Hungary. Marcus had already proved that he specialised in perfecting river ambushes with his annihilation of the Marcomanni in 171, and now he repeated the trick with even more devastating effect. In what seems like a pre-echo of Alexander Nevsky's famous battle on the ice with the Teutonic knights in 1242 (though on a far larger scale), he timed his attack perfectly and destroyed the enemy force.[142] It was a great victory, and on this occasion Marcus agreed to be acclaimed as *imperator* for the sixth time by his troops, without waiting for the customary vote in the Senate. He probably did this to earn favour with the troops, having disappointed them over the donative. But it was typical of Marcus to play down all overripe triumphalism. Unlike Lucius Verus, he never had commemorative coins struck unless there actually had been a great victory. Even when victorious, he liked to speak of 'mixed success' and 'cautious optimism'.[143] To put his modesty in perspective, it might be noted that the emperor Claudius, with at most one-seventh of Marcus's military achievements to his credit, 'allowed' himself to be acclaimed no fever than twenty-seven times.[144]

It should not be thought that the seemingly endless wars against the Marcomanni, Quadi and Iazyges were wholly affairs of set-piece battles, such as the four mentioned by Cassius Dio. Much of the fighting consisted of hard-fought skirmishes in dark forests and dank marshes, a brutal slugging affair, with no quarter given or asked. Marcus's famous Aurelian column, later erected in Rome to depict his successes in the German wars, convey the reality only too vividly. Its iconography has been well described as conveying 'visible tenseness, anguish in the muscles and facial expressions as Marcus inspects the captured or when a barbarian chief pleads for admission'.[145] Among the horrors depicted on the column are barbarians begging for their lives; Romans clearing villages and massacring all the adult males; the gutting and torching of entire settlements; Germans praying to the gods for divine intervention and rescue; long lines of unarmed men being decapitated as they step up to the executioner's sword; the mass murder of prisoners thrown into open pits, which they had been forced to dig themselves; head-hunting by Roman troops who display trophy heads to an admiring emperor; the abuse and murder of prisoners; the death-marches; the rape of women; the seizure of cattle and killing of infants.[146] Contemporary sensibility would have it that these horrors were painful for Marcus and were sadly portrayed on the column, but this is a strictly modern view. The horrors of war are outside the ambit of meaning to be found on a Roman triumphal monument, and Romans would have seen the atrocities as just punishment exacted by a dutiful emperor.[147] The correct analogy is not something like Picasso's *Guernica*, but the matter-of-fact report of executions and mutilations of Gauls and Germans during Caesar's Gallic Wars.[148] Evidence of a sort for Marcus's attitudes can be found in Books Two and Three of the *Meditations*, written 'among the Quadi' on the Danube in 170–3, where death was omnipresent. He himself later refers almost casually to the severed heads, decapitated torsos and truncated limbs of the dead in war.[149] Roman iconography dealing with the war is concerned with far different things from alleged war crimes. We realise that Marcus's victories have given Rome confidence, that the Germans are no longer feared, as in the past; Marcus is often portrayed as a heroic figure, a giant, with the barbarians as dwarfs.[150]

The year 174 was notable for a two-pronged Roman offensive, one army directed against the Iazyges, the other given the task of crushing the treacherous Quadi once and for all. In June, Marcus himself was at the head of his forces when they again decisively defeated the Iazyges.

By now the Romans regarded him as a man favoured by the gods. Also in June of that year, when hard pressed by the Iazyges, he was said to have summoned a thunderbolt from heaven, which destroyed an enemy siege engine. This was later built up as the 'Lightning Miracle' by Roman propaganda on the Aurelian column and on coinage, which shows Marcus in general's uniform being crowned by the goddess Victory; in his hand he holds Jupiter's thunderbolt, which the president of the immortals had presumably loaned to him to strike terror into the detested Sarmatians.[151] It is possible that the story has some kind of basis in fact, with the emperor's prayers for victory before the engagement being answered by an opportune lightning strike. Meanwhile, the campaign against the Quadi seems to have been entrusted to Pertinax, who came perilously close to defeat; all the evidence in the sources suggests that, of the three main enemies, the Quadi were, man for man, the most formidable. There followed an even more wondrous event, the so-called 'Rain Miracle'. In July 174, about a month after Marcus's victory over the Iazyges in the 'Lightning Miracle', Pertinax, commanding an elite task force, found himself surrounded by the Quadi and desperately short of water.[152] The spectre of another disaster like that of the Teutoburg forest loomed. Realising that the Romans were prevented from reaching fresh-water supplies, the Quadi held back, waiting for them to become dehydrated and demoralised, and thus easy prey. By all accounts the day was blisteringly hot; the Romans had many wounded, they were exhausted, outnumbered and above all parched and thirsty. Suddenly, out of a clear blue sky, a cloud bank appeared as if from nowhere, and a summer storm sent a veritable monsoon of rain down onto the combatants. The Romans held their mouths up to the sky to gulp down the rain, then caught and stored copious amounts of the precious liquid in their helmets and inverted shields.[153] Seeing the enemy relieved from immediate peril by the downpour, the Quadi staked all on a mass charge. Furious fighting ensued, but the morale of the Romans was now high, convinced as they were that the gods were on their side. Even so, some of the legionaries were so obsessed with continuing to gulp down water that they allowed the Quadi to penetrate gaps in their ranks.[154] Cassius Dio speaks of a confused welter of blood and rain, with the Romans continuing to drink as they fought, and in the process glugging down blood (both their own and the enemy's) along with the rain. Then the secondary manifestation of the 'miracle' occurred. The Quadi's charge was broken up not so much by the stout Roman resistance as by a series of hailstorms and lightning strikes. Finally they broke and fled, leaving the field to the victorious legions.[155]

Since success has a hundred fathers and failure is an orphan, it is not surprising that virtually every religious sect in the Roman empire claimed credit for the victory, which we can unhesitatingly set down to Pertinax and a relatively small Roman force.[156] Prayers to the gods that turned the tide were claimed by a number of people with a hotline to the immortals, including Egyptian thaumaturges, Chaldean maguses and representatives of the official Roman religion. The Aurelian column and the imperial coinage clearly identify Jupiter and/or the divine Marcus as the miracle-workers, although the numismatic evidence is probably ultimately inconclusive.[157] An Egyptian priest named Anuphis (or Harnouphis) claimed that he was responsible, and that he had invoked several deities, but principally Hermes in his Egyptian guise as Hermes Aerios, a Romanised version of the native Nile god Thoth-Shou.[158] The Chaldean magus Julianus was another who put himself forward as prime mover, and his candidacy has likewise attracted scholars.[159] The real problem about identifying the god responsible as Hermes comes from the Aurelian column itself, which provides a series of sharp sketches as a guide to the 'miracle'. The downpour is presented in godlike form as a frightening, semi-human figure with a gloomy, threatening face and long beard, straddling the battlefield and taking grim satisfaction in the mounds of barbarian dead and mangled horses beneath him. Since this deity is quite unlike any other Roman representation of Mercury (the Roman version of winged-footed Hermes), it seems likely that it may be a nature-god, perhaps the rain-bearing god of the north wind, Notus, who is described in Ovid's *Metamorphoses*.[160] The most bare-faced attempt to appropriate the 'Rain Miracle' came from the Christians. They claimed that the prayers of the Christian soldiers in XII Fulminata had brought the rain, and that Marcus himself had later praised and congratulated the Christians for their role in this victory. Unfortunately, Christian propaganda was on this occasion rather too transparently fraudulent. The alleged letters from Marcus to the Christians are crude and obvious forgeries.[161] As for the Twelfth Legion, it has been conclusively established that it was nowhere near the Danube at the time and was in fact stationed in Cappadocia, after sterling service in the Parthian war. The legend 'Fulminata' or 'Thundering' was a very old one, given because its emblem was Jupiter's thunderbolt; it had nothing to do with the 'Rain Miracle'.[162] Nevertheless Christians and their apologists have been very reluctant to relinquish their hold on this 'miracle'. It is of course not impossible that Christians were serving in Pertinax's task force, though one would have expected any who had overcome the usual aversion to military service to be stationed in the East, since Christianity was a religion that spread to Rome from the Middle East.[163]

After the victory of the 'Rain Miracle' Marcus was immediately acclaimed as *imperator* for the seventh time by his troops.[164] This time Marcus was reluctant to accept the honour, but acquiesced so as not to give offence to the legions. Scrupulous as ever, he realised that the 'Rain Miracle' was a minor engagement that had been inflated by propaganda far beyond its intrinsic importance. He knew he had the Quadi on the run, but still respected their fighting qualities.[165] For the rest of 174 he gradually wore them down with grim, slugging attrition; there were no spectacular pitched battles. The Quadi hoped the Marcomanni would rise again or that the Iazyges would relieve the pressure on them, but neither event happened. In fact by the end of the year the Iazyges were so hard pressed that the peace party momentarily got the upper hand. Their leader Bandaspus made overtures to the Romans – which Marcus contemptuously rejected – but, when this was discovered, the war party led by Zanticus imprisoned Bandaspus and renewed the war with greater vigour.[166] Yet they could make little impact on the legionary veterans, now convinced that Marcus was a great war leader and that victory was theirs. The Roman mood at the end of the Marcomannic wars was yet another vindication of the moral over the material, though of course one should not underrate the wearying effect on the enemy of what seemed like Rome's inexhaustible resources. By early 175 the Quadi had had enough. They sued for peace on the same terms as the Marcomanni. Marcus granted this but made it clear that the Quadi were in net terms receiving harsher conditions by lightening the impositions on the Marcomanni, readmitting them to certain limited Roman markets and reducing the demilitarised zone to five miles instead of the original ten; this was the classic reward for good behaviour.[167]

By April 175 the Quadi had signed the peace and were out of the military picture. Able now to devote all his resources against the Iazyges, Marcus announced that his new war aim was the total extermination of these vexatious nomads.[168] In contrast to the German tribes, whom he planned to disperse throughout the empire, the Iazyges were roving horsemen who were in principle incapable of absorption in the Roman empire. It is important to be clear that Marcus did not at this stage contemplate two new provinces of Marcomannia and Sarmatia, as has sometimes falsely been alleged. This was an idea that came *later* – specifically on the renewal of the northern war in 178–80.[169] Geography and logistics worked against such an idea, because Sarmatia lacked the homogeneity of Bohemia and Moravia, with their boundaries well defined by highlands and hill ridges, or even of Transylvanian Dacia inside the arc of the Carpathians. Besides, those areas contained mines and minerals whereas the Hungarian plain, the heartland of the Iazyges, was in those days largely swampland. Such a province, if created, would have extended 200 miles from the Danube bend to the line of the Carpathians in modern Ruthenia, with a flank exposed to the unreliable Quadi and other tribes in Moravia and western Slovakia. Another reason why annexation of Sarmatia made no sense was that it was defensible only if Slovakia and Bohemia were also absorbed into the empire, thus resting the new frontier on the northern arc of the Carpathians, but this would have destroyed the peace treaties Marcus had already made with the Quadi and Marcomanni; it would have been feasible only if in 175 Marcus was still at war with all three enemies.[170]

Little has come down to us about the final stages of the campaign against the Iazyges in 174–5, but the Romans must have made significant progress, for by June 175 Zanticus himself, the erstwhile warmonger, approached the Romans with a desperate plea for peace.[171] Marcus, still set on his programme of extermination, would have none of it and was about to send the embassy away with a humiliating rebuff when the sensational news arrived that the empire in the East was aflame, and that Avidius Cassius had proclaimed himself emperor. This changed everything overnight. Quickly changing tack, but inwardly furious that the scheming Avidius had prevented him from destroying the Sarmatian menace for ever, Marcus granted the Iazyges peace on the same terms as the Quadi, except for settlement rights.[172] The Roman propaganda machine presented the end of the war as a total triumph by Marcus, but he ruefully accepted that it was not; on

the brink of total victory in the north, the problems of the East had
returned to haunt him. Nevertheless, he was acclaimed as *imperator*
for the eighth time and given the title 'Sarmaticus'.[173] To salve his
wounded pride, Marcus also insisted on the return of all prisoners
and Roman deserters in Sarmatian hands and the provision by the
vanquished of 8,000 horsemen, to serve as mercenaries in the Roman
empire at the emperor's discretion. Similar levies were taken from the
Quadi, Marcomanni and Naristae, earmarked for the imminent civil
war in the east.[174] If the East could stymie his plans for total conquest
in the north, Marcus would redress the oriental balance by calling in
the power of the northern tribes. His forces were presumably also
swelled by the vast numbers of prisoners and deserters returned by
the Iazyges. The ancient sources speak of 100,000 such men and, even
if we allow for the usual irremediable hyperbole over numbers by
Greek and Roman historians, the numbers involved must have been
huge.[175] This alone underlines how hard fought the northern wars
were.

There were thus three main aspects to the general peace on the
northern frontier signed in mid-175. The Quadi and the Marcomanni
were kept away from the Danube by a ten-mile demilitarised zone
(five miles in the case of the Marcomanni) and were forbidden to sail
ships or otherwise voyage on the Danube itself.[176] Their chiefs were
taken as hostages and dispersed throughout key points in the empire,
following the example set by the deposed 'king' of the Quadi,
Ariogaesus, who was already in exile in Alexandria.[177] The rank and
file, together with the German prisoners already in Roman hands,
were offered the option of working as indentured peasants on great
estates within the empire, with the prospect of becoming free peasants at the end of the indenture period. It must be conceded that this
was not an original notion of the emperor's; the Julio-Claudians had
already experimented with the idea.[178] This was supposed to be an
economic quid pro quo for the denial to the Germans of full membership of the imperial free-trade area, but it was actually machiavellianism
on Marcus's part. Labour shortages arising from the war, and above
all from the devastation of the plague, made Roman proprietors and
leaseholders desperate for hands to work the estates.[179] The German
labourers, who attained the status of peasants on Roman soil, after
some years acquired Roman ways and attitudes, which drew them

closer to Rome and ensured that their primary loyalty was to the empire rather than to Germany – and this too may have been part of Marcus's intentions.[180] The process was not always smooth: a large number of Quadi were transplanted to Ravenna and ended up having to be expelled after (allegedly) having tried to take over the city. Naturally absorption of Sarmatian nomads into the empire was not feasible, hence the demand for mercenary horsemen. It is noticeable that the Iazyges made no objection to a demand that must have gelded them militarily. Of the 8,000 horsemen handed over to Marcus, 5,500 were sent immediately to Britain, which suggests that the situation there was serious.[181] It is likely that the British tribes seized the obvious opportunity presented by the German wars to rise in rebellion once more. All the evidence suggests that the Sarmatian horsemen in Britain were a striking success; some have even proposed that the presence of unusually armoured cavalrymen may have been the genesis for the legend of King Arthur.[182]

Marcus personally handled all these complex negotiations and did so with great skill, ably concealing the extent of the crisis both from his own troops and the enemy envoys. His achievements in nearly six years of war were impressive – all the more so given his total lack of military background. He had shown courage, endurance and true leadership, and all of this while suffering grievously from continued ill-health. With reason, Cassius Dio said that 'he not only possessed all the other virtues but was also a better ruler than anyone else who had ever been ruler'.[183] Marcus's dispositions on the northern frontier, which he left so unwillingly, had been shrewd and his approach to the troubled province of Britain also commands admiration. He abandoned Scotland and the Antonine Wall, concentrating his strength at Hadrian's Wall and reinforcing the legions with his shock force of 5,500 Iazyges. How significant a reinforcement they were can be gauged by the judgement, standard since Vespasian's time, that just three legions sufficed to hold all of the north as far as Hadrian's Wall, and only an extra legion to dominate the entire Lowlands of Scotland as far as the Antonine Wall.[184] A lesser man might have been tempted to use the Sarmatians to fulfil Antoninus's dream, but not Marcus. Moreover, there were several desirable spin-offs from the Marcomannic wars, not least the outstanding performances by Claudius Pompeianus, Pertinax and Didius Julianus, who finally left his long and successful guardianship of the Rhine frontier in 175 to take up a consulship.[185] Perhaps the most brilliant success of all was that of Valerius Maximianus, who now left for the East with the German contingents as the vanguard of Marcus's counter-offensive.[186] Marcus also showed his sure touch by associating his wife and son with his victories and using them to dig himself deeper into the affections of his troops. Faustina, who had been at her husband's side since the winter of 174, was acclaimed as *mater castrorum* – honorary mother of the entire army.[187] Commodus meanwhile was summoned from Rome (he left on 19 May 175) to adopt the *toga virilis*, the formal recognition that at fourteen he was now a man, not a boy. Since this was a ceremony usually performed at the Capitol in Rome, Marcus intended the gesture as a signal mark of honour for his legions. On 7 July – the day when according to Roman tradition, Romulus had mysteriously disappeared from the Earth – Commodus was inducted into the ranks of Roman citizens under the auspices of Rome's founder. Having already been co-opted to all priesthoods, he was given the rank of *princeps iuventutis*, or leader of the knights, and his position as heir apparent was publicly proclaimed.[188] Avidius Cassius had justified his rebellion on the grounds that Marcus was dead and his son too young to succeed him. Marcus now intended to prove him wrong on both counts. It was time for the long journey to Asia Minor.

15

Marcus's reponse to the crisis in the East was rapid: his greatest immediate fear was that Egypt's defection would cut Rome's corn supply and lead to rioting in the city, which the anti-war party would capitalise on. One of his first actions was to send a large body of *vexillationes* to Rome under his reliable acolyte Vettius Sabinianus.[1] That there was a powerful anti-war party at Rome and elsewhere in the empire was not in doubt; to an extent it merged with the Ceionius faction and the family of Lucius Verus, whose commitment to the campaign against the Germans had always been lukewarm.[2] Marcus saw the revolt in the East as a rerun of Antony and Cleopatra versus Augustus and was determined to end it, if necessary, with his own version of the battle of Actium. He was full of confidence, thinking (with justification) that his troops adored him and his reputation was sky-high.[3] His great mistake, he now saw, was to appoint proconsuls whose power became entrenched and who thought of themselves as absolute rulers, unanswerable to Rome.[4] Naturally the rebels saw it differently. They portrayed themselves as the champions of the true interests of Rome, needlessly sacrificed by an emperor whose obsession with the German frontier had gone to his head. They pointed to the massive desertion rates, the consequent rise in banditry and, above all, the sheer cost of the war in casualties. The exiguous sources do not allow us to give accurate tallies for Marcus's losses through battle, wounds and disease, but studies for the years 200–168 BC in the Roman republic turn up average combat mortalities of 8.8 per cent (4.2 per cent being the figures sustained in the average victory and 16 per cent in defeat).[5] If such figures were replicated in the Marcomannic wars, and bearing in mind also the ferocity of German warriors and the impressionistic evidence of high levels of carnage, it is likely that at least 10 per cent of Marcus's troops (anywhere between 100,000 and 140,000 at any given moment) perished – and this at a time when the plague was also cutting fearful swathes through both military and civilian populations.[6]

Yet it was not just the high cost in human lives and in taxes – imposts that the eastern provinces resented, on the grounds that the German wars were fought entirely for the interests of the western half of the empire – that depressed the anti-war faction. It also seemed to them that the empire, both west and east, was in serious danger of implosion while Marcus pursued his fantasies of conquest on the Danube. The North African frontier had always been unstable, particularly in Antoninus's reign,[7] but now the ancient enemy, the Moors of the Atlas mountains, made a dramatic incursion into Spain, usually considered the most tranquil corner of the Roman domain. Many factors were involved in this dramatic challenge to Roman power by armed horsemen who were considered by Pausanias superior even to the Scythians, the Alans and the Sarmatians.[8] They could rely on a sympathetic native population in North Africa, for the Roman ruler there was unpopular and oppressive. Large tracts of the province were crown lands or imperial domains supervised by procurators. Much of it was confiscated land: Nero had been particularly good at expropriation, for Pliny the Elder tells us that he executed six Roman grandees who owned half the empire.[9] Crown lands, an important source of imperial revenue and food supplies, were leased to tenants-in-chief or *conductores*, who received rents in kind from the peasants who worked the soil, and drove them hard, just this side of starvation. Although in theory there was a system of appeals to the emperor if the landlords were too extortionate, what poor peasant could afford to go to law?[10] Assured of a sympathetic peasantry, among whom they could swim, in Mao's famous formulation, like fish in the sea, the Moors looked with envious eyes on the wealth of Roman Spain, just a short voyage away across the strait at the Pillars of Hercules.

Spain – and particularly the province of Baetica – luxuriated in an embarrassment of riches: corn, wine, olive oil, wax, honey, pitch, dyes, wool, cattle, game and seafood, to say nothing of the mines of copper, iron, silver and gold.[11]

Sallying out from their strongholds in the Atlas mountains, the Moors swept into southern Spain in 171, landing first on the coast of Baetica. They chose a favourable moment to attack, since Rome was not only preoccupied on the Danube, but there was only one legion in the whole of Spain, and that was stationed hundreds of miles from Baetica, at León; because of sympathy for the Moors in North Africa, the single legion there could not be safely transferred across the straits.[12] To hold the line in Spain Marcus relied heavily on C. Aufidius Victorinus. Baetica was temporarily switched from senatorial to imperial control and was joined to Hispania Tarraconensis, both governed by Victorinus. Publius Cornelius Anullinus was appointed commander of the Legio VII Gemina and sent south from León to contain the invasion. Additionally, Marcus sent a special task force of 5,000 troops to Spain under the procurator Julius Julianus.[13] It took hard fighting by veterans equivalent to two legions to expel the invaders, but not before they had laid waste to Baetica and raided into Tarraconensis and Lusitania as well. The situation in North Africa remained tense, as can be gauged by a probe 250 miles south of the African frontier by a force of Roman cavalry in 174.[14] The Moors were checked, but not beaten. In 177 they mounted an even more serious raid on Spain, this time attempting a clean sweep of the Guadalquivir valley and effecting a serious breakdown in security and communications there. Landing at Malaga, they laid siege to the town of Singilia Barba (Antequera) and were on the verge of victory. Then they were taken in the rear by the African legion of Mauretania Tingitana (which had dogged the trail of the invaders all the way from the Atlas mountains), commanded by C. Vallius Maximianus, who had been given temporary military jurisdiction over Baetica.[15] Since the Danube frontier was quiet in 177 and there was peace in the rest of the empire, it has been conjectured that the depressive gloom apparent from Roman coinage minted that year must relate to the situation in Spain.[16] Some authorities, indeed, claim that the two raids by the Moors triggered a kind of anxiety neurosis in the three provinces of Spain, which became a general crisis in the third century and led to their decline and eventual conquest by the Vandals and Visigoths.[17]

The second major outbreak of violence while Marcus was at the front occurred in Egypt. This was potentially much more serious, as no external enemy was involved; the trigger was grievances between capital and labour. Egypt supplied Rome with grain, linen, papyrus, glass, hemp and manufactured goods from Alexandria, but it was a breeding ground of profiteering entrepreneurs in search of superprofits and consequent wage reductions and immiseration of the toiling classes.[18] Egypt, in short, was a byword for exploitation: taxation was oppressive, the method of collection brutal and unfair, officialdom corrupt and the entire weight of forced labour borne by an impoverished peasantry. As the yield from the land declined, discontent rose, and villagers increasingly refused to pay taxes or perform forced labour. Many simply went on strike or fled to live as refugees and bandits in the delta swamps of the Nile.[19] Another group that felt the sharp edge was the herdsmen and shepherds of the Nile, but they were made of sterner stuff, with the warlike propensities of all pastoral societies.[20] These herdsmen, the so-called *boukouloi*, lived mainly in the Nile delta, with a particular concentration in the marshes behind Alexandria. They lived a dismal, wretched life, existing mainly on fish. In 172 a trivial dispute over taxation escalated rapidly. Taking up arms, the *boukouloi* killed two Roman soldiers (one a centurion) to show they meant business. The killers then swore an oath of eternal enmity on the slain men's intestines, which they proceeded to eat. A priest named Isidorus arose as a saviour, doubtless the forerunner of the Mahdi and other similar eastern thaumaturges.[21] Evidently a charismatic individual, Isidorus soon gathered around him an army of tough herdsmen, well used to bearing arms. They began by defeating a Roman legion sent against them and soon seemed to be threatening Alexandria itself.[22] The spectre of Spartacus instantly flashed across Roman minds, but Marcus's proconsul Avidius Cassius was determined not to make the mistakes the Romans had initially made in the great gladiatorial revolt 250 years earlier. It was a reflex action for Roman commanders to move swiftly to put down rebellion – to nip the rising in the bud, to extinguish hopes and depress morale by suggesting that the Romans were bound to win and even to march recklessly against superior numbers, to show how superior they were man for man.[23] Avidius Cassius thought that this usual way of suppressing rebellions was a mistake. He declined to meet the rebels in pitched battle, but instead wore them down by a sustained campaign of attrition, waging a war of raid and ambush, as if the Romans (not the herdsmen) were the guerrillas. This was part of the wisdom the Romans had learned from their dreadful errors in the Bar-Kochba revolt. Eventually he was able to detach portions of Isidorus's army by making false promises and appealing to the 'moderates'. It was essentially the technique Henry VIII would use centuries later to put down the Pilgrimage of Grace – and here, as there, it worked perfectly. By the end of 173 the army of the *boukouloi* was no more.[24]

In raising the standard of revolt in 175, Avidius Cassius was able to appeal to all the sceptics who believed that Marcus was pursuing a chimera on the Danube while elsewhere the empire was falling down around his ears. Yet the ancient authorities unanimously convicted Avidius of being driven primarily by raw ambition. Born in 130, he was the son of Gaius Avidius Heliodorus of Cyrrhus, an Epicurean philosopher and friend of Hadrian, who served as Prefect of Egypt in 137–42.[25] Although he had a normal senatorial career, entering the Senate as quaestor in 154 or 155 and as praetor six years later (160 or 161), he suffered a certain amount of prejudice and snobbery because of the anti-imperial reputation of his family: the Cassii were one of the families who had conspired against Julius Caesar, were reputed to loathe the whole idea of emperors and suspected of having plotted against Antoninus Pius.[26] He himself had a reputation as a ferocious martinet. When he commanded troops in Germany, he routinely crucified soldiers for looting. Romans normally reserved crucifixion as a punishment for slaves, so Avidius's reaction was draconian to say the least. On one occasion a band of auxiliaries, urged on by their centurions, slaughtered 3,000 peaceful Sarmatians on the banks of the Danube. Avidius arrested and crucified the centurions, justifying his behaviour as follows: 'It might have been an ambush and, if so, all barbarian fear of us would have been lost.'[27] On another occasion there was a mutiny in his camp, and he emerged from his tent clad only in a wrestler's loincloth. He then allegedly said, 'Strike me if you dare, and add the crime of murder to indiscipline' – a histrionic act of derring-do that was said to have hugely impressed the German camp-followers.[28] Avidius was said to go far beyond Roman norms of severity – which were strict enough – and to delight in refinements of cruelty. One story told of him was that he built a pole 180 feet high and used it to kill criminals in three different ways: by direct burning, by suffocation from smoke and by inducing heart attacks through sheer terror of the ordeal to come. Other stories had him binding men in chains and throwing them into rivers or the sea. He maimed and mutilated deserters, declaring that a hideously wounded criminal left alive had more exemplary effect than a dead one.[29] Although historians treat the biography of Avidius in the *Historia Augusta* at arm's length, and some of these stories are clearly tall tales or expedient exaggerations, it is clear that no one could acquire such legendary infamy who was not actually more than usually contemptuous of the dignity of human life, and perhaps even driven by sadistic urges. An alternative reading is that Avidius was really incapable of controlling his troops, and had these 'tough' stories bruited about as 'compensation' and to save face.[30]

The historian is on firmer ground when it comes to Avidius's service in the East during the Parthian war of 161–6, but here again there is controversy. Avidius was credited with being the military genius of the campaign, but some think he was a mere glory-snatcher, and that his alleged eminence was entirely due to the patronage of Lucius Verus.[31] To his peers he came across as all things to all men: both severe and mild, savage and gentle, a drunkard and a temperance man, a glutton who could do without food, a libertine who oscillated between bouts of sexual excess and celibacy. He was said to take it as a great compliment when he was accused of being a second Catiline.[32] It was during the Parthian war that clearer evidence emerged for his disciplinarian profile: Avidius was said to insist on weekly manoeuvres and daily target practice.[33] Certainly by the end of the war he had a greatly enhanced reputation as a military tactician and strategist, and his rapid rise seems to have upset Lucius Verus, his erstwhile patron, who, as we have seen earlier (see pp. 164–66) wanted to take all the credit for victory in Parthia himself. The correspondence between Verus and Marcus on Avidius's vaulting ambitions has been declared by all the best experts to be a forgery, but it does nonetheless convey a 'Thucydidean' or 'Aristotelian' kind of truth.[34] Verus was said to have warned Marcus that Avidius ultimately aimed at the purple, that he was popular with the troops and therefore dangerous, and that Marcus should look to himself and the interests of his children. The apocryphal correspondence ends with a rejoinder from Verus's colleague that, as cod-Aurelius, is quite brilliant and very much chimes with his real cast of mind:

> If the empire is divinely decreed to be his, we cannot slay him even should we so desire. Remember what your great-grandfather used to say: 'No one ever kills his successor'. And if this is not the case, he himself will fall into the toils of fate without any act of cruelty on your part . . . And as for your statement that I should take heed for my children by killing him, by all means let my children perish if Avidius be more deserving of love than they, and if it profit the State for Cassius to live rather than the children of Marcus.[35]

The reality is that Marcus did not fear Avidius's ambitions, but promoted him as a counter-balance to Claudius Pompeianus. It was not just with Germans and Sarmatians that Marcus played 'divide and rule'. He granted Avidius proconsular powers (*imperium maius*) in the East so that he himself could concentrate on the German wars and so that Pompeianus, whom he was grooming for stardom, would not grow too powerful. His thinking was that since both Pompeianus and Avidius were Syrian, if there was a revolt in the East it would be literally half-hearted, since Avidius did not control all the power and patronage there.[36] As for Avidius, it seems that his personal attitude to his emperor was always ambivalent. To his cronies he lamented that the old republican spirit of Lucius Cassius (he who famously plotted against Julius Caesar) and Cato the Censor was dead, snuffed out by imperial tyranny. Although claiming to find Marcus 'the best of men', Avidius appears to have despised him for weakness. In his view, Marcus tried to make a virtue of being merciful in the wrong contexts: he habitually pardoned the unpardonable. As for his Stoic philosophy, that was at best an eccentricity and at worst an abomination; who needed an emperor who meditated on philosophical principles instead of the interests of the state? It was not philosophy Rome needed, but practical wisdom and, above all, the sword.[37] Moreover, he considered that Marcus's appointments were always poor; they produced a raft of second-rate provincial governors, men who thought they had a God-given right by reason of birth to become rich by soaking the provinces and practising extortion. In Avidius's view, the insurgency of the *boukouloi*, which he had been so hard pressed to put down, was over-determined both by military weakness – since Marcus had drained away most of the military manpower to the Danube – and by the exactions of his officials, which had pushed the peasants to snapping point.[38]

We cannot trace all the thoughts that revolved in Avidius's mind between his suppression of the *boukouloi* in 172 and his eruption into revolt three years later. Some say that he had vaulting ambitions to restore the kingdom of Commagene (a small Hellenised Armenian kingdom in southern Anatolia near Antioch, which had had a monarchy from 163 BC to AD 72 until annexed by Rome) and that this ambition had early been inculcated by his father. Others said that he was influenced by the examples of Gaius Julius Vindex, first governor to rebel against Nero, or Antonius Saturninus, who led a rebellion against Domitian. But two crucial immediate factors seem to have encouraged him to rebel. One was his genuine conviction that Marcus Aurelius was dead, though it remains a mystery why Avidius should have thought this. True, Marcus was a notorious valetudinarian, but such 'creaking gates' notoriously outlive the hale and hearty. Convinced, then, that the emperor was no more, he responded to the overtures of Faustina, who proposed that he declare himself regent so as to secure the succession for her beloved Commodus; it is possible that Faustina also proposed a marriage to cement the union.[39] Her abiding fear was that if Marcus died while Commodus was still a minor, Rome (averse to 'boy emperors' at this date) would look elsewhere for its supreme ruler, and the obvious choice was the detested Claudius Pompeianus. There are those who dismiss the idea of a conspiracy between Faustina and Avidius, on the grounds that Faustina could have found more obvious willing helpers among the generals on the Danube if she wished to be rid of Marcus; after all she was mother of the army (*mater castrorum*).[40] But this overlooks the obvious objection that Marcus's standing among such men was sky-high and Faustina would never have been able to persuade them to such a step. It is also probable that Avidius and Faustina were old acquaintances, being the same age; it is even possible that they were close friends.[41]

There was, then, a certain rationality to Avidius's actions, even though Herodes Atticus dismissed his ambitions with a personal note containing a single word (in Greek): 'you are mad'.[42] Herodes was basing his judgement on certain glaringly obvious facts: no Roman aristocrat of any standing supported the revolt and there was no organised anti-war faction – a political party in waiting, as it were.[43] Moreover, in a straight fight, the legions of the Danube were bound to prevail over their Syrian counterparts, even if Avidius had not already weakened his position by sending the cream of his troops to the German frontier.[44] Nevertheless, at first Avidius's rebellion looked deadly serious. Syria, Palestine and Egypt all hailed him as emperor, with the adherence of the Prefect of Egypt, C. Calvisius Statius, being especially important. Ominously for the Avidius cause, though, two important eastern governors remained loyal to Marcus: Decimus Clodius Albinus, proconsul of Bithynia, and Publius Martius Verus, governor of Cappadocia, whose immediate message to Marcus alerted him to the emergency as early as May 175.[45]

On learning the stupefying news of the rebellion, Marcus instinctively opted for secrecy, mainly because he did not wish the Iazyges to know that the Romans were divided and on the brink of civil war.[46] But as rumour piled on rumour and alarming canards drifted through the camps, Marcus decided he had no option but to address the troops at a mass meeting. The speech was something of a masterpiece, displaying no anger or animosity, but merely sadness and resignation. He began by lamenting that a man he had admitted into the inner circles of government should have displayed such disloyalty and ingratitude.[47] He told the men he could feel no anger, as what had happened had to be part of a divine plan, however bizarre it appeared at first sight. What appalled him was the prospect of civil war and, if the danger Avidius posed was purely to him (Marcus) personally, and not the empire, he would have been prepared to hand the entire issue over to the Senate; perhaps he and Avidius would each make his case, and the Senate would decide between them.[48] Alas, the issue concerned the Roman state and every last one of his listeners; it was not just a personality contest. It was therefore necessary for him to travel east to put down the rebellion, which he was confident he could do, for how could the pampered legions of the Orient withstand the battle-hardened veterans of brutal campaigns against the Germans and Sarmatians? Besides, Avidius's rebellion was already doomed, for he faced a better general in Martius Verus. The reality was that, once Avidius heard that Marcus was alive, he would probably be plunged into despair at his stupid and reckless act and might even contemplate suicide.[49] But Marcus did not want him dead, either by self-slaughter or hostile action. His dearest wish was that the rebellion would be wrapped up quickly, without revenge or reprisals. He intended to pardon Avidius and indeed all the rebels, except for those who had already committed genuine war crimes or atrocities. The address was perfectly judged, exactly the right mixture of toughness and compassion, realism and self-effacement.[50]

In a letter sent at around the same time to the Senate, Marcus was even more explicit. He announced his intention to pardon the rebels, to punish Avidius solely by banishment and not to take reprisals against his family, who had done nothing wrong. He claimed that he would feel compelled to commit suicide if the Senate could not promise him this. It was a point of honour for him that no senator – no matter how treasonous – should be put to death during his reign.[51] 'For there is nothing which endears a Roman emperor to mankind as much as the quality of mercy.' Bloodshed achieved nothing (a curious argument for one who had just completed the sanguinary German wars). 'Would that I could also recall many others from the grave! Vengeance for a personal wrong is never pleasing in an emperor, for the juster the vengeance the harsher it always seems.'[52] Marcus took an Olympian stance towards the rebellion itself. It had never been feasible, he wrote, that Avidius could succeed, since he (Marcus) had done nothing to offend the gods; it was very different with Caligula, Nero and with Galba, Otho and Vitellius (the failed emperors in the 'year of the four emperors', 68–9), who had all deserved to die.[53] He pointed out to the senators that no rebellion had ever succeeded against good and just emperors (he instanced Augustus, Trajan and Antoninus Pius); indeed, Antoninus had expressly forbidden the death-penalty for senators, even for express acts of treason.[54] Marcus cunningly wound up by asking the senators to accept his son-in-law Claudius Pompeianus as next year's consul. Yet it seems that Marcus's policy of clemency was not at all pleasing to his wife. The mix-up over Marcus's 'death' seems to have occurred because Faustina travelled south from the Danube at the beginning of 175, en route for the family villa in the Alban hills. There is correspondence in which she talks of possibly failing to link up with her husband at an agreed rendezvous at Formiae and going on instead to Capua. It is uncertain whether all this is to do with early news of the Avidius rebellion or simply the illness of their daughter Fadilla.[55] But when she learned that Marcus did not intend to pursue Avidius and the conspirators, she wrote to him angrily, accusing him of putting strangers before his own family and showing mercy to people who would have shown no mercy to Marcus's wife and children.[56] This outburst, arguing for a tough line against Avidius, has seduced the unwary into claiming that it is proof that Faustina and Avidius never colluded. It could equally well be read as the despair of a woman who realised that the conspirators were not going to be killed and therefore that her own role in the plot would be revealed.

Unfortunately for Marcus's pacific intentions, his letter to the Senate crossed with news that the 'Conscript Fathers' had spontaneously declared Avidius Cassius as a public enemy, the first person to be so described since Galba.[57] To be declared a public enemy bore the mandatory implication that the entire property of the malefactor and his family was confiscated. Later Marcus would make this good by restoring half of the patrimony to the family, giving gold and jewels to Avidius's daughters and treating the entire clan indulgently.[58] Meanwhile Avidius had not replied to Marcus's overtures in which he offered him generous peace terms and promised to spare his life.[59] Thinking he had many supporters in the Senate and unaware of the proscription by that august body, Avidius sent a papyrus letter to the people of Alexandria, promising them a new era of prosperity under his principate, and pointing out that his actions were no mere *coup d'état*, since he had been spontaneously elected emperor by his troops.[60] He seemed to have been confident of mass support in Egypt as early as April 175, but was not proclaimed emperor until 3 May. Avidius's golden dream lasted just three months and six days. Suddenly word reached Rome that the rebellion was over and Avidius was dead, slain by a centurion named Antoninus and a fellow non-commissioned officer. The two men eventually brought the dead man's head to

Marcus, but he refused to look at it and ordered it buried.[61] He told his councillors that he took no pleasure in this denouement to the drama, but was grieved that he had lost an opportunity to show mercy; his intention had been to take Avidius alive and then lecture him for ignoring all previous kindnesses, before sparing him in a public act of theatre that would demonstrate the vigour of the Stoic code.[62]

In retrospect, the revolt of Avidius Cassius looks like the proverbial storm in a teacup, an *opéra bouffe* botched coup by an army officer anticipating the putschist tendencies of Latin American generals 1,800 years later, but it did not appear so to participants in the drama of 175. It is likely that if Marcus really had been dead when Avidius raised his standard, then Avidius would have been successful, possibly cementing his position by marriage to Faustina. Marcus certainly learned the lesson about over-mighty proconsuls and immediately rushed through a law that no senator could become governor in the province where he had been born.[63] He gave special titles to the loyal legions whose actions had persuaded Avidius's centurion to strike him down, dubbing Legio XV Apollinaris 'Loyal and True' and XII Fulminata 'Sure and Steadfast'.[64] But he was excessively lenient with most of Avidius's associates, particularly protecting rebels of senatorial rank. Nevertheless, a few death sentences were carried out to the letter, to show that Marcus was not just a soft touch and could be tough and ruthless when necessary. The praetorian prefect of Egypt, whose defection could conceivably have led to food riots in Rome, was executed, as was Avidius Cassius's son Maecianus; but, in a rank display of inequity, the real traitor C. Calvisius Statianus, of senatorial rank, was punished only by exile, as was Avidius's other son Heliodorus. Marcus ordered all Avidius's correspondence burned, to protect all treasonous senators and, most importantly, to cover up all evidence that Faustina was involved in the plot.[65] Further circumstantial evidence for the empress's collusion came in the reign of Commodus, when Avidius's *ab epistulis* was finally apprehended and offered to reveal the contents of these letters, copies of which he had made. Not wishing to incriminate his mother, Commodus burned these also.[66] The wider Cassius family was also protected by the confiscation of Avidius's domains in northern Syria, but the restoration of their holdings in Italy.[67] It is doubtful, however, if Marcus intuited the long-term lesson from the Avidius revolt that, in subtle ways, power was shifting to the eastern empire. After the 'year of the four emperors' the military centre of gravity had shifted from the Rhine to the Danube, but it was soon to shift from the Danube to Rome's eastern empire.[68]

Although Avidius Cassius's revolt had fizzled out unexpectedly, and news of this certainly reached Marcus while he was still on the Danube, nevertheless he thought it was extremely important to continue with his journey to the East. If the provinces of Asia Minor and Egypt had felt themselves sidelined and neglected, expected to pay for a northern war that had nothing to do with them or their interests, then it was necessary for Marcus to appear in person, to explain his policies and co-opt the unwilling; also to demonstrate to the eastern empire that he valued its crucial role in the stability of the Roman state and, as it were, to apologise for having seemed to neglect it. It was also important to have Commodus at his side, so that the Greek-speaking portions of the empire could have a close view of their future emperor and even form an affective bond with him.[69] To make the point even clearer, Marcus had coinage minted that explicitly named Commodus as his heir.[70] With the ultra-loyalists Didius Julianus and Pertinax as consuls for 175 (needless to say, the latter appointment reawakened all the old jealousy and snobbery),[71] his position in Rome was guaranteed. Valerius Maximinianus had been sent ahead in command of the mixed force of Quadi, Marcomanni and Naristae (maybe 20,000 strong) to smite Avidius's disloyal Syrian legions, though there was no longer any need for such a task force. Nonetheless, the Germans were on a one-way trip to permanent stations in the East, for one of Marcus's purposes in the general Germanic diaspora was to drain the potential manpower available to any future king of the Quadi or Marcomanni. He may even have raised 'divide and rule' to new heights, whereby, if the experiment with German warriors in the East was successful, he would devise a pan-imperial system, securing the Parthian border with Germans and the Danube frontier with recruited Parthians.[72] The German garrison in the East was anyway a crafty way of avoiding having to transfer legions to the Orient, which was what had happened in 162, thus encouraging the great German revolt in the first place. Marcus was determined not to make this mistake twice.

Sometime around the end of August 175 Marcus assembled the retinue he intended to take east with him.[73] The presence of Claudius Pompeianus can be assumed, and Pertinax was certainly one of the party, along with the governor of Cappadocia, C. Anius Antoninus.[74] By now Faustina had rejoined him, and for the first time one notices among the inner group of *comites* leading scions of the Quintilius family, a Latin sept whose power base was Alexandria Troas, a Roman colony near the site of ancient Troy. The Quintilii had made their mark under Antoninus Pius, when the brothers Maximus and Condianus had been consuls together (in the year 151). Their sons, Maximus (curiously he was the son of Condianus, while Condianus was the son of Maximus) and Condianus, achieved similar eminence in the early 170s under Marcus.[75] Now the family really achieved eminence, for the venerable elder duo accompanied the emperor to help him with their known expertise on Asia Minor, while the sons stayed behind as governors in the two Pannonian provinces. Also in the party was the prefect of the guard, Bassaeus Rufus, commanding a strong detachment of elite fighters. Bassaeus, like Pertinax, was one of Marcus's meritocrats, a tough warrior, reputedly illiterate, and sprung from the very lowliest origins in the Italian countryside; like Pertinax, he had his snobbish critics.[76]

When all was ready, Marcus set off at a speed that pointed up the tardiness of Lucius Verus when similarly eastward-bound thirteen years earlier. A meticulous and scholarly reconstruction of his itinerary shows a route, at first by boat, down the Save to the junction with the Danube at Singidunum, then down the Danube as far as Novae.[77] Thereafter Marcus struck south across the Balkans into Thrace and crossed to Byzantium. A traverse of the Bosphorus to Chalcedon was followed by a south-westerly journey across Bithynia to Ancyra, whence Marcus headed south-east towards the Taurus mountains.[78] Nothing has been recorded of his thoughts during this long journey, though it would be strange if he and his captains had not discussed the amusing and bizarre events during the late war, as old soldiers do, rather than the savagery and butchery. Two of them were thought by Cassius Dio to be worth saving for posterity. A German boy was taken prisoner in the dead of winter and brought before Marcus, who promised him freedom if he would give him accurate intelligence about the enemy. The shivering boy replied that he would do so only if the Romans wrapped him in a coat so that he could get warm. On another occasion a soldier standing sentry-go on the Danube heard a shout from the other side of the river and thought he recognised the voice of a friend who had been taken prisoner by the Germans. Although the opposite banks were held by the enemy, he swam across, released his friend and several other captives and brought them all back safely.[79]

Suddenly tragedy struck. Marcus was just a little way beyond Tyana in Cappadocia, at a village called Halala, when Faustina was taken ill and died.[80] The death seemed just a bit too convenient and suspicious, coming so close on the heels of the Avidius Cassius revolt, so the rumour mills began to grind. It was whispered that Marcus himself had done away with a disloyal and treacherous wife, or that Faustina, racked with guilt and mortification, made away with herself; another possible motive for suicide might have been if she feared her correspondence with Avidius was about to be made public.[81] None of these suggestions has found favour with modern scholars and, indeed, they do not seem to fit what we know of the character either of Faustina or of Marcus. Aged forty-five and the bearer of fourteen or fifteen children, Faustina had reached an age where death would not have been unexpected, given the short life-spans even of Roman aristocrats. Some say she was pregnant yet again and this time her great heart could no longer take the strain. Two other considerations are salient. No death of an emperor or his family, or indeed of any great man in this era, was ever regarded by the ancients as natural or accidental; everything had to be the result of poisoning, plots or other conspiracies.[82] On principle, therefore, we should discount stories of secret assassination unless there is truly compelling evidence. The other point is more obvious. The Romans had virtually no protection against disease, and Faustina and Marcus – never having travelled outside Europe before – were in terrain where they were prey to new viruses and diseases against which they had acquired no immunity. Marcus had trained himself since reaching adulthood to take a steely attitude if his loved ones died;[83] there was none of Herodes Atticus's over-emotionality in his make-up. His tribute in the *Meditations* is brief, but telling: 'Such a fine woman, so obedient, so loving, so simple.'[84]

Modern sceptics say that Marcus's real attitude to Faustina may have been far more complex. Three negative aspects of her personality may have weighed with him. The first was her meddling in political affairs, which led to difficulties as she had pronounced likes and dislikes, Claudius Pompeianus and Herodes Atticus being in the latter group; she overtly supported the citizens of Athens in its many jousts and lawsuits with Herodes, even when Marcus was doing all he could for him behind the scenes.[85] That might have been tolerable, but it was her determination to have a say in the world of high politics that led to the conspiracy with Avidius Cassius. Here an at least partial defence of Faustina is possible. She may well have written to Avidius to declare himself emperor *if*, and only if, Marcus was dead, but the headstrong Avidius read this as definite information that Marcus had died.[86]

Second, there is much circumstantial evidence that Marcus found his free-spirited, assertive and sometimes abrasive (the modern euphemism would be 'feisty') wife a trial, curiously echoing the experience of another philosopher, Socrates, with *his* allegedly shrewish wife Xanthippe.[87] Certainly the busts of Faustina in the National Museum at Rome show the transition from a young beauty to a coarsened figure of matronly petulance (perhaps hardly surprisingly after fifteen pregnancies).[88] Moreover, the absolute predominance of the image of the goddess Venus in the coins struck in her honour suggests a strong, ardent and ambitious personality.[89] Renan's inter-pretation was that Faustina enjoyed the high life and fast society of Rome and rapidly grew bored with her dutiful, solemn husband. In short, she found him a bore: 'His austere virtue, his perpetual melan-choly, his aversion from all that resembled a court, might well seem tedious to a young, capricious woman of ardent temperament and marvellous beauty . . . she did not like her husband's friends; she did not enter into his life; she had her own tastes apart from his.'[90] The ancient writers may well have viewed Faustina with disdain, since she did not conform to Roman notions of femininity. An aristocratic wife was supposed to be seen, not heard, and anything else was considered 'uppity'. Besides, Faustina was an intriguer, and this tapped into a deep well of Roman misogyny, according to which women were excessively lustful and excessively treacherous crea-tures. The archetypal story, showing Roman fear of women and their ability with poisons, concerns Antony and Cleopatra. Pliny the Elder related that Mark Antony, obsessed with being poisoned, employed

a squad of samplers and foretasters. Even so, Cleopatra demonstrated to him how she could evade them all and poison her consort,
if she had a mind to.[91]

The third aspect of Faustina was her alleged sexual promiscuity.
Her defenders say that her general hedonism and zest for life were
written up by hostile critics to make her appear a second Messalina.
Nevertheless, it is not so easy to dismiss the charges against her on
this count. Cassius Dio says that her libidinous character was well
known to everyone in Rome, and that she scandalised Roman high
society by taking low-born characters like gladiators as lovers.[92] The
Historia Augusta, a generally reliable source for Marcus's reign, if not
for other emperors, actually names four of her lovers: Tutilis, Ortitus,
Moderatus and Tertullus – all of whom Marcus promoted, even
though he had once caught Tertullus *in flagrante* with his wife.[93] Here
we must remember that Roman aristocrats, with their functional,
pragmatic 'heir and a spare' attitude that seems to characterise
oligarchs in all eras, took a relaxed attitude to adultery, provided it
was done discreetly. Pertinax was another emperor who took a
complaisant view of his wife's adultery, even though it was with a
'low-life' – in this case a flute-player.[94] What Roman public opinion
objected to was the scandal caused by Faustina's overt, insouciant
sexual liaisons. Tertullus was openly mentioned as her lover in a
lampoon on stage, and on another occasion the mob shouted out
its disapproval for the emperor's forbearance towards his wife's
behaviour.[95]

The fact that Commodus later turned out to be such an unlikely
son for a philosopher-king soon became the orthodoxy that Marcus
was not the father; from Commodus's passion for the arena, it was
inferred that he must have been sired by a gladiator – one of
Faustina's casual 'flings'. One story was that she had an affair with
a gladiator and later confessed the crime to Marcus when she was
ill and thought she was dying. Marcus then consulted Chaldean
magicians, who advised that Faustina should bathe in the gladiator's
blood and then have intercourse with Marcus. This was said to have
cured the passion, but by that time she was already pregnant with
Commodus, which explains his later behaviour in the arena.[96] Others
said that she slept with sailors while at Caieta, but that Marcus,
when informed, said, 'If we send her away, we must also send away

her dowry.' His reasoning was that the marriage to Faustina was part of a general package bequeathed by Antoninus Pius, whereby he (Marcus) had acquired the empire; he could not legitimately tamper with one part of the legacy without affecting the whole.[97] It is impossible to be precise about Faustina's infidelities, though we can work out that her halcyon days were probably 169–72, when Marcus was away at the Danube front.[98] It is particularly important to avoid a simplistic 'either/or' in evaluating Faustina: either she was a Roman madonna or an out-and-out whore. In the French Revolution Marie-Antoinette was lampooned as a man-eater of insatiable appetites, when she was in fact a timid, unadventurous person. On the other hand, she *had* been an unfaithful queen, albeit with good reason.[99] The most judicious judgement would be that Faustina did have affairs, but that Marcus was uninterested in knowing the details; he did, after all, find the entire topic of sexuality a bore. But any suggestion that he should divorce her was always indignantly rejected.[100]

Although Marcus knew the truth, it was essential for the stability and credibility of the Roman state that the myth of Faustina as perfect matron be cultivated. He insisted on deification by the Senate, together with the striking of commemorative coinage, on which she received the mystical title '*sideribus recepta*' ('received among the stars'); on the erection of statues in the temple of Venus at Rome and in theatres, and on the renaming of Halala, where she died, as Faustinopolis.[101] A new alimentary institution – the *puellae novae Faustinianae* – was added to the one that already bore her mother's name. Altars testifying to the worship of the deified Faustina sprang up all over the empire, and her cult worship became quite extensive. The coins commemorating her deification show her veiled, holding a sceptre and seated on Juno's peacock, which is carrying her to heaven.[102] As for Faustina's real nature and attributes, these have always been a matter of controversy and will doubtless continue so.[103] Her death inevitably tempted other ambitious women to chance their arm with the emperor. Ceionia Fabia, sister of Lucius Verus, and the woman Hadrian had originally intended Marcus to marry, made it known that she was willing to be empress, but Marcus would have none of it.[104] Apart from his by now pronounced distaste for the Ceionius clan, he regarded a second marriage as an obvious threat to already established succession arrangements that benefited the children of his marriage to Faustina. It would be folly to introduce the traditional 'wicked stepmother' into such a delicate set-up. In these circumstances, following the example set by previous emperors such as Vespasian and Antoninus Pius, Marcus took a concubine of a lower social order.[105] The woman chosen was the daughter of one of Faustina's stewards. Given Marcus's contempt for sexual intercourse, it cannot be imagined that his new bedfellow's duties were especially onerous.

After the enforced long stopover in Halala, Marcus headed south through the Cilician Gates to Tarsus, where he heard the latest 'boy genius' in action. Hermogenes, a fifteen-year-old sophist, turned out to be both precocious and prodigious, enchanting the emperor with his mastery of the formal techniques of rhetoric and his ability to improvise brilliantly on basic themes. Marcus always liked to reward talent, and Hermogenes was a delighted recipient of his largesse.[106] Logically, the next stop should have been the great city of Antioch, the headquarters of the Avidius Cassius rebellion, with its massive population of 600,000. But Marcus pointedly snubbed the place and, moreover, punished it by banning all public games, spectacles and assemblies – an interdict that remained in place until Commodus repealed it in 181. Marcus's loathing for the Antiochene Syrians seems to have been visceral, but he was persuaded by Claudius Pompeianus to pay it a brief visit on his return trip in 176.[107] The imperial trail goes cold for a while, but it seems likely that Marcus simply looped round Syria by sea and put in again at Palestine, before resuming his overland trek. The so-called Holy Land did not impress him, and he found the inhabitants dirty, unhygienic, boorish, troublemaking, defiant and self-pitying. He was said to have remarked sardonically that he had finally found a more highly strung and belligerent people even than the Quadi and the Marcomanni.[108] Yet the most interesting tradition concerning Marcus's brief sojourn in Palestine claims that he met the legendary Jewish rabbi Juda I and struck up an immediate rapport with him. The two were said to have discussed philosophy and found they agreed on most things.[109] If true, this shows Marcus in a rare ecumenical mood at a time when the gulf between the official Roman religion and other beliefs was beginning to yawn impossibly wide.[110] If true, it also shows him much more tolerant and accommodating to Judaism than he ever was to Christianity.

Marcus's next destination was Alexandria, where he would spend the winter of 175–6. The jewel of Roman Egypt, with a population of 300,000, the city was not just the port through which the grain of Egypt reached Rome, but also prided itself on its status as an intellectual centre.[111] Founded by Alexander the Great, it was already a glittering megalopolis under Alexander's heir in Egypt, Ptolemy, who founded the first university and built a magnificent library, one of the academic glories of the ancient world. Alexandria also boasted the famous lighthouse or Pharos at the entrance to the harbour, 400 feet high and one of the Seven Wonders of the Ancient World. Alexandria was also *the* centre of Greek science and mathematics. Euclid had taught there, Archimedes had been a student there, and it was there that Eratosthenes, librarian of the museum, calculated the circumference of the Earth (in 220 BC), estimating it surprisingly accurately to be 28,500 miles (it is actually nearer to 25,000 miles). The mathematician Hero (first century AD) had invented both a steam turbine and a dioptra for surveying land, sharing with Eratosthenes the credit for prising Greek mathematics out of its cocoon of desiccated abstract theory. There too the first alchemists and experimental chemists had worked, while Alexandria also witnessed the first real breakthroughs in surgery, albeit with vivisection on convicted criminals.[112] Famously, the city was also the scene of the celebrated dalliance between Antony and Cleopatra. Lovers of dramatic irony might relish the thought that it would later be the scene of a great slaughter (AD 215) ordered by the emperor Caracalla, when among the victims would be Pertinax's son and Marcus's grandson Pompeianus, son of Lucilla and Claudius Pompeianus.[113] There were few such sombre vibrations in the city in the winter of 175–6; at this juncture it simply basked in its great wealth. Marcus found it to be a delightful base in which to rest and recuperate, even receiving an embassy from Parthia there. Rather oddly, though Alexandria had supported Avidius Cassius just as vociferously as Antioch, Marcus forgave it instantly and imposed no sanctions. He enjoyed his time there, avoiding all imperial pomp, living quietly as a private citizen or one of the jobbing philosophers with which the city teemed.[114]

In the spring of 176 Marcus commenced a long, arduous and

circuitous return journey to Rome. Once again the details of his
itinerary are not entirely clear, but he seems to have travelled northwards overland as far as Antioch, which he now reluctantly deigned
to visit.[115] Heading west by Tarsus, his route probably ran through
Cilicia and Lycia-Pamphylia as far as Ephesus. Then he decided to
make a long stopover at Smyrna, before the protracted sea voyage
to Greece. At Smyrna he renewed the acquaintance of Aelius Aristides,
whom he had not seen since 144, when Aristides, then a young orator,
delivered his famous speech in the presence of Antoninus Pius. This
meeting has sometimes been compared to that between the emperor
Julian and Libanus,[116] but was in many ways an odd thing for Marcus
to interest himself in; it was almost as if he deliberately set himself
quasi-Stoic tests of fortitude by seeking out the company of people
whom he must have found antipathetic. Aelius Aristides, born three
years before Marcus in 118 and taught by one of the same tutors
(Alexander of Cotiaeum), was poles apart from Marcus in personality, temperament and sensibility. Where the emperor was humble
and self-deprecating, Aristides was boastful and vainglorious; where
Marcus believed in eliminating the self as an object of worship,
Aristides raised narcissism and egomania to new heights.[117] A native
of Smyrna, he had enjoyed a gilded youth and a pampered existence
as a young man. After finishing his formal education, he set out on
a sightseeing tour of Egypt, Greece and Italy, where, at twenty-six,
he delivered his famous address in Rome. Believing himself to be in
direct contact with the god Asclepius, he claimed to receive instruction from him in dreams, in one of which he was crowned at the
temple of Zeus for the brilliance of his speeches – 'for he is invincible
in rhetoric'.[118]

Apparently launched on a career as the new Demosthenes, Aristides
was suddenly struck down in his prime by a series of mysterious
illnesses. His symptoms included breathing difficulties, fever, swollen
stomach, chest pains, deafness and toothache – all of which continued
to plague him for the rest of his life. His syndrome has been convincingly explained as the psychosomatic maladies of a neurotic, with
megalomaniac self-compensation making up for his basic insecurity,
physical weakness and thwarted ambition. One analyst has written:
'Most, if not all, of his ailments were of the psychosomatic type:
among the medley of symptoms which he reports we can recognise

those of acute asthma and various forms of hypertension, producing violent nervous headaches, insomnia and severe gastric troubles.'[119] Another has spoken of his narcissism, inferiority complex and exhibitionist masochism.[120] Aristides tried various remedies, but the physicians he consulted could not help him, and neither could the Egyptian healing god Serapis. It was on his return from Rome, at Warm Springs near Smyrna, that he received his first 'visitation' from Asclepius, who told him to write down all his dreams – these would later be published as the *Hieroi Logoi* or Sacred Tales, the first religious autobiography.[121] In 145 he went to Asklepeion in Pergamum and stayed for two years in the sanctuary there. The second-century rest home and place of pilgrimage had been founded in the fourth century BC as an offshoot from the parent temple at Epidauros, and lay in a little valley outside the city. There were buildings along the eastern side of a large rectangular plaza enclosed on the other three sides by colonnades, and a theatre was attached to the western end of the northern colonnade. In the south-western corner was a luxurious suite of flushing latrines, and within the plaza were altars, wells, springs, the altar of Asclepius and temples of Apollo, Hygeia and Telesphorus.[122] One way of conveying the atmosphere might be to say that Asklepeion was the Lourdes of its day.

During his two years at Asklepeion, Aristides consulted the physician Theodotus and told him his dreams, which simply nonplussed the doctor.[123] Aristides and the other rich patients lived in an atmosphere of pampered hypochondria, surrounded by servants and retainers alive to their every whim. Bored and idle with a surfeit of self-indulgence, Aristides started a craze whereby all the patients told each other their dreams.[124] His personal regime consisted of walking barefoot, riding on horseback, taking cold baths and submitting to blood-letting, sweating under blankets and incessant but inconsequential medical probes and examinations. Galen, who regarded the patients at Pergamum as neurotics, cynically remarked that when physicians told their charges not to drink, they ignored the advice, but heeded it if Aristides's 'god' told them not to.[125] Galen's star pupil Satyrus was one of the physicians who was consistently overruled in favour of 'Asclepius', who on one occasion ordered sixty pints of blood to be let; among Aristides's other attributes, he was what in modern parlance would be called an 'operation freak'.[126]

However, Galen did later diagnose him as a genuine consumptive: he remarked that whereas most people had a strong body but a weak soul, Aelius Aristides had the opposite: a weak body but a strong soul.[127] Aristides finally abandoned his futile regime after two years, but his psychosomatic ailments and visitations from the 'god' continued for the rest of his life.[128] Ironically, he was in real danger of his life on three separate occasions, which in most other people might have concentrated the mind. He was caught in two bad storms on the Aegean, in 144 when returning to Smyrna from Rome and again in 149. And in 165 he contracted the plague, but survived two near-fatal bouts and was left with (this time probably genuine) intestinal problems.[129]

After travelling widely in Greece – he visited Epidauros in 155 and gradually clawed back some of his fame as an orator – Aristides returned to Smyrna, where he spent most of his time litigating to avoid having to fill offices that the citizens insisted he should fill. Convinced of his rights to immunity on the grounds of being an orator and a great sage, he successfully refused to serve as high priest of Asia in 147, as tax collector in Smyrna in 152 and later as chief of police.[130] On the face of it, it is a complete mystery why the dutiful, careworn and courageous Marcus would have wanted anything to do with this scrimshanking, duty-dodging exponent of hypertrophied egotism, but Marcus as a politician felt he had to have lines out to all the notables in the Greek-speaking areas of the empire; similar consideration inspired his tolerance for the even more insufferable Herodes Atticus. Moreover, Marcus later made it clear that he had nothing but contempt for 'Asclepius's' remedies such as cold baths.[131] One of the problems, of course, was that Marcus, Galen and Aelius Aristides were all playing the same game of 'who is Asclepius's favourite?' – all of them claiming a hotline to the 'god' via dreams.[132] So it was hardly surprising that when Marcus eventually arrived in Smyrna in the early autumn of 176, his encounter with Aristides was less than satisfactory. Initially peeved that Aristides did not come to meet him, and becoming even more irritated when he did not appear after three days, Marcus eventually sent the Quintilii brothers to demand the orator's presence. He came in the next day with the lame explanation that he had been so deeply sunk in meditation that he could not be disturbed. Marcus asked to hear him declaim. 'Give me my subject today and hear me speak tomorrow' was the boastful answer. But the valetudinarian prima donna insisted on conditions: his pupils were to be in the audience and they should be allowed to cheer and applaud. Marcus readily agreed to the first condition, 'for that is democratic,' but was terser in his reply to the second: 'That is your business.'[133] One imagines that Marcus was glad to take his leave and embark for Athens. But it would turn out that he had merely exchanged one preening egomaniac for another. In Athens he would encounter the even more egregious Herodes Atticus.

16

The voyage to Greece was uneventful, and in this Marcus was lucky, for it was already past the date of 14 September, after which Roman mariners thought it foolhardy to try conclusions with the Mediterranean. It is a fair inference that on the passage through the Aegean, Marcus often thought of Herodes Atticus, as his name was linked to that of Athens by a kind of inevitable association of ideas. By now Marcus had reached the limits even of his formidable tolerance when it came to the narcissistic Greek billionaire. Herodes Atticus saw himself as a genius who had been dogged by ill-luck, on the grounds that his wife, most of his children and three of his foster sons had all pre-deceased him.[1] The truth was that it was only his vast wealth that made him a player in imperial politics. Self-pitying, with a tendency to public demonstrations of excessive grief that repelled even those observers who did not share Marcus's Stoic disdain for such behaviour,[2] Herodes was both litigious and aggressive, with a tendency to violence when he did not get his way. Marcus had already papered over one major scandal in Herodes's life, right at the beginning of his principate. In the year 160 Herodes's wife Annia Regilla, a relation of Faustina the Elder, died in controversial circumstances after being kicked in the stomach when pregnant. It was a moral certainty that Herodes had attacked her in one of his rages – it was well known that he and his wife of twenty years did not get on, since she, wealthy in her own right, was too independently minded for his despotic taste.[3] The affair was quickly hushed up, and the blame for the fatal blow fastened on Alcimedon, Herodes's freedman, though no one could explain why, in that case, Alcimedon remained in Herodes's employment; the obvious inference was that the freedman knew the truth and was blackmailing Herodes.[4] Regilla's brother Bradua accused Herodes of murder, and the subsequent trial was a cause célèbre. Since there were no witnesses apart from the accused and Alcimedon, the charge was likely to have failed for lack of evidence, but since the Athenians hated Herodes, Marcus thought it proper to exert his influence behind the scenes.[5] Herodes was acquitted and celebrated with one of his public demonstrations of grief, so unconvincing that one student of the trial has called it 'tantamount to a confession'.[6]

Too arrogant to be a good politician, Herodes learned nothing from this brush with the law and was soon involved in several long-running disputes with the burghers of Athens. He deprived the city of part of his father's legacy and deducted from it debts allegedly owed to the estate. When feelings ran high over this, his political rival T. Claudius Lysades used Herodes's unpopularity as an excuse to take over the high priesthood of the Augusti, which had belonged to Herodes's father. Athenians, angry at their exclusion from political participation by Herodes's high-handedness, were now eager for a showdown.[7] Whereas in the past he had always been able to count on Marcus's support, whatever the emperor's private misgivings – even to the point where Marcus had 'leaned on' Fronto on Herodes's behalf – by the early 170s he had managed to alienate the powerful Quintilius family, who were the new favourites at court. Although Maximus and Condianus Quintilius had been appointed the emperor's special commissioners in the province of Achaea, Herodes treated them with contempt and thought it a great joke to refer to them openly as 'the Trojans' (because they came from Troas).[8] He then made the mistake of bringing charges against the Quintilii on the grounds that they had conspired to set the people of Athens against him. Actually there was no need for them to do that; Herodes managed the task perfectly well on his own. His political adversaries Demostratus, Praxagoras and Mamertinus saw a chance to trump his ace and appealed to Marcus, who was then based at Sirmium in Pannonia, directing the Marcomannic wars. The Athenian trio were as adept at politics as Herodes was deficient. They travelled to the Danube and made a point of ingratiating themselves with the royal family prior to the hearing (this clearly indicates that this trial was held in 174).[9] Faustina and her little daughter Vibia Aurelia Sabina, then aged three, took a liking to them, and soon the little girl was heard lisping in her childish way to her father that he must 'save the Athenians'. Soon Marcus himself was sending the Athenians food and other delicacies and inquiring whether there was anything more he could do for them.[10] Already disillusioned with Herodes over the Regilla affair and tired of his ceaseless litigiousness, Marcus was now swayed against the tiresome billionaire both by his favourites the Quintilii and by his own family. Someone less pig-headed than Herodes might have read the runes and settled the dispute out of court.

Evidently Herodes thought he would make his own affective appeal to the emperor by bringing to Sirmium with him twin girls he had brought up from childhood, who were actually the daughters of his freedman Alcimedon; officially the twins were employed as cup-bearers and cooks. But just before Marcus convened his tribunal, the two girls were killed in a freak accident. Herodes and his party had hired a tower as lodgings in the suburbs of Sirmium, but in Roman times lightning-conductors were not used. A bolt of lightning struck the tower, with fatal results. Convinced more than ever now that he was cursed with supernatural ill-luck, Herodes succumbed to another of his surges of hysterical grief, which had not abated when the day of the hearing came.[11] To universal astonishment, he launched a vituperative personal attack on the emperor. Among the words reported were these: 'This is all I get in return for my hospitality to Lucius [Verus], though it was you who sent him to me!' – a reference to the lavish hospitality he had laid on during the Parthian war. 'These are your reasons for judging me: you are sacrificing me to the whim of a woman and a three-year-old child.'[12] By all accounts Herodes's body-language was so threatening and his aggression so manifest that when he made a step towards the emperor, the praetorian prefect Bassaeus Rufus drew his sword and was on the point of cutting him down, believing Marcus's life to be in danger.[13] Herodes was saved from death only by Marcus's swift reflexes when he waved Rufus away. Poker-faced and betraying no emotion, Marcus rose from his chair and made the enigmatic remark, 'My good fellow, an old man fears little' – doubtless meaning that Herodes could not browbeat him. He then swept from the court and said that he would hear the other side's case tomorrow, adding the sardonic parting shot: 'even though Herodes does not give you leave'.[14] When the Athenians made their case, it was so powerful that the emperor was moved to tears. He found for them and ordained punishment for Herodes's freedmen and minions, albeit the mildest the law allowed. Alcimedon was pardoned absolutely – which suggests that he threatened to reveal the truth about Regilla if Marcus tried to scapegoat him this time. Marcus was tempted to pronounce sentence of exile against Herodes, but found a Solomonic way to save his face.[15] He 'suggested' that Herodes take an extended holiday at his villa in Oricum in Epirus, where he was popular after his many financial gifts to the municipality, and undergo a cooling-off period for a couple of years. This was banishment in all but name, but allowed Herodes to escape a formal sentence.

When Marcus was in Asia Minor in 176 Herodes wrote to him, asking why he no longer corresponded with him. The diplomatic Marcus replied that he was still well disposed towards him and that Herodes had no cause to feel aggrieved, since his freedmen (the guilty party at the hearing two years earlier) had been treated very leniently. However, since he himself now intended to be inducted into the Eleusinian mysteries when he reached Athens, he suggested that if Herodes had any complaints he should make them in the temple of Athena just before the initiation ceremony. As a sweetener, he asked Herodes, already a member of the magic circle of initiates, to supervise his own induction.[16] This was in effect a recall of the exile from Epirus to Athens. To try to settle the nerves of the Athenians, who would scarcely welcome the old despot back among them, Marcus wrote to them as follows:

I think that I have shown through my pronouncements that I have made every effort to ensure, by my concern rather than my power, that in future Herodes should be able to join gladly with the Athenians in their religious and secular celebrations with his well-known concern for education and culture; and that the Athenians, recalling the generosity which the excellent Herodes had already displayed to them, should renew their warm mutual friendship for him, on account of which they do not require me as mediator.

He added in a postscript: 'Would it not be possible for them to love my Herodes, who is also their Herodes?'[17] Marcus also held out an olive branch to Herodes by appointing his protégé Hadrian of Tyre to a chair of rhetoric in Athens and asking Herodes to nominate four candidates for philosophy chairs. Yet he never felt the same about him again and remained detached and cool for the remaining short period of the billionaire's life. Herodes was pointedly excluded from the list in the *Meditations* of those who influenced Marcus.[18]

Once in Greece, Marcus and Commodus were duly initiated in the Eleusinian mysteries, although the emperor's sponsor was not Herodes Atticus, but a certain Julius; the officiating priest was the selfsame L. Memmius who had inducted Lucius Verus fourteen years earlier.[19] Quite what these mysteries were has always been a matter of debate, but the essentials were a fertility rite relating to the myth of Demeter and her daughter Persephone, who had been condemned to spend six months of every year in the Underworld. The elaborate ritual for initiates contained quasi-masonic esoteric ceremonies concerning a sacred chest and a sacred basket, said to contain, respectively, a mystical serpent and a holy phallus. In the final part of the ceremony priests were said to reveal a vision of life after death. It has been speculated that an essential priming pump for the vision was the use of psychedelic drugs, perhaps magic mushrooms, but more likely a drink of ergot-parasitised barley that contained lysergic acid.[20] Others claim that a trance-like state was induced by mantras or quasi-Buddhist aids to meditation. Not surprisingly, modern Jungian theorists have annexed the ceremonies as a primitive form of the Jungian 'individuation' process aimed at achieving spiritual integration.[21] Whatever the exact contents of the ceremony, members of the Roman elite concurred in regarding the initiation as a transcendental experience, akin to a personal audience with the gods.[22] The initiation was important to Marcus for two main reasons, apart from the honour of being enrolled in the most sought-after elite association in the ancient world – emperors now routinely aimed at the honour, and Marcus and Commodus joined Hadrian and Lucius Verus on the roll of honour.[23] First, since it was thought that only the pure in heart were acceptable to the goddesses at Eleusis, Marcus wished to show that he was innocent of all wrongdoing – so that he could not be accused of compassing the deaths of Lucius Verus or Faustina – and that neither he nor the

Roman empire was being punished (by plague or German invasions) for any unexpiated guilt.[24] Second, his initiation set the seal on post-war recovery, since the original temple of Eleusis had been destroyed by the Costoboci and Roxolani during their sensational raid in 170.

Marcus's main aim in Athens was to ensure that the aristocratic principle was upheld there. Wanting to cut back the influence of wealthy freedmen, he and Lucius Verus had reimposed the old *trigonia* rule, requiring that those holding political office should have free-born ancestry for three generations and expelling those who did not meet these criteria. The result was said to have been chaos during the years 167–70 when Marcus's attention was elsewhere. Forced to modify his demands, he now ratified a new arrangement whereby a member of the Council of Five Hundred had to be free-born and future entrants had to have both parents born free. He still retained his right to decide so-called 'appealed suits' from Athens – those involving priesthoods, membership of the Areopagus and of the pan-Hellenic council founded by Hadrian, as well as issues involving Athenian citizenship and property disputes.[25] But he wished to stress that he was no mere interventionist, micromanaging emperor, and sugared this administrative pill by endowing four new chairs of philosophy at a salary of 60,000 sesterces a year each, one each in the four great schools of Platonism, Aristotelianism, Stoicism and Epicureanism.[26] Perhaps as a sop to Herodes Atticus, Marcus put him on the advisory panel to recommend appointments to these chairs, whose successors would thereafter be selected by the Areopagus.[27] It is to be assumed (though the sources do not make it explicit) that two of these positions were occupied by Alexander of Damascus, then the leading Aristotelian in Athens,[28] and Atticus, the leading Platonist. Diogenes Laertius is mentioned as the star of the Epicureans, but the Stoics do not seem to have had a leader of the same calibre. The truth is that by this time both Stoicism and Epicureanism were fading in their appeal, and Platonism was the most vital philosophical creed. On the one hand, Stoicism's notion of an immanent, rather than transcendent, god was increasingly seen as a weakness; on the other, Platonism had the advantage that it could address intellectual problems at a higher level than either Stoicism or Epicureanism, with a world view that located reality outside the physical universe.[29] Marcus was confident that in these professors he now had a credible transmission belt between Rome and the centre of

Greek culture. Although he had earlier personally approved the appointment to a chair of rhetoric of Herodes Atticus's protégé Hadrian of Tyre, he left Herodes in no doubt as to who was running things by appointing a vociferously anti-Herodes candidate, Theodotus, to a rival chair in the same discipline.[30]

It was now perilously late in the season to make the crossing to Italy, but Marcus and his party embarked (presumably at the Gulf of Corinth) for a crossing of the Ionian Sea to Brindisi. As if to underline the risks of autumn sailings, his ship was overtaken by a violent storm and seems at one stage to have been in danger of being overwhelmed by huge waves. When the vessel limped into Brindisi, Marcus swapped his philosopher's garb for the toga required by Roman gravitas and his imperial station.[31] His re-entry into Rome had none of the triumphalism of previous emperors returning home and seems to have been low-key at every level. When he addressed the citizen body, he simply stated that he had been away from the capital for 'a number of years'. The crowd yelled out 'eight' in response. Their exact calculation of Marcus's absence, however, owed little to sentiment; by vigorous and repeated hand gestures they made it plain that they felt entitled to a *congiarium* of eight gold pieces or 800 sesterces.[32] Marcus may have refused a donative to the troops during the German wars, but he knew better than to refuse the mob when in money-grubbing mood. The largesse was granted, but Marcus rationalised the forced generosity by dovetailing it into the general celebrations for Commodus's rapid promotion as co-emperor. As soon as he returned to Rome, Marcus accelerated this process. On 27 November 176 he conferred the title *imperator* on his son, and followed this on 23 December by granting him a triumph (somewhat absurdly) as conqueror of Germany; during the ceremony Marcus trotted alongside Commodus's triumphal chariot.[33] On 1 January 177 Marcus had the fifteen-year-old Commodus appointed consul, forcing the Senate to waive the law that stipulated the minimum age at which magistracies could be held. To keep the consulship in the family, Marcus had Commodus's brother-in-law, M. Peducaeus Plautius Quintillus (Fadilla's husband and nephew of Lucius Verus), appointed as his colleague. Commodus thus became the youngest consul in Roman history – younger even than Nero, who was eighteen when he took up the same office in AD 55, the year after he became emperor.[34] To underline the fact that Commodus was now co-emperor and thus had the same powers that Lucius Verus used to have, Marcus set the seal on his son's elevation by giving him the tribunician power (*tribunicia potestas*) and, a little later, naming him Augustus (later in 177); the Senate chipped in by bestowing the title of father of the fatherland (*pater patriae*).[35]

By unilaterally imposing his son as his successor, without any reference to the wishes of the Senate or indeed any consultation, Marcus was accused of undermining the legitimacy and credibility of the entire Roman state and of making a nonsense of his frequent protestations of respect, honour and deference for the Senate. The unhesitating choice of Commodus seemed even odder, as his base character was already evident and had been so since childhood. From the earliest years he had appeared naturally cruel and dishonourable, and to these vices he added a lewd, foul-mouthed, debauched character as he grew older. Such abilities as he possessed seemed almost perversely the opposite of those looked for in a putative emperor: he could dance, sing and whistle well, could mould goblets, fight in the arena and generally act the buffoon.[36] Sexually precocious, as soon as he became capable of intercourse he kept an informal harem of pressganged or dragooned women. His deep character was fully on display at the age of twelve when he found his bath too cool and ordered his bath-keeper burned alive. It was said that his household staff conspired to deceive him: a slave threw a sheepskin in the furnace and the resulting stench convinced Commodus that his vile orders had been carried out.[37] The best of everything was provided for him. As tutors he had Onesicrates for Greek, Antistius Capella for Latin and Ateius Sanctus for rhetoric, but his attitude to learning is well conveyed by Renan: 'The best philosophers lectured before the youth and he listened, almost as might a young lion being instructed, allowing his teachers to have their say, yawning and showing them his long teeth the while.'[38] Marcus naively believed that a loving environment would ensure that all evil was driven out of the boy – a 'nurture over nature' illusion to which many have been prey when dealing with wayward offspring, but one unsupported by the best genetic studies. It was perhaps singularly unfortunate that Marcus was on the Danube and away from home during the youth's key formative years (from the age of eight onwards).

Many excuses have been made for Commodus's intolerable character and behaviour. Some say that the weight of expectations on him, as the only surviving son of eight male children, was too heavy and was laid on him too early. Others amplify this by claiming that he might have been exceptionally lonely and alienated, deprived of his twin brother at the age of four,[39] his younger brother just four years later and his mother when he was fourteen. Marcus was aware of his son's less-than-desirable personality, but excused it – as so many fond parents do in similar circumstances – by claiming that he kept bad company and was subject to bad influences, but would soon grow out of it.[40] Still others claim that posterity has overrated Marcus at every level and that there was a less rational and less admirable Marcus Aurelius who makes it eminently plausible that Commodus was indeed his son. Among the bizarre inclinations that could conceivably have emerged as madness in his son was the golden bust that Marcus had made of himself, and the doting father fantasy that could have influenced Commodus for life when in 166 (when the lad was five) he commissioned a statue of Commodus, showing him as a young Hercules strangling two serpents in his cradle.[41] There is perhaps less excuse for twentieth-century commentators who have opined all the following: the *Historia Augusta* exaggerates; Commodus's faults were venial and his attributes might in certain circumstances have been considered desirable; and the bath-keeper he condemned to death did not die. This incident 'would not be revealing of a sensationally evil and odious character, merely of impetuous bad temper. After all, the order was not carried out, and was probably only shouted out in a tantrum.'[42] The truth is that Commodus was excessively spoiled; developed no moral sense, notions of duty or responsibility; and worshipped at a temple of the self, where only his will and his pleasures counted. This hedonistic and egotistic personality explains one famous conundrum: the alleged absence of Commodus from the Aurelian column. A meticulous investigator has concluded that it was simply Commodus's utter lack of interest and total indifference to the Marcomannic wars that accounts for his non-appearance.[43] We should, however, be aware that this entire issue is highly controversial; some scholars have detected Commodus's presence in the base frieze.[44]

Most ancient authorities had little time for Commodus and no patience with attempts to exculpate or extenuate his behaviour, though Julian the Apostate – who liked to think of himself as Marcus Aurelius reborn, and as such claimed to be able to interpret his thought processes – veered between forgiving Marcus on grounds of natural affection for a child and censuring him for making Commodus his successor.[45] Another emperor, Septimius Severus, was blunter and more brutal: he thought Marcus should have quietly done away with such an unpromising specimen.[46] But while Marcus was away at the front, young Commodus was cosseted and indulged by his sisters Fadilla, Cornificia and Annia Faustina. His so-called moral tutor, in overall charge of the heir apparent, was one Pitholaus, who seems to have given the youth no guidance whatsoever. Nature almost did the job that Septimius Severus thought should have been done by the family. Some time around 173–4 Commodus succumbed to a fever just after leaving the wrestling school where he liked to disport himself; a high temperature gave rise to concern. Galen was called in, took the boy's pulse, diagnosed inflammation of the tonsils and prescribed a throat gargle.[47] The useless Pitholaus annoyed Galen by querying how the physician could make such a diagnosis merely from feeling the pulse. On hourly standby, Galen soon decided that the gargle he had prescribed was too strong and concocted a new potion, a solution of honey and rosewater. Whether this was mere quackery and nature simply ran its course is uncertain, but on the third day the danger was over and Commodus was making a rapid recovery.[48] The boy's aunt, Annia Fundania Faustina, called to see the patient and was mightily impressed by Galen's expertise. She spread word of his amazing skill through her extensive oligarchic network, and soon Galen's reputation was higher than ever. He added to his laurels shortly afterwards by another 'miracle' cure, this time of Quintilius Condianus the younger. Since the Quintilii were the clan currently in great favour with Marcus, Galen had added several feathers to an already well-plumed cap.[49]

Why did Marcus favour Commodus when abundant evidence of his unsuitability for the highest office was extant? Some say that Marcus was always naive and otherworldly, which is allegedly why he could not see through Faustina and Avidius Cassius, either. This is unconvincing. Although Marcus's world view could sometimes appear Panglossian, he had no illusions about many of those who tried to cosy up to him – Fronto, Aelius Aristides and Herodes Atticus being obvious cases in point. At the simplest level, he had a visceral feeling for blood kin and was determined that his son was going to succeed him, whatever the objections.[50] Moreover, Marcus had to be consistent with his own principles, which led him to emphasise *philostorgia* (family and human warmth) rather than mere expediency.[51] Then there were 'structural' considerations. Roman emperors were habitually family members, and even the adoptions came from a network of close kin; Nerva's adoption of Trajan was the only known case where family connections did not play a part.[52] The reasons for keeping the throne 'in the family' were partly financial. Since imperial wealth subdivided into the private property of the emperor (*fiscus*) and the funds in the public treasury (*aerarium*), and thus this wealth was in turn at least partly linked to the imperial family rather than the 'job' of emperor, it was extremely hard for a reigning emperor to exclude a son from the succession without at the same time disinheriting him.[53] Finally, there were prudential reasons. Meritocracy was all very well, but a meritocratic appointment to the purple would risk almost certain rebellion from the excluded kin of the late emperor. To appoint an emperor on mere talent and ability, then, was to hand him a poisoned chalice. When an emperor finally did exclude his own son (in 306), the result was eighteen years of civil war.[54] Septimius Severus was being ruthlessly pragmatic in his recommendation. Once Commodus survived infancy, Marcus was faced with a stark choice: he either had to make him his heir or kill him.

Yet it would be an elementary fallacy to assume that because Marcus confirmed Commodus as his heir for all these weighty reasons, he was totally convinced of his suitability for the principate and had no reservations whatsoever. There is much evidence that he took the step with great reluctance. At one time he may have had hopes that his two sons-in-law, Claudius Pompeianus and Claudius Severus, might be able to rule as joint emperors, much as he and Lucius Verus had done. But when the two men shared the consulate in 173, they proved a spectacular mismatch, divided as much by ideology and policy as by background and culture.[55] Where Pompeianus was a soldier of 'low birth' from Antioch, Severus was an aristocrat from an ancient family and his main interest was Aristotelian philosophy. Baulked of that hope, Marcus also sounded Pompeianus on his attitude to a possible principate, but he, wisely, was having none of it.[56] Too old for the keenest pangs of ambition, he preferred to be a live also-ran rather than a dead hero, and for prudential reasons would later refuse to share the throne with Pertinax. As a Syrian, he was too closely identified with the East, and the East was deeply suspect in the wake of the Avidius Cassius rebellion. Pompeianus was aware that he had many powerful enemies at Rome, starting with his own wife, who had grown fat on the diet of hatred that had also nourished Faustina, for whom Pompeianus was also a bête noire. Most obviously, he knew that for him to accept the throne would mean certain civil war with Commodus.[57] The accelerated programme of promotion that Marcus speeded Commodus through on their return from Asia Minor and Greece in late 176 was simply the recognition of necessity, the acceptance that there was no other option. Yet many of Marcus's asides show that he feared for the future. When he spoke of those who would rejoice at his death,[58] it is hard to imagine that he did not have Commodus on his list. To his confidants Marcus admitted that his son was turning out badly and said that he felt the same way about him that Philip of Macedon felt about Alexander the Great – which did not prevent Alexander from going on to immortal glory.[59] Marcus hoped that this would be the case with Commodus, but this was surely one instance of the triumph of hope over expectation.

The late 170s were a time when Marcus tried to consolidate the nexus of immediate family around him, so that he could die content with his private arrangements, if not with the problems of empire. Only two of his six surviving children now remained unmarried – the two youngest, Commodus himself and Vibia Aurelia Sabina. Lucilla, who had borne a daughter to Lucius Verus (two other children were born, but only this one survived), produced a son for Claudius Pompeianus.[60] Annia Faustina was married to the C. Claudius Severus who had such a disastrous consular partnership with Claudius Pompeianus.[61] Fadilla was married to Verus's nephew Plautius Quintillus, son of Ceionia Fabia and descended through his father from the Avidii and Plautii families; he served as consul in 177.[62] Cornificia was married to Petronius Suza Mamertinus, grandson (or possibly grand-nephew) of Antoninus Pius's praetorian prefect Petronius Mamertinus and also a kinsman of Fronto.[63] After Marcus's death Vibia Aurelia would marry L. Antistius Bursus, son (or nephew?) of the commander of the *praetentura*.[64] Marcus gradually allowed his daughters to marry husbands at a higher social level than Pompeianus and even of consular status, while making sure that none of them had any military ability that would enable them to mount a rebellion against Commodus.[65] In 178 Marcus decided that reasons of state required Commodus to be married also. Somewhat hastily a wedding was arranged with Brutta Crispina of the Praesens family. Her grandfather had been a protégé of Hadrian and had shared a consulship with Antoninus Pius, while her father (a couple of years older than Marcus) had been consul in 153; to celebrate the wedding he was offered a second consulship for the year 180.[66] Marcus insisted that the marriage be a low-key affair, and it was said to have been celebrated with no pomp, almost as if the bridal pair were two ordinary middle-class Roman citizens. Yet it was impossible for a Roman emperor to sneak through an entirely private wedding, for the immediate outcry from the Roman crowd would be that he was being tight-fisted. Some kind of largesse, though stopping short of a formal *congiarium*, was arranged for the people, commemorative coinage was struck, and the sophist Julius Pollux wrote a wedding hymn for Commodus, which pleased the heir apparent so much that he later appointed Pollux to a chair of rhetoric at Athens.[67]

Marcus wanted to put his family affairs in order, for he had a presentiment of approaching death. Sometime early in 177 the fifty-six-year-old suffered a serious illness, which his doctors diagnosed as a fever. He took his daily dose of aloes and then, five hours later, the beloved theriac. At sunset he had a bath and ate a little food, but was then hit by stomach ache, diarrhoea and a raging temperature. His doctors came to him at dawn and gave him porridge and gruel, advising him to rest. When his condition was no better that evening, Galen was summoned and the physicians explained the case history.[68] Galen puzzled them by saying nothing, and when they asked why he did not take the emperor's pulse, he replied that they knew the medical history better than he did; this was presumably heavy irony. Pressed to take the pulse, he finally did so and said that the illness was no fever, but merely a stomach bug. This seemed to please Marcus, who sat up in bed and said, 'That's right. It's exactly as you said. I feel as though I'm weighed down by some cold food.' Galen explained that in this case he would normally prescribe wine flavoured with pepper, but, as an emperor's illness had always to be considered a grave matter, he intended to apply to the rectum a pad of red wool with warmed spikenard ointment.[69] Marcus said he had had such a remedy before and asked his doctor Pitholaus to prepare it. He then had his feet massaged and drank some Sabine wine mixed with pepper. Soon he was fully recovered. It seems that his physicians had panicked and overreacted and the emergency was little more than gastric flu or enteritis. Nevertheless, Marcus acclaimed Galen's treatment as yet another miracle cure and, as previously mentioned, referred to him as 'first among physicians and unique among philosophers'.[70]

In 177 Marcus was able for a short time to turn his attention almost exclusively to questions of law and administration – it had been ten years since he was last in this position. Nevertheless, even at the height of the Marcomannic wars, he never neglected this aspect of his principate. At Sirmium he often put in an eleven- or twelve-hour day on a single lawsuit and then spent the same number of days on it, even holding sessions at night. Cassius Dio reports that he had a standing order for a supply of water for the water clocks used in court to ensure that no one exceeded the time allotted for speaking.[71] Marcus was a devotee of the old adage *festina lente* ('make haste slowly'), trying to get through the press of business while still being meticulous over detail, to the point where he would spend an entire day getting the minutiae of a case absolutely right. And he did all this while suffering very poor health, forever plagued by mysterious complaints in the chest and stomach, using his beloved theriac as a panacea.[72] As ever, family law was his chief interest. In one case a woman married to a senator from Sparta had left a substantial legacy to her two sons, with the proviso that they could receive it only when their father was dead and they were no longer under his legal control. The senator proposed to emancipate his sons formally so that they could inherit at once, and argued before Marcus that his late wife had framed her will as she did to ensure that her sons (and not her husband) got the money. The senator, Brasidas by name, pleaded that in law his emancipation of his sons was tantamount to his death, as it released them from his control and they were therefore entitled to receive the legacy at once.[73] Marcus granted the plea, even though cynics whispered that the emancipation was an obvious 'stitch-up': clearly the father had secretly agreed with the sons to carve up the legacy in a three-way split in return for his emancipating them.

From 177 onwards legal and administrative decisions were made in the names of the co-emperors Marcus Aurelius and Commodus. It is interesting that, despite his official disdain for sexual passion, Marcus was prepared to accept a plea of *crime passionnel* in his court.[74] A man killed his daughter's lover and thought he had killed the daughter also when he caught them in bed, but the daughter survived. Roman law clearly stated that *crime passionnel* would be accepted as a plea only if there was no appearance of premeditation or favouritism; the survival of the daughter therefore looked suspicious. But since the woman was seriously wounded in the attack, Marcus concluded that it had been the clear intention of the father to kill both the daughter and the lover.[75] In another court case Marcus accepted the very modern-sounding plea of diminished responsibility by reason of insanity in the case of a man – admittedly an upper-class male – who had murdered his mother, concluding with the Solomonic judgement: 'insanity itself is punishment enough.' This was not modern liberalism, however, for Marcus recommended that the man be closely confined and even kept in chains.[76] The emperor's judgement tends to give new meaning to the word 'meticulous'.

> If, as often happens, he has intervals of sanity, you must ascertain whether or not he committed the crime during those lucid intervals, in which case he would have no right to mercy on grounds of diminished responsibility. If this turns out to be the case, refer the case back to me and I will decide the appropriate punishment . . . I also want you to find out why those who were in charge of him at the time were so remiss, and to examine each person individually to see whether they were negligent and, if so, whether there was any excuse for their negligence.

Marcus also wanted to know whether the murderer was being treated as insane at the time of the homicide. 'Those who have charge of the insane have a twofold duty: not just to stop the mentally ill from harming themselves but to make sure they don't harm others. If this happens, as in this case, the obvious question arises: are the minders to blame, and is their negligence the prime cause of the tragedy?'[77]

The most controversial law-giving done in the name of Marcus and Commodus in the years 177–80 concerned gladiatorial spectacles, which Marcus had always detested – a loathing partly inspired by Antoninus

Pius and partly by the tenets of Stoicism. Yet Marcus was not a free agent, and something of a social crisis had been caused by the Marcomannic wars, which drained away most of the trained gladiators from the empire to the theatre of war, and left the people without one of their entertainment mainstays. With a diminished supply of gladiators, those that remained in the cities of the empire could command a high price, so the cost of such shows rocketed. Increasingly, the upper classes, whose duty it was to provide games to keep the mob quiet, refused to put on these spectacles; the lower classes grew restive, and it was rumoured that the alleged shortage of gladiators was simply a case of Marcus manipulating the market to clamp down on something he disapproved of.[78] The emperor could live with defamatory remarks about being a spoilsport or 'party-pooper', but the discontent of the proletariat was potentially very dangerous, and it made no sense either to alienate the oligarchy when the empire was in danger. He therefore authorised municipal and provincial authorities to press criminals already condemned to death into service in the arena and, moreover, committed the state to meet the cost of providing them.[79] The costs of gladiatorial shows plummeted, upper-class sponsors once more appeared, and the mob was appeased. Some relate the persecutions of the Christians directly to this edict rather than to some general ideologically based purge. The legal power of an *oratio* is made clear by the following joint reply by Marcus and Commodus to a request from Miletus about celebrating games: 'Having received your message about the festival, we thought it fitting to consult the sacred assembly of the Senate, to gain its acceptance of your request. There were many other matters to speak to it about too. Since, therefore, it did not ratify individually each item which we raised, but its decree was, instead, a joint, collective one about matters on which we had spoken that day, we have attached to this answer for your information the section of the speech delivered by us relevant to your request.'[80]

Marcus always sent the accused from the senatorial class for trial in the Senate, and reserved his own court for others, unless senators expressly asked for a hearing before the emperor. He was usually lenient and avoided the death-penalty except in extreme cases; his habitual method was to remove people from office or demote them.[81] Overwhelmingly his interest centred on what would be termed nowadays family and employment law. He forbade a guardian to marry his ward or give her in marriage to a son or grandson, thus ending an obvious scam.[82] Another law gave a woman's children prior rights to inheritance if she died intestate. The significance of this was that it was a step forward for women's rights; henceforth a woman was not merely the creature of her family, to be battened on by siblings and other relatives.[83] Although some of Marcus's measures might seem liberal to a modern eye, his essential temperament was always conservative, and his abiding concern was to maintain the existing class structure. Yet another *oratio* issued in his name and that of the co-emperor Commodus prohibited marriage between members of the senatorial class and certain other classes.[84] It has often been claimed that Marcus promoted the interests of the equestrian class, but this is a misconception. It is true that the equestrian class made great strides under Marcus, but this was mainly because of heavy losses in the senatorial class, both in the Marcomannic wars and in the Antonine plague. To have a credible political administration and a well-run army, Marcus simply had no choice but to make rapid promotions at all levels. The rise of Pertinax is the classic example,[85] but there were many others. Two army commanders particularly made their mark. Vespronius Candidus, another martinet in the Avidius Cassius mould, was hated by his men as much for his low birth in Mantua as for his disciplinarian tendencies. Even more notorious was Ulpius Marcellus, who believed so strongly in the old Spartan virtues that, when governor of Britain, he insisted that his daily bread be brought out from Rome so that it was stale and tough when he ate it.[86]

In the years 177–8 Marcus also began a building programme, though on nothing like the lavish scale of previous emperors like Nero and Hadrian. The equestrian statue and triumphal arch were completed by 177, but the Aurelian column, consciously built to rival Trajan's, had to wait until Commodus's reign to be completed. The few years of relative peace between 175 and 178 also enabled Marcus to begin tentatively to put the economy on a sounder footing. Emulating Hadrian's actions in 118, he cancelled all debts owed both to the throne (*fiscus*) and the treasury, which had been incurred in the previous forty-six years.[87] Yet even outside wartime there were always demands on the public purse. In 177 a disastrous earthquake devastated Smyrna, and the citizens appealed to Rome for assistance. Aelius Aristides, the city's leading son, composed an address to the emperor that was said to have moved Marcus to tears. He told the emperor that he now had a chance to surpass the famous benefactions of Alexander and Lysimachus. Whereas Domitian had famously brought about the destruction of an entire tribe in Libya by simple fiat, Marcus had a unique opportunity of doing something in the opposite direction, as praiseworthy as Domitian's action was despicable. After rehearsing the long history of Smyrna's loyalty to Rome, he concluded, 'When I consider the magnitude of the disaster, it seems to me that no speech would be adequate, but that all possible words would fall short of what is appropriate; but when I consider your virtue and character and readiness to grant benefactions, it occurs to me to be afraid lest I seem to have gone on too long.'[88] Aristides need not have worried. When he said of Smyrna, 'She is a desert, and the west winds blow through her', Marcus was visibly moved. He already had the example of Antoninus Pius, who had provided earthquake relief for cities in Caria, Lycia, Cos and Rhodes, and needed no prompting. He at once asked the Senate to provide all funds necessary for the rapid rebuilding of Smyrna, and this was done.[89] The city was virtually rebuilt from scratch by 179.[90] As Cassius Dio scathingly remarked, this was the reality of a man who, simply because he was financially prudent, was habitually accused of being a skinflint and a tightwad.[91]

By the beginning of 178 Marcus was coming to the reluctant conclusion that he was once again needed at the Danube frontier. Robbed by the Avidius Cassius revolt of a total victory in Germany, he had hoped that only minor mopping-up operations would be required by the Quintilii brothers whom he had left in charge. Unfortunately, the Quadi and Marcomanni took advantage of the crisis in the East to go on the warpath once more. This time they made a point of avoiding pitched battles and instead opted for guerrilla warfare. The Romans responded by crossing the Danube, penetrating beyond the demilitarised zone and establishing forts in enemy territory. Despite what Cassius Dio calls the 'shrewdness, courage and experience' of the Quintilii, they could not put an end to hostilities.[92] Whether there was enemy collusion in 176–8, with the Marcomanni directing far-flung risings, or whether the unrest was simply spontaneous combustion is unclear, but in these years there was a massive upsurge in brigandage, piracy and other manifestations of irregular warfare. Banditry was of course an endemic problem in the Roman empire,[93] but it had never before reached such a pitch of intensity. Didius Julianus had his hands full in Dalmatia, fighting robber bands in the mountains of Albania and Montenegro, while the situation became so serious in Thrace and Macedonia (roughly where modern Greece, Bulgaria and the old Yugoslavia intersect) that the great hero of the Marcomannic wars, Valerius Maximianus, was dispatched there in 176 with a strong force of *vexillationes* to deal with the problem.[94] Another indication that matters were serious on the northern frontier comes from the rather panicky switching of Pertinax from one key position to another, first as governor of Upper and Lower Moesia, then as supremo in Dacia.[95] Moreover, new tribes, never heard from in the wars of 167–75, now made an appearance as Rome's enemies, chief among them the Hermunduri.[96] Further indirect evidence of the toll exacted on the empire by the troublesome northern frontier comes in the continuing devaluation of the currency carried out by Marcus at this time and the disappearance of the titles *Germanicus* and *Sarmaticus* on the coinage issued in 177.[97] Clearly Marcus was deeply unhappy about developments in the north.

He and Commodus left Rome for the north on 3 August 178 on what was officially termed the Second German Expedition. Perhaps sensing that he would never see the Eternal City again, Marcus symbolically put his effects in order by insisting on swearing a solemn oath on the Capitol that he had never been responsible for the death of any senator and would have spared all the rebels in the Avidius Cassius rebellion if he had been able to commute the few death sentences actually passed.[98] One can take this declaration with a pinch of salt – as Albert Camus has fittingly remarked in another context, 'it was too late – it is always too late, thank God'[99] – and even more so the emperor's extravagant declaration to the Senate about his wealth and possessions. He went through the charade of asking the Senate for funds for the war when he had access to them in any case, and then added this piece of humbug: 'As for ourselves, we are so far from having any possessions of our own that even the house we live in is yours.'[100] This from a man who had vast inherited riches and who was always meticulous, as Antoninus Pius had been, in making the distinction between private and public imperial wealth. But Marcus was grandstanding, as he made clear by casting the bloody spear kept in the Temple of Bellona into the ground there symbolically regarded as enemy territory.[101] This once again showed his devotion to the traditional Roman religion, for he was one of the *fetiales* or priests given the duty of declaring war. Another story about Marcus on the eve of his departure is more dubious, but has the strength of abiding tradition. It is said that the philosophers with whom he liked to debate were so cast down by his abrupt departure for the front that they asked him for some *ex cathedra* pronouncements on obscure questions of theory and ethics. They lamented that the demands of war should have deprived them of their consoling sage and wanted his last words of wisdom – Marcus's 'Blue Book', as it were. It was thought to underline the glory of Rome that, with the empire in crisis, its ruler could take the time to devote himself to eternal verities as well as ephemeral blood-letting.[102]

Marcus took with him to the Danube most of his important advisers and *comites*, among them Claudius Pompeianus, Vitrasius Pollio and Bruttius Praesens, relatives by marriage.[103] Another important consular in the party was Iunius Maximus, who formally presented Lucius Verus's victory address to Marcus in 166 after the Parthian war.[104] Bassaeus, the bluff, no-nonsense prefect of the guard who had come within an ace of scything Herodes Atticus down at the imperial audience in Sirmium, had now retired and his place was taken by Tarruttienus Paternus, the rising star of the late 170s, with Tigidius Perennis as his deputy.[105] With Pertinax and Valerius Maximianus already in action at the front and the reliable Aufidius Victorinus as proconsul in Asia, Marcus felt confident that he had the right team for the task ahead. But what was that task? Amazingly, it seems that Marcus intended to convert the territory of the Quadi and the Marcomanni into a new, permanent Roman province, his own version of Trajan's Dacia, so to speak; some say he also intended to create a second province out of some of the Sarmatian land.[106] These quixotic plans, which to Marcus were deadly serious, have been criticised by modern scholars who assert that Marcus 'cannot' have intended such impracticable folly.[107] It is important to state his intentions with the utmost care. Whereas annexation was never part of his policy during the first German war of 167–75, this time he saw it as the best long-term solution. The perplexity of modern scholars arises from a hard-headed cost-benefit analysis, which Marcus himself may not have undertaken. Besides, the motives for annexation seem obscure. Normally empires annex new provinces out of land-hunger. Not only was this never a motive in Roman expansion, but it makes no sense at all in the context of the late 170s. The empire faced severe manpower shortages becauses of the losses in the Antonine plague, which was why Marcus allowed German tribes to migrate and resettle *within* the empire.[108] Not only was there no land-hunger to justify the expansion into a new province of Marcomannia, but it would have been next to impossible to find colonists to found new settlements there.

Marcus's thinking about the new province was purely military and administrative, aiming to eliminate all border tribes who were a potential threat. The new frontier line would presumably have rested at the foot of the Sudeten–Tatra chain of mountains and would have included territory that is now in modern Bavaria.[109] This would have created a bulging ur-Czechoslovakia, complete with a vulnerable salient, as in Dacia. To make the new province militarily secure, Marcus would have to annex also the territory of the Hermunduri west of Bohemia, which was feasible, as well as the territory of the Iazyges south-east of Slovakia, which was not, unless his plans were truly grandiose and included the vision of a second province of Sarmatia.[110] To create the second province he would have to wage war to the knife against both the Iazyges and their cousins the Roxolani. Could it be that this was his ultimate intention? If so, he would be one of the arch-Machiavellians of history, for his first step on arrival at the Danube was to negotiate allegedly permanent peace terms with the Iazyges. There were always those who said that Marcus's 'I'm a pretty straight guy – what you see is what you get' persona, promoted so assiduously in the *Meditations*, was a mask.[111] Scholars who cannot accept that such a character could be attributed to the 'real' Marcus tend to work backwards from the alleged impossibility of Sarmatia to the implausibility of Marcomannia. This implies either a straightforwardness or a clarity of thought that Marcus may not have possessed. He might have been devious, or he might have been unable or unwilling to think his projects for annexation through. We cannot say for certain that he never had annexation projects, and indeed the sources argue otherwise.[112]

The argument for a 'machiavellian' Marcus is strengthened by his initial actions once he reached the Danube. Parlaying his penchant for 'divide and rule' almost into grand stategy, Marcus pulled off something of a political masterpiece by concluding an alliance with the Iazyges that kept them out of the war. He was pleased with the way the Iazyges had kept out of the resurgent war with the German tribes and wished to show them that it made sense to be on friendly terms with Rome. The terms they received were the best any barbarians had yet been presented with. Marcus offered Roman citizenship, immunity to taxes and in addition a one-off payment of tribute and the firm promise of annual subsidies thereafter.[113] The Iazyges were now allowed free access to Roman markets, no longer had to respect the old ten-mile demilitarised zone, and, in an extraordinary sign of Marcus's confidence, were allowed to cross Dacia to communicate with their kinsfolk the Roxolani in the East. The only matter on which Marcus dug in his heels was the Danube itself. The Iazyges were bound by the treaty not to sail in their own ships on the river or to occupy any of the islands. They were allowed riverine trade only in Roman freighters and could only put in at towns that had a Roman garrison.[114] Marcus assured the Iazyges that he intended to campaign solely against the Quadi and Marcomanni and their allies. They responded by saying they would be only too happy to join in on the Roman side, provided they were allowed to wage a war of extermination against the Germans. Delighted with this response – or had he set it up and thus produced the result he had aimed at all along? – Marcus said that he would not take up the offer immediately, but would prefer to keep the Iazyges on ice, until he saw how the German campaign progressed. He informed the Iazyges that his first move would be against the Cotini, on their flank, but that they should not be alarmed, since it was merely his intention to displace this troublesome tribe, who were now leagued with the Quadi and Marcomanni.[115]

Thus confident that he had neutralised the Iazyges, Marcus moved against the Cotini. A quick campaign drew their military teeth, and the survivors were transplanted away from the Sudeten–Tatra line to Lower Pannonia.[116] It was made clear to the Cotini that this was their punishment for the way they had treated Tarruttienus Paternus in 166–7, and it may well have been Paternus in person who oversaw the chastisement of this tribe. The pill was, however, sweetened with an offer of Roman citizenship.[117] Aiming further to cut down on the resources available to the enemy, Marcus allowed the most important elements of the Naristae and their families to cross the Danube and relocate within the empire.[118] Alarmed that their putative allies were being gelded, the Quadi broke ranks with the Marcomanni and decided on a great trek north to join their kinsmen the Semnones on the middle Elbe. But Marcus had no wish for his new province of Marcomannia to be a depopulated desert and sent orders that Roman armies were to block this attempted migration.[119] By now the territory of the Quadi was firmly under the Roman heel, with 40,000 legionaries in permanent occupation in massive, stone-built forts and a series of blockhouses and watchtowers that effectively controlled every inch of territory on the plains.[120] The Quadi were in a desperate plight, unable to leave their territory and unable to defeat the Romans. It was at this juncture that the Germans were offered a possible respite. For reasons that are unexplained, but possibly because Marcus saw no reason to offer the same generous terms he had given the Iazyges to their Sarmatian cousins, the Roxolani sent an army to aid the beleaguered Germans.[121] Thus reinforced, the Quadi and Marcomanni finally felt confident enough to abandon their guerrilla hideouts and face the Romans in pitched battle. The result was utter disaster. In a day-long battle with the legions, commanded by Tarruttenius Paternus, the enemy army was utterly routed; there were huge numbers of dead and wounded, and 40,000 Germans were taken prisoner. This decisive battle can be fairly confidently dated from coinage issues to April 179.[122]

This victory brought Marcus his tenth (and last) salutation as *imperator*, while Commodus, still in his teens, notched up his third. The Roxolani, dismayed by the rout of their forces and perhaps influenced by the lavish terms that their cousins, the Iazyges, had received, pulled out of the coalition. The Quadi and the Marcomanni were forced back into guerrilla warfare. Determined to finish them off once and for all so that his new province of Marcomannia could be a reality, Marcus quartered 45,000 men on their territory in permanent stations, equipped with every convenience including hot baths, and pursued a scorched-earth policy. Cassius Dio reported: '[The Romans] would not allow them to pasture their flocks, till the soil or do anything else in security, but kept receiving deserters from the enemy's ranks and captives from their own.'[123] The contrast with the early years of the first Marcomannic war, when the traffic in deserters and prisoners had been entirely the other way, was clear. The war of attrition was even grimmer than before, and the savagery and atrocities visited on the guerrillas even more horrible than in 171–5. The Aurelian column provides graphic evidence of this, with all the action after Scene 55 tending to deal with beheadings, imploring captives and weeping women; it is significant that there is no counterpart on Trajan's column to the plethora of decapitation scenes after Scene 55.[124] Cassius Dio asserted that Marcus felt sorry for the barbarians (and some have claimed to see him stretching out his hands in pardon on the column),[125] but a realistic assessment of this is that Marcus was displaying his sorrow for the human condition in general (*lacrimae rerum*), as he did when he wept over the Smyrna earthquake, rather than evincing pity for individuals.

Still, in purely pragmatic terms 179 was a great year for Roman armies and was capped by a signal honour to the man who, even more than Pertinax, was regarded as *the* great military hero. Valerius Maximianus was made a senator, appointed legate of Legio I Adiutrix and chosen as one of the select band of men to receive the emperor's Most Honourable Order (roughly the equivalent of the modern British Order of Merit).[126] The army was in high spirits in its winter quarters at Trencin on the River Waag (about 100 miles beyond the Danube in southern Slovakia) during 179–80,[127] with the general feeling prevalent that the final mopping-up campaign would be completed the following spring.

The first German war had been halted on the very brink of success when Avidius Cassius raised the standard of revolt. The second war came to a similar end, but this time because of the death of the emperor. Early in March 180 Marcus fell seriously ill, a victim of the Antonine plague – in reality smallpox. Since all the symptoms matched those that he and Galen had observed in all the victims since 166, it was obvious that the end could not be long delayed. Marcus at once sent for Commodus and stressed that it was imperative that the German war be brought to a successful completion. He put the maximum pressure on his son, saying that if he did not obey his last wishes, this would constitute a betrayal of the interests of the Roman state. Commodus equivocated in a manner that in a later era would have been called Jesuitical. He promised to do what he could, but said that his own health had to be the prime consideration, for everyone knew that smallpox was contagious. Marcus got him to agree to wait in camp for a few days. Commodus rationalised his apparent lack of filial deference by muttering that even men in good health could achieve things only gradually, but 'a dead man can achieve nothing'.[128]

Marcus then decided to accelerate the inevitable by abstaining from food and drink. On the sixth day of self-starvation, he summoned his friends and intimates. Those who gathered round the sickbed were Claudius Pompeianus, Claudius Severus, Bruttius Praesens, Vitrasius Pollio and Aufidius Victorinus, the men Marcus hoped would provide continuity in the new reign.[129] When he saw them grieving, Marcus reproached them with taking such an unphilosophical attitude; they should instead be thinking about the implications of the Antonine plague and pondering death in general.[130] It was a particular sadness to him that the only men who might have prevented Commodus's succession, Pompeianus and Severus, had always been at daggers drawn. Perhaps it was this that drew from him the rueful remark that he feared his son would become another Caligula, Nero or Domitian.[131] Nevertheless, he had no option but to make a formal commendation, and then he called for Commodus to come in, at which point he made the address that the historian Herodian reported as follows:

> Here is my son, whom you brought up, who has just reached the age
> of adolescence and stands in need of guides through the tempests and
> storms of life . . . You who are many must be fathers to him in place
> of me alone . . . You must give my son this sort of advice and remind
> him of what he is hearing now. In this way you will provide yourselves
> and everyone else with an excellent emperor and you will be showing
> your gratitude to my memory in the best of all ways. Indeed, it is the
> only way you can keep my memory alive for ever.[132]

When the troops learned that the emperor was dying, they were grief-stricken. Despite starting as a despised philosopher, Marcus had over a decade of hard fighting won his army's respect, and even more than that; by this time 'they loved him as no other'. On the seventh day Marcus sent for Commodus, but sent him away after a brief audience, for fear that he would become infected. He then covered his head and went to sleep, and during his brief slumber slipped away. His last recorded words were to recommend Commodus to the army. When a tribune asked him for the day's watchword, he replied: 'Go to the rising sun. For I am already setting.'[133] It was 17 March 180, and Marcus was just a month short of his fifty-ninth birthday. Inevitably, as when any great man died, the rumour mills bruited it about that the death had not been natural. Commodus was said to have bribed the emperor's doctors to poison the emperor in such a way that the symptoms of smallpox could be simulated, but this canard is unconvincing, even though Cassius Dio claimed to have it from unimpeachable sources: 'murder – as I have been plainly told', to cite his words.[134] Dio's remark that Marcus did not die of the disease from which he was suffering has also been thought indicative of a concealed assassination, but it probably simply means that Marcus died of something other than his chronic chest and stomach ailments – which would certainly be the case if the cause of death was smallpox. The ancients always liked to make a mystery out of the deaths of their celebrities, and it is somehow typical of Roman historiography that the authorities could not even agree on the *place* of death, with some claiming that it was at Vindobona (modern Vienna) and others, much more plausibly, that it was at Sirmium or nearby, possibly at Bononia on the Danube.[135] At all events we are justified in stating that Marcus died a noble death, not a squalid one as the victim of homicide. His best epitaph was provided by Cassius Dio: 'He always tolerated the faults of others, neither inquiring too closely into them nor chastising the perpetrators.'[136]

17

'My father has gone up to heaven and now sits as a companion of the gods. We must concern ourselves with human matters and govern affairs on earth.'[1] Commodus's 'concern' was ultimately to pitchpole the Roman empire into a tailspin from which it never recovered; everyone agrees that he was the most disastrous of emperors. Any overall estimate of Marcus Aurelius as man or ruler cannot avoid consideration of the salient fact that he bequeathed his empire to an inadequate and a monster.

Almost the first thing Commodus did after his father's death was to announce that he intended to wind up the war in Germany and not pursue Marcus's policy of annexation.[2] He claimed that he was playing Hadrian to Marcus's Trajan, the enlightened intellect that clears up after the misguided conqueror. Since Hadrian was a man Marcus disliked, one is justified in construing this as a transmogrified form of 'revenge' by Commodus on his father. Others said that the proper analogy was with Lucius Verus, a man who had gone to war reluctantly and then raced back to Rome as fast as he could. Since Verus was known to have been friendly with Faustina, some even whispered that it was Verus, not some unknown gladiator, who was the new emperor's true father, and that Commodus's famous relish for the arena was an echo of Verus's mania for the circus factions.[3] The hedonism of Verus was also cited, and it was alleged that Commodus was prepared to sign *any* terms with the Germans that would release him to enjoy the fleshpots of Rome.[4] At all events,

Commodus's desire to have immediate peace on the Danube was regarded by the pro-war party as a blatant betrayal of his father and his policy.[5] The announcement of the new bearing in frontier affairs caused dismay and bitterness in the Senate, and from this moment dates the intolerable relationship between that august body and the new emperor. With hindsight, we can declare with confidence that Commodus's elevation to the purple was the end of the line for the Senate.[6]

However, although Commodus was a disaster in almost every respect, one must always give the devil his due. Influential voices have been raised to claim that Commodus's German policy has been much maligned, that his withdrawal from this arena actually made more sense than his father's annexationist policy, and that finance, manpower and logistics would have made the project for a greater 'Marcomannia' impracticable anyway, even had Marcus lived.[7] These are weighty objections that command much respect. Let us examine the case for Commodus in Germany in ascending order of importance. In the first place, he was criticised for showing scant honour to his father's burial rites by remaining in Germany instead of returning to Rome with the catafalque. This might have been acceptable if he was staying in Germany to complete his father's work, but he remained there simply to wind it up.[8] While Marcus had a funeral in Rome, was deified and given the title *Pius* to go with *Divus*, Commodus bided his time in Germany, initially trying to marginalise Claudius Pompeianus, who led the hawks on the imperial war council.[9] Pompeianus roundly declared that a retreat from Germany would mean that the past dozen years of warfare and all Marcus's efforts would turn out to have been in vain, and moreover the barbarians would regard the Romans as cowards. Far, far better to fight all the way to the 'Ocean' (the Baltic or the North Sea) and bring back every last German king in triumph. Nothing less was required by Rome's honour and greatness. Pompeianus and the overwhelming majority on the general staff thought in terms of a code of honour rather than pragmatism. Like all Marcus's *amici*, they had been 'formed' in a certain ethos of duty, bolstered by Latin literature and rhetoric, in terms of which 'banausic' considerations like costs and resources did not come into it. For Pompeianus and his fellow-hawks the debate was all about credibility.[10]

Doubtless too polite to say so openly in the council, Commodus thought all this romantic nonsense. There were many compelling reasons why an early settlement with the Germans was essential. It was never a good thing for a new emperor to be proclaimed except in Rome; therefore he needed to return to the capital as soon as possible to head off the machinations of any possible pretenders (there had already been rumours of a plot)[11] and to win over the Senate and the people. Commodus needed to calm the plebs, guarantee food supplies, receive embassies and, above all, establish first-hand contacts with the hundreds of senators who were just names to him. As for Germany, the choices were stark: peace, extermination or annexation, of which the third was the least preferable.[12] Besides, to annex Marcomannia was a chimerical project. There would be massive logistical and political problems in creating a new province, for it would need new roads, cities and political institutions to be viable, especially if the old tribal aristocracy was to be Romanised. The entire scheme was anyway ruinously expensive. Commodus argued that the benefits of continuing military action in Germany were not clear, but the risks were. He could not afford to lose a campaign when he had barely entered the principate, and the continuing losses from plague made this a distinct possibility.[13] To continue fighting into the winter of 180–1 was to invite devastation from the plague, always most deadly in winter, as Galen had noted.[14] Continual warfare would also have meant the introduction of the draft, extra taxation and thus, as an inevitable corollary, more banditry.[15] Pompeianus had spoken of credibility; well, Commodus had his own, more pressing realpolitik version of credibility. Finally, Commodus attempted to turn the tables on his critics by claiming that Marcus had not really been aiming at annexation, but simply at protectorate status for Marcomannia, and that his overtures towards friendly Germans had all been for the purpose of creating a Romanised local elite – the future aristocracy of a new Roman protectorate.[16] Here Commodus was being disingenuous, since Marcus's plans for annexation had been clear to the point of transparency, but modern scholars have been prepared to follow him on this point.[17] Nonetheless, the arguments Commodus deployed were powerful; it is by no means self-evident that on German policy Marcus was right and his son wrong.

Moreover, Commodus made it clear that he did not intend simply to cut and run, to end the war on giveaway terms. Before he left Germany, he conducted a lightning campaign against the Buri tribe, defeated them and sealed his victory with a generous peace, which, however, kept them away from the Dacian border.[18] Seeing this, the remnants of the Quadi and Marcomanni finally decide to surrender.[19] The terms they received were also magnanimous. The Romans dismantled all their forts and fastnesses north of the Danube and withdrew across the river. All the German tribes had in return to give up their ships and agree to a ten-mile demilitarised zone around the Danube and its islands. The Quadi and the Marcomanni were expressly forbidden to make war on the Iazyges, Buri or Vandals or to support any enemies of Rome whatsoever. They had to return all prisoners and deserters, pay an annual tribute in grain, and agree to large forced levies of their fighting men for service elsewhere in the empire.[20] They were not allowed to make war on each other without Roman say-so and were restricted in freedom of assembly to a monthly meeting, supervised and overseen by Roman centurions, thus making effective decision-making by assembly impossible.[21] The centurion was authorised to put a stop to any meeting at which treason was talked or anti-Roman sentiments expressed and to take the names of troublemakers. Commodus then had his commanders conclude similar terms with the Iazyges and Roxolani.[22]

The peace treaties worked remarkably well, and Commodus's instincts seemed confirmed. Roman manpower shortages were improved by the return of tens of thousands of prisoners and deserters and by the recruitment of 13,000 Quadi and 10,000 Marcomanni.[23] There was no further serious trouble on the German frontier until the reign of Valerian in the 250s. Caracalla campaigned in Germany in the early years of the third century, but more to make a show of his strength and to glory-hunt than because the empire was in danger; no serious battles were reported. When Caracalla intervened to impose a new king on the Quadi, there was scarcely a squeak out of them.[24] To some extent, of course, Caracalla drew the teeth of German resentment by his famous decree of 212, which made all 'internal barbarians' Roman citizens and thus provided a massive incentive for Germans to settle inside the empire as agriculturalists.[25] But the real credit for peace in Germany must go to Marcus Aurelius. It was his remorseless campaigns of 169–80 that exhausted Germany's military potential. Marcus's achievement was all the more remarkable in that he campaigned there while the Antonine plague was at its height – a smallpox epidemic that both reduced his numbers and had a numbing effect on military morale.[26] Commodus, though, did not acknowledge his father's crucial role in the pacification of Germany, but ascribed all the credit to his own peerless diplomatic skills. His basic attitude to Germany and the northern frontier was boredom. Devoid of Marcus's sense of duty, he adopted a purely prudential attitude to this part of the empire, though he was alert for any signs of trouble and even fought a minor campaign in Dacia in 182–3.[27] He had absolutely no personal interest in Germany, and the titles *Germanicus* and *Sarmaticus* never appeared on his coinage, though *Britannicus* did, even though it denoted a country where he had never been.[28]

Commodus was aware that his return to Rome after concluding such a controversial peace was a make-or-break affair, that he would not be able to please everyone, and especially not the 'hawks'; even the opinion of the Roman 'chattering classes' and professional philosophers inclined to the view that the settlement with the German tribes was a mistake.[29] He decided to aim his appeal at the army and the common people, rather than the Senate (as his father always had), and the historian Herodian confirmed that the tactic was initially successful.[30] Commodus entered Rome on 22 October 180 in an atmosphere of spurious triumphalism. His early speeches to the Senate were universally considered flat and unconvincing. Against this, he delighted the masses by distributing his third *congiarium* and followed this up with a fourth and a fifth in 181 and 182.[31] With no knowledge whatsoever of finance, Commodus had not the remotest idea how to pay for such liberality. When it was pointed out to him that one could not simply coin money at will, he hit on the idea of declaring wealthy figures treasonous and confiscating their estates, thus ensuring a healthy flow of revenue. To the war-weary army he posed as the apostle of peace and made a point, in October 180, immediately on his return to Rome, of signing a treaty with Canarta, King of the Baquatar in North Africa, whereby Canarta agreed to be a client-king of Rome, attached to the province of Mauretania Tingitana.[32] Then Commodus issued two sets of coinage, one for the deification of Marcus and the other to commemorate his 'victory' in Germany, wherein he was hailed as *Adventus Augusti Fortuna Redux* (literally, 'With the advent of a new Augustus, Fortune returns').[33]

On paper, Commodus's position as emperor was unassailable. He was the first ever supreme ruler actually born to the purple, as he was fond of boasting. The sixth emperor in a dynasty founded with a series of adoptions by Nerva in 96 (the Julio-Claudian dynasty by contrast produced only five emperors), he was not only the son of the divine Marcus, but by the series of adoptions could call himself the great-great-great-grandson of Nerva, the founding father. He revelled in being able to describe himself as the most nobly born of all the princes of the empire.[34] But under this carapace of nobility lurked a gliding monster, a seeming avatar of all the deadly sins. Pathologically idle, and thus a born delegator even of the most important decisions, a drunkard and lecher, Commodus was also venal and would sell anything if the price was right, even allowing murder as part of the transaction if it suited his book.[35] Sinister, cruel, obscene and scandalous, he was an obvious psychopath – or some would say sociopath, on the grounds that his early socialisation in bad company had vitiated a normal moral personality.[36] Murderous and lustful towards members of either sex, he had always been, as the *Historia Augusta* reports, 'From early boyhood, cowardly, dishonourable, cruel, lecherous, foul-mouthed and debauched.'[37] It was all very well for Julian the Apostate to state, 200 years later, that Commodus was not even worth ridicule,[38] but few of those who suffered under his tyranny could afford to take such an Olympian stance. The vicious aspects of his character were obvious from the very beginning of his reign, for he purged the supporters of Avidius Cassius, whom Marcus had publicly pardoned, and had some of them sent to the stake.[39] However, at first he successfully obfuscated his homicidal personality by 'balancing' it with an apparent act of statesmanship. When Manilius, one of the conspirators of the year 175, was hauled before him and offered to divulge the full secrets of the conspiracy in return for his life, Commodus waved him away and had his papers ostentatiously burned to try to show that he was not bent on vengeance.[40]

Opinions were divided on the physical appearance of the new emperor. Herodian's verdict was favourable: 'Most attractive to look at because of his well-proportioned body and the manly beauty of his face. His eyes had a commanding look and flashed like fire. His hair was natural, blonde and curly. When he walked in the sunlight it shone like fire (so that some thought he sprinkled it with gold dust before going out) while others regarded it as a sign of divinity, saying that a heavenly light shone out above his head. And the first down was just beginning to appear on his cheeks.'[41] However, others thought that the most distinctive thing about his appearance was the unsightly growth or hernia on his groin, which he tried to disguise, but which was visible through his robes. Critics thought his arbitrary change of hairstyle from the long hair of Antoninus Pius and Marcus to a short cut was a bad mistake.[42] Most significantly, Commodus never *looked* intelligent. Influenced by his long years at the theatre of war, Marcus had come to see excessive specialisation in rhetoric, law and philosophy as an unbalanced training for an emperor (he secretly blamed Antoninus Pius for this) and had over-compensated by favouring 'on-the-job' training at the front for Commodus. The consequence was, as one authority has put it, that 'Commodus had no higher education.'[43] Once he took to the bottle, the combination of a vacant look, slurred speech and the lack of an inner mental life often made Commodus appear as the merest *stupidus*.[44] A modern observer, after examination of the bust of Commodus in the Conservatori Museum in Rome, commented: 'The smooth and effeminate emperor with his weak arms, his flaccid, feeble face in its aureole of drilled and over-barbered hair, reeking of pomade, the property [*sc*. trademark] lion-scalp and club and tiny "apples of the Hesperides" in that tenuously manicured hand, is indicative of a delicate but brutally expressive charade.'[45]

Nevertheless, for about a year Commodus did not really reveal his true colours. In 181 he was consul for the third time with his brother-in-law Antistius Burrus. Cocooned in his palace on the Palatine, he maintained good relations with his father's old guard: Claudius Pompeianus, C. Aufidius Victorinus and Tarruttienus Paternus, prefect of the praetorian guard. There was peace throughout the empire, the corn supply was undisturbed, and all the omens for a successful reign seemed auspicious. Lavish in the shows and spectacles he provided for the public, Commodus celebrated them with the legend *Magnificentia* on his coins.[46] The only cause for concern was the

growing influence of his male lover and freedman Saoterus, an object
of disgust to those of senatorial rank.[47] Saoterus had disgusted the
Roman aristocracy almost as soon as Commodus returned to Rome
from Germany. During the 'triumph' held for the victory in Germany,
Saoterus stood behind Commodus on the chariot during the caval-
cade and, at the end of the ceremony, was kissed by the emperor in
full view of everyone, scandalising senators and suggesting that his
reign would indeed be a return to the worst days of Nero. Thoughts
of a coup must have arisen as early as Commodus's first days in
Rome. However, the fate of Avidius Cassius was a dire warning to
any military commander rash enough to chance his arm. Moreover,
Marcus Aurelius had deliberately chosen nonentities to marry his
daughters so that there could never be any credible pretenders to
Commodus's throne. Despite Commodus's youth, inexperience and
obvious ineptitude at so many levels, the discontent caused by his
abandonment of Germany and the daily scandal of Saoterus, it was
difficult to see the potential focus around which any group of plotters
could form.[48]

But Marcus had forgotten his daughters, some of whom were
evidently made of tougher stuff than their husbands. The secret opposition of the Senate was the core around which, in the winter of 181–2
Lucilla (widow of Lucius Verus and wife of Claudius Pompeianus)
began to weave a conspiracy. Evidently with some of her mother's
drive and ambition, Lucilla was especially animated by hatred of
Commodus's young wife Crispina, who may have been pregnant at
this time. It seems that the last straw was when her powerful rival
caused her to lose her front-row seat at the theatre.[49] Since she, a
good hater, also detested her husband and always had, she looked
elsewhere for her accomplices and found the first one in the shape
of her lover Ummidius Quadratus, the adopted son of Marcus's
nephew and stepson of Commodus's eldest sister. Together they
enlisted Lucilla's prospective son-in-law Claudius Pompeius
Quintanus, a young senator, nephew of her husband Pompeianus
and said also to be Lucilla's lover.[50] They managed to plan the time
and place of an assassination, and Quintanus took up his concealed
position in the shadows of the Flavian amphitheatre. Unfortunately,
he had none of the deadly efficiency of which successful hitmen are
made. Emerging from the shadows, he surprised Commodus but,

instead of plunging a dagger into his heart, found time for some
histrionic effusions. 'See, this is what the Senate sends you!' were his
words, evidently hoping that Commodus would enjoy a few seconds
of despair before the end. But the precious interval gave the emperor's
bodyguard time to react; Quintanus was overpowered, tortured and
revealed the full details of the plot.[51] The outcome of Lucilla's abortive
scheming was both clear-cut and confused. It was clear-cut in that
the main conspirators, Ummidius Quadratus and Quintanus, were
executed. Lucilla was banished to Capua where Commodus later had
her done away with, but her family was not harmed.[52] The scandal
ruined Claudius Pompeianus, who retired from public life on the
pretext of failing eyesight.[53] But the outcome was confused in that it
evidently had much wider ripples than the botched assassination
attempt by Quadratus, and indeed his thespian's boast about the
Senate was a giveaway.[54] Two who escaped immediate detection were
Tarruttienus Paternus, who had colluded with his colleague Tigidius
Perennis to implement the second half of the plot, for while Quadratus
was supposedly striking Commodus down, this pair (using the secret
police) had Saoterus murdered.[55] Incandescent with anger about the
loss of his favourite, Commodus was a willing listener when a few
days later Perennis double-crossed Tarruttienus Paternus, who had
been 'kicked upstairs' to the Senate to avoid suspicion – though some
say Commodus promoted him so that he could not raise the praetorians, and then arrested him when he was a mere civilian.[56] Others
say that Paternus was actually given the job of investigating the
conspiracy, but proved too clever by half; he attracted Commodus's
suspicion by finding all the obvious parties to the intrigue – his friends
and fellow-soldiers – not guilty.[57] Perennis ingeniously revealed to
Commodus evidence of a second plot, linked to Salvius Julianus,
commander of the army of Upper Germany. Some historians think
this second plot was a phoney, a pure fabrication by the machiavellian
Perennis, but it was probably real enough. Paternus had close links
to Julianus, whose son was betrothed to his daughter; but, even worse,
Salvius Julianus's kinsman, Didius Julianus, governor of Lower
Germany, was also said to be involved.[58] As a result of Perennis's revel-
ations, Paternus, Salvius Julianus, Vitruvius Secundus and two of the
consuls for the year 182 were executed. Vitruvius Secundus was *ab
epistulis*, the head of the secretariat, and through him Paternus had

been trying to inveigle all the provincial armies in the plot. Didius Julianus was lucky to escape with his life: found not guilty, he was nevertheless forced to retire to Milan under a cloud. Commodus suspected him of treason, but lacked the hard evidence to convict him.[59]

There were in fact even more consequences from the second conspiracy. Commodus used the plot as a pretext to sweep away all the old guard who had been appointed to high positions by Marcus, especially those who had attained high military command in the Marcomannic wars. Pertinax and Septimius Severus were the next important generals to join Didius Julianus on the scrapheap, but not before they had fumbled a task assigned to them by the young emperor.[60] The Quintilius family was the next obvious target for Commodus's rage. The elder brothers, the ex-consuls, were executed on trumped-up charges and Quintilius Condianus, the leading family scion in the next generation, fled to Syria, where Pertinax and Severus were given the task of hunting him down. It is unclear whether what happened next occurred in collusion with Pertinax and Severus or on Condianus's own initiative. At any rate he feigned death by drinking the blood of a hare and then histrionically falling from his horse, vomiting and appearing to spew up dark gore, which the onlookers were supposed to construe as his life-blood. Carted off as if dead, he then made good his escape, and a dead ram was cremated in his place.[61] Somehow the story got out, and there was a general hue and cry throughout Asia Minor, with anyone who looked even vaguely like Condianus being executed and the heads sent to Commodus in Rome to identify. Condianus's eventual fate is unknown, but Commodus suspected that his 'miracle' escape owed much to Pertinax and Severus.[62] Now in a state of raging paranoia, he sacked all his top commanders and winnowed the army down to centurion rank. Other victims of the executioner – evidently notables at the time, but obscure figures to historians – were Norbanus, Norbana and Paralius and the ex-consuls D. Velius Rufus Julianus and Atilius Severus. By this time Commodus was not even bothering with niceties like trials, but was ordering executions by fiat. He had no mercy on the gentler sex, and the noble lady Vitrasis Faustina was another caught up in the post-Lucilla purge.[63] Already the full tsunami of Commodus's mad rage was bursting over Rome and he was executing

anyone to whom he happened to take a dislike: because they were
too rich, because they came from too ancient a family, because they
were too intelligent, because he did not like the cut of their jib – in
fact for any reason whatsoever. His most notorious exploit was the
hiring of paid assassins to 'take out' any senators who particularly
annoyed him.[64]

After the blood-letting of 182, Commodus settled into a three-
year binge of pleasure and debauchery, effectively leaving the running
of the empire to Tigidius Perennis, the supremely cunning survivor
of the Lucilla purges. Commodus never left Rome or its environs
after 180, allowing the hub of the empire no respite from his malign
presence. He would make occasional political interventions,
swamping the Senate with his cronies both to geld it and make it a
laughing-stock in the eyes of the people. Virtually all senators were
removed from his inner circle and replaced with knights. He detained
at Rome the children of those provincial governors he did not trust.
He downgraded the office of consul, both by serving himself in the
office an unconscionable number of times (in 181, 183, 186, 190 and
192) and by expanding the annual number of people who held the
post.[65] But most of the time Commodus was wallowing in pleasure,
indulging his voracious bisexual appetites. He kept a harem of beautiful women, said to be 300-strong and ranging from lubricious
matrons to virgins seized from all classes by his pressgangs for their
looks.[66] He was said to have taken 'revenge' for Lucilla's plot by
debauching his other sisters. Like all pleasure-lovers, he soon became
bored with the normal processes of heterosexuality and sought out
ever more abstruse perversions. He developed a taste for voyeurism
by having his political favourites and his current concubines couple
in front of him.[67] He took a string of male lovers and, if ever he
was baulked of his prey, punished the family, as in the case of the
Julianus *gens*, who suffered when the son of Salvius Julianus rebuffed
his advances.[68] The quest for the El Dorado of pleasure took
Commodus into further realms of depravity; he fully satisfied
Voltaire's dictum 'once a philosopher, twice a pervert' by a taste for
finding a new perversion and then slaking his appetite to the point
of boredom.

Meanwhile Perennis was given a free hand to purge the Senate
and settle old grudges. He proved an able lieutenant for Commodus,

mocking the 'Conscript Fathers' by appointing freedmen to the Senate and equestrians to roles traditionally filled only by members of Rome's Brahmin class. He and Commodus positively revelled in the political chaos they caused, changing the prefects of the guard almost daily and appointing twenty-five consuls in one year.[69] But whereas Commodus acted mainly out of simple madness, tinged always with that super-calculation and manipulative brilliance that psychotics so often possess, Perennis seems to have been more of a Robespierre *avant la lettre*, intent on permanent revolution. Although the historian Herodian tries to tar him with Commodus's mad brush,[70] the reality was that Perennis, though wildly ambitious, was both incorruptible and a good financial manager; it is significant that during his three-year hegemony no *congiaria* were distributed. Perennis was also highly efficient as *praefectus annonae*, making sure that the supply of bread to Rome was constant and assured, and thus heading off trouble from the lower depths.[71] And so, until 185, the empire limped along under this curious two-man rule, yet another Roman example of 'dyarchy' of the Hitler–Goebbels type. There were continuing skirmishes along the Danube, and in 182–3 Commodus was saluted as *imperator* for the fifth and sixth times. The Romans also scored a few successes in Mauretania.[72] Yet the most serious disturbances occurred in Britain. In 184 the Britons north of Hadrian's Wall invaded and cut up a detachment of legionaries. They were defeated by Ulpius Marcellus, giving Commodus the opportunity to take the title *Britannicus*,[73] but the victory over the natives simply inflamed pre-existing army grievances. Perennis was deeply unpopular with the troops, both because of his policy of financial austerity (he had not allowed them a donative) and because he – horror of horrors – appointed equestrians to lead the legions as part of his 'permanent revolution'. Taking matters into their own hands, the troops in Britain sidelined Ulpius Marcellus and acclaimed one Priscus (no other name is known) as emperor. Priscus wisely refused the offer, but a panic-stricken Commodus had to recall Pertinax and send him to Britain before the crisis could be calmed.[74]

The disturbances in Britain lit a fuse that led rapidly to Perennis's downfall in 185. Commodus's 'prime minister' had made a bad mistake by not neutralising or buying off the army, which in the years 180–5 stewed in a resentful atmosphere of perennial crisis.[75] Perennis thought he had been astute by making over the praetorian guard so that he could not be ousted, meanwhile laying all the blame for the regime's failings on his master's debauchery and dissipation. But he had neglected the army, and especially the soldiers in remote outposts of the empire.

Angry at the lack of donatives and the 'insult' of having the legions led by knights, the army petitioned Commodus to allow a delegation of their number to come to Rome from Britain to put before him their grievances against Perennis. At the limit Commodus was prepared to sacrifice Perennis to prevent another rising in Britain, so he consented.[76] Observers marvelled at the anarchic innovation whereby 1,500 armed men were allowed to proceed unchecked and unhindered through the empire to complain about Perennis. This was the first sign of the military indiscipline that was to overwhelm the empire in the third century, and also an unintended consequence of the militarisation of the Roman state under Marcus Aurelius as a result of the Marcomannic wars.[77] Commodus was too stupid or too alienated to realise that he was setting a very dangerous precedent, but everything about the debauched emperor always reeked of short-termism. By amazing luck, and the incompetence of the conspirators, he survived a dozen years of non-stop plots and intrigues, seemingly unaware of the thin ice on which he daily stood.[78] When the unruly deputation reached Rome, the soldiers accused Perennis of plotting to become emperor. Their supporters had meanwhile whipped up senatorial anger about equestrian over-promotions in order to foment a whispering campaign from the Senate. Smeared by both the elite and the army, Perennis sudenly found himself dangerously exposed. A serpent arose in his rear in the shape of the imperial chamberlain M. Aurelius Cleander, who increasingly had the ear of the emperor and produced circumstantial evidence of a plot by Cleander's own son, the army commander in Pannonia. Soon Cleander had persuaded the gullible Commodus of the ultimate absurdity – that Perennis intended to make himself emperor.[79] Although the tarnishing of Perennis was the most obvious of 'frame-ups' – an unholy alliance of envious rivals, disgruntled senators and avaricious legionaries, Commodus chose to abandon his erstwhile favourite. Perennis, together with his wife, two sons and sister, was turned over to the tender mercies of the mob.[80]

Commodus's cynical sacrifice of Perennis did little to quell the continuing crisis in the empire. There was unrest in Upper Germany in 185 – both brigandage and large-scale attacks on cities – which it took two legions until the summer of 186 to put down.[81] Having been initially placated by the acceptance of their deputation, the legions in Britain soon found fresh reasons for grievance and rebelled again. This time they offered the throne to Pertinax, who not only refused the offer, but wrote in a panic to Commodus requesting to be recalled; his fear was that he would be asked again and, next time, when he refused the legionaries would kill him. He was allowed to return to Rome and put in charge of the *alimenta*.[82] Yet in some ways even more serious than the non-stop disturbances in Britain was the so-called War of the Deserters in 185–6. A man named Maternus, a common soldier in Gaul, deserted his legion and persuaded many others to desert with him. Aiming to be a second, more successful Spartacus, he began a guerrilla campaign.[83] Beginning with raids on farms and villages, the guerrillas graduated to the sacking of large towns, specialising in breaking into prisons so that they could release the most dangerous criminals to join them. The 'madness' soon infected all Gaul and Spain, where the largest cities were besieged by groups claiming allegiance to Maternus. Embarrassed by this tumult, Commodus flew into a rage and accused his provincial governors of incompetence. He appointed three new governors (all significantly salient personalities after 192): Pescennius Niger in Syria, Clodius Albinus in Britain and Septimius Severus in Upper Pannonia. Pescennius Niger defeated Maternus's tatterdemalion army in Gaul, but this did not end the revolt. Regrouping with the survivors of battle, Maternus shifted his base of operations to Italy, again waging a very successful guerrilla war and making it plain that his ultimate aim was the purple. Aping Spartacus, he announced a march on Rome.[84] Successfully evading all the legions sent against him, Maternus and his men infiltrated themselves into Rome itself. Their master plan was to disguise themselves as praetorians during the festival of Hilaria (a Roman Mardi Gras held at the time of the spring equinox), hoping to get close enough to Commodus to assassinate him. Sadly for the ambitious Maternus, his very success hitherto had attracted envy in his own ranks. One of his men, with an obscure personal grudge against his leader, betrayed the plot to Commodus; Maternus was seized and executed.[85]

The years 185–9 saw Cleander installed as court favourite and 'prime minister'. More and more Commodus was inclined to ape Tiberius and retreat from the day-to-day governing of the empire, this time not to Capri, but only as far as the Palatine, spending his day racing horses, fighting in the arena, killing animals and generally showing off his skill with a javelin, before retiring for a night of orgies and carousing. But whereas in the Perennis years he had a skilful captain on the bridge of the ship of state, with Cleander in charge all was disaster. Perennis and Commodus had had spheres of influence, sometimes overlapping, but Cleander put himself in the business of direct competition with his emperor, each trying to plumb previously unsounded depths of depravity.[86] The competition had two main facets, one sexual, the other political. Sexually Commodus and Cleander liked to have women in common, either in mass orgies or by sharing the same concubines; one of Commodus's principal concubines was Demostratia, Cleander's wife.[87] Politically they tried to outdo each other in devising new insults with which to outrage men of senatorial rank. Cleander gave imperial freedmen a free hand to rob, steal, defalcate, debauch, rape, live riotously and sell privileges and places. Commodus responded by overt demonstrations of contempt for the Senate, pointedly excluding senators from his palace banquets and inviting depraved cronies instead.[88] He allowed freedmen to become senators on payment of a set fee. No office-holder any longer had security of tenure. The role of praetorian prefect became a laughing stock. One lasted just six hours, another five days and a third was executed on a Commodus whim. Even Cleander eventually tired of the instability and in 187 assumed the office himself, appointing two notorious dagger-men assassins as his under-prefects.[89] Commodus meanwhile decided that he needed more money from the Senate and issued a decree that every senator had to pay him annually two *aurei* a head for each member of his family, the sum to be payable on his birthday. One of his most outrageous scams was to ask the Senate for money for an expedition to North Africa; this was duly voted, but Commodus bare-facedly pocketed the money and did not go.[90] The craven Senate responded by voting the fraudster the title of father of the Senate (*pater Senatus*).

For the first two years of his ascendancy Cleander was involved in a brutal struggle with the Burrus family, the only focus of opposition left. L. Antistius Burrus and his Libyan kinsman Arrius Antoninus, proconsul of Asia, certainly built up a formidable anti-Cleander coalition, but the sources do not permit us to state definitely that he was also aiming at the purple.[91] Burrus had many powerful allies, including at one time the guard prefect Atilius Aebutianus, but does not seem to have been a very skilful intriguer. At any rate he sounded out Pertinax about joining the conspiracy, when Pertinax owed his recall from disgrace and reinstatement to Cleander. Pertinax, at that time still in Britain, wrote to Commodus with full details of the plot.[92] It is unlikely that Pertinax had any great love for Commodus, but he was a slippery customer, nothing like the fool he pretended to be, and may have made his decision to reveal the conspiracy out of hard-headed calculation.[93] In short, he doubted that Antistius Burrus had the right stuff for a successful coup, and wanted it made clear at an early stage to the likely winners that he himself was not one of the conspirators. He was rewarded by being appointed proconsul in Africa. By 187 Cleander had the upper hand and made a clean sweep of the plotters. Burrus, Arrius Antoninus and Atilius Aebutianus were all executed, while another notable, C. Aufidius Victorinus, cheated the headsman by committing suicide.[94] Commodus's wife Crispina seems to have been tainted with this conspiracy, for she too joined the ranks of the fallen this year. Allegedly caught *in flagrante* with her lover, she was banished to Capri by Commodus and then put to death shortly afterwards; exactly the same procedure had been followed with Lucilla.[95]

It was fortunate indeed for Rome that no powerful external enemies appeared during the years of Commodus's chaotic reign. It appears that there was a minor rising of the Quadi in 188, and at first Commodus contemplated a third German war.[96] How serious this intention ever was is doubtful. Some historians claim that the Senate persuaded him not to undertake a fresh German expedition, but, since the Senate was now packed with his creatures, such a gesture would have been a 'put-up job', with Commodus masking his own disinclination to campaign with a bogus show of deference to an assembly he had already gelded.[97] Elsewhere, apart from the disturbances in North Africa, the empire was tranquil. This may be the explanation for the paradox that Commodus tried to put Italy at the centre of the world, but was deeply unpopular there, although he was popular in the East, which he neglected.[98] It was Commodus's continual presence in Rome that was so oppressive; outside Italy his reality was tenuous. In this instance the old French saying *les absents ont toujours tort* is itself wrong. It was because he was a distant, unreal presence that Commodus received the accolades of communities in far-flung corners of the empire; the epigraphy and archaeology of the Greek-speaking empire would not enable us to infer the existence of a mad emperor.[99] And, before we follow Commodus on his steep descent into paranoid psychosis, it may be as well to mention the few areas where he has grudging supporters. Christians preferred him to Marcus Aurelius because he did not persecute them; the martyrdom of Apollonius sometime between 183 and 185 was an isolated case. Of course the Christians benefited greatly from the fact that Commodus's favourite mistress Marcia was one of them and could influence the emperor and divert his wrath.[100] Other scholars claim that Commodus had certain gifts as a poet, and a genuine understanding of the ways in which art, iconography and other visual motifs could create a distinctive imperial image and could be used as a powerful propaganda tool.[101]

Yet in the main all was madness, paranoia and cruelty. Priding himself on his prowess with the javelin and the bow and arrow, he waged a one-man war on the dumb beasts, killing thousands of all species, evincing a particular hatred for elephants, doubtless for their 'objectionable' qualities of great size and great nobility.[102] But his lust for killing was not assuaged by his helpless victims in the animal world. Casual homicide was a mundane pastime, which he liked to spice up with cruel and sadistic refinements. Often he would amuse himself by cutting off a person's foot or blinding someone in one eye.[103] He said he had learned much from Galen, and 'proved' this by callously going to work on his victims with a scalpel and allowing them to bleed to death.[104] He liked to demonstrate his surgical prowess by slicing a fat man down the middle, so that the intestines poured out. It amused him to surround himself with freaks, and he included in his entourage a man with a penis larger than that of every known animal except the elephant – so perhaps that was the motive for his hatred of the tuskers.[105] Like all bored psychopaths, he sought ever more recondite varieties of cruelty. Noticing a man who had a few white strands among a healthy head of black hair, he ordered that a starling be fixed to his head, which pecked away at the white hairs, thinking they were worms. The man's head festered and he, presumably, became yet another sacrifice to the emperor's whims.[106] Commodus had yet another detestable trait, often found in individuals of great power who rationalise their essential humourlessness: he was a practical joker. He liked to seat people at a banquet and then serve expensive food mixed with excrement, delightedly observing the inevitable reaction. At another feast he displayed two misshapen hunchbacks on silver platters, first smearing them with mustard to make the 'dish' more delectable.[107] Anyone with a physical peculiarity was fair game for Commodus's 'amusing' stunts. Anyone tall enough to be classified as a giant was likely to be forced to wear leggings shaped to look like serpents, with protruding heads and fangs that made walking impossible; anyone dwarfish sustained an opposite fate. As the *Historia Augusta* put it: 'Certain men who were lame in their feet, and others who could not walk, he dressed up as giants, encasing their legs from the knee down in wrappings and bandages to make them appear like serpents; he then dispatched the "beasts" with arrows.'[108] Psychologists will no doubt ponder the deep meaning of his 'compensatory' ablutions, for he insisted on bathing seven or eight times a day.[109] But the madness was not limited to the harm he doled out on other hapless humans. He decided it would be a good idea to rename all the months: and so August was retitled Commodus, September Hercules, October became Invictus, November Exsuperaorius, December Amazonius, and so on.[110]

How did such a crazed individual manage to remain in power? There were three main factors at play: his handling of the Senate, his popularity in the army, and his assiduous courting of the Roman mob. After ten years on the throne, Commodus had largely finished his sport with the Senate and began aiming at a balance of power, no longer gratuitously alienating the senatorial class, but always ensuring that none of them could ever be a threat to him, cleverly giving key positions to knights and freedmen. He eventually worked out a system where he gave senators honorific positions, but devoid of all real power.[111] Senatorial grandees were still secretly incensed that the emperor had broken down the 'natural order' and irate that they had to defer to equestrians. In patrician circles it was increasingly whispered that Commodus was a second Tiberius, not just because he lived in isolation, as Tiberius had done on Capri, but because he encouraged a raft of favourites – Saoterus, Perennis and Cleander – who were all carbon copies of Tiberius's notorious favourite Sejanus.[112] But, partly because Commodus now humoured them and partly because so many plots against him had failed, the Senate was by and large prepared to mark time. Besides, senators were cowed by Commodus's periodic purges of patrician ranks. On one occasion he executed six ex-consuls and all their families (Allius Fuscus, Caelius Felix, Lucceius Torquatus, Lartius Eurupianus, Valerius Bassinaus and Pactumerius Magnus). In the provinces the emperor's hitmen liquidated Sulpicius Crassus, proconsul of Asia, plus Julius Proculus and ex-consul Claudius Lucianus (both of Asia). In 190 he purged Gratus Julianus, the two Silani brothers and their families, the senator M. Antonius Antius Lupus and his kinsman M. Pertonius Sura Mamertinus, together with his brother M. Petronius Sura Septimanius and his son Petronius Antoninus.[113] The case of Julius Alexander, a patrician of Emesa in Syria, particularly evoked comment. Alexander attracted Commodus's hatred and jealousy simply because he was a mighty hunter and had killed a lion with a javelin from horseback. Since Commodus regarded himself as the only true Nimrod in the empire, he at once proscribed Alexander as a 'rebel' and sent his assassins after him. Alexander turned the tables, killed the hitmen and then fled to the Euphrates, hoping to find sanctuary in Parthia. He would certainly have got clean away but for his concern for his boyfriend. When his gay partner became exhausted during the flight in the desert, and it seemed likely that Commodus's new team of assassins would overhaul them, Alexander killed his lover and then fell on his own sword to escape the fate the emperor had prepared for them.[114]

As well as his effective castration of the Senate, Commodus had the important advantage that he was very popular in the army.[115] The soldiers liked a man who had ended the toilsome wars on the Danube and who pandered to their whims, making promotion easier, listening to their complaints and, above all, being lax about discipline. It was Pertinax's insistence on strict discipline that did for him later in his career when he became a short-lived emperor.[116] Commodus was also generous with his handouts, often awarding an individual largesse of 140 denarii.[117] Superficially it might appear that he was in danger of alienating the mob by awarding only three *congiaria* after the fall of Perennis (the sixth, seventh and eighth, in 186, 190 and 192), but Commodus was diverting all his spare cash to pay for his lavish spectacles and games, which seemed to provide ample compensation.[118] Nevertheless, Commodus's social control was far from complete, and by the late 180s there were some ominous clouds on the horizon. In 187–8 Rome experienced a disastrous recrudescence of the Antonine plague, which killed 2,000 people a day in Rome alone.[119] Additionally, Rome was becoming more and more run-down for, with money short and Commodus continually debasing the currency to pay for his gladiator and animal spectacles, little building work was undertaken. The only public monuments of Commodus's reign were some baths, a temple to Marcus Aurelius and, later, the modification of a statute to the sun so that it resembled Hercules. The famous column of Marcus Aurelius took the whole of the twelve-year reign to complete.[120] Perhaps because of the insouciance over its infrastructure, Rome was hit by a series of fires. Those of 189 compelled a reluctant Commodus to order some rebuilding. The far more serious inferno of 192, however, which devastated the district east of the Forum and a portion of the Palatine, was clearly a spontaneous combustion; there can be no excuse for laying this at Commodus's door and making him out to be another Nero-like incendiarist.[121] Hard on the heels of the new outbreak of plague came a famine, caused initially by the plundering, hoarding and price-fixing of the cronies to whom Cleander had farmed out the grain supply.[122] This developed into a full-blown crisis that toppled Cleander.

After winning the power struggle with Antistius Burrus and Arrius Antoninus, Cleander was confident that he had disposed of all rivals for the foreseeable future. But events turned against him sooner than he could reasonably have expected. For the disgruntled senatorial class, Cleander was now a marked man; if they could not overthrow Commodus, they would at least make an end of his detested favourite. The execution of Burrus and Antoninus was angrily resented, even though some scholars insist that this was a personal initiative by Commodus and that Cleander had nothing to do with it.[123] Cleander nonetheless gave hostages to fortune by his extreme greed and venality; it was his excessive sale of offices that resulted in the ultimate absurdity in 190 when there were no fewer than twenty-five consuls.[124] Meanwhile Pertinax, who had returned from Africa in 189 (where he had been proconsul) and taken up the post of prefect of the city, was drawn into the anti-Cleander conspiracy.[125] Yet the main precipitant for Cleander's downfall was the hatred of M. Aurelius Papirius Dionysius, who loathed the favourite and could not forgive him for demoting him from the prefecture of Egypt to the lesser post of *praefectus annonae*, where he superintended the corn supply. Soon there was a powerful triumvirate of conspirators: Dionysius, Pertinax and Julius Julianus, prefect of the guard. Papirius Dionysius cunningly schemed to engineer a shortage of grain, intending it to spark a riot among the volatile Roman mob.[126] Commodus, ignorant of economics and unaware of the gravity of the situation, tried to impose price controls for food and fresh taxes to pay for fresh shipments of grain. This served only to exacerbate the situation, as food supplies dried up completely at the threat of controls. As the plotters had foreseen, the Roman proletariat went on the rampage, thirsting for the blood of Cleander, whom they blamed for the debacle.

Discontent boiled over on 19 April 190 during a race at the Circus Maximus, a reliable cauldron of mob fury, with its 150,000 spectators.[127] Since the prefect of the *annona* controlled the seating for shows there, Dionysius had all his agents placed in key positions. The riot was beautifully stage-managed. First, a crowd of children ran out onto the racetrack and began chanting anti-Cleander slogans, which were taken up vociferously by the crowd. The enraged spectators then burst out of the Circus and made for the villa of the Quintilii on the Appian Way, where Cleander then was, demanding his head. Cleander succeeded in unleashing the praetorians on them, and great slaughter ensued, but, when he called for back-up from Pertinax and the 1,500 men of his city cohort, it was obvious that it would not be forthcoming. Indeed, Pertinax infiltrated his men into the crowd to stiffen their resistance to the baffled praetorians.[128] News that Rome was in uproar reached Commodus at his country villa outside Rome. At the prompting of Marcia (or, some say, his sister Fadilla), who persuaded him that civil war was imminent, Commodus agreed to sacrifice Cleander to save himself. The mob swarmed all over the grounds of the villa on the Appian Way, dragged Cleander out and killed him, before hauling his body by chariot through the streets of Rome. They then sought out the entire extended family of Cleander, complete with children, and massacred them all.[129]

Publicly Commodus shrugged off the insolence of the mob, ordered another *congiarium* distributed and 'celebrated' with a new coinage issue.[130] The riot over Cleander would have alerted a more intelligent man to mend his ways, but Commodus simply plunged deeper into madness. Suspecting that Julius Julianus had had something to do with the downfall of his favourite, Commodus set out to humiliate him. While embracing him in public and calling him 'father', in private he submitted Julianus to all kinds of petty indignities. Commodus pushed him into a swimming pool in his formal toga and in front of his staff.[131] Then Julianus had to dance naked before the emperor's concubines, clashing cymbals like a corybant or maenad. Finally, bored by mere humiliation, Commodus had him murdered. This ended the hope that Pertinax, Dionysius and Julianus might have been able to form a sensible triumvirate to replace the trio of personal favourites who had all ended up murdered.[132] Yet Commodus simply decided that he no longer needed a second-in-command and instituted his own troika, consisting of his favourite concubine Marcia (whose husband consequently became a power behind the scenes), his bedchamber servant Eclectus and the praetorian prefect Q. Aemilius Laetus. All of the trio had chequered careers: Eclectus, significantly, had been an old crony of Lucius Verus; Marcia had once been the mistress of Ummidius Quadratus who was executed in 182; while Laetus, a man of no distinction, was simply Commodus's sop to the important North African elite, who had to be conciliated because they were so vital to the corn supply, but who had been alienated after the executions of Burrus and Antoninus.[133] Since none of these was capable of running the empire the way the three ill-starred favourites could, Commodus was reluctantly forced to rouse himself from his sybaritic slumbers and take a more active part in affairs of state. This inevitably meant a fresh round of purges, pogroms, proscriptions and bloody massacres. The years 190–1 saw a reign of terror, with fifteen senators executed (including twelve ex-consuls) and their families murdered also. Rome was already demoralised and panic-stricken with the fresh outbreak of plague, and the reign of terror simply compounded this.[134] It was in any case difficult to know whether death was from smallpox or homicide, since political factions used the cover of the Antonine plague to settle old scores, kill off rivals and pursue private vendettas. It got to the stage where professional hitmen were hired to stab victims with sharp needles coated with plague spores, so that the murdered could then be passed off as natural victims of the pestilence.[135]

Commodus's final descent into total insanity is thought to rest heavily on two issues: his 'coming out' as a gladiator; and his self-identification with the god Hercules – both of which were increasingly in evidence from about the middle of 190. Commodus had trained as a gladiator even when Marcus Aurelius was alive, but his father had dismissed the boy's obsession as a youthful craze that would soon pass.[136] It did not. Gladiatorial combat became crucial to Commodus's self-image. Behind his back his senatorial enemies expressed the utmost contempt for this aspect of the young emperor.[137] Not only were his appearances in the arena a farce, since his opponents would not dare to harm him and therefore had to let him win every time, but Commodus was a stupid boy who had never grown up, and a humbug to boot, because it would require more energy than the lazy emperor could ever summon to try out his skill by hunting in the countryside.[138] To say nothing of the further farce whereby he fought with iron weapons while his opponents were given lead ones.[139] Above all, there was a deeply rooted tradition that for a high-born Roman it was the ultimate disgrace to enter the arena, not least because becoming a gladiator normally meant exchanging freedom for bondage.[140] By performing in the arena as a gladiator, a citizen became infamous and could even be deprived of his citizenship; it was considered that the higher the status of the person in the arena, the greater the offence against nature – an impious reversal of the cosmic order.

Commodus cared nothing for such scruples. He wanted to establish himself as a great warrior, having already, to his own satisfaction, proved that he was a mighty hunter. In the years 180–90 he had regularly enjoyed the Roman version of 'turkey shoots' in which he shot down 100 lions with javelins – or sometimes 100 bears – or shot the heads off ostriches with special crescent-headed arrows. In those years he had massacred the dumb beasts in the morning and then fought in the arena in the afternoon.[141] Now he preferred to concentrate on gladiatorial combat and could be found every day in the arena, always accompanied by Aemilius Laetus and Eclectus. Whenever Commodus the gladiator was victorious – which is to say always – he would kiss his two favourites through the visor of his helmet. All senators and knights were obliged to watch the emperor fighting, on pain of death; no excuse for absence was tolerated. The senators were also forced to chant moronic hymns or paeans to the emperor-god. Some of the words of these exercises in mass humiliation have been preserved: 'You are the lord; you are the first of all men and the most fortunate. You will conquer; you will conquer Amazonius; you will conquer for all eternity.'[142]

Revisionist historians, while conceding Commodus's psychosis, have nevertheless insisted that there was method in his gladiatorial madness. Commodus had decided on a policy of peace, playing Hadrian to his father's Trajan, but all pacific emperors then had a problem with their image, given the importance in Roman culture of the martial ethos. Hadrian had tried to get round this by portraying himself as a mighty hunter, which was why Commodus felt he had to transcend even this and project himself as a great warrior. He also considered that spectacles enhanced stability in subtle ways: the Roman people had a right to see the emperor who was protecting them and assure themselves that he was man enough to merit his supreme position. In short, Commodus used gladiatorial spectacles to promote his ideology of himself as the great God of Plenty who would usher in a new Golden Age.[143] He was proclaiming his special status, not yet seated on Olympus with the immortals, but still no mere human. He was a being outside and above society, not bound by normal rules of morality or social hierarchy.[144] Beyond this, Commodus was fully aware that in the Roman mind the arena was perceived as a shadowland between normality and abnormality, between order and the chaos world, and that games represented a kind of metaphysical theatre in which the nature of ultimate reality could be symbolised and social life harmonised dialectically, so that the gap was bridged between the apparent antinomies of 'is' and 'ought', 'appearance' and 'reality', existence and essence.[145] Gladiatorial games symbolised the triumph of order over chaos, culture over biology (or, as we might say, superego over id), Roman over barbarian, and thus symbolised the nature of the cosmos itself.[146] Utimately, gladiatorial games played the key consolatory role of all religion, since Rome triumphing over the barbarians could be read as an allegory of the triumph of immortality over death. Just as by winning a contest in the arena, a condemned man could win his life on the whim of the emperor, so by conquering chaos humans could hope to receive the ultimate gift from the president of the immortals.[147] It may be that some Roman emperors felt that the 'offence against nature' committed when a patrician entered the arena was trumped by the symbolic conquest of death achieved when the emperor himself donned sword and helmet; this could explain why Caligula, Hadrian and Lucius Verus were all rumoured to have performed at games and spectacles.[148] In Commodus's case, he became a gladiator to enhance his claim to be able to conquer death, already implicit in his self-deification as the god Hercules.

From a minute examination of coinage, scholars have detected a gradual drift towards monotheism during the Antonine era, culminating with Commodus.[149] At the beginning of his reign Commodus was content to identify himself closely with Jupiter, shunting the other Olympians into limbo. Then he developed a taste for the mystical religions of the East, and particularly the cult of Mithras, which had been brought back by Lucius Verus and his entourage after the Parthian war. Mithraism appealed to Commodus as it was a warrior's religion and implicitly contemptuous of the heritage of Greek culture, ultimately the foundation of traditional Roman religion. Commodus relished this contempt, as it served to distance him from his father, to whom Greek in all its manifestations had been supremely important.[150] But Commodus was eclectic: he had time for all mystical religions and particularly liked the syncretism whereby, say, the cult of Isis often merged with that of Anubis, the Egyptian god.[151] Christianity benefited from this tolerance, since to Commodus it was not a deadly threat to the entire traditional religion and culture of Rome, as it had been for Marcus Aurelius, but simply another obscure Eastern sect. The other thing that appealed to him about the mystery religions was that they provided more of

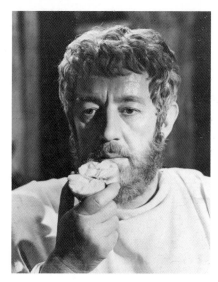

Marcus in myth and legend. (*Above left*) An Irish hellraiser with a roistering 'feedback image' was a curious choice to play Marcus Aurelius in the film GLADIATOR (2000). The movie did not help matters by depicting the emperor's death in a ludicrous and implausible way. (*Above right*) Much more convincing in terms of dignity and gravitas was Alec Guinness, who played Marcus in THE FALL OF THE ROMAN EMPIRE (1964). Sadly, the movie subscribes to the discredited legend that Marcus was assassinated when he ate half of an apple that had been poisoned.

Lucius Verus, Marcus's short-lived co-emperor. Is it one's imagination or can one actually discern something of the dissolute character of Verus in this statue preserved in the Vatican Museum?

Although this image of a Parthian warrior, taken from a bronze statue at Shami, Iran, relates to the century before Marcus, little changed in warfare or iconography in the five-hundred year life of the Parthian empire.

The Triumph of Marcus Aurelius. Admiration for Marcus Aurelius reached a peak in the eighteenth century when Gibbon identified his reign as the 'golden age' of the Roman empire. It was, then, entirely appropriate that the greatest painter of the high eighteenth century should have chosen Marcus as a subject. This is a typical product of the Tiepolo imagination, whereby history becomes high theatre. In its eschewal of the painter's usually early morning colours it is, however, a somewhat untypical product of the Venetian master.

Throwing Christians to the lions has become one of the dominant motifs in the story of early persecuted Christianity. It was, however, not that easy to tempt lions to attack humans unprovoked, so the Romans had to devise various 'incentives' for the king of beasts.

One of the key elements in Christianity, allowing it to survive and become a world religion, was the support given it by women. Even high-born Roman ladies were prepared to pay the ultimate sacrifice of martyrdom.

Marcus sets out for Aquileia at the start of his campaign against the Germans. We can be reasonably certain that this *profectio* (setting out) – a typical convention in Roman imperial art – was at the start of his German wars rather than those against Parthia, since the reclining figure is a personification of the Via Flaminia, the most important road to the north and the main artery from Rome to Rimini.

This relief from the Capitoline Museum in Rome shows Marcus on horseback granting clemency to the defeated Germans in the immediate aftermath of battle, as shown by the trees in the background. Marcus's attitude would harden over twelve years of warfare, so that by 180 the merciful emperor was no longer in evidence.

Marcomannic prisoners plead for their lives before the emperor. The image is blatant propaganda, identifying Marcus with Justice. In all such images the emperor is seated on a podium, the legendary 'seat of justice'.

Marcus's wars with the German tribes were sustained, bloody and pitiless. At least 50,000 men perished in nine years of warfare, excluding the fatalities from the simultaneous Antonine plague.

The so-called 'Rain Miracle' during a battle between the legions and the Quadi in summer 174, which gave the Romans an unexpected victory. The downpour appears in the guise of a grim and terrifying Nature god.

Transport of German prisoners and booty. The German wars were not as 'cost effective' as the Parthian campaign, since the northern tribes had no fixed stores of wealth or treasure to loot. The 'spoils of war' were therefore exiguous, but the fresh supply of slaves helped to mitigate the Empire's increasing manpower shortage.

The beheading of German nobles. By the end of the war Marcus's attitude had hardened. It is pure sentimentalism to imagine that he would have felt sorry for his victims. What we see as atrocities or war crimes the Romans viewed as just punishment meted out to 'rebels' by a dutiful emperor.

an excuse for violence, sadism and cruelty than worship of the Olympians did. The devotees of the esoteric cults soon found they had got more than they bargained for, when imperial interest and favour turned nasty. He ordered the priests of Isis to beat their breasts with pine cones until their flesh was in shreds, and ordered the orgiastic worshippers of the Bellona cult to cut off an arm apiece. He himself killed a man during a Mithraic rite.[152] Commodus's defenders claim that there was method in his madness, that he was rejecting the hidebound, class-fixated conservatism of his father in favour of new, future-looking experimental modes of thought and emotion; he represented, in short, the movement from a discredited intellectualism to a new world of instinct.[153] Yet Commodus was serpentine in his cunning and trod warily at first. After 190 he adopted the titles *Pacator Orbis* (Pacifier of the World), *Conditor* (Founder), *Invictus* (Undefeated), *Amazonius* and *Exsuperatorius* (The Man of Superlative Excellence, Surpassing All Mankind).[154] The last title was a nod to the old religion, but denoted a Jupiter quite unlike the limited figure in the traditional Olympian pantheon, a mere state god. The new Jupiter or *Exsuperatorius* was to be considered the chief and only god of the universe. *Amazonius* was a further step away from traditional theology, referring as it did both to his mistress Marcia – now portrayed as an Amazon – and to his own overweening gladiatorial ambitions.[155]

Yet all these flirtations with mystery religions and new cults faded into insignificance beside the mania for the figure of Hercules, which first became overt and finally overwhelming and all-pervasive in 191. In that year thirty-year-old Commodus completed his numismatic rejection of his father by dropping the appellation *Marcus Antoninus* and by referring to himself on coins as *Lucius Aelius Aurelius Commodus Augustus Felix*. This was merely the prelude to his assumption of the title *Herculius* and finally, in the last six months of his reign, *Hercules Commodianus*.[156] Many rulers had associated themselves with Hercules (or the Greek Herakles) in the past, especially Alexander the Great, who claimed that the hero-god (not Philip of Macedon) was his true father. More significantly, all the great Roman tyrants – Caligula, Nero and Domitian – had chosen the title of Hercules to go with their other appellations, since Hercules was the first man to become a god.[157] The difference between them and Commodus was that they had chosen

Hercules as a paradigm or model; he claimed that he was *literally* the incarnation of Hercules. Commodus insinuated that he was truly the lord of the universe, not just a reincarnation of Hercules the man-god, but also an emergent super-deity, rather like the Zeus of the Stoics. All the Olympian gods and all the Eastern deities were co-existent manifestations of this supreme spirit – and this was because humans understood polytheism more easily than monotheism. So Sol Invictus, Mithras, Cybele, Serape, Isis and all the rest of them were really just aspects of the supreme god Commodus. He liked to use so many different manifestations of this supreme being on his coinage to show the people that he was the earthly counterpart of all of them; the heterogeneity of the coins masks a fundamental unity.[158] His appearance as Hercules on all coins and statues went far beyond the earlier assimilations of Jupiter, Sol Invictus, Mithras and the rest. He took to appearing in a lion skin, brandishing a club, on public occasions. He laid about him with a 'club of Hercules'. Still masquerading as Hercules, he had a procession of gout-sufferers file past him draped in saddlecloths and made up to look like dragons, and then demonstrated his Herculean prowess as a dragon-slayer by shooting arrows into them.[159]

As with the mania for combat in the arena, Commodus's modern interpreters insist that, beneath the obvious madness, there was a purposive intelligence at work. All the Hercules nonsense went down well with the army, especially when Commodus told the legionaries that henceforth they could use the axe in battle as the Germans did – something forbidden them hitherto.[160] Yet the real trigger for the Hercules mania seems to have been the events surrounding the fall of Cleander, which were deeply disturbing to Commodus. Having already alienated the Senate to the point of no return, Commodus could not risk losing the support of the fickle Roman mob as well.[161] In promoting his identity with a reincarnated Hercules (possibly an idea suggested by the Christian Marcia), Commodus tried to stress that he was superhuman and hence invulnerable and indispensable if Rome was to see the dawn of the promised new Golden Age.[162] Sociologically, it was a rich irony that he returned to the centralising ideology of the earlier Antonines, stressing Hercules as a peculiarly Roman and Italian deity at the precise moment when Italy was in objective terms declining vis-à-vis the rest of the empire.[163]

The combination of Hercules and a gladiatorial champion was sure to be a crowd-pleasing stunt, and Commodus announced that, as proof of his new divine status, he was prepared to defeat 12,000 gladiators with one arm tied behind his back.[164] Had he shared his father's love of books, he might have pondered what Artemidorus had to say about dreams. A simple dream of Hercules was auspicious, but anything more than that – spending time with the hero, helping him in his work, sharing his meals, his lion skin, club or other weapon – was not. 'For the life that Hercules led is one that he imparts to the dreamer, and the life that he led, when he lived among men, was a life full of trials and misery, athough he himself was very famous and esteemed. Frequently the dream signifies that the man will find himself in situations that the god was in when he was carrying those weapons.'[165]

Having already taken so much imbecility from Commodus, the Roman aristocracy could doubtless have lived with the latest manifestation of psychosis, provided it was restricted to the religious domain. But Commodus's delusion that he really was a god and the reincarnated Hercules increased the levels of his homicidal paranoia. As more and more patrician 'names' – L. Julius Vehilius, Q. Aemilius Laetus and others well known at the time (named as Gratus, Regillus and Motilenus) – were led away to execution, more and more property plundered by the predatory praetorians, and instant death meted out to anyone lampooning, satirising or even in the mildest way criticising the emperor, Commodus created his own critical mass of opposition. The patrician class came together in a conviction that they must make an end to Commodus before he made an end of them.[166] As if to enhance their misgivings, 192 was a year of ill omen. The Great Fire in Rome that year destroyed the Temple of Peace, most of the imperial palace and the grain warehouses and state archives; many of Galen's writings perished in the conflagration. The Roman people read this as a portent of impending disaster, and it began to be whispered that Commodus's usurpation of the personality of Hercules had offended the gods.[167] Commodus added to the atmosphere of gloom and chaos by ratcheting his obsession up another notch. He cut off the head of the sun god outside the Colosseum and replaced it with his own portrait, adding a club and a bronze lion at the foot of the new monument to make the figure appear like the reborn

Hercules. He then announced that he wished to be known as the divine founder of Rome and to rename the city *colonia Commodiana*.[168]

In vain did Marcia, Laetus and Eclectus plead with the emperor that the combination of 'Hercules' and the gladiatorial mania was seriously alienating all classes in Rome. Commodus responded to this 'impertinence' by laying plans for the liquidation of this presumptuous trio. Learning of this, Laetus and Eclectus began plotting against him and inveigled Pertinax into their conspiracy; Marcia too was invaluable as she had constant access to the emperor. But they proceeded cautiously. There had been too many unsuccessful attempts on Commodus's life and he had survived them all, so this time the coup would have to be planned meticulously.[169] Word reached them that Commodus now intended to kill both new consuls (Erucius Clarus and Sosius Falco) on New Year's Day 193 and take their place in his eighth consulship, after which he would descend on Rome from the Caelian hill with a picked force of gladiators to cow all opposition. It was clear that Commodus was becoming over-confident, that he felt he had nothing to fear from his immediate circle, as they owed everything to him. The conspirators cleverly reasoned that the best time to strike would be the day before Commodus's planned New Year's Day purge. On the one hand, Commodus would be so involved with his own conspiracy plans that it would not occur to him that his enemies might get their blow in first. On the other, the praetorians, revelling in the festivals of Saturnalia and Sol Invictus, would be lax and probably drunk.[170]

But first it was necessary to destroy any vestige of pity or regret that might attach to an assassinated emperor. With this in mind, Laetus and Eclectus encouraged Commodus to hold a great slaughterous spectacle in the arena just before the planned coup.[171] A fourteen-day killing spree was arranged, during which the demented Commodus slaughtered every conceivable species of wild animal, with lions and bears particularly to the fore. The orgy of animal massacre culminated in an ostrich hunt. Commodus was equipped with a bow whose arrows had blades shaped like a half-moon, which cut through the birds' neck, so that the unfortunate ostriches went on running without their heads. Commodus the god already seemed to be in heaven, and in his arrogance he approached the senatorial box to threaten and browbeat the 'Conscript Fathers'. This is how an eyewitness described the scene: 'After killing an ostrich and cutting off its head, he came up to where we were sitting, holding the head in his left hand and raising the bloody sword in his right. He said nothing, but nodded his head with a grin, showing he would treat us likewise.'[172] The same eyewitness claimed that the senators actually chewed laurel leaves to keep their mouths moving, so as not to burst into the spontaneous laughter of shocked contempt. Some say that Commodus added to his sins by displaying the old racehorse champion of the Greens, Pertinax, and giving his club to the human Pertinax, the city prefect. Whatever the truth, the effect of his antics on the credulous and superstitious crowd was to whip them into a highly volatile and inflammable state, where they viewed their emperor with danger. One of the conpirators' agents provocateurs brilliantly stirred up the mob by spreading the word that Commodus, as Hercules, intended to massacre some of the spectators, putting them in the role of the Stymphalian birds in the Herculean labours.[173] Then the troika of Marcia, Eclectus and Laetus put their plan into action. Pertinax was in on the conspiracy, but was told to remain in the background so that he could emerge as an innocent observer at the end.[174] On the night of 31 December 192 the trio gave Commodus poison, but, possibly because he was such a hardened drinker and vomited the potion up, the toxin did not work. Switching to Plan B, they had him strangled by his personal trainer, an athlete named Narcissus.[175] Then Pertinax, the sleeping partner in the conspiracy, finally emerged from the shadows. First making sure that Commodus really was dead, he addressed the people, saying that the emperor had died a natural death and that he had been invited to succeed him by Laetus and Eclectus; to celebrate he was offering a donative of 12,000 sesterces for every man in Rome. The idea that Pertinax had not been involved in the plot fooled no one, and at first there was no response. Finally, with a judiciously placed claque, Laetus engineered Pertinax's acclamation as emperor.[176]

Unfortunately too much damage had been done to the empire during the twelve-year incumbency of Commodus. Apart from anything else, he had charged one million sesterces for each of his appearances in the arena and had clocked up 735 of these by 192 (including a suspiciously annotated 365 during Marcus's reign), thus bankrupting the treasury. As Cassius Dio said, he transmuted Rome 'from a kingdom of gold to one of iron'.[177] Commodus was in fact wrong to think that his cronies owed him too much to turn against him, but his reasoning was sound, because very few of them long survived him. Pertinax did not last long as emperor, since the praetorians, now accustomed to being above the law, murdered him when he tried to reintroduce discipline.[178] The end of the empire was prefigured when it was auctioned off to the highest bidder, being temporarily won by Didius Julianus, who offered a larger donative than his rivals.[179] The only true survivor was the veteran Claudius Pompeianus, now in his eighties, who was brought back into the Senate by Pertinax after a decade in obscurity. His son (and Marcus's grandson), Aurelius Commodus Pompeianus (b. 177), had survived all Commodus's murderous purges simply because Claudius Pompeianus was manifestly no threat; indeed, Commodus actively considered the young man as his successor.[180] But it was the younger Pompeianus's fate to avoid Scylla only to be sucked down by Charybdis. After becoming consul in 209, he was liquidated by Caracalla.[181]

Yet for the Senate it was a matter of no importance who survived and who did not. The important thing was that the great tyrant was no more, and they no longer had to endure his daily insults, such as the deliberately needling substitution of *Populus Senatusque* for the normal SPQR (*Senatus Populusque Romanus*). The Senate ordered all Commodus's statues and portraits destroyed. The mere mention of Hercules thereafter was enough to set alarm bells ringing; Caracalla, for instance, expressly forbade his men to call him Hercules after he had killed a lion.[182] There were no deification ceremonies for Commodus. Instead the Senate branded him: 'More savage than Domitian, more foul than Nero. Let the memory of the foul gladiator be utterly wiped away.'[183] It has always been considered a strike against Marcus Aurelius that he allowed paternal feelings to overrule good sense and thus permit a monster to succeed to the purple. We have seen the many reasons why Marcus felt he had no other choice, but later generations have always been uncomfortable with the thought of their beloved philosopher-king acting so irresponsibly, hence the absurd canards that Marcus intended to will the succession away from Commodus and was murdered by his son in consequence before he could implement the decision. Commodus *was* a monster; there can be no gainsaying that, and modern scholars have perhaps been too keen to dismiss the damning portrait of him in the *Historia Augusta* as mere propaganda. But Marcus could not have imagined the depth of hatred that his son evidently entertained for him. Those who doubt that this was part of Commodus's psychology will be hard put to explain his actions otherwise. Father–son hatred is not perhaps so strange to us now, after Freud and Strindberg, and indeed is a constant in dynasties, as witness the Hanoverian kings or the Young and Old Pretenders. Alexander the Great allegedly said that he was more grateful to Aristotle for giving him knowledge than to Philip for giving him life. Marcus gave Commodus both, and summoned the best teachers for him from the four corners of the globe, but all in vain.[184] Sadly, this was yet another case of a wise Solomon being succeeded by a useless Rehoboam.

18

Marcus Aurelius's moral stature is secure. He remains an example to the ages or, as Matthew Arnold put it, with understandable exaggeration: 'perhaps the most beautiful figure in history'.[1] Unquestionably he was the greatest of Roman emperors, but that is not saying a lot, given how many of them were crazed psychopaths, warmongering expansionists or inadequates clearly out of their depth. As for being a philosopher-king, the sceptic would no doubt argue that this is another variant on Dr Johnson and the woman preacher, that we tend to overrate Marcus because he was a thinker and not a foaming-mouthed crackpot like his son. But, on a cold analysis, how successful was Marcus Aurelius as an emperor? Was he really, as some claim, a truly Promethean figure, or has he been overrated simply because he wrote philosophy in his spare time? Was he perhaps, as the sceptics allege, 'a pathetic product and powerless actor in a great historical drama'?[2]

Even to attempt to answer this question, we need to distinguish three levels at which Marcus functioned as a historical player. There was the narrow cultural and social milieu within which every emperor operated, which it would have taken an imaginative and original genius of the highest order to have transcended – and not even his most fervent advocates have been prepared to put Marcus in that class. There were the events that we can classify under the 'whirlwind of history', which would have swept away or overwhelmed *any* leader, even an Alexander the Great or a Julius Caesar. And there were the social changes that Marcus might, could and should have made (all within the realm of the possible), but did not, thus revealing an inadequate grasp on the problems of empire. In the last category, the knee-jerk response is to say that Marcus was a dilettante philosopher who should have devoted his energies to the problems of empire. As Robert Louis Stevenson ungraciously replied when Gladstone reported that he had been up all night reading *Treasure Island*, perhaps it would have been better if Mr Gladstone had spent the night attending to affairs of state.[3] All these issues need to be addressed if we are to assess Marcus as emperor.

The question of milieu and culture is crucial. Perhaps the most famous and most quoted of all passages from Edward Gibbon's *Decline and Fall* is the following: 'If a man were called to fix the period of history during which the condition of the human race was most happy and prosperous, he would, without hesitation, name that which elapsed from the death of Domitian to the accession of Commodus.'[4] There are not many propositions of the famous historians that one can unhesitatingly dismiss as nonsense, but this is one. Hobbes's famous categorisation of the life of Man in the State of Nature – 'nasty, brutish and short' – applies just as well to the Roman empire. Out of the dozens of poignant testimonies to the horror of life for the vast majority of people during the 'grandeur that was Rome', we will quote just three, to avoid becoming wearisome. Here Galen describes the usual plight of the Roman peasantry in a 'normal' year, one not officially characterised as a year of crisis because of plague, famine or pestilence:

Immediately summer was over, those who lived in the cities, in accordance with their usual practice of collecting a sufficient supply of corn to last a whole year, took from the fields all the wheat, barley, beans and lentils and left to the rustics only pulses and some vegetables, for they took away a good portion of these as well. So the people in the countryside, once they had consumed the meagre pittance left to them and with still half the winter to get through, were forced to eat all kinds of unhealthy fodder. Spring found them eating twigs, shoots of trees, bulbs and roots or noxious plants and wild vegetables, which they boiled and reboiled to make them taste less like green grass. I myself saw some of them at the end of spring covered with ulcers which ate into their skin, and these ulcers were of many different kinds: some people were suffering from erisypelas, others from inflamed tumours, and others from boils that spread all over their body, while others had a noisome eruption on their trunks that looked like lichen, and the more advanced cases had developed scabs and leprosy.[5]

The lot of the urban proletariat may have been better, but not by very much. Here is Apuleius's description of slaves in a baker's mill in *The Golden Ass*:

O my God, what kind of poor slaves were in there! Some had their skin bruised all over black and blue, some had their backs striped with lashes and were covered – I won't say clothed – with torn rags, while some had only their private parts hidden by a narrow loincloth. All wore such rags and tatters that you could see clearly through them to their naked bodies. Some had been marked and burned in the forehead with hot irons, some had their hair half clipped so that they appeared semi-shaven, some had shackles on their legs and chains round their ankles, ugly and ill-favoured as they were, while others were effectively blind, their eyes and faces so black and dim with smoke, their eyelids all cankered with the darkness of that reeking place, groping around and sprinkled black and white with dirty flour, like boxers who carry on fighting when they are befouled with sand.[6]

And there is no reason whatsoever to think that landlord–peasant relations were any different under Marcus Aurelius than when John Chrysostom described them in the fourth century:

What could be more oppressive than landlords? If you look at the way they treat their miserable tenants, you will find them more savage than barbarians. They lay intolerable and continual taxes and burdens on men who are weakened with hunger and toil throughout their lives and they put upon them the burden of oppressive services. They use their bodies like asses and mules, or rather like stones, hardly letting them breathe, and they strain them equally in good years and bad, never giving the slightest relief. They make them work all through the winter in cold and rain, they deprive them of sleep, and send them home with empty hands, indeed with debts still to pay. Moreover, the tortures of beatings, exactions and ruthless demands for services which such men suffer from the agents are worse than hunger. Who could recount the ways in which these agents use them for profit and then cheat them? Their labour turns the agent's wine-press but they receive not a scrap of the produce which they are compelled, illegally, to bottle for the agent, receiving only a tiny sum for this work. Moreover, the agent extorts even more oppressive interest than even pagan law allows, not 12% but 50% from a man with a wife and children, who is filling the agent's barn and wine-store by his own labour.[7]

The absurdity and myopia of Gibbon will be clear, but his Panglossian comments alert us to an important point about Marcus and the empire. Eighteenth-century England had clear parallels with the Roman empire, even though the grandees of the Hanoverian period chose to see themselves as Periclean Athenians, battling against either Persia or Sparta in the shape of the great Satan, France. Gibbon, Hume, Adam Smith, Johnson, Boswell and the other great figures of London's salons and the Scottish Enlightenment resembled Marcus and his coterie in that they discussed knotty philosophical problems that still trouble us today. They lived in an Augustan elegance and privilege, based on the fruits of an expansionist and predatory empire, which they took to be the natural order of things, yet their society was one characterised by the most draconian legal codes, the Waltham Black Act, the Riot Act and above all the Bloody Code, which could consign a starving man to the gallows for stealing an apple.[8] This schizoid nature of Georgian society in England found a pre-echo in the Rome of the Antonines. Marcus was a man who could preach wisdom, enlightenment and tolerance in the privacy of his diaries while being quite content to sanction hideous deaths – in the arena, in the jaws of wild beasts, on the cross – in the everyday life of Rome. His career highlights, above all, a failure of imagination – a failure imbricated in the very education, culture and assumptions of the aristocratic Roman. The Roman upper class had so little imagination that, even when the senatorial class plotted against an emperor, their only thought was to replace him with another one.[9] Root-and-branch social change was beyond their universe of discourse. As has been well said. 'We must not expect to find emperors concerned to *change* their world, in the way that many modern governments are. Innovation was some-

thing the Roman classes always dreaded.'[10] Yet another aspect of
Marcus's unimaginative approach to the problems of empire was his
background as a cloistered, pampered heir to the throne, never ranging
far beyond the environs of Rome (or being allowed to by Antoninus
Pius). Even rulers tend to take the line of least resistance and draw
facile conclusions from what is apparent in their immediate environment, but which may be completely atypical. Marcus was not the only
culprit. Tertullian, from his eyrie in North Africa, produced a pre-echo
of Gibbon when he said that the world in his day was better known,
better cultivated and more civilised than ever before: he spoke of cities
where there had once been only cottages, and of roads and trade
everywhere in evidence.[11]

When faced with obvious threats to the empire, such as those from
Parthia and the German tribes, Marcus acted decisively and probably
wisely. In a military sense he certainly restored the status quo ante.[12]
The judgement of his contemporaries – even of those with good cause
to detest him, like Tertullian – was universally favourable. Cassius Dio,
who observed the reign at first hand, thought that the only strike
against Marcus was that he failed the Napoleonic test: he was not
lucky. 'He did not have the good fortune that he deserved, for he was
not physically strong, and for almost his whole reign was involved in
a series of troubles. But I for my part admired him all the more for
this very reason, that amid unusual and extraordinary difficulties he
both survived himself and preserved the empire.'[13] But Marcus never
saw beneath the surface of events. His defenders say that even if he
had or could have done, the travails that assailed Rome by the end of
his reign were those of 'systemic failure'. Rome, in a word, stopped
getting bigger, better, more integrated, more complex, more meritocratic and more socially fluid, and simply ossified into changelessness.
There is a considerable consensus that things started to go badly wrong
during his reign, but that these lay beyond the scope and grasp of any
emperor, no matter how far-sighted.[14] To use the Churchillian phrase,
it was not yet the beginning of the end, but it was the end of the
beginning – that Golden Age of 'good emperors' that had begun in
AD 96 with Nerva. Rome was not yet in the terminal stages of decline,
as evidenced by the fact that the empire could absorb a Commodus
and survive, as it would not have been able to do post-260. For a little
while, too, military conquest and the subsequent import of looted

wealth and new slaves could compensate for the lack of technological innovation and a stagnant economy.[15] But the writing on the wall
was there for those who chose to read it. Under Marcus the delicate
equilibrium of the imperial system was disturbed: that between the
power of frontier defence and barbarian incursion; between the exigen-
cies of war and the resources of the state; between production and
consumption and town and country; between the authority of the
Senate and unbridled imperial power; between old republican residues
and new Antonine modalities; and between the classical tradition and
the birth of irrationality.[16] The last point is particularly important, for
some discern a new malaise and an intellectual crisis to match that in
the objective conditions of the empire; on one view, the increasing
urbanisation of the empire was already producing those seemingly
modern phenomena of rootlessness, anomie and anxiety, all exacerbated by natural and military disasters, the crisis of religious belief
and population implosion in urban areas.[17] Yet since the diagnosis of
'systemic failure' is vague, mysterious and misleading (in its jettison
of human actors), a clear narrative account of the structural problems of the Antonines is necessary.

While not seeking to interpret the 'decline and fall of the Roman
empire' monocausally, we can argue strongly that there was a hierarchy of causes, and in first place was the Antonine plague, an event
of devastating proportions. Since I propose to put great weight on
the impact of this 'plague', against the evidence of a powerful phalanx
of critics, it is necessary to contextualise the events of 166–80 in the
broader ambit of disease in the ancient world. All diseases in the
history of Rome were called 'plagues' – hardly surprisingly, since
before about AD 1600 there was little appreciation that diseases were
separate entities, let alone that they tend to bifurcate into insect-
borne and viral types.[18] From internal evidence we can understand
that smallpox, malaria, tuberculosis, measles, leprosy and typhus, diph-
theria, tetanus and poliomyelitis were all features of the ancient world,
alongside the two scourges properly called plague, the pneumonic
and bubonic types. Against these demons Romans had few defences.
Ancient medicine was crude and primitive, with many thinking that
'plague' was the effect of changes in the body caused by changes in
temperature; even the 'father of medicine', Hippocrates, favoured
'making the air right' with huge bonfires. Much of Roman medicine

sounds to modern ears like quackery, but medical science (like science in general) had no great cachet in Roman culture. Physicians enjoyed low status, many being Greek freedmen, cure rates were low – most soldiers wounded in battle died of septicaemia; and both the common people and the oligarchy were sceptical of doctors' claims to expertise.[19] The greatest problem for the ancient historian is the extreme difficulty of differentiating between the different 'plagues'. We know from the chroniclers and from the great letter-writers like Cicero and Seneca that deadly disease was a constant in the Roman world. There was a particularly bad plague in 174 BC and, in the republican period, others in 142, 87, 58, 46 and 43 BC.[20] During the principate there were similar outbreaks in 23–22 BC, AD 65, 79–80, 90 and in Arabia under Antoninus Pius.[21] Mainly Romans regarded diseases as a manifestation of the anger of the gods, though Orosius tried to turn this argument on its head by claiming that plagues always followed the persecution of Christians.[22]

Without doubt the disease that most consistently menaced the Romans was malaria, that perennial scourge of mankind spread by the bite of the anopheles mosquito. Of the three most common types of malaria – the benign tertian (*Plasmodium vivax*), quartan fever (*P. malariae*) and malignant tertian (*P. falciparum*) – it was the last (malignant tertian, sometimes called semitertian fever) that was the killer. In Marcus Aurelius's time it was common throughout the empire, but particularly prevalent in Rome, as Galen noted.[23] One mark of Galen's great ability was that he was able to classify the three types of malaria, from which he inferred that quartan fever generally followed other fevers, instead of arising spontaneously on its own; he also noticed that the semitertian variety attacked men in their prime, while the lesser tertian seemed to home in on young men.[24] High levels of mortality from malaria had been noted since the earliest days of Rome, and by the early days of the empire were reluctantly accepted as a fact of life.[25] The disease struck above all in large cities, also indirectly worsening food supplies, and in army encampments, particularly when troops were packed together in winter quarters. It was endemic in Rome, particularly in the most deadly form, the malignant tertian.[26] Among soldiers, the fortress of Carnuntum on the Danube, adjacent to extensive wetlands, had a particularly bad reputation, but there were no safe areas, since even in Scotland in 208 Caracalla's troops succumbed to the dreaded disease.[27] What linked the military camps and the large cities was of course the high density of populations; army encampments, with their contaminated food and water, were a notorious breeding ground for all kinds of diseases, including dysentery and typhoid fever. What made the cities of the empire particualrly vulnerable was that the epoch of the Roman empire, relative to the eras that preceded and followed it, was a period of global warmth and, as such, even more vulnerable to malaria.[28] Naturally, Romans had not the remotest idea of the connection between malaria and mosquitoes; even Victorian explorers in Africa thought the fever was conveyed by 'miasmata'. Avoidance of the disease was to some extent possible for the elite, who decamped from Rome and isolated themselves on their country estates. Needless to say, the burden of malaria fell on the urban poor and the slaves. The proletariat unwittingly went in harm's way by growing vegetables in irrigated gardens during the heat of summer, thus exposing themselves to maximal ravages from mosquitoes. Pliny the Elder noted the phenomenon of vegetable-growing, but lacked the knowledge to connect it with mosquitoes, as indeed did everyone until the beginning of the twentieth century.[29] The best the ancients could do was note down those areas in Italy and elsewhere where malaria was rampant.[30] Unquestionably it was Rome's slave population that was hardest hit by the fever, mainly because they were dragooned to work in pestilential areas where free labour would not toil. It was no accident that the first recorded slave revolt in Roman history (in 198 BC) took place in the Pontine marshes.[31]

Horrific as malaria and all the other deadly diseases were, Romans absorbed them as part of daily existence; slaves and the other wretched of the Earth were already living a death-in-life, so may not have been unduly perturbed by the approach of the Reaper. But the 'plague' that hit Rome under Marcus Aurelius was entirely different, both in degree and kind, from anything that Romans had experienced before. By common consent there were just three great pestilences in the ancient world: the plague recorded by Thucydides in Athens at the beginning of the Peloponnesian War (431–29 BC), the plague of Justinian in the sixth century AD and what has become known as the Antonine plague or 'the plague of Galen' (because he so minutely described its symptoms).[32] Thucydides, who claimed to have contracted the disease and survived, describes heavy mortality among an Athenian population artificially packed within the walls of their city because the Spartans were laying waste their land outside. The symptoms he describes include headaches, fever, rashes, insomnia, diarrhoea, stomach cramps, unquenchable thirst and coughing up blood. Those who died tended to expire on the seventh or eighth day of the illness. He provides no precise figures for the dead, but says that some sufferers did recover, even though some of these in turn were blind, amnesiac or partially paralysed.[33] The usual explanation is that the 'plague' was actually smallpox, but there are difficulties with this diagnosis. Smallpox is associated with scarring and scabbing on the face, but Thucydides makes no mention of this; additionally, haemorrhagic smallpox, the only variety likely to produce such a death toll among an adult population, has a mortality rate close to 100 per cent, yet Thucydides speaks of many survivors, including himself.[34] Since the Athenian plague or 'plague of Pericles' does not satisfy all the criteria for an ideal-type smallpox epidemic, some epidemiologists have speculated that the pestilence that convulsed Athens might have been ebola. This is a revolutionary suggestion, since ebola is customarily believed to have appeared for the first time in the Congo in 1976. Nonetheless, its classical symptoms do match Thucydides's descriptions uncannily: headache, muscle, joint or abdominal pain, sore throat, nausea, dizziness, fever, vomiting, diarrhoea and external and internal bleeding (caused by a chemical reaction between the virus and the platelets). Death from organ failure occurs within three to twenty-one days, with ten days being the mean. All this is compatible, just, with Thucydides, and the ebola theory has the further merit that it would account for the Athenian survivors, since the mortality rate is between 50 and 80 per cent, according to the viral subtype.[35]

The next great pestilence of the ancient world was the Antonine plague of 165–80, occupying most of Marcus Aurelius's reign. This was a distinctive event: 'in a world where epidemics were frequent, the plague of Marcus stood out for its severity'.[36] Some say the nursery of the disease was central Asia, whence the virus spiralled out westwards towards the Roman empire and eastwards towards China, since there was a similar outbreak in the Chinese empire at roughly the same time, with the worst manifestations a little later.[37] Brought back from the East as a by-product of the Parthian war, this epidemic soon

overwhelmed the western empire like a tsunami, as the regular westward voyages across the Mediterranean by vessels with eastern cargoes
brought the virus to Rome in whole battalions. It then spread north
as far as the Rhine and the English Channel.[38] The vectors of the
disease were mainly waterborne: both shipping in the Mediterranean
and riverine traffic on the great arteries – Nile, Rhine, Rhône, Danube
and so on. Rome paid the price of its vast conquests since the military, and particularly soldiers travelling on home leave, were prime
carriers.[39] Although archaeology has left few traces of the Antonine
plague, unlike for example the evidence left by the fourteenth-century
Black Death (insect-borne bubonic plague), its impact can occasionally be gauged by physical evidence, as in the significant drop in the
volume of Mediterranean shipwrecks dating from this period.[40] The
fact that Marcus Aurelius was at war with the Germans for almost
exactly the period the pestilence was at its height exacerbated matters,
reducing the protection normally given to pre-industrial societies by
their sheer inertia, which generally restricted the speed of infectious
disease. Some authorities have even linked the greater state interven-
tionism under Marcus and Commodus to the general decline of trade
in these reigns caused by the plague and the subsequent decline in
population.[41]

That the 'Antonine plague' was a major disaster, unlike any other
pestilence to have hit Rome in its 900-year history, is very clear from
the sources. The study of travel patterns, government business, religious activities, city administration, grain distribution and many other
indices all point in the same direction: major social breakdown,
involving war and disease in a symbiotic relationship and portending
general, apocalyptical crisis. In the words of Aurelius Victor: 'Never
was there a rest from arms. The entire East was ablaze with war.
Cities were destroyed by earthquakes; rivers overran their banks; there
were frequent epidemics and fields were plagued by locusts, so that
almost none of the most distressing afflictions of which one could
speak or contemplate did not run riot during Marcus Aurelius's reign.'[42]
To many the plague seemed the final refutation of Stoicism, so that
increasingly people turned for consolation to ideas, motifs and religions that offered the consolation of a future life, or at least suggested
that the implacable evil of disease could be conquered by magic.
Alexander of Abonoteichos predictably got in on the act by marketing

a totally useless method of averting pestilence, involving pinning charms to doorposts in the manner of the biblical shibboleth.[43] In his writings Marcus affected a contempt for the plague, claiming that 'to lie down with evil' was worse than any pestilence (which he tellingly attributed to 'tainted air or an unhealthy climate') and that disease could only threaten your life while moral evil attacked one's humanity.[44] As an emperor, however, he could not afford to be so cavalier, especially as hundreds of dead were being carried away daily in carts and wagons.[45] Many laws came onto the statute-book to deal with the crisis. No one was allowed to build a tomb in a private villa, statues were erected to all notables killed by the plague, and the common people were to be allowed funerals at public expense. It was forbidden to transport the bodies of victims through towns, and an edict was passed to punish severely the increasing practice of appropriating other people's graves, disinterring the corpses and substituting the bodies of the recently dead. The entire undertaking business experienced hyper-inflation and the cost of burials became astronomical. Heirs to aristocratic fortunes, bound by the terms of wills to provide a suitably magnificent funeral for the deceased benefactor, tried to evade the responsibility – which made a considerable dent in the legacy they received – by coming to 'private arrangements' for the disposal of the body. Marcus tried to forbid this evasion of the terms of the will by yet another decree, but with what success is uncertain. He also attempted to deal with the growth in land speculation, as people bought and sold land for sepulchres, and issued a rescript excusing those attending funerals from answering court summonses.[46]

Even the Romans, who had been hardened over the centuries to the impact of deadly disease, could scarcely comprehend what had hit them. Undoubtedly one of the deep causes of the persecution of the Christians in Marcus's reign, and certainly not discouraged by the emperor, was the perception that they had caused the plague, either by the black magic of their Christian god or by angering the Olympians with their blasphemy. Epidemics and pandemics always produce outbreaks of scapegoating: in previous eras Spartacus and the slave rebels had been accused of poisoning wells, and Roman matrons of engineering the mass death of the Roman patriarchy by deadly toxins. It was rumoured that this time around the criminal classes were spreading the disease with poisoned needles – just as, during the

medieval period, the Black Death was blamed on Jews and lepers.[47]
Yet the horrors of smallpox (which is what the plague actually was)
were so vivid that such overreaction is understandable. Two examples of its ravages, one from the modern era and one from ancient
times, may be cited to explain the terror it caused. During his journey
through Ashangoland in West Africa in 1863–5 the French explorer
Paul du Chaillu described 'the Great Suffering' (as Africans called it)
as follows:

> Every village was a charnel house. Wherever I walked the most
> heartrending sights met my view. The poor victims of the loathsome
> disease in all its stages lay about in sheds and huts. There were hideous
> sores filled with maggots and swarms of carrion flies buzzed about
> the living but putrid carcasses. The stench in the neighbourhood of
> the huts was insupportable. Some of the sick were raving, and others
> emaciated with sunken eyes, victims of hunger as well as of disease.
> Many wretched creatures from other villages were left to die in the
> bush.[48]

And this is the poet and Epicurean philosopher Lucretius on the
Athenian plague of 431–29 BC:

> Here, between stifling walls, death crams his heap of victims high.
> Along the roads by the drinking fountains lay the bodies of those who
> died of thirst or of a glut of water. The city teemed with the wasted
> frames, covered by no flesh, but only skin, of those who lay dying in
> filth and rags virtually already buried by their loathsome sores. Death,
> too, had filled every holy shrine with corpses – yes, those heavenly
> temples once filled with worshippers now lay waste with dead bodies.
> Reverence had no further place: all that was banished in the imme-
> diacy of agony. Proper burial was no longer possible, the nation was
> in terror, each family abandoned its dead, amidst shrieks of fear, as
> best it might. People flung their spouses, children, parents on pyres
> built by others for their own. Sometimes they fought rather than leave
> their dead.[49]

The two burning issues surrounding the Antonine plague are: what
was the nature of the disease; and what was the total mortality it engen-

dered? Many answers to the former question have been given over the years, including genuine (bubonic) plague, anthrax, exanthematic typhus and malaria.[50] Yet the minute observations of Galen enable us to say with near-certainty that the pestilence was smallpox. Epidemiologists differentiate between two genera of smallpox (*Variola major* and *V. minor*) and four species in turn of the much more deadly *major*.[51] The virus localises in the small blood vessels of the skin, mouth and throat, and the most obvious consequences are a rash and fluid-filled blisters. Of the four species of *Variola major* (ordinary, modified, flat and haemorrhagic) it is the haemorrhagic variety that is thought to have been rampaging through the Roman empire. After an incubation period of about twelve days between contraction of the disease and first symptoms, a flu-like syndrome develops – fever, high temperature (greater than 101°F or 38.3°C), muscle pain, headache, backache, nausea and vomiting. Typically lasting two to four days, this initial phase gives way after about two weeks to the first visible lesions: small reddish spots called exanthems appear on the mucous membrane of the tongue, palate and throat. The lesions enlarge and rupture, the temperature disappears but then, some twenty-four to forty-eight hours later, a rash appears on the skin, first on the forehead and face, then the proximal parts of the extremities, then the trunk and finally the rest of the extremities. The lesions then become pustules, which feel like small beads in the skin, and after seven to ten days they reach their maximum size. By days sixteen to twenty scabs form over the lesions and then fall off, leaving a rash. In flat smallpox, which most often affects children, patients suffer from prolonged fever and severe symptoms of toxaemia.[52] Haemorrhagic smallpox, the most deadly kind, is accompanied by extensive subcutaneous bleeding, and bleeding into the mucous membrane and gastrointestinal tract. The bleeding occurring under the skin makes it appear black and charred. Death usually occurs five to seven days after the appearance of the illness, caused by massive haemorrhage in all the vital organs, though the proximate cause of death is heart failure or pulmonary oedema. The mortality rates are almost 100 per cent in the case of haemorrhagic smallpox and 90 per cent in the flat type.[53]

If we correlate all this with Galen's observations, we can easily appreciate the high degree of probability of a diagnosis of smallpox for the pandemic of 165–80. With his usual care, Galen detected the presence of fever, even though this was not apparent to those who touched the patient. Stomach upsets were a constant feature of every case he investigated; there was vomiting, foetid breath, diarrhoea, the coughing up of blood and of the membrane lining the larynx and pharynx, internal ulceration of the windpipe and trachea (which left the patient unable to speak) and, above all, the presence of black exanthema and black excrement. Galen noted that the black exanthema did not appear in all fatal cases, but that those who were going to survive always developed black exanthema; he also concluded that excreting black stools was an inevitable sign of approaching death.[54] The skin rash was black because of the amount of blood putrified in the fever blister. Also, in smallpox, the rash usually becomes vesicular and there are pronounced haemorrhagic 'extravasations' into the lesions. In haemorrhagic smallpox there is frequent intestinal ulceration and bleeding, and in some cases the entire circumference of the bowel may be black for several inches from the widespread 'extravasations' of blood beneath the mucous membrane. Although there is not a complete 'fit' between Galen's notes and modern knowledge of smallpox, it is the only disease that answers to all his descriptions; because of his careful evaluation of the symptoms we can rule out bubonic plague and typhus.[55] For example, while it is true that haemorrhagic extravasations of the skin occur in typhus, the crucial difference is that smallpox produces the already noted vesicular and pustular lesions, whereas the lesions associated with typhus are flat and never pustular – which is how Galen describes them.[56] The only thing that has given medical historians pause is that we know the survival rate was reasonably high (Aelius Aristides was one of the famous survivors),[57] and yet haemorrhagic smallpox is not supposed to allow so many to escape its deadly embrace. This has led some scholars to speculate that the 'Antonine plague' may have been over-determined, and in particular that there was a simultaneous epidemic of measles and smallpox.[58] On this hypothesis Aristides and the survivors may have sustained measles, while those observed by Galen were genuinely afflicted by smallpox. The thesis of over-determination or simultaneous pestilences may seem far-fetched until we remember that at the end of the sixth century the Rome of Pope Gregory the Great was hit simultaneously by malaria and bubonic plague.[59]

Even if we establish the aetiology of the Antonine plague, we then have to confront a far more impassioned and embattled area of academic debate: the mortality from the pestilence. Just as the subject of Christianity has sharply divided those who see Marcus as a fairly convinced persecutor (the argument advanced in this book) and those who see him taking no interest whatever in the new religious sect, so the plague in his reign finds commentators divided between those who think it was yet another disease in Roman history that has been exaggerated in importance and those who consider that it was an almost apocalyptic breakdown. Estimates of the empire-wide mortality range from a low of 1–2 per cent of the population to a high of 25 per cent.[60] Even if we split the difference between the most impressive scholarly studies, we cannot get lower than a total mortality of ten million empire-wide, assuming a total population of seventy million; it is not inconceivable that as many as eighteen million perished altogether. Such a fatality is by no means impossible *a priori*, especially if we embrace the thesis of a combined pandemic. Smallpox was estimated to have killed 400,000 people every year in the eighteenth century, while measles is thought to have carried off 200 million worldwide in the nineteenth and twentieth centuries. The final figure for the plague's mortality cannot, unfortunately, be pinned down with exactness, as too many unknown variables are involved.[61] The middling range of ten million deaths is estimated by an extrapolation from smallpox outbreaks in Mexico and Prussia, but the Antonine case is peculiarly complex, for a number of reasons. Different parts of the empire show significant variations, with Egypt, Dacia, Nisibis, Smyrna, Aquileia and Rome itself being particularly badly hit, while Spain and most of North Africa seem to have got away lightly.[62] As against this, all the evidence shows the mortality in cities to have been particularly severe. Even in urban areas calculation is difficult, since the death rate varied according to the level of crowding, the sanitary conditions, the seasons, the severity of secondary infections, the methods used to combat the pestilence, and pure chance; mortality rates were particularly high if the disease hit a 'virgin' population with no previous immunity.[63] Scholars have attempted to compute statistics for deaths based on the chronological distribution of army discharges, dated inscriptions in the city of Rome, the state of public and imperial buildings in Italy and even the levels of brick production, marble-quarrying and coin output.[64] The fate of Roman Egypt, in particular, has become a notable academic battlefield.[65] But when all factors are taken into account, it is difficult to escape the conclusion that the Roman empire suffered a catastrophic setback in 165–80. Not only was the 'plague' prolonged into the reign of Commodus, with a particularly severe outbreak in 189, but it became endemic. The population of the empire was just beginning to recover when, in the 250s and 260s, it was hit by another pandemic, this time probably measles.[66]

If the Roman empire lost between ten and eighteen million of its inhabitants, it does not need a historian of genius to conclude that it must have experienced a severe manpower shortage.[67] Rome's growing economic crisis was compounded by particularly severe manpower losses in two key areas of productivity: the vast agricultural estates, or *latifundia*, and the mines. The *latifundia* were found mainly in Italy, Sicily and North Africa, with a few outposts in mainland Greece proper and southern Gaul, which has sometimes seduced the unwary into the assertion that the great estates cannot have been a significant factor in Rome's decline.[68] The process on the *latifundia* was complex, but a number of convergent factors can be identified: the use by landlords of the lowest class of slaves, the decline in their numbers, the existence of gross exploitation (landlords extracting the maximum surplus from their labour force), the emergence of serfdom and the decline of Italian agriculture. In the first century AD there was a dual pattern of land-holding. Some entrepreneurs diversified their real-estate portfolio and owned a number of smallholdings, not necessarily in one district or part of the country. But the dominant mode of production was the great estate or *latifundium*, depending on slave labour, which gradually squeezed out both free peasantry and small farms.[69] It is for this reason that Pliny the Elder waged his famous propaganda campaign against the *latifundia*, arguing that they would eventually be the ruin of Rome.[70] Both he and the agriculturalist Columella particularly objected to the use of chained slaves (*vincti, conpediti, alligati*, as they were variously referred to) on the big estates. Such slaves were popular with landlords as they were cheaper than other kinds of slaves; they were usually convicts, ex-criminals or demoted slaves.[71] Pliny argued that the practice of using chained slaves was morally repugnant, economically disadvantageous and disastrously short-sighted, for all the labour was done by men without hope.[72] Columella took a more nuanced view, opining that slavery might at a pinch work in vineyards and olive groves, but was hopelessly inefficient when it came to growing cereals or legumes – the type of agriculture some considered definitional of the *latifundium*.[73]

When the Roman empire ceased to expand, the supply of slaves diminished and in general the slave population failed to reproduce itself.[74] The crisis was particularly severe in Italy, where the agricultural sector was already struggling to cope with competition from elsewhere in the empire. Italy was not faring well even before Marcus Aurelius. To arrest the twin evils of depopulation and decline in Italian agriculture, Trajan had forbidden emigration from Italy and forced the senatorial class to acquire land in the home country, even supplying cheap credit to landowners large and small. But still Italian entrepreneurs struggled in some key sectors, with the over-production of wine a particular problem. Italian vintages could not compete in the eastern market with the wine of the Greek Islands, Asia Minor, Syria and Palestine, while in the west only northern Italy had a ready commercial outlet – in Germany and the Danube lands. It was too expensive for landlords in western Italy to ship their vintages to those northern markets, but on the western flank they were being challenged by Spain and North Africa, which were also outpointing them in the production of olive oil.[75] Manpower shortages could not have come at a worse time. When this diminishing workforce was further decimated by the plague, the severe fall in numbers produced a crisis in the countryside, exacerbated by the crudely exploitative mindset of the landlords. Increasingly the estate owners aiming at maximisation of profits tended to be knights and freedmen rather than senators, who preferred the more easy-going lifestyle of the absentee rentier.[76] Equestrians and the nouveaux riches were drawn to the *latifundia* both by the superprofits that could be engendered and the (comparatively) low cost of acquiring one, estimated by Pliny the Elder to be 1,300,000 sesterces.[77] With the disappeaance of small, independent landowners, land came to be concentrated in fewer and fewer hands; some have even linked the change in ownership from city bourgeoisie to big capitalists (the classical *latifundistas* of the imperial aristocracy) with a decline in scientific agriculture.[78]

But the harsher the employer, the greater the problems – not just for the reasons Pliny had mentioned, but because a large estate employing chained slaves was a haven for malaria; it was even estimated that building contractors putting up a villa in the countryside had to add 25 per cent to their basic estimate of costs because of the factor of disease.[79] Although the decline in slave numbers in the countryside was always relative, by the end of Marcus's reign more and more free citizens were working the land and becoming downgraded to a form of debt-bondage. They started out as settlers and homesteaders (*coloni*), to whom the big landlords, finding slaves harder and harder to come by, leased out parcels of land. Full-blooded serfdom was the logical next step, and some see the Roman economy of the third century as one characterised by a gradual transition from slavery to serfs tied to the soil.[80] A flight from the land became apparent, and was quickened rather than retarded by the Antonine plague, thus adding a multiplier effect to the pestilence by increasing overcrowding in the cities.[81] In theory the financial powers of the Roman state could have been employed to arrest the crisis in the countryside, but the Roman grasp of economics was shaky. When there was a conflict between the demands of the army and the imperial bureaucracy on the one hand and the needs of Gross National Product on the other, it was always the 'parasitic' agencies who prevailed. Italy, then, was hit by an over-determined crisis: population implosion to the cities, the competition of the provinces, declining slave numbers, low levels of human repro-duction, malaria, lead poisoning, soil erosion and finally the plague itself.[82] Rural labour shortages were the paramount overall factor (as compared, say, with soil erosion), but beyond this the crisis in agri-cultural slavery in the late second century bore out Pliny's worst fears. He had pointed out that the slave mode of production made the *latifundia* particularly brittle and vulnerable and that it was a struc-tural defect in the economy, but even he could not have foreseen that the dread hand of pestilence would exacerbate the situation so dramatically.[83]

Apart from agriculture, the other great component in the economy of Rome was mining, especially of precious metals. Roman mining was carried on almost exclusively outside Italy, in Spain, Macedonia, Asia Minor, Noricum, Dalmatia and Gaul. Different regions tended to specialise: lead came from Sardinia, Britain, the Iberian peninsula and the Attica region of Greece; iron from Gaul, Noricum, Dacia, Asia Minor and the Iberian peninsula; copper from Gaul, Cyprus and Spain; gold from Dalmatia, Dacia and Spain; silver from Asia Minor and Spain.[84] The three Spanish provinces were at the heart of Roman mining enterprises. Iron was used for making tools, lead for sealing roofs, for bath systems, water tanks and pipes in the water supply; copper (especially in alloyed form) for the bulk of the coinage, cheap jewellery, fittings for vehicles, armour and furniture. Bronze (lead and tin alloyed with copper) was the norm for statuary.[85] Particularly in Spain, Greece and Britain the Romans used all known methods to extract ore, from simple surface working among the detritus of rivers and the fallen debris of mountains to deep-cast mining in sunken shafts. Water released from dams fed by aqueducts was used to clear away surface soil and loose rock in open-cast sites. Fire-setting was particularly effective in open-cast mines or tunnels; the rock was heated by fire and then flooded so that thermal shock would shatter it, making the ore easier to remove. Pliny the Elder personally witnessed the process by which water eroded tunnels in the workface of an open-cast mine until it collapsed.[86] Obviously underground mining called for greater investment of capital and labour – deep tunnels and shafts were required as well as drainage and ventilation – which was why it was regarded as a last resort, reserved for precious metals. But even when seeking gold, the Romans tended to opt for open-cast workings, exploiting patches or veins of ore lying near the surface with pits or trenches.[87]

The labour force used in the mines consisted overwhelmingly of slaves; the situation in Dacia, where unskilled free labourers worked for two sesterces a day was unusual and extraordinary.[88] Once again it was chained slaves who bore the brunt, particularly in the deep mines, where they ran the risks of collapsing tunnels and noxious gases. Criminals, convicts and Christians were chosen for the really dangerous tasks, and in the deep-shaft mines they would often not see daylight for months on end, some of them emerging blind into the sunlight.[89] Roman emperors and provincial governors were particularly delighted to consign the followers of Jesus Christ to this fate worse than death, and we learn of Christians condemned to the deep shafts of Cilicia, the copper mines of Palestine and the porphyry quarries of Egypt.[90] In addressing Romans, Tertullian remarked sardonically on this practice, 'we are condemned to the mines, whence your gods have their origin'.[91] Even by the not noticeably compassionate standards of the Roman empire, conditions in the mines were considered atrocious. But the exploitation of slave labour was enhanced by the profits available to entrepreneurs in this sector. All mines were imperial property, controlled by procurators, but the actual working of them was farmed out or leased to individual capitalists or their consortia on a 'sharecropping' basis – usually 50:50.[92] Permission to mine metal cost 4,000 sesterces – not something the Roman man in the street could afford, but within the reach of an army veteran.[93] Some statistics will help to clarify the opportunities available in mining and the revenues produced. In Cyprus it was estimated that sixty million tons of charcoal were needed to produce 200,000 tons of copper. In the silver mines of Nova Carthago in Spain 40,000 men were employed, and the Roman state received a revenue of four talents (25,000 drachmae) a day, generating 400,000 sesterces a year. In normal times Spanish silver mines produced 300 pounds of silver a day, while the gold mines of Asturia, Lusitania and Callaecia generated 20,000 pounds of gold annually.[94]

Without question, Rome's mining Mecca was the Iberian peninsula, even though agriculture still employed more people. Gaul was originally earmarked as the El Dorado of the empire, but it was soon realised that its precious metals were negligible when compared with Spain's.[95] Some 231 different mining sites have been identified in the three Spanish provinces, and mining here was conducted on a spectacular basis, with gold, silver and copper only the most prominent of the ores extracted; perhaps as a corollary, working conditions in Spanish mines were regarded as the most terrible in the empire, exceeding even the legendarily bad ones in the Egyptian gold mines.[96] Slavery in the mines was regarded as akin to death and, in contrast to the situation on the *latifundia*, where after the Antonine era debt-bondage serfs increasingly replaced scarce slaves, there was, both literally and figuratively, no light at the end of the tunnel. Domestic slaves could look forward to manumission, even though it was often a mixed blessing and they found themselves worse off than under servitude, while the serfs were at least secure against the ultimate sanction that owners could bring to bear against slaves – the break-up of the family.[97] The labour supply in the mines was, therefore, precarious and brittle, so that it was not surprising that the first segment of the economy to totter from the impact of the Antonine plague and the catastrophic manpower shortages that resulted was mining. But there was worse to come. For obvious reasons, the mines were particularly vulnerable to enemy action and barbarian invasion. Almost the first sign of the crisis in the north in 168 was when the Dacian mines ceased to operate, and during the war the mines of the Danube virtually dried up.[98] The two Moorish invasions of Spain in the 170s had even more calamitous repercussions. The famous Rio Tinto silver and gold mines, which had supplied these metals and many others (copper, tin, lead, iron, zinc, mercury) to the entire empire, plummeted into a steep decline, hit both by marauding Moors and by dire shortages of manpower.[99] The whole of Spain went into economic freefall at the end of Marcus Aurelius's reign, with senatorial families decamping en masse to Italy.[100]

The disappearance of precious metals, and particularly the shortage of gold, had dire consequences for the Roman empire. Rome's 'balance of payments' was seriously distorted by the aristocratic mania for the luxury items of the East, especially Chinese silk. Pliny the Elder was the first to put together a comprehensive critique of the coexisting phenomena of gold fever and a passion for oriental luxury, although individual writers and commentators had already noticed some aspects of this. Pliny explained that, paradoxically, the true Golden Age existed when gold itself was unknown or rare, such as in the early days of the Roman republic; his ideal was the era of the Trojan war when goods were bartered. 'The worst crime against human life was committed by the person who first put gold on his fingers . . . next in degree was the crime committed by the person who first coined a gold *denarius*.'[101] He famously praised Spartacus for forbidding his followers the possession of gold and silver. According to Pliny, the first real villain in Roman history was Sulla, who in 81 BC amassed 15,000 pounds of gold and 115,000 pounds of silver as the proceeds of his victories. This set a pattern whereby conquerors measured themselves, so to speak, in precious metals. Julius Caesar, on entering Rome during the civil war with Pompey, drew from the treasury 15,000 pounds of gold in ingots, 30,000 silver ingots and thirty million sesterces in coin.[102] The worship of gold was well established by the time Augustus inaugurated the empire. But, as a parallel development, Roman aristocrats developed a craze for the produce of the Orient, which had to be paid for in gold. The East alone produced the luxury goods that wealthy Roman consumers craved, and while some of these could be supplied from within the empire (glass and purple dye from Phoenicia; linen and textiles from Egypt; fine woollens and leather goods from Asia Minor; rugs from Mesopotamia), it was the extra-imperial products that were most sought-after: cosmetics from Arabia, ivory from Africa, ebony from India and, above all, silk from China. The problem was that Rome had little that China wanted, and Chinese silk (exported via India) always had to be paid for in gold.[103] At one time there was talk of a silk industry on the island of Cos in the Aegean, but the high hopes for this soon fizzled out.[104]

The result was economic madness. Nothing – not exhortations from the emperor, the condition of the finances of the Roman state or even inflation itself – halted the craze for Eastern luxury goods, partly of course because the buyers were aristocrats who counted their wealth in land rather than money and so were not deterred by inflating commercial prices. In vain did Tiberius denounce the mania for Chinese silk that was causing such headaches for the current account of the Roman state. Tacitus complained fruitlessly that 'ladies and their baubles are transferring our money to foreigners'.[105] Pliny the Elder denounced the fashion whereby young Roman women dressed in silk and flaunted themselves in transparent clothing. He also reported having seen Lollia Paulina, the former wife of Caligula, seated at a banquet covered in pearls and emeralds valued at forty million sesterces.[106] From the Christian vantage point Tertullian joined in too, criticising the insatiable appetite of women for jewellery and professing outrage at the value of necklaces, rings and earrings; how much real estate or money out on loan, he asked, hung suspended from a frail neck or delicate ears in the shape of Eastern jewels?[107] Pliny actually maintained that the export of gold to India and China to pay for these luxuries was just as much a threat to the Roman state as the *latifundia*. He estimated that 100 million sesterces a year in gold was being exported to China via India to pay for the silk trade, and that the entire luxury trade outside the empire was worth as much as 550 million sesterces, with India exporting to the Roman empire goods marketed at 100 times their actual cost.[108] Modern scholars have sometimes tried to query these figures, but they are borne out by circumstantial evidence.[109] One consignment from Musiris to Alexandria contained 700–1,000 pounds of nard (an aromatic balsam), 4,700 pounds of ivory and 790 pounds of textiles, the whole valued at 131 talents and enough to purchase 2,400 acres of the best farmland in Egypt. It must be remembered that the average Roman cargo ship could have held about 150 such consignments. The Romans, short-termists always, cynically encouraged the massive trade with India and beyond, as they could levy 25 per cent tax on all exports to the East at the Red Sea port of Lecce.[110]

All luxury goods from the East had to be paid for in silver and gold, as the value of Roman coinage was not guaranteed by the Roman state beyond the frontiers of the empire. Once gold became scarce in the Roman empire, and particularly when the rich gold and silver mines at Rio Tinto in Spain went into decline during the reign of Marcus Aurelius,[111] the question obviously arose: how were the luxury goods of the East, whose importation the Roman oligarchy regarded as its 'right', to be paid for? There were two answers: with other precious commodities, and by currency depreciation. Such was the mania for luxury goods that the Romans finally abandoned their own essentially mercantilist policy and went in for a bizarre form of 'export substitution'. Grain from Egypt, which was supposed to go to Rome, and whose supply was thought vital for Rome's survival, actually began to be exported to India in place of the diminishing specie.[112] Yet increasingly Roman emperors opted for depreciation of the currency. Rome had used silver coinage (replacing copper) since the sack of Tarentum in 272 BC and gold coins ever since the destruction of Carthage and Corinth in 146 BC. By the time of the ascendancy of Julius Caesar in 47 BC the ratio of gold to silver was about 1:9. Under Augustus the monetary system was stabilised, with the gold *aureus* worth about twenty-five silver denarii, and 100 copper or bronze sesterces having the equivalent value of twenty-five denarii or one *aureus*.[113] Nero was the first emperor to confront the financial implications of the Roman empire as an empire of conquest. With the conquests over and no new territories being acquired (complete with their land, gold and cheap labour), pressure on the currency soon manifested itself. Nero accordingly reduced the silver content of the denarius to 90 per cent, adding a copper alloy. This was the beginning of a slippery slope. Under Trajan the alloy percentage reached 30 per cent, under Septimius Severus 50 per cent and by the time of Elagabalus in the third century the denarius had become almost wholly copper.[114] Trajan, however, was able to arrest further decline because of his conquest of Dacia, which brought in a fresh influx of gold. Marcus Aurelius, beset with problems on all sides and in dire need of money, decreased the amount of gold in the *aureus* to 75 per cent, the silver content of the denarius to 75 per cent and debased the *orichalcum* in the brass coinage to 65 per cent zinc.[115]

No government in history has ever been able to tinker with its currency in this way without severe repercussions. The inevitable results of currency debasement were inflation, hoarding and a switch to barter. Following the iron dictates of Gresham's law, Romans tended to hoard the older, higher-content silver coins and pay their taxes with the debased ones, and the situation got worse in the third century, when the denarius ended up with a silver content of just 5 per cent. When currencies are not backed by gold, there is a tendency for them to become valueless and, when a currency loses credibility, people in general opt to barter for objects of real value.[116] As for inflation, the emperors' attempt to deal with the shortage of precious metals by debasing the currency simply increased the price both of gold itself and of that asked for luxury goods by the 'hard-currency' traders of the East. The Romans were trying to get away with paying over the same amount of silver, but just spreading it over millions more coins, and shrewd traders were having none of it; they increasingly rejected the *aureus* and asked for payment in bullion.[117] Financial instability was just part of the wider pattern of economic crisis under Marcus Aurelius. Despite the absurdly exaggerated estimates of the sums left in the treasury by Antoninus Pius (see p. 190), the truth is that Marcus did not inherit a healthy legacy. Faced by the twin evils of plague and the Danube war, and reluctant to impose new taxes, he was forced into emergency requisitions, such as the extraordinary tax on Asia Minor and the forced loans extracted from the richest cities in the empire – loans that the city bourgeoisie could not pay off without selling their landed property.[118] Additionally, Marcus had to abolish debts to the *fiscus* and *aerarium* while facing continual demands from cities for gifts or the remission of taxes. Marcus even had to take the extraordinary risk of refusing a donative to his troops, and thus putting his own position in danger, because he knew how parlous the condition of the Roman state really was. Imperial expenditure was always heavy and under Marcus it increased noticeably, not just as a result of war, plague, earthquake and flood, but because of the demands of the *annona*, the generous *congiaria* and the innumerable subsidies and remissions of taxes, including the thirty million sesterces a year tax on gladiatorial contests, which Marcus rejected as blood-money. Finally, there was the cancellation of debts in 178.[119] Within the limits of the impoverished economic thought of the time, Marcus could not have conceived of any alternative to the debasement of the gold, silver and even bronze coinage. An embargo on the import of luxury goods would have been a step too far even for a Stoic emperor.

It will thus be appreciated that the crisis of Marcus Aurelius's reign contains a curious mixture of events and factors, presenting a threefold appearance. We may describe the 'acts of God' that befell the empire as Category One phenomena; the serious but contingent military crises are Category Two events; while in Category Three are those instances where the emperor could clearly have acted otherwise. In sum, there were factors absolutely beyond Marcus's control; those theoretically within his control, but which he and his advisers lacked the imagination to deal with because of the cultural limits and parameters of the Antonine age; and finally those where he unquestionably made bad decisions. No emperor could do anything about the plague, and none of any credibility could ignore the military challenges on both frontiers. There were other 'structural', environmental and even ecological issues that would have taxed the ingenuity of the greatest political minds of the ages. A German historian in the 1980s famously listed no fewer than 600 factors involved in the 'decline and fall of Rome'.[120] Among these were the hypothesis of lead poisoning, which has generated so much controversy.[121] Whatever weight we give to the 'charge of the six hundred', in most cases they lay well beyond Marcus Aurelius's capacity to deal with. For much of the time he was in the position of a luxury liner (for as man and emperor we can put Marcus in that class) caught in the coils of a hurricane or typhoon and so potentially at risk, even though the vessel was state-of-the-art. The dire manpower shortage, which in turn impacted on both agriculture on the big estates and on the mining industry, led to a catastrophic decline in the real wealth being generated by the empire, to balance-of-payments crisis and general financial uncertainty and lack of confidence.[122] Only a political genius could have found an answer even to the day-to-day problems generated by all this. But before we follow Marcus and the empire into the vicious circle of economic decline, higher taxation, further decline and even more draconian taxation, we need to investigate some of the unintended consequences of the Category Two events, of which the most important was the rise of the army.

The wars with Parthia and, especially, with the Germans, which occupied the whole of Marcus's reign virtually non-stop, increased the financial burden on the state and hence on taxpayers, diminished imperial productivity through the manpower demands on the peasantry and, by making the military the virtual arbiters of Roman destiny, increased the arrogance, indiscipline and mutinous tendencies of soldiers. Long gone were the days of a citizen army: Italians had made up 68 per cent of the army in the days of Augustus, 48 per cent by the reign of Claudius and just 22 per cent by the year 100; by the time of Marcus's principate just 2 per cent of the legionaries were Italian.[123] Because the veterans tended to settle in distant provinces, Italian agriculture suffered and the peninsula itself became depopulated. Trajan attempted to deal with the problem by forbidding emigration from Italy and forcing senators to acquire land in the home territories; he also tried to tempt landowners of all sizes by making cheap credit available. But whatever steps emperors took, it was increasingly plain that Italy was no longer the core of the Roman empire.[124] As more and more soldiers were foreigners or mercenaries and Rome could no longer recruit freely from the peasantry, more perceptive observers began to be alarmed at what the real commitment of such troops might turn out to be in a real emergency. At the same time, the costs of maintaining an army of 500,000 men escalated frighteningly.[125] Whereas Augustus needed to find 380 million sesterces annually to finance the army, Domitian's famous pay rise took the bill to 600 million sesterces; and by the time of Caracalla's reign, early in the third century, 800 million sesterces were needed.[126] Whereas the cost of the army under Domitian and Trajan probably consumed half the total state revenues, by the time of Marcus Aurelius the true figure was nearer three-quarters.[127] The days when military conquest allowed the army to be virtually self-financing were far in the past. Additionally, legionaries demanded ever higher levels of donatives. Marcus Aurelius and Lucius Verus had tried to ensure the loyalty of the army with a payment of 20,000 sesterces, but when Pertinax tried to get away with just 12,000 sesterces, he soon paid the price for his 'meanness'.[128] Later emperors, however

short-lived, took the lesson to heart. Didius Julianus awarded the
legionaries 30,000 sesterces each, but then found himself unable to
pay as the treasury was empty.[129] Septimius Severus gave the incredible sum of 100,000 sesterces each to the troops when he was hailed
emperor – not just an unprecedented sum, but one that made wars
of foreign conquest imperative.[130] After defeating Parthia and looting
Ctesiphon, he paid the sum, but then announced that henceforth
there would be no more donatives, but a pay rise and an annual
review. However, the logic of that step was still more conquest.[131]
Never was it made clearer that the Roman empire always had to
expand and annex merely to survive.

Military operations required tax to be piled on tax, like the mythical Ossa on Pelion. But Rome was caught in a dilemma. On the one
hand, foreign wars against the barbarians of the north made no sense
on a cost-benefit analysis and represented a net drain on the economy
– unlike, say, wars with Parthia, where there were rich pickings. On
the other hand, the German tribes were becoming ever more menacing
as Rome's potential enemies, which was what impelled Marcus to act.
Yet once the genie of militarisation was let out of the bottle, it could
not be put back in. Because of the huge mortality of the Antonine
plague, maintaining an army of 500,000 with a seriously reduced population meant both that soldiers loomed larger in the everyday life of
the empire and that they took a bigger real slice of the budget.[132] Their
ubiquitous impact had other deleterious economic consequences. Even
had there been a will for technological innovation or economic
improvement, there was a straight conflict between the army's need
to recruit fresh troops and the demands of the agricultural sector. No
putative Roman capitalist could innovate through systems of enclo-
sure or maximise the profit motive, simply because the state needed
the 'surplus' of peasant labour to recruit for its armies.[133] Moreover,
the competing demands of the army for food often brought Roman
provinces to the brink of starvation. Italy had been able to divert
almost the entire corn supply of Sicily, Sardinia, Spain and Egypt to
feed itself, because Greece and Asia Minor could rely on supplies of
corn from southern Russia. But as a result of Marcus's German wars,
the army increasingly appropriated these supplies at the very moment
when the Ukraine, for reasons that are unclear, suffered a cut in wheat
production.[134] The financial circle was then closed as the famine-stricken

cities appealed to Rome for aid – not so much *la ronde de l'amour* as a vicious circle of hunger. The threat of famine was a constant in the history of the Roman empire.[135]

By the end of the third century the situation would be reached whereby no emperor could trust his own troops or feel safe from them.[136] The army in the era of Marcus Aurelius had not yet reached that stage, but the long years of warfare increasingly engendered indiscipline, volatility and thuggish behaviour – perhaps not surprisingly, given that Marcus had had to conduct an emergency recruitment drive among gladiators, bandits and slaves, all the most 'unsocialised' elements of society. Even before the German wars it was a constant lament that no civilian in conflict with the army could hope to win justice, and that the military was a law unto itself: this motif appears in the work of Petronius, Apuleius and, especially, in the unfinished sixteenth satire of Juvenal.[137] The brutality of the 'licentious soldiery' was notorious, and it was often given a legal cloak. The lower classes had to perform all manner of 'liturgies' or public services, such as providing food, lodging and transport to imperial troops, and to do unpaid physical labour or corvée. When this system predictably produced riots and revolts, army regulars were sent in to enforce a governor's orders.[138] Soon troops decided that if they could be used in this way at another's behest, they could use force on their own account. Extortion, blackmail, shakedowns, protection money and arbitrary seizures became commonplace, with blackmail of Christians being an especial favourite.[139] Epictetus taught that the course of wisdom was to raise no protest when soldiers came to requisition your mule; all that would happen is that you would get beaten and then they would take the mule anyway. He added that the most egregious malefactors were the praetorian guards, who were already the best paid of all troops.[140] The army always acted on the side of privilege and against the wretched of the Earth. Michael Rostovsteff has hypothesised that in the third century the rural peasantry and urban proletariat formed an alliance with the army to defeat the urban bourgeoisie in an example of open class war. This is not a theory that has commanded any assent, for there are too many strikes against it. The urban bourgeoisie's decline was at the hands of big money, not the dispossessed. The army had no reason to help the peasantry at this epoch, because it was no longer recruited from their ranks. All the

evidence overwhelmingly suggests that army raids disrupted the countryside more than the cities, and that the chief victim of military
depredations was the peasantry in its role as food producers.[141]

It is a truth universally observed that the aftermath of wars gener-
ates high levels of criminality.[142] It is only a slight exaggeration to say
that Marcus Aurelius's German wars turned endemic banditry into an
epidemic. In the reign of Hadrian there were famous bandit leaders
like Tilliboras, defiant in his mountain fastness of Mount Ida in the
Troad.[143] Even under Antoninus Pius brigandage was a serious problem,
with cattle-stealing at a high pitch in Spain and strikes of artisans
turning ugly and resulting in the flight of workers to the hills and a
life of outlawry. Masons struck at Pergamum and Miletus, bakers at
Ephesus, and in Egypt there was the phenomenon known as *anachoresis*
– an over-determined breakdown of law and order, involving everything from petty crime to outright banditry.[144] In the reign of Marcus
Aurelius the common opinion was that brigandage was rampant, especially in Macedonia, Thrace, Pannonia and Numidia (eastern Algeria);
Marcus had to send a special army commander to Moesia Superior
to deal with the problem there. In the end he gained a temporary
respite from the problem by recruiting many of these outlaws for his
army on the Danube, paying them special bounties.[145] The Roman
empire always had to tolerate a high level of highway robbery and
banditry. Nowhere was absolutely safe – and in this respect the *pax
Romana* contrasts very unfavourably with the *pax Mongolica* of the
thirteenth century. Pliny the Younger in his *Letters* provided an almost
exact pre-echo of Horace Walpole in eighteenth-century England.
Where Walpole complained of highway robbery taking place in
peaceful Twickenham in the environs of London, Pliny lamented the
famous 'disappearance' of an aristocratic party on the Via Flaminia
just north of Rome.[146] But it was the same story elsewhere, with other
notorious instances reported in south-eastern Anatolia, northern Syria
and Judaea.[147] Commentators were divided about the causes. Some
blamed the lax attitude to law and order in the Greek part of the
empire.[148] Others said that the lenient attitude to army desertions was
at the root of the problem. Given the usual brutality with which
Romans met any attempt by the lower orders at 'social defiance', their
attitude to desertion – at least in peacetime – was remarkably lenient.
Dishonourable discharge was the usual punishment, and Hadrian

allowed even deserters in wartime to escape with impunity, provided they captured bandits or informed on other deserters.[149]

This somewhat dismal situation went through a multiplier process during and after the wars on the Danube, as can be inferred from the huge numbers of soldiers either deserting to the enemy or forming guerrilla bands. Inscriptions on tombstones reveal the large numbers of citizens killed by the new marauders. Gaul and Spain were full of deserters and bandits, and the incidence of brigandage in Italy itself shot up.[150] There was little of the ideologically fuelled anti-war protest of later history; self-interest, survival and self-preservation were the spurs. When the provinces of Spain refused to send troops to serve on the Danube, Marcus concluded there was nothing he could do about it.[151] But he was criticised, then and later, for ordering too strong a draft and then concentrating pressed men in particular theatres, thus encouraging subsequent mass break-outs and desertions.[152] Security in the empire, even on well-travelled roads or actually within the cities, was non-existent, causing what in later eras would be called 'moral panic'. The task of the provincial governor overwhelmingly became that of putting down bandits,[153] which meant making further obeisance to the arrogant army, and a new breed of men, professional bounty-hunters, arose in the lawless climate – Fronto mentioned a pilot version of this new manifestation in his letters to Marcus: a man named Julius Senex.[154] Marcus himself was responsible for a raft of legislation attempting to deal with the problem. Although bandits were officially regarded as beyond the pale, a lower form of life even than the worst criminals, Roman ingenuity had yet to devise more cruel forms of death than crucifixion or being torn apart by wild beasts. Taking his usual pragmatic line with bandits, Marcus favoured easing the labour shortage in the mines by condemning them to eternal toil in the darkness of the deepest shafts.[155] Such was the prevalence of banditry that new laws had to be devised to accommodate the tricky problems it threw up. If someone already condemned to the mines, quarries or saltworks was captured by bandits and then sold as a slave, and if this were uncovered, the 'slave' had to be sent back to the hard labour to which he had originally been consigned; the slave owner was then compensated by the state.[156]

A breakdown of the social composition of the guerrilla bands and gangs of brigands helps to underline the severe problems that Marcus faced. There were a number of different kinds of bandits. There were veterans inured to violence but with inadequate army pensions, and those who simply refused to return to peasant farming; there were deserters, those who joined guerrilla bands opposing the Romans and those who had backed the wrong side in a war (as, for example, many had during the 'year of the four emperors' in 68–9). Then there were those used to a life of casual violence because they lived in the equivalent of the 'Wild West', in remote areas of the empire where the imperial writ did not run. Another notable group was ex-shepherds, again inured to violence because pastoralism entails cattle-rustling and the defence of livestock by main force. Finally there were common criminals who at sea would have become pirates or privateers, but who inland made common cause with the deserters and others.[157] Although it is tempting to see these groups as 'social criminals' or 'primitive rebels', it is probably simpler to view them as alternative societies of the kind that spring up when the state itself is undergoing 'systemic' failure.[158] An analogy might be with eighteenth-century England of the 'half-state', when the regime is not yet fully formed or unable to deal with endemic crime because of backward technology.

In the reign of Marcus and his successors, many of these men attained a fame that in their own day would have been equivalent to that of a Dick Turpin, a Robin Hood or a Jesse James. The leading figure after the reign of Commodus was Bulla Felix, who led 600 men and plundered Italy for two years in the very early third century under Septimius Severus.[159] Bulla achieved celebrity through his superb intelligence service (based around Brundisium) and for his habit of confiscating only part of his victim's wealth. He liked to detain artisans and skilled workers on compulsory service with his men for lengthy periods, always rewarding them at the end with a parting gift. Bulla combined the attributes of Zorro and the Scarlet Pimpernel (he could never be caught) with a Robin Hood-like concern for social justice. Stories about Bulla concentrated on his talent for disguise, his confidence trickery and his ability to pull the wool over officialdom right in the panting heart of Rome itself. It has been ingeniously speculated that such larger-than-life bandits function as a kind of Jungian 'shadow' to 'bad' emperors, revealing clearly to onlookers the real character of the regime, much as John Gay in *The Beggar's Opera* used his highwayman hero as a 'shadow' for the corrupt Robert Walpole.[160] The irony of the Bulla insurrection, as long-lived as the famous revolt of Spartacus, was that in 193 Septimius Severus had made it one of the key points in his manifesto as emperor that he would be 'an enemy to bandits everywhere'. His critics say he himself was responsible for the Bulla uprising when he stopped recruiting Italians into the praetorian guard.[161] But Bulla was simply the shape of things to come: the later bandit rebellion of Gallienus was widely considered even more serious than the Spartacus rebellion.[162]

The militarisation of the Roman state, the increasing tendency of the military to intervene in politics by *coup d'état* and the spin-off of banditry arising from large-scale desertion from the army were all unintended consequences of Marcus Aurelius's German wars. But he can be held directly responsible for the increasing class antagonisms in the Roman empire, which manifested themselves in multifarious modes. The most obvious was the way in which Roman citizenship itself became a depreciated asset. In the first century AD, as we see clearly from the experiences of St Paul, Roman citizenship was a much-prized privilege, conferring substantial benefits. By the time of Antoninus Pius, 'by a process that is not at all clear',[163] the value of citizenship became negligible. The first obvious sign of the change came with Antoninus's decree underlining the different legal status of so-called *humiliores* and *honestiores* – the legal equivalent of the economic distinction between poor and rich.[164] This formalised a growing legal practice best described as inequality before the law. In most modern societies lip-service is paid to 'equality before the law', when everyone knows that a millionaire has in effect superior legal rights to a slum-dweller, if only through access to highly priced lawyers. Roman society did not believe in obfuscation, mystification or political camouflage: it was made sparkingly clear that higher wealth and social status conferred significant legal benefits. And so Antoninus's rescripts established that the social groups regarded as *honestiores* – senatorial, equestrian and curial families plus army veterans and their kin – would always receive lighter legal penalties than the 'great unwashed' (*humiliores*).[165] If sentenced to capital punishment, they would be beheaded instead of crucified or thrown to the wild beasts; if interrogated, they would not be put to torture or subjected to corporal punishment. The usual penalty for the privileged sector in the new two-tier justice system was exile rather than death. *Humiliores*, by contrast, found it much harder to be released on bail or to have their evidence taken seriously by the courts; they could be tortured, scourged, crucified, put to hard labour or forced to become gladiators. Had St Paul lived in the reign of Marcus Aurelius, he would not have been sent to Rome to plead his case before the emperor, but would have been flogged and condemned to a summary trial in Judaea, where the governor would have been advised by a council of hostile Jews.[166] Perhaps the most sinister thing about the new *honestior–humilior* distinction was that it classed soldiers among the first-class citizenry, in a sense anticipating the situation where they would eventually displace the Senate as the political factor of prime importance. The rationale for the shift from citizen/non-citizen to *honestior/humilior* was clearly economic. The gap between rich and poor, which had previously been disguised and obfuscated by reliefs, *alimenta* and *congiaria*, widened alarmingly when the state was faced by economic recession, and when rising prices and inflation eroded the value of state handouts. The financial factor too lay behind Caracalla's decree of AD 212 making all free men – even the 'internal barbarians' who had been settled within the empire – Roman citizens.[167] This was a revenue-raising measure making 'aliens' (*peregrini*) liable to taxes that only Romans had previously paid. Any previous advantage of citizenship was now subsumed in the *honestior–humilior* distinction; the Roman state simply moved the goalposts while apparently displaying statesmanship and magnanimity.

The indifference to the class antagonism caused by the *honestior/humilior* divide was an organic aspect of Marcus's greatest weakness as emperor: his knee-jerk conservatism, lack of imagination and failure to think through the social implications of imperial policy, and here surely we once again see the baneful influence of the Stoic doctrine of 'indifferents'. Marcus was always on the side of the status quo, which meant essentially the interests of the senatorial class. He allowed senators to acquire more land outside Italy than had previously been permissible and generally bolstered the socio-economic position of the elite sectors. He disliked seeing freedmen in positions of authority and in Athens debarred descendants of freed slaves from such positions; all this was in a hallowed oligarchic tradition.[168] The only area where he really permitted meritocracy was in the army,

where individual military prowess was at a premium, hence the meteoric rise of Pertinax. In the clash between wealth and birth, Marcus
unhesitatingly took the side of birth. Men of great wealth, especially
freedmen, ran into a brick wall or 'glass ceiling' of snobbery if they
tried to convert their money into status; the only way they could hope
to break through was by marrying impoverished aristocratic women.[169]
It is true that knights did well under Marcus, and imperial officials of
the equestrian class even received titles such as *egregius* for the
emperor's procurators and *eminentissimus* for praetorian prefects.[170] But
the rise of the equestrians was mainly caused by manpower losses (in
plague and war) among the senators. The empire continued to be a
place where the wealthy ruling classes did largely as they liked.

Yet the senatorial order wanted it every which way round. Although
hugging to themselves the privilege of paying for gladiatorial games
– which excluded the lesser orders from demagogic influence through
the brute exercise of wealth – they continually complained about the
expense of this 'chore', which was already 720,000 sesterces per games
by the year 53 BC. And they were deeply resentful about the way praetorian prefects were gradually edging them out of positions of power
and privilege. It seems that they retaliated by cutting back on all
public philanthropy, which is why donations for baths and amphitheatres seem to come to an end after the death of Antoninus Pius.[171]
Here we come to one of the central 'contradictions' about Marcus's
imperial policy. Marcus realised that the only way not to make state
policy coincident with the interests of an irresponsible cabal of plutocrats was to create a countervailing class of bureaucrats, but these
civil servants soon became a drain on the treasury, second only to
the army.[172] The senatorial order depended for its wealth on extracting
a surplus from the rural peasantry, given that slave numbers were
declining. But this same peasantry was also the source of the new
army recruits desperately needed for the wars and recruited accordingly by Marcus's bureaucrats. In this way there arose a conflict
between senators and the imperial administration that had never been
there before.[173] Disgruntled senators alleged that Marcus did nothing
to arrest the growth in centralisation and bureaucracy begun by
Trajan and Hadrian, which was another way of saying that his stewardship of public finances was reckless and unwise.[174] However, if the
senators gradually lost their political power both to the imperial civil

service and to the military, they seem to have preserved their wealth largely intact: it has been estimated that senators in the western empire in the fourth century were five times richer than they were in the first century.[175]

If Marcus's aristocratic critics complained that he sacrificed their interests to those of the army or the civil service, most of the evidence shows the big landowners and giant capitalists thriving during his reign, at the expense both of the city bourgeoisie and the rural population. Rostovsteff was right to identify a kind of euthanasia of the prosperous middle classes, but was led to construct the extraordinary scenario of an unlikely alliance between the peasantry and the army to account for it. The true explanation was that the middle classes could not compete with big capital, largely because the declining population made slaves more expensive and their quality inferior. Squeezing out the urban middle sectors was a disastrous turn of events.[176] The Roman economy could be revived only by an injection of what modern economists would call 'effective demand', but where was this to come from, if both the peasantry and the bourgeoisie were too impoverished, while there were too few great landowners and multi-millionaire entrepreneurs to generate demand? In rural areas meanwhile the trend was overwhelmingly towards the elimination of free agriculturalists and the spectre of men tied to the soil.[177] Debt bondage had not been unknown before the reign of Marcus Aurelius,[178] but it was the scale of the problem by the end of the second century that was so alarming. Increasingly, exploitation in the economic sense (the extraction of a surplus) became more overt and the relationship of cities to the countryside became blatantly parasitic; even the doles paid to the city mob had to be paid for, ultimately, by the sweated labour of rustics.[179] Successive emperors allied themselves with the plutocrats against the settlers or *coloni*, unconcerned about the appearance of serfdom. Class divisions became too acute and the gap between city and countryside too wide. As has been well said, 'The existence of two castes, one ever more oppressed, the other ever more idle and indulging in the easy life of men of means, lay like an incubus on the Empire and arrested economic progress.'[180]

As the empire's financial crisis deepened, beginning with Marcus successive emperors turned the screw even tighter on the taxes they expected from their unfortunate citizens. While not yet at the crippling meltdown level of the late third and early fourth centuries,[181] taxation was both oppressive and climbing. It was the responsibility of provincial governors, but was chaotic, with all kinds of different imposts, a bewildering variety of types of tax collectors, differential rates of tax and a general air of a localised, ramshackle ad hoc approach. Imperial officials in Rome tended to be cynically uninterested in everything except the final aggregate yield – how much could they suck out of each province in a given year?[182] Officials proliferated, adding further strain to the imperial treasury, and tax evasion and many other forms of corruption were rife. When Trajan appointed Pliny the Younger as his special imperial representative in Bithynia, bypassing the Senate, which in normal circumstances would have appointed a one-year governor, his main objective was to clamp down on large-scale pervasive graft and bribery.[183] Tax collection was almost entirely in the hands of the equestrian class and there was always huge corruption (maybe 'relative deprivation' envy of the senatorial class by the knights) – an inevitable consequence of any social system with a steep pyramid of stratification. As a notable student of corruption has remarked, 'Governors could do almost anything they chose, off in their provinces . . . The classes from which [they] were recruited under the empire generally protected their mentors from harsh punishment.'[184] In Marcus's reign there was a famous instance of venal collusion in North Africa between procurators and *conductores* (holders of prime leases on imperial lands), aimed at extracting more than the legal six days' labour and taking more than the legal amount of the sharecrop.[185] Many of the empire's inhabitants 'solved' the problem of excessive taxation by simply decamping to join the barbarians. Rome had a slender hold on the affections of its far-flung people. In the Dacian wars large numbers had defected to Decebalus,[186] and the enormous figure of 100,000 prisoners and deserters retrieved by Marcus at the end of the German wars tells its own story, even if the weight of the tax burden was not anyway apparent from the official records.[187] Marcus was not unaware of the problem, but he had a delicate balancing act to pull off: securing corn and money for his troops while reining in the worst excesses of the *conductores* and thus preventing an outbreak of rioting (or worse) among the tenants. Meanwhile the tax collectors themselves were under pressure from the imperial administration to come up with results. Not surprisingly, this was a circle that Marcus could not square.[188]

The core problem about the Roman economy was that it was brittle and fragile even *before* the impact of the Antonine plague. The existence of slavery was the main reason for backwardness and the inability for the most part to advance beyond a Gandhi-like village mode of production, simply because slavery worked against technical innovation.[189] Some revisionist scholars have disputed the slavery-as-fetter-on-technology thesis, pointing to the great achievements in road-building and bridge-building and the number of industries not covered by the mining nexus, especially the marble and brick trades.[190] Other defenders of the grandeur that was Rome argue that the Roman economy matched the urbanisation and living standards of the former Hellenistic west – with mining technology more advanced than anything seen until the eighteenth century – and argue that it is absurd to compare ancient Rome with industrialised economies of the post-1800 'take-off' period.[191] But denial of slavery as a salient factor works only for the years when Rome was still an expansionist empire of conquest.[192] In any case, alongside effective demand from a consuming middle class, the economy suffered from lack of competition, since emperors tried to impose a division of labour instead of being guided by the market. And since the commercial sector accounted for only about 5 per cent of Gross Domestic Product,[193] the rise in entrepreneurship that some have identified in the Antonine era took place only on the periphery. Besides, opportunities for entrepreneurship were limited: the barbarians beyond the frontier could not generate effective demand – and in any case were likely to opt for raiding rather than commerce to get what they wanted – while the East of India and beyond was very choosy about what it took from Rome, having many competing industries of its own.[194] In this regard the signs of an inchoate global economy, symbolised by the journeys of the Phoenicians – found anywhere from Britain to Sierra Leone and from Arabia to the Malabar coast, and marked by the entry of Vietnam, Thailand, Malaysia and Indonesia into an Indian Ocean economy that Rome could access – did not help the Roman empire very much.[195] The other drawback about ancient entrepreneurship was that it all too readily degenerated into mere corruption and profiteering, which was why Marcus had to address this specific problem, which was particularly acute during the chaos of the Antonine plague.[196]

Successive emperors were vaguely aware that all was not well, especially in Italy, and hence the many bungling and amateurish ad hoc measures taken from time to time. Petronius relates how Tiberius ordered workshops of flexible glass destroyed for fear that gold, silver and copper would lose value; Suetonius relates that Vespasian suppressed the invention of a machine that would haul large pillars, on the grounds that it would increase unemployment; and Domitian ordered many Italian vineyards destroyed to prevent the overproduction of wine.[197] The Antonines were not exempt from such economic paranoia. Precious metals were perceived to be so important that Antoninus Pius ruled that those who stole gold or silver from imperial mines should be condemned either to exile (if they were *honestiores*) or to hard labour in the mines and quarries (if they were not).[198] The basic tendency of the economy all through the Antonine period was for Asia Minor and the eastern provinces to grow richer relative to Italy and Greece; Spain held up well until the 170s and then joined in the general decline in the west.[199] At the same time people in the eastern part of the empire increasingly resented the control from Rome. They reasoned that the emperors' refusal to make tackling banditry a priority affected their commercial prosperity, while the increasing tendency to try to tax the decurial class in Asia encouraged them to opt out of political participation.[200] Since the bureaucrats in Rome dealt with a diminishing tax yield by trying to force municipal councillors and officials to make good the shortfall, they in turn refused to serve. The central administrators then had no choice but to use coercion, further eroding Rome's popularity in the far corners of the empire. It is in this context that we should read the constant jockeying for minor reliefs from taxation and the somewhat hysterical response when such lobbying was successful.[201] Already the groundwork was being laid for the eventual split that would see the Roman empire divided into two by the end of the fourth century, with rival capitals in Italy and at Byzantium. Roman society was at the crossroads under Marcus Aurelius, for the end of all empires is presaged when its subjects no longer believe in the imperial ideal.

Marcus aspired to encourage agriculture and to achieve 'improvement' through public works, but these aims were always vitiated by the countervailing demands of military expenditure. He began his reign with an ambitious programme of aqueducts, viaducts, sewers, roads, temples, palaces, irrigation and drainage works. He even managed to reclaim 247,000 acres of the Pontine marshes, a notorious breeding ground for mosquitoes (whose danger was not appreciated) and brigands and highwaymen (whose danger was).[202] But all these projects had to be abandoned when the war in Germany broke out and military funding claimed priority. Towards the end of his reign he ingeniously tried to dovetail agriculture, the manpower shortage and security concerns by embracing the thing he had initially set his face against: the settlement of barbarians within the empire. Although this was not the first time aliens had been given land, Marcus's gifts to the Marcomanni, Naristae and others set in train an unstoppable 'barbarisation' of both the countryside and the Roman military.[203] Marcus's ploy of using tribes previously outside the empire to defend frontiers and fight enemy tribes at first seemed a great success (not least because on a cost-benefit analysis he was providing labour and solving the manpower shortage without incurring the child-rearing expenses of raising from birth to adulthood)[204] – and by the mid-third century there was little ethnic difference between Roman armies and the foes they confronted – but it led to numerous problems, quite apart from the insidious 'barbarisation' of Roman culture. The status of the barbarians in Roman law was not entirely clear. As free men voluntarily incorporating themselves in the empire, they were given land under the system of *emphyteusis* (the long-term leasing of public lands). But as prisoners they were tenants, as much tied to the soil as other peasants in debt-bondage. The free men were demanding, requiring good land to farm and tax-exempt status in return for their military obligations to fight for Rome. Yet tribal solidarities and kinship ties could not be dispensed with at the stroke of a bureaucrat's pen. The ex-prisoners tied to the soil perceived their primary loyalty to be to their free brethren, and vice versa. But Roman law contradicted this. The legal code clearly stated that anyone bequeathing *inquilini* (tenants) without the lands to which they were attached was making an invalid bequest and, if this was done, the heir must pay the legatee an equivalent sum in compensation.[205] But what if they were barbarian settlers? Were they really tied to the land like their Italian counterparts? Did they have obligations to military service, which would align them with the free Germans, or were they like domestic serfs, in which case they had no obligation to bear arms?[206] If the barbarian tenants insisted on being treated like their more fortunate brethren, what would be the upshot? If the legions were sent to enforce their obedience to landlords, the entire barbarian clan would then rise in revolt. Once again we see Marcus and other emperors torn between their putative loyalty to the great landowners and to the needs of the army. If they enforced the strict letter of the law to require serfdom, they would have a war on their hands. The uncertainty thus engendered meant that legions could never be sent away from the colonised area anyway, thus destroying the original objective of the barbarian settlement.

The problems of the Roman empire were by this time anyway intractable and Marcus was not temperamentally the right sort of person to deal with them. Economists have usually poured scorn on the later emperor Diocletian's attempt to freeze prices, but at least the doomed attempt showed glimmerings of an understanding of some of the socio-economic problems. For all kinds of reasons, both Marcus's education and the legacy he had inherited from Antoninus Pius did not encourage radical thinking on social problems. There may be cultural factors at work too. Like the rest of the Antonines, Marcus probably seriously believed that there were limits to what any individual action could achieve because the destinies of the world were in the lap of Zeus (as a proper name for the god suffusing the universe, not the Olympian bounder).[207] In cultural terms the late second century was afflicted by a twofold mental crisis. On the one hand Romans were insecure, full of fear and hatred, sceptical about the old gods, not yet committed to a new universal belief system. As G.K. Chesterton famously observed, men who cease to believe in religion will believe in *anything*, hence the rise of magic, astrology and Eastern mystery religions.[208] Failure of nerve and the decline of rationalism was one aspect of the late Antonine disease, but the other was a scepticism about the scope of individual action and a consequent dissolution into the collective myth, whereby the traditional and the customary become king. In such a world view the gifted individual is suspected of sorcery and trivialisation, while pedantry and showmanship function as an escape from reality and society becomes 'pathologically traditionalist'.[209] Some commentators have linked this mindset to an over-emphasis on the concept of *philotimia*. A difficult concept, famously used by Plutarch to describe the Athenian statesman Themistocles, *philotimia* originally meant 'love of honour' in the sense that one achieved prestige by performing useful services for others.[210] But by the late Antonine period it denoted simply the desire for prestige and reputation for whatever reason, the wish to appear superior, and that superiority usually came down to simple wealth and social status. The sharpening of class divisions and the accumulation of wealth into fewer and fewer hands, already noted, would be the 'objective correlative' of this attitude.[211]

Marcus Aurelius was caught up in the whirlwind of history. Although he could have done more to increase a wider commitment to the Roman empire – it is noticeable how far short he fell of his own aspiration in the *Meditations* to make Rome a true 'city of God' – so that people continued to believe in the imperial ideal, most of the problems he confronted were beyond the reach of any individual, however gifted. Rome was caught in the 'expand or die' dilemma, but by Marcus's time even survival through expansion was problematical. Septimius Severus made a bold attempt to return to the glory days of Trajan with his war on Parthia, during which he thoroughly plundered Ctesiphon and finished off the Parthians, and it is thought that the treasure he brought back postponed Rome's financial crisis for another forty years.[212] But by this time even military expansion was not enough. By Marcus's time, Rome could no longer meet its frontier expenses even in a 'steady state' universe, and the German wars forced a huge increase in such expenses. As Cassius Dio correctly saw, it was stupid to make war on Parthia or try to annex provinces beyond the Danube, for you would then have to maintain an even larger army to hang on to the conquests.[213] Any treasure accumulated by Rome would have to be used up in suppressing risings in the conquered territories, to say nothing of the balance-of-payments crisis caused by the drain of specie to the East to settle the cost of luxury imports. In the case of the Parthian conquests of Septimius Severus, an even more serious unintended consequence was engendered, for the Parthian regime collapsed in 226 and was replaced by the altogether more formidable Sassanid dynasty of Persians, a fanatical theocracy of zealots, as hell-bent on conquest as the armies of Islam would later be; Rome was thereafter condemned to permanently maintaining 25 per cent of its army on the eastern frontier.[214] Cassius Dio explicitly contrasted the glory-hunting of Septimius Severus and Caracalla with Marcus's German wars, essential to Rome's very survival.[215] Marcus's record as emperor, though not perfect, was honourable. Most of all he was unlucky. The core factor during his reign was the Antonine plague, its huge mortality and the resulting manpower shortage, whose effects were felt everywhere throughout social and economic life. It was the final irony for a Stoic philosopher who believed in 'holism' that a truly holistic, octopus-like phenomenon such as the pandemic should have made null and void all the objectives for which he strove.

19

Marcus was largely a failure in politics and government, overwhelmed by circumstances mostly beyond the scope of any human being; even so he qualified as the best-ever Roman emperor and, to use Shakespeare's phrase, was 'the noblest Roman of them all'. It is as a thinker that he transcends the ages and lives on as a true 'immortal'. His reputation among his successors was high, but not perhaps as elevated as it should have been. Most of the notables of late antiquity rated Trajan, the drunkard conqueror, ahead of him, while probably going along with the opinion of Pescennius Niger that Trajan, Antoninus Pius and Marcus Aurelius were the three most outstanding emperors, and Hadrian, Lucius Verus and Commodus were in the category of 'puppets or monsters'.[1] Diocletian, who also persecuted Christians, was said to have revered Marcus.[2] Yet it was only when Julian the Apostate, emperor from 361 to 363, wrote his comparative study of the Caesars that Marcus was definitively awarded the palm as enlightened ruler. Finding only Alexander the Great as another figure from the past to rank alongside him, Julian praised Marcus's godlike patience, his instinctive knowledge of when to speak and when to remain silent and his aspiration, through philosophy, 'to turn men into gods'. 'Four-square and without a blemish', Marcus was not just more morally admirable than all other emperors, but also wiser. He even looked the most dignified of the princes and showed the effect of his long studies in the expression in his eyes and the furrow in his brows.[3] He had but three flaws – his indulgence of Lucius Verus,

Faustina and Commodus – but this showed his humanity and, after all, the paternal partiality for his son could be construed as both a human and a divine flaw, since it was sanctioned by Homer himself.[4] It is easy to see why Julian should have been so fascinated by Marcus. Like him, he was an intellectual emperor (he, Cicero and Marcus are the only three Romans fully to disclose the workings of their minds); he loathed Christianity; he fought wars on two fronts, and was preoccupied by the problem of the 'barbarians'. Intriguingly, too, Julian had a fondness for sacrificing to the traditional Olympian gods.[5] The list of similarities can be almost endless. They both disliked chariot races, were both inducted into the Eleusinian mysteries and were both alleged to have died mysteriously (though the allegation has much more circumstantial weight in Julian's case).

Julian scouted the idea that mere military talent allowed one into the pantheon of the truly great. Rome's greatest warriors were Julius Caesar, Augustus and Trajan, but at this level they were hopelessly eclipsed by Alexander the Great. Whereas he had convulsed the Persians in three great battles, none of the Roman trio had worked out how to defeat the Parthians; Julian found Trajan's victories against Parthia unconvincing, and not even as impressive as those gained under Marcus.[6] In Julian's *Caesars* the gods are asked to choose the greatest figure of antiquity, and they select Marcus. But because he was pronounced victor by a majority verdict and not a unanimous one, some modern critics have alleged that Julian was not really very influenced by Marcus.[7] Some claim that Julian's real objective was a critique of Constantine for allowing the Christian tide to overwhelm the Roman world, but that he had to choose his words carefully, so opted for praise of Marcus, hoping that his more intelligent readers would construe this as a coded message of approbation for his harshness towards the followers of the 'Galilean'.[8] Others claim that many aspects of Julian's personality work against the idea that he regarded himself as Marcus *redivivus*. For one thing, Julian was acknowledged to have a good sense of humour, while Marcus was almost humourless.[9] For another, if Julian had wanted to copy Marcus so closely, why did he choose to look so different? Where Marcus had a short, stubby beard, Julian had a long one trimmed in goatee fashion, which attracted particular ridicule in Antioch, that bane of both Marcus and Julian.[10] Again, Marcus fought the Germans as he perceived it to be a necessity, but Julian's campaign against the Persians in 363 seemed to have been mainly glory-hunting. The most ingenious suggestion is that Julian modelled his portrait of Marcus on himself rather than modelling himself on Marcus.[11] Although Julian and Marcus shared a taste for pantheistic mysticism, it has to be conceded that Julian's Neoplatonism was a long way from Marcus's Stoicism. Yet at the most basic level, both emperors were concerned not so much to persecute Christianity in Nero's way, but to deny the detested religion all influence among the ruling class and its decision-making. In this sense Julian was a true heir of Marcus, beyond the possibility of reasonable dispute.[12]

Once Christianity became the world religion of the Roman empire (and its prolongation in the eastern empire at Byzantium), it became problematical for thinkers to admit the influence or similarity of Marcus's teachings. Some solved the problem by claiming that Marcus was really a 'premature Christian', guilty of a culture-bound 'false consciousness' in persecuting the true faith. Others, while using his insights, effectively wrote him out of their script. This 'Christianity in denial' factor makes very difficult the comparison between Marcus and St Augustine that is often touted as a natural convergence.[13] It seems best to deal with the issue by enumerating the many instances where there was congruence between Marcus and Augustine, and then contrast them with the many more where the two were poles apart.

Augustine (354–430) enjoyed a long life, most of it spent in North Africa. He began his career as a Manichaean, converted to Christianity, was baptised by the famous Christian father Ambrose, became Bishop of Hippo near Carthage and remained there until his death, mainly engaged in theological feuds with heretical sects such as the Donatists, Manichaeans and Pelagians. Augustine is famous for his *Confessions*, which at many points do resemble Marcus's *Meditations*,[14] although Marcus's writings are a spiritual odyssey while Augustine's are more conventionally autobiographical, at least for the first ten chapters. St Augustine began the trend for 'warts-and-all' memoirs that would culminate in Rousseau and Tolstoy. It is sometimes claimed that in this he was a complete original, though the best authorities agree that he took his cue from the *Meditations* and that the character studies in the *Confessions* – far richer than was normal in lives of the saints – were influenced by Marcus's example.[15] What differentiates him most clearly from Marcus is the concept of sin, one of the axes of Christianity, but totally unknown in the Stoic tradition. Possibly the most famous story in Augustine's *Confessions* (if only because he writes about it at such unconscionable length) is the boyhood exploit when he 'scrumped' some pears from a neighbour's orchard. Augustine regarded this as the apogee of wickedness and besought God piteously for forgiveness; the quasi-pathology in his reaction to a venial juvenile fault is thought to be because of the association between the stolen pears and the forbidden fruit in the Garden of Eden.[16]

Superficially, the similarities between the *Meditations* and *Confessions* are legion, and it is easy to cherry-pick passages showing remarkable harmony of outlook. Augustine and Marcus agree, albeit for different reasons, that evil is not-being or the mere absence of good. Both stress the importance of rationality as against passion, and agree that the offended party who bears a grudge is morally worse than the offender. Both agree on the unreality of time and its purely subject status as a mental construct. Only the present exists, and the meaning of past and future is that they are both present phenomena, the former connected to the here and now by memory, the latter by expectation. Augustine's reflections on time have become famous: 'If no one asks me what it is, I know; but if I wish to explain it to him who asks, I don't know.'[17] Both are linked by an extreme emphasis on subjectivity, though for Marcus this is a result of the spiritual exercises expected of a Stoic, while for Augustine it is the result of his excessive emphasis on sin.[18] In terms of life experience, one might also mention that both survived with dread and horror the experience of storm-tossed seas. While on his way to Rome to study as an orator, Augustine's ship was caught in huge seas; the experience meant that, once back in North Africa after his sojourns in Rome and Milan, he never ventured abroad again.[19] Both men detested games and the arena, though Augustine slightly spoiled his record in this area by a never finally abated taste for hunting and cock-fighting – the very same 'quail fancying' that Fronto had long ago denounced to his pupil.[20]

Yet whatever similarities can be cited in the thought and lives of the two men, they are easily eclipsed by the salient differences. Augustine, especially in his *Sermons*, was a showy writer who deployed gaudy phraseology, which Marcus never did. Augustine had a 'complex' about his mother (St Monica), as Marcus never did about his, and is altogether a more exciting case for psychoanalysis. At the very simplest level is the fact that Marcus (and Julian the Apostate) wrote in Greek, while Augustine hated the language from childhood and never mastered it.[21] At a more profound level Augustine's City of God is the Christian Heaven, from which sinners are excluded, whereas Marcus's conception of the transcendental city is something that represents the entire world; in a word, it is monistic where Augustine's is dualistic. Finally, Marcus and all the Stoics were pantheists, whereas Augustine believed in a personal, transcendental deity.[22] For Augustine, as for so many Christian thinkers, Plato and Aristotle were the only philosophers of note, and the Stoics were epigones, if not outright charlatans.[23] But when it came to a conflict between Neoplatonism and Genesis, Augustine opted for the Bible. Whereas Christians believed in creation out of nothing, for the Greeks this was an impossibility. The Greek – and Stoic – view was that everything in the world was part of God, that God and the world are not distinct. Above all, Augustine rejects the Stoic argument from cosmic design, since this denies the transcendence of a biblical Creator. He believed that the Stoic conception of Fate was mistaken, since both angels and men had free will.[24] According to Augustine, the fact that God has foreknowledge of our sins has nothing to do with the matter, for we do not sin because of his foreknowledge but because of Original Sin. It is with Augustine that this key concept enters the Christian lexicon. He opted for a middle path between the Fate of the Stoics and the true free will of his great rival Pelagius. He wanted the concept of Free Will to explain human sinfulness, but he also wanted Predestination and the notion of an elite Elect who entered Heaven – exactly what so appealed to Calvin a thousand and more years later.[25]

Probably the difference that most strikes the layman (as opposed to the theologian) when considering the two thinkers is their differential attitude to sexuality. It is not an exaggeration to say that Augustine was obsessed with sexuality and with carnal lust, which he thought particularly shameful since it was independent of the will. In his early pre-Christian days he lived in Carthage with a mistress and even had a son with her, though he later referred to the 'hell of concupiscence'.[26] When his mother arranged a suitable marriage for him, Augustine discarded the broken-hearted mistress, but then, as his intended wife was very young, took another mistress until the young girl came of age.[27] Always beset by sexual longings – perhaps his most famous saying is 'give me chastity, but not yet'[28] – Augustine, like so many reformed libertines, could not leave the subject alone. His pre-occupation with sin – and his conviction that sexual desire was a large part of this – distorted his writings. Because of sin, he over-emphasised libido, and here the contrast with Marcus is clear. Marcus always despised those who attached too much importance to sex, which he regarded as much ado about nothing, an insignificant physical function.[29] In this he was remarkably like his admirer Julian the Apostate, of whom Ammianus Marcellinus related: 'He was splendid, first of all, for his unvarying continence. After his wife's death (when Julian was twenty-five), all agree that he eschewed sex, taking to heart Plato's remark about the tragedian Sophocles who, when asked if he was still capable of intercourse in old age, said no, and added that it was a great relief to escape that species of love, as one flees from a crazed and ruthless despot.'[30] Roman society was disfigured by its routine cruelty, bloodshed and exploitation, but took a relaxed attitude to sexuality and never got it out of proportion, as Christianity continued to do throughout its history.

Marcus's *Meditations* have also been compared to another famous book dating, like Augustine's writings, from the end of the Roman empire in the West: Boethius's *De Consolatione Philosophiae*. Both works were composed in circumstances of great stress, Marcus's 'among the Quadi' (that is, on campaign in Germany) and Boethius's while awaiting execution as part of the Arian King of Italy Theodoric's persecution of orthodox (Athanasian) Christians. The *Consolations of Philosophy* take the form of a dialogue between Boethius (480–524), who speaks in prose, and the goddess Philosophy, who speaks in verse.[31] The aphoristic style in which many of the propositions are framed is heavily redolent of Marcus, and most of the sentiments are similar, yet there is no mention of the emperor in the entire work. Although Boethius goes out of his way to stress that the only true philosophers are Socrates, Plato and Aristotle and that the Stoics were 'usurpers', in fact his thinking draws heavily on Stoicism. So: Nature is more important than any individual;[32] happiness is not the same as pleasure; evil is mere absence, not-being; virtuous men are always powerful and wicked men weak; in wise men there is no place for hatred; and so on. It is the supreme illusion that the highest goods are riches, prestige, power, fame or pleasure; real power and real happiness are his who meets a highwayman on the road with no purse and empty pockets.[33] In an argument that would later appeal to C.G. Jung, Boethius argues that wicked men are actually happier when punished for their transgressions than if they get away scot-free.[34] He denies that Free Will and Destiny are in collision and asserts that there is no such thing as pure chance. He distinguishes Providence from Fate by positing that Providence is divine reason, while Fate is what the divine reason arranges; it follows that all fortune is good and we should practise *amor fati* (Love of fate/Destiny).[35] The truly curious thing about the *Consolations* is that, though written by a Christian, it is almost entirely pagan in sensibility. With Augustine, the Bible trumps Neoplatonism, but in Boethius Neoplatonism is yoked with Stoicism. There is a quite evident pantheism that pervades the work, especially in the 'holistic' statement that unity is synonymous with good,[36] but pantheism was regarded in Boethius's time as heresy. The pagan sensibility of the work recalls Marcus as much as the oracular style and the Stoic sentiments, but, although Boethius quotes classical authors copiously, there is no mention of Marcus; the Stoic influence cited is Seneca.[37]

Nearly one thousand years ensue before we can identify any real influence of or homology with Marcus's *Meditations* in the history of thought. Scholars have never (so far as I am aware) suggested any reason for this, but the obvious explanation is the decline in classical learning and the lessening importance of motifs from the old Roman empire in the West.[38] From Constantine to Boethius, Christian thinkers still largely framed their thoughts with reference to the empire, as we see clearly in the works of the saints Augustine and Jerome. Thereafter these concerns diminished and doubtless, with them, interest in philosopher-kings. Although the idea of the 'dark ages' has been over-done – for one thing the eastern empire based on Byzantium survived until 1453 – it is true that from the time of Augustine to Thomas Aquinas in the thirteenth century most of the best work in philosophy was done outside the Christian world: by Avicenna and Averroes, for example.[39] The dominance of Aquinas introduced another dimension, for he elevated Aristotle to the stature of *the* philosopher, displacing Plato. For Marcus, on the other hand, Platonism was always important and the Aristotelian school negligible. There are frequent references to Plato in the *Meditations*, but none to Aristotle.[40] Given that Plato was a philosophical idealist and a political philosopher, while Aristotle was a realist and a political *scientist*, Marcus's preference was obvious.[41] Clearly the coming of the Renaissance, the revival of classical learning and the re-assumption by Plato of number-one spot in the philosophical pantheon had something to do with the revival of interest in Marcus Aurelius in the sixteenth century. In this context it is surely significant that the Christian thinker most obviously influenced by Marcus was the fifteenth-century mystic Thomas à Kempis (1380–1471), although, as in the case of Boethius, there is no explicit reference to the emperor – hardly surprisingly, as Kempis is dedicated to extravagant praise of the Almighty.

Thomas à Kempis is often hailed as the greatest single influence on Christians after the Bible itself. If he had not read Marcus when he wrote his *Imitation of Christ*, then the parallels with the *Meditations* are truly astonishing. Just from the first three books of the *Imitation* alone we can excerpt the following sayings, which can be matched almost precisely by similar passages in Marcus's reflections: set no value on worldly things, for all things will pass away; solitude and silence are to be treasured; it is pointless to envy the rich and powerful, for life on Earth is inherently miserable; carnality is an illusion; never boast of riches or influential friends; avoid all interest in, or asking questions about, the lives of others; do not strive for fame or be concerned if others like you; don't fear the foolish judgements of public opinion; have contempt for all temporal honours; it is better to get advice than to give it; do not talk too much or use too many words; learn to turn adversity to your advantage; when judging others you are striving in vain, but when judging yourself you are doing something useful; the proud and avaricious man is never at rest, while the poor and lowly of heart abide in an ocean of peace; we should always love truth; love no contemplation that leads to pride; revel in the joys of a good conscience; if you cannot conquer small things, how can you conquer big ones? be thankful for the least gift, so that you are worthy to receive a greater one; don't be angry that you cannot make others as you wish them to be, since you cannot make yourself as you wish to be; no one has a harder fight than he who is striving to overcome himself; beware the dangers of familiarity, don't open up to everyone, love all men but never make close companions of others.[42]

Sometimes the echoes are almost uncanny, as when Kempis recommends that we should make preparations as if we are to die today; when it is morning reflect that you may not see evening, and when it is evening that you may not see next morning.[43] Like Marcus, Augustine and Boethius, Kempis recommends subjecting passions and emotion to reason, arguing that a passionate man will turn even good into evil; he says what he should not and does not say what he should.[44] In almost identical language to that in the *Meditations* Kempis recommends that we should develop the ability to perceive our own faults, and should treat praise and flattery as impostors.[45] In Book Three of the *Imitation* Kempis sings a paean to Love that recalls Marcus's pantheism, and it is this book that most resembles Buddhism, and hence Marcus himself in his 'Eastern' manifestation. Kempis preaches that perfect freedom means self-denial, the avoidance of all selfishness, and finally the extinction of the self. Patience is all-important and the realisation that on Earth we are in a veil of illusion: 'like smoke those who are rich in this world will pass away, and no record shall remain of their past joys'.[46] Naturally, Kempis leaves Marcus behind when he plunges deeply into Christology: Book Four is taken up almost entirely with the subject of Holy Communion, though even here he sounds an Aurelian note, as when he condemns laughter.[47] When he mocks death and the ambition to live a long life, Kempis flavours the thought with a Christian sauce: 'On an hour which is not to be thought about, the Son of Man will come.' Even the moral prescriptions often come with a tint of Christianity: 'At the Day of Judgement we shall not be asked what we have read but what we have done.'[48] Most divergent of all Kempis's thoughts is his opposition to 'following Nature'. He tells us that Nature is deceitful and is always inferior to Grace; a long section in Book Three sets out to prove that Grace will always trump Nature.[49]

The massive revival of both classical learning and Stoicism itself (albeit in a Christianised form) in the Renaissance is most clearly seen in the *Essays* of Montaigne, himself a Renaissance man and one, like Marcus, who aimed at wisdom rather than proficiency in technical philosophy. However, it was initially Cicero and Seneca, of all the classical authors, who made the biggest impact. This can clearly be seen in Montaigne's writings, for in more than fifty long essays he refers to Marcus and Epictetus just once each, while making twenty-one references to or citations from Seneca. In Montaigne we see classical learning in its 'overkill' mode, for he is barely capable of making the most commonplace observation without bringing in a plethora of Greek and Roman authors to buttress it. Even though we search in vain for many traces of Marcus in his *oeuvre*, except for the aside that his own father quoted the emperor frequently,[50] it is hard not to see a distinct Aurelian flavour, in treatment and sensibility, in Montaigne's meditations on death in the essay 'That to study philosophy is to learn to die'. There is also the fulmination against lying and the Marcus-like reflections on dreams ('Life is a dream; when we sleep we are awake and when awake we sleep'), which we do not find in Seneca, to say nothing of the following: 'A man who fears suffering is already suffering from what he fears.'[51] However, Marcus was not yet making his full impact in the new liberalised era, where the Church had been forced to renounce its stranglehold on thought and specu-lation, partly because, whereas the revival in the study of Epictetus had begun in the fifteenth century, Marcus's *Meditations* were not widely available in translation until the reign of Elizabeth I in England, with the first printed edition appearing in Zurich in 1559.[52] Yet already Marcus had several doughty champions. His spirit hovers over Thomas More's *Utopia* – the finest treatment of philosopher-kings since Plato's *Republic*. Another important supporter was the Franciscan scholar Antonio de Guevara.[53] Yet another was Thomas Gataker (1574–1645), who far preferred Marcus to Seneca and wrote as follows: 'I give Seneca the first place for chronological reasons, though I consider him inferior to the others [Epictetus and Marcus] in dignity and true worth. He does indeed have some excellent, useful, bold, sublime, penetrating and subtle things to say, and he is well worth a careful, if critical, reading by students of theology as well as of the human-ities. But he is variable and often inconsistent – I don't just mean his hypocritical life, for which Dio Cassius attacked him . . . but in his writings themselves.'[54]

Stoicism continued to make inroads on European thought in the seventeenth century, though still largely shackled to Christian ortho-doxy. Its influence is palpable in the ethical system of Spinoza, who espoused the most thoroughgoing version of determinism and reason operating through logical necessity. Like the Stoics, he denies the reality of evil and of time (these are 'partial' and hence illusory phenomena when seen from the vantage point of God, *sub specie aeternitatis*). But he decisively parts company from the Stoics in not denying the utility of *all* emotions, but instead drawing a careful distinction between 'higher' and 'lower' feelings or, as he puts it, between proper emotion and mere *passion*. Reason yoked to emotion will lead us to God, as it never will if mere passion is at play.[55] Yet it is in two works of mysticism in this century that we most clearly see the growing influence of Stoicism, even if it is Epictetus rather than Marcus who still holds pride of place. Sir Thomas Browne, who was to be such an influence in the nineteenth century, with devotees as various as Coleridge, de Quincey and Herman Melville, was one of those who pushed to the very edges of orthodox belief, incorporating ideas from Gnosticism, occultism and abnormal psychology.[56] While subscribing to Christianity, he shows his ambivalence in many asides, such as the remark that atheists have been the only true philosophers, praising Lucian, Euripides and Julian the Apostate for their unbelief.[57] Again, we find few overt references to Marcus, except an inconsequential one in an essay discussing the age of the planet Earth,[58] but many of the maxims are Aurelian in tone – 'we term sleep a death, and yet it is waking that kills us', 'we carry within us the wonders we seek without us; there is all Africa and her prodigies in us' – and the best authorities are adamant that Browne's aphoristic style derives from Marcus.[59] Yet one cannot push too hard at this particular door, for many of Browne's remarks on Stoicism are very jaundiced. 'The Stoics who condemn passion and command a man to laugh at Phalaris's bull cannot endure without a groan a fit of stone or the colic . . . the sceptics that affirmed they knew nothing even in that opinion confute themselves and thought they knew more than all the world beside . . . Diogenes I hold to be the most vainglorious man of his time, and more ambitious in refusing all honours than Alexander in rejecting none.'[60]

The other great seventeenth-century Christian mystic was Pascal, who incorporates much Stoic wisdom while ultimately deriding it as far inferior to Christianity. As with Montaigne, his writings teem with classical references: Horace, Seneca, Cicero, Virgil, Tacitus, Terence, Quintilian. His intention was to find another way to God, distinct from the so-called metaphysical proofs of St Anselm and Thomas

Aquinas, which were remote from human experience and so complex that they bypassed the human imagination.[61] Pascal's intellectual strategy was to contrast and interpenetrate the thoughts of Montaigne and Epictetus in such a way that the reader would ultimately become utterly confused and in the end opt for conventional belief in a Christian God. The last seven of the fourteen books of his *Pensées* are given over to recondite issues in theology and Christian apologetics, but in the first seven his 'dialectical' method is everywhere in evidence: the *locus classicus* is perhaps: 'It is not certain that everything is uncertain.'[62] First there are the copious references to Montaigne and Epictetus, supposedly representing respectively the sceptical and Stoical positions. Montaigne receives especially rough treatment for his lewdness, ignorance, indifference to salvation and his views on suicide.[63] Then come a number of propositions that could easily come from Seneca, Epictetus or Marcus: attacks on human vanity and the lust for glory (interestingly, Pascal thinks that the quest for glory stems from the admiration we had from our parents in infancy); on the war between passion and reason; on the hollowness of pleasure.[64] The following could all be construed as amended or borrowed Epictetus: 'All men naturally hate each other.' 'Do you wish people to believe good of you? Then don't speak.' 'If all men knew what each said of the other, there would not be four friends in the world.' 'The only thing that consoles us for our miseries is diversion, and yet this is the greatest of our miseries, for it stops us reflecting.' 'Reason commands us far more imperiously than a master; for in disobeying the one we are unfortunate, and in disobeying the other we are fools.' 'It is not good to have too much liberty. It is not good to have all one wants.' 'Let us imagine a number of men in chains and all condemned to death, where some are killed each day in the sight of others, and those who remain see their own fate in that of their fellows and wait their turn, looking at each other sorrowfully and without hope. It is an image of the condition of men.'[65]

But Pascal 'compensates' for his use of Stoic wisdom by savage attacks on the doctrine in general. All the principles of the Stoics, he says, as also of sceptics and atheists are true, but their conclusions are false, because the opposite principles are also true.[66] This is a favourite dialectical device of Pascal. Stoicism is both difficult and foolish: 'The Stoics lay down that all who are not at the high degree of wisdom are equally foolish and vicious.'[67] *Pace* the Stoics, the deaths of the 300 Spartans at Thermopylae (480 BC, in the Persian Wars) were pointless, but those of the Christian martyrs were not.[68] Curiously, although he cites Epictetus only to refute him, Pascal never mentions Marcus, yet incorporates many of the emperor's cosmological insights into his world view. Pierre Hadot has pointed out that Marcus's beloved triads (see p. 214) are mirrored in the Pascalian tripartite order of flesh, spirit and will.[69] Man's insignificance in the universe is a theme common to both Pascal and Marcus,[70] and they share the conviction that only the present is real, whereas human 'false consciousness' consists of thinking always either of the past or the future.[71] Pascal also shares Marcus's amused contempt for the 'great men' of history, taking delight in pointing out that the great conqueror Oliver Cromwell was hastened to his end by a urinary infection.[72] Where Marcus's main target was Alexander the Great, Pascal lays into Julius Caesar: his desire to conquer the world when he was in his fifties showed exceptional immaturity; such ambition is understandable in the young, which is why Pascal could forgive it in Alexander or Augustus, but a man of Caesar's years should have known better.[73] The absurdity of seeking fame when one will not be alive to enjoy the judgement of posterity is another theme common to both.[74] Most striking is Pascal's venture into the world of dreams, which is Marcus's territory rather than Epictetus's. Pursuing Marcus's favourite 'Are we dreaming all the time?' conundrum, Pascal offers the following thought. If an artisan were to dream every night for twelve hours non-stop that he was a king, he would be as happy as a king who dreamed every night for twelve hours that he was an artisan, for either man would then have the same quotient of 'reality'.[75]

Signs that Marcus was beginning to overtake Epictetus as *the* Stoic philosopher whom all men of letters and thinkers quoted came at the beginning of the eighteenth century in the shape of three men: Bishop Joseph Butler (1692–1752), Anthony Ashley Cooper, 3rd Earl of Shaftesbury (1671–1713) and the poet Alexander Pope (1688–1744). Bishop Butler attempted to defend orthodoxy against the rising tide of Deism, but headed in exactly the opposite direction from Pascal, trying to ground a general theory of ethics in Stoicism before arguing that it needed to be 'topped up' by Christianity. In his work he paid particular attention to Book Nine of Marcus's *Meditations*.[76] A far better writer, but perhaps hampered by a certain aesthetic dilettantism, was

Shaftesbury, who adored Marcus only just this side of idolatry. His *Characteristics of Men, Manners, Opinion, Times*, which enjoyed a great vogue in the eighteenth and nineteenth centuries, quoted the emperor copiously and eagerly.[77] From the twenty-first-century perspective perhaps the most impressive endorsement of Marcus was given by Alexander Pope, another devotee who had a statue of his hero in his villa at Twickenham. *An Essay on Criticism* raises the Stoic standard with the famous lines:

> First follow Nature, and your judgment frame
> By her just standard, which is still the same.[78]

In 'The Temple of Fame' he praises Marcus explicitly:

> And Wise Aurelius in whose well-taught mind,
> With boundless power unbounded virtue join'd
> His own strict judge and patron of mankind.[79]

Yet it is in the *Essay on Man*, dilating on the 'Great Chain of Being', that the embrace of both the Stoics and Marcus Aurelius reached its apogee and ended with a whole-hearted embrace of the 'holism' that Marcus preached so assiduously:

> Who noble ends by noble means obtains
> Or, failing, smiles in exile or in chains,
> Like good Aurelius let him reign, or bleed
> Like Socrates, that man is great indeed . . .
>
> All are but parts of one stupendous whole
> Whose body nature is, and God the soul . . .
>
> All nature is but art, unknown to thee;
> All chance, direction which thou canst not see
> All discord, harmony not understood;
> All partial evil, universal good;
> And, spite of pride, in erring reason's spite
> One truth is clear, whatever is, is right.[80]

As the eighteenth century wore on, the fame of Marcus increased, eclipsing the reputation of Epictetus. There were two main reasons for this. The Age of Enlightenment made deism, atheism and pantheism much more popular and acceptable, with the result that Stoicism – hitherto invariably yoked to Christian belief – gradually became a philosophy of scepticism and unbelief rather than an adjunct to orthodoxy.[81] Because Marcus had persecuted Christians, apologists for the faith always preferred to cite Epictetus, and this tendency is seen most clearly in the work of Pascal. Second, the eighteenth century saw a widespread fascination with the idea of the philosopher-king. Pope Benedict XV was hailed by his supporters as one such figure, and even stronger claims were adduced for Frederick the Great of Prussia, a man who consciously modelled himself on Marcus Aurelius. Additionally, the sages of the Enlightenment liked to fancy themselves as Plato at the court of Dionysius of Syracuse: Voltaire for a while played this role with Frederick the Great until the experiment ended in tears, as did Diderot with Catherine the Great of Russia. They were consequently far more interested in the mental processes of an emperor than a slave (Epictetus). Voltaire said that the Stoic praise for humility made perfect sense for Epictetus: he was a slave and had a limited range of choices. But it was more difficult to explain in the case of Marcus Aurelius, especially given the constraints of human nature: 'the master of the known world recommends humility; but propose humility to a musician, and see how he will laugh at Marcus Aurelius'.[82] The growing power available to rulers, as military technology advanced in the eighteenth century, made Marcus seem even more remarkable to the *philosophes* of the Enlightenment. Montesquieu wrote: 'Search through all Nature and you will not find greater objects than the two Antonines . . . Nothing can make us forget the first Antoninus except the man he adopted – Marcus Aurelius. We feel a secret pleasure within ourselves in speaking of this emperor; we cannot read his life without experiencing a kind of tenderness. Such is the effect it produces that we have a better opinion of ourselves because we have a better opinion of men.'[83]

The *philosophes* of the Enlightenment worked mainly in the rationalist tradition of Descartes, Spinoza and Leibniz, so that it might have been expected that their enthusiasm for Marcus would not necessarily have been shared by the more empirically minded thinkers of the Scottish Enlightenment, that remarkable effloresence of original work on philosophy and political economy that lasted from about 1740 to 1790. Yet, if anything, Marcus was even more influential on this group, with Francis Hutcheson, Adam Ferguson and Adam Smith being particular devotees of the Stoic emperor.[84] Adam Smith was especially impressed by Marcus's analogy between the work of God and the work of the physician. If we understand God as a physician, we clearly understand it when a doctor tells one man to ride on horseback, another to go barefoot and another to take cold baths. Similarly, God as the world's physician has ordered that one man will have a disease, another lose a limb and another lose a child.[85] Smith says of Marcus: 'The good-natured emperor, absolute sovereign of the whole civilised part of the world, who certainly had no peculiar reason to complain of his own allotment, delights in expressing his contentment with the ordinary course of things, and in pointing out beauties even in those parts of it where vulgar observers are not apt to see any.'[86] But Marcus's influence was not just confined to the French men of the Enlightenment (*les lumières*) and their Scottish equivalents. It may have been the example of Frederick the Great that triggered the impact on German culture, but the best critics are adamant that Goethe's *Faust* is animated by Marcus's holistic concerns. Perhaps the greatest influence of Marcus and the Stoics was on Kant, at least in his ethical writings (the major stimulus to his epistemology was self-confessedly Hume, *the* key figure of the Scottish Enlightenment). Many scholars see Kantian idealism as the working out of inchoate ideas of Epictetus and Marcus. His conception of the pre-eminent value of the Good Will, his moral indifference to external circumstances, the concern to examine whether our principles can become a universal law, and the cosmological speculations – all these breathe the spirit of Marcus Aurelius.[87]

The nineteenth century saw the cult of Marcus Aurelius at its zenith. What other figure could simultaneously appeal profoundly to Darwin, Nietzsche, Schopenhauer, Ernest Renan, Matthew Arnold and John Stuart Mill, especially as Nietzsche notoriously referred to the English empiricist as 'that blockhead Mill'? Darwin cited Marcus in his *The Descent of Man* to explain the origin of the moral sense and the influence of habitual thoughts, endorsing the emperor's view that whatever makes any bad action familiar also makes its performance much easier.[88] Renan's biography of Marcus is shrewd and insightful, still valuable today even in an era of specialised technical academic scholarship. He makes the emperor out to be a sceptic very much in the mould of Renan himself, and this view reappears in Matthew Arnold, especially in the poems 'Empedocles on Etna' and 'In Utrumque Paratus', where the Aurelian influence is palpable. Marcus is also the subject of one of Arnold's best essays where he sums him up à la Renan as follows: 'He remains the especial friend and comforter of all clear-headed and scrupulous, yet pure hearted and upward-striving men, in those ages most especially that walk by sight, not by faith, and yet have no open vision.'[89] Arnold is particularly concerned to rescue Marcus from the opprobrium of being a persecutor of Christians and suggests, in his favour, that the Romans of the late second century probably viewed Christianity much as the Victorians viewed the Mormons. His Stoic message was a gloomy one, only for the strong, and it is obvious that the new religion of Jesus Christ, with its promise of universal salvation, was more optimistic and appealing. Yet, Arnold claims, Marcus was always an 'unconscious' Christian: 'What an affinity for Christianity had this persecutor of the Christians!'[90] Arnold rates him as the greatest of the Stoics: 'the sentences of Seneca are stimulating to the intellect; the sentences of Epictetus are fortifying to the character; the sentences of Marcus Aurelius find their way to the soul'.[91]

There is a very similar attitude in John Stuart Mill's writings. Mill often has Marcus in the back of his mind (and sometimes in the forefront), as when he says that on the philosophical principle of induction, Marcus would have had every reason to suppose that Commodus would turn out virtuous.[92] For Mill, Marcus was the man who did what other Stoics merely talked about, which is what makes him superior to Epictetus.[93] Yet Mill was clearly troubled by his hero's role as the persecutor of Christians, which he often seems reluctant to admit.[94] He takes very much the Arnold line, that Marcus must have been in some sense an unconscious Christian, since his writings differ scarcely at all from the teachings of Jesus Christ – to the point where the *Meditations* and the Sermon on the Mount could be regarded as companion teachings. Mill is then led to a vigorous defence on this score. Clearly Marcus was a better Christian than most nominal Christians who have ever lived, and Mill laments that he failed to see that the new religion was an ultimate good; there was a particular irony that Christians have always regarded atheism as the great enemy, yet it was on precisely those grounds that they themselves were persecuted by the Romans.[95] Mill consoles himself with counterfactual musings on what would have happened if Christianity had been adopted as the state religion under Marcus, instead of 150 years later under Constantine. Metaphorically shaking his head, he concludes:

> The gentlest and most amiable of philosophers and rulers, under a solemn sense of duty, authorised the persecution of Christianity . . . Unless anyone who approves of punishment for the promulgation of opinions flatters himself that he is a wiser and better man than Marcus Aurelius – more deeply versed in the wisdom of his time, more elevated in his intellect above it, more earnest in his search for truth, and more singleminded in his devotion to it when found – let him abstain from that joint infallibility of himself and of the multitude which the great Antoninus made with so unfortunate a result.[96]

It was the persecution of the Christians that in Victorian England was the only thing that stood between Marcus and virtual canonisation, and it was this issue that drew out his rare critics, such as Walter Pater, aesthete and friend of Oscar Wilde. In his well-known historical novel *Marius the Epicurean*, tracing the career of a boy who was twelve when Marcus came to the throne and who eventually converts to Christianity after trying out Stoicism and Epicureanism, Pater criticises the emperor for his polytheism and his failure to see the future. Some critics view the novel as an allegory for Victorian imperialism, implicitly criticising the conduct of the British empire while apparently condemning the Roman one.[97]

In contrast to the sadness of Mill and Arnold, Marcus's attitude to the Christians was one of the many things that positively commended him to Friedrich Nietzsche, who in turn drew on Schopenhauer. In many respects Schopenhauer is as far from Marcus's stoical mental universe as is conceivable. Where Marcus, along with so many subsequent Christian thinkers, held that evil was unreal, a mere negation, not-being, the absence of good, Schopenhauer believed that Good was an illusion and that under the mask of phenomena there was only the Universal Will, which he identified with Evil. To make matters worse, he did not even allow humans the consolation of suicide, as the Stoics did, for the doctrine of eternal recurrence, which he clung to, implied in his view reincarnation and the transmigration of souls.[98] Schopenhauer was deeply influenced by Buddhism and Hindu mysticism (principally the Upanishads), which at one level should have aligned him with Marcus, but he had as much contempt for Stoicism as for Christianity (and for Islam, for that matter), famously dismissing Jesus's Law of Love by stating, 'the ancient wisdom of the human race will not be displaced by what happened in Galilee'.[99] Where Marcus often allows himself a somewhat facile and flippant attitude to death – at least we won't have to be bored by the Circus Maximus or the amphitheatre[100] – Schopenhauer espouses the darker view of Marcus's predecessor Lucretius, who claimed that even if a man was immortal, he would continue to experience the same things.[101] Schopenhauer adds to this by saying you are doomed to experience the same things even if you die, as you will be incarnated as part of the process of eternal recurrence:

> From the beginning to the end, it is repetition of the same dream, with different costumes and names . . . This identical element, which persists throughout all changes, consists in the basic qualities of the human heart and head – many of them bad; a few of them good. History's overall motto ought to be *Eadem sed aliter* [the same things only differently arranged]. One who has read Herodotus has, from a philosophical point of view, already studied enough history, for his work already contains everything which constitutes the subsequent history of the world.[102]

From the philosophical point of view, Schopenhauer – dealing with many of the same concerns as Marcus – was more logically consistent: it is indeed extremely difficult to embrace eternal recurrence *and* maintain Marcus's high-minded philosophical detachment.

It has been said that Friedrich Nietzsche, who regarded himself as Schopenhauer's successor, thought of Marcus's *Meditations* as the 'fifth gospel', but this seems unlikely given Nietzsche's contempt for Christianity and his preference for the smiting Yahweh of the Old Testament. Nevertheless, the influence of Marcus can be found in many areas of Nietzsche's thought, though naturally the emperor cannot be held responsible for Nietzsche's notorious exaggerations. Both men shared a deep admiration for Heraclitus, though in Marcus's case this went together with a reverence for both Socrates and Plato, both of whom the German sage despised.[103] What most drew Nietzsche to Marcus was his reputation as a persecutor of Christians, for in Nietzsche's view Christianity – a religion for cowards, mediocrities and (horror of horrors) women – was the scourge of mankind.[104] Like Nietzsche's other bêtes noires, democracy, liberalism, socialism and Kantianism (he loathed Kant in the same vociferous way that Schopenhauer loathed Hegel),[105] the entire thrust of Christianity is towards weakness and hatred of the strong and gifted, whom it attempts to destroy insidiously by introducing anxiety, neurosis and other poisons into social life. It follows that a man who condemned its practitioners to the beasts was, in Nietzsche's view, a true 'superman' (to use his debased term). Nietzsche is also in agreement with both Schopenhauer and Marcus on the reality of eternal recurrence, and assails organised religion for its ludicrous attempts to provide consolation for mortality. The desire for immortality and the refusal to face death are simply a specialised form of the 'sentimental senility' that is a feature of Christianity as a whole.[106] Most Aurelian of all is the embrace of destiny, where Nietzsche was directly influenced by the emperor.

> My formula for what is good in mankind is *amor fati*: not to wish for anything other than that which is; whether behind, ahead or for all eternity. Not just to put up with the inevitable – much less to hide it from oneself, for all idealism is lying to oneself in the face of the necessary – but to love it . . . Everything that is necessary when seen from above and from the perspective of the vast economy of the whole, is in itself equally useful. We must not only put up with it, but love it . . . *Amor fati*: that is my innermost nature.[107]

The Victorian era was the high-water mark of Marcus's reputation. One can see why he was so much admired by enthusiasts for the British empire like Cecil Rhodes, and why, by contrast, a Stoic ruler had far less to offer the twentieth and twenty-first centuries.[108] No one any longer takes seriously the idea of benevolent empires, and the *pax Britannica* is usually considered just as much an engine of exploitation as the *pax Romana*. The co-optation by Arnold, Renan and other Europeans in the nineteenth century led Americans to swing away from Marcus and towards Epictetus, who seemed a Stoic untainted by 'imperialism': certainly it is striking that it is Epictetus who features as the major influence on Walt Whitman, whose 'holistic' thought might otherwise be thought more in line with Marcus.[109] Despite its occasional irruption on the silver screen, the Roman world in general seems less interesting to the modern sensibility. The Victorians prized duty as the highest moral responsibility, whereas the entire thrust of modern thinking is towards rights, usually so-called 'rights' with no duties attached. The entire modern therapy industry would be in danger if people took seriously the idea that only fools blame others for their failure. To an egotistical, hedonistic modern audience, Marcus's strictures on pleasure and the indulgences of sleeping, copulating and over-eating seem neurotic, and Stoicism itself seems over-rational and joyless. Marcus still has a certain vogue, but only because his so-called modern admirers tend to cherry-pick the convenient bits of his doctrine and ignore the rest. Moreover, the twentieth century was par excellence the century of the great dictators. Max Weber made a famous threefold distinction in types of ruler: the traditional, the rational-legal and the charismatic. Whereas Marcus was the best example of a traditional ruler, all the great dictatorial figures of the twentieth century (Lenin, Stalin, Mao, Castro, Perón, Hitler, Mussolini, Franco, and so on) were charismatic rulers. In such a context studying Marcus Aurelius as a guide to how to rule well seems merely absurd.

This connects with a more general consideration. Rationalism, or the idea that reason (rather than feelings, sense-experience or authority) is the only true guide to knowledge, probably reached a peak with Kant and Hegel, and has been in decline ever since. This is why the distinguished American philosopher Brand Blanshard, himself a rationalist, chose in his book *Four Reasonable Men* to lament the decline of such men in ethical theory, instancing Renan, John Stuart Mill, Henry Sidgwick and Marcus himself as the finest of this breed.[110] The decline of Marcus can be charted at a more general philosophical level. To a large extent the post-1900 trends in philosophy have all been in directions where Marcus's thought seems irrelevant: pragmatism in the USA, logical positivism in continental Europe, linguistic analysis in

Britain. Only in three philosophical areas can one discern a continu-
ation of the themes of Marcus Aurelius: in the work of 'time-obsessed'
philosophers such as Henri Bergson (experienced time is duration, not
a sequence of moments) and J.M.E. McTaggart (the differentiation of
time into three distinct series, A, B and C, allegedly thus proving its
unreality);[111] in the neo-utilitarian and deontological work of Henry
Sidgwick and his handful of followers,[112] and in some of the recalcitrant metaphysicians like Samuel Alexander and A.N. Whitehead.[113] It
has been suggested in some quarters that the end of the road that
leads from Epictetus and Marcus is Freud, but this seems less than
convincing.[114] In modern literature, however, Marcus's influence
continues strong: here one might mention such figures as Maurice
Maeterlinck, Anatole France, Theodore Dreiser, Joseph Brodsky and
Tom Wolfe, but there are many others.[115]

If Marcus's influence on thinkers and writers down the ages is
palpable, there is more controversy about his place in the history of
autobiography, and this is not only because of conceptual problems
inherent in the genre, to say nothing of the obvious consideration
that many memoirs are simply self-serving packs of lies, designed to
show the hero as wise, underrated, neglected or unfairly maligned.[116]
Some students of the problem claim that Marcus's *Meditations* cannot
really be classed as an autobiography at all. Here is one such view:

> One must distinguish autobiography . . . from philosophical reflections
> on the self, static analysis and the self-portait – as in Marcus Aurelius,
> Boethius or Nietzsche's *Ecce Homo*, and many journals which note down
> the changing aspects of a character, like the tortured confessions of
> many pietists. What is common to all these methods is the attempt,
> by means of introspection, at a static representation of the personality.
> The autobiography is on the contrary historical in its method, and at
> the same time the representation of the self in and through its rela-
> tions with the outer world. Perhaps one might say that it involves the
> philosophical assumption that the self comes into being only through
> interplay with the outer world.[117]

But such a definition seems unacceptably purist and narrow. Far
preferable is the judgement of the distinguished classical scholar Gilbert
Murray, when speaking of Marcus Aurelius: 'Amid all the harshness

and plainness of his literary style, Marcus possessed a gift which has
been granted to few, the power of writing down what was in his heart
just as it was, not obscured by any consciousness of the presence of
witnesses or any striving after effect. He does not seem to have tried
deliberately to reveal himself, yet he has revealed himself in that short
personal notebook almost as much as the great inspired egotists,
Rousseau and St Augustine.'[118] There have been many distinguished
autobiographies that light up an era or illumine a particular historical problem – one thinks of those by Frederick Douglas, Henry Adams,
Benjamin Franklin, Thomas Huxley or even Arminius Vámbéry.
Among the important 'spiritual' autobiographies, we may list those
of St Teresa, Benvenuto Cellini, Berlioz, Tolstoy, Oscar Wilde in *De
Profundis* or George Santayana in *Persons and Places*. But Marcus's niche
in autobiography can be pinned down only if we compare him to
writers who had genuinely philosophical concerns. In this category
there are only three indisputably great autobiographies: those by
Rousseau, J.H. Newman and John Stuart Mill.

John Stuart Mill's *Autobiography* gives us a clear line on the issue of
whether the *Meditations* can be considered a true autobiography, and
the ways in which they are like and unlike conventional memoirs. Mill
was brought up on the classical authors, even studying some of the
selfsame ones in his childhood that Marcus had read. Famously, he
was put to Greek at the age of three, but did not start Latin until
eight; the contrast between him and Marcus on the one hand and the
Virgil-loving St Augustine on the other is clear. Like Marcus, Mill
claims that he was not exceptionally gifted intellectually – he did not
have a great memory, was not quick-witted or fast-thinking and lacked
energy – attributing his superiority over his contemporaries simply to
the early hothouse training by his father James Mill.[119] His father
educated him in a narrow logic-based way, emphasising reason and
social utility, with Jeremy Bentham and utilitarianism as gods, though
without cramming his mind with facts or insisting on rote learning.
James Mill strongly disliked Christianity and brought his son up without
any religious belief, espousing a form of deism. He had a strongly
Stoic personality (in the ancient sense) and in some ways could have
been a figure from the ancient world, being a curious mixture of the
Cynic, the Stoic and the Epicurean. In the Mill household intellectual
enjoyment was always rated above pleasure. Moreover, James was

vehemently anti-Romantic and regarded passionate emotions as a form of madness; 'intense' was his favourite 'boo' word.[120] John Stuart Mill had no proper childhood in any recognisable sense, but in compensation was intellectually precocious, and was an established political journalist by the age of twenty. In many ways he would have appeared as a young Marcus Aurelius. But he moved in a precisely opposite direction from Marcus, who gave up the simple joys of youth for the austerity of Stoic philosophy. At twenty Mill experienced a Pauline conversion, which he describes as follows: 'It occurred to me to put the question directly to myself, "Suppose that all your objects in life were realised; that all the changes in institutions and opinions which you are looking forward to, could be completely effected at this very instant: would this be a great joy and happiness to you?" And an irrepressible self-consciousness distinctly answered, "No!"'[121]

Mill came to feel that he had little to live for: 'I frequently asked myself, if I could, or if I was bound, to go on living, when life must be passed in this manner. I generally answered to myself, that I did not think I could possibly bear it beyond a year.'[122] He saw himself as a mere reasoning machine, not a proper human being. Indeed, his later mentor Thomas Carlyle thought that Mill's memoirs were 'the autobiography of a steam engine'.[123] In this frame of mind, in full revolt against rationalism and utilitarianism, Mill read the memoirs of Jean-François Marmontel, which convinced him he was on the wrong track. He found Wordsworth to be the perfect antidote to Bentham: 'What made Wordsworth's poems a medicine for my state of mind, was that they expressed, not mere outward beauty, but states of feeling, and of thought coloured by feeling, under the excitement of beauty. They seemed to be the very culture of the feelings, which I was in quest of. In them I seemed to draw from a source of inward joy, of sympathetic and imaginative pleasure, which could be shared in by all human beings; which had no connection with struggle or imperfection . . . From them I seemed to learn what would be the perennial source of happiness, when all the greater evils of life shall have been removed.'[124] From Wordsworth, he graduated to Coleridge, philosophically a more profound poet and also the perfect antidote to Bentham. Later there were other salient influences, principally Thomas Carlyle and the Saint-Simonians, from whom he learned to shift his political and social viewpoint from a utilitarian to an organic one.

It is tempting to see Marcus Aurelius as a kind of prefiguring of Bentham and James Mill, remorselessly repressing emotions in favour of reason, though this hardly squares with the mature John Stuart Mill's high regard for the emperor, implausible in the case of a mere 'reasoning machine'. In fact there are many points of similarity between Mill and Marcus as autobiographical writers. Many of Mill's later apothegms could have come straight from the *Meditations*: 'Those only are happy . . . who have their minds fixed on some object other than their own happiness.' 'Ask yourself whether you are happy, and you cease to be so. The only chance is to treat, not happiness, but some end external to it, as the purpose of life.'[125] Moreover, Mill's *Autobiography* is structured in terms of Marcus's beloved triads, and in a form that can be called Hegelian. First is the 'thesis' of the loveless education under James Mill; then comes the mental crisis, the repudiation of utilitarianism and the 'antithesis' when Mill turns to poetry; finally, there is the synthesis incorporating Carlyle, the Saint-Simonians and the best of Bentham and Coleridge.[126] It has been objected that Mill's autobiography evinces change and transformation, that it is existential, whereas in Marcus's work we have the model of a man already set in his views and ideas – essentialism in a word.[127] A further criticism of the *Meditations* is that, whereas someone like Girolamo Cardano, self-confessedly strongly influenced by Marcus, in his *Book of My Life* tries to tell the truth about who he is, Marcus tells us what he ought to be, but not whether he actually measures up to the paradigm, or how far short he falls. For instance, Cardano agrees with Marcus that yearning for fame is pointless, but admits he still does so; in Marcus's case we get the sermon and the moral lesson, but not the struggles and conflicts of the person behind it.[128] However, the strength of this criticism is blunted when we realise that in the *Meditations* there is still another triadic structure: the dialogue of Marcus with himself or his alter ego, and the third party in the form of the alien 'they' (others) who are so often referred to. There is conflict and transformation in the *Meditations*, but we do not see the year-by-year process, as we do in Mill's *Autobiography*. But the theme of re-education is present in both cases. Unlike St Augustine, who gave up sin to receive Spirit, Mill gave up some of his early learning to gain new values; Marcus gave up rhetoric for Stoicism. What we find in St Augustine and Mill, but not in Marcus, is genuine *redemption*.[129]

Another figure whose autobiography is relevant to the *Meditations* is John Henry Newman. Not so much philosopher-king as theologian-prince (late in life he received a cardinal's hat and thus became a prince of the Catholic Church), Newman had a sensibility in some respects like Marcus's. Introverted, withdrawn, celibate, he shared Mill's and Marcus's dislike of games, but most of all resembled the emperor in that he was a deeply conservative, and even reactionary, figure: he could not bear to look at the French tricolour flag as it was an emblem of the French Revolution.[130] Another devotee of duty and a workaholic, he composed his autobiography in long shifts, standing at his desk, often in tears, once putting in sixteen hours non-stop on the writing. If Newman's arch-critic Charles Kingsley was right, Newman possessed 'feminine' qualities and an aesthetic sense very like Marcus's. Kingsley's hypothesis was that the Reformation was the triumph of the masculine principle of Protestantism, as represented by the English and Germans, over 'feminine' Catholicism, as practised by the inferior Celts and Latins. For Kingsley, those who repudiated life and turned to solitude or meditation – and especially celibates such as nuns and priests – were in effect rebels against Nature and thus 'unnatural', perverted.[131] The one thing that clearly distinguishes Newman from Marcus is that the future cardinal had a reputation for being 'economical with the truth'. Kingsley famously accused him of covering up for Jesuitical casuistry and supporting the Roman Church, whose aim was expediency, but never truth. This could be set down as the obvious malice of an inveterate enemy, but for the fact that Newman was also suspect in the Catholic Church itself. Lord Acton called him 'a sophist, a manipulator, and not the servant of truth'.[132] His great rival Cardinal Manning, primarily concerned with social issues and social justice, detested Newman's ascetic and otherworldly detachment; like Marcus, Newman had absolutely no interest in socio-economic matters. The consensus opinion is that Manning gave paper support to the campaign to make Newman a cardinal, while really working behind the scenes to make sure this would not come about. While publicly supporting Newman's elevation to the cardinalate, he secretly thought him a heretic and condemned him as 'the most attractive and most colossal egotist that ever lived'.[133]

Having gone through three stages of Anglicanism – what one critic has called the Evangelical, Noetic and Tractarian modes – Newman converted to Catholicism in 1845 at the age of forty-four. Victorian England, which took religion with deadly seriousness, was convulsed by the event. The two great political rivals, Gladstone and Disraeli, concurred in finding the conversion seismic. 'A storm which left a wreck on every shore,' was Gladstone's characterisation, while Disraeli twenty years later called it a blow from which the Church of England still reeled.[134] Newman was branded a traitor, not just to his Church but to his country. The received view was that he should not have spent so many years working in the reform movement of the Church of England if he was finally going to abandon the Church for Rome; also that he should not have dithered for years, even leaving the Anglican communion to live as a layman, before announcing the momentous conversion. The resentment reached a head when Kingsley in effect accused him of being a hypocrite and liar, thus prompting Newman to reply with his *Apologia pro Vita Sua* in 1864. Part theological broadside, part patient argumentation and part autobiography, the *Apologia* (its Christian message apart) was in many ways reminiscent of the *Meditations*. Newman admitted that the intellectual arguments for the existence of God, provided by Anselm, Aquinas and others, did not impress him and that the one thing that prevented him from being (like Marcus) a pantheist was his belief in a transcendent deity. In his *Grammar of Assent* he would later elaborate an idiosyncratic argument for God's existence from conscience, but in the *Apologia* he declared that the 'traditional proofs' of theology 'do not warm me or enlighten me; they do not take away the winter of my desolation, or make the buds unfold and the leaves grow within me, and my moral being rejoice. The sight of the world is nothing less than the prophet's scroll, full of "lamentations, and mourning, and woe".'[135]

There are many more such 'Aurelian' passages in the *Apologia*. Like Marcus, Newman agonised over the relationship between dreams and waking life. 'I used to wish the *Arabian Nights* were true; my imagination was on unknown influences, on magical powers, and talismans . . . I thought my life might be a dream, or I an angel, and all this world a deception, my fellow-angels by a playful device concealing themselves from me, and deceiving me with the semblance of a material world.'[136] Interestingly, one of the criticisms of the *Apologia* as autobiography is that, like the *Meditations*, it enables us to get to know the author intellectually, but not directly or imaginatively. Certainly the most striking passage in all the *Apologia* is one that, on a blind reading, could be assumed to be one of the longer passages from the *Meditations*:

> To consider the world in its length and breadth, its various history, the many races of man, their starts, their fortunes, their mutual alienation, their conflicts; and then their ways, habits, governments, forms of worship, their enterprises, their aimless courses, their random achievements and acquirements, the impotent conclusion of long-standing facts, the token so faint and broken of superintending design, the blind evolution of what turn out to be great powers or truths, the progress of things, as if from unreasoning elements, not towards final causes, the greatness and littleness of man, his far-reaching aims, his short duration, the curtains hung over his futurity, the disappointment of life, the defeat of good, the success of evil, physical pain, mental anguish, the prevalence and intensity of sin, the pervading idolatries, the corruptions, the dreary hopeless irreligion . . . all this is a vision to dizzy and appal; and inflicts upon the mind the sense of a profound mystery, which is absolutely beyond human solution.[137]

Marcus, Mill and Newman were all highly talented men, morally strenuous, learned, with firm moral purpose and all in their own way writers with a striking way with words. But to none of them could one apply the word 'genius', which so easily fits the brilliant autodidact and visionary Jean-Jacques Rousseau. His *Discourse on Inequality* and *The Social Contract* have a profundity as political theory excelled only by Marx and rarely, if ever, since. He was a musicologist and composer of high talent, and his opera *Le Devin du Village* has survived to be recorded by digital technology. As to the measure of Rousseau's genius, it has been well said that 'it took Kant to *think* Rousseau's thoughts and it took Freud to "think" Rousseau's feelings'.[138] The price Rousseau had to pay is the one hallowed by cliché, for 'mad genius' is the facile tag by which original creativity is so often summed up. In Rousseau's case, sadly, the cliché was appropriate. He was a character whose psychological complexity only Dostoevsky could do justice to. As for the roots of his madness, there have been almost as many theories as commentators. The nineteenth century tended to dismiss him with vague bromides such as 'a degenerate', a 'morbid genius', a man with a 'neuropathic constitution'. With more precision the twentieth century has tried to pin him down with various diagnostic labels. Rousseau himself mentioned a mysterious problem with his bladder or urethra, which some have interpreted as uraemia, producing delusional incidents. Others have opted for schizophrenia, itself perceived as increasingly problematical as a diagnosis. Inevitably, that old favourite 'latent homosexuality' has also made its appearance in the literature.[139] What seems clear from Rousseau's own *Confessions* is that he had an appetite for suffering and talk of suffering, hinting at a sadomasochistic personality, and that he was terribly afflicted by persecution mania and paranoia. In the words of a leading Rousseauist: 'The *Confessions* are the plea of a hunted man who feels, rightly or wrongly, that terrible accusations hang over him.'[140]

What has drawn modern critics so irresistibly to the *Confessions* is that Rousseau wrote it like a novel and devoted a good deal of attention to his childhood. His mother died giving birth to him, and he himself was nearly rejected as stillborn. This fact alone seems to have engendered a curious ambivalence in him, almost as though, having survived, it was his duty to ensure that no one similarly circumstanced should ever survive again; he tells us that he would never take responsibility for a sick child, even if guarantees were given that it would live to the age of eighty;[141] actually, as we shall see, he would not even take responsibility for healthy ones. Taught as a child that sex was repulsive and always thereafter sexually confused, he 'was incapable of desiring an actual woman or seeking to possess her. Desire was a sort of effervescence, and ardour, without object, or with too many objects.'[142] He derived an odd satisfaction from being punished. When chastised by his aunt, Rousseau reported that he sought by fresh offences 'a return of the same chastisement; for a degree of sensuality had mingled with the smart and shame, which left more desire than fear of a repetition'.[143] However, he was less than pleased to be beaten by his uncle for a misdemeanour he did not commit, for the sense of injustice overwhelmed the basic sadomasochistic urges. Born and bred in Geneva, he left school at twelve and the city itself at sixteen, fleeing to Savoy, where he made an opportunistic and insincere conversion to Catholicism. He worked as a lackey for a Madame de Vercelli, but at her death was accused of having stolen a ribbon from her. He fastened the blame for this on a quite innocent maid.[144] Next he was befriended by Madame de Warenne, like himself a convert from Protestantism. Combining an exaggerated need for tenderness with a ruthless and unscrupulous personality, Rousseau called her 'maman' and continued to do so, even after he became her lover. Madame de Warenne was herself a psychological oddity who could not exist outside a *ménage à trois*. When the third partner died some years later – for Rousseau spent nine years in the household of Madame de Warenne – he consoled himself with the thought that he would inherit the man's wardrobe.[145]

When Madame de Warenne took another lover, Rousseau could stand the situation no more and struck out on his own. There followed a picaresque series of adventures and amours: for a while he was private secretary to a mysterious figure who represented himself as an archimandrite on the way to the Holy Land; on another occasion he had an affair with a rich woman while posing as a Scottish Jacobite named Duddington.[146] An episode when he was secretary to the French ambassador in Venice ended disastrously and then, in 1745 at the age of thirty-three, Rousseau took up with a servant named Thérèse de Vasseur, with whom he lived for the rest of his life, though not in state of monogamous fidelity. She bore him five children, all of whom he callously took at once to the foundling hospital, which in those days was a virtual sentence of death.[147] In 1749 Diderot persuaded him to enter a competition, with a prize offered by the Academy for an essay on the benefits conferred on mankind by the arts and sciences. Rousseau's negative and nihilistic essay won him the prize. At first he was euphoric: 'The news that my Discourse on the Arts and Sciences had won the prize of the Dijon Academy reawakened all the ideas that had dictated it to me, animated them with new force, and finally set fermenting in my heart that first yeast of heroism and virtue that my father, my fatherland, and Plutarch had planted there in my childhood. I judged nothing greater or more beautiful than to be free and virtuous, lofted above fortune and men's opinion, and to be sufficient unto myself.'[148]

But the triumph turned out to be a false dawn. Rousseau proved unable to stomach criticism and his paranoia became overt as he related that 'My discourse had no sooner appeared than the defenders of letters fell upon me as they had agreed with each other to do.'[149] He identified the ringmasters in the conspiracy against him as Diderot, d'Holbach and Grimm, but thought others were involved, including Voltaire. Almost by pre-established harmony, his health broke down with what he calls 'nephritic colic' and bladder problems, which modern critics identify as uraemia. He fully expected to die: 'I forever abandoned all projects of fortune and advancement, and resolved to pass in independence and poverty the little time I had to exist. I made every effort of which my mind was capable to break down the fetters of prejudice, and courageously to do everything that was right without giving myself the least concern about the judgement of others.'[150] Convinced that he had lost all his friends simply because he had committed the 'crime' of achieving literary success, and overwhelmed by the thought of an 'odious conspiracy' being directed against him, Rousseau retreated further and further into madness. Hume tried to befriend him, but the brief friendship ended in disaster when Rousseau's persecution mania engulfed him. He managed to make just one friend in later life, another singular oddity, George Keith, Earl Marischal, the Scottish confidant of Frederick the Great, but Rousseau remained convinced that his real life had ended for ever when Diderot, by encouraging him to enter for the Dijon prize, tempted him with the apple of fame out of the Eden of simplicity.[151] He now saw himself as a man alone, a perfect Ishmael, at war with the *philosophes*, who in his view wanted to throw out the bath water of social solidarity with the baby of corrupt social institutions. Even the success of his later writings, including his masterpiece. *The Social Contract* and his opera *Le Devin du Village*, could not console him.

Rousseau had read Epictetus and been particularly impressed by the Stoic sage's advice that we should live life as if we were acting on a stage.[152] Marcus had added to the insight, advocating bringing imagination to the role we are assigned by Fate or God. If we are actors, the script is fixed and the director knows the general effects he wishes to achieve. But it is still open to us as actors to turn in a brilliant performance or be content with a dud one; we should aim to steer between too much pride and too much resignation. Rousseau took this to heart when trying to come to terms with the wrong turning he had taken while listening to Diderot's encouragement about the Dijon prize in the Bois de Vincennes in 1749.[153] He tried to become another man, as Epictetus suggested, but ended up merely alienated and inauthentic. He continued being 'another person' until 1756 when he made the Thoreau-like decision to abandon city life and live in the forest.[154] Yet as soon as he tried to return to the 'state of Nature', he experienced violent mood swings and found himself unable to recapture the tranquillity of his pre-literary existence. Rousseau was in fact, by Epictetus's lights, a very bad actor. He had not merely played a role, but lost himself in falsehood. By trying to return to a false past in 1756, he became the thing he had elsewhere condemned – a zealot – for now he was a self-confessed zealot for virtue, a man who saw everything in black or white with no irony, detachment, nuance, ambiguity or what Keats would later call 'nega-tive capability'. In this disabled state he found himself unable to lie.[155] The final irony was that the man who once travelled under pseudo-nyms as Vassore or Duddington, forgot how to conceal his own name, once a warrant was issued for his arrest after falling foul of European governments for 'blasphemy'. Even though his very freedom was at stake, he found himself unable to disobey virtue and tell so much as a white lie. 'I must tell you . . . that in passing from Dijon I had to give my name, and that, although I picked up the pen with the inten-tion of substituting my mother's name for my own I could not go through with it. My hand trembled so much that I was obliged to put the pen down twice. In the end, the name Rousseau was the only one I could write, and my only dishonesty was to eliminate the initial J. from one of my first names.'[156]

We have come a long way from Marcus Aurelius and the world of the *Meditations*. No Stoic would have any time for Rousseau's posturings and preenings, his self-pity, exhibitionism and self-deceptionism. Cicero and Epictetus would have gulped when reading Rousseau's egoistic effusions, liberally scattered through the *Confessions*. 'I have entered upon a performance which is without precedent, whose accomplishment will have no imitator. I intend to present my fellow-mortals with a man in the integrity of nature; and this man shall be myself.' 'I know my heart and have studied men; I am not made like any one I have met, perhaps like no one in existence. If not better, I at least claim originality, and whether Nature did wisely in breaking the mould with which she formed me, can only be determined after reading these books'. 'My confessions are necessarily connected with those of many other people: I write both with the same frankness in everything that relates to what has happened to me; and I am not obliged to spare any person more than myself, although it is my wish to do it. I am determined always to be just and true, to say of others all the good I can, never speaking of evil except when it relates to my own conduct, and there is a necessity for my so doing.' 'Since my name is to live, it is my duty to endeavour to transmit with it to posterity the remembrance of the unfortunate man by whom it was borne, such as he really was, and not such as his unjust enemies incessantly tried to describe him.'[157] We have spoken of acting, and the appropriate comment on this must at one level be: what a performance! Marcus would have been horrified by the self-pity and paranoia, the illusion of searching for the self when the proper task of the Stoic is to extinguish the self, the humbug and hypocrisy of a man who set himself up as a theorist of education, yet acted so cruelly and callously to his own children, who were not as vulnerable to early mortality as Roman children. Marcus teaches us to despise the opinions of others and not to strive for posthumous fame, yet Rousseau is desperately preoccupied by both. In fleeing to the forests, he tries to recapture the past[158] – the very definition of 'false consciousness' by Marcus on about half a dozen different counts. Most of all, he would have been horrified at the elevation of passion and emotion above reason. 'The heart has its reasons which the mind knows nothing of' – originally a thought of Pascal, but at the core of Rousseau's thought – would have struck any Stoic as the most egregious fallacy.

Yet it is not just that we can shed light on Marcus by studying Rousseau, following what Mill called the 'method of difference'. Nor is it necessarily valid to say that Rousseau's insights are likely to be more cogent, since he often knew what it was like to be hungry and penniless, as Marcus never did. At a superficial level, it is true that to come to Rousseau after Marcus is to encounter the world turned upside down. At a deeper level, however, we can even build sympathetic links between these two figures, seemingly so unlike. The detestation of cities and the praise of solitude in Rousseau is an echo of similar thoughts in the *Meditations*.[159] The fanatical dislike of injustice in Rousseau could be sanctioned too in Marcus's writings, even though no Roman would take it to the Rousseau extent of chasing cockerels and other 'alpha male' animals who tried to lord it over their inferiors in herds and barnyards.[160] Duty too is a watchword common to both. Finally, a list of Rousseau's apothegms might well puzzle the reader as to their source, which could well be from a Stoic philosopher. 'Nothing vigorous or great can come from a totally venal pen.' 'The thirst after happiness is never extinguished in the heart of man.' 'There is no true felicity without virtue.' 'Those in a superior situation are never better nor happier than those they command.' 'Having found so many good people in my youth, why do I find so few in my age? Is their race extinct?' 'We should always carefully avoid putting our interest in competition with our duty, or promise ourselves felicity from the misfortunes of others.'[161] Although Rousseau was self-deceiving, a humbug, a liar, a ruthless, unscrupulous and even cruel man, in his own confused way he aimed at what Plato called The Good, just as Marcus did. There is a peculiar honesty even in his pathological ravings. It is doubtful if Marcus himself would have dissented from Rousseau's most basic ambition: 'To be beloved by everyone who knew me was my most ardent wish.'[162]

To be an influence on the ages and a precursor of the art of autobiography would be enough fame for anyone, but Marcus has still more strings to his bow. He was also one of that rare breed of men who have been soldier, statesman and writer; many have been two of the three, but few have attained the triple. Very few historical figures truly qualify for this accolade: for example, to admit Churchill, we would have to accredit his youthful experiences in the Sudan and South Africa as true soldiering. Trotsky is another problematical figure. There can be no doubts about his credentials in politics and literature, but, simply as founder and commander of the Red Army and People's Commissar of War, does he really qualify as a soldier, even if he did weld the Soviet fighting men into a professional and disciplined force? There can of course be no doubts about the claims of Julius Caesar, and in many ways he makes the most realistic and credible point of comparison with Marcus. His merits as one of the great captains of the ages and as a supremely talented politician (whatever estimate we put on his ultimate ends) are unchallengeable. He is also famously a writer of clear and direct prose, but here he loses much stature when placed alongside Marcus. As writers, Churchill and Julius Caesar make a natural pair. Churchill's six volumes on the Second World War are worthless as history, full of falsehood and distortions, uninformative or ignorant about the Eastern Front or the war in the Pacific, and always making the writer out to be all-wise and foreseeing. If mistakes were made, it was always the fault of incompetent subordinates: notoriously Churchill concealed the fact that he was receiving Ultra intercepts, to make his decisions appear all the more sagacious and statesmanlike.[163] Julius Caesar is in the same mould. His main aim in writing his *Gallic Wars* was not to present an objective history of his conquest of Gaul, but to burnish his image, to make propaganda and promote his ulterior political aims. As with Churchill, he blames all setbacks and defeats on subordinates and claims that all his enemies were driven by a lust for power, but he alone by the pursuit of virtue.[164] As a writer Caesar had two main aims. Since he was absent from Rome for ten years from 58 BC, he had to keep his name constantly before the Roman people. This he did by writing dispatches from the front in serial form, rather as Dickens would later write his books in this manner. The serialisation accounts for the famous Homeric nods, as when Caesar tells us that the Nervii were annihilated in 57 BC, only for them to reappear magically with a population of 60,000 in 51.[165] A highly talented manipulator, orator and propagandist, Caesar knew how to tap into the 'collective self-image' of the literate Roman, how to reinforce all the traditional motifs and raise them to a new height.[166] He aimed for the equilibrium point at all levels, cleverly using a vocabulary of no more than 1,300 words, avoiding all Greek on the one hand and colloquialisms on the other, to produce a 'universal' classless form of Latin.[167]

Where Caesar's writings functioned as a propagandist newspaper, full of both *suppressio veri* and *suggestio falsi*, Marcus's writings, never intended for publication, were utterly truthful. Given that Caesar was a man who worshipped power and ambition, his high talents as general and politician are to some extent diluted by his tendentious writings, even if the quality of his prose is peerless. Marcus Aurelius had only modest success as a statesman, and no one could accuse him of being a great literary stylist. Yet his achievements in warfare were more durable than Caesar's and his writing more truthful. The 'mixed' achievements of Marcus in the triple role of soldier, statesman and author are probably more closely parallelled by the career of Ulysses S. Grant: greater than Marcus as a general, but a far lesser figure as a politician, and usually considered one of the worst US presidents ever. Yet as a writer of prose Grant is in Caesar's class. Interestingly, though, he sprinkles his *Personal Memoirs* with some very Aurelian observations. His dislike of bullfights, which he calls 'sickening', recalls Marcus's distaste for the arena.[168] He has no relish for mindless violence and, recording his disappoval of 'the code of honour', says: 'No doubt a majority of the duels fought have been for want of moral courage on the part of those engaged to decline.'[169] Many of his experiences and reactions recall those of Marcus, with the cholera outbreak that attacked his regiment on the way from New York to California via Panama (leading to the death of one-third of them) standing in for the Antonine plague.[170] In a deserted one-room shack on the slopes of Popocatapetl in Mexico he shared experiences surely similar to those endured by Marcus on the Danube in the depths of winter. 'It was very cold and the rain fell in torrents. A little higher up the rain ceased and the snow began. The wind blew with great velocity. The log-cabin we were in had lost the roof entirely on one side, and on the other it was hardly better than a sieve. There was little or no sleep that night.'[171]

Many of his observations are more elegantly expressed versions of sentiments found in the *Meditations*: 'Experience proves that the man who obstructs a war in which his nation is engaged, no matter whether right or wrong, occupies no enviable place in life or history. Better for him, individually, to advocate "war, pestilence and famine" than to act as obstructionist for a war already begun . . . The most favourable posthumous history the stay-at-home can hope for – is oblivion.'[172] 'My later experience has taught me two lessons: first, that things are seen plainer after the events have occurred; second, that the most confident critics are generally those who know the least about the matter criticised.'[173] Grant, though a fine general, was no glory-hunter. He confesses that he felt out of his depth when appointed to command a regiment in 1861, and it is hard not to imagine that Marcus felt similarly at the beginning of the German campaign.[174] Marcus stretching out his hands in pity to the German captives on the Aurelian column seems echoed by Grant's reflections: 'While a battle is raging one can see his enemy mowed down by the thousand, or the ten thousand, with great composure; but after the battle those scenes are distressing, and one is naturally disposed to do as much to alleviate the suffering of an enemy as of a friend.'[175] Finally, Grant could almost have been thinking of Marcus and the Christians when he wrote: 'If a sect sets up its laws as binding above the State laws, whenever the two come into conflict this claim must be resisted and suppressed at whatever cost.'[176]

The fourth and final category in an assessment of Marcus as a man for the ages is in some ways the most intriguing: that of the philosopher-king. Rulers with significant cerebral publications to their credit are rare indeed. Perhaps the most obvious comparisons are the ones that both Arnold and Renan made: with Alfred the Great and Louis IX of France, better known as St Louis. Alfred is a creature of myth in more senses than one, and both his political and literary careers are controversial.[177] But it is certain that he translated Boethius's *The Consolation of Philosophy* into prose and then used it as the basis for his own poem 'The Lays of Boethius' before producing his idiosyncratic work of musings, *Blostman* or 'Blooms'.[178] Certainly influenced by St Augustine and Boethius, and hence by Marcus, Alfred has been accused of 'a curious lack of historical imagination',[179] but then this is a fault that could be laid at the door of all classical authors, and indeed all medieval ones up to and including Machiavelli. A more interesting comparison in many ways is that between Marcus and St Louis. Like his great forerunner, St Louis always suffered bad health, but shared the hatred of his Church for the body, a motif detectable in Marcus's writings. His saintliness is thought analogous to Marcus's Stoic resignation; his hostility to the Jews mirrors that of Marcus towards the Christians; and, like Marcus, he campaigned extensively for what he thought a vital cause, going on two separate crusades.[180] After St Louis one has to move forward to the eighteenth century to find other possible candidates as philosopher-king. Frederick the Great is often cited and he has claims, both because he expressly modelled himself on Marcus and because he surrounded himself with other philosophers, or at least *philosophes*, most notably Voltaire. His 1739 work the *Anti-Machiavel* was meant to be in the Aurelian idiom. A vigorous attack on Machiavelli for his advocacy of murder, plunder, the occupation or annexation of foreign lands, scorched-earth policies and all the other atrocities that the Florentine prescribed, Frederick's work aimed to decant all that was valuable from Machiavelli's thought and jettison the rest: he supported him, for example, in his glorification of militarism and detestation of mercenary armies. The irony, of course, was that Frederick was exactly the kind of ruler Machiavelli had yearned for in *The Prince*.[181] A better candidate as philosopher-king was probably Frederick's contemporary Pope Benedict XIV, a liberal pontiff, able politician and author of a learned book on miracles. However, it is difficult to see any overlap in his case with Marcus if only because, like Abe Lincoln, he had a highly developed sense of humour.[182]

The historical personage who has most closely approached the Marcus model of philosopher-king is the South African statesman Jan Christian Smuts, though opinions differ on his merits both as ruler and philosopher. After a brilliant career as a lawyer, he led Boer forces in a 'commando' in Transvaal during the South African War of 1899–1902 before emerging as a notably pro-British politician. In the First World War he directed the operations that captured German South-West Africa, and as General Smuts he was British Army supremo in the East Africa campaign. From 1917 to 1919 he served in Lloyd George's War Cabinet. Becoming Prime Minister of South Africa, he also served in Churchill's 1940–5 War Cabinet and was given the rank of field marshal in the British Army in 1941. A founding father of the Royal Air Force, the League of Nations and the United Nations, Smuts was the only person to sign the peace treaties ending both World Wars.[183] The main political criticisms of Smuts are twofold. In his own country he was considered too close to the British Establishment, and this fact caused him to be unseated in 1948 by the Nationalist Party, which introduced the policy of apartheid. More generally, he was considered a humbug, forever orating to international audiences about problems of world peace while neglecting the dire problems of South Africa itself. By modern standards a racist, Smuts did not believe in equality for what he habitually referred to as 'coloured people', but had no coherent conception of what the future for a racially divided South Africa might be. Smuts is interesting as fulfilling also the Caesar-Grant criteria of soldier-statesman-writer mentioned above, even if his promotion to field marshal in 1941 was made on political rather than military grounds, and was the British Establishment's reward to a loyal servant who was in all senses *plus royaliste que le roi*. His many critics say that, like Marcus, he spent too much time speculating on abstract philosophy when he should have been attending to pressing matters of state.

In philosophical terms, Smuts was the modern figure who, more than anyone, carried forward that part of Marcus's ideas that we can call 'holism'. To establish his significance, we have to return for a moment to Epictetus and Marcus. In the words of Epictetus: 'God has made everything that is in the universe and the universe in its entirety free of constraint and independent: but he made the parts of the Whole for the sake of the Whole. Other beings lack the capability of understanding the divine administration: but rational beings possess the inner resources which allow them to reflect upon this universe. They can reflect that they are part of it, and on what kind of a part they are; and that it is good for the parts to yield to the whole.'[184] Marcus took over this view – later to be given a dramatic facelift by Hegel – that, properly considered, all phenomena in the universe ultimately link with everything else. The *Meditations* contain the first explicit reference to what would later be considered the vitalist or holistic view of the universe, as against the mechanised atomism of Democritus.[185] The Stoics took over the belief from early Ionian philosophy that all bodies are animated, that a spirit runs through the whole universe, and that each part of the whole, besides participating in the life of the world, contains its own vital principles; even Galen, no orthodox Stoic, believed in holism.[186] In Marcus's work we can even see an anticipation of Hegel's famous ternary form, for at many points in the *Meditations* we see one triad intersecting with another. So, for example, the three activities of the soul (justice, desire and impulse) interpenetrate with the three domains of reality and the three principal rules of Stoicism. So when the faculty of judgement links to the domain of reality, the correct inner attitude engendered is objectivity. When desire links to universal nature in the domain of reality, the correct inner attitude emerges as the acceptance of destiny. Similarly the impulse towards action links with human nature and produces the correct inner attitude of justice and altruism.[187] The idea of the subtle interrelatedness of all phenomena is what Pope was referring to in his 'Vast chain of Being, which from God began'[188] and what the physicist Sir Oliver Lodge referred to when he wrote: 'Things which appear disconnected, like stars, are ultimately connected or united by something which is by no means obvious to the senses and has to be inferred.'[189] The idea has had a long history both in philosophy and poetry. The eighteenth-century poet Edward Young spoke of:

> Connexion exquisite of distant worlds
> Distinguished link in Being's endless chain.[190]

William Blake famously praised the ability:

> To see a World in a grain of sand
> And a Heaven in a wild flower
> Hold Infinity in the palm of your hand
> And Eternity in an hour.[191]

And the nineteenth-century poet Francis Thompson, anticipating modern 'chaos theory', wrote:

> All things by immortal power
> Near or far,
> Hiddenly,
> To each other linked are
> That thou canst not stir a flower
> Without troubling of a star.[192]

The 1920s in philosophy was what one might call the golden age of metaphysics, and Smuts's book *Holism and Evolution* (1926) was part of a process that embraced Alexander's *Space, Time and Deity* (1920), Lloyd Morgan's *Emergent Evolution* and Whitehead's *Process and Reality*. All these metaphysical systems were an attempt to fuse the Hegelian tradition of Absolute Idealism with the new scientific findings, especially those coming from biology and physics, and to square the most attractive ideas from idealism (for example, on the nature of relations) with philosophical realism. All were agreed that metaphysics could not aspire to be supra-scientific and transcend science (as in Hegel); any metaphysics worth its salt must accord with science and differ only in its greater comprehensiveness. Smuts was nothing if not intellectually audacious. He claimed that Bergson, then all the rage, went wrong in elevating Time above Space, but Alexander went wrong in elevating Space above Time.[193] As Smuts saw it, Alexander's notion of Space-Time was not the space-time of Einstein's relativity theory, but simply an updating of the theory of motion in Heraclitus. Alexander had tried to solve the mind/body problem by pointing out that the very same experience that can be 'enjoyed' as a mental process can be 'contemplated' as a neural one. But Smuts argued that this 'neural monism' did not go far enough. The mind/body problem was simply a manifestation of a more fundamental reality – holism. The idea of systematic interpenetration made more sense than the idea of mind and body as primary realities interacting, or of pre-established harmony as preached by Leibniz, or even the attempt to solve the problem by postulating a mediating agency, whether 'ether', extra-sensory perception or something else.[194] As for Lloyd Morgan's vitalism, this was simply Aristotle's entelechy brought up to date. Vitalism offended against Ockham's razor by producing a *deus ex machina*, which is not needed once the concept of holism is grasped.[195] Smuts also thought his version of holism was superior to Whitehead's process.

Having finished throat-clearing, so to speak, and shown to his own satisfaction at least that he was the greatest metaphysician of the 1920s, Smuts proceeded to outline how the theory of holism, as old as the Stoics, made sense of modern science. Marcus had loved his triads, but now Smuts introduced one of his own: matter, life and mind.[196] Matter was largely the province of the theory of relativity and quantum theory, perhaps especially Einstein's breakthrough. Smuts argued, following Whitehead, that a general theory of relativity was deducible from philosophy without recourse to Einstein's clocks, measuring rods, tensors and constants like the velocity of light. Even Einstein's General Theory of Relativity was, on this analysis, merely a Special Theory of Holism and, as such, secondary to Smuts's own general theory.[197] Smuts argued, first that the 'instants' or 'moments' seemingly required by physics were a mere abstraction from the fundamental process of duration, but that Bergson had gone wrong in trying to reduce all reality to the single concept of Duration; duration itself was only part of the whole. Another name for the whole was Space-Time, not as conceived by Einstein or Alexander, but as a dialectical process of Nature, which also replaced the either-or of Newton's objective and independent universe or Kant's ultimate reality of the subjective categories of experience.[198] Life was principally represented by Darwin and the theory of evolution, and Smuts claimed to be smoothing off the rough edges of neo-Darwinism. Properly understood, the atoms of physics correlated with the cells of biology, though the cell was more complex.[199] What was valuable about the theory of evolution was its projection into the future. Most previous metaphysics had located the explanation of the universe in the past, and evolution (though that word was not used) was simply the unfolding of a pre-determined structure, as in Hegel's Idea. Evolution, properly considered, was emergent and created new forms, it was a 'nisus' into the future, and was on the side of freedom against determinism. Although Smuts agreed with Hegel that ultimately everything links with everything else, he thought there was operating in Hegel a mechanistic logic, whereas future-looking evolution replaced this with 'process'.[200]

If Smuts was content to have Einstein as the prophet of physics (Matter) and Darwin of biology (Life), he reserved for himself the role of interpreter of Mind, the third aspect of his ternary metaphysic. Philosophical idealism, he thought, went astray in simply excerpting one aspect of the whole and mistaking it for the entirety. But both Western and Eastern philosophy are at fault for devaluing the body.[201] Mind is simply one aspect of holism, but has no privileged position. Truly to understand Nature is to understand that no one feature of its multifaceted mosaic is primary; here Smuts edges very close to Marcus's pantheism.[202] Sure enough, Smuts is soon invoking the poets, especially Wordsworth, as the only true interpreters of reality, emphasising the fluidity and plasticity of the universe. 'The intimate rapport with Nature is one of the most precious things in life . . . the emotional appeal of Nature is tremendous, sometimes almost more than one can bear.'[203] According to holism, there is no conflict between science and poetry or even between science and the numinous, so long as we are not talking about organised religion. Soon Smuts is talking very much like an Eastern sage: 'There is not a problem of Metaphysics, of ethics, of Art, and even of Religion which will not benefit enormously from contact with the concept of holism.' 'Holism comprises all the wholes in the universe.' 'The Einstein standpoint of relativity is not only the soundest science, it is fundamental to psychology.'[204] Smuts comes close to the Platonic view of the 'world soul' that would later so heavily influence C.G. Jung – and we should remember that this was one of the aspects of Platonism that Marcus too had taken over.[205]

It would be a mistake to over-emphasise the points of similarity between Marcus and Smuts. Science had no cachet in the ancient world, and Smuts's optimistic anticipation of the future fusion of science and philosophy, engendering a general synthesis whereby the particular became reconciled to the general and the concrete to the universal,[206] would have been meaningless to a Stoic sage. There is a Panglossian quality in Smuts (perhaps derived from Leibniz, who influenced him so deeply) that is alien to Marcus. Nor would he have understood Smuts's insistence (which he shared with Jung) that holistic speculations were 'scientific'.[207] Smuts's tirade against academic specialisation would not have meant much either in the second century, an era of limited knowledge. One of Smuts's favourite arguments was that the great men of the past – Goethe, Shakespeare, Leonardo da Vinci, Aristotle – all straddled a continuum composed of what for lesser men would comprise discrete academic disciplines; this is alien to the holistic personality.[208] But the enthusiasm for Nature would have struck a chord, as would Smuts's belief that evil is unreal and partial when considered from the standpoint of the Whole.[209] The implicit pantheism and pan-psychism would, moreover, have been received enthusiastically, for Smuts insisted that holism was a unitary principle that explained not only chemistry, biology, physics and psychology, but also the 'absolute' values of truth, beauty and goodness.[210] Many of Smut's apothegms could have come from the *Meditations*. 'Beauty in Nature is holistic.' 'If you substitute "whole" for matter, life and the soul, you can explain them all better.' 'When we speak of Nature or the Universe as a Whole or The Whole, we merely mean Nature or the Universe considered as organic.'[211] Smuts's views were severely criticised, and not just for being a seam-bursting eclectic melange of Plato, Leibniz, Darwin, Einstein and Wordsworth. If everything is a whole, it was objected, knowledge becomes impossible, for we would have to know everything before we could know anything. More generous critics will be intrigued by the echo that Marcus's ideas struck in an inter-war statesman. When one considers that very similar ideas were entertained by Buddha on the banks of the Ganges in the fifth century BC, by Marcus on the banks of the Tiber (or Danube) in the second century AD and by Smuts in the twentieth century, it is hard not to agree that there is something in the idea of holism. Truly Marcus Aurelius was a man for all ages.

Appendix One: Stoicism

What was the attraction of this Stoic philosophy that Marcus embraced so avidly? Fully to penetrate the world of the Stoics, one needs a deep background in the theories of Plato and Aristotle, not to mention the so-called Presocratic philosophers, but certain guidelines are clear. To understand Stoicism, we have to appreciate that the ancients viewed the world in a fundamentally different way from most moderns. The notion that the universe, and human life within it, might be meaningless was to them almost incomprehensible; their mental world was obsessed with the quest for meaning, based on the conviction that there really were keys that could unlock the secrets of the cosmos. The philosopher was paid, and given university chairs, in the expectation that he could explain to lesser mortals what these secrets were. How did the world come about? What is the meaning of history? Who or what is God and what are his attributes? What should we do to be happy and live the good life? This was the ancient meaning of philosophy, which still survives in demotic usage today, but which is repudiated by all modern philosophers, who concern themselves with technical issues of no interest to the man in the street and expect each individual to answer the traditional questions himself. Ancient philosophers were all convinced that life must have some purpose – hence the ubiquity of the concept of *logos*, a favourite Marcus Aurelius notion (and one to which we will return later). Only after the Romantic movement could people conceive of unhappy endings as the natural end of human life and accept that the entire human experience might be meaningless; the most famous expression of this viewpoint is Friedrich Nietzsche's 'God is Dead'. Ancient philosophy, then – including Stoicism – was close to what we would think of as religion or theology.

Another fundamental tenet of ancient philosophy was that in some sense all phenomena must interconnect – the belief that in modern parlance would be called holism. Although the ethical dimension of Stoicism was its most important aspect, the founders of the doctrine thought it axiomatic that before you could proceed to ethics, you had to lay out a cosmological stall in which there would also be a complementary theory of physics and logic. The originator of Stoicism, Zeno of Citium (335–263 BC), whose writings survive only in fragments, said that philosophy is like an orchard, in which logic is the walls, physics the trees and ethics the fruit; or like an egg, in which logic is the shell, physics the white and ethics the yolk.[1] It cannot be said that the Stoics ever did any important work in physics, apart perhaps from Posidonius (c. 135–51 BC), a Syrian Greek who did original work in astronomy (his estimate of the distance of the sun from the Earth is the best in the ancient world) and worked out that one could sail westwards from Cadiz and eventually reach India.[2] There were many other early followers of Zeno: Cleanthes, Panaetius and Aristo of Chios, who caught the imagination of the young Marcus Aurelius. But it was Chrysippus (280–207 BC), to whom Fronto often refers disparagingly, who put Stoicism on a systematic basis. Supposedly the author of 705 books, he laid out the basic cosmology behind the theory. The fundamental element in the universe is fire, and the human spirit or soul is composed of fire and air (*pneuma*) – the breath of life; the body is made of earth and water.[3] There was no uniformity among the Stoics on whether the soul survives death. Some said the bodily elements remained on Earth after death, but the fiery part of the soul would rejoin the fire burning in heaven; others, such as Zeno himself, were thoroughgoing materialists, impatient with all such speculation.[4] But fire was a central motif in the metaphysics of the Stoics, which has led some scholars to believe that the origin of the doctrine was Eastern, and that Stoicism represented a syncretism of Chaldean religion and Greek philosophy. The fire motif is clear in the Stoic belief that the world would ultimately be destroyed by fire. But far more Eastern – Buddhist even – is the accompanying notion of eternal recurrence: after the destruction, the whole process would begin again, and so ad infinitum; everything that happens has already happened before hundreds of times and will recur in the future.[5] Stoicism was at root a pantheistic belief-system, but there is a lack of clarity in the thinking about God and gods that is one of its internal weaknesses.

Interesting as such ideas are to specialists, it was only the ethical ideas of Stoicism that enabled it to survive and not be simply another obscure mystery religion. The expression 'virtue is its own reward' has become a cliché, but to the Stoics virtue was the sole good; morality consisted in being virtuous, and virtue meant willing oneself to live according to Nature, to accept whatever happened as God's providence, never to use a utilitarian calculus or think about the consequences of one's actions. For example, if a wise (that is, virtuous) man saw his child in danger of drowning, he would try to save it, but if he failed he would accept the outcome without tears, lamentation, distress or self-pity.[6] Since everything that happens is governed by divine providence, his failure, and the drowning, must have been for the best, even if he could not see why. Since moral virtue is the only good, and wickedness the only evil, by definition the child's death could not have been evil. Since moral virtue is the only good, the wise and virtuous man has already done all he could, so there is nothing for him to regret. From the point of view of virtue, suffering and joy are equivalent; there are lots of pleasures we *prefer* to pain, but they are not good in themselves. Happiness is virtue, it has nothing to do with pleasure or joy. Not losing one's children does not make us more virtuous, therefore it does not make us happier. Stoicism is thus the extreme version of a morality of *intention*; consequences are unimportant from the ethical standpoint. Stoics do not believe that 'the road to hell is paved with good intentions' because they consider intentions irrelevant, so they are at least immunised against the law of unintended consequences. The modern mind thinks of morality and happiness as being, at least potentially, in conflict, but the Stoics denied that happiness and morality could ever collide, for by definition you can only be happy if you live morally. The 'holistic' approach of the Stoics also found expression in collapsing discrete notions, so that happiness, security, morality and virtue all mean the same, whereas in modern philosophy their difference is a staple of philosophical analysis.[7]

It will be appreciated immediately that the modern word 'stoical' is very different in connotation from the Stoicism of the ancients. Common expressions that have come down to us in a transmogrified way from Stoicism are such as the following: 'Be a man'; 'take what's coming to you'; 'roll with the punches'; 'what will be, will be'; 'show some guts'; 'make the best of it'; 'go down fighting'; 'don't be a wimp'; 'we had this coming to us'; 'try to be philosophical'; 'just my luck'; 'go with the flow'; 'don't make things worse'; 'you'd better face up to it'; and so on.[8] But these are all bastardised forms of 'stoicism', to do with fatalism, realism and resignation rather than Stoicism properly considered. Stoicism does not require us simply to accept whatever happens, but to be *happy* about it – a completely different thing. The ancient idea of happiness was that it could never be self-assigned; it was what others – the state or your peers – said it was. In contrast to modern liberalism, which stresses relativism and self-definition, the ancients thought that notions like happiness were an *objective* category that had nothing to do with individual perception. Since the rise of the Romantic movement it has become axiomatic for the modern mind that happiness must be self-defined. The only modern philosophical dispensation, as opposed to organised religion, that shares the Stoic view of objective categories is Marxism. Under Stoicism, individuals were in effect exhorted to sacrifice themselves for the good of the cosmos, just as the revolutionists of the nineteenth century were urged by Marx to sacrifice themselves for the good of *future* generations.[9] The modern liberal notion of self-interest would say that both propositions are nonsense.

Stoicism aimed at the elimination of the emotions, even though its defenders say it is only *passions* that they tried to abolish. Marcus Aurelius's teacher Sextus fought hard to maintain the distinction, saying that one could be passionless, but still full of affection: in his book the passions to be avoided were fear, lust, mental pain (envy, jealousy, grief, pity) and 'mental pleasure' – by which he meant such things as the pleasures of serendipity, the misfortunes of others or pleasure caused by deceit or magic. It seems clear, though, that the Stoics went way beyond Aristotle, who wanted only to moderate emotion, because they thought of emotion as a kind of malfunctioning in the engine of reason. In the words of La Fontaine:

> Ils ôtent à nos coeurs le principal ressort
> Ils font cesser de vivre avant que l'on soit mort.[10]

Both Plato and Aristotle said that one part of the soul, reason, should keep passions within bounds, but the Stoics could not take up such an approach because for them the soul was unitary and could not be divided; once again their stress on 'holism' and the unity of everything worked against the reasonable compromises that might have avoided many intellectual cul-de-sacs. Plato had the dualism of appearance and reality, the contrast between the empirical world and the world of the Forms. Stoics committed the fundamental fallacy of thinking that the emotions could be the handmaidens of reason; as the great eighteenth-century philosopher David Hume later pointed out, the reality is the other way about: emotions are primary and reason is the moderator.[11] The Stoic condemnation of pity has, rightly, been much criticised, but here again the Stoics were caught in the coils of their own doctrine: if sorrow is not allowed for one's own misfortunes, logically it cannot be felt for those of others.

Fundamentally, Stoicism was a narrow doctrine that elevated 'virtue' above all other considerations; most of the other goals, values, ideals of human beings were dismissed as 'indifferents'. It taught that the ultimate end for rational beings was happiness, that this meant being virtuous and living according to Nature, and that virtue was always to be chosen for its own sake and preferred to any possible combination of items of a non-moral nature.[12] Its flavour is best caught by listing a number of different tenets, which of course all turn out to be variations on the one central theme. So: do not bother about things that don't depend on our moral liberty and free choice; to be bothered by such things is an illusion. Humans make themselves unhappy by desiring things beyond their reach – the world is at it is, and there is no changing it. The body, being in the realm of the physical and hence of determinism, is beyond our control: birth, death, pleasure and pain are all beyond us. The apparent goods and evils of the world – wealth, health, poverty, sickness – do not depend on us and are likewise part of the determinism of the universe, so we should renounce these illusions and concentrate only on moral good. Even if we acquire wealth and honours, we should understand that worldly success never depends on us, but on a series of events and factors superior to us; in this realm determinism will always trump so-called free will. It is the soul, not the body, on which we should concentrate, for that is the centre of moral operations and only there can true freedom and moral good be located.[13]

Politics, family, health are all 'indifferent' phenomena. Even if you are rich, healthy and brave, you will still be unhappy if you are unjust or intemperate. It is a fallacy that you can live an evil life, as tyrants do, but still have a lot of fun and pleasure along the way; this is because happiness and morality are indivisible. We should concentrate instead on the four virtues of temperance, courage, justice and prudence. All we really need – food, water, shelter – is readily at hand and we should not fear the gods. The only calamity is to have acted shamefully by choice; if you come to grief you get consolation from the thought that no real harm can come to a good man; the quest for moral improvement is a function of reason, which is itself a spark of the divine substance ruling the universe. The only happiness is ascetic happiness and the conviction that misfortune, humiliation and even death are nothing; 'the only happiness worthy of the name is that which nothing can impair'.[14] Suffering is either long but bearable, or hideous but brief. Grief over mortality is unseemly, as death is the most natural thing in the world and leaves the scheme of the universe unchanged. Death is anyway unreal: if we are dreading it, by definition we are still alive and death is absent; if death has come, then by definition we are no longer conscious. We should leave life with the same serene indifference that we leave a banquet where a boorish guest is in full flight or where the drink has run out. Again and again the Stoic writers insist that death should not be considered evil; moral evil is attributable purely to humans, for it is people who make irrational choices and assent to the wrong propositions. We cannot choose to be immortal or avoid death, and the only thing properly to be called evil is something whose elimination depends on us.[15]

If we accept that the Stoic world view, and its detailed presciptions for ethical conduct, are so at variance with common sense, we are entitled to ask how it is, in the Stoic view, that the majority of mankind sees things differently. This brings us to the favourite Stoic doctrine of 'representations'

– seeing the world as other than it is – a forerunner of the many critiques of empiricism and 'sense data'. The Stoics did not, like Plato, deny the ultimate reality of perception, but thought that the categories of the mind could easily warp the truth of what sense-experience presented. There is a famous story, often cited against the Stoics in the ancient world, but actually showing that their theory of perception was well warranted. The philosopher Sphaerus, a disciple of Zeno, was invited to dinner by King Ptolemy of Egypt, who offered him a pomegranate made of wax. When Sphaerus ate it, Ptolemy laughed at the absurdity of philosophers, their gullibility and unworldliness. Sphaerus answered gravely that he did not really think the pomegranate was real, but thought it unlikely that anything inedible would be served at the royal table.[16] He was underlining the Stoic distinction between things that can be known with certainty by perception and those that are only probable. Most of the time, though, Stoics applied the doctrine of 'representations' to explain the *ethical* mistakes people made. Most so-called misfortunes, like death, are 'representations' or judgements that have no basis in reality; they are not objective, they are *value-judgements*. Most of these false perceptions or 'representations' arise from the failure to grasp the basic message that happiness is only to be found in moral virtue and misfortune in moral evil. Exercising proper judgement means making our 'representations' conform to objective reality: in conducting an inner dialogue we must never confuse the subjective with the objective. It is only our value-judgements that make us fear death. A proper stoical training will strip objects and events of the false values we attribute to them and which prevent us from seeing things as they really are.[17]

The Stoics preached what later thinkers called a morality of strenuousness – that is, they were not resigned and hermit-like, but combative in their goal of bringing mankind into conformity with Nature. Since this is a Promethean task, it calls for special gifts and special human beings, and Stoic literature is full of references to 'the sage' – the ideal-type of Stoic philosopher, a kind of super-guru or perfect master needed to teach his benighted mortal brethren. Seneca said that the true Stoic sage must have merits surpassing even God's, for all God has to do is exist as He is.[18] The sage is a figure conceived as being at the midway point between ordinary humans and God. The gods are wise and they know it, but men think they are wise and are not. The sage at the beginning is a kind of trainee Socrates, who knows he is not wise, but nonetheless strives for wisdom. At the end of his life the true sage should have evolved beyond the status of a mere philosopher. The philosopher is at a midpoint between the ordinary man and the sage; ordinary humans are foolish and the philosopher is not, but he has not yet acquired transcendental wisdom. The philosopher is someone who can fill public office, as Junius Rusticus would do in the years 162–8, and is merely someone who lives in a certain way and according to certain tenets. He is not necessarily a writer or even someone with original thoughts.[19] The true sage goes far beyond this, and the Stoics themselves were uncertain whether such a person had ever existed or ever could: he remained nonetheless an aspiration and an inspiration. The would-be sage must live within himself as in a fortress under a permanent state of siege. Every day must be spent building up 'character armour' to reinforce the idea that poverty and death are nothing, and his reading should inculcate the same lesson. Since every second is precious, the sage must never waste time – on this basis Pliny the Elder, the ancient world's most famous workaholic, was on the road to sagehood, though not a Stoic. Understanding true happiness means asceticism, self-training and self-restraint; the sage should always metaphorically live on bread and water, even if not actually. The would-be sage must undergo spiritual exercises (of the kind later made famous by Ignatius Loyola), read philosophy books, attend lectures, write philosophical tracts, conduct a daily examination of conscience and keep a journal of meditations. The sage must be like a courtier to a queen who allows her entourage no absences from her presence. Finally, when his consciousness is raised to the highest level and our understanding is fundamentally transformed, he becomes a god in his own right; he realises that there are no beings superior to him and becomes co-equal with God.[20]

The doctrine of the sage obsessed Marcus Aurelius and he strove to put it into practice, and to become this godlike creature. But was it plausible to think that a Roman aristocrat, trainee emperor and heir apparent to world dominion could be such a person? Marcus took comfort from the example of Seneca, a man he disliked personally, but who provided a role-model as the Stoic oligarch. Like Marcus, Seneca (c. 3 BC–AD 65) was a Roman Spaniard and, like him, was immensely rich. Where Aristotle had had Alexander the Great as a pupil, Seneca was unlucky enough to get Nero, a byword for tyranny. When Nero's excesses gradually got out of hand, Seneca fell from favour, was accused of being complicit in a conspiracy to assassinate the emperor, and was eventually invited to commit suicide in the famous Roman way, by opening his veins in a hot bath.[21] Because of his aristocratic status and the fact that he wrote in Latin, Seneca was the most influential of all the Roman Stoics, and his martyrdom under Nero recommended him to the Christians, who even concocted a supposedly genuine correspondence between him and St Paul. Seneca's importance to Marcus was that he purported to show how a man could be both rich and a Stoic, though no two individuals could have been more dissimilar.[22] Just as rich bishops caused moral problems for *ancien régime* France, so the conundrum of a wealthy philosopher puzzled Stoic theorists. Seneca grasped this bull by the horns and explicitly declared there was no conflict, adducing a number of arguments. First, to refuse the gifts of an emperor, such as those of Nero to Seneca, was both dangerous and a political insult. Then there was the fact that in all societies before the nineteenth century occupants of high political office expected to benefit financially from it; Seneca pocketed several bequests on the ground that it was considered praiseworthy in Roman culture to be rich. Since banking in the Roman empire was primitive and there were no banks in the modern sense, Roman society thought that the rich and powerful performed a public service by lending money at interest. It is certainly true that attitudes to interest-bearing loans have fluctuated enormously over the centuries: a person who would be considered a shameless usurer by medieval scholastic philosophy would today be considered a 'wealth-creating' entrepreneur.[23]

Seneca could also use in his defence the undoubted fact that Chrysippus, the great codifier of Stoicism, authorised materialism and profiteering, and also advocated private property and the market.[24] The notion of the rich Stoic was one part of Seneca's original (if dubious) contribution to the movement's theory. Another was the justifiability of suicide, which Seneca was the first to emphasise; the Stoics hitherto had been ambivalent about it, justifying it in principle as against, say, Plato, but never making it a central plank in their programme.[25] Seneca argued for suicide in all the following cases: if your fatherland or friends required it of you; if a tyrant forced you to do dishonourable things; if, afflicted by an incurable disease, the body was letting the soul down; if you were destitute or indigent; or if you went mad.[26] The Stoics in general tended to say that the issue of self-slaughter was open-ended: in some circumstances it could be the right thing, but they were reluctant to issue moral blueprints. The fact that different Stoics gave different answers to common everyday ethical questions showed that there was always an uncertainty in their doctrine between clear moral objectives and the appropriate actions needed to attain them.[27] Chrysippus seemed to think that suicide was inappropriate for wise men, but Diogenes Laertius thought it was permissible to kill yourself for your country or friends. Cicero, more a Stoical fellow-traveller than a paid-up Stoic, argued that it was sometimes the duty of the wise man to depart from this life, while Epictetus, *the* great influence on Marcus Aurelius, remarked gnomically on suicide: 'the door stands open'.[28] Seneca argued that opening one's veins was the final, instantaneous way to achieve wisdom; trying to become a sage was a utopian dream, but dying one had an immediate, permanent and irrefutable reality.[29] Some have argued that the doctrine of suicide as *the* act par excellence of the wise man was an idiosyncrasy of Seneca himself and not typical of Stoicism in general.[30] It may in some sense have been his rationalisation of the high levels of suicide in the Rome of the first century AD that are reminiscent of the cult of *hara-kiri* or *seppuku* in Tokugawa Japan. It is clear, however, that Seneca's prescription of suicide is not Romantic melancholy *avant la lettre*, but simply common sense when considering the alternative in Nero's Rome.

In Seneca's defence, it should be said that he was not a total humbug and did try, albeit unsuccessfully, to live out the meaning of the Stoic creed. He famously faced his own worst fears and tried to conquer his claustrophobia when passing through the dark and gloomy tunnel connecting Naples with Pozzuoli. He once arrived at his villa faint with hunger and, finding no white bread there, forced himself to eat the coarse brown loaves of his tenants. He contented himself with the thought that enduring unexpected trials was more of a challenge than those for which one had time to prepare. On one occasion he deliberately set out in a peasant cart with just two slaves, dressed like a poor peasant, so that he could experience the contempt of those who looked down on him, thinking this was his real station in life. Another time he tried to emulate the great sages who had proved themselves indifferent to noise (Buddha was famously supposed to be able to meditate while tigers roared around him) by renting an apartment next to a bathhouse in Naples, but was soon driven out by the hubbub and confessed himself defeated in his Stoic principles.[31] Always a faint-hearted Stoic, Seneca knew that his money was an obstacle to the life of a philosopher and tried to meet the obvious objections. He was personally generous, lived austerely, requested a simple funeral and handed over perhaps half of his wealth to Nero to enable him to rebuild Rome.[32] But he was always vulnerable to the charge that he had obtained much of his wealth from the tyrant-emperor in the first place and must have listened in horror in the year 58 when a man on trial tried to inveigle him by exclaiming: 'What philosophical principles had caused him to acquire three hundred million sesterces in less than four years of imperial favour?'[33] His accuser did not exaggerate. Seneca's fortune was seventy-five million denarii, perhaps one-tenth the annual revenues of the entire Roman state. The fact that much of it came from usury was often held against him. The historian Cassius Dio claimed that the famous British revolt of the Iceni under Boudicca was caused because Seneca made the Britons a loan of ten million denarii at usurious rates, and then called it in all at once.[34]

Seneca's would-be Stoic humanism also evaporates when put under the microscope. He burst into laughter at the decrepitude of an old slave who had brought him up lovingly, jeering at the old man as if he were dealing with a dog.[35] The best he ever rises to is to say that we should treat slaves as humble friends, but he echoes Chrysippus's formula that slaves are merely 'wage workers in perpetuity', that Providence has assigned us all our roles and there is nothing to be done.[36] As has been well said: 'If the Stoics had been masters of society and could have remodelled it to their liking, they would have retained slavery, albeit under another name.'[37] The Stoic Musonius thought it better to spend money on human beings rather than architecture and public works, and Seneca agreed; but his notion of charity did not extend to the poor and needy and never transcended the limitations of clientelism.[38]

He expounded the very convenient doctrine – which all societies have espoused – that what is murder in an individual case is a public duty when the state says so; it is quite clear that pacifism formed no part of Stoic doctrine. He believed in 'pre-emptive' warfare and said, 'The best way to love Asian barbarians is for Rome to maintain them under her hegemony, for their own good.'[39] He even iced his own cake, so to speak, by putting forward a doctrine of Roman 'particularism': Roman conquests were always good, but those of Alexander the Great were always wicked.[40] Although Marcus Aurelius never surmounted the basic limitations of Stoicism and accepted many of Seneca's ideas about the relationship between Stoic theory and Roman state power, he disliked the man himself, much as he had disliked Hadrian, because he saw them both as apologists for tyranny. He pointedly ignored Seneca's writings, as did Epictetus.[41] He allowed Fronto to inveigh against him at full throttle. Fronto thought Seneca a humbug, insincere, a windbag who repeated the same stock sentiments a thousand times, but dressed them up in different language. 'There are certainly some acute and weighty sayings in his books,' he wrote to Marcus. 'But little pieces of silver are sometimes found in sewers; and is that a reason for us to undertake the cleaning of the sewers?'[42]

The basic problem with Marcus Aurelius's embrace of Stoicism was that all his objections seemed to be *ad hominem*, directed at particular practitioners of the theory he did not care for, such as Seneca. He never questioned or even seemed to appreciate the glaring self-contradictions in the doctrine. Some of them are obvious, some less so, but, properly considered, even more damaging to the overall system. At the very simplest level, Stoicism threw up large numbers of phoneys, charlatans and confidence men; even Seneca admitted that the doctrine attracted too many tricksters on the make.[43] Lucian, who basically thought all philosophy spurious and its practitioners humbugs, often has fun with a rogues' gallery of 'sages', 'sophists' and 'perfect masters' and singles out the Stoics as egregiously absurd for spending their entire lives trying to learn how to live – an obviously self-defeating and self-contradictory process. In the *Hermotimus* he lashes out at a rebarbative Stoic philosopher who preaches poverty, but sues his pupils when they don't pay his fees.[44] A man named Antiochus, realising that there was money to be made from an affectation of Stoicism, won both cash and honours from the emperor Septimius Severus in the early third century by rolling in the snow, demonstrating his indifference to physical discomfort; he repeated the feat for Septimius's successor Caracalla.[45]

Beyond the bogus credentials of so many 'Stoics' who were individual charlatans, critics fastened on an essential dishonesty in the Stoics' social thought, if we may call it that. Stoicism was supposed to be an egalitarian doctrine. It stressed that slaves were reasonable and, in a masterpiece of condescension, announced that even women – creatures of emotion par excellence – were educable, even if the process was strenuous.[46] Yet all this is in conflict with an elitism that is imbricated into the very system of Stoicism, with its emphasis on the sage as the highest form of human life. If value is to be accorded to human beings strictly in accordance with the moral excellence of each individual, it follows logically that Stoicism can never be a creed for all men.[47] Where Plato, in *The Republic*, was concerned with the training and discipline necessary to be a Guardian, which he envisaged as a real social possibility, in the writings of the Stoics the figure of the sage is an ideal as remote as Plato's Forms. Given that the search for the perfect sage is the quest for an impossible dream, what emerges is the paradox of an ideology (Stoicism) existing without any real practitioners (Stoic sages). If the ideal is beyond human nature, what does that tell us about the project in the first place? The Stoic Musonius 'solved' this dilemma by saying that sages do not yet exist, but they may – some day.[48] We have already mentioned the conflict between the actual Stoic attitude to slaves and what the doctrine really requires that attitude to be. If the human race is one, and all men are equal by virtue of possessing reason, how can there be slaves? Stoicism provides no answer. Cicero pointed out that there was a flat contradiction between the allegedly 'universal' views of Stoicism and the privileges of Roman citizenship itself; this special privilege, he alleged, destroyed 'charity, liberality, kindness and justice'.[49] The reality is that Stoicism operated a dual system: an elitist doctrine for the ruling class and a cut-price version for the masses. In the cut-price version slaves, women and other 'inferiors' could be accepted as equals, but in the true doctrine it was only rich, educated Romans who could aspire to ultimate truth. Stoicism, which by its implications preached political quietism as well as a bogus egalitarianism, was, not surprisingly, a favourite doctrine both with the Hellenistic kings who succeeded Alexander the Great and with the Roman emperors.

To put it another way, Stoicism as a social doctrine was vacuous. As a social philosophy, the creed suffered from the unconquerable disability that it never viewed human beings as *social* animals, but merely as atomic individuals. That was why it had so little to say about politics and unthinkingly accepted slavery as a datum, as if it were equivalent to the law of gravity. Even the Cynics, allegedly the 'left-wing Stoics', did not believe in 'share the wealth' or any form of communitarianism or socialism; they simply restricted themselves to saying that Mammon was an obstacle to self-realisation. Stoicism prescribes no solution to any of the problems of social organisation or says what kind of *society* would be just.[50] The total lack of any political theory placed the Stoics in the same kind of untenable position as Dickens and the benevolent Victorians: while deploring poverty and recommending individual charity, they drew the line at any radical restructuring of society that would eliminate indigence (or, in the Roman case, slavery). Even worse, Stoicism was vacuous when it came to Rome's self-interest. The monomaniacal emphasis on individual morality and virtue, and the disregard for consequences, was part of the political nullity of Stoicism. Since winning victories over Rome's enemies (like losing one's children to sudden death) does not make us more virtuous, it follows that whether or not Roman arms prevail in the field against its enemies is unimportant: it can make no difference to our happiness because only virtue can do that.[51] Once again we see the dual system in action: Stoics prescribe actions that, if universally adopted (which they would have to be if the doctrine was egalitarian), would inevitably lead to the destruction of Rome. It is more than a little curious that a trainee emperor would imbibe a doctrine with such baneful implications: one can only assume that the young Marcus Aurelius did not spot this contradiction.

At a more general philosophical level, Stoicism was impaled on the classic free will/determinism dilemma. If the world is completely deterministic, as the doctrine says it is, the freedom that virtue is supposed to provide is not possible. On the deterministic view, natural laws will decide whether an individual is virtuous or not; if he is wicked, this is because Nature has compelled him to be wicked. An allied point is that if the world is determined by divine Providence, as in Stoic doctrine, why is it that there so many sinners in the world, so much cruelty and injustice? The determinism of Providence certainly does not seem to be aimed at producing virtue, yet according to the Stoic, virtue is the only good. Paradoxically, a malevolent Providence makes more sense of the world as we experience it, since the existence of cruelty and injustice gives the good man or the sage more opportunities for being virtuous. There is therefore a contradiction both between the idea of perfect freedom through the exercise of virtue and a deterministic universe *and* between virtue as the supreme good and a divine Providence that produces so little of it. Both dilemmas are ultimately insoluble, but modern defenders of Stoicism, whether explicit or implicit, have tried to square the circle in a number of ways. One is to attack the very idea of determinism as an intellectually vacuous concept, on the ground that it breaks down into heterogeneous components: physical determinism – the relationship between cause and effect; logical determinism, dealing with reasons and conclusions; ethical determinism, stressing the preconditions of human decisions; and teleological determinism, or the determination by an overall end or purpose.[52] The suspicion arises here of a desire to rescue Stoicism by mere verbal legerdemain, and a similar criticism applies to those who espouse 'compatibilism' – the idea that there is no necessary conflict between free will and determinism, that the entire problem results from semantic confusion. According to the compatibilists, a free action is one where the agent could have chosen otherwise, and in such a case the agent is morally responsible even if determined; this is because there is not one true definition of 'free', but merely two different conceptions.[53] It will be clear that 'choice' does nothing to dispose of the essential problem of determinism, so the Stoic's dilemma remains.

In many ways the ancients wrestled more honestly with the age-old conundrum of free will and determinism, but then they did not suffer from the modern delusion that all philosophical problems are verbal ones. Cicero tried to argue his way out of the dilemma by a contrast between the *données* of our birth and our roles in life. He claimed that all humans have four roles: the common identity as human beings; the differences in physique, looks, abilities and temperaments; our lot in life – what Fate throws up – which has nothing to do with innate abilities; and the specific person we choose to be: in jobs, professions, attitudes, lifestyles (needless to say, he was speaking of the experience of the free-born Roman). We are all constrained by our parental, genetic, nurtural, cultural and environmental legacy, but we are not rigidly determined: there are good emperors and bad emperors; the son of a pauper can have extraordinary abilities; and even the slave Epictetus became a Stoic philosopher.[54] Marcus Aurelius himself later attempted his own version of 'compatibilism' by stating that a roller or cylinder, if started, will roll down a slope because its motions are determined by its shape, but, when set free in this way, will pursue its own path; within limits, therefore, it is free.[55] Others tried to argue that Stoic providence applies only to the cosmos, but not to persons. It guarantees the prosperity of the cosmos, but not of individuals, cities, kingdoms or empires. God, or the ruling principle of the universe, supervises everything, but has no time to deal with particulars. It (He) organises Nature for the good of mankind and gives him the gift of reason, but is otherwise non-interventionist. However, all attempts to differentiate between levels of reality (atomic/human, appearance/reality, providence/determinism) founder not only on the Stoic insistence that reality is unitary, but on the simple logical principle of the law of excluded middle: something is either the case or it is not, it cannot both be p and not-p. Stoics habitually emphasised the need to play well the cards you were dealt.[56] But if everything is written, it is not just that Destiny hands you your cards; it must also have predetermined how you are going to play them. Moreover, it is far from clear how there can be a doctrine that is supposedly centred on individuals and human morality, but which at the same time stresses a universal, impartial reason that makes no allowance for individuals.

The free will/determinism, providence/morality conundrum is the most serious intellectual flaw in Stoicism, but it is far from the only one. The mind/body problem, one of the constants in the history of philosophy, is never addressed systematically by the creed, which tacks in and out of different perspectives, at one moment materialist, at another Gnostic; nor is there any agreement on where the core of the human personality should be located.[57] There is also a contradiction between the idea that a genuinely good action should be spontaneous, like an animal instinct, and the countervailing Stoic idea that you should be acutely conscious of what you are doing. The conscious pursuit of virtue seems to rule out the famous Christian attitude expressed in the Gospels: 'When you give alms, let not your left hand know what your right hand is doing.'[58] There is also the central contradiction in Stoicism that its practitioners assert simultaneously that natural goods such as health are desirable if we are to be happy, but that reason shows we can do without them. But surely either man is an animal and cannot forego animal pleasures and remain happy, or he is pure reason and his animal nature does not matter. Seneca tries to evade this trap by remarking lamely that because we are at the top of the animal chain we must become paragons of rationality.[59] To say that it is more natural to be healthy, but health does not guarantee happiness – the usual Stoic answer – is simply an evasion of the self-contradiction in the doctrine.[60] Moreover, the 'elitist' conception of Stoic doctrine, which allows it to reinforce official Roman culture, holds that to be honoured and sublime in the state or to be a military hero is also to be happy – a notion in glaring contradiction to the usual tenets.

Another source of interminable confusion is the Stoic conception of God. Stoicism is basically a pantheistic creed, but this simple approach is vitiated by any number of caveats and cavils that different Stoics enter in their explication. First of all there is the conflict between theism and pantheism, and then between monotheism and polytheism. The Stoics sometimes referred to the ruler of the universe as God, but also as Zeus, to be carefully distinguished from the Olympian deity of that name, synonymous with Roman Jupiter. Seneca, out of deference to the official polytheism of the Roman state religion, liked to say that the Olympian Zeus was a real being, but he was subordinate to 'Zeus', aka God or the supreme ruler of the universe. But if God is the spirit that informs the universe – the pantheistic *logos* – it is difficult to see how he can be personalised, whether we call him Zeus or by some other name. Even worse intellectual chaos is introduced by the idea that God is not really a transcendental being, but part of our soul – properly understood, God is the 'god within us' – the notion that so appealed to the Buddhists and modern-day mystics like C.G. Jung.[61] Moreover the Stoic sage is supposed to be equal to God, but elsewhere we are told that humans are distinct from gods, and in any case how could the sage equal God if we understand the deity as 'god within'? Stoicism uses so many different conceptions and meanings of 'God', and slips between them without ever explaining the elision from one sense to another, that the entire doctrine bids fair to become gibberish. Even the most enthusiastic defenders of Stoicism have been inclined to throw up their hands in despair at this point. Here is the most eminent modern authority on Stoicism:

> Stoic theology was a complex amalgam of pantheism and theism . . . God was conceived as being both an omnipresent physical force embodied in fire or fiery breath [*pneuma*] *and* the world's governing mind or soul . . . This combination of pantheism and theism raises enormous questions . . . Such pantheism makes it hard to understand how God can be present in an exemplary or specially refined way in the human mind. Moreover, if our minds are simply and directly 'parts' of God's mind, it is hard to see how we individuals are capable of thinking for ourselves and able to assume responsibility for our own lives.[62]

The Stoic doctrine of 'following Nature' also engenders myriad problems. Does the prescription mean that we *have* to follow Nature, or only that that is preferable? Do we have a choice or not? The exercise of a virtuous will cannot affect Nature if it is predetermined. Stoics tend to say lamely that Nature has marked out an obvious path for humans, and those pursuing self-interest are bound to find it. But, as always with this doctrine, there is an element of wanting to have it both ways, to practise 'compatibilism'.[63] Once again one can see a resemblance between Stoicism and Marxism – we are enjoined to do what is going to happen anyway. At least Marxism, in urging revolutionary struggle towards an end that is historically determined, has the excuse that one could affect the *timing* of the revolution. With Stoicism there is the obvious problem that there is no proof that Nature acts in a benevolent and purposive way. Like all arguments from design, it assumes what has to be proved, but then the cynic (in the modern sense) would say that begging the question is the name of the Stoic game. 'Following Nature' does not solve the moral problem Stoicism sets itself by the dogma of 'indifferents'. There is an innate self-contradiction in the creed that the things we are guided to do by reason, following Nature, must also be 'indifferent' since they do not depend entirely on us. Quite apart from the difficulty of identifying self-evidently 'appropriate' actions (and it is worth noting that any doctrine of 'self-evidence' is always suspect), we face the insoluble problem that, strictly speaking, all our actions will be 'indifferent' and thus incapable of generating morality.[64] Stoics never face this implication of 'following Nature' head-on. Epictetus, for example, evades the issue by broad-stroke pragmatism, providing prescriptions that are fine as a guide to everyday life, provided they are detached from the general doctrine, and which do nothing whatever to elucidate the basic problems of Stoicism. 'Eat like a human being, drink like a human being, get spruced up, get married, have children, lead the life of a citizen, learn how to put up with insults, tolerate an un-reasonable brother, father, son, neighbour or travelling companion. Show us these things, so that we can see if you have really learned anything from the philosophers.'[65] Fine, but what does any of this have to do with the finer points of Stoic doctrine? One could just as well derive this cracker-barrel philosophy from the maxims on old-fashioned tea chests.

Following Nature is vitiated by circularity. If you argue that whatever is, is right, and also argue for design in the cosmos, the only logical conclusion is that our minds must be in error when we see injustice in the so-called divine order. Stoics invented the idea that freedom is the recognition of necessity, and branded as absurd those who railed against the world as it was. Many modern notions of freedom are exactly contrary: for the existen-tialist, absurdity consisted in the recognition that the world was *not* deter-mined, that it could be otherwise. To assent to the world as is is also potentially dangerous, for it means embracing the blind cruelty of the cosmos. Once you assent unquestioningly to what is, it becomes a moot point, especially in view of Stoicism's 'holistic' view, why you should accept only the rational. Nietzsche, for one, accepted the logic of this and opted for the will to power, beyond good and evil. Galen, a Stoic fellow-traveller, professed himself furious with Epicurus, who said that the anus and the urethra would have been better placed on the foot than where they were – both more practical and more aesthetic.[66] Galen, of course, shared the Stoic view of those who thought the body a marvellous organism rather than those, like Hume, who thought it the botched work of an 'infant or superannuated deity'.[67] The Stoics were neither humanists, dedicated to man's mastery of Nature, nor sceptics who thought of the natural order as in some sense hostile. The idea of Nature being on mankind's side was largely accepted until Voltaire devastated it in *Candide* (1759), but was not fully overthrown until the high noon of the Romantic movement (with Shelley as a notable critic). The modern sensi-bility finds 'following Nature' merely bizarre.

Although one can find dozens of objections to Stoicism at a theoretical level,[68] the most telling criticism of the creed is that it discounts human nature and elaborates a theory that flies in the face of all the wisdom culled from art, literature and psychology. The entire discussion of happiness and morality in Stoic texts is a mess. A number of discrete propositions will, I hope, make this clear. Stoicism fails to distinguish necessary conditions – having what is necessary for happiness – from sufficient conditions, since it obviously does not follow that he who has everything necessary for happi-ness is thereby happy.[69] The doctrine advanced the bizarre view that men and women attain happiness by satisfying certain approved criteria, regard-less of whether they were actually happy. Stoicism assumes, with the utilitarians, that the search for happiness was the spur for all human actions and ignored other motivations: conscience, individual existentialist morality, altruism, masochism, love, the will to power, admiration, ideological zeal, libido, *élan vital*, and so on. As Nietzsche remarked: 'Men do not seek happiness but power; that is, for the most part, unhappiness.'[70] Stoicism advocates conquering passions, whereas the best minds of the ages, from Aristotle to Hume, have always considered this impossible; the best you can do is moderate passions by reason. The idea of the soul as unitary, with passion and reason working together, denies the entire history of the 'divided self' in cultural history, which can be illustrated with hundreds of examples, from Robert Louis Stevenson to Freud.[71] The idea of love as mere friction between bodies is a joyless tenet and the enemy of all significant art and literature. Stoicism, with its 'all-or-nothing' approach to psychology and philosophy, lacks all nuance. It denies human nature by recommending what most sane people would regard as chimerical: braving torture, mocking death, conquering sexual passions.[72] It subscribes to the dreadful doctrine that if someone suffers misfortune, he himself is responsible.[73]

Appendix Two: The reign of Antoninus Pius

As already mentioned, many of Marcus's chores as Antoninus's deputy concerned the imperial council. This council of thirty-one members was formally the supreme decision-making body for the empire – though naturally it often simply rubber-stamped a personal decision by Antoninus. The emperor showed his conservatism both by keeping on large numbers of Hadrian's old councillors and by evincing his well-known preference for Italians over provincials. Of the sixteen senators on the council, eight were Italian, four African and four Asian. The bias of the knights who served was even more pronounced: nine Italians, two Africans, two from Spain and two from Asia.[1] The same system was applied in imperial administration. Antoninus overwhelmingly used Italian senators to govern the provinces and only ever used eastern senators in the Greek-speaking world.[2] It should be emphasised that to become governor of a senatorial province was very much a best-case scenario. Most senators served as quaestors, tribunes, aediles or praetors, but got no further and were not employed in the imperial household. Even for those senators who got as far as consul, their careers usually fizzled out thereafter. Only the very privileged got appointments to the eleven imperial consular provinces (Britain, Cappadocia, Dalmatia, Hither Spain, Lower Germany, Upper Germany, Lower Moesia, Upper Moesia, Upper Pannonia, Syria, Palestine). Theoretically, fifteen years after a consulate a senator's name could go into a draw to decide by lot who got the plum proconsulates of Asia and Africa, but in practice only the emperor's favourites went into the draw.[3] A senator's chances may have been marginally better in the twelve imperial praetorian provinces (Arabia, Dacia, Numidia, Pannonia, Aquitaine, Belgica, Sicily, Galatia, Lusitania, Lycia-Pamphylia, Lugdunum and Thrace), but even to get as far as the consulate it was a distinct advantage to be an Italian.[4]

As an administrator Antoninus ran a tight ship. There was stringent financial control from Rome, increased use of *curatores*, meticulously audited accounts, and the emperor kept his officials on their toes by writing frequently to them, nudging and herding them in the desired direction. He liked to check back through accounts for the previous twenty years, rooting out embezzlement and making sure that all expenditure, even recurrent, was properly approved by the authorities at Rome.[5] Particularly interested in the administration of the provinces of Asia Minor, where he had had personal experience, Antoninus was good as a fund-raiser and knew how to lean on local bigwigs to get them to cough up for local building projects.[6] He tried hard to end the racket of immunities and exemptions from taxes enjoyed by rhetoricians, philosophers and doctors, especially in the Eastern cities. He fixed an exemptions quota of five doctors, three teachers of grammar and three teachers of rhetoric in the small cities, of seven, four and four respectively in medium-sized ones and of ten, five and five in the large conurbations.[7] He liked to keep people at their posts for a long time to increase stability and continuity, keeping on five of Hadrian's governors for an extended period and then putting in long-lived appointments of his own, such as Q. Lollius Urbicus, governor of Britain 140–5 and C. Popilius Carus Pedo, governor of Upper Germany 152–61. One of his prefects, M. Gavius Maximus, served for twenty years (138–58).[8] Antoninus pioneered the approach, later claimed by Pescennius Niger as an original innovation of his own, that all governors of provinces – not just imperial legates, but also proconsuls – should remain in office for five years.[9]

Antoninus attempted no reform of the administrative structure and basically depended on Italian senators and knights to carry out the main functions of empire. But he rarely allowed senators a second consulate, and even more rarely allowed knights jobs as prefects or procurators.[10] This might suggest a certain distance from the Senate, but, as he had been a senator for twenty-five years himself, he always showed great outward respect and deference for the assembly.[11] His concern, as always, was to promote Italians and Italian hegemony. The place of origin of some 30 per cent of senators in the years 138–61 is unknown, but of those whose origin is certainly known, it has been established that 46 per cent were Italian and 54 per cent provincial. The Italians should by now have been eclipsed, since Trajan and Hadrian had made it a policy to increase the numbers of Eastern senators (they were thought more reliable politically), but the new breed had not yet come through the system in sufficient numbers. For a while, under Antoninus, Italian senators enjoyed their last moment in the sun.[12] By suppressing the previous 'consulars' who ruled Italy and handing back the administration of the peninsula to the Senate, Antoninus kept that august body happy. He was even prepared to flatter it, as when he struck coins showing the genius of the Senate with a sceptre in its right hand; the Senate responded in the same way with numismatic homage in 143.[13] Antoninus made a big fuss about his claim that no senator would ever be executed in his reign and, with this in mind, marooned a confessed senatorial parricide on a desert island, reasoning that on the one hand he did not want to tarnish his record with such a killing, but, on the other, it was against the laws of nature to let such a man live.[14] Yet the relations of even 'good' emperors with the Senate were always necessarily tense. Antoninus did not allow the Senate any true role in making imperial policy and, at the limit, he was prepared to face it down by brute power, as in the dispute over the deification of Hadrian. The Senate for its part was reserved. Even under a benign ruler like Antoninus, its mood was still essentially republican, always hankering for the golden age when that assembly was (at least theoretically) sovereign. We know of at least three major plots during his reign: that of ex-consul T. Atilius, that of Rufus Titianus who was proscribed by the Senate, and a major eruption in 151 when three senators were deported for conspiracy.[15]

Two of the most striking aspects of Antoninus's reign were his building programme and his legislative onslaught. His road- and bridge-building schemes were famous, and most of the empire's milestones bore the legend of Antoninus Pius.[16] But he was not a great one for lavish public buildings, purely on the grounds of expenditure; Antoninus realised he could not cut down on public spectacles and so risk the wrath of the mob, and indeed his shows tended to be richer, with greater pomp and more novelties, but in compensation for this he cut down on extravagance in architecture.[17] The contrast with Trajan and even Hadrian is clear. In Trajan's reign there had been a veritable building frenzy, with the reconstruction of the House of the Vestal Virgins, Caesar's Forum and the Temple of Venus Genetrix. Trajan had ordered massive new developments along the Tiber and at Ostia and had built splendid new baths on the Esquiline. Trajan's Frank Lloyd Wright, so to speak, was Apollodorus of Damascus, previously the architect of a magnificent bridge over the Danube. Under his aegis Trajan's Market – a commercial complex – was built on the Quirinal, and also Trajan's Column, commemorating the Dacian wars, a 125-foot-high obelisk of white Carrara marble with 185 internal steps.[18] Hadrian made his mark in his usual idiosyncratic and bloody manner, switching to a more modern style of architecture and executing Apollodorus of Damascus into the bargain. He completed the Temple of the Deified Hadrian in the Roman Forum, rebuilt Augustus's

Pantheon and constructed the Temple of Venus in a neo-Grecian style, then capped his achievements with the imperial mausoleum at Castel Sant'Angelo and his own magnificent villa at Tivoli.[19] This was not Antoninus's style at all. After building temples to the deified Hadrian and Faustina the Elder (overlooking the Forum) – matters over which he had no choice – and then restoring the Pons Sublicius, the Graecostadium and the Colosseum, he decreed that all new expenditure had to go on conserving existing buildings.[20]

Yet Antoninus was not able to secure significant retrenchment in his building programme, since the obstacles were legion. Although he made clear that he preferred rich patrons to build something useful in their cities rather than gain easy and instant popularity by providing games, the provincial oligarchs either ignored him or built monuments and 'follies' of their own.[21] In Ephesus, where he wanted an extensive programme of public building, he was warned by his advisers that the mob insisted that all available funds had to be spent on games, shows or money handouts; to make any headway at all in his plans he had to keep the provincial notables on side by granting them exactly the kinds of favours, sinecures and exemptions he was in general trying to stamp out.[22] In the end, to get any useful building done, he had to earmark special hypothecated funds. As if to get his revenge on the foot-draggers in the provinces, he spent most of the money in Italy, on baths at Ostia and Puteoli and an amphitheatre at Capua; the aqueduct at Athens was his only real sop to the Greek-speaking world. Most of all, though, natural disasters conspired against him and forced him to build where he had not wanted to. There were earthquakes in the Greek islands and in Asia Minor (in 140 and 151): major tremors destroyed cities in Lycia, Caria, Cyzigus, Ephesus, Nicomedia, Bithynia and the Hellespont region as well as on the islands of Rhodes and Cos; in each case Antoninus paid for the rebuilding of the ruined cities.[23] Fire was another frequent hazard: there were major blazes during his reign at Narbonne, Antioch and Carthage as well as in Rome itself, where 340 seven-storey tenements or *insulae* were destroyed along-side hundreds of houses. The Circus Maximus collapsed, with more than 1,000 victims, and the Tiber, that reliable scourge, continued to overflow its banks, with a particularly vicious flood in the year 142.[24] In all these cases Antoninus was forced to disgorge funds for rebuilding. Against his will, he presided over a change of face in Rome.[25]

It has been suggested that as a legislator Antoninus Pius was on the lazy side, since he introduced so few pieces of legislation in the Senate compared with the deluge in Hadrian's reign.[26] But this is to concentrate excessively on the senatorial side of things. In fact Antoninus was energetic in the legal field, but he liked to work in extra-senatorial ways, of which four main ones can be identified. There were the imperial edicts, either relating to the whole empire or to specific territories; the imperial decrees entered after appeal on individual cases; the administrative instructions or *mandata* addressed to magistrates and civil servants; and the rescripts, or written replies to queries and requests from governors, magistrates and other municipal authorities.[27] As a lawyer, Antoninus's spheres of interest were fairly clear-cut. His main themes were the problems of slavery, the rights of women and the rights of the accused, but he also took a great interest in the law of bequest, as well as in esoteric subjects like the ownership of sea coasts, the laws governing bird-hunting and the *ius alluvionis* – the ownership of land added to or subtracted from estates by the natural alteration in the course of rivers. In modern terms Antoninus would be characterised as primarily a family lawyer. He brought in legislation to safeguard children in cases of dubious paternity or legitimacy; insisted that greater weight be given to the wishes of daughters in the choice of a marriage partner; and scrutinised closely the realm of guardianship and the issue of dowries.[28] He tried to reduce the power of fathers in the family, and decreed that a father could no longer compel a son to divorce. Always interested in balancing acts, Antoninus palliated this by a provision that if a father returned a deserting son to the army, the son could not then be put to death.[29] Since Romans were obsessed with bequests, Antoninus steered a careful course between safeguarding inheritances and keeping family estates intact, on the one hand, and denying the rights of bequest to criminals on the other. In the case of those sentenced to hard labour or the mines, they lost the right to inherit or (if they were slaves) to become free, but Antoninus forbade the confiscation of their property. He decreed that bequests should be limited to three-quarters of an estate, that soldiers' wills be made less complex, and that Greeks who were Roman citizens should be allowed to transmit property to children who were not themselves Roman citizens.[30]

Above all, Antoninus made his mark in the laws relating to slavery. Naturally he was not opposed to that institution – 'the power of masters over slaves must remain intact and no man must have his rights diminished'[31] – but he was in net terms an improver. Once again he sought the equilibrium point, in this case between the master's rights and duties. On the one hand, he took a very serious view of runaway slaves – and how not, since manpower shortages were an endemic problem for the Antonines. He decreed that runaways, whether slaves or gladiators, must always be returned to their masters and made this obligation absolute, even in cases where, to escape slavery, men had opted instead to fight in the arena. He even allowed his police to enter private dwellings to check that absconding slaves had not taken refuge there.[32] He also tightened up the rules on torture so that people could not free slaves to prevent them being tortured.

With an eye to over-benevolent owners, he insisted that all trials must take place in the location where the crime occurred, not in the master's baili-wick, where he could conceivably defend slaves and allow them to evade justice. But he was also mindful of the problems of wicked owners. During his reign it became a crime to kill a slave without good reason, and in extreme cases, if it was proved that egregious oppression had taken place, the right to flight could be sustained. At the limit a tyrannical owner could even be ordered to sell all his slaves. Antoninus once publicly reprimanded a slave owner in Baetica (Spain) for not providing the right paternal example to his slaves.[33] He also allowed manumission to proceed if such a request was in the will of a master, but written by the hand of a freedman – some-thing that until his reign had been prohibited by the full force of the law. In general he made all legal enfranchisement of slaves irrevocable and, where legal problems arose, he recommended obeying the spirit rather than the letter of the law.[34]

If Antoninus was liberal in family law, his attitude to slavery and his response to natural disasters, he was a deep-dyed conservative in his reli-gious views. He believed sincerely in Rome's official polytheistic religion, never viewing it as a metaphor as Marcus did, and had an almost fanatical attachment to the official myths and legends of early Rome. A series of coins issued in 139–47, designed to culminate in the 900th anniversary celebrations (in 148) of Rome's founding, commemorates all the traditional stories: the landing of Aeneas in Italy, Hercules and Cacus in Italy, Mars and Rhea Silvia, the she-wolf and the twins Romulus and Remus, the rape of the Sabine women, Attus Navius, Horatius Cocles, the arrival of the serpent of Aesculapius on the island in the Tiber, and so on. One coin showed him and Marcus sacrificing to the Penates, the household gods.[35] Keen on the local cults of Latium and a member of all the local priestly colleges, he sacrificed daily to the gods, never failing to do so unless seriously ill, and insisted that Marcus join him in setting this good example. Antoninus saw himself as a second Numa Pompilius, the founder of the Roman religion, and in his coinage liked to portray himself as pious almost in the modern sense, the latest in a series that included Aeneas, Romulus, Numa and Augustus.[36] There was method behind the fanaticism, for in political terms Antoninus was using religion to promote the imperial cult, associating the emperors with the Olympians so that they became minor gods themselves. Given the emphasis on traditional Roman religion, it therefore comes as something of a surprise to find that the iconography of Antoninus's reign tends towards religious eclecticism and even syncretism. Not personally attracted by Eastern mystery cults, such as those of Attis, Mithras or Sol Invictus, he was liberal towards them, especially the cults of Dionysus, Isis and Cybele. In the case of Cybele and Isis, he even tried to associate his dead wife Faustina with them and conflate her with the idea of the Great Mother. His later coinage shows Jupiter cohabiting quite happily with Cybele.[37] Tolerant even of magic, astrology and belief in the supernatural that was rampant under the Antonines, unlike Marcus, Antoninus had no idea of the threat posed to the Roman system by the new religion devoted to the worship of Jesus Christ. Under Antoninus it really was the case that only local initiatives were taken against Christianity.[38]

The energy Antoninus displayed in domestic matters contrasted sharply with his lack of interest in foreign policy, where his main preoccupation seemed to be to ensure that all the frontiers were properly mapped and delimited. Antoninus fulfilled Hadrian's best hopes by being just as firmly set against imperial expansionism as his predecessor. For Antoninus, Rome's imperial policy was an open-and-shut case. Rome lacked the troops and general military capability to control any more territory; the economic advantages of admitting any more peoples into the empire were negligible; and he was already committed to subsidising and subventing a host of client kings and did not want to add to the number.[39] Any pacific interest shown in him by foreign powers was politely rebuffed. Indians, Bactrians and Hyrcanians all sent him fruitless embassies, and he was on several occasions offered the submission of various peoples wishing to be admitted into the empire, only to refuse the offer.[40] He argued that true strength meant peace and tranquillity, not martial glory, and reinforced the message on his coinage, which showed Mars the war god as principally a bringer of peace.[41] He liked to quote Scipio to the effect that he would rather save a single citizen than slay a thousand foes.[42] Of Antoninus it could be said that, alone of the Roman emperors, he took no measures that led to the spilling of blood; blood was spilled in his reign certainly, but not on his initiative.[43] Just as Hadrian was thought to have chosen a successor with no military experience to make sure his non-expansionist policy was continued, so Antoninus made sure that *his* heir apparent never saw a spear cast in anger.

His champions claimed that he fought no wars, yet intimidated Rome's enemies by his reputation.[44] The facts say otherwise. From the very beginning of his reign Antoninus was plagued by frontier disturbances, some of them very serious. The rising of the Brigantes in Britain in 140–1 was put down only with difficulty by Q. Lollius Urbicus. He deported some of the defeated warriors to Germany and, with the emperor's permission, started work on the Antonine Wall, a thirty-seven-mile fortification stretching from the Clyde estuary to the Firth of Forth.[45] Controversy has always attended the Antonine Wall, with military experts unclear about its ultimate purpose; some say it was merely a prestige project to show that Antoninus was truly in charge, while others claim that he seriously intended a permanent conquest of the Scottish Lowlands. The Wall did not even overawe the Brigantes, who rose again in 154–5. They were defeated once more, but not before Roman reinforcements were sent to Britain from Germany.[46]

The second most serious theatre of war was North Africa, which continued troubled throughout the reign, with frequent incursions by Moorish armies into Mauretania (in 145 and 152).[47] There was also a revolt in Egypt (Alexandria) in 142–3, and minor risings in Greece and Palestine. Antoninus headed off trouble in the East by writing a letter to the King of Parthia, dissuading him from an attack on Armenia, though his generals had to campaign vigorously against the nomadic and powerful Alans on the borders of Bithynia.[48] Finally, there is good reason to believe that Dacia was also a hotspot. It is well known that there was a revolt there in 158–9, as a result of which the province of Dacia Superior was divided into two, but Russian historians believe there were two previous rebellions, one in 139 and the other in 143–4.[49] Always nervously eyeing his frontiers, Antoninus decided to make the career of an auxiliary (that is, a non-legionary soldier) in the Roman armies more attractive by an astute reform: henceforth those who completed auxiliary service would receive citizenship, and so would any future children, but the privilege was denied to auxiliaries' children already born. This was a complete volte-face from his earlier stance, which was to *cut down* on the privileges of the auxiliaries so as to widen the differential between them and the legionaries.[50]

The empire under Antoninus Pius received its most glittering eulogy in the year 144, when the young Greek orator Aelius Aristides, the most talented pupil of Herodes Atticus, made a famous speech of praise for the *pax Romana*.[51] There were five main arguments in the oration. First, Rome, unlike the Macedonian and Persian realms, was a truly 'universal' empire, combining all the virtues of a city state with the power, magnificence and sense of duty of a great empire. The Roman genius had discovered the secret of combining the very best of democracy, aristocracy and monarchy. Aristides claimed that the whole world was now one gigantic city state, but it would have been more accurate to describe it as a vast confederation of city states. Second, the army was the empire's showpiece, its Platonic 'work of perfection'. Its methods of recruitment, conditions of service, training, discipline and techniques all spoke of its excellence, and its power was now so great that only a handful of lunatics or benighted barbarians like the Moors or Dacians dared to oppose it. Third, Roman imperial policy was itself a masterpiece. Lesser people surrounded their cities with walls, but Rome chose to girdle its empire with the 'walls' of natural frontiers. Fourth, Rome's golden age was not in the age of Aeneas or even of Augustus, but was happening right now; and, unlike other so-called golden ages, this one would last for ever. Finally, Rome was famous for Roman justice, whereby the emperor protected the weak, which had not happened in the old Greek city states.[52] In a second speech, addressed to the emperor himself, Aristides went in for gross flattery of Antoninus, archly hinting at the many points of comparison with his 'lesser' predecessor Hadrian. He praised the emperor for staying in Rome and doing the hard work instead of promenading around the empire. Antoninus, he said, governed by letters 'which arrive at their destination almost as soon as they are written, as though borne by winged messengers'. The emperor achieved the remarkable paradox of never travelling, but still contriving matters so that his position as the apex and source of the entire imperial system was openly exalted and recognised as never before with previous wearers of the purple. Antoninus, he pointed out, had abolished the death-penalty for senators, and was a model of prudence, justice and piety. It was as if the gods had decanted all evil into certain madmen and given Antoninus all the virtues.[53]

At first reading, Aelius Aristides's speech seems a cliché-ridden collection of stereotypes, trite commonplaces mixed with ludicrous flattery. The idea of the impregnable 'walls' of the natural frontiers would have been news to those toiling on the Antonine Wall or in the deserts of North Africa. The speech related solely to the experience of upper-class Romans or oligarchic Italians and would have drawn ribald guffaws from anyone else. The 'golden age' idea would have been meaningless, and worse to slaves, peasants and anyone who was not of Italian or Greek origin. And there was a deal of humbug in Aristides's praise for Antoninus's eschewal of his predecessor's peripatetic existence. Like all the important writers of the Antonine period – Lucian, Galen, Pausanias, Artemidorus, and so on – Aristides was himself a great traveller. Yet beneath the froth we can discern two important ideas. One was an inchoate version of the 'divine right of kings'.[54] Aristides argued that a divine mind was at work in the person of the emperor and this gave him a sacred, almost religious character. Antoninus was not so much Plato's philosopher-king as the Platonic logos made flesh. This alerts us to one of the hidden motifs of this emperor's reign, sufficiently hinted at in the coinage.[55] The other important idea was first noticed by the great Russian historian Michael Rostovsteff, who scouted the idea that Aristides's oration was flummery, and instead regarded it as the most accurate extant picture of the Roman empire in the second century. For Rostovsteff, the idea of a confederation of city states matched his idea of a great engine of Roman capitalism, which provided an early example of globalisation. Roman commerce and Roman goods reached Scandinavia and the Baltic; through the Black Sea cities, Roman trade penetrated southern Russia;

the Canaries, Iceland, China, Indochina, Indonesia and East Africa were all known about and traded with. Indeed, in the entire world only Japan, the Pacific, the Americas and southern Africa remained outside the commercial orbit of the Roman empire.[56]

Appendix Three: Solitude

Marcus's praise of solitude and his sometimes expressed desire that he would rather be a hermit than an emperor have been very influential and have produced a number of distinguished descendants. One of the most famous solitaries in history was Henry Thoreau, the New England mystic and dissident who denounced the Mexican-American war of 1846–8 as grotesque imperialism and regarded John Brown, the abolitionist martyr of Harper's Ferry, as a true saint. During the years 1845–7 Thoreau built a rude house on the shore of Walden Pond near Concord, Massachusetts and lived there as a hermit for two years and two months. The ideas brought to light by this experience had a peculiarly Aurelian timbre, which only extensive quotation can convey. But any reader of the *Meditations* is bound to pick up the conscious or unconscious references in *Walden* as follows: 'What a man thinks of himself, that it is which determines or rather indicates his fate.' 'The mass of men lead lives of quiet desperation.' 'There can be no very black melancholy to him who lives in the midst of nature, and has his senses still. There was never yet such a storm but it was Aeolian music to a healthy and innocent ear.' 'The thrills of joys and the thrills of pains are indistinguishable. How peaceful the phenomena of the lake! Again the works of Man shine as in the spring – aye, every leaf, and twig and stone, and cobweb sparkles now at mid-afternoon, as when covered with dew in a spring morning. Every motion of an oar or an insect produces a flash of light; and if an oar falls, how sweet the echo!' 'When we are unhurried and wise, we perceive that only great and worthy things have any permanence and absolute existence, that petty fears and petty pleasures are but the shadow of reality.' 'Goodness is the only investment that never fails.' 'He is blest who is assured that the animal is dying out in him day by day, and the divine being established.'

'Rather than love, than money, than fame, give me truth. I sat at a table where were rich food and wine in abundance, and obsequious attendance, but sincerity and truth were not; and I went away hungry from the inhospitable board.'[1]

Yet another 'artificial' American solitary was the polar explorer Admiral Richard Byrd. For five months in 1934 Byrd lived alone in a tiny wooden shack at Advance Base on the Ross Ice Shelf during the Antarctic winter – for meteorological research, he claimed, but mainly to test himself. Remaining alone from 19 March to 11 August, he nearly died and hovered at times on the brink of madness. Byrd's self-inflicted ordeal also produced a wealth of sayings and observations that could have come from the *Meditations*. 'The tolerable quality of a dangerous existence is the fact that the human mind cannot remain continuously sensitive to anything . . . the threat of sudden death can scare a man for only so long; then he dismisses it as he might a mealy-mouthed beggar.' 'A man doesn't begin to attain wisdom until he recognises that he is no longer indispensable.' 'His [Man's] view of life is no more than a flash in time.'[2] As with many ascetics and recluses, he found that loneliness bred a mystical outlook. 'Freed from materialistic distractions, my senses sharpened in new directions, and random or commonplace affairs of the sky, the earth and the spirit, which ordinarily I would have ignored if I had noticed them at all, became exciting and portentous.'[3] Consoling himself with a reading of the philosopher Santayana, Byrd learned that one can live even more fully without possessions; he felt more alive than ever; he experienced Nature more intensely; and he had a profound sense of oneness with the universe. 'I could feel no doubt of Man's oneness with the universe. The conviction came that the rhythm was too orderly, too harmonious, too perfect to be a product of blind chance – that therefore there must be purpose in the whole and that Man was part of that whole, and not an accidental offshoot.'[4] It is most of all Marcus Aurelius's 'holism' – the conviction that all things are interconnected – and his pantheism that are in evidence in Byrd's reflections: 'The universe was a cosmos, not a chaos; Man was as rightfully a part of that cosmos as were day and night.'[5]

Some have said that both Thoreau and Byrd misinterpreted Marcus and took a wrong turning into a blind alley. Critics of Byrd stress that he did not have the Stoic emperor's concern for truth. Like his fellow-countryman Frederick Cook, Byrd was a genuinely great polar explorer, but his own undoubted achievements were not enough for him: he wanted immortality. And so, in 1926 he claimed that he and his co-pilot Floyd Bennett had flown from Spitzbergen to the North Pole and back in fifteen and a half hours, thus making Byrd the first person incontestably to have reached the Pole (since both Cook's and Peary's claims to have reached it overland were widely discredited). In fact it turned out that Roald Amundsen, the first man to the

South Pole, achieved a unique 'double first' when he flew over the pole in the airship *Norge* shortly afterwards. When Byrd's plane developed an oil leak, he instructed Bennett to fly back and forth off the coast of Spitzbergen until enough time had elapsed that they could plausibly claim to have been to the North Pole and back.[6] Byrd, in short, lacking Marcus's dedication to the truth, was not a real heir to the emperor, though the truly significant thing is that he aspired to be. Thoreau, too, was accused of being disingenuous. Robert Louis Stevenson thought him an effeminate skulker, peevishly avoiding social life, chafing at having to work for a living and resenting that 'Apollo must serve Admetus'. Stevenson wrote scathingly: 'Marcus Aurelius found time to study virtue and between whiles to conduct the imperial affairs of Rome; but Thoreau is so busy improving himself that he must think twice about a morning call.'[7]

Bibliography

1 Works by contemporaries or near-contemporaries

Apuleius, *Metamorphoses* (*The Golden Ass*); *Apologia*

Cassius Dio, *History of Rome*

Galen in C.G. Kuhn (ed.), *Claudii Galeni Opera Omnia* (Leipzig 1833)

Herodian, *Roman History*

Justin Martyr, *Apology 1*; *Apology 2*; *Dialogue with Trypho*

Lucian, *Toxaris*; *Demonax*; *Alexander*; *Icarousenippus*; *Peregrinus*; *Hermotimus*; *Philopseudus*; *Quomodo historia* (*How to Write History*): *Charon Sees Life*; *A Portrait Study*

Pausanias, *Description of Greece*

Tertullian, *Apologeticum pro Christianis*; *De Cultu Feminarum*; *De Carne Christi*; *De Fuga in Persecutione*; *Ad Martyres*; *Accedit ad Scapulam liber*; *Libri duo ad Nationes*

2 Sources in classical literature

Caesar, *De Bello Gallico*

Cicero, *De Officiis*; *De Finibus Bonorum et Malorum*; *De Natura Deorum*; *De re publica*

Columella, *De Re Rustica*

Diodorus Siculus, *Bibliotheca historica*

Horace, *Epistulae* (*Letters*)

Josephus, *The Jewish War*; *Jewish Antiquities*

Juvenal, *Satires*

Livy, *History*

Lucan, *Pharsalia* (*Civil War*)

Lucretius, *De Rerum Natura*

Martial, *Epigrams*

Musonius Rufus, *Diatribes*

Ovid, *Fasti*; *Metamorphoses*

Petronius, *Satyricon*

Philo, *Legatio ad Gaium*; *On Creation*; *On Allegorical Interpretation*; *On the Cherubim*; *On Husbandry*; *Who Is the Heir of Divine Things?*

Pliny the Elder, *Natural History* (NH)

Pliny the Younger, *Letters*

Plutarch, *Lives*; *Moralia*; *On Superstition*

Ptolemy, *Geography*

Quintilian, *Institutio Oratoria*

Seneca, *Epistulae morales ad Lucilium* (*Letters to Lucilius*); *Ad Helviam matrem*; *De Consolatione*; *De Constantia Sapientis*; *De Beneficiis*; *Naturales Quastiones*

Strabo, *Geographica*

Suetonius, *The Lives of the Caesars*

Tacitus, *Annals*; *Histories*; *Germania*; *Dialogus de oratoribus*

Thucydides, *History*

Varro, *De lingua latina*; *Rerum rusticarum*

Virgil, *Aeneid*

3 Works in Latin and Greek by authors in the third century and later

Ammianus Marcellinus, *Res Gestae*

Augustine, *Confessions*; *City of God*; *De Ordine*

Aurelius Victor, *De Caesaribus*; *Epitome de Caesaribus* (attrib., but really just a precis of the first work)

Ausonius, *Gratiarium Actio Dicta Domino Gratiano Augusto*

Diogenes Laertius, *Lives and Opinions of Eminent Philosophers*

Eusebius, *Historia Ecclesiastica* (HE)

Eutropius, *Breviarium historiae romanae*

Festus, *Breviarium*

Jerome, *Chronicle*

Julian, *The Caesars*; *Contra Galilaeos*

Minucius Felix, *Octavius*

Origen, *Contra Celsum*

Orosius, *Historiae adversum paganos*

Philostratus, *Vitae Sophistorum* (VC) (*Lives of the Sophists*)

Notes

Guide to abbreviations used in the notes

Throughout the Notes classical texts are referred to by book, section and sub-section. Where no place of publication is given, the title in question was published in London.

AE	*L'Année Épigraphique* (Paris 1888–)
AHR	*American Historical Review*
ANRW	*Aufstieg und Niedergang der römischen Welt*
BHAC	*Bonner Historia Augusta Colloquium*
BMC	H. Mattingly, *Coins of the Roman Empire in the British Museum* (1940)
CAH	*Cambridge Ancient History*, Vol.II (Cambridge 2000)
CIL	*Corpus Inscriptorum Latinorum* (Berlin 1863)
CQ	*Classical Quarterly*
Digest	Theodore Mommsen & P. Krueger (eds), *Justinian's Digest of Roman Law*, trans. A. Watron, 4 vols (Philadelphia 1985)
EA	*Epigraphica Anatolica*
Farquharson	A.S.L. Farquharson (ed.), *The Meditations of Marcus Aurelius*, 2 vols (Oxford 1944)
Galen K	C.G. Kuhn (ed.), *Claudii Galeni Opera Omnia* (Leipzig 1833)
GR	*Greece and Rome*
Haines	C.R. Haines (ed.), *The Letters of Fronto to Marcus Aurelius* (Loeb 1919)
HA	*Historia Augusta*
IGR	*Inscriptiones Graecae ad Res Romanas Pertinentes*
IL	A. Degrassi (ed.), *Inscriptiones Italiae* (Rome 1947)
ILS	H. Dessau (ed.), *Inscriptiones Latinae Selectae* (Berlin 1916)
JRS	*Journal of Roman Studies*
JTS	*Journal of Theological Studies*
KS	G. Alföldy, *Konsulat und Senatorenstand unter den Antoninen* (Bonn 1977)
Meds	*The Meditations of Marcus Aurelius*

PBSR	*Proceedings of the British School at Rome*
PIR2	E. Groag, A. Stein & L. Petersen (eds), *Prosopographia Imperii Romani* (Leipzig 1933–)
PP	*Past and Present*
RIC	H. Mattingly & E.A. Sydenham (eds), *The Roman Imperial Coinage*, 4 vols (1936)
Rostovsteff	Michael Rostovsteff, *The Social and Economic History of the Roman Empire* (1926 & 1957)
RP	Ronald Syme, *Roman Papers*, 7 vols (Oxford 1979–89)
Rutherford	R.B. Rutherford (ed.), *The Meditations of Marcus Aurelius* (Oxford 1989)
SEG	J.J. Hondius & A.G. Woodhead (eds), *Supplementum Epigraphicum Graecum* (Leiden 1925–)
ZPE	*Zeitschrift für Papyrologie und Epigraphik*

Notes to Introduction

1. Higgledy-piggledy Marcus Aurelius
   Guiding his life by a rule of thumb
   Gaining the nickname of IMPERMEABILE

   Meaning both 'Stoic' and, possibly, 'dumb' (Anthony Hecht & John Hollander, eds, *Jiggery Pokery. A Compendium of Double Dactyls* (1966) • 2. James Stockdale, *Courage under Fire. Testing Epictetus's doctrines in a laboratory of human behaviour* (1993) • 3. For the influence of self-help books see, for example, Albert Ellis, *How to Refuse to Make Yourself Miserable about Anything* (1998) • 4. Philip L.Barbour, *The Three Worlds of Captain John Smith* (1964), p.14; E. Keble Chatterton, *Captain John Smith* (1927) pp. 19–20 • 5.Robert I.Rotberg, *Rhodes,The Founder* (Oxford 1988) pp. 95, 100, 122, 384–85 • 6. All these propositions are discussed at length in Chapters Nine and Ten above. • 7. Peter Stothard, *Times Literary Supplement* 9 October 1998 • 8. Marcus Aurelius, *Meditations* 3.2
   • 9. There was a time when meadow, grove and stream
   The earth, and every common sight,
   To me did seem
   Apparell'd in celestial light,
   The glory and the freshness of a dream . . .

   The rainbow comes and goes
   And lovely is the rose
   The moon doth with delight
   Look round her when the heavens are bare

Waters on a starry night
Are beautiful and fair
The sunshine is a glorious birth.
(Wordsworth, *Intimations of Immortality* i–ii)
10. Matthew Arnold, 'Marcus Aurelius' in R.H. Super, ed. *The Complete Prose Works of Matthew Arnold* (Ann Arbor 1962) iii. p. 149 • 11. Katha Upanishad 2; Taittireya Upanishad 3.10 • 12. F.L. Woodward, *Some Sayings of the Buddha* (2002) p. 8 • 13. Sri Aurobindo, *Essays on the Gita* (Pondicherry 1987) • 14. *Bhagavad-Gita* 2.27 • 15. J.J.Clarke, *Oriental Enlightenment.The Encounter between Asian and Western Thought* (1997) • 16. For Rousseau see Chapter 19 below. Cf. Wordsworth, 'How gracious, how benign is solitude.' *The Prelude* iv. 357; 'Then stirs the feeling infinite,so felt in solitude when we are least alone.' (Byron, *Childe Harold's Pilgrimage* iii. 90) • 17. Bacon, 'Of Friendship', Essay 26. • 18. See Appendix 3.

Notes to Chapter One   *pp. 1–23*

• 1. Augustus (27 BC–AD 14); Tiberius, 14–37; Caligula (Gaius), 37–41; Claudius, 41–54; Nero, 54–68; Galba, 68–9; Otho, 69; Vitellius, 69; Vespasian, 69–79; Titus, 79–81; Domitian, 81–96; Nerva, 96–8; Trajan, 98–117; Hadrian, 117–38; Antoninus Pius, 138–61. • 2. It is only fair to add that this intense academic debate between 'maximalists' and 'minimalists' produces wildly divergent figures, anywhere from a low of fifty-four million to a high of some 130 million. The debate is in some ways an uncanny pre-echo of the very similar controversy over the population of pre-Conquest Mexico. The sanest estimate is somewhere near the high end of the 'minimalists' figures (see the eighty million produced by Brent Shaw in 'Rebels and Outsiders', *Cambridge Ancient History* (Cambridge 2000) – hereinafter CAH – 11, p.361. It may be of interest to the reader briefly to review the figures given in some classic studies. Julius Beloch, *Die Bevölkerung der Griechisch-römischen Welt* (Leipzig 1886), pp.50–7, gave a figure of fifty-four million and was supported in this by P. Salmon, *Population et dépopulation dans l'empire Romain* (Brussels 1974), pp.22–39, who estimated twenty-eight million souls living in the eastern empire and twenty-six million in the west. Some minimalists are prepared to go as low as forty-five million for AD 14 (at the end of Augustus's reign) – see J.C. Russell, *Late Ancient and Medieval Population* (Philadelphia 1958), pp.81–3; G. Charles-Picard, *La civilisation de l'Afrique romaine* (Paris 1959), pp.45–59; cf. also C. McEvedy & R. Jones, *Atlas of World Population History* (1978). Slightly more realistic totals of seventy million at the time of Augustus are provided by Ernst Stein, *Geschichte des spätzrömischen Reiches* (Vienna 1928), pp.1–3, though Stein does think that the total declined to fifty million by AD 250. H. Delbrück, *Geschichte der Kriegkunst* (Berlin 1927), ii, pp.237–8, estimates 90–100 million around 150 – interesting, as Delbrück was usually a 'downsizer'. It should be stated that the authoritative article by W. Fier in the CAH ('Demography', CAH II, pp.811–14) is even more downsizing and favours a figure of 61.4 million at Marcus Aurelius's accession. • 3. J.D. Durand, *Historical Estimates of World Population. An Evaluation* (Philadelphia 1974), pp.15, 61. •4. Beloch, *Die Bevölkerung* op. cit, p.411; P.A. Brunt, *Italian Manpower 225 BC–AD 14* (Oxford 1987), pp.382–3. • 5. Keith Hopkins, *Conquerors and Slaves* (Cambridge 1978), pp.68–9; Duncan Jones, *The Economy of the Roman Empire* (Cambridge 1982), p.317; Nicholas Purcell, 'Rome and Italy', CAH II, p.423. • 6. Diodorus 17.52.6; Herodian 7.16.1; Aurelius Victor, *De Caesaribus* 40.19; Strabo 16.2.5; 17.9.8.1; Galen K.5.49; D. Delia, 'The population of Roman Alexandria', *Transactions of the American Philological Association* 118 (1988), pp.275–91. • 7. Garnsey, 'Land', CAH II, pp.687–8. • 8. ibid., p.682. • 9. Columella, *Rustica* 1.2.3.; Strabo 4.177, 207; 5.235. •10. For the greed, see Pliny, *Natural History* 11, 118, 125; Juvenal, *Satires* 14.ll.275–84. On the dangers of the Mediterranean, see J. Rouge. *Recherches sur l'organisation du commerce maritime en Mediterranée sous l'empire Romain* (Paris 1966), pp.31–9; A.W. Crosby, *Ecological Imperialism: The Biological Expansion of Europe 900–1900* (Cambridge 1986), pp.104–31. For the cost ratios, see Keith Hopkins, 'The transport of staples in the Roman Empire', *Trade and Staples in Antiquity* (Budapest 1982), pp.81–7 (at p.86). • 11. W.V. Harris, 'Trade', CAH II, pp.724–37; Greene, 'Industry and Technology', CAH II, pp.752–6; Jean-Jacques Aubert, *Business Managers in Ancient Rome* (Leiden 1994), pp.227–39; John Ward-Perkins, 'The marble trade and its organisation', in J.H.D. Arms & E.C. Kopff (eds), *The Seaborne Commerce of Ancient Rome* (Rome 1980), pp.326–8. •12. R.W. Goldsmith, 'An estimate of the size and structure of the National Product of the early Roman empire', *Review of Income and Wealth* 30 (1984), pp.263–88; A.H.M. Jones, *The Later Roman Empire* (1964), p.465. • 13. For the quasi-theological fervour with which this somewhat pointless academic battle is waged, see (on the primitive side) M.I. Finley, *The Ancient Economy* (Berkeley 1973, revised 1999); Peter Garnsey & Richard Saller, *The Roman Economy, Society and Culture* (1987); Peter Garnsey, *Food and Society in Classical Antiquity* (Cambridge 1999). For the pro-marketeers, see Peter Temin, 'A Market Economy in the Early Roman Empire', *JRS* 91 (2001), pp.169–81; Peter Temin, 'The Economy of the Early Roman Empire', *Journal of Economic Perspectives* 20 (2006), pp.133–51; Peter Temin, 'The labour market and the early Roman empire', *Journal of Interdisciplinary History* 34 (2004), pp.513–38; Kevin Greene, 'Technological innovation and economic progress in the ancient world: M.I. Finley reconsidered', *Economic History Review* 53 (2000), pp.29–59. See also Jean Andreas, 'Commerce and Finance', CAH II, pp.769–87; Richard Duncan-Jones, *Money and Growth in the Roman Empire* (Cambridge 1994); Joseph Manning & Ian Morris (eds), *The Ancient Economy. Evidence and Models* (Stanford 2002); D.J. Mattingly and John Salmon (eds), *Economies beyond Agriculture in the Classical World* (2000);

Aldo Sciavone, *The End of the Past. Ancient Rome and the Modern West*, trans. Margaret J. Schneider (Harvard 2000); Michael E. Smith, 'The Archaeology of Ancient State Economies', *Annual Review of Anthropology* 33 (2004), pp.73–102. It may be amusing to note that Marxists, who love a synthesis, have even considered classifying the Roman empire as one of Marx's classical 'Asiatic modes of production'. • 14. Keith Hopkins, 'Taxes and Trade in the Roman Empire', JRS 70 (1980), pp.101–25. • 15. P.A. Brunt, 'The Revenues of Rome', JRS 71 (1981), pp.161–72. • 16. Hopkins, 'Taxes' loc. cit. • 17. Keith Hopkins, *Conquerors and Slaves: Sociological Studies in Roman History* (Cambridge 1978). • 18. K.R. Bradley, *Slavery and Society at Rome* (1994); cf. also R.W. Barrow, *Slavery in the Roman Empire* (1928); W.L. Westermann, *The Slave Systems of Greek and Roman Antiquity* (Philadelphia 1955). • 19. Tacitus, *Annals* 14.42–5. • 20. Epictetus, *Discourses* 3.26.21–3. • 21. Jo-Ann Shelton, *As the Romans Did. A Sourcebook* (1988), p.170. • 22. S. Treggiani, 'Jobs for Women', *American Journal of Ancient History* 1 (1976), pp.76–104 (at pp.91–4). • 23. M.I. Finley (ed.), *Classical Slavery* (1987). • 24. Keith Hopkins, 'Novel evidence for Greek slavery', in Robin Osborne, *Studies in Ancient Greek and Roman Society* (Cambridge 2004), pp.206–25. • 25. For the slave trade, see W.V. Harris, 'Trade', CAH II, p.721; W.V. Harris, 'Towards a Study of the Roman Slave Trade', *Memoirs of the American Academy in Rome* 36 (1980), pp.117–40; Keith Hopkins, 'Conquerors and Slaves: The Impact of Conquering an Empire on the Political Economy of Italy', in Craige B. Champion (ed.), *Roman Imperialism: Readings and Sources* (Oxford 2004), pp.108–28; for Phrygia, see Philostratus, *Vita Apollonii* 8.7.12. • 26. Columella, *Rustica* 1.8.4; 1.18.19. • 27. John Madden, 'Slavery in the Roman Empire. Numbers and Origins', *Classics Ireland* 3 (1996). • 28. Josephus, *Jewish Wars* 6.4.20; 6.9.3. • 29. M. Crawford, 'Republican Denarii in Romania: the suppression of piracy and the slave trade', JRS 67 (1977), pp.117–24. • 30. Suetonius, *Augustus* 32.1; *Tiberius* 8.2; Columella, *Rustica* 1.6.3. • 31. Cassius Dio – hereinafter Dio – 54.16; Tertullian, *Apology* 9.7; Tertullian, *Ad Nat.* 1.15; Minucius Felix, *Octavian* 30.2; Justin Martyr, *Apology* 1.27; W.V. Harris, 'Child Exposure in Ancient Rome', JRS 84 (1994), pp.1–22. • 32. M. Hammond, 'The composition of the Senate, AD 68–235', JRS 47 (1957), pp.74–81; R.J.A. Talbert, *The Senate of Imperial Rome* (Princeton 1984). • 33. P.A. Brunt, 'The administrators of Roman Egypt', JRS 65 (1975), pp.124–7. • 34. O.F. Robinson, *Ancient Rome. City Planning and Administration* (1992), p.211. • 35. Keith Hopkins, 'Contraception in the Roman Empire', *Comparative Studies in Society and History* (1965), pp.124–51. • 36. Hopkins, *Conquerors and Slaves* op. cit., pp.3–6. • 37. Garnsey & Saller, *The Roman Economy* op. cit., pp.64–5. • 38. ibid., pp.51–2. • 39. B. Dobson, 'The centurionate and social mobility during the principate', in C. Nicolet (ed.), *Recherches sur les structures sociales dans l'antiquité classique* (Paris 1974), pp.99–115. • 40. P.A. Brunt, 'Pay and Superannuation in the Roman Army', PBSR 18 (1950), pp.50–71. •

41. Dio 48.36. • 42. Richard Duncan-Jones, *The Economy of the Roman Empire*, p.4. • 43. P.A. Brunt, 'Two Great Roman Landowners', *Latomus* 34 (1975), pp.619–35. • 44. Pliny, *Natural History* – hereinafter NH – 8.37. • 45. Apuleius, *Apology* 23, 71, 77. • 46. Duncan-Jones, *Economy* op. cit., p.348. • 47. W.L. Westermann, *The Slave System of Greek and Roman Antiquity* (1955), pp.100–1. • 48. Pliny, NH 7.128. • 49. Dio 61.10.3; Tacitus, *Annals* 13.42. • 50. Galen K. 13.636; Duncan-Jones, *Economy* op. cit., p.343. • 51. S. J. Bastomsky, 'Rich and Poor: The great divide in Ancient Rome and Victorian England', GR 37 (1990), pp.39–43. • 52. E. Groag, A. Stein & L. Petersen (eds), *Prosopographia Imperii Romani* (Berlin & Leipzig 1933) – hereinafter PIR2 – A.630, 637, 677, 701. • 53. HA Marcus 1.1–2. • 54. *Corpus Inscriptorum Latinorum* (Berlin 1863) – hereinafter CIL – xiv, 3579. Cassius Dio states quite clearly that there was a tie of kinship between the Annii and Hadrian's family (Dio 69.21.2), but more straitlaced scholars prefer to hedge their bets ('it cannot be ascertained' etc. in Ronald Syme, *Roman Papers* – hereinafter RP – i, p.244). • 55. For the origin of the fortune, see Pliny the Younger, *Letters* 8.18. • 56. *The Meditations of Marcus Aurelius* – hereinafter Meds – 1.2. • 57. PIR2 D.183; *L'Année Épigraphique* – hereinafter AE – 1955, 3; HA Didius Julianus 1.3.4; E. Champlin, *Fronto and Imperial Rome* (1980), pp.108–9; Farquharson, *Marcus Aurelius* i, p.270. • 58. Meds 1.3. • 59. HA Marcus 1.7; 1.9; Meds 1.4; Syme, RP ii, pp.682–3; iii, p.1174. • 60. As a young man he was a friend of Pliny the Younger (Pliny, *Letters* 7.24). For his career, see Syme, RP iii, pp. 1158–78. • 61. Syme, RP iii, pp.1175–6. • 62. Tacitus, *Dial* 28–9; Quintilian, *Inst.* 1.1.12. • 63. H.R. Bradley, *Discovering the Roman Family* (Oxford 1991), pp.13–36; S.B. Pomeroy, *Goddesses, Whores, Wives and Slaves: Women in Classical Antiquity* (New York 1975), pp.168, 212. • 64. Bradley, *Discovering* op. cit., p.160. • 65. B. Rawson et al. (eds), *The Family in Ancient Rome* (Ithaca 1986), pp.31–7; J.F. Gardner & T. Wiedemann, *The Roman Household. A Sourcebook* (1991), pp.1–29. • 66. J. Marquardt, *Das Privatleben der Römer* (Berlin 1964), pp.80–1. • 67. HA Marcus 1.5.7; C.R. Haines (ed.), *The Letters of Marcus Aurelius to Fronto*, 2 vols (Loeb Classical Library 112) (1919), i, p.242. • 68. Meds 1.1; 1.17.2. • 69. HA Marcus 4.1; Michael Grant, *The Antonines* (1994), p.26. • 70. HA Marcus 1.10; 4.1–2; Dio 69.21.2; H. Dessau (ed.), *Inscriptiones Latinae Selectae* (Berlin 1916) – hereinafter ILS – 6305; Brian K. Harvey, 'Two Bases of Marcus Aurelius and the Roman Imperial Succession', *Historia* 54 (2004), pp.46–60. • 71. G.J. Szemler, *The Priests of the Roman Republic: A study of the interactions between priesthoods and magistracies* (1973). • 72. Livy 1.20; Cicero, *Rep* 2.14; Lucan 9.478. • 73. Ovid, *Fasti* 3.384, 387; Horace, *Epistles* 2.1.86; Dionysius ii.70, 71, 83; Virgil, *Aeneid* 8.286; Varro, *De lingua latina* 6.45; 7.2; 7.26; Quintilian, *Inst.* 1.6.54. • 74. Tacitus, *Annals* 2.83. • 75. Suetonius, *Claudius* 33. • 76. HA Marcus 4.2–4. • 77. A.S.L. Farquharson (ed.), *The Meditations of Marcus Aurelius*, 2 vols (Oxford 1944) – hereinafter Farquharson – i, p.276; cf. Richard H. Millington (ed.), *The Cambridge*

Companion to Nathaniel Hawthorne (Cambridge 2004). • 78. Meds 1.4. • 79. Quintilian, *Inst.* 1.2.4; Pliny, *Letters* 3.3. • 80. S.F. Bonner, *Education in Ancient Rome* (Berkeley 1977), pp.32–3, 105, 332–3; cf. P. Ginestet, *Les organisations de la jeunesse dans l'Occident romain* (Brussels 1991). • 81. Bonner, *Education* op. cit. pp.20–33, 104–10. • 82. Meds 1.5. • 83. Meds 1.6. • 84. HA Marcus 2.6. • 85. Martial 10.62.5; 14.223; Juvenal, *Satires* 7.27. • 86. Bonner, *Education* op. cit., pp.87–8. • 87. ibid., pp.213–15. • 88. Meds 1.10. • 89. Dio 72.36.2. • 90. Meds 1.17.2; 1.17.11.

Notes to Chapter Two   *pp. 24–44*

• 1. HA Marcus 1.9; 4.5; Dio 69.21.1–2. • 2. Tacitus, *Annals* 3.55.4; 16.5.1; Martial 9.73.7–10; Petronius, *Satyricon* 58. • 3. Syme, RP v, p.670. • 4. HA Marcus 4.5; Syme, RP i, pp.325–32; iii, pp.1172–8. • 5. Tertullian, *Apology* 5.7. • 6. Dio 69.11.2–4; HA Hadrian 14.5–7; R. Lambert, *Beloved of God. The Story of Hadrian and Antinous* (1984). • 7. HA Hadrian 17.10; Tacitus, *Annals* 2.26.3; *Epitome de Caesaribus* 4.10; Haines, *Fronto Letters* op. cit., ii, p.206; Eutropius 8.6.2. • 8. Miriam Griffin, 'Trajan', CAH 11, pp.130–141. • 9. Martial, *Epigrams* 93.2. • 10. HA Hadrian 5; 17; 21. • 11. Hadrian and his travels have attracted a lot of attention. Apart from the famous novel *Memoirs of Hadrian* by Marguerite Yourcenar, there are the scholarly volumes by A.R. Birley, *Hadrian* (1997); R. Chevallier & R. Poignault, *L'Empereur Hadrian* (Paris 1998); Elizabeth Speller, *Following Hadrian* (2003); M.T. Boatwright, *Hadrian and the City of Rome* (Princeton 1987). More popular, but entertaining, is Danny Danziger & Nicholas Purcell, *Hadrian's Empire* (2005). See also Fergus Millar, *The Emperor in the Roman World* (1977), pp.28–40, and Syme, 'The Journeys of Hadrian', RP vi (Oxford 1991), pp.346–57. • 12. Julian, *The Caesars* 311D. This recalls Tertullian's remark that the restless travelling of Hadrian was the sign of a man in search of mysteries that could not be known (Tertullian, *Apology* 5.7). • 13. HA Hadrian 3.11; 26.1–3. • 14. M.T. Boatwright, *Hadrian and the City of Rome, passim*; cf. Birley, *Hadrian*, pp.110–11. • 15. Dio 69.6.3. Needless to say, sceptics insist this was a story told about a variety of emperors (Millar, *The Emperor in the Roman World* op.cit., pp.3–4). A similar story was told about Philip of Macedon, Demetrius Poliorcetes and Serenus of Antipater (Plutarch, *Moralia* 179 C–D; Plutarch, *Life of Demetrius* 42.7; Stobaios, *Florilegium* 2.13.48). See in general Richard P. Saller, 'Anecdotes as historical evidence', GR 127 (1980), pp.169–84. • 16. HA Hadrian 20.7–11. • 17. Dio 69.8.1; HA Hadrian 5.7; Birley, *Hadrian*, pp.97–8. • 18. HA Hadrian 1.5; 13.1; 21.4; 22.10; Syme, 'Hadrian as Philhellene', RP v, pp.546–62. Tetrapharmacum or, in its expanded form, pentapharmacum, was also a favourite dish of the emperor Alexander Severus, who reigned 222–35 (HA Alexander Severus 20.6). • 19. HA Hadrian 6.1–2; 22.1.2; Birley, *Hadrian*, p.102; Syme, 'Hadrian and the Senate', RP v, pp.295–324. • 20. Michael Rostovsteff, *The Social and Economic History of the Roman Empire*

(1957), pp.365–71. • 21. HA Hadrian 9.1.2. • 22. HA Hadrian 8.1–11; Syme, 'Hadrian and the Senate', RP v, pp.295–324. • 23. HA Hadrian 11.1; 20.3. • 24. HA Hadrian 19.3–7. • 25. HA Hadrian 11.4–7. • 26. Aurelius Victor, *Epitome de Caesaribus* 14.6; cf. HA Hadrian 14.11. • 27. HA Hadrian 15.10–13. • 28. HA Hadrian 2.4; 14.8–10; 16.3–4; 16.7; Syme, 'Hadrian the Intellectual', RP vi, pp.157–81. • 29. A.R. Birley, 'Hadrian', CAH 11, pp.138–149. • 30. Dio 69.4.6; HA Hadrian 16.2; 16.5–6. • 31. HA Hadrian 16.8.9. • 32. Galen K.5.17. • 33. HA Hadrian 14.1. • 34. HA Hadrian 15.9. • 35. HA Hadrian 15.1–8. • 36. HA Hadrian 26.10. • 37. Artemidorus, *Dream Interpretation*, ed. Robert J. White (New Jersey 1992), 2.12 (p.95); 4.56 (p.208). • 38. HA Hadrian 5.1–2. • 39. Warwick Ball, *Rome in the East* (2000), p.59. • 40. Dio 68.32.1–3; Orosius 7.12.6. • 41. P. Schäfer, *Der Bar Kockba-Aufstand. Studien zum zweiten jüdischen Krieg gegen Rom* (Tübingen 1981); cf. also Schäfer, 'Hadrian's policy in Judaea and the Bar Kokhba revolt: a reassessment', in P.R. Davies & R.T. White (eds), *A Tribute to G. Vermes* (1990), pp.281–3; L. Mildenberg, *The Coinage of the Bar Kokhba War* (Frankfurt 1984), esp. pp.17–49; T.D. Barnes, 'Hadrian and the Jews', *Journal of Jewish Studies* 36 (1985), pp.145–62. • 42. Dio 69.12.2; Eusebius, *Historia Ecclesiastica* 4.6.2; 4.8.6; Justin, *First Apology* 31.6; Jerome, *Chron.* 201. • 43. Birley, *Hadrian*, pp.272–4. • 44. Dio 69.12.3; 69.13.1–2; 69.14.3; M. Gichon, 'New insight into the Bar Kokhba war and a reappraisal of Dio Cassius 69.12–13', *Jewish Quarterly Review* 77 (1986), pp.15–43; Gichon, 'The Bar Kochba war – a colonial uprising against imperial Rome', *Revue Internationale d'histoire militaire* 42 (1979), pp.82–97. • 45. Eusebius HE 4.6.2–4.6.3; Schäfer, *Der Bar Kochba Aufstand* op.cit, p.138. • 46. Dio 69.13.3. The casualties were certainly enormous, but unquantifiable. The Bar-Kochba campaign resembled the American Civil War in that deaths from disease, starvation and wounds were far greater than battle losses, perhaps in a ratio of three to one. On Dio's figure of 580,000 battle casualties Ronald Syme remarks scathingly: 'The total of Palestinian population which this figure implies would make Karl Julius Beloch [see Ch. 1 Note 2 above] turn in his grave' (Syme, RP i, p.60). • 47. Syme, RP i, pp.325–32; iii, pp.1172–8; cf. Dio 69.1.5; HA Hadrian 7.1. • 48. HA Hadrian 23.3–6. • 49. The case for Hadrian's paternity is put by J. Carcopino, *Passion et politique chez les Césars* (Paris 1958), pp.143–82, but is convincingly refuted by H.G. Pflaum, 'Le règlement successoral d'Hadrian', BHAC (Bonn 1963), pp.95–122. For the idea of Aelius as the lover, see Dio 69.171.1; HA Hadrian 23.10. • 50. T.D. Barnes, 'Hadrian and Lucius Verus', JRS 57 (1967), pp.65–79; P. Grimal, *Marc Aurèle* (Paris 1991), p.54; J.P. Martin, *Providentia deorum. Recherches sur certains aspects religieux du pouvoir impérial romain* (Rome 1982), pp.298–304. • 51. CIL iii.4366, 10366; Dio 69.17; HA Aelius 3.8–9; 4.1–5; HA Hadrian 16.7; 23.14. • 52. HA Marcus 4.5. • 53. Eutropius 8.11; Birley, *Hadrian*, pp.289–90. • 54. Tacitus, *Annals* 4.36; Suetonius, *Nero* 7. • 55. HA Marcus 4.5. • 56. Dio 69.17.1–3; HA Hadrian 15.8; 23.1–6; 25.8. For

Servianus, see Pliny, *Letters* 6.26. • 57. Syme, RP v, p.671. • 58. Dio 69.20.1–4;
HA Hadrian 24.1; 26.6–10; Syme, RP ii, p.681. • 59. H. Lindsay, 'Adoption and
its function in cross-cultural contexts', in S. Dixon (ed.), *The Roman Family*
(Johns Hopkins 1992), pp.190–204. • 60. A. Wallace-Hadrill, 'Family and inher-
itance in the Augustan marriage laws', *Proceedings of the Cambridge Philological
Society* 27 (1981), pp.58–80; P. Csillag, *The Augustan Laws on Family Relations*
(Budapest 1976). • 61. H. Lindsay, 'Adoption and succession in Roman Law',
Newcastle Law Review 3 (1998), pp.57–81. • 62. Dio 69.20.5; *Epitome de Caesaribus*
12.3; HA Antoninus Pius 1.4; 4.4. • 63. HA Antoninus 4.6; HA Marcus 5.6; 6.2;
HA Lucius Verus 2.3; HA Aelius 6.9. • 64. Dio 69.21.1–2; HA Antoninus 4.5;
HA Marcus 5.1; HA Verus 2.1–2; HA Hadrian 15.7; 24.6–7; Syme, RP iii,
pp.1175–8. • 65. HA Marcus 5.4. • 66. HA Hadrian 24.8–13. • 67. The entire
story of the succession struggle in 136–8 is extraordinarily complicated and
could fill a book in itself. Besides the sources already cited, one might mention
J.P. Martin, *Providentia deorum. Recherches sur certains aspects religieux du pouvoir
impérial romain* (Paris 1982), pp.298–302; A. Chastagnol, *Le Sénat romain à
l'époque impériale* (Paris 1992), pp.63–4; F. Chausson, 'Deuil dynastique et
topographie urbaine dans la Rome antonine', in N. Belayche (ed.), *Rome, les
Césars et la ville aux deux premiers siècles de notre ère* (Rennes 2001), pp.293–342.
• 68. Dio 72.36.1; HA Marcus 5.2; Artemidorus in White (ed.), *Dream
Interpretation* op.cit., 1.31 (p.32); 2.39 (p.123). • 69. E.R. Dodds, *Pagan and
Christian* (1965), pp.8, 29. The attempt by Pierre Hadot in *The Inner Citadel*
(1998), pp.245–7, to refute this is unconvincing: it amounts to a mere assertion that psychology and psychoanalysis can have nothing to do with the
ancient world. Hadot does not tell us how he knows this 'certainty', apart
from another *a priori* assertion that we can interpret dreams from the ancient
world only within their own limited context. Two comments are in order.
First, Hadot's position is the familiar liberal fallacy whereby things can only
be what people perceive them to be, that there can be no objective interest
or reality beyond their perceptions. So: 'he is not acting in his own interests'
must be meaningless to Hadot – which is a strange position for a
Wittgensteinian concerned with ordinary language to take up. Second,
although it may be objected against writers like Erich Fromm that, equally,
we cannot be certain that the unconscious remains constant over time, the
mere fact that consciously in the twenty-first century mortals have the
same drives, lusts, ambitions and greeds as those in the second century
suggests, on a common-sense basis, that the unconscious may be similarly
constant. A similar example of using a mere assertion to counter the (admittedly intellectually reckless) stance of the Freudian school occurs in Simon
Price, 'The future of dreams: from Freud to Artemidorus', in Robin Osborne
(ed.), *Studies in Ancient Greek and Roman Society* (Cambridge 2004), pp.226–59.
• 70. HA Marcus 5.6–8; HA Antoninus 6.9–10. • 71. A.R. Birley, *Marcus Aurelius*

(1987), p.51; B. Baldwin, 'Hadrian's farewell to life. Some arguments for authenticity', *Classical Quarterly* 20 (1970), pp.372–4 • 72. HA Hadrian 25.6–7; 25.11; Dio 69.23.2; B. Baldwin, 'Hadrian's death in the Historia Augusta', *Gymnasium* 90 (1983), p.546. • 73. Dio 69.22–3; HA Marcus 6.1. • 74. Birley, *Hadrian* op. cit., p.303. • 75. R.B. Rutherford edition of *The Meditations of Marcus Aurelius* (Oxford, 1989) – hereinafter Rutherford – p. 108; Julian, *Caesars* 311. One is reminded of similar criticisms (albeit for heterosexual philandering) of US president John F. Kennedy. • 76. Meds 1.16.4; 6.30.3; Julian, *Caesars* 311D. • 77. HA Hadrian 16.10; Rutherford op. cit., p.8. • 78. *Epitome de Caesaribus* 4.10; Eutropius 8.6.2; Haines, *Fronto Letters* op. cit., ii, p.206. • 79. Haines, op. cit., ii, pp.110, 206–8. • 80. Champlin, *Fronto* op. cit., pp.95–7; C.P. Jones, 'Aelius Aristides' Eis Basileia', JRS 62 (1972), pp.134–52 (at pp.145–6); Fergus Millar, *A Study of Cassius Dio* (1964), p.60; R.W. Davis, 'Fronto, Hadrian and the Roman Army', *Latomus* 27 (1968), pp.75–95. • 81. Meds 10.8; HA Hadrian 15.1–2; 16.8–9; Meds 1.16.2.

Notes to Chapter Three   *pp. 45–68*

• 1. Meds 1.12. • 2. Meds 1.10; C.A. Behr, *Aelius Aristides and the Sacred Tales* (1968), pp.10–16; Behr, *Complete Works of Aelius Aristides* op. cit., pp.158–65. • 3. Philostratus, VS 1.22.3; PIR2 C.368. • 4. HA Marcus 3.8; Dio 60.27.2. • 5. Meds 1.9; Dio 71.1.2; Philostratus, VS 2.1.9. • 6. Meds 1.13. • 7. HA Antoninus 10.4. • 8. HA Marcus 3.1; Meds 1.8; 1.17.5. • 9. Philostratus, VS 2.5.571; HA Marcus 3.2–3; G.W. Bowersock, *Greek Sophists in the Roman Empire* (Oxford 1969), pp.53–4. • 10. Meds 1.14. • 11. Apuleius, *Apology* 19–20; PIR2 C.933–4; G. Alföldy, *Konsulat und Senatorenstand unter den Antoninen* (Bonn 1977) – hereinafter KS – pp.143, 208, 236. • 12. Meds 1.15. • 13. Juvenal, *Satires* 7.11.148–9. • 14. Champlin, *Fronto and Antonine Rome* op. cit., esp. pp.2, 9, 21–4, 52–3. • 15. The search for this verbal Holy Grail was precisely what made Fronto so ponderous, leaden and pettifogging. One is reminded of Ogden Nash's quip: 'The *mot juste*, the less speed.' • 16. Fronto to Marcus, AD 139 in C.R. Haines (ed.), *The Letters of Fronto to Marcus Aurelius* (Loeb 1919) – hereinafter Haines – i, pp.5–13 • 17. Fronto to Marcus, 139, Haines i, pp.13–15. • 18. Marcus to Fronto, 139, Haines i, pp.15–17. • 19. Bonner, *Education* op. cit., pp.79–89, 250–87 (esp. 265–70). • 20. Quintilian *Inst*. 1.1.12–14; J. Kaimio, *The Romans and the Greek Language* (Helsinki 1979). • 21. Marcus to Fronto, 139, Haines i, pp.19–21. • 22. Juvenal, *Satires* 6.187–9. • 23. Fronto to Marcus, c. 140–3, Haines i, pp.71–5. • 24. Marcus to Fronto, 139, Haines i, pp.31–3. • 25. Fronto to Marcus, 143, Haines i, pp.83–91. • 26. Haines i, pp.75, 77, 91, 109, 113, 115, 189. • 27. Amy Richlin, whose *Marcus Aurelius in Love* (Chicago 2007) is an expanded version of a thesis first argued in Matthew Knefler & John Boswell (eds), *History and Homosexuality* (Chicago 2005), pp.111–29, has fallen into this trap, but is by no means the first. Rictor Norton, *My Dear Boy. Gay love letters through the centuries* (1997), made similar erroneous assumptions. Nevertheless, in some quarters Richlin's 'findings' have been greeted with rapture. David Konstan of Brown University says: 'She has discovered something that was lying right out in the open.' Thomas Hubbard, of the University of Texas, Austin, is more cautious: 'Whether one interprets them [the Marcus–Fronto letters] as evidence of a genuine student–teacher romance, over-elaborated rhetoric of friendship or the precocious young prince playing the manipulative tease, the letters of Marcus Aurelius and Fronto are sure to fascinate.' Hubbard's second and third choices are spot-on, but the first is 'absurd', to use the words of Fronto expert Edward Champlin in a communication to the author. See also the review of Richlin's book by Pascal Fleury in *Bryn Mawr Classical Review*, 6 December 2007. For what it is worth, my own reading on the subject of Roman homosexuality makes Marcus a very unlikely candidate indeed. See Eva Cantarella, *Bisexuality in the Ancient World* (Yale 1992); Craig A. Williams, *Roman Homosexuality: Ideologies and Masculinity in Classical Antiquity* (New York 1999); Ramsay MacMullen, 'Roman attitudes to Greek love', in Wayne R. Dynes & Stephen Donaldson, *Studies in Homosexuality: Homosexuality in the Ancient World* (New York 1992). • 28. The misunderstanding of different cultural modes is one of the banes of historical interpretation. Two young women in the same bed in the Victorian era, as in Meredith's *Diana of the Crossways*, does not imply lesbianism; nor does the fact that Pierre in Herman Melville's eponymous novel addresses his mother as 'sister' mean that he entertains incestuous thoughts or feelings of sibling rivalry towards her. • 29. Meds 1.16.5. • 30. Lucian, *True History* 2.28. • 31. Meds 1.11. • 32. Haines i., pp.33–9, 54–5, 81–3. • 33. Marcus to Fronto, 140–3, Haines i, pp.50–1. • 34. Fronto to Marcus, 140–3, Haines i, pp.52–3. • 35. Fronto to Marcus, 139, Haines i, pp.45–9. • 36. A.J. Papalas, 'Herodes Atticus: An Essay on Education in the Antonine Age', *History of Education Quarterly* 21 (1981), pp.171–88; Fotini Skenteri, *Herodes Atticus reflected in the occasional poetry of Antonine Athens* (Stockholm 2005); W. Ameling, *Herodes Atticus* (Hildesheim 1983); Jennifer Tobin, *Herodes Attikos and the City of Athens* (Amsterdam 1997); E.L. Bowie, 'Greek sophists and Greek poetry in the Second Sophistic', ANRW ii.33.1 (1989), pp.209–58. • 37. Philostratus VS 2.554 • 38. Philostratus VS 1.25.3; 2.1.4–8; 2.1.14. • 39. Aulus Gellius, *Noctes Atticae* 1.2. • 40. ibid., 19.12. • 41. ibid., 9.2. • 42. Marcus to Fronto, 140–3, Haines i, pp.59–63. • 43. W. Ameling, *Herodes Atticus* op. cit., ii, pp.30–5; Champlin, *Fronto* op. cit., pp.63–5; Bowersock, *Greek Sophists in the Roman Empire* op. cit., pp.93–5. • 44. Marcus to Fronto, 140–3, Haines i, pp.58–62. •45. Fronto to Marcus, 140–3, Haines i, pp.63–7. •46. Marcus to Fronto, 140–3, Haines i, pp.67–9. As Amy Richlin has pointed out, Fronto uses a clever method to indicate his true feelings. When talking about the 'good' Herodes he uses the subjunctive; when talking about the 'bad' Herodes he uses the indicative mood (Richlin op. cit., p.57). • 47. *King Richard the Third*, Act Two, Scene One, Lines 7–22. • 48. Champlin, *Fronto* op. cit., pp.104–5. • 49. Millar, *The Emperor in the Roman World* op. cit., pp.26–7. • 50. Fronto to Marcus, 143, Haines i, pp.84–5. • 51. Ausonius, *Grat. Act.* 7.32.3. • 52. Fronto to Marcus, 143, Haines i, pp.145–7. • 53. Antoninus Pius to Fronto; Marcus to Fronto; Fronto to Domitia Lucilla; Fronto to Marcus (all 143), Haines i, pp.109–13, 125, 127–37, 145–51. • 54. Bonner, *Roman Education* op. cit., p.265. • 55. Marcus to Fronto, 143, Haines i., pp.91–7. • 56. Fronto to Marcus, 143, Haines i, pp.97–103. • 57. Fronto to Marcus, August 143, Haines i., pp.119–21. • 58. Fronto to Marcus, 143, Haines i, pp.104–7. • 59. Marcus to Fronto, 143, Haines i, pp.107–9. • 60. Marcus to Fronto, 143, Haines i, pp.117–19, 139–41. • 61. Philostratus, VS II, 534–45; cf. W.W. Reader (ed.), *The Severed Hand and the Upright Corpse: the Declamations of Marcus Antonius Polemo* (1998). • 62. Marcus to Fronto, Naples, 143, Haines i, pp.142–5. • 63. Described by Pliny in *Letters* 2.27.3. • 64. Marcus to Fronto, 143, Haines i, pp.150–2. • 65. Marcus to Fronto, 144–5, Haines i, pp.180–3. • 66. Marcus to Fronto, 144–5, Haines i, pp.155–62. • 67. Marcus to Fronto, 144–5, Haines i, pp.178–81. • 68. Fronto to Marcus, 144–5, Haines i, pp.163–9. • 69. Lucian, *Demonax* 24, 25; Philostratus, VS 2.42 • 70. Fronto to Herodes, 144–5, Haines i, pp.169–71. • 71. Fronto to Marcus, 144–5, Haines i, pp.170–1, 186–7. • 72. Marcus to Fronto, 144–5, Haines i, pp.180–3. • 73. Galen K.14.216. • 74. Marcus to Fronto, 144–5, Haines i, pp.186–7. • 75. Marcus to Fronto, 144–5, Haines i, pp.184–5, 186–9. • 76. Haines ii, p.79. • 77. Haines i, pp. 206, 308. • 78. Champlin, *Fronto*, p.92. • 79. Meds 6.30.2; 2.5.1; 11.18.18. • 80. Meds 1.7. • 81. Galen K. 19.61. • 82. This was undoubtedly one factor in the decline of rhetoric from the mid-second century on. Sociologically one can compare it to the decline of parliamentary oratory in twentieth-century Britain, as mastery of the mass media became the important politician's weapon, with only 'outsiders' like Jimmy Maxton of the ILP and Sir Oswald Mosley still keeping up the old traditions of rhetoric. • 83. Marcus to Fronto, n.d., Haines i, p.124. • 84. E. Champlin, 'The Chronology of Fronto', JRS 64 (1974), pp.136–59; Rutherford, op. cit., p.109; P. Hadot, *The Inner Citadel* (1998), pp.12–24; H. Görgemanns, 'Der Bekehrungsbrief Marc Aurels', *Rheinische Museum für Philologie* 134 (1991), pp.96–109. • 85. Meds 1.7.5; G. Downey & A.F. Norman (eds), *Themistius, orationes quae superaesunt* i, p. 307; ii, pp.218, 226; A.D. Nock, *Essays on Religion and the Ancient World*, ed. Z. Stewart (Oxford 1972), p.472. • 86. Meds 1.7.1–2. • 87. Haines ii, p.10. • 88. Haines i, p.196. • 89. Haines ii, p.36. • 90. Meds 1.17.5; Dio 72.35.1. • 91. Meds 1.7.3; 1.17.7; Hadot, *Inner Citadel* op. cit. • 92. See Appendix One. • 93. But see Lawrence C. Becker, *A New Stoicism* (Princeton 1998), esp. pp.63–8; Martha C. Nussbaum, *The Therapy of Desire* (Princeton 1994), pp.212–23. • 94. Sextus Empiricus, *Against the Schoolmasters* 5.149; *Outlines of Pyrrhonism* 1.29; 3.237; 5.156. • 95. Cicero, *De*

582 FRANK MCLYNN

Finibus. • 96. More sympathetic views of Stoicism are available in John Sellars, *Stoicism* (Berkeley 2006), and Steven Strange (ed.), *Stoicism: Traditions and Transformation* (Cambridge 2004).

Notes to Chapter Four
pp. 69–98

• 1. HA Hadrian 26.6; HA Antoninus 4.2.3; Dio 69.20.4–5; 70.1; Aurelius Victor 14.11; Syme, RP ii, p.681. • 2. HA Antoninus 1.1.8; 2.9–11; 4.1.7; Eutropius 8.8.3; CIL xv. 92–5; Rémy, *Antonin le Pieux* op. cit., pp.94–5. • 3. HA Hadrian 27.1–4; HA Antoninus 5.1–2; 6.6–7; 8.1; 10.1; HA Marcus 6.1. • 4. HA Antoninus 5.1; Dio 69.23.1–3; 70.1.2–3; Aurelius Victor 14.11; 14.13–14; Eutropius 8.7.3. • 5. HA Antoninus 6.6; Aurelius Victor 14.14; A.R. Birley, 'Antoninus Pius', CAH 11, p.153. • 6. HA Hadrian 24.3–5; 27.4; Pausanias 8.43.4–5; A. Chastagnol, *Le Sénat romain à l'époque impériale* (Paris 1992), p.84; J. Beaujeu, *La religion romaine à l'apogée de l'Empire. La politique religieuse des Antonines* (Paris 1955), p.288; J.P. Martin, *Providentia deorum. Recherches sur certains aspects religieux du pouvoir impériale romain* (Rome 1982), pp.308–12. • 7. H.G. Pflaum, 'Tendances politiques et administratives au 2e siècle de notre ère', *Revue des Études Latines* 42 (1964), pp.112–21. • 8. Dio 73.3; Eutropius 8.8.3. • 9. HA Antoninus 7.11. • 10. HA Antoninus 1.1–7; 4.10; E. Bryant, *The Reign of Antoninus Pius* (Cambridge 1895), pp.34–5. • 11. HA Antoninus 4.8. • 12. L. Vidman, *Fasti Ostienses* (Prague 1982), pp.49–52; R. Duncan-Jones, *Money and Government in the Roman Empire* (Cambridge 1994), pp.248–50. • 13. HA Antoninus 2.8; 4.9; 8.1; 10.2; Rémy, *Antonin le Pieux* op. cit., pp.76, 211. • 14. HA Antoninus 4.9–10; 6.1; 7.1–2; 8.1; 10.8–9; L. Richardson, *A New Topographical Dictionary of Ancient Rome* (Baltimore 1992), pp.184–5. • 15. HA Antoninus 13.2; Meds 6.30; Aurelius Victor, *Epitome de Caesaribus* 15.4–5. Many Romans believed in the efficacy of dry bread (see Pliny, NH 22.139). • 16. HA Antoninus 2.1; 13.1.2; Dio 69.20.4; Aurelius Victor, *Epitome* 15.2–4; Malalas of Antioch, *Chronographia*, ed. E. Jeffreys, M. Jeffreys & M. Salt (Melbourne 1986), 11.21; Ammianus Marcellinus 16.1.4; 30.8.12; Pausanias 8.8.1–2. • 17. Rémy, *Antonin le Pieux*, pp. 100–2. • 18. HA Antoninus 3.6; Julian, *Caesars* 312A; CIL v.7167; vi.33840; vi.2075, vi.1340; vi.9797; xi.1617. • 19. H. Mattingly, *Coins of the Roman Empire in the British Museum* – hereinafter BMC – iv.xcvii. • 20. ILS 6898; Albino Garzetti, *From Tiberius to the Antonines* (1974), p.441. • 21. W. Weber in *Cambridge Ancient History* (1936 edn) 11, p.328. • 22. Syme, RP iii, p.1178. • 23. Meds 1.16. • 24. ibid. • 25. HA Antoninus 2.1; 7.11; 11.2; 11.7. • 26. Meds. 1.17.3. • 27. HA Antoninus 6.8; Dio 71.35.5; HA Marcus 6.3; CIL vi.32; ILS 360. • 28. HA Marcus 3.6; HA Pertinax 5.6; HA Alexander 1.3; HA Prob. 12.8; L. Vidman, *Fasti Ostienses* op. cit., p.50. • 29. Fronto to Marcus, 145–7, Haines i, pp.206–7; AE 1940, 62. • 30. Haines, *Fronto Letters passim.* • 31. HA Marcus 7.2. • 32. Pliny, *Letters* 6.31. • 33. Fronto to Marcus; Marcus to Fronto, 144–5, Haines i, pp.172–7. • 34. HA Antoninus 10.5. • 35. Philostratus, VS 2.5. • 36. ibid., 2.548, 545. • 37. ibid.,

2.548. • 38. ibid., 2.535. • 39. RIC iii.99.538. • 40. HA Antoninus 11.8. • 41. HA Marcus 6.9. • 42. *Digest* 27.1.6.7. • 43. Juvenal, *Satires* 10.80. • 44. HA Septimius Severus 18.3; HA Aurelian 35.2; 48.1. • 45. P. Garnsey, 'Grain for Rome', in Garnsey, K. Hopkins & C.R. Whitaker (eds), *Trade in the Ancient Economy* (1983), pp.118–30, estimates that Rome needed 200,000 tonnes annually. G.E. Rickman, *The Corn Supply of Ancient Rome* (Oxford 1980), p.10, estimates 250,000 tonnes. L. Foxhall & H.A. Forbes, 'Sitometreia: The role of grain as a staple food in classical antiquity', *Chiron* 12 (1982), pp.41–90, opt for an intermediate figure of 212,000 tonnes, while L. Casson, *Ancient Trade and Society* (Detroit 1987), p.97, plumps for a high of 400,000 tonnes. • 46. Peter Garnsey *Famine and Food Supply in the Graeco-Roman World* (Cambridge 1988), pp.247–8; Rickman, *Corn Supply* op. cit., pp.27–8. • 47. Rostovsteff, *Social and Economic History* op. cit., p.145. • 48. Rickman, *Corn Supply*, pp.40–2; A.J.B. Sirks, *Food for Rome* (Amsterdam 1991), p.21; cf. also Paul Erdkamp, *The Grain Market in the Roman Empire: A Social, Political and Economic Study* (Cambridge 2005). • 49. Rickman, *Corn Supply*, p.10; Garnsey (1988), pp.191, 231; C.R. Whitaker, 'Africa', CAH 11, p.535. • 50. P. D'Escurac, *La préfecture de l'annone: service administratif impérial d'Auguste à Constantin* (Paris 1976). • 51. Duncan-Jones, *Economy* op. cit., pp.364–5. • 52. Galen K.6.511–15. • 53. Celsus, *On Medicine* 4.2–28; HA Hadrian 22. • 54. Martial 1.59; 3.30; 6.88; 8.42; 9.100; 10.70; 10.74–5; Juvenal, *Satires* i, pp.127–8. By the second century cash handouts had become the norm. Pliny the Younger, when governor of Bithynia, reported that cash payments of four to eight sesterces were regularly made to town councillors and others at marriage, coming-of-age ceremonies and public rituals; ditto in Tripolitania under Antoninus Pius (Pliny, *Letters* 10.11; Apuleius, *Apology* 87). • 55. HA Antoninus 11.2; 12.4; Dio 72.17.4. • 56. Seneca, *Letters* 83.7; 90.45; Pliny, *Letters* 9.6.2; Martial 10.48.23; Tacitus, *History* 1.72. • 57. HA Pius 10.2; 10.9; Pausanias 9.21; Aurelius Victor 15.4. • 58. Meds 1.16; Vidman, *Fasti Ostienses* op. cit., pp.49–51. • 59. Galen K.11.14.9. • 60. M.-C. Amouretti, *Le pain et l'huile dans la Grèce antique* (Paris 1986), pp.177–96. • 61. A. Tchernia, *Le vin de l'Italie romaine: essai d'histoire économique d'après les amphores* (Rome 1986), pp.61–7, 76–7, 201–3, 277–8. • 62. Pliny, NH 14.57; 17.8; 15.40; Suetonius, *Tiberius* 34. • 63. Columella, *Rustica* 8.8.9–10. • 64. Pliny, NH 10.53; Pliny, *Letters* 5.6.12; 10.8.6. • 65. Martial 12.3.1; 10.96; Juvenal, *Satires* 3.171–4. • 66. Columella 7.3.22; 7.3.13; 7.9.4; Varro, *Rerum Rusticarum* 1.16.3; 3.2.7; 3.2.14; 3.2.15; 3.2.17. • 67. Juvenal, *Satires* 3.223–7; Apuleius, *Metamorphosis* 11.28; Duncan-Jones, *Structure* op. cit. • 68. See Richardson, *New Topographical Dictionary* op. cit.; Eva Margarita Steinby, *Lexicon Topographicum Urbis Romae*, 5 vols (1999). • 69. Samuel Ball Platner (revised Thos. Ashby), *A Topographical Dictionary of Ancient Rome* (Oxford 1929), pp.126–7. • 70. Plutarch, *Crassus* 2.4–5. • 71. H. Lavagne (ed.), *Hadrien. Trésors d'une ville impériale* (Milan 1999), pp.27–36; cf. also the article by M.Th. Raepset-Charlier in *Klio* 75 (1993), pp.257–71. • 72.

HA Antoninus 3.6; PIR2 A.716; CIL v.7167; vi.33840; vi.2075; vi.1340; vi.1617; vi.9797. • 73. HA Marcus 6.2; HA Lucius Verus 2.4; Dio 69.21.1; CIL vi.988–9. For the (simple) process of dissolving betrothals, see P.E. Corbett, *The Roman Law of Marriage* (1930), pp.1–23. For the blow to the Ceionii, see Syme, RP ii, pp.681–2. • 74. Vidman, *Fasti Ostienses* op. cit., pp.49–50, 122–3; Rémy, *Antonin le Pieux* op. cit., pp.129–33. • 75. Judith P. Hallett, *Fathers and Daughters in Roman Society* (Princeton 1984), pp.230–1, 237–40. • 76. R. MacMullen, 'Women in Public in the Roman Empire', *Historia* 29 (1980), pp.208–18; Richard Saller, 'Status and Patronage', CAH 11, p.833. • 77. Tacitus, *History* 1.73; Pliny, *Letters* 7.24. • 78. HA Antoninus 10.2; Aurelius Victor 15.4; RIC iii.49.191; 94.506; 79.422–4; 81.432; 171.1206; 174.1234; 74.1238; 175.1241; Vidman, *Fasti Ostienses* op. cit., pp.49–51. • 79. RIC iii. 93.494; 94.503; 95.50; 95.505, 509, 511; 191.1367, 1372; 192.1380; S. Treggiani, *Roman Marriage: 'Iusti Conjuges' from the time of Cicero to the time of Ulpian'* (Oxford 1991), pp.401–3; P. Veyne, 'La famille et l'amour sous le Haut-Empire romain', *Annales* 33 (1978), pp.35–63. • 80. Birley, *Marcus Aurelius* op. cit., p.53. • 81. Marcus to Fronto; Fronto to Marcus, 145–7, Haines i, pp.190–6. • 82. Marcus to Fronto, 145–7, Haines i, pp.196–7. • 83. Keith Hopkins, 'Age of Roman Girls at Marriage', *Population Studies* 18 (1965), pp.309–27; R. Syme, 'Marriage ages for Roman senators', *Historia* 36 (1987), pp.318–32; R.P. Saller, 'Men's age at marriage and its consequence in the Roman family', *Classical Philology* 82 (1987), pp.21–34; B.D. Shaw, 'The age of Roman girls at marriage: some reconsiderations', JRS 77 (1987), pp.30–46. • 84. Possibly the risks of overpopulation outweighed those of the reverse. 'The Roman population was fairly delicately poised between the risks of under- and overpopulation; in this respect, of course, it resembles all pre-modern societies.' (Bruce W. Frier, 'Demography', CAH 11, p.805.) • 85. Tacitus, *Germania* 19.5; Juvenal, *Satires* 6.592–8. • 86. B. Rawson (ed.), *The Family in Ancient Rome. New Perspectives* (1986), pp.201–29. • 87. W. Frier, 'Demography', CAH 11, p.795; Thomas Wiedemann, *Adults and Children in the Roman Empire* (1989), p.15. • 88. M. Hombert & C. Préaux, 'À propos des chances de survivre dans l'empire romain', *Latomus* 5 (1946), pp.91–7; J.C. Russell, *British Medieval Population* (Albuquerque, New Mexico 1948), pp.180–8. • 89. Keith Hopkins, 'The probable age structure of the Roman population', *Population Studies* 20 (1966–7), p.245; W. Scheidel, 'Roman age structure: evidence and models', JRS 91 (2001), pp.1–26; W. Scheidel, *Measuring sex, age and death in the Roman empire: explorations in ancient demography* (Ann Arbor 1996), pp.97–116. • 90. Jerome O. Nriagu, *Lead and Lead Poisoning in Antiquity* (New York 1983), esp. pp.309–415. • 91. Jackson, *Doctors and Diseases* (1988), pp.103–6. • 92. Keith Hopkins, *Death and Renewal* (Cambridge 1983), p.225; M. Bar-Ilan, 'Infant Mortality in the land of Israel in Late Antiquity', in S. Fishbane & J.N. Lightstone (eds), *Essays in the Social Scientific Study of Judaism and Jewish Society* (Montreal 1990), pp.3–25. Some think the Romans did better than early modern societies. Figures for London in the 1760s show 50 per cent of children dying before the age of two (Jackson, *Doctors and Diseases*, p.104). • 93. K.R. Bradley, 'Wet-Nursing at Rome: A study in social relations', in B.M. Rawson (ed.), *The Family in Ancient Rome. New Perspectives* (Ithaca 1986), p.220; Hopkins, *Death and Renewal* op. cit., pp.224–6; cf. S. Dixon, *The Roman Mother* (1988). • 94. Keith Hopkins, 'Contraception in the Roman Empire', *Comparative Studies in Society and History* 8 (1965), pp.124–51; E. Eyben, 'Family Planning in Graeco-Roman Antiquity', *Ancient Society* 11–12 (1981–2), pp.5–82. • 95. Wiedemann, *Adults and Children* op. cit., p.36. • 96. Hopkins, *Death and Renewal* op. cit., pp.79–81. • 97. J.A. Crook, *Law and Life of Rome* (1967), pp.111–12; Hopkins, *Death and Renewal*, p.41. • 98. Garnsey & Saller, *The Roman Economy* op. cit., pp.144–5. • 99. Richard Saller, 'Family and Household', CAH 11, pp.873–4. • 100. Duncan-Jones, *Economy* op. cit., p.144; P. Garnsey, 'Trajan's Alimenta: Some problems', *Historia* 17 (1968), pp.367–81. • 101. Duncan-Jones, *Economy*, pp.133, 306–10; cf. also Duncan-Jones, 'The Purpose and Organisation of the Alimenta', PBSR 32 (1964), pp.123–46. • 102. Pliny, *Letters* 1.8.10–12; Tacitus, *Germania* 19.5; W.V. Harris, 'Child Exposure in the Roman Empire', JRS 84 (1994), pp.1–22. • 103. Pliny, *Letters* 8.10. • 104. Jackson, *Doctors and Diseases* op. cit., p.106; J.R. Goody, *Production and Reproduction* (Cambridge 1976), pp.133–4. • 105. Frier, 'Demography', loc. cit., CAH 11, p.804. • 106. ibid., p.800. • 107. A. Degrassi, *Inscriptiones Italiae* (Rome 1947), 13.1.207; H. Fittschen, *Die Bildnistypen der Faustina Minor und die Fecunditas Augustae* (Göttingen 1982), pp.23–7. • 108. Marcus to Fronto, 147, Haines i, pp.198–201. • 109. Marcus to Fronto, 147, Haines i, pp.202–3. • 110. Fronto to Marcus, Haines i, pp.202–9. • 111. ibid. • 112. Marcus to Fronto, Haines i, pp.218–19, 224–5. • 113. Fronto to Marcus, Haines i, pp.218–23. • 114. Marcus to Fronto, Haines i, pp.212–13, 224–5; *Inscriptiones Italiae* op. cit. – hereinafter IL – 13.1.207; *Inscriptiones Graecae ad Res Romanas Pertinentes* – hereinafter IGR – iv.1379. • 115. PIR2 A. 707, 714; IGR i.1509; W.A. Ameling, 'Die Kinder des Marc Aurel und die Bildinstypen der Faustina Minor', *Zeitschrift für Papyrologie und Epigraphik* – hereinafter ZPE – 90 (1992), pp.147–67; R. Bol, *Das Statuenprogramm des Herodes-Atticus-Nymphaeums* (Berlin 1984), pp.31–5. • 116. AE 1951, 184; AE 1940, 71–2. • 117. CIL xv.1090; Meds 1.17.7. • 118. IL 13.1.207; HA Marcus 7.4; PIR V 601, 604; Syme, RP ii, pp.685–9. • 119. Mark Golden, 'Did the ancients care when their children died?', GR 25 (1988), pp.152–63. • 120. Epictetus, *Discourses* 3.24.88–9. • 121. Meds 8.49. • 122. Meds 9.40. • 123. Meds 10.35. • 124. Meds 11.34. • 125. Wiedemann, *Adults and Children* op. cit., pp.8–10. • 126. Fronto to Marcus, ii, p.34; Wiedemann, *Adults and Children*, pp.6, 11, 93–9; Birley, *Marcus Aurelius*, p.107. • 127. For Antoninus's reign, see Appendix Two. • 128. RIC iii.99.538. • 129. RIC iii.112.642; 116.691a; 34.73; 165.1149; Duncan-Jones, *Economy* op. cit., pp.288–319, 333–41. • 130. Meds 1.16; 6.30. • 131. Pausanias 8.43; AE 1966, 423; AE 1967, 446; AE 1967, 480. •

132. AE 1927, 49; AE 1951, 257; AE 1957, 279. • 133. Syme, RP v, p.674. • 134. J.H. Oliver, *Greek Constitutions of Early Roman Emperors from Inscriptions and Papyri* (Philadelphia 1989) pp.325–6. • 135. Meds 6.30. • 136. Meds 1.16.7. • 137. The inevitable cliché 'rearranging deckchairs on the *Titanic*' is almost irresistible. • 138. Fronto to Marcus, 154–6, Haines i, pp.248–53. • 139. Fronto to Marcus, Haines i, p.234; Syme, RP iv, pp.325–46. • 140. Fronto to Marcus, Haines i, p.236. • 141. Fronto to Marcus, 154–6, Haines i, pp.254–63. • 142. Philostratus VS 2.1.8–9; Ameling, *Herodes Atticus* op. cit. i., pp.100–2; ii, pp.7–9. • 143. Fronto to Antoninus Pius, 157–61, Haines i, pp.262–5; Albino Garzetti, *From Tiberius to the Antonines* (1974), p.449. • 144. Dio 71.33.3–5; HA Antoninus 12.7. • 145. HA Antoninus 12.4–8; Dio 71.33.4–5; HA Marcus 7.3; Aurelius Victor 15.3–4; Eutropius 8.8.4; Orosius 7.141.1: Malalas, *Chronographia* op. cit. 11.21; 11.26–7. • 146. Fronto to Marcus, 161, Haines i, pp.302–5.

Notes to Chapter Five   *pp. 99–117*

• 1. Galen K.5.14. Much of the food listed in the ancient sources would not be available to the non-elite. How many of the following fruits listed by Artemidorus would the average Roman slum-dweller have seen: apples, quince, almonds, walnuts, hazelnuts, white figs, black figs, white grapes, black grapes, pomegranates, pears, apricots, cherries, mulberries, peaches? (Artemidorus 1.73 in White (ed.), *Dream Interpretation*, op. cit, p.54) • 2. Julian, *Caesars* 317C. • 3. J.M.C. Toynbee, *The Art of the Romans* (1965), pp.65–6; C.C. Vermeule, *Roman Imperial Art in Greece and Asia Minor* (Harvard 1968), pp.95–123. • 4. HA Hadrian 26.1. • 5. Epictetus, *Discourses* 1.16.9–14. • 6. Herodian 5.2.3–4. • 7. Meds 6.33; 7.33; 7.64; 9.26. • 8. Galen K.14.3. For the early-rising Romans, see Pliny, *Letters* 3.5.9. • 9. Meds 5.1. • 10. Meds 8.12; 10.9; 10.13. • 11. Dio 72.6.3–4; 77.24.4; 72.34.2; 72.36.2–3. • 12. G. Bowersock, *Greek Sophists in the Roman Empire* (1969), pp.71–2. • 13. Meds 2.1; 6.2. • 14. Meds 1.17.7. • 15. J.E.G. Whitehorne, 'Was Marcus Aurelius a hypochondriac?', *Latomus* 36 (1977), pp.413–21; R. Dailly & H. Van Effenterre, 'Le cas Marc-Aurèle. Essai de psychosomatique historique', *Revue des États Anciens* 56 (1954), pp.347–65 (at p.354); cf. also J.A. de Groot, 'Karakter structuur van een Keizer', *Hermeneus* 20 (1948), pp.17–24, 33–41. • 16. Galen K.14.2–3; K.14.216–17; Dio 72.6.3. • 17. Galen K.14.1–5, 24, 29, 82, 103, 161–3, 210–18, 230–310; 11.404, 421, 596, 751, 757; 19.736. One is reminded of one of Voltaire's quips: 'Physicians pour drugs, of which they know little, to cure diseases, of which they know less, into humans, of which they know nothing.' In fairness, it should be pointed out that Marcus himself had a somewhat Shavian view of doctors (see Meds 3.3; 4.48). • 18. Thomas de Quincey, *Confessions of an English Opium Eater*, ed. A. Hayter (1971), p.71. • 19. T.W. Africa, 'The Opium Addiction of Marcus Aurelius', *Journal of the History of Ideas* (1961), pp.97–102; also in R. Klein, *Marc Aurel* (Darmstadt 1979), pp.133–43. • 20. P. Hadot, 'Marc-Aurèle, était-il opiomane?', in E. Lucchesi & H.D. Saffrey, (eds), *Antiquité païenne et chrétienne* (Geneva 1984), pp.33–50. For Plotinus's visions, see E.R. Dodds, *Pagans and Christians* (1965), p.9; cf. also Edward Witke, 'Marcus Aurelius and Mandragora', *Classical Philology* 60 (1965), pp.23–4. • 21. See also the contribution by J. Kraye, 'Marcus Aurelius and his Meditations from Xylander to Diderot', in J. Kraye and M.W.F. Stone (eds), *Humanism and Early Modern Philosophy* (2000), pp.107–34. My own position is that, while one can only state that Marcus *might* have become an opium addict, the arguments to this effect are marginally more convincing than those of the opposition. Hadot's article (cited above) in particular contains this author's certainty on all issues on which he pronounces. • 22. Meds 6.31. • 23. Behr, *Complete Works of Aelius Aristides* op. cit. ii, p.279. • 24. Galen K.6.832–5. • 25. In some respects Artemidorus out-sexualised Freud. The penis, for example, can symbolise one's parents, children, wife, mistress or brothers. It can symbolise eloquence or education (since both are fertile) and is also a sign of wealth and possessions, secret plans, poverty, servitude, enjoyment of dignity and respect and enjoyment of civil rights (Robert J. White (ed. & trans.), *Oneirocritica of Artemidorus* (New Jersey 1992), pp.38–9 (*sc.*I.45)). It is therefore difficult to imagine what the penis does *not* signify. • 26. Artemidorus in White (ed.), *Dream Interpretation* op. cit., pp.14–15. • 27. Artemidorus claimed to be able to interpret all the following symbols as they appeared in dreams: the head, the foot, the eyes and the ears (White, pp.17–19, 27–9), names (ibid., p.19), pregnancy and childbirth (p.24); hair and beards (pp.27–31), crucifixion (p.127) and fighting with wild beasts (p.128). • 28. See in general D. Shulman & G.G. Stroumsa (eds), *Dream Cultures: Explorations in the Comparative History of Dreaming* (Oxford 1999); M. Andrew Holowchak, *Ancient Science and Dreams. Oneirology in Greco-Roman Antiquity* (Lanham, Maryland 2001). S.R.F. Price, 'The Future of Dreams: From Freud to Artemidorus', PP 113 (1986), pp.3–37, is too dogmatic in his dismissal of the Freudian approach to the ancient world as 'anachronistic'. But it is not just Freud who feels the purists' lash. Eric Osborne, *Tertullian, First Theologian of the West* (Cambridge 1997), pp.28–9, attacks Jung's views as 'anachronistic' – that word again. He falls into the trap of all such critics, which is to assume that which has to be proved, not to mention using a clichéd tag to avoid close argumentation. Much better on Freud and Artemidorus is Beat Näf, *Traum und Traumdeutung im Altertum* (Darmstadt 2004), esp. pp.124–8, 182–7. It is surely an elementary fallacy to *assume* that a dream recorded by an ancient can be interpreted only in terms of ancient culture. This is the reverse fallacy of the one attributed to psychoanalysis, which allegedly assumes the constancy of the unconscious throughout historical time (though admittedly Erich Fromm, for one, is guilty of this in his writings). Price, Hadot and those who are primarily ancient historians always assume that the unconscious is a mere mirror of contemporary culture and is thus in a permanent state of flux. Such a view appears one-dimensional: for one thing, it overlooks the phenomenon of 'overdetermination' – the notion that the generation of a dream symbol may be multi-causal. • 29. I am obliged to dissent from the ecstatic praise usually accorded to Pierre Hadot's contribution to Marcus Aurelius studies. Two of Hadot's propositions are particularly problematical. 1) He says that psychological interpretations 'anachronistically' project back modern interpretations onto ancient texts. But how does he know they are 'anachronistic'? One might just as well say that a Marxist interpretation of the economy of the ancient world was 'anachronistic' because nobody in ancient Rome used Marxist categories in their thought. Hadot's 'anachronism' is a classical example of a prime intellectual error: the assumption of that which must be proved. The Christian argument for the existence of God from design is the *locus classicus* of this sort of thing, but there are many more. 2) He (in defiance of his own alleged tenets, canons and beliefs) attributes motives to the psychologisers. They must either be examples of 'tall poppy syndrome' – cutting down to size the great figures of the past like Marcus Aurelius – or they are a reductionist version of psychology, emphasising the morbid and the abnormal, insinuating a world view in which everything is explained by sex or drugs. Hadot is so concerned to circumscribe Marcus purely within a formal Stoic tradition of 'intellectual exercises' and formulaic utterances, procedures and modalities that one suspects that, even if Marcus had written a signed confession that he was a neurotic or a neurasthenic, Hadot would have sought a precedent in Epictetus or Seneca to show that this was merely a Stoic trope, topos or conceit. More reliable than Hadot are Beat Näf, *Traum und Traumdeutung* op. cit., pp.114–23; cf. Rutherford, op. cit., pp.196–8. • 30. Meds 5.5.1. • 31. Meds 5.5.2. • 32. Meds 11.18.6; 12.26–7. • 33. Meds 11.9.2. The similarity of the *Meditations* to oriental philosophy has often been remarked on. Marcus's statement that the consequences of anger are always more serious than the causes has a pre-echo in the sayings of Buddha: 'Holding on to anger is like grasping a hot coal with the intention of throwing it at someone else. You are the one who gets burned.' (Anne Bancroft, *The Dhammapada* (2001).) • 34. Meds 9.1; 11.1; 12.29. • 35. P.A. Brunt, 'Marcus Aurelius and his Meditations', JRS 64 (1974), pp.1–20 (at pp.8–9). • 36. Meds 1.15.8; 2.1; 3.5.4; 7.12; 11.15; HA Marcus 12.2. • 37. HA Marcus 20.5. • 38. HA Marcus 20.5; 22.4–5. • 39. Meds 10.36. • 40. Meds 2.6; 9.18; 10.34; 12.4. • 41. Meds 5.5. • 42. Dio 72.16; 73.5; 73.8.4; Ramsay MacMullen, 'The Emperor's Largesses', *Latomus* 21 (1962), pp.154–66; R. MacMullen, 'The Roman Emperor's Army Costs', *Latomus* 43 (1984), pp.571–80. • 43. HA Marcus 7.4; Syme, RP ii, pp.685–9; Garzetti, *From Tiberius to the Antonines* op. cit., p.521. • 44. HA Marcus 29.6; for the 'kingship' quote, see Meds 7.36. • 45. For this dislike, see Meds 6.46; 6.20. • 46. Philostratus, VS 2.557. • 47. Dio 72.30.2;

72.34.4–5. • 48. Meds 11.6.3–4. • 49. Meds 7.38–41; 11.6.1–2. • 50. Meds 11.2. • 51. Rutherford op. cit., pp.119–20; Herodian 1.2.3–4. • 52. Meds 5.11. • 53. Meds 9.21. • 54. P. Wendland, *Die Hellenistische-römische Kultur in ihren Beziehungen zu Judentum und Christentum* (Tübingen 1972), p.238; cf. Rutherford, op. cit., p.123. • 55. M. Grant, *The Antonines* op. cit., p.58. • 56. Ernest Renan, *Marcus Aurelius*, ed. William G. Hutchinson (1903), p.6. Certainly it could never be said of him what was said of the hero of Rafael Sabatini's *Scaramouche*: 'He was born with the gift of laughter and a conviction that the world was mad.' • 57. Meds. 6.42.2. For this aspect of Haig, see Walter Reid, *Architect of Victory: Douglas Haig* (Edinburgh 2007) p.75. • 58. John Steinbeck, seeking to explain the personality of the Mexican revolutionary Emiliano Zapata, is one of many who have argued this (Steinbeck, *Viva Zapata* (1993). • 59. Renan, *Marcus Aurelius* op. cit. • 60. Syme, RP v, p.688; cf. also Dailly & Van Effenterre, 'Le cas Marc-Aurèle', loc. cit., pp.349–54. • 61. Sandbach, *The Stoics* op. cit., p.169. Truly there is merit in H.L. Mencken's quip: 'There is no record in history of a happy philosopher.' • 62. Epictetus, *Discourses* 1.9.10–11; Long, *Epictetus*, p.157. • 63. Meds 3.3; 5.28; 6.32. • 64. Meds 2.2; 8.24; 9.36. • 65. Epictetus, *Discourses* 3.1.43–4. • 66. Epictetus, *Discourses* 3.21.5. • 67. Epictetus, *Discourses* 2.18.8–26; 2.4.4. • 68. Epictetus, *Enchiridion* 33.8. • 69. Meds 1.16.1; 1.17.2; 1.17.6. • 70. Meds 5.10; 6.34; 8.21. • 71. Meds 6.13; 10.19; 10.26. • 72. Meds 10.13; 11.18.2; 9.41. • 73. Artemidorus 1.78–80 in White (ed.), *Dream Interpretation* op. cit., pp.58–65. • 74. Meds 1.17.6; 1.17.8. • 75. Rutherford op. cit., p.93. • 76. Meds 1.16.2; cf. Craig Williams, *Roman Homosexuality* (Oxford 1999); R. MacMullen, *Paganism in the Roman Empire* (New Haven 1981). • 77. For the hostility, see Meds 2.8; 4.32; 4.18; 6.16.3. • 78. Meds 2.13. Whether Stoicism and psycho-analysis really are compatible, there is no doubt that Stoicism would provide the psychoanalytical enquirer with a field-day, exhibiting as it does symptoms of obsession, escapism, ritualisation, overcompensation, narcissism, defence mechanisms and masochism. 'Divided-self' theorists would doubt-less point to the incompatibility of its political conservatism, stressing duty and conformism, with the coexisting contempt for politics and all other mani-festations of the quotidian world. • 79. Meds 1.17.11; 1.17.2; 6.21; 7.1; 7.5; 7.7; 7.38; 8.16; 10.1; 11.18.7; 12.16. • 80. Meds 8.42. • 81. Meds 11.13. • 82. Marcus's view, indeed, goes against the wisdom of the ages. See H.L. Mencken's remark: 'The older I grow, the more I distrust the familiar doctrine that age brings wisdom.' • 83. Dio 72.34.4. • 84. ibid. • 85. Meds 10.15.3. • 86. Meds 5.10.4. He adds thieves, perverts, parricides and dictators to the list (Meds 6.34). • 87. Meds 5.5; 6.30.4; 11.18.10. • 88. Herodian 1.2.4; Dio 71.35.2; Meds 1.16.5; 9.29. • 89. Meds 6.2; 9.37; 10.3; 4.3.1; cf. Rutherford op. cit., pp.121–3. • 90. Meds 5.16.2; 8.9. • 91. Meds 10.15.2. • 92. Meds 3.16.1; 6.30.1; 3.16; 12.27; 4.28; 4.32–7. • 93. Suetonius, *Nero*, 27, 31; A. Boethius, *The Golden House of Nero* (Ann Arbor 1960); M.T. Griffin, *Nero* (1984), pp.125–42. • 94. Meds 1.16.2.

• 95. Hadot, *The Inner Citadel* op. cit., pp.296–8. • 96. Epictetus, *Discourses* 1.3; 1.9.7; 1.14.15–17; 1.29.61; 1.19.7–15. • 97. Epictetus, *Discourses* 4.6.20; Meds 7.36. • 98. Epictetus, *Discourses* 1.25.15; 2.22.22; 3.13.9–13. • 99. Meds 8.30; HA Marcus 10.1.7; 11.2; Dio 71.17.11; 71.33.2; 71.35.3; 71.35.5. • 100. Meds 1.17.3. • 101. Meds 1.16; 4.12; 3.4; 7.5. • 102. Meds 3.5. • 103. Meds 11.18.1. • 104. Meds 9.29. • 105. Dio 71.34.2; 71.36.3; cf. Herodian 1.2.1. • 106. Renan, *Marcus Aurelius* op. cit., p.3. • 107. HA Marcus 13.6. • 108. HA Marcus 20.4; 22.3.8; Dio 71.3.4; 71.30.2. • 109. Klaus Rosen, 'Die angebliche Samtherrschaft von Marc Aurel und Lucius Verus', in G. Bonamente & N. Duval (eds), *Historiae Augustae Colloquium Parisinum* (Macerata 1991), pp.271–85; Joseph Vogt, *The Decline of Rome* (1967), p.203. • 110. Plutarch, *Demetrius Poliorcetes* 3.5. • 111. H.G. Pflaum, 'Les gendres de Marc Aurèle', *Journal des Savants* (1961), pp.28–41. For the trio of Agrippa Postumus, Tiberius Gemellus and Britannicus, see, respectively, Suetonius, *Tiberius* 32; Josephus, *Jewish Antiquities* 8.6; Anthony Barrett, *Agrippina: Sex, Power and Politics in the Early Empire* (Yale 1999). • 112. Syme, RP ii, p.690. Herodian, always a naive critic, said that Marcus Aurelius chose men of virtue for his daughters, not wealthy patricians, as the 'wealth of the soul' was the only real wealth (Herodian 1.2.2). • 113. PIR2 A.714; C.1024. • 114. J. Keil, 'Kaiser Marcus und die Thronfolge', *Klio* 31 (1938), pp.293–300. • 115. HA Marcus 21.2.5; see also Walter Pater, *Marius the Epicurean*, Chapter 18 (ii, p.61). • 116. Epictetus, *Discourses* 3.24.88–9. • 117. Wiedemann, *Adults and Children* op. cit., p.17; Lucian, *Demonax* 24. • 118. Meds 8.25; 8.31; 8.37; 7.41; 9.31. • 119. Meds 8.49; 11.34; cf. also 9.40. • 120. In Leonato's speech in Shakespeare's *Much Ado About Nothing*, Act Five, Scene One, Lines 1–37; cf. also Samuel Johnson, *Rasselas*, Chapter 8. That blood ties meant more to Marcus than was permitted by Stoicism is evident from the following: 'If you had a stepmother and a real mother, you would pay your respects to your stepmother, yes . . . but it's your real mother you'd go home to' (Meds 6.12).

Notes to Chapter Six   *pp. 120–140*

• 1. M. Nilsson, *Imperial Rome* (1926), p.59; Barnes, 'Hadrian and Lucius Verus', JRS 57 (1967), pp.65–79. • 2. Doubtless on the analogy of the Third Reich 1939–45, when Goebbels ran the country while Hitler ran the war. • 3. Dio 71.1.2–3. For the Ceionii, see E. Groag, A. Stein et al., *Prosopographia Imperii Romani saec. I,II,III* (2nd edn., Leipzig 1939) – hereinafter PIR2 – C.603, 78, 106, 136; Syme, RP v, p.671. • 4. One is reminded of Lyndon Johnson's famous dictum: 'I'd rather have him in the tent pissing out than outside pissing in.' • 5. HA Verus 4.1. • 6. HA Verus 2.5–7; 2.8; 2.9; ILS 1740. • 7. J.H. Oliver, *Greek Constitutions* op. cit., pp.334–6. • 8. HA Verus 2.5; 3.5; 3.7. • 9. Birley, *Marcus Aurelius* op. cit., p.108. • 10. Eutropius 8.9; HA Verus 3.3–5; 4.2. • 11. HA Verus 10.6–8. • 12. HA Verus 4.4; 4.10; Syme, RP i, p.327. • 13. HA Verus 4.6–7. • 14. Suetonius, *Caligula* 55.2; *Nero* 22. • 15. HA Verus 4.8; 6.2–6. • 16. HA Verus

5.3–5; Gellius 13.11.2. • 17. HA Verus 5.2. • 18. HA Verus 5.6. • 19. Galen K.1.32–8; 4.628. • 20. For varying assessments, see Syme, RP v, pp.692–3; W. Zwikker, *Studien zur Markussäule* (Amsterdam 1941), pp.61–2. Galen's remarks are at K.14.650 and K.19.18. Other ancient sources largely back up the *Historia Augusta*. See Ammianus Marcellinus 23.5.17; 23.6.24; 27.6.16. The classical attempt to rehabilitate Lucius Verus is 'L'Empereur Lucius Verus: Essai de réhabilitation', *L'Antiquité classique* 3 (1934), pp.173–201; also in R. Klein, *Marc Aurel* (Darmstadt 1979), pp.25–60. • 21. Justin, *Apology* 1. • 22. Champlin, *Fronto* op. cit., p.112. • 23. ibid., pp.113–14. • 24. Mattingly, BMC iv, p.cxii; RIC iii. 250.444; 316.1276; AE 1966, 206, 517, 4976. • 25. Dio 72.35.2; Galen K.19.228–33. • 26. Meds 1.17.4. • 27. HA Marcus 7.9; HA Verus 4.3; Mattingly, BMC iv, p.109; F. Carrata Thomes, *Il Regno di Marco Aurelio* (Turin 1953), pp.64–8. • 28. HA Marcus 7.10; Rémy, *Antonin le Pieux* op. cit., p.279. • 29. HA Marcus 7.10–11; 8.2; HA Antoninus 13.3–4; Rémy, *Antonin le Pieux*, p.280. • 30. HA Marcus 7.7; H. Mattingly & E.A. Sydenham, RIC iii (1930), Nos 1–14. • 31. W. Eck, *Die staatliche Organisation Italiens in der hohen Kaiserzeit* (Munich 1979), pp.146–55. • 32. HA Commodus 1.3–4; BMC iv, p.cxxvi. • 33. In the light of this, the theories of Artemidorus are very interesting. A serpent in his system was meant to denote a king (because of its strength) as well as wealth and possessions (as serpents traditionally guard treasure). So if a pregnant woman dreamed of giving birth to a serpent, this tended to mean that the child would be outstanding, possibly an orator, high priest or prophet (Artemidorus 2.13 – in White (ed.), *Dream Interpretation* op. cit., p.97). However, Artemidorus added this cautionary tale. Six pregnant women all had the same serpent dream, and three of them had *bad* experiences. One had a child who became a robber and was beheaded; another had a son who became a runaway slave; while the third child turned out to be 'undisciplined and wanton; he committed adultery with many of the women in the city' (Artemidorus 4.67 – in White, op. cit., p.213). • 34. HA Marcus 8.1. • 35. Verus to Fronto, 161; Fronto to Verus, 161, Haines i, pp.294–301. • 36. Champlin, *Fronto* op. cit., p.115. • 37. Pliny, NH 3.5.53–6. • 38. Suetonius, *Augustus* 30; Tacitus, *Annals* 1.76–9; Tacitus, *Histories* 1.8.6. • 39. O.F. Robinson, *Ancient Rome. City Planning and Administration* op. cit., pp.83–9; CIL vi.31553–4. • 40. HA Marcus 8.4–5; Sallares, *Malaria at Rome* (Oxford 2002), pp.109–12. • 41. ILS 429; CIL xiv.172,5345; AE 1948, 75; AE 1951, 1826C. • 42. Dio 39.61.1–2; 53.33.5; 54.1.11;56.4;79.25.5; Ammianus Marcellinus 29.6.17–18; Orosius, *History* 4.11.5–7; Aurelius Victor, *Epitome* 13.12.13; Pliny, *Letters* 5.6.11–12; 8.17. See also L. Quilici, *Roma primitiva e le origini della civiltà Laziale* (Rome 1979), pp.66–8; J. Le Gall, *Le Tibre: fleuve de Rome dans l'antiquité* (Paris 1953), pp.29–34, 120–5. • 43. Champlin, *Fronto* op. cit., p.93. • 44. Jozef Wolski, *L'empire des Arsacides* (Louvain 1993); B.P. Lozinski, *The Original Homeland of the Parthians* (1959); M.A.R. Colledge, *The Parthians* (1967). • 45. Arthur Keaveney, 'Roman Treaties with Parthia *c.*95–*c.*64 BC', *American Journal of Philology* 102 (1981), pp.195–212; A.Keaveney, 'The King and the Warlords: Romano-Parthian Relations *c.*64–53 BC', *American Journal of Philology* 103 (1982), pp.412–28. • 46. 'The invasion of Parthian Mesopotamia by the proconsul Marcus Crassus was the first instance of Roman aggression in the eastern regions for which no Roman writer could find any vestige of justification' (A.N. Sherwin-White, *Roman Foreign Policy in the East* (1984), p.279). Cf. also Joseph Poirot III, *Perceptions of Classical Armenia. Romano-Parthian relations 70 BC–220 AD* (Baton Rouge, Louisiana 2003). But some Iranian specialists see Crassus's motives primarily as supporting a pro-Roman pretender, rather than as naked aggression (A.D.H. Bivar, 'The Political History of Iran under the Arsacids', *Cambridge History of Iran* (Cambridge 1983) 3.1, pp.21–99 (at pp.49–50). • 47. Plutarch, *Crassus* 23–7; Dio 40.16.3; 40.21–7; Jérôme Gaslain, 'La bataille de Carrhae', *Histoire Antique* 10 (2003), pp.60–5; Kurt L. Regling, 'Crassus' Partherkrieg', *Klio* 7 (1907), pp.357–94. • 48. The classic account of the story is in Pliny, NH 6.47. This is not easy to discount, as Pliny was singularly well informed. Nonetheless, scholars are divided on the veracity and reliability of the story and a huge amount of academic ink has been spilled on this issue. See Samuel Lieberman, 'Who were Pliny's Blue-Eyed Chinese?', *Classical Philology* 52 (1957), pp.174–7; H.H. Dubs, *A Roman City in Ancient China?* (1957); L. Boulnois, *The Silk Road* (1966), pp.64–6; H. Ferguson, 'China and Rome', ANRW 2.9.2 (1978), pp.581–603 (at pp.599–601); I.M. Franck & D.M. Brownstone, *The Silk Road. A History* (New York 1986), pp.114–15; M.A. Yong & Sun Yutang, 'The Western Regions under the Hsiung-Nu and the Han', in D. Harmatta (ed.), *History of the Civilizations of Central Asia. Vol. 2 The Development of Sedentary and Nomadic Civilizations, 700 BC–AD 250* (Paris 1994), pp.227–46 (at pp.240–3); Y.A. Zadneprovsky, 'The nomads of Central Asia after the invasion of Alexander', in Harmatta, *History* op. cit., pp.457–72 (at pp.463–8); N. Ishjamts, 'Nomads in Eastern Central Asia', in ibid., pp.151–70 (at pp.163–4); B.J. Staviskij, 'Central Asian Mesopotamia and the Roman World. Evidence of Contacts', in A. Invernizzi (ed.), *In the Land of the Gryphon. Papers on Central Asian archaeology and antiquity* (Florence 1995), pp.191–203 (at pp.200–2); M.G. Rashke, 'New Studies in Roman Commerce with the East', ANRW 2.9.2 (1978), pp.604–1378 (at pp.679–81). • 49. Dio 48.40.2; J. Segal, *Edessa, 'The Blessed City'* (Oxford 1970), p.12; Stephen Kirk Ross, *Towards Roman Edessa 114–242 AD* (1997). • 50. Suetonius, *Julius Caesar* 44; Suetonius, *Augustus* 8; Dio 43.51.1–2; Propertius 3.4; Adrian Goldsworthy, *Caesar. The Life of a Colossus* (2006), pp.491–2. • 51. Justin 41.2.6. • 52. Moses of Khorenats, *History of the Armenians*, trans. R.W. Thompson (Harvard 1978) 2.22–3. • 53. Plutarch, *Antony* 37–41. • 54. Justin 42.5; Dio 49.33. • 55. Sherwin-White, *Roman Foreign Policy* op. cit., pp.311–19. • 56. ibid., p.320. • 57. Dio 49.32.2. • 58. Josephus, *Antiquities* 18.2.4; Justin 43.5; Dio 51.18; 53.33; A. Oltramare, 'Auguste et les Parthes', *Revue des Études Latines* 16 (1938), pp.121–38;

Charles Brian Rose, 'The Parthians in Augustan Rome', *American Journal of Archaeology* 109 (2005), pp.21–75. • 59. Some historians think the Greek–Parthian issue was overlaid with a quite separate class war between rich and poor (Tacitus, *Annals* 6.34.35). • 60. Tacitus, *Annals* 6.31; 12.45; Josephus, *Antiquities* 20.81–91; Suetonius, *Augustus* 8; Propertius 3.4; B. Isaac, *The Limits of Empire. The Roman Army in the East* (Oxford 1990), p.142. • 61. Rose, 'The Parthians in Augustan Rome' loc. cit; Otto Kurz, 'Cultural Relations between Parthia and Rome', *The Cambridge History of Iran* op. cit. 3.1, pp.559–67. • 62. Tacitus, *Annals* 15.6.17; Tacitus, *Histories* 11.6; Strabo 16.1.28; Suetonius, *Nero* 19. • 63. Tacitus, *Histories* 4.51; Tacitus, *Annals* 15.29–31; E.M. Sanford, 'Nero and the East', *Harvard Studies in Classical Philology* 48 (1937), pp.75–103; Fergus Millar, *A Study of Cassius Dio* (Harvard 1964), pp.142–3. • 64. Suetonius, *Domitian* 2.2; C.R. Whitaker, 'Frontiers', CAH 11, p.309; R. Frye, *The History of Iran* (1984), p.360. • 65. Marie-Louise Chaumont, 'L'Arménie entre Rome et l'Iran. De l'avènement d'Auguste à l'avènement de Dioclétien', ANRW 2.9.1 (1976), pp.71–194; J. Texidor, *Un poste romain du désert. Palmyre* (Paris 1984); Kevin Butcher, 'A vast process: Rome, Parthia and the formation of eastern "client" states', *Journal of Roman Archaeology* 7 (1994), pp.447–53. • 66. These views are represented, respectively, in J. Guey, *Essai sur la guerre Parthique de Trajan* (Bucharest 1937); F.A. Lepper, *Trajan's Parthian War* (Oxford 1948); and, significantly, in an ancient view in Dio 68.17.1; cf. also the review by M.I. Henderson of the Lepper book in JRS 39 (1949), pp.121–31. See also George Robert Constable, *The Development of Trajan's Political Program in the Coin Releases of the Roman Mint* (Chapel Hill, North Carolina 1981). • 67. Dio 68.17.2. • 68. Dio 68.7.5; 68.17.1; Haines ii, p.213; Isaac, *The Roman Army in the East* op. cit., pp.50–3, 119; J. Bennett, *Trajan, optimus princeps* (1997), p.190; G.W. Bowerstock, *Roman Arabia* (1983), pp.82–5. • 69. Eutropius 8.3.1; Festus, *Breviarium* (ed. John W. Eadie, 1967) 20; Arrian, *Periplus* 11.2; Dio 68.18.2; 68.19.2. • 70. Eutropius 8.3.1; Dio 68.191.1–68.20.4. • 71. Griffin, 'Trajan', CAH 11, p.126. • 72. Dio 68.22.2–68.26.4; Lepper, *Parthian War* op. cit., pp.44–54. • 73. Arrian, *Parthian Fragment* 67; Eutropius 8.3.2; Festus, *Brev.* 14.20; Dio 68.28.1–2. • 74. Dio 68.28.3–68.29.3; 68.30.1. • 75. Dio 68.29.4; 68.30.1–3; 75.9.6. • 76. Isaac, *Limits of Empire* op. cit., p.30; C.S. Lightfoot, 'Trajan's Parthian War and the Fourth Century Perspective', JRS 80 (1990), pp.115–26; R.P. Longden, 'Notes on the Parthian Campaigns of Trajan', JRS 21 (1931), pp.1–35; Bivar, 'Political History', *The Cambridge History of Iran* op. cit., pp.586–91; Graham Wylie, 'How did Trajan succeed in subduing Parthia where Mark Antony failed?', *Ancient History Bulletin* 4 (1990), pp.37–43. • 77. Arrian, *Parthian Fragment* 46.85; Dio 68.21.1–3; 68.22.1–2; R. Syme, 'The Career of Arrian', *Harvard Studies in Classical Philology* 86 (1982), pp.181–211. • 78. Aurelius Victor, *Epitome* 13; Malalas, *Chronicles* op. cit. 11.4.7. See also M.H. Dodgeon & S.N.C. Lieu, *The Roman Eastern Frontier and the Persian Wars. A Documentary History* (1991), p.176;

R.N. Frye, *The History of Ancient Iran* (Munich 1984), p.242. • 79. HA Hadrian 13.8–9; 21.10–12; Birley, *Hadrian*, pp.153–4; Bowerstock, *Roman Arabia* op. cit. • 80. Dio 68.9.10; 68.30; 68.33; 69.15.2; F.A. Pennachietti, 'L'Iscrizione bilingue grego-parthica dell' Eracle di Seleucia', *Mesopotamia* 22 (1987), pp.169–85. • 81. HA Antoninus 9.6–7; Rémy, *Antonin le Pieux*, pp.247–9. • 82. *Digest* 4.8.8.11. • 83. HA Antoninus 12.7; HA Marcus 8.6; ILS 1076; CIL ix.2457. • 84. G.W. Bowersock, 'La Mésène (Maishan) Antonine', in T. Fahd (ed.), *L'Arabie préislamique* (Leicester 1989), pp.159–68. • 85. David Sellwood, *An Introduction to the Coinage of Parthia* (1980); J. Dilmaghani, 'Parthian Coins from Mithradates II to Orodes II', *Numismatic Chronicle* 146 (1986), pp.216–24; Robert H. McDowell, *Coins from Seleucia on the Tigris* (Ann Arbor 1935); H.E. Mathiesen, *Sculpture in the Parthian Empire. A Study in Chronology*, 2 vols (Aarhus 1992); Daniel Schlumberger, 'Parthian Art', in E. Yarshater (ed.), *The Cambridge History of Iran. The Seleucid, Parthian and Sassanian Periods*, Vol. 3, Part 2 (Cambridge 1983), pp.1027–54. • 86. Alföldy, KS op. cit., p.244. • 87. AE 1981, 648. • 88. Lucian, *Quomodo historia (How to Write History)* 21, 24, 25; Lucian, *Alexander* 4, 27, 30. • 89. A.R. Birley, *The Fasti of Roman Britain* (Oxford 1981), pp.220–1. • 90. HA Antoninus 12.7; HA Marcus 8.6; Dio 71.2.1. For Cornelianus, see PIR2 A.1341; HA Pertinax 1.6. See in general Sencer Şahin, 'Statthalter der Provinzen Pamphylia-Lycia und Bithynia-Pontus in der Zeit der Statusänderung beider Provinzen unter Mark Aurels und Lucius Verus', EA 20 (1992), pp.77–90. • 91. Birley, *Fasti of Roman Britain* op. cit., pp.123–7; D.J. Breeze and B. Dobson, *Hadrian's Wall* (1987), pp.124–5. • 92. Alföldy, KS op. cit., pp.219, 232, 234–6; Birley, *Fasti* op. cit., pp.106–25. • 93. AE 1956, 123; ILS 8974, 1057, 5864. • 94. Dio 71.1.3. • 95. HA Verus 5.8–9; HA Marcus 8.9. • 96. Birley, *Marcus Aurelius* op. cit., p.122.

Notes to Chapter Seven   *pp. 141–167*

• 1. CIL iii.6169; ILS 2311, 1091, 1097–8; E.N. Luttwak, *The Grand Strategy of the Roman Empire* (1976), pp.81–4. • 2. ILS 1102, 1098; CIL iii. 12091, 6169; viii.7050; Lucian, *Quomodo historia* 31; H.M.D. Parker, *The Roman Legions* (Oxford 1928), p.167; R. Saxer, *Untersuchungen zu den Vexillationen des Römischen Kaiserheeres von Augustus bis Diokletian* (Berlin 1967), pp.3, 123; J. Beneš, *Auxilia Romana in Moesia atque in Dacia* (Prague 1978), pp.76–8. • 3. Syme, RP v, p.683; G. Camodeca, 'La carriera del prefetto del pretorio S. Cornelius Repentinus in una nuova iscrizione puteolana', ZPE 43 (1981), pp.43–56; ILS 8977, 1098, 1091, 9002; CIL iii.6169; AE 1956, 123. • 4. ILS 1094, 1092, 1100, 9002. • 5. ILS 394, 9117, 9492; AE 1972, 576; Lucian, *Quomodo hist.* 31; Dio 71.2.1. • 6. HA Verus 6.7; Champlin, 'The Chronology of Fronto', JRS 64 (1974) loc. cit. • 7. HA Verus 6.8–9; HA Marcus 8.1. • 8. Fronto to Lucius Verus, 162, Haines ii, pp.84–7. • 9. AE 1940, 30; AE 1960, 314; J.H. Oliver, 'The Eleusinian Endowment', *Hesperia* 21 (1952), pp.381–99. • 10. Fronto to Lucius Verus, Haines ii, pp.232–4.

• 11. AE 1959, 13–14; Millar, *Emperor in the Roman World* op. cit., p.36. • 12. HA *Lucius Verus* 6.9; Halfmann, *Itinera Principum*, pp.210–11. • 13. Dio 71.2.2; Eutropius 8.10.2; HA *Verus* 7.1–3; 8.11; HA *Marcus* 8.2. • 14. N.C. Debevoise, *A History of Parthia* (1937), pp.209–10; S. Braund, 'Juvenal and the East: Satire as an historical source', in D. French & C.S. Lightfoot (eds), *The Eastern Frontier of the Roman Empire* (Oxford 1989), pp.45–52. • 15. Pliny, NH 8.35.87; 14.28, 144, 148; Josef Wiesehöfer (ed.), *Das Partherreich und seine Zeugnisse* (Stuttgart 1998). • 16. The caveat is necessary for 'was Parthia feudal?' is essentially a futile argument hinging on terminology. Not only did the Parthian empire change considerably over 500 years, and was never based on any one economic system, but our sources, being Western, are almost entirely limited to the western part of the empire. See Josef Wiesehöfer, *Ancient Persia from 550 BC to 650 AD* (1996). • 17. J. Wolski, 'L'aristocratie foncière et l'organisation de l'armée parthe', *Klio* 63 (1981), pp.105–12. • 18. Warwick Ball, *Rome in the East. The Transformation of an Empire* (2000), p.9; Ben Isaac, *The Limits of Empire: The Roman Army in the East* (Oxford 1990), p.403. • 19. Isaac, op. cit., pp.19–53; J.R. Campbell, 'War and Diplomacy: Rome and Parthia 31 BC–AD 235', in J. Rich & G. Shipley, *War and Society in the Roman World* (1993), pp.213–40. • 20. Dio 40.16.1–20. • 21. Fergus Millar, *The Roman Near East* (Harvard 1993), p.244. • 22. Justin 41.2.6; Plutarch, *Crassus* 21. • 23. Edward Dabrowa, *La politique de l'état parthe à l'égard de Rome d'Artaban II à Vologase (c.79 de N.E.) et les facteurs qui la conditionnaient* (Cracow 1983); Gennadii A. Koshelenko & V.N. Pilipko, 'Parthia', in Janos Harmatta (ed.), *History of the Civilisations of Central Asia* (Paris 1994) ii, pp.131–50; see also Heidemarie Koch, *A hoard of coins from Eastern Parthia* (New York 1990). • 24. Hermann Kulke & Dieter Rothermund, *A History of India* (1998), p.365; Robert H. McDowell, 'The Indo-Parthian Frontier', AHR 44 (1939), pp.781–801; cf. also Joseph E. Schwartzberg (ed.), *A Historical Atlas of South Asia* (Oxford 1992); B.J. Staviski, *La Bactriane sous les Kushans* (Paris 1986). • 25. Aurelius Victor, *De Caesaribus* 15.4. • 26. M. Rashke, 'New Studies in Roman Commerce with the East', ANRW 2.9.2 (Berlin 1978), pp.604–1361 (esp. pp.751, 800); Derek Williams, *The Reach of Rome. A History of the Roman Imperial Frontier, 1st–5th Centuries* (New York 1997). • 27. Ptolemy 7.2.15; 6.14.7–14. • 28. Ptolemy 7.1.55; W. Tarn, *The Greeks in Bactria and India* (1951), pp.223–4, 291–2; P. Daffinà, *L'Immigrazione dei Saka nella Drangiana* (Rome 1967); Robert H. McDowell, 'The Indo-Parthian Frontier', AHR 44 (1939), pp.781–801. • 29. *The Cambridge History of Iran* op. cit. 3.1, pp.192–7. • 30. Lionel Casson (ed. & trans.), *Periplus Maris Erythraei*, p.186; Schoff, *Periplus* (1989), pp.166–7; Michael Mitchiner, *Indo-Greek and Indo-Scythian Coinage*, 9 vols (1975), esp. Vols 5–9. • 31. J.I. Miller, *The Spice Trade of the Roman Empire, 29 BC to AD 641* (Oxford 1969); Helen Wang, *Money on the Silk Road* (2004); Gary K. Young, *Rome's Eastern Trade. International commerce and imperial policy, 31 BC–AD 305* (2001); Emmanuel

Choisnel, *Les Parthes et la Route de la Soie* (Paris 2004). • 32. Herodotus, Book 4; Bernard S. Bachrach, *A History of the Alans in the West* (Minnesota 1973); Agusti Alemany, *Sources on the Alans. A Critical Compilation* (2000); Marcelo Tilman Schmitt, *Die Römische Aussenpolitik des 2 Jahrhunderts* (Stuttgart 1997). • 33. Ammianus Marcellinus 30.2.21; 31.2.1–35; Ptolemy 3.5.15; 3.19.21; 6.14.3; 6.9.11; Lucian, *Toxaris* 51. • 34. Josephus, *Jewish Wars* 7.4.244–8; Josephus, *Antiquities* 18.4.96; Strabo 23.11.5.8; Bachrach, *History of the Alans* op. cit., pp.4–5; Tessa Rajak, 'The Parthians in Josephus', in Wiesehöfer, (ed.), *Das Partherreich* op. cit., pp.309–24; Marek J. Olbrycht, *Parthia et ulteriores gentes: die politischen Beziehungen zwischen dem arsakidischen Iran und den Nomaden der Euraischen Steppen* (Munich 1998). • 35. Suetonius, *Domitian* 2.2. • 36. HA Hadrian 17.11.12; 21.13; Dio 69.15.12. • 37. Dio 69.15.3; M. Sartre, *L'Asie Mineur et l'Anatolie d'Alexandre à Dioclétien* (Paris 1995), p.182; M. Chaumont, 'L'Arménie entre Rome et l'Iran. De l'avènement d'Auguste à l'avènement de Dioclétien', ANRW 2.9.1, pp.71–194 (at pp.145–6); D. Braund, *A History of Colchis and transcaucasian Iberia 550 BC–AD 562* (Oxford 1994), pp.213–14. • 38. Arrian, *Tactica* 32.3; 44.2–3; E.L. Wheeler, 'The occasion of Arrian's *Tactica*', *Greek, Roman and Byzantine Studies* 19 (1978), pp.351–66; Wheeler, *Flavius Arrianus. A Political and Military Biography* (Ann Arbor 1977), pp.223–7; M. Karras-Klaproth, *Prosopographische Studien zur Geschichte des Partherreiches auf der Grundlage antiker literarischer Überlieferung* (Bonn 1988), p.85; Birley, *Fasti* op. cit., p.220. • 39. Dio 69.18.2. • 40. HA Antoninus 5.5; Rémy, *Antonin le Pieux*, p.245. • 41. Dio 69.15.3; HA Antoninus 9.6; Vidman, *Fasti Ostienses* op. cit., p.50; F. Carrata Thomes, *Gli alani nelle politica orientale di Antonino Pio* (Turin 1958), pp.25–30. • 42. Martial 7.30; Dio 69.15. • 43. Mark Hassall, 'The Army', CAH 11, p.341. • 44. Adrian Goldsworthy, *The Roman Army at War 100 BC–AD 200* (Oxford 1996), pp.12–38, 121–4; cf. G. Alföldy, *Die Legionslegaten der Römischen Rheinarmeen* (Cologne 1967). • 45. Hubert Devijver, *The Equestrian Officers of the Roman Army*, 2 vols (Amsterdam 1992); Brian Dobson, 'Legionary Centurion or Equestrian Officer? A comparison of pay and prospects', *Ancient Society* 3 (1972), pp.193–207. • 46. Webster, *The Roman Imperial Army* (Norman, Oklahoma 1998), pp.113–14. • 47. P.A. Brunt, 'Pay and Superannuation in the Roman Army', PBSR 18 (1950), pp.50–71; Webster, *Roman Imperial Army* op. cit., pp.264–8. • 48. M.P. Speidel, *Roman Army Studies* (Stuttgart 1992) ii, pp.101–2. • 49. Ramsay MacMullen, 'How Big was the Roman Army?', *Klio* 62 (1980), pp.451–60. • 50. Ben Isaac, *Limits of Empire* op. cit., p.383. • 51. J.B. Campbell, *The Emperor and the Roman Army* (Oxford 1984), p.165–71. • 52. E. Badian, *Private Enterprise in the Service of the Roman Republic* (Cornell 1983), pp.16–25; cf. Jonathan P. Roth, *Logistics of the Roman Army at War, 264 BC–AD 235* (Leiden 1998). • 53. Mark Hassall, 'The Army', CAH 11, p.323. Marcus Aurelius had the same number of legions (twenty-eight) – ILS 2288. • 54. Hassall, 'The Army' op. cit., pp.320–1; Webster, *The Roman Imperial Army* op. cit., pp.99–105. • 55. Goldsworthy, *The Roman Army* op. cit., p.246. • 56. Lazlo Torday, *Mounted Archers: The beginnings of Central Asian history* (Durham 1997); Mariusz Mielczarek, *Cataphracti and Clibanarii; Studies on the heavy armoured cavalry of the ancient world* (Lodz 1993); Alfred S. Bradford, *With arrow, sword and spear: A history of warfare in the ancient world* (Westport, Connecticut 2001); A.D.H. Bivar, 'Cavalry equipment and tactics on the Euphrates frontier', *Dumbarton Oaks Papers* 26 (1972), pp.273–91. • 57. Goldsworthy, *Roman Army* op. cit., pp.61–8. • 58. Dio 40.1.5; 49.20.1–4. • 59. Goldsworthy, *Roman Army* op. cit., p.229. • 60. Plutarch, *Antony* 38, 42–3; Tacitus, *Annals* 13.36–40; 15.9. • 61. Sherwin-White, *Roman Foreign Policy* op. cit., p.315. • 62. Plutarch, *Antony* 39.9; 40.1; 45.8; Dio 49.26.4–27.1. • 63. Tacitus, *Annals* 15.11. • 64. AE 1966, 4976; Brian Campbell, 'War and Diplomacy: Rome and Parthia 31 BC–AD 235', in John Rich & Graham Shipley (eds), *War and Society in the Roman World* (1995), pp.213–40; K. Jakubiak, *The Development of the Defence System of Eastern Anatolia* (Rome 2003). • 65. ILS 1097–8; 394; 9117; for Zeugma, see Pliny, NH 5.21; Strabo 16.2.3; Polybius 5.43.1. • 66. For the rigours, see Tacitus, *Annals* 13.35.5–8. For the richness of this area, see Strabo 11.13.4. • 67. HA Marcus 9.1–2; Dio 71.14.2; 71.3.1; ILS 1092; Haines, ii., pp.144–5; Alföldy, KS, pp.221, 240. • 68. Also with having killed precisely 70, 236 of the enemy (Lucian, *Quomodo historia* 20). • 69. ibid., 24, 31. For more detail on these absurd stories, see Millar, *The Roman Near East* op. cit., pp.111–18. • 70. See J.A. Hall, *Lucian's Satire* (New York 1981); C.P. Jones, *Culture and Society in Lucian* (1986). • 71. Birley, *Fasti of Roman Britain* op. cit.; Alföldy, KS, p.221. • 72. ILS 1097–8, 2311, 1102. • 73. Lucian, *Quomodo historia* 20, 29; Haines ii, pp.212–13. • 74. Lucian, *Quomodo historia* 29; Ammianus Marcellinus 23.3; M.L. Astarita, *Avidio Cassio* (Rome 1983), p.41; Syme, RP v, pp.693–4. For Nicephorium, see Pliny, NH 5.21.30; Strabo 16.1.3. • 75. Nazarius, *Panegyric* 24.6; Haines ii, pp.128–50; 212–13. • 76. HA Verus 9.11. • 77. HA Verus 9.2–4. But Syme refuses to believe that Libo was sent out at all, and identifies Marcus's agent as one Julius Verus (RP v, p.693). • 78. HA Verus 7.1–6; Dio 71.2; Lucius Verus to Fronto, 163, Haines ii, pp.116–19. • 79. HA Verus 7.10. • 80. Lucian, *A Portrait Study* 1–2, 6, 8–9, 22. • 81. HA Marcus 7.5–11. Marcus refers to Panthea in dismissive terms at Meds 8.37. • 82. PIR2 C.602; AE 1939, 109; Syme, RP i, p.326. Among other members of Marcus's circle who were also Aristotelians, one should mention Sergius Paulus (proconsul in Asia, 166–7, and Prefect of Rome in 168) and Flavius Boethius, governor of Palestinian Syria in 166–8 (Bowerstock, *Greek Sophists* op. cit., p.82); V. Nutton, *Galen on Prognosis* (Berlin 1979), pp.163–4; J. Hahn, *Der Philosoph und die Gesellschaft* (Stuttgart 1989), pp.29, 148–9. • 83. Halfmann, *Itinera Principum* op. cit., p.211; Barnes, 'Hadrian and Lucius Verus', JRS 57 (1967), pp.65–79 (at p.72). • 84. Fronto to Marcus Aurelius, 162–3, Haines ii, pp.20–30. • 85. Champlin, *Fronto* op. cit., pp.112–17. • 86. Haines ii, pp.216–17. • 87. Eutropius 8.10; AE 1936, 153. • 88. Eutropius 8.3;

Festus 20.2; H.J.W. Drivjers, 'Hatra, Palmyra and Edessa', ANRW 2.8 (1977), pp.799–906. • 89. Dio 68.28.3–4. See also D.C. Braund, *Rome and the friendly king. The character of client kingship* (1984); cf. C. Chad, *Les dynastes d'Émèse* (Beirut 1972); R.D. Sullivan, 'The Dynasty of Emesa', ANRW 2.8 (1977), pp.198–219. • 90. Dio 71.22.2. • 91. HA Avidius Cassius 5.2–12; 6.1–2. • 92. Reliable sources for Verus's Parthian campaign are, sadly, meagre. Two valiant attempts have been made to impose a credible narrative sequence on events: C.H. Dodd, 'The Chronology of the Eastern Campaigns of the Emperor Lucius Verus', *Numismatic Chronicle*, 4th series II (1911), pp.209–67; K. Strobel, 'Zeitgeschichte unter den Antonine: die Historiker des Partherkrieges des Lucius Verus', ANRW 2.34.2 (1994), pp.1315–60. • 93. Lucian, *Quomodo historia* 22; Pliny, NH 5.85; Stephen Kirk Ross, *Towards Roman Edessa 114–242 CE* (1997). • 94. Lucian, *Quomodo historia* 15, 19–20. • 95. B.P. Reardon (ed.), *Collected Ancient Greek Novels* (1989), p.783. • 96. HA Marcus 9.1; HA Verus 7.1–2; Dio 71.2; Lucian, *Quomodo historia* 20, 24, 28. For the crossing of the Euphrates, see Anthony Comfort, 'The crossing of the Euphrates in Antiquity', *Anatolian Studies* 50 (2000), pp.99–126 and *Anatolian Studies* 51 (2001), pp.19–41. • 97. Nigel Pollard, 'The Roman Army as a total institution; in the Near East? Dura-Europos as a case study', in David Kennedy (ed.). *The Roman Army in the East* (Ann Arbor 1996), pp.211–27; J.F. Gilliam, *Roman Army Papers* (1986), pp.207–27; Millar, *The Roman Near East* op. cit., pp.445–52. • 98. Pliny, NH 5.20.83–8; 6.30–1; Strabo 16.1.9. • 99. A.R. Birley, *Septimius Severus* op. cit., pp.181–202. • 100. Strabo 21.1.16; Pliny, NH 6.30.122–4. • 101. Debevoise, *History of Parthia* op. cit., p.xli. • 102. HA Verus 8.3–4; Eutropius 8.10; Dio 71.31; R.H. McDowell, *Coins from Seleucia on the Tigris* (1935), p.234; Syme, RP v, p.690. • 103. Josephus, *Antiquities* 18.9.9; Millar, *Roman Near East* op. cit., p.445. • 104. Ammianus Marcellinus 23.6.24. • 105. Millar, *Roman Near East*, p.114. • 106. Pliny, NH 6.17; 6.29.114–17. • 107. Strabo 11.13.1; 16.1.16; Tacitus, *Annals* 15.31; Curtius Rufus 5.8.1. • 108. Pliny, NH 6.14; 6.17; Strabo 11.13.6. • 109. W. Szaivert, *Die Münzprägung der Kaiser Marcus Aurelius, Lucius Verus und Commodus, 161–192* (Vienna 1989), pp.199–200. • 110. Dio 75.3.2–3. • 111. RIC iii.1360, 861–8, 1429, 915, 9126. • 112. HA Marcus 9.2. • 113. Lucius Verus to Fronto, 165, Haines ii, pp.196–7. • 114. Fronto to Lucius Verus, 163–5, Haines ii, pp.144–5, 148–9, 208–9. • 115. Tacitus, *Annals* 13.35; Dio 75.12.3; Everett Wheeler, 'The laxity of the Syrian legions', in D. Kennedy (ed.), *The Roman Army in the East* op. cit., pp.229–76. He claims the propaganda has 'much to do with Roman morality, if not also ethnocentrism, and very little to do with the reality of the Syrian legions' (ibid., p.237). • 116. Fronto to Lucius Verus, 165, Haines ii, pp.196–211. See also J.C. Baltry & W. van Rengen, *Apamea in Syria: The Winter Quarters of the Legio II Parthica* (Brussels 1993). • 117. Fronto to Avidius Cassius, 165, Haines ii, pp.190–3. • 118. C.G. Starr, *The Roman Imperial Navy* (1975), pp.188–9. • 119. Alföldy, KS, pp.24, 180–3, 240, 243. • 120. Dio 71.3.1; Philostratus, VS

2.563. • 121. Dio 75.1.2–3; Millar, *Roman Near East* op. cit., p.113. • 122. AE 1913, 170; Birley, 'Marcus', CAH 11, p.165. • 123. Ammianus Marcellinus 23.6.23–4. • 124. The *reductio ad absurdum* comes in Warwick Ball, *Rome in the East* op. cit., pp.17, 453, where he doubts that Ctesiphon, which fell to Trajan, Avidius Cassius and Septimius Severus, was *ever* taken and suggests that Rome's successes were due to a smallpox epidemic among the Parthians. Certainly the Romans experienced more problems in Parthia, both at this juncture and under Septimius Severus, than they were prepared to admit. See D.B. Campbell, 'What happened at Hatra? The problems of the Severan siege operations', in P. Freeman & D. Kennedy (eds), *The Defence of the Roman and Byzantine East* (Oxford 1986), pp.51–8. • 125. Septimius's campaign featured another *reductio ad absurdum*, this time of the 'imitation of Alexander' topos. Having visited Alexander's tomb, he ordered it locked up so that no one in future could see the great conqueror's body (Dio 75.13.2). See also Z. Rubin, 'Dio, Herodian and Severus's Second Parthian War', *Chiron* 5 (1975), pp.419–41.

Notes to Chapter Eight   *pp. 168–203*

• 1. Fronto to Praecilius Pompeianus, 162, Haines ii, pp.88–91. • 2. Fronto to Marcus, 162, Haines ii, pp.62–71. • 3. Fronto to Marcus, 162, Haines ii, pp.34–7. • 4. Fronto to Marcus, 161, 163, Haines i, pp.302–5; ii, pp.126–7; cf. Dio 71.35. • 5. Fronto to Marcus, 162, Haines ii, pp.28–9. • 6. Fronto to Marcus, 162, Haines ii, pp.8–9, 12–13. • 7. Marcus to Fronto, Fronto to Marcus, 161–2, Haines i, pp.300–3; ii, pp.2–7, 18–19. • 8. Fronto to Marcus, Haines ii, pp.118–21. Some claim, with not a shred of evidence, but on the strength of poetic licence, that the boy holding the white bread was Commodus. • 9. Champlin, *Fronto* op. cit., p.71. For Matidia, see PIR2 M.368. • 10. Fronto to Marcus, Marcus to Fronto, Fronto to Aufidius Victorinus, 162, Haines ii, pp.94–101. • 11. Tacitus, *Annals* 4.5. • 12. Tacitus, *Annals* 13.18. • 13. Dio 79.14. • 14. Suetonius, *Augustus* 25; Dio 55.26. • 15. Tacitus, *Annals* 1.7; Dio 55.24; Herodian 3.13.4; L. Keppie, *The Making of the Roman Army* (1984), p.188. • 16. Campbell, *The Emperor and the Roman Army* op. cit., p.114; cf. also L.L. Howe, *The Pretorian Prefect from Commodus to Diocletian* (1942); A.H.M. Jones, *The Later Roman Empire* (1964), pp.448–62, 586–92. • 17. HA Hadrian 22.13; HA Antoninus 2.11. • 18. HA Marcus 11.6; C.L. Lepelley (ed.), *Rome et l'intégration de l'empire. 44 av. J.-C.–260 ap. J.-C. Approches régionales du Haut-Empire romain* (Paris 1998). • 19. Dio 53.12; Strabo 17.3.24. • 20. Strabo 3.4.19; 17.3.25. • 21. Dio 53.13.2–3; Campbell, *The Emperor and the Roman Army* op. cit., pp.348–52. • 22. Dio 53.15.4. • 23. Alföldy, KS p.218; W. Eck, 'Empire, Senate and Magistracies', CAH 11, p.225. • 24. S.J. Keay, *Roman Spain. Conquest and Assimilation* (1991). • 25. M. Todd, *Roman Britain 55 BC–AD 400* (1997). • 26. Lennox Manton, *Roman North Africa* (1988). • 27. AE 1956, 123. • 28. M. Sartre, *D'Alexandre à Zénobie. Histoire du Levant antique* (Paris 2001), p.606. • 29. *Digest* 50.2.3.2; 48.18.1.27; 2.14.60; 1.18.14; 25.4.1.

• 30. 'A large number of Praetorian prefects met sudden and violent deaths. It is one of the clearest signs of the relative stability of the imperial regime in the middle of the period that none is recorded as having done so between 97 and the reign of Commodus.' (Millar, *Emperor in the Roman World*, p.126) • 31. W. Eck, 'The Growth of Administrative Posts', CAH 11, pp.240–1. • 32. J. Schwendemann, *Der historische Wert der Vita Marci bei den scriptores Historiae Augustae* (Heidelberg 1923), pp.28–51; W.W. Williams, 'Individuality in the Imperial Constitution: Hadrian and the Antonines', JRS 66 (1976), pp.67–83 (at pp.71–8). • 33. H.G. Pflaum, *Les carrières procuratoriennes équestres sous le Haut Empire romain* (Paris 1950), iii, pp.1019–20. • 34. Birley, 'Marcus Aurelius', CAH 11, p.159. • 35. Eck, 'Administrative Posts', loc. cit. CAH 11, pp.242–4. • 36. Suetonius, *Claudius* 24.1; Dio 53.15.5; H.G. Pflaum, *Abrégé des procurateurs équestres* (Paris 1974), p.63; Eck, 'Administrative Posts', p.259; Syme, RP v, p.687. • 37. M. Hammond, 'The Composition of the Senate, AD 68–235', JRS 47 (1957), pp.74–81. The process accelerated under Septimius Severus (Campbell, *The Emperor and the Roman Army*, pp.404–8). • 38. Eck, 'Administrative Posts', p.256. • 39. Dio 55.4.1–2. • 40. Eck, 'Administrative Posts', pp.263–5. • 41. W. Eck, 'Emperor, Senate and Magistracies', CAH 11, p.227. • 42. Eck, 'Administrative Posts', p.245. • 43. AE 1954, 138; Champlin, *Fronto* op. cit., p.79. • 44. During the reign of the Flavians there were usually six consuls a year. Trajan had six to eight, Hadrian eight, Antoninus Pius eight to ten. With Marcus the figure was ten and rising, and by 190 Commodus was appointing twenty-four a year (Talbert, *Senate* op. cit., p.21). • 45. HA Marcus 11.8. • 46. Pliny, *Letters* 9.5. • 47. Marcus signs off: 'Farewell, my Marsianus, dearest to me.' (H.G. Pflaum, 'Une lettre de promotion de l'empereur Marc Aurèle pour un procurateur ducenaire de Gaulle Narbonne' *Bonner Jahrbuch* 171 (1971), pp.349–66); cf. AE 1960, 167; 1962, 183. • 48. Eck, 'Administrative Posts', pp.259–60. • 49. HA Marcus 6.6. • 50. Dio 71.17.1; Talbert, *Senate*, p.366. • 51. HA Marcus 10.7–9; HA Pertinax 2.9; Dio 71.33.2. • 52. Talbert, *Senate*, pp.166–71. Technically, the right of veto derived from the tribunician power (*potestas tribunica*), which Augustus had cunningly included in the wide-ranging powers of an emperor (ibid., pp.170–1). • 53. *Digest* 49.4.1.7. • 54. As when the inhabitants of Miletus requested a special tournament of physical games (AE 1977, 801; AE, 1989, 683). • 55. Talbert, *Senate*, pp.290–1. • 56. Anthony Everitt, *Augustus. The Life of Rome's First Emperor* (New York 2006); Pat Southern, *Augustus* (1998); Werner Eck, *The Age of Augustus* (Oxford 2003). • 57. 'We might almost come to believe that the primary role of the emperor was to listen to speeches in Greek' is the waspish comment of Fergus Millar (*The Emperor in the Roman World* op. cit., p.6). • 58. H. Halfmann, *Die Senatoren aus dem Östlichen Teil des Imperium Romanum* (Göttingen 1979). • 59. Millar, *The Emperor in the Roman World*, has a section (pp.110–22) that, with its nuances and differences, irresistibly recalls the Mafia distinction between 'a friend of mine' and 'a friend of ours'. • 60. Theodore Mommsen, *Gesammelte Schriften* (Berlin 1905), iv, pp.311–22. For Domitian's *amici*, see the aside in Juvenal, *Satires* iv.37. • 61. HA Marcus 1.16. • 62. M. Royo, *Domus Imperatoriae. Topographie, formation et imaginaire des palais impériaux du Palatin* (Rome 1999). • 63. Herodian 1.6.5. • 64. Meds 8.4. • 65. Dio 72.6.2; W. Williams, 'Individuality and the Roman Constitution', JRS 66 (1976), pp.78–82. • 66. *Digest* 2.12.1.2. • 67. HA Marcus 24.12. • 68. *Digest* 49.1.1.2. • 69. *Digest* 23.2.57, quoted in Millar, *The Emperor in the Roman World* op. cit., p.548. • 70. *Digest* 37.14.17. • 71. *Digest* 28.4.3. • 72. *Digest* 36.1.23; 32.27.1. • 73. Tacitus, *Annals* 3.17; 13.43; *Digest* 48.20.1. • 74. HA Marcus 10.11–12; Haines i, pp.11–13; *Digest* 26.2.191; 47.191.1; 26.5.1.1; 2.15.8. • 75. Richard Saller, 'Family and Household', CAH 11, p.859. • 76. *Digest* 27.1.1.4. • 77. *Digest* 26.5.14. • 78. W. Williams, 'Individuality in the Roman Constitutions', loc. cit., p.80. • 79. HA Marcus 9.7. • 80. *Digest* 29.5; Tacitus, *Annals* 13.52; 14.142–5. • 81. Cicero, *Republic* 3.25; Juvenal, *Satires* 6.480; *Digest* 47.10.15.42. • 82. *Digest* 50.6.6.10–11. • 83. *Digest* 11.4.1.1–2. • 84. HA Marcus 9.7–9; *Digest* 40.16.2.4. • 85. F. Schulz, 'Roman registers of birth and birth certificates', JRS 32 (1942), pp.78–91; JRS 33 (1943), pp.55–64. • 86. AE 1971, 534; M. Christol, 'Une correspondance impériale: testimonium et suffragatio', *Revue historique de droit français et étranger* 66 (1988), pp.31–42. • 87. W. Eck, 'Provincial administration and finance', CAH 11, pp.271–2. • 88. Millar, *The Emperor in the Roman World* op. cit., pp.482–3. • 89. *Digest* 49.4.1.7. • 90. *Digest* 28.3.6–9; 48.12.2.1. • 91. *Digest* 17.2.52.10; 20.2.1; 20.3.2. • 92. Horace, *Satires* 2.6.10. • 93. HA Hadrian 18.6; *Digest* 49.14.3.10. • 94. *Digest* 1.18.14. • 95. *Digest* 40.15.1.3. • 96. *Digest* 50.6.6.6. • 97. HA Marcus 23.8. For the background to the decree abolishing 'unisex' bathing, see Garrett V. Fagan, *Bathing in Public in the Roman World* (Ann Arbor 1999). • 98. Meds 10.8.2. • 99. For the games in general, see A. Cameron, *Circus Factions* (1976); Michael Grant, *Gladiators* (1971); E. Rawson, 'Chariot Racing in the Roman Republic', PBSR 49 (1981), pp.1–6; E. Rawson, 'Theatrical Life in Republican Rome and Italy', PBSR 53 (1985), pp.97–113. • 100. HA Marcus 15.1; Dio 69.1.4; Meds. 6.46. • 101. Suetonius, *Augustus* 44; Suetonius, *Claudius* 21; Tacitus, *Annals* 15.32; Dio 60.7. • 102. *Digest* 40.19.17. • 103. HA Marcus 11.4; 27.6; Dio 71.29.4. • 104. CIL vi.31420; F.M. de Robertis, 'Dispensa del munus venatorium in una costituzione imperiale de recente scoperta', *Historia* 9 (1935), pp.248–60. • 105. HA Marcus 24.1; 10.10; 11.10; 11.1; 12.5; Dio 71.6.1. • 106. HA Marcus 10.1–9. • 107. Dio 71.38.2; J.E. Allison & J.D. Cloud, 'The Lex Julia Maiestatis', *Latomus* 21 (1962), pp.711–31. • 108. HA Marcus 11.1. • 109. HA Marcus 11.10. • 110. W. Williams, 'Formal and historical aspects of two new documents of Marcus Aurelius', ZPE 17 (1975), pp.37–78. • 111. Herodian 1.2.3–4. • 112. HA Marcus 8.1; 12.1; 22.3; Dio 72.33.2; Meds 1.6; 1.16; 6.21; 6.30. • 113. HA Marcus 12.3. • 114. HA Marcus 12.12. • 115. *Digest* 4.2.13; 48.7.7. • 116. P. Noyen, 'Divus Marcus princeps prudentissimus et iuris religiosissimus', *Revue Internationale de Droit de l'Antiquité*, 3rd series I (1954), pp.349–71. • 117. See, for example, Pliny, *Letters* 9.5.3; 7.29; Tacitus, *Annals* 13.26–7. • 118. For full details on this, see J.H. Oliver, *Greek Constitutions* op. cit. • 119. HA Marcus 27.3; Dio 71.33.3. • 120. HA Marcus 10.1–3; 10.7–9; 11.10. • 121. Michael Grant, *The Antonines* op. cit., p.39. • 122. For examples of the employment of men of merit rather than rank and family, see AE 1934, 155; AE 1956, 123–4; AE 1957, 121; AE 1958, 261. • 123. Dio 71.19.1. • 124. ILS 5841, 5864, 5868; T. Pekary, *Untersuchungen zu den Römischen Reichstrassen* (1968), pp.16–17. • 125. HA Marcus 11.5; 23.8. • 126. O.F. Robinson, *Ancient Rome. City Planning and Administration* (1992), p.22. • 127. HA Marcus 11.7. • 128. ILS 375; HA Marcus 11.3; *Digest* 27.1.26. For the many rescripts to provincial governors, see *Digest* 1.18.14; 2.14.60; 25.4.1; 48.18.1.27; 50.2.3.2. • 129. AE 1937, 246; AE 1949, 27; AE 1952, 88; AE 1957, 264; AE 1960, 114, 200, 342. See also SEG 9 (1944), 170–2; SEG 13 (1956), 291; SEG 15 (1957), 231. For the literary peccadillo, see Haines i, pp.178–9. For confirmation of Marcus's early popularity, see Ammianus Marcellinus 15.7.3; 16.1.4; 21.16.11; 22.5.5; 25.4.17; 30.9.1; 31.10.19. • 130. Dio 73.8; HA Antoninus 13.4; Eutropius 8.8.3. See also L. Vogel, *The Column of Antoninus Pius* (Cambridge 1973). • 131. D.R. Walker, *The Metrology of the Roman Silver Coinage, Vol.2 From Nerva to Commodus* (Oxford 1977), pp.55–60; cf. also Vol.3 (Oxford 1978), p.125; R. Duncan-Jones, *Structure and Scale in the Roman Economy* (Cambridge, 1990), p.44. • 132. Hopkins, 'Taxes and Trade in the Roman Empire', loc. cit., pp.116–25. • 133. P.A. Brunt, 'Pay and Superannuation in the Roman Army', PBSR 18 (1950), pp.50–61. • 134. ILS 2288; B. Dobson, 'The significance of the centurion and primipilari', ANRW loc. cit., pp.392–430. • 135. HA Marcus 7.9; Webster, *The Roman Imperial Army* op. cit., pp.264–8; Campbell, *The Emperor and the Roman Army* op. cit., p.171. • 136. Dio 72.32.3. • 137. PIR2 A.1512. • 138. Fronto to Marcus, 165, Haines ii, pp.224–7. • 139. *Cymbeline*, Act Four, Scene Two, Lines 258–62. Or, in a similar vein: 'Be absolute for death; either death or life / Shall thereby be the sweeter. Reason thus with life. / If I do lose thee, I do lose a thing / That none but fools would keep; a breath thou art / Servile to all the skyey influences (*Measure for Measure*, Act Three, Scene One, Lines 5–9). • 140. Fronto to Marcus, 165, Haines ii, pp.226–33. • 141. Fronto to Lucius Verus; Verus to Fronto, 165, Haines ii, pp.233–6. • 142. Marcus to Fronto, 165, Haines ii, pp.223–4. • 143. Lucius Verus to Fronto, 166, Haines ii, pp.238–41. • 144. Fronto to Verus, 166, Haines ii, pp.236–8. • 145. Artemidorus 4.22 (in White (ed.), *Dream Interpretation* op. cit., p.195). • 146. R. MacMullen, *Enemies of the Roman Order* (1967), pp.121–2. • 147. Millar, *The Emperor and the Roman World* op. cit., p.203. • 148. Meds 3.16; 4.28; 6.30; 12.27. • 149. HA Marcus 12.7–11. • 150. HA Verus 8.11. • 151. HA Verus 9.8–11. • 152. P. Kneissl, *Die Siegestitulatur der Römischen Kaiser* (Göttingen 1969), pp.200–2. • 153. Campbell, *The Emperor and the Roman Army* op. cit., pp.136–7; Nicholas Purcell, 'The City of Wonders', CAH 11, p.411. • 154. ILS 375. • 155. C.H. Picard, 'Le monument aux victimes de Carthage et l'expédition orientale de Lucius Verus', *Karthago* 1 (1950), pp.65–94; M. Hammond, 'Imperial Elements in the Formula of the Roman Emperors', *Mem. American Academy at Rome* 25 (1957), pp.17–64. • 156. HA Verus 7.9. • 157. HA Marcus 12.7–8. • 158. HA Marcus 12.9–12; Dio 71.29.4. On games expenditure, see ILS 5163, 9340. For the Roman fascination with lions, see Pliny, NH 8.17–21; Epictetus, *Discourses* 4.1.24–8; 3.22.6. For further thoughts on Romans and wild animals, see H. Scullard, *The Elephant in the Greek and Roman World* (Ithaca, New York 1974). Some scholars are sceptical about the numbers of animals allegedly slaughtered at the games. Syme, RP ii, p.646, thinks the totals in the *Historia Augusta* are simply plucked from the air, as in the case of the 1,000 bears said to have been exhibited in one day by the emperor Gordian. • 159. There is a considerable literature on the Silk Road. See David Christian & C. Benjamin (eds), *Realms of the Silk Road: Ancient and Modern* (Turnhout, Belgium 2000); Emmanuel Choiseul, *Les Parthes et La Route de la Soie* (Paris 2004); J. Thorley, 'The Silk Trade between China and the Roman Empire at its height, circa AD 90–130', GR 18 (1971), pp.71–80. But see the contrarian, hyper-sceptical view of Warwick Ball: 'The existence of the "Silk Road" is not based on a single shred of historical or material evidence . . . Both ancient Rome and China had only the haziest notions of each other's existence and even less interest, and the little relationship that did exist between East and West was usually one-sided, with the stimulus coming mainly from the Chinese' (Ball, *Rome in the East* op. cit., p.139). • 160. Pliny, NH 37.67; 21.8; Ammianus Marcellinus 23.6; Tacitus, *Annals* 2.33. • 161. Seneca, *Declamation* 1. • 162. Ptolemy 1.11.4–8; 1.12.2–10; 6.16.1–8; 6.21.1; J. Thompson, *History of Ancient Geography* (Cambridge 1948), pp.177–81, 306–12; Aurel Stein, 'On Ancient tracks past the Pamirs', *The Himalayan Journal* 4 (1932), pp.1–24. • 163. P.M. Fraser, *Cities of Alexander the Great* (Oxford 1996), pp.88–93; Michael Grant, *A Guide to the Ancient World* (1986), p.163. • 164. N. Kramer, 'Das stathmoi Parthikoi des Isidor von Charax. Beschreibung eines Handelsweges?', *Klio* 85 (2003), pp.120–30. • 165. Strabo 11.13.1; 16.1.16; 21.1.16; Tacitus, *Annals* 15.31; Curtius Rufus 5.8.1. • 166. Wilfred H. Schoff, *Periplus Maris Erythraei* (1912), p.172. • 167. Pliny, NH 6.52; Strabo 11.7; Schoff, *Periplus* op. cit., p.277. • 168. Martin R. Charlesworth, 'Roman trade with India: A Resurvey', in Paul R. Coleman-Norton (ed.), *Studies in Roman Economic and Social History in Honor of Allan Chester Johnson* (Princeton 1951), pp.131–43; George Woodcock, *The Greeks in India* (1966), pp.140–1. • 169. Lionel Casson, *Mariners* (1964) pp.9–11. • 170. Pliny, NH 6.24–6; Ptolemy 7.4.1; Strabo 15.691. • 171. Casson, *Periplus* op. cit., p.89. • 172. E.H. Warmington, *The Commerce Between the Roman Empire and India* (Cambridge 1928), pp.57–64; Thani Nayagam (ed.), *Tamil Culture and Civilization* (1970), pp.145–50; Woodcock, *The Greeks in India* op. cit., p.145. • 173. G.S.P. Freeman-Grenville, 'Some recent archaeological works on the Tanganyika coast', *Mars* 58 (1958), pp.106–12;

Freeman-Grenville, *The Swahili Coast: 2nd to 19th Centuries: Islam, Christianity and Commerce in East Africa* (1988), p.5. • 174. Casson, *Periplus* op. cit., pp.283–91. • 175. And hence the coins of Antoninus Pius found in southern India (see P.J. Turner, *Roman Coins from India* (1989)). • 176. Pliny, NH 12.8.9; 12.26; 35.25.27; 37.9–42; Athenaeus 3.46; Strabo 16.4.6; 2.5.12; 17.1.3; 15.1.4. Cf. Casson, *Periplus*, pp.17, 21–2, 63, 65, 67, 77, 79, 101–2, 118–20, 122–4, 134–6, 181, 193–4; Schoff, *Periplus*, pp.120–8, 136–41, 213–16, 222–7, 263–8. • 177. Pliny, NH 12.26; Strabo 15.1.13; Schoff, *Periplus*, pp.269–70; Joseph Needham, *Science and Civilisation in China* (Cambridge 1954) i, pp.173–82. • 178. Pliny, NH 35.28; H.A. Maraudian, *The Trade and Cities of Armenia in Relation to Ancient World Trade* (Lisbon 1965). • 179. Pliny, NH 32.11; Schoff, *Periplus*, p.128. • 180. Pliny, NH 9.54–8. • 181. The Chinese sources can be found in John E. Hill (ed. & trans.), *The Western Regions according to the Hou Hansu* (2004), and Hill (ed.), *The People of the West from the Weilue* (2004). Cf. also D.D. Leslie & K.H.J. Gardiner, *The Roman Empire in Chinese Sources* (1996). • 182. Strabo 11.11.1; Pomponius Mela, *De Situ Orbis* 1.2; 3.7; Ptolemy 1.11.4–8; 1.12.2–10; 6.16.1–8; 6.21.1. • 183. Raymond Grew, 'The case for comparing histories', AHR (1980), pp.763–8; Richard A. Olson, 'Parthia, China and Rome: Perspectives along the Great Silk Route', in M.A. Powell & R.H. Sack (eds), *Studies in Honor of T.B. Jones* (1979), pp.329–39; John Frederick Teggart, *Rome and China: A Study of correlations in historical events* (Berkeley 1969). • 184. It used to be thought that China's western expansion was in pursuit of trade (CAH 10 (1934), pp.880–1). This view has largely been abandoned (Casson, *Periplus* op. cit., pp.36–7). Some scholars are even more sceptical: 'The whole story of Rome–China trade has been vastly exaggerated by the myth of the Silk Route' (Ball, *Rome in the East*, p.138). See also Gary K. Young, *Rome's Eastern Trade* (2001); H.H. Dubs, 'A military contact between Chinese and Romans in 36 BC', *T'Oung Pao* 36 (1940), pp.64–80. • 185. The pioneering study of these inchoate contacts was Frederick Hirth, *China and the Roman Orient* (Leipzig 1885). More modern scholarship is contained in a plethora of works: E.G. Pulleybank, 'The Roman Empire as known to Han China', *Journal of the American Oriental Society* 119 (1999), pp.71–9; Manfred G. Raschke, 'New Studies in Roman Commerce with the East', ANRW 2.9.2 (1978), pp.604–1378; Christian Gizewski, 'Römische und alte Chinesische Geschichte in Vergleich zur Möglichkeit eines gemeinsamen Altertumsbegriffes', *Klio* 76 (1994), pp.271–302. • 186. Schoff, *Periplus* op. cit., p.276; Thomson, *A History of Ancient Geography* op. cit., p.312. • 187. H. Ferguson, 'China and Rome', ANRW 2 loc. cit., pp.581–603. • 188. Michael Mitchiner, *Oriental Coins and Their Values. The Ancient and Classical World 600 BC–AD 650* (1978), pp.105–23. • 189. E.H. Warmington, *Commerce between the Roman Empire and India* op. cit., pp.130–1, 262, 394; L. Boulnois, *The Silk Road* (1966), p.71; D.E. Graf,

'The Roman East from the Chinese Perspective', *Annales Archéologiques Arabes Syriennes* 42 (1996), pp.199–216. • 190. ILS 8869; Webster, *The Roman Imperial Army* op. cit., p.83.

Notes to Chapter Nine   *pp. 204–225*

• 1. Augustine, *City of God* 18.18. For general discussions of Marcus as philosopher-king, see G.A. Stanton, 'Marcus Aurelius. Emperor and Philosopher', *Historia* 18 (1969), pp.570–87; Klein (ed.), *Marc Aurel* op. cit., pp.359–88; Peter Franz Mittag, 'Kaiser oder Philosoph? Zur Münzprägung Marc Aurels', *Schweizerische Numismatische Rundschau* 73 (1994), pp.61–75. • 2. Renan, *Marcus Aurelius* op. cit., pp.23–4; cf. Hadot, *Inner Citadel* op. cit., pp.52–3. • 3. Herodian 1.2.3. • 4. Philostratus, VS 2.12; Philostratus, *Dialogues* ii.58. • 5. Meds 7.35; 7.44–6; 10.23. • 6. Some have interpreted Meds 6.11–12 in this way, but this is highly speculative. For a much purer example of this mystical Neoplatonism, see Thomas à Kempis, *Imitation of Christ* 1.11.1. • 7. Meds 7.66; Rutherford op. cit., p.216. Nonetheless, there are many references in the *Meditations* to Socrates personally (Meds 7.19; 7.26; 11.23; 11.25; 11.28; 11.39). • 8. See Charles Kahn, *The Art and Thought of Heraclitus* (Cambridge 1979); Jonathan Barnes, *The Presocratic Philosophers* (1982); M. Dragona-Monachou, *The Stoic Arguments for the Existence and Providence of the Gods* (Athens 1976). • 9. Meds. 3.3; 4.46; 6.42; 6.47; 8.3. See in general A.A. Long, *Stoic Studies* (Cambridge 1996), pp.35–57 (esp. pp.56–7). • 10. Meds 5.36–7; 7.27. • 11. Meds 4.46.4. • 12. Meds 4.36; 5.10; 5.13; 6.57; 10.26. • 13. Meds. 4.42; 4.23; 5.23. • 14. Meds 3.3. The legend got a new lease of life when the third-century biographer Diogenes Laertius popularised it. Actually, in this passage Marcus can be accused of trying to be too clever by half, for he pairs Heraclitus with Democritus and confuses Democritus's death with that of Pherecydes, thus destroying his argument twice over (Farquharson op. cit. ii, p.553). • 15. Gilbert Murray, *Five Stages of Greek Religion* (1935), pp.113–19. • 16. Luis Navia, *Diogenes the Cynic. The War against the World* (2005). • 17. Keimpe Algra, Jonathan Barnes, Jaap Mansfield & Malcolm Schofield (eds), *The Cambridge History of Hellenistic Philosophy* (Cambridge 1999), pp.625–6. 'Big thieves are arresting a little one' sounds like a gloss on Aesop's remark: 'We have petty thieves and appoint great ones to public office.' • 18. Epictetus, *Discourses* 3.21.18–19. • 19. Epictetus, *Discourses* 2.13.24. • 20. Meds 8.3. • 21. Epictetus, *Discourses* 3.23.29. • 22. Galen, K.20, p.44. For Arrian, see R. Syme, 'The career of Arrian', *Harvard Studies in Classical Philology* 86 (1982), pp.171–211; S.L. Wheeler, *Flavius Arrianus: A political and military biography* (Duke, North Carolina 1977); P.A. Stadter, *Arrian of Nicomedia* (Chapel Hill, North Carolina 1980). • 23. Sandbach, *The Stoics* op. cit., p.169. • 24. Long, *Epictetus* op. cit., p.119. • 25. Epictetus, *Discourses* 4.1.46; 1.1.7–13; 3.24.3. • 26. Epictetus, *Discourses* 1.18.3; 1.28.9; 2.22.36; 4.1.47; 4.12.19. • 27. Epictetus, *Discourses* 1.18.11. • 28. Epictetus, *Discourses* 2.14.23–9.

• 29. Epictetus, *Discourses* 1.29.9–12. • 30. Meds 4.23. • 31. Meds 11.17. But, as the best modern scholar of the Stoics has remarked: 'Such a thesis would be as repugnant as it is implausible' (Long, *Epictetus*, p.154). See also Paul Veyne, *Seneca: The Life of a Stoic* (2003), p. 20: 'Stoic philosophy had no content other than to forbid the emperor from tyrannising his subjects; it was devoid of any reformist program. Searching for originality in Marcus Aurelius's politics would be just as futile.' The Marcus view on politics was famously summed up by Alexander Pope: 'For forms of government let fools contest,/Whate'er is best administered is best' (*An Essay on Man* iii.303). • 32. Epictetus, *Discourses* 3.24.31–6. • 33. Epictetus, *Discourses* 2.5.26; Meds 6.44.6. See also Hadot, *Inner Citadel* op. cit., pp.211–14. • 34. Epictetus, *Discourses* 3.24.31. • 35. Epictetus, *Discourses* 1.13.4–5. • 36. Epictetus, *Discourses* 1.18.5–9. • 37. Epictetus, *Discourses* 1.18.11–16. • 38. Meds 2.1; 4.3; 5.25. • 39. Epictetus, *Discourses* 4.4.11–18. For further light on Epictetus, see William O. Stephens, *Stoic Ethics: Epictetus and Happiness as Freedom* (2007). • 40. Rutherford op. cit., pp.225–55 (esp. pp.229, 232). • 41. Ramsay MacMullen, *Enemies of the Roman Order* (Cambridge, Massachusetts 1966), pp.70–94. • 42. The alleged link is emphasised by Long, *Stoic Studies* (Cambridge 1996), p.276. But this seems in conflict with the passage where Epictetus explicitly attacks the value of the things Freud thought were the natural goals of the 'normal' male: wealth, power and beautiful women (Long, *Epictetus*, pp.137–9). • 43. J.M. Rist, 'Are you a Stoic? The case of Marcus Aurelius', *Jewish and Christian Self-Definition* (1983), pp.23–45. • 44. Rutherford op. cit., pp.240–1, 248. Some see Marcus as occupying a middle position between Seneca and Epictetus. Epictetus 'does not flirt, as Seneca for instance does, with Plato's other-worldly metaphysics and eschatology' (Long, *Epictetus*, pp.166–7). • 45. Hadot, *Inner Citadel*, p.103. • 46. Epictetus, *Discourses* 2.14.25–6. • 47. Rutherford, p.236; Hadot, *Inner Citadel*, p.128. Cosmology was a much more important part of Marcus's work than that of all former Stoics. See J. Annas, *The Morality of Happiness* (Oxford 1993), pp.161–75. • 48. G.E. Moore, *Hellenistic Philosophers* (Princeton 1925), pp.94–171. • 49. Galen K.5.17. • 50. Long, *Epictetus*, p.18; Algra, Barnes, Mansfield & Schofield, *Cambridge History* op. cit., pp.770–80. • 51. Long, *Epictetus*, p.161. • 52. Hadot, *Inner Citadel*, p.70. • 53. ibid, pp.98–115; *Cambridge Companion to the Stoics* op. cit., pp.37–43. • 54. Meds 5.25; 6.58; 9.31; 11.13.4; 12.32.3. • 55. Meds 3.16; 2.17; 12.3. • 56. Meds 3.6.1; 3.9.2; 8.32.2; 9.1; 12.15; 12.33. • 57. Meds 11.10.4. • 58. Meds. 8.27. • 59. Meds 9.40. • 60. Meds 12.10. • 61. Meds 12.24; 12.15. • 62. T.H. Irwin, 'Stoic Naturalism and its Critics', *Cambridge Companion to the Stoics* op. cit., pp.345–64. • 63. G.R. Stanton, 'Marcus Aurelius, emperor and philosopher', *Historia* 18 (1969), pp.570–87. • 64. Hadot, *Inner Citadel*, p.122. • 65. Meds 4.46.4; 6.42.1. • 66. Meds 4.3.11; 4.36; 5.23; 8.6–7; 10.11; 12.11; cf. Rutherford, pp.86–8; Harold Skulsky, *Metamorphosis. The Mind in Exile* (Harvard 1981). For Marcus's limited grasp of logic and metaphysics, see

Cambridge Companion to the Stoics, p.37. As noted elsewhere, the Roman Stoics tended to be dismissive of these aspects of Stoicism (see Seneca, *Letters* 45.5; 49.5). • 67. Meds 4.24; 4.29–30; 4.46; 5.9; 5.14; 5.27; 5.32; 6.1; 6.5; 6.22–3; 6.35; 7.9–11; 7.53–5; 8.40; 9.8–12; 9.42; 10.7; 10.12a; 10.31–3; 11.1; 11.9; 11.29; 12.31; 12.35. • 68. Heraclitus, *Fragments* 1, 2.64, 118, in P. Wheelwright, *Heraclitus* (Princeton 1959), pp.19, 68, 102; Plutarch, *Isis and Osiris*, pp.377–8; Sextus Empiricus, *Against Logicians* i, p.131; Diogenes Laertius 7.134, 136, 149. • 69. Philo, *On Creation* 5.20; 10.36; 48.139; 51.146, in C.D. Yonge, *The Works of Philo* (Peabody, Massachusetts 1993), pp.4, 6, 20, 21; Philo, *On Allegorical Interpretation* 3.31.96; Philo, *On the Cherubim* 1.11.35; Philo, *On Husbandry* 12.45; Philo, *Who is the heir of divine things* 27.140; 38.188; 48.234, in Yonge, ibid., pp.61, 84, 178, 287, 292, 296. • 70. Meds 2.14.1; 5.13; 10.27; 12.26; cf. also 6.37; 9.35; 11.1.3. • 71. Lucretius, *De rerum Natura* 3.947; 3.1090. • 72. There is an interesting variation on some of the implications of this notion in Milan Kundera's novel *The Unbearable Lightness of Being*. • 73. Sir Thomas Browne, *Religio Medici* 1.59. • 74. Meds 7.29; 2.13; 3.10; 6.37; 7.68.3; 8.36; cf. also 7.8; 7.29; 2.14; 12.1–4; 12.26.2. • 75. Meds 2.5.2; 11.34; 7.69. • 76. Seneca, *Letters to Lucilius* 78.14. 'A soul obsessed with the future is miserable indeed; it is unhappy even before any mishap' (Seneca, *Letters to Lucilius* 98.6). • 77. Meds 6.7. • 78. Victor Goldschmidt, *Le système stoicien et l'idée de temps* (Paris 1953), p.195. • 79. Meds 11.34. • 80. e.g. Meds 9.21. • 81. For some typical discussions, see T.B. Mabbott, 'Our Direct Experience of Time', *Mind* 60 (1951), pp.153–67; Bernard Mayo, 'Is there a sense of Duration?', *Mind* 59 (1950), pp.71–8; Heather Fotheringham, 'How Long is the Present?', *Stoa* 1 (1999), pp.56–65. • 82. William James, *The Principles of Psychology* (1902) i, p.609. • 83. Gerald Myers, 'James on Time Perception', *Philosophy of Science* 38 (1971), pp.353–60; C.D. Broad, *Scientific Thought* (New York 1923); Henri Bergson, *La Pensée et Le Mouvant* (Paris 1934), pp.168–9. The following quasi-oracular proposition from the early Wittgenstein seems to lend comfort to Marcus and the Stoics: 'If we understand by "eternity" not an infinite temporal duration but a lack of temporality, then he who lives within the present lives eternally' (*Tractatus* 6.4311). • 84. For Epicurus and Democritus, see Eugene O'Connor, *The Essential Epicurus* (New York 1993); Benjamin Farrington, *Science and Politics in the Ancient World* (New York 1965); G.S. Kirk, J.E. Raven & M. Schofield (eds), *The Presocratic Philosophers* (Cambridge 1983). • 85. Galen K.19.306–8. • 86. Galen K.2.28–29. • 87. Meds 9.39.2. • 88. Meds 4.27; 6.10; 6.44; 7.75; 8.18; 9.28; 9.39; 10.6–7. • 89. Meds. 2.3; 4.3; 4.27; 6.10.1; 8.17; 9.28; 9.39; 10.6; 11.18; 12.44.4. The idea that whichever is right, Providence or atoms, does not affect the rule of reason is already in Seneca (*Letters to Lucilius* 16.4). • 90. Epictetus, *Discourses* 2.28.24–6; 3.12.15. • 91. Epictetus, *Discourses* 4.26. • 92. Meds 5.16. • 93. Epictetus, *Discourses* 4.1.42–6. Epictetus passed on to Marcus the preoccupation with what the emperor thought and did and how difficult it was for him to avoid tyranny. See C.G.

Starr, 'Epictetus and the the Tyrant', *Classical Philology* 44 (1949), pp.20–9. • 94. Epictetus, *Discourses* 1.28.12–13. On this A.A. Long comments: 'Paris's lust for Helen, Helen's compliance, and Menelaus's desire for revenge were all instances of misjudging the value of what their representations or thoughts presented to them' (Long, *Epictetus*, p.254). Cf. also Long, *Stoic Studies* op. cit., pp.73–83. • 95. Epictetus, *Discourses* 3.24.17–19. • 96. C.J. Gill, 'Did Chrysippus understand Medea?' *Phronesis* 28 (1983), pp.136–49. Seneca wrote a tragedy on the subject. • 97. Epictetus, *Discourses* 1.28.6–8; 2.17.19; 4.13.14. • 98. The original story is found in Appollonius Rhodius and Apollodorus. • 99. Meds. 4.7; 5.2; 5.19; 6.52; 7.2; 7.14; 7.16; 8.40; 8.47; 9.13; 9.15; 11.11; 11.16; 12.22; 12.25. • 100. Meds 8.29; 8.47. • 101. Meds 9.13. • 102. Meds 4.39. • 103. Meds 4.3.10; 5.19; 6.52; 9.15. • 104. Epictetus, *Discourses* 1.28.10. • 105. Long, *Stoic Studies* op. cit., pp.265–71. This is a generous interpretation, and I prefer the iconoclasm of R.D. Hicks, *Stoic and Epicurean* (1910). • 106. Meds 12.18. • 107. Meds 3.11.3; 12.18; 6.13; 6.57; 10.35.

Notes to Chapter Ten   pp. 226–255

• 1. Meds 6.4; Chrysippus is mentioned by name at ibid. 6.42; 7.19. • 2. Meds 5.24. • 3. Meds 5.17. • 4. Meds 6.43. • 5. Meds 6.51. • 6. Meds 6.57. • 7. Meds 6.19. • 8. Meds 8.22a. • 9. Meds 9.41. • 10. Meds 11.33. • 11. Meds 12.9. • 12. Meds 12.6. • 13. G.J. Szemler, *The Priests of the Roman Republic. A study of the interactions between priesthoods and magistracies* (Brussels 1972). • 14. Millar, *The Emperor in the Roman World* op. cit., pp.355–61; Françoise van Haeperen, *Le collège pontifical, 3ème s.a.C–4ème s.p.C.* (Brussels 2002), pp.186–8, 197–201. • 15. Van Haeperen, *Le collège* op. cit., pp.47–77. • 16. Athaneus 1.26; Purcell, 'Rome and Italy', CAH 11, p.426. • 17. See C. Koch, *Religio* (Nuremberg 1960). • 18. Farquharson i, p.422. • 19. Meds 4.34; 11.18; 4.23; 8.27; 11.8; 5.7–8; 6.43. • 20. RIC iii.235.28; 248.1070. • 21. Cornelius Motschmann, *Die Religionspolitik Marc Aurels* (Stuttgart 2002), pp.58–68; G.W. Bowerstock, *Julian the Apostate* (1997), • 22. P. Petit, *La paix romaine* (Paris 1982), p.194. • 23. Renan, *Marcus Aurelius* op. cit, p.9. • 24. Motschmann, *Die Religionspolitik* op. cit., p.81; J.E. Lendon, *Empire of Honour. The Art of Government in the Roman World* (Oxford 1997), pp.72, 160; cf. I. Gradel, *Emperor Worship and Roman Religion* (Oxford 2002). • 25. F.H. Cramer, *Astrology in Roman Law and Politics* (Philadelphia 1954), p.208; *The Cambridge History of Hellenistic Philosophy* op. cit., pp.597–9. For a contrary view, see Rutherford op. cit., pp.58, 180, 211, 217–18, 219, 229, 261 and especially the volumes by Peter Brown, *Religion and Society in the Age of St Augustine* (1972), pp.74–81; *The Making of Late Antiquity* (1978), pp.4–11 and *Society and the Holy in Late Antiquity* (1982), pp.103–52. Cf. also A.D. Nock, *Essays on the Religion of the Ancient World* (Oxford 1972), pp.440–56. • 26. Lucian, *Alexander passim*. P. Mummius Sisenna Rutilianus, proconsul in Asia 160–1, was his father-in-law, having married Alexander's daughter at the age of sixty.

He died aged seventy, possibly in 171. He survived Alexander, whose death was slow and lingering, long enough for him to be able to arbitrate in the dispute over the leadership of his own cult (Lucian, *Alexander* 34, 35, 59–60). For the date of Rutilianus's death, see Alföldy, KS, pp.215, 330. • 27. L. Robert, 'Le serpent Glycon d'Abonouteichos à Athènes et Artémis d'Éphèse à Rome', *Comptes rendus de l'Académie des inscriptions et belles-lettres* (1981), pp.513–30. • 28. *The Cambridge History of Hellenistic Philosophy* op. cit., pp.795–6; cf. J. Fontenrose, *Didyma: Apollo's Oracle, Cult and Companions* (Berkeley 1988). • 29. Lucian, *Alexander* op. cit.; L. Robert, *À travers l'Asie Mineure* (Paris 1980), pp.393–421. • 30. C.R. Jones, *Culture and Society in Lucian* (1986), pp.133–48. • 31. Athenagoras, *Apology* 26; J. Eckhel, *Doctrina Nummorum Veterum* (Vienna 1792) ii, pp.383–4; cf. also William Godwin, *Lives of the Necromancers* (1834, reissued 2004); Renan, *Marcus Aurelius* op. cit., p.25. • 32. Lucian, *Alexander* 58; B.V. Head, *Historia Nummorum* (1911), p.550. • 33. Epictetus, *Discourses* 2.17.25. • 34. Epictetus, *Discourses* 1.24.1–2. • 35. Epictetus, *Discourses* 4.1.100–1. • 36. Epictetus, *Discourses* 4.1.103–4; 1.16.15–21. • 37. Epictetus, *Discourses* 3.5.10. This is very like the 'testament of acceptance' in Father Mapple's sermon in Melville's *Moby Dick*, Chapter Nine: 'O Father – chiefly known to me by Thy rod – mortal or immortal, here I die. I have striven to be Thine, more than to be this world's, or mine own. Yet this is nothing; I leave eternity to Thee; for what is man that he should live out the lifetime of his God?' • 38. Epictetus, *Discourses* 2.18.12–13. • 39. Epictetus, *Discourses* 1.16.20–1. For further panthe-istic thoughts, see ibid. 2.14.25–7. • 40. Epictetus, *Discourses* 3.26.28. • 41. Meds 4.26; 4.34; 5.8; 5.12; 10.5. • 42. Meds 5.27. Epictetus also seems to lean towards the 'guardian angel' version of transcendence (*Discourses* 1.14.11–14), except that in his version it could also be construed as an alter ego or 'superego', to use the Freudian term, which takes us back to square one of the conun-drum. Cf. also Long, *Epictetus* pp.163–4; Farquharson i, pp.291–2. • 43. See Appendix One. • 44. Meds 5.27. • 45. Rutherford, pp.228–9. • 46. Long, *Epictetus*, p.178; cf. also Alistair MacIntyre, 'Pantheism', in P. Edwards (ed.), *The Encyclopedia of Philosophy* (New York 1967) v, pp.31–5. • 47. Meds 6.44; 9.40; 7.9; 8.54; 9.1. • 48. Meds 1.17.1; 9.27. • 49. 'Of all the Stoics Marcus is the one whose theology comes closest to a strict pantheism' (Long, *Epictetus*, p.178). • 50. Epictetus, *Discourses* 1.1.12; cf. Farquharson i., p.290. • 51. Long, *Epictetus*, p.146. 'But when God is conceived pantheistically as physically present in all things, it is hard to understand what property he could have that would constitute the paradigm of a virtuous *human* character' (ibid., p.170). • 52. Meds 4.23; 5.7. • 53. Meds 7.70. • 54. Meds 12.2; 12.28. 'People ask "Have you ever seen the gods you worship? How can you be sure that they exist?" I answer . . . "I've never seen my soul either . . . That's how I know the gods exist"' (Meds 12.28). This reminds one of the way C.G. Jung would make the statement, 'I don't just believe God exists, I know', apparently giving comfort to orthodox Christians, but really meaning that he knew the 'God image', the God archetype or the 'god within' existed (see Frank McLynn, *Jung. A Biography*, p.526). • 55. Rutherford, p.219. • 56. Specifically *The Tempest*, Act Two, Scene One, and Tennyson, 'Crossing the Bar' (Farquharson ii, p.529). • 57. Farquharson i, pp.392–3. • 58. Meds 2.1.3; 4.3.6; 12.8. • 59. Meds 7.73–4; 11.4. • 60. Meds 7.22.1–2; 9.9; 11.1.4. • 61. Meds 5.6. • 62. Meds 11.18. • 63. Meds 3.4.3; 2.17. • 64. Meds 6.47; 2.1; 7.22; 11.9.2. • 65. Epictetus, *Discourses* 1.18.3; 1.28–9; 2.22.36; 4.1.47; Meds 9.9; 9.11. • 66. Meds 2.2; 7.3; 12.19. • 67. Meds 3.14. • 68. Meds 5.9.3–5; 6.7; 8.26; 10.33; 12.29.3. Cf. Father Mapple's sermon in Chapter Nine of Melville's *Moby Dick*: 'Delight is to him – a far, far upward and inward delight – who against the proud gods and commodores of this world ever stands forth his own inexorable self. Delight is to him whose strong arms yet support him, when the ship of this base, treacherous world has gone down beneath him. Delight is to him who gives no quarter in the truth, and kills, burns and destroys all sin though he pluck it out from under the robes of Senators and Judges. Delight – topgallant delight – is to him, who acknowledges no law or lord but the Lord his God and is only a patriot to Heaven.' • 69. Meds 2.1; 4.3; 12.8. • 70. Epictetus, *Discourses* 3.24.17. • 71. For a discussion of these points, see Elizabeth Azmis, 'The Stoicism of Marcus Aurelius', ANRW 2.36.3 (Berlin 1989), pp.2228–52; T.H. Irwin, 'Stoic Naturalism and its Critics', *The Cambridge Companion to the Stoics* op. cit., pp.345–64; J.M. Rist, 'Seneca and Stoic Orthodoxy', ANRW 2.36.3 (1989), pp.1993–2012; Mark P.O. Morford, *The Roman Philosophers* (2000). • 72. Epictetus, *Discourses* 3.22. • 73. Meds 2.1. • 74. Meds 4.3; 4.34; 7.63; 11.18.4–5; 11.18.10; 12.8; 12.12; 12.22; 12.26. • 75. Epictetus, *Discourses* 2.8.11–14. For evil as 'error' in Epictetus, see also ibid. 1.28.4–9; 2.22.36. • 76. Plato, *Protagoras* 345d; *Gorgias* 509e; *Timaeus* 86d. Plato's view was endorsed by his most brilliant student. See Aristotle, *Ethics* 7.3.1145b; 21–7. • 77. Meds. 2.13; 5.28.3; 6.27.3; 6.50.1;7.26; 8.59; 9.11; 9.42; 10.4. • 78. Meds 3.2. Marcus seems to have derived this notion from Aristotle (*Parts of Animals* 644.6.31). One is reminded of Robert Louis Stevenson's striking aphorism: 'The mark of beauty's in the touch that's wrong.' • 79. Meds. 6.15.2. • 80. Meds 6.36a. • 81. Meds 8.55. • 82. Cicero, *On the Nature of the Gods* 3.35.86; 2.66–167. • 83. Meds 12.32; cf. Epictetus, *Discourses* 1.12.26. • 84. Meds 6.41. • 85. J.S. Mill, 'Nature' in *Three Essays on Religion* op. cit., pp.35–8. • 86. Epictetus, *Discourses* 1.29.62; 1.9.33; 1.24.1–2; 3.25.3–4; 4.7.17. • 87. Epictetus, *Discourses* 1.4.20. • 88. Meds 5.30; 9.1.1. But, as so often with Marcus, there is a conflict between two very different notions, this time of justice. 1) Everything that happens is just (Meds 4.10). 2) Injustice exists: 'Evil men often live in pleasure, and obtain the means to do so, while the good encounter only misery and that which causes misery' (Meds 9.1). • 89. Dostoevsky, *The Brothers Karamazov*, Book Five, Chapter Four 'Rebellion'. • 90. Meds 7.41. • 91. Meds 8.50. • 92. Meds 12.5. • 93. Meds 8.34. • 94. Or, as Hume puts it: 'If the evil in the world is from the intention of the Deity, then he is not benevolent. If the evil in the world is contrary to his intention, then he is not omnipotent. But it is either in accordance with his intention or contrary to it. Therefore either the Deity is not benevolent or he is not omnipotent' (*Dialogues Concerning Natural Religion*, Part Ten). • 95. William James, *The Varieties of Religious Experience* (1902), p.199. • 96. Malory, *Morte d'Arthur*, Book Fourteen, Chapter Six. • 97. Thomas Browne, *Religio Medici* 1.6. • 98. Seneca, *Natural Question 6*; *Letters* 53. • 99. Quoted in Veyne, *Seneca* op. cit., p.41. • 100. A.N. Whitehead, *Science and the Modern World* (1925), p.56. • 101. Meds 7.1; 8.40; 9.1; 9.42; 10.7. • 102. Wallace I. Matson, *The Existence of God* (Ithaca, New York 1965), pp.142–3. • 103. Martin Heidegger, *Being and Time* (1962); cf. A. de Waelheus, *La philosophie de Martin Heidegger* (1942). • 104. McLynn, *Jung* op. cit., p.476. • 105. L. Kolakowski, *Main Currents of Marxism* (2005), p.338. • 106. Meds 4.3; 4.5; 11.18; 9.3; 9.28; 9.32. Cf. Montaigne *Essays* i: 'Your death is part of the order of the universe. It is a part of the life of the world.' Or, to take a modern example: 'There is no cure for birth and death but to enjoy the interval' (George Santayana, 'War Shrines', *Soliloquies in England* (1922)). But though the *Meditations* are often compared to Eastern philosophy, Marcus does not allow himself the usual oriental consolation of reincarnation. See, for example, the *Bhagavad Gita*, Chapter Two: 'For certain is death for the born and certain is birth for the dead. Therefore over the inevitable thou shouldst not grieve.' • 107. Meds 4.26.4; 10.5. Cf. Ahab's remarks in *Moby Dick*: 'The whole act's immutably decreed. 'Twas rehearsed by thee and me a billion years before this ocean rolled' (Chapter 131) and: 'By, heaven, man, we are turned round and round in this world, like yonder windlass, and Fate is the handspike.' (Chapter 133) • 108. Meds 8.2; 2.14. • 109. Meds 7.49. • 110. Meds 12.23; 4.48.4. • 111. Meds 2.2. This idea of a 'soul carrying a corpse' can be found in Epictetus (*Discourses* 2.19.27; 3.10.15; 3.22.41; 4.7.31). The idea that we die daily through decay is a key notion in Freud's famous *Todestrieb* or death-drive. • 112. Meds 2.6; 5.31; 10.15; 12.1–2. Or, to use the argument adduced by Sophocles in *Electra*: 'Death is not the worst; rather in vain to wish for death, and not to compass it.' • 113. Cicero, *De Senectute* passim; Juvenal, *Satires*. 10.188–288. • 114. Meds 4.50. • 115. Meds 3.2; 10.36. • 116. Lucian, *Charon Sees Life*. • 117. St Augustine, *Confessions* 4.10–11. • 118. Meds 2.12; 4.50. This calls to mind Montaigne's remark in the *Essay on Death* when he says: 'Death's sad array, not death itself, alarms me.' • 119. Meds 6.28; 6.48; 6.56; 7.29; 7.56; 8.21; 8.58; 9.1; 10.29. • 120. The same theme appears in Lucian, *Icarousenippus* (4 and Charon passim pp.17–24). • 121. Meds 4.47. • 122. Meds 9.3. • 123. Meds 9.21. • 124. Meds 7.23; 4.48; 5.4. • 125. Rutherford, pp.244–6. • 126. Epictetus, *Discourses* 2.1.17–19. • 127. Epictetus, *Discourses* 4.1.106. • 128. Lampedusa, *The Leopard* (the final words of Chapter Six). • 129. Kant, *Critique of Practical Reason* (last pages). • 130. Meds 4.33. This probably influenced the

similar list by François Villon in his *La ballade des seigneurs du temps jadis*. •
131. Meds 4.32; 8.5. • 132. Meds 3.3; 6.24; 8.3; 6.47. • 133. Meds. 4.19; 6.18. This
is probably the earliest version of 'What has posterity ever done for me?',
which is usually attributed either to the essayist Joseph Addison or to Sir
Boyle Roche (1743–1807). • 134. The point is hammered home again and again
(Meds 4.3.7–8; 4.21; 7.21; 7.29.6; 8.11; 8.21; 9.37; 9.25; 11.18.6; 12.18; 12.21). • 135.
The 'vanity' quote is at *Ecclesiastes* 34. As for the other, like any successful
offspring, it has a hundred parents. The first clear usage is by Abraham
Lincoln in an address to the Wisconsin State Agricultural Society, Milwaukee,
on 30 September 1859: 'It is said that an Eastern monarch once charged his
wise men to invent him a sentence, to be ever in view, and which would be
true and appropriate in all time and situations. They presented him with the
words "And this too shall pass away." How much it expresses! How chas-
tening in the hour of pride! How consoling in the depths of affliction!' (R.P.
Basler (ed.), *Collected Works of Lincoln* (New Brunswick, New Jersey 1953) iii,
pp.481–2). • 136. Meds 7.3. • 137. Meds 7.40. • 138. Meds 10.34. • 139. One of
the elements in Marcus's horrified fascination with death is the process of
physical decomposition and decay, which links with his loathing of the body.
This motif is perhaps the only one where the influence of Roman Stoics, as
opposed to the Greek Epictetus, can be discerned. See Lucretius, *De rerum
Natura* 3.881; Seneca, *Letters* 14.6.24; 14.120.18. • 140. For studies placing Marcus's
reflections on death in a wider context, see J. McManners, *Death and the
Enlightenment* (Oxford 1981); Elizabeth Kübler-Ross, *On Death and Dying* (1969);
E.M. Cioran, *The Temptation to Exist* (Chicago 1998). • 141. Seneca, Letter 77;
Veyne, *Seneca*, p.85. • 142. Epictetus, *Discourses* 2.15.4–12; 1.25.20; 2.1.19; 3.8.6;
3.13.14; 3.23.24; 3.24.101–2. As the foremost modern authority on Epictetus has
remarked: 'By attaching the conditional justifiability of suicide to Socrates's
famous statement, Epictetus contrives to remain loyal to both camps . . .
Epictetus shows none of Seneca's fascination with suicide, nor does he treat
it, like Seneca, as the supreme test of a Stoic's freedom' (Long, *Epictetus*,
p.204). • 143. Meds 7.33; 10.3; 10.22; 10.32. This line is endorsed by Sir Thomas
Browne, who so often follows Marcus closely (*Religio Medici* i.44). See also
M. Seidler, 'Kant and the Stoics on Suicide', *Journal of the History of Ideas*
(1983), pp.429–53. • 144. Meds 3.1; 5.29. • 145. Meds 5.29; 8.47. • 146. Meds 9.2;
10.8.1–2; 10.22; 10.32. • 147. For a discussion, see Rutherford, pp.248–50. • 148.
Meds 4.14; 4.21; 5.33; 6.4; 7.34; 8.25; 8.28. • 149. Rutherford, p.255. • 150. Meds
10.1; 10.36. • 151. Meds 12.5.2. • 152. Meds 10.7. • 153. Meds 3.3.2. • 154. Meds
7.27. • 155. Meds 5.31.2. • 156. Meds 12.36. • 157. Epictetus, *Discourses* 3.24.21;
3.24.31–4; 3.24.36. • 158. Meds 5.8; 5.16. • 159. Meds 4.3.5; 5.8; 7.9; 4.2.7; 6.10; 7.7.5;
9.28; 9.39; 10.6–7. • 160. Meds 6.44. • 161. Meds 9.29; HA Marcus 27.7. • 162. Meds
4.23. • 163. Thomas à Kempis, *Imitation of Christ* 4.3.15. Others liken it to Milton's
Sonnet 7.4.24; cf. also Henri Bordeaux, *La Peur de Vivre*. All the quasi-mystical

passages of the *Meditations* where Marcus seems to advocate a Neoplatonic withdrawal into the self link easily with Thomas à Kempis (see, for example, Meds 6.11, as compared with *Imitation of Christ* 1.11.1). • 164. Meds 10.21. • 165. Meds 12.24; cf. Milton, *Paradise Lost* 4.677; Sir Thomas Browne, *Religio Medici* i.33: 'Millions of spiritual creatures walk the earth unseen.' • 166. Dio 53.6–7. See Karen Armstrong, *Buddha* (New York 2001); J. Brockington, *The Sanskrit Epics* (Leiden 1998); Fritjof Capra, *The Tao of Physics* (1975); S. Lebell, *Epictetus. The Art of Living: The Classic Manual on Virtue, Happiness and Effectiveness* (San Francisco 1995), p.xi. See also the *Rubáiyát of Omar Khayyám*, esp. stanzas 59–64, for a sensibility very like Marcus's. • 167. H.D.M. Parker, *History of the Roman World AD 138–337* (1935), p.16. • 168. *The Oxford Classical Dictionary* (2003), p.152. • 169. Michael Grant, *The Antonines* op. cit. • 170. Hadot, *The Inner Citadel* op. cit. • 171. Renan, *Marcus Aurelius* • 172. The familiar phrase *de gustibus non disputandum (est)* was formerly attributed to Cicero, but it nowhere appears in his *oeuvre* and appears to be one of those 'invention of tradition' Latin tags, though the essential thought behind it often appears in the classical authors. The only genuine phrase featuring 'taste' that is clearly attributable to a Latin author is the famous description of Petronius by Tacitus as *elegantiae arbiter* (*Annals* 16.18). • 173. Meds 7.27. • 174. Meds 9.27.3; 9.11.2. • 175. And, as Cassius Dio pointed out, Marcus's personality in this regard was formed before he ever took up Stoicism (Dio 71.35.2). • 176. Dio 62.34.2–3. • 177. To use Renan's words: 'As St Louis did not suffer a moment's uneasiness in his faith by reason of clerical disorders, Marcus Aurelius never felt disgusted with philosophy, whatever the vices of philosophers' (Renan, *Marcus Aurelius*, pp.18–19).

Notes to Chapter Eleven   *pp. 256–279*

• 1. Meds 7.22.1–2; 11.1.4; 9.9. • 2. Philippians 3.14; 1 Timothy 6.12; 2 Timothy 4.7; cf. Rutherford, pp.232–3. • 3. Hebrews 5.7; Mark 14.36; Mark 15.34; 1 Corinthians 6.16; 15.26. • 4. Long, *Epictetus*, p.144. • 5. W.R. Halliday, *The Pagan Background of Early Christianity* (Liverpool 1925); M. Spannent, *Le Stoïcisme des Pàres de l'Église* (Paris 1957). • 6. The writings of G.A. Wells are the *locus classicus*. See *The Jesus Legend* (1996). More nuanced views are available in Robin Lane Fox, *The Unauthorised Version. Truth and Fiction in the Bible* (1991), and Graham Stanton, *The Gospels and Jesus* (Oxford 2002). • 7. Michael Grant, *Saint Paul* (2000), is a good introduction. • 8. Tacitus, *Annals* 15.44; cf. H. Fuchs, 'Tacitus über die Christen', *Vigiliae Christianae* 4 (1950); Charles Saumagne, 'Tacite et Saint Paule', *Revue Historique* 232 (1964), pp.67–110. • 9. Pliny, NH 10.96. • 10. Suetonius, *Nero* 38; Dio 62.16.18; Tacitus, *Annals* 15.38–44. • 11. Gerhard Baudy, *Die Brande Roms. Ein Apokalyptisches Motiv in der antiken Historiographie* (1991). A recent biography of Nero suggests: a) it was unlikely Nero started the fire; b) it may not have been the orthodox Christians who started it, but the hardline Jewish followers of Peter (who had clashed violently with Paul at the Jerusalem council), who still practised circumcision (Richard Holland, *Nero. The man behind the Myth* (2000), pp.163, 175); cf. also Charles Saumagne, 'Les incendaires de Rome et les lois pénales des romains', *Revue historique* 227 (1962), pp.337–60. • 12. Edward Champlin, *Nero* (Harvard 2003), pp.178–209. • 13. Josephus, *Jewish Antiquities* 20.200; I. Epstein, *The Babylonian Talmud* (1935). • 14. L.W. Barnard, 'Clement of Rome and the panic of Domitian', *New Testament Studies* 10 (1964), pp.251–60; Robin Lane Fox, *The Unauthorised Version* op. cit., p.433; Barnard, *Justin* (1967). • 15. Pliny, *Letters* 10.96. • 16. ibid., 10.97. • 17. Tertullian, *Apologeticum* 2.6. • 18. Timothy Barnes, 'Legislation against the Christians', JRS 58 (1968), pp.32–50; JRS 57 (1967); Paul Keresztes, 'The Imperial Roman Government and the Christian Church. I. From Nero to the Severi. II. From Gallienus to the Great Persecution', ANRW 2 (1980), pp.247–315; 375–86. • 19. G. de Ste Croix, 'Why were the early Christians persecuted?', 26 (1963), pp.6–38 (esp. pp.11–12). • 20. Keresztes, loc. cit., p.285. See also Rudolf Freudenberger, *Das Verhalten der Römischen Behörden gegen die Christen im 2. Jahrhundert* (Munich 1967). • 21. Pliny, *Letters* 10.34. • 22. Tertullian, *Apol.* 39.14–21. • 23. Tertullian, *Apol* 7.3; cf. Robert L. Wilken, *The Christians as the Romans saw them* (Yale 1986), pp.31–47. • 24. Tacitus, *Histories* 5.5; 5.13; Suetonius, *Nero* 16. • 25. Robin Lane Fox, *Pagans and Christians* (1986), op. cit.; R.M. Ogilvie, *The Romans and Their Gods* (New York 1969). • 26. L.F. Janssen, '"Superstitio" and the Persecution of the Christians', *Vigiliae Christianae* 33 (1979), pp.131–59; J.J. Walsh, 'On Christian Atheism', *Vigiliae Christianae* 45 (1991), pp.196–211; Stephen Benko, 'Pagan criticism of Christianity during the first two centuries AD', ANRW 2.32.2 (Berlin 1980), pp.1055–118; William R. Schoedel, 'Christian "Atheism" and the Peace of the Roman Empire', *Church History* 42 (1973), pp.310–11. • 27. Ste Croix, 'Why were the early Christians persecuted?', loc. cit., p.18; A.N. Sherwin-White, 'Why were the early Christians persecuted – an Amendement', PP 27 (1964), pp.23–7; Ste Croix, 'A Rejoinder', PP 27 (1964), pp.28–33. • 28. Dio 52.36.1–2. • 29. Wilken, *The Christians* op. cit., p.62. • 30. Cicero, *De legibus* 2.25.26; Apuleius, *Apol.* 65. • 31. Ramsay MacMullen, *Paganism in the Roman Empire* (New Haven 1981), pp.2, 40. • 32. Keresztes in ANRW 2 loc. cit., p.284; Lane Fox, *Pagans and Christians*, op. cit., p.428. • 33. Tacitus, *Histories* 5.5; 5.13; Juvenal, *Satire* 14. • 34. W.H.C. Frend, *Martyrdom and Persecution in the Early Church* (1965), p.334; Frend, 'The Persecutions: Some links between Judaism and the Early Church', *Journal of Ecclesiastical History* 9 (1958), pp.141–58. • 35. Josephus, *Jewish Antiquities* 20.8.11. • 36. J. Juster, *Les Juifs dans l'empire Romain* (Paris 1914), i, pp.213–14. • 37. Philo, *Legatio ad Gaium* 157, 317. • 38. Tacitus, *Histories* 5.1; Edward Gibbon, *The Decline and Fall of the Roman Empire* (1776), ii.16.74. • 39. Cicero, *De Natura Deorum* 1.3–4; 2.8; Plutarch, *On Superstition*. • 40. Peter Brown, *The Making of Late Antiquity* op. cit., p.39. • 41. That the Christians were vulnerable to such charges is clear from a reading of the New Testament. See Mark 15.2; 12.26; Luke 23.2; John 19.12; Revelation 14.8; 16.19; 17.18. Even Tertullian acknowledged the force of the claims (*Apol.* 10.1; 10.2.28.1; 10.2.28.2–35. • 42. Ste Croix, 'Why were the Christians?' loc. cit., p.24; Lane Fox, *Pagans and Christians*, p.434. • 43. See René Girard, *Things Hidden Since the Foundation of the World* (1978). • 44. Lane Fox, *Pagans and Christians*, p.425. • 45. Tertullian, *Apol.* 40.1–2; D. Stockton, 'Christianos ad leones', in B. Levick (ed.), *The Ancient Historian and His Materials* (Farnborough 1975), pp.199–212. • 46. R.J. Hoffmann, *Celsus on the True Doctrine* (Oxford 1987), pp.75, 102, 57.53, 54, 108, 75, 91, 71, 124. On Jesus: pp.59, 60, 61, 62, 63, 65, 116. • 47. M.P. Nilsson, *Geschichte der griechischen Religion* (Munich 1950) ii., pp.465–85; A.M. Tupet, 'Rites magiques dans l'antiquité romaine', ANRW 2.16 (1986), pp.2591–675; F.H. Cramer, *Astrology in Roman Law and Politics* (Philadelphia 1954). • 48. J. Tontain, *Les cultes païens dans l'empire romain* (Paris 1920) ii, pp.179–206. • 49. Lane Fox, *Pagans and Christians*, p.304. • 50. J.G. Griffiths, *Apuleius of Medauros. The Isis Book* (Leiden 1975); P. Walsh, *The Roman Novel* (1970), pp.186–9. • 51. Acts 9.36–9; 16.14–15; Romans 15.1; 16.1; 1 Corinthians 9.5; 16.15; 2 Timothy 4.19–21. • 52. J.E. Salisbury, *Perpetua's Passion. The Death and Memory of a Young Roman Woman* (1997). • 53. Warwick Ball, *Rome in the East* op. cit., p.433. • 54. Lane Fox, *Pagans and Christians*, pp.308–11, 323. • 55. Artemidorus 1.78–80; 4.65; 5.62–8; 5.87, 95. • 56. Lane Fox, *Pagans and Christians*, pp.351–74. • 57. 1 Corinthians 11.6–10; 14.34–5; 1 Timothy 2.12; 5.11–13. • 58. This is a huge subject and we have not even scratched the surface. See Brent D. Shaw, 'The Passion of Perpetua', in Robin Osborne (ed.), *Studies in Ancient Greek and Roman Society* (2004), pp.286–325; Peter Brown, *The Body and Society: Men, Women and Sexual Renunciation in Early Christianity* (New York 1988); D. Sawyer, *Women and Religion in the First Christian Centuries* (1996); M. MacDonald, *Early Christian Women and Pagan Opinion* (Cambridge 1996); Mary Lefkowitz, 'Motivations for St Perpetua's Martyrdom', *Journal of the American Academy of Religion* 44 (1976), pp.417–21; Andrzej Wypustek, 'Magic, Montanism, Perpetua and the Severan Persecution', *Vigiliae Christianae* 51 (1997), pp.276–97. • 59. Origen, *Contra Celsum* 2.55; 3.44. It was notable that if a married woman converted to Christianity, the husband would denounce both her and her converters to the authorities (Justin, *Second Apology* 3–4; Tertullian, *Apol.* 8.4). • 60. Tertullian, *Ad Scap.* 5.2; Lane Fox, *Pagans and Christians*, pp.317–21. • 61. ibid, pp.295–9; Ste Croix, *The Class Struggle in the Ancient Greek World* (1981), pp.234–6; K.R. Bradley, *Slaves and Masters in the Roman Empire* (Oxford 1987); Bradley, *Slavery and Society at Rome* (1994); R.H. Barrow, *Slavery in the Roman Empire* (1968). • 62. Friedrich Engels, *Die Neue Zeit* (1894–5), pp.4–13, 36–43; Karl Kautsky, *Der Ursprung des Christentums* (1908). • 63. R.Stark, *The Rise of Christianity: A sociologist reconsiders history*

(Princeton 1996); R.A. Markus, *The End of Ancient Christianity* (Cambridge 1990); R. MacMullen, *Christianising the Roman Empire* (Yale 1984). • 64. Ste Croix, 'Why were the Christians?' loc. cit. p.17. • 65. Tertullian, *De Fuga in Persecutione* 5.12–14; 13.5. • 66. S.J. Harrison, *Apuleius. A Latin Sophist* (Oxford 2000). • 67. Eusebius, HE 4.9; Justin, *Apology* 1.68; E. Bickermann, 'Trajan, Hadrian and the Christians', *Rivista di Filologia e di Istruzione Classica* 96 (1968), pp.290–315; Gerhard Krodel, 'Persecution and Toleration of Christianity until Hadrian', in S. Benka & J.J. O'Rourke (eds), *The Catacombs and the Colosseum* (Valley Forge, Pennsylvania 1971) pp.255–67; L.W. Barnard, *Justin Martyr. His Life and Thought* (Cambridge 1967), pp.173–4; cf. also Marta Sordi, *The Christians and the Roman Empire* (Oklahoma 1987); Stephen Benko, *Pagan Rome and the Early Christians* (Indiana 1984). • 68. Eusebius, HE 4.13. • 69. Origen, *Contra Celsum* 5.25–7; 5.33–5. For Celsus in general, see Gerard Watson, 'Celsus and the philosophical opposition to Christianity', *Irish Theological Quarterly* 58 (1992), pp.165–79; Michael Frede, 'Celsus' attack on the Christians', in Jonathan Barnes & Miriam Griffin (eds), *Philosophia Togata, Vol.2 Plato and Aristotle at Rome* (Oxford 1997), pp.218–40. • 70. Origen, *Contra Celsum* 21.4. • 71. Justin Martyr, *Dialogue with Trypho* 10. • 72. Julian the Apostate later used the same argument (Julian, *Contra Galileos* 306a; 356c). • 73. Origen, *Contra Celsum* 7.58; 6.15. • 74. Cicero, *Laws* 2.10.27; Plato, *Phil.* 16c. • 75. Origen, *Contra Celsum* 1.14. • 76. Justin, *Apology* 1.30–54. • 77. Origen, *Contra Celsum* 8.68. • 78. ibid., 8.73–5. • 79. Epictetus, *Discourses* 4.7.6. • 80. Origen, *Contra Celsum* 1.9; 3.17; 4.10. • 81. ibid., 3.55. • 82. ibid., 8.55. • 83. ibid., 7.62. • 84. ibid., 8.14. • 85. Matthew 6.24. • 86. Origen, *Contra Celsum* 8.2; 7.68. • 87. ibid., 1.28. • 88. ibid., 1.32. • 89. Mark 1.23, 34; 3.11; 4.35; 6.35; 2.8. • 90. Origen, *Contra Celsum* 1.6; 6.40. • 91. ibid., 7.18. • 92. ibid., 2.4; 2.8; 2.11. • 93. ibid., 7.53. • 94. ibid., 8.14–15. • 95. Lewis Ayres, *Nicaea and its legacy* (2004); Richard E. Rubenstein, *When Jesus became God: The Epic Fight over Christ's Divinity in the Last Days of Rome* (2003). Since the Greek for 'identity' is *homoousia* and for 'likeness' *homoiousia*, it has been well said that the entire bitter battle at the Council was fought over the single letter 'i'. • 96. Origen, *Contra Celsum* 6.34. • 97. ibid., 2.55. • 98. ibid., 5.14. • 99. One is reminded of Einstein's famous saying that God does not play dice with the universe. • 100. Origen, *Contra Celsum* 4.2–3. • 101 ibid., 4.7–8. This was a point that particularly appealed to Julian the Apostate. Why, asks Julian, should God have manifested himself only in Judaea? And if Jesus is the God of us all, why did he neglect everyone but Judaeans? (Julian, *Contra Galilaeos* 141e; 106d). • 102. Origen, *Contra Celsum* 4.10. • 103. ibid., 4.2. • 104. ibid., 4.14. • 105. J. Bidez, *Vie de Porphyre* (Ghent 1913); P. Hadot, *Plotin, Porphyre – études néoplatoniciennes* (Paris 1999). • 106. T.D. Barnes, 'Porphyry and the Christians', *Journal of Theological Studies* 24 (1973), pp.424–42. • 107. Mark 6.3. • 108. W. den Boer, 'A Pagan Historian and His Enemies: Porphyry against the Christians', *Classical Philology* 69 (1974), pp.198–208. • 109. W. den Boer (ed.), *Romanitas et Christianitas* (Amsterdam 1973). • 110. R.J. Hoffmann (ed. & trans.), *Porphyry against the Christians* (Guildford 1994); Wilken, *The Christians as the Romans saw them* op. cit., pp.126–63 (esp. p.161); for the claims of Christian evangelists that irked Porphyry, see Mark 16.18 and Matthew 17.20. • 111. Richard Walzer, *Galen on Jews and Christians* (Oxford 1949), pp.44–5. • 112. Galen K.3.237–41. • 113. Galen K.3.238–40. • 114. Galen K.3.364, 471, 904. • 115. Walzer, *Galen* op. cit., pp.26–7, 83–90; Galen K.4.649; 5.86.13; 8.637–98; 19.339. • 116. Matthew 19.26; Luke 1.37. • 117. Walzer, *Galen* op. cit., pp.28, 31. • 118. ibid., pp.61–3. • 119. ibid., pp.65, 79–80. • 120. Apuleius, *Metamorphosis* 9.14. • 121. Lucian, *Peregrinus* 11–16. • 122. Augustus de Morgan, *A Budget of Paradoxes* (New York 1872) p.377.

Notes to Chapter Twelve *pp. 280–305*

• 1. On the imminence of the *parousia*, see Justin, *Dialogue with Trypho* 31; L.W. Barnard, *Justin Martyr. His Life and Thought* (Cambridge 1967). For his demonology, see Jeffrey Burton Russell, *The Birth of Satan: Tracing the Devil's Biblical Roots* (2005); cf. also Alan E. Bernstein, *The Formation of Hell: Death and Retribution in the Ancient and Early Christian Worlds* (Cornell 1993). • 2. J. Daniélou, *The Theology of Jewish Christianity* (1964), pp.101–92. • 3. Justin, *Dialogue with Trypho* 31. • 4. Justin, 2 *Apology* 13; Barnard, *Justin* op. cit., pp.89–90. • 5. Grant, *The Antonines* op. cit., p.120. • 6. Justin, 1 *Apology* 17. For Justin's *Apology*, see also Anthony J. Guerra, 'The Conversion of Marcus Aurelius and Justin Martyr. The Purpose, Genre and Content of the First Apology', *Second Century* 9 (1992), pp.171–9; Gary Bisbee, 'The Acts of Justin, Martyr', *Second Century* 3 (1983), pp.129–57. • 7. Barnard, *Justin* op. cit., p.53. • 8. Respectively 1 *Apology* 31, 33, 14 (also *Dialogue with Trypho* 78), 47, 49. • 9. Justin, 1 *Apology* 2, 7, 8, 10, 11, 14, 15, 25, 27, 29, 39, 45, 49, 51, 57, 67; Justin 2 *Apology* 47. The charges of cannibalism and incest were habitually brought against the Christians. See Eusebius, HE 5.1; Tertullian, *Apol.* 9.8; Minucius Felix, *Octavius* 9.5–6; Origen, *Contra Celsum* 6.27; cf. also Stephen Benko, *Pagan Rome and Early Christianity* op. cit., p.68; Andrew McGowan, 'Eating People. Accusations of Cannibalism against Christians in the Second Century', *Journal of Early Christian Studies* 2 (1994), pp.413–42; Champlin, *Fronto* op. cit., pp.65–6. Some of the Gnostic sects may have been guilty of these practices. Clement claimed that the Gnostic sect of Carpocraticus practised free love and orgies, while there was another sect called the Phibionites who indulged in ritual sexual intercourse, the eating of foetuses and the drinking of menstrual blood. It may not always have been easy for the Romans to distinguish these sects from the Christians proper (Wilken, *The Christians as the Romans saw them* op. cit., pp.19–20). • 10. Justin, 1 *Apology* 6, 7, 9, 10. • 11. Justin, 2 *Apology* 13; cf. C. Andresen, *Logos und Nomos* (Berlin 1955). On Socrates, see Justin, 1 *Apology* 46; 2 *Apology* 10. • 12. Justin, 1 *Apology* 2; cf. Peter Brown, 'Late Antiquity', in P. Veyne, *A History of Private Life, Vol. 1 From Pagan Rome to Byzantium* (Cambridge, Massachusetts 1992), pp.235–311 (at p.243). • 13. Justin, 1 *Apology* 14. • 14. Justin, 2 *Apology* 10. • 15. Jerome, *De viris illustribus* 53; Eusebius, HE 2.4; Claude Briand-Ponsard, *L'Afrique Romaine* (Paris 2006), p.261. • 16. Christine Trevett, *Montanism: Gender, Authority and the New Prophecy* (Cambridge 1996). • 17. Tertullian, *De Cultu Feminarum* 1.1.2; cf. also T.D. Barnes, *Tertullian* (Oxford 1985), pp.100–1, 137–40. • 18. Tertullian, *Apol.* 1. • 19. 'certum, quia impossibile est' (Tertullian, *De Carne Christi* 5.4). This is usually bowdlerised into the form *credo quia absurdum*. • 20. Barnes, *Tertullian* op. cit., pp.94–5. • 21. Justin, 1 *Apology* 55. • 22. Tertullian, *De Carne Christi* 9; Justin, *Dialogue with Trypho* 88; Clement of Alexandria, *Paedogogus* 3.1.3; Irenaeus, *Adversus Haereses* 4.33.12; Origen, *Contra Celsum* 6.75. • 23. Barnes, *Tertullian*, pp.107–12. • 24. Tertullian, *Apol.* 13, 17, 39. • 25. Tertullian, *Apol.* 21. • 26. Tertullian, *Apol.* 7.1–2; 9.2–3; Artemidorus i.70 (White (ed.), *Dream Interpretation* op. cit., p.53). • 27. Porphyry claimed that human sacrifice still went on in Carthage (*De Abstinentia* 2.27). In the late second century Sextus Empiricus said men were still sacrificed to Chronos (*Hypotheses* 3.208, 221). Officially, of course, the Roman state had set its face against human sacrifice and, under Claudius, had fought a brutal campaign to suppress this favourite practice of the Druids in Britain. • 28. Tertullian, *Apol.* 35.9. • 29. Tertullian, *Apol.* 30.4; 32.1; 39.2. It is a moot point whether Tertullian was more contemptuous of the Jews or the Greeks. 'For Tertullian . . . Judaism was an unchanging, fossilised faith, not to be taken seriously or deserving proper attention' (Barnes, *Tertullian*, p.92). • 30. F. Cumont, *Lux perpetua* (Paris 1949), pp.55–108; J.H.W.G. Liebeschuetz, 'Religion', CAH 11, pp.1006–7. • 31. Barnes, *Tertullian*, pp.132–4. • 32. Tertullian, *Apol.* 42.1–2. • 33. Tertullian, *Apol.* 43.1. • 34. Tertullian, *Apol.* 44.1. • 35. Tertullian, *Apol.* 23.4. • 36. Tertullian, *Apol.* 37.6. • 37. Barnes, *Tertullian*, 99, 134–5. • 38. ibid., p.136. • 39. Eusebius, HE 4.17. • 40. H. Musurillo (ed.), *The Acts of the Christian Martyrs* (Oxford 1972), pp.40–1. • 41. Quoted in Ste Croix, 'Why were the Christians?' loc. cit., p.21. • 42. Eusebius. HE 4.15.48. • 43. Musurillo, *Acts* op. cit., pp.22–5. • 44. ibid. pp.26–7. • 45. ibid., pp.28–9, 34–5. • 46. Tertullian, *Ad Scap.* 4.2. • 47. Justin, 2 *Apology* 3. • 48. Eusebius. HE 4.16.7–8; P. Keresztes, 'The "so-called" Second Apology of Justin', *Latomus* 14 (1965), pp.858–69. • 49. G.W. Bowerstock, *Martyrdom in Rome* (Cambridge 1995), p.72; cf. Arthur Droge & J. Tabor, *A Noble Death: Suicide and Martyrdom among Ancient Jews, Christians, Greeks and Romans* (San Francisco 1992). • 50. Meds 1.7; PIR2, pp.243, 535. • 51. Musurillo, *Acts* op. cit., pp.42–61. • 52. There is a massive and long-running controversy about the exact date of Polycarp's martyrdom, with some opting for a date in the years 156–9. But the best scholarship places his death firmly in Marcus Aurelius's reign. Although both Eusebius and Jerome (*De viris illustribus* 17) tell us categorically that Polycarp was martyred under Marcus, modern scholars claim to know better. Vast amounts have been written about the disputed dates (155–6, 157–8 or 166–7). It is way beyond our remit to pursue this controversy – we are far enough away from Marcus Aurelius as it is – but for a few pointers, see: J.D. Barnes, 'A Note on Polycarp', JTS 18 (1967), pp.433–7; Barnes, 'The Pre-Decian *Acta Martyrum*', JTS 19 (1968), pp.510–14; W. Telfer, 'The date of the martyrdom of Polycarp', JTS 3 (1952), pp.79–85; A. Strobel, *Ursprung und Geschichte des frühchristlichen Osterkalenders* (1977), pp.245–50; P. Keresztes, 'Was Marcus Aurelius a Persecutor?' *Harvard Theological Review* 61 (1968), pp.321–43 (at pp.325–6). • 53. Eusebius, HE 14.1–46; Musurillo, *Acts* op. cit., pp.8–19; Irenaeus, *Adv. Haer.* 5.33.4; 3.3.4. • 54. Leonard L. Thompson, 'The Martyrdom of Polycarp: Death in the Roman Games', *The Journal of Religion* 82 (2002), pp.27–52. • 55. Musurillo, *Acts*, pp.14–15. • 56. PIR2, p.559; Tertullian, *Apol.* 2. • 57. Frend, *Martyrdom and Persecution* op. cit., pp.1–21. • 58. Musurillo, *Acts*, pp.66–7. • 59. Eusebius, HE 5.1. • 60. Musurillo, *Acts*, pp.68–75. • 61. Eusebius, HE 5.1.42–52. For more on the horrors of the arena, see Carlin Barton, 'The Scandal of the Arena', *Representations* 27 (1989), pp.1–36; Donald Kyle, *Spectacles of Death in Ancient Rome* (1998). • 62. Musurillo, *Acts*, pp.78–81. • 63. Eusebius, HE 5.1.56; 5.1.60–3. There is a huge literature on the Lyons persecutions. See the collectaneous volume *Les martyres de Lyon* (Paris 1978); M. Reginold, 'The Martyrdom of Prominent Martyrs of Lyons and Vienne', in Franklyn Balasundaram (ed.), *Martyrs in the History of Christianity* (Delhi 1997); C. Bruno (ed.), *The Book of Christian Martyrs* (1990). See also Robert McQueen Grant, *Irenaeus of Lyons* (1997); Eric Francis Osborn, *Irenaeus of Lyons* (Cambridge 2001). P. Keresztes, 'The Massacre at Lugdunum in 177 AD', *Historia* 16 (1967), pp.75–86, is a convincing refutation of the bizarre idea in J. Colin, *L'empire des Antonins et les martyrs gaulois de 177* (Bonn 1964), that the persecution took place in Asia Minor. See also Keresztes, 'Das Christenmassaker von Lugdunum im Jahre 177', in Klein, *Marc Aurel* op. cit., pp.261–78. • 64. Eusebius, HE 5.1.47; Tertullian, *Ad Scap.* 4.3–4; cf. Ramsay MacMullen, 'Judicial savagery in the Roman Empire', *Chiron* 16 (1986), pp.147–66. • 65. Quoted in Ste Croix, 'Why were the Christians?' loc. cit., p.10. • 66. Musurillo, *Acts*, pp.86–9. • 67. H. Karpp, 'Die Zahl der Scilitanischen Märtyrer', *Vigiliae Christianae* 15 (1961), pp.165–73. • 68. Barnes, *Tertullian* op. cit., pp.60–3. • 69. Justin, 1 *Apology* 57. • 70. Tertullian, *De Anima* 55.4–5. As the martyrs put it: 'Today we are in heaven' (Musurillo, *Acts*, p.89). On the psychology of martyrdom more generally, see W. Ameling (ed.), *Märtyrer und Märtyrerakten* (Stuttgart 2002). • 71. Fergus Millar, 'Condemnation to hard labour in the Roman Empire, from the Julio-Claudians to Constantine', PBSR 52 (1984), pp.124–47; cf. Lane Fox, *Pagans and Christians* op. cit., p.434. • 72. H.W. Attridge, 'Philosophical Critique of Religion', ANRW 2.6 (1978), pp.45–78; J.P. Brown, 'The sacrificial cult and its critics in Greek and Hebrew', *Journal of Semitic Studies* 24 (1979), pp.159–74, and 25 (1980), pp.1–21; E. Ferguson, 'Spiritual Sacrifice in Early Christianity and Its Environment', ANRW 2.23 (1980), pp.1151–89; R.C. Hanson, 'The Christian attitude to pagan religions up to the time of Constantine the Great', ANRW 2.23 (1980), pp.910–73 (esp. pp.913–18). • 73. Frend, *Martyrdom and Persecution* op. cit., pp.268–314. See also Frend, 'The Failure of the Persecutions in the Roman Empire', PP 18 (1959), pp.10–27. For Antioch as the urban fount, spreading Christianity from East to West, see G. Downey, *A History of Antioch in Syria* (Princeton 1961), pp.272–316. • 74. Wilken, *The Christians* op. cit. p.31; Lane Fox, *Pagans and Christians* op. cit., p.269. • 75. Ste Croix, 'Why were the Christians?' loc. cit., pp.28–9. • 76. Eusebius, HE 6.1.1; 6.6. • 77. K. Rudolph, *Gnosis* (Edinburgh 1985). And hence the kernel of truth behind Peter de Vries's brilliant quip: 'It is the final proof of God's omnipotence that he need not exist in order to save us' (*Mackerel Plaza*, Chapter One). • 78. Eusebius, HE 5.16.3–4; W. Tabbernee, 'Early Montanism and Voluntary Martyrdom', *Colloquium* 17 (1985), pp.33–44; Frederick Klawaiter, 'The role of martyrdom and persecution in developing the priestly authority of women in early Christianity. A Case Study of Montanism,' *Second Century* 49 (1980), pp.251–61; Daniel Boyarin, 'Martyrdom and the Making of Christianity and Judaism', *Journal of Early Christian Studies* 6 (1998), pp.577–627. • 79. Eusebius, HE 5.16.12–23; 5.18.3. • 80. Eusebius, HE 4.14.10–15; cf. also Herbert Brook Workman, *Persecution in the Early Church* (Oxford 1988); E.A. Livingstone, *The Oxford Dictionary of the Christian Church* (1997); Paul Keresztes, 'War Marc Aurel ein Christenverfolger?' in Klein, *Marc Aurel* op. cit., pp.279–303. • 81. Orosius 7.15, 4; Origen, *Contra Celsum* 8.69; Eusebius, HE 4.23.2; 4.26.3; cf. also R.W. Burgess, 'The date of the persecution of Christians in the army', JTS 47 (1996), pp.157–8. • 82. Eusebius, HE 4.3; Keresztes, 'Was Marcus Aurelius a Persecutor?' loc. cit., p.334. • 83. Eusebius, HE 4.26.1. • 84. Eusebius, HE 26.1–10; 5–6, 7–9; Jerome, *Chronicle* (ed. Helm), p.206. • 85. Leslie Barnard, *Athenagoras: A study in second century Christian Apologetic* (Paris 1972); cf. W.R. Schoedel, *Athenagoras. Legatio and De Resurrectione* (1972); Millar, *Emperor in the Roman World* op. cit., p.565. • 86. L.W. Barnard, 'The Embassy of Athenagoras', *Vigiliae Christianae* 21 (1967), pp.88–92; T.D. Barnes, 'The Embassy of Athenagoras', JTS 26 (1975), pp.111–15. • 87. Eusebius, HE 4.26.1; 4.27.1; Tertullian, *Apol.* 39.1–2. • 88. Lane Fox, *Pagans and Christians* op. cit., p.450; Barnes, *Tertullian* op. cit., p.149. 'Until the third century at any rate it is better not to think of persecutions primarily in terms of emperors' (Ste Croix, 'Why were the Christians?' loc. cit., p.15). 'The emperor's words in a letter (or any other form of pronouncement) could not of themselves determine what was done in a province' (Millar, *Emperor in the Roman World*, p.559). • 89. Eusebius, HE 5.21.1; Keresztes, 'Was Marcus Aurelius a Persecutor?' loc. cit. Timothy Barnes in *Tertullian* (pp.149–56) makes a spirited attempt to claim that there was nothing special about the level of persecution under Marcus, and that it continued at the same level under Commodus ('The thirteen years of Commodus's rule have a higher frequency of well-attested instances of persecution'). Unfortunately his argument seems to me both disingenuous and poorly constructed. Disingenuous, in that he includes the Scillitan martyrs as one of Commodus's persecutions. Though these executions (July 180) took place in the first months of Commodus's reign, they were obviously the result of inquiries set in train during the previous reign. As Garzetti remarks: 'The martyrdom of nine Numidian Christians, beheaded on 17 July 180, though it occurred under Commodus, is also to be ascribed to the enduring hostility of Marcus's reign' (Garzetti, *From Tiberius to the Antonines*, p.526, and see also ibid., p.546). Barnes does not cite any further evidence of the alleged four instances of persecution in thirteen years (which he contrasts with five in nineteen years under Marcus). Commodus's persecutions are evidently so 'well attested' that they need no further documentation. Poorly constructed, in that Barnes dismisses all contrary evidence as 'circumstantial' and says that Marcus's collusion with Fronto to damn Justin is 'pure fantasy'. No evidence whatever is produced for the author's *ipse dixit*. He relies heavily on hunch theory, evinced by the recurring phrase 'need not'. It is perhaps not insignificant that Barnes is the biographer of Tertullian, for it was Tertullian who made the absurd attempt to deny the obvious, of which he was perfectly well aware, and claim Marcus as a protector of Christians (Tertullian, *Apol.* 5.6).

• 90. For these points, see Motschmann, *Die Religionspolitik* op. cit., pp.81, 272–3, and Ste Croix, 'Why were the Christians?' loc. cit., p.10. For emperor worship, see I. Gradel, *Emperor Worship and Roman Religion* (Oxford 2002); J.E. Lendon, *Empire of Honour. The Art of Government in the Roman World* (Oxford 1977), pp.160–72. • 91. Ste Croix, loc. cit., p.14; Lane Fox, *Pagans and Christians* op. cit., p.424. • 92. Tertullian, *Apol.* 40.1. • 93. T.D. Barnes, 'Legislation against the Christians', JRS 58 (1968) loc. cit., p.39, claims that this is the explanation for the Lyons persecution. • 94. Eusebius, HE 4.26.5. • 95. Eusebius, HE 4.12.13; 4.26.10; G.W. Bowerstock, 'The Proconsulate of Albus', *Harvard Studies* 72 (1967), pp.289–300. • 96. Eusebius, HE 5.1.44–52. • 97. Garzetti, *From Tiberius* op. cit., p.524. • 98. See, for example, Duchesne, *Histoire ancienne de l'Église* (Paris 1906), p.210. • 99. On the competing religions and their status in Christian eyes, see M. Beard, J. North & S. Price (eds), *The Religions of Rome* (Cambridge 1998); S. Price, *The Religions of the Ancient Greeks* (Cambridge 1999). • 100. Justin, 1 *Apology* 59; 2 *Apology* 10.8. • 101. Tertullian, *Apol.* 46.4. • 102. Tertullian, *Apol.* 23.4–5. • 103. For example, Justin 1 *Apology* 43; 2 *Apology* 7. • 104. Meds 6.54; Origen, *Contra Celsum* 4.23. • 105. James Rives, 'The Piety of a Persecutor', *Journal of Early Christian Studies* 4 (1996), pp.1–25. • 106. Eusebius, HE 8.1; G. Geffken, *The Last Days of Greco-Roman Paganism* (Amsterdam 1978). • 107. See M. Beard & J. North (eds), *Pagan Priests* (1990).

• 108. H. Lewy, *Chaldean Oracles and Theurgy. Mysticsm, Magic and Platonism in the Later Roman Empire* (Paris 1978), pp.259–359; A.J. Festugière, *La révélation d'Hermès Trismégiste*, 4 vols (Paris 1954), esp. Vol. 2; J.M. Dillon, *The Middle Platonists* (1977); R. MacMullen, *Paganism in the Roman Empire* (Yale 1981), pp.67–8, 86–94; M.P. Nilsson, *Geschichte der Griechischen Religion* (Munich 1950) ii, pp.546–62; F. Dunand & P. Leveque, *Les syncrétismes dans les religions de l'antiquité* (Leiden 1975). • 109. For further pointers on this, see C. King, 'The organisation of Roman religious belief', *Classical Antiquity* 22 (2003), pp.275–312; Jason P. Davies, *Rome's Religious History. Livy, Tacitus and Ammianus on their Gods* (Cambridge 2004); H.F. Mueller, *Roman Religion in Valerius Maximus* (2002). • 110. R. MacMullen, *Christianising the Roman Empire*, AD 100–400 (Yale 1984), pp.16–42. • 111. Keresztes, 'Was Marcus Aurelius a Persecutor?' loc. cit., p.329. • 112. *Digest* 48.19.30. • 113. Keresztes, 'The Massacre at Lugdunum' loc. cit., pp.75–86. • 114. Meds 11.3. • 115. P. Brunt, in 'Marcus Aurelius and the Christians' in C. Deroux (ed.), *Studies in Latin Literature and Roman History* (Brussels 1979), pp.483–520, argues that it is a clear case of doctoring and that the words 'like the Christians' are a later addition. Some even think it a reference to the events at Lyons related by Eusebius in HE. 5.1 et seq. (see the discussion in Farquharson ii, pp.859–60). But Brunt's view has been comprehensively and meticulously refuted by A.R. Birley (*Marcus Aurelius*, pp.264–5) in a masterpiece of close textual analysis – quite the finest example of this sort of thing I have ever seen. • 116. Possibly Meds 1.6; 7.68; 8.48; 8.51; but, most tellingly, 3.16. But this is unlikely (see Farquharson ii, p.587). • 117. Keresztes, 'Was Marcus Aurelius a Persecutor?' loc. cit., p.329. • 118. M.L. Astarita, *Avidio Cassio* (Rome 1983), pp.123–5.

Notes to Chapter Thirteen *pp. 308–335*

• 1. Meds 4.3. • 2. Epictetus, *Discourses* 1.25.15. According to Epictetus, peace means 'no wars any more, no battles, no large-scale brigandage; we can travel by land at any hour, we can sail from sunrise to sunset' (Epictetus, *Discourses* 2.22.22). • 3. '*Coelum non animum mutant qui trans mare currunt*' (Horace, *Epistles* 1.11.27). • 4. Heraclitus, *fragment* 80 in H.A. Diels, *Fragmente der Vorsokratiker* (6th ed. 1952). • 5. The possible motives for German migration are exhaustively discussed in Burns, *Rome and the Barbarians* (2003), pp.42–87. • 6. T. Carney, *A Biography of C. Marius* (Chicago 1970), pp.30–8; cf. also Richard J. Evans, *Gaius Marius. A Political Biography* (Pretoria 1994). • 7. Plutarch, *Marius* 11.2–3. • 8. Adrian Goldsworthy, *Caesar* op. cit., pp.224–32. • 9. ibid., pp.272–5. • 10. 'Julius Caesar's "Germans" were a political invention, a device to account for his own "Gallic" wars which took him as far as the Rhine.' C.R. Whitaker, 'Frontiers', CAH 11, p.313; cf. also G. Walser, *Caesar und die Germanen. Studien zur politischen Tendenz Römischer Feldzugsberichte* (Wiesbaden 1956), p.21. • 11. Caesar, *De Bello Gallico* 1.50–3; H. Schutz, *The*

Prehistory of Gemanic Europe (1983), pp.338–43. • 12. W. Jobst, *Provinzhauptstadt Carnuntum* (Vienna 1983), pp.31,37,44. • 13. Tacitus, *Annals* 2.44.3; 2.62.3; Strabo 7.1.3; Velleius Paterculus, *Compendium of Roman History* 2.108.2. • 14. E. Hornemann, *Römische Geschichte* (Stuttgart 1982), p.141. • 15. Dio 66.18.2–4; Tacitus, *Annals* 2.44; 2.62–3. • 16. Velleius Paterculus, *Compendium* op. cit. 2.118.2; Tacitus, *Annals* 2.10.3; 1.58.1–5; 1.55.2–3; Dio 66.19.3; Florus 2.30.33; Strabo 7.1.4. • 17. Dio 56.19–22. Cf. Peter S. Wells, *The Battle that Stopped Rome* (2003); Adrian Murdoch, *Rome's Greatest Defeat: Massacre in the Teutoburg Forest* (2006). • 18. Suetonius, *Augustus* 23. • 19. Burns, *Rome and the Barbarians* op. cit., p.209; P. Fitzinger, D. Planck & B. Cämmerer (eds), *Die Römer in Baden-Württemberg* (Stuttgart 1976), p.26. • 20. Tacitus, *Annals* 2.16–21; E.A. Thompson, *The Early Germans* (Oxford 1965), pp.72–108. • 21. Strabo 7.4.1; Tacitus, *Annals* 1.58.2. • 22. Tacitus, *Annals* 1.59–60; 2.17.18; 2.21.2; 2.44.3; 2.45.4; 2.62.2; 2.88.1; Dio 67.5.1. • 23. Tacitus, *Annals* 2.88.1–3; 11.16.1. • 24. Tacitus, *Annals* 11.16; 12.28–30; 13.56; Tacitus, *Germania* 29, 42; H. Schönberger, 'The Roman Frontier in Germany: An archaeological survey', JRS 59 (1969), pp.144–97 (esp. pp.158–61); Schönberger, 'Recent research on the *limes* in Germania Superior and Raetia', in *Limeskongress* 12 (1980), pp.54–62. • 25. Thompson, *The Early Germans* op. cit., pp.87–8. • 26. Suetonius, *Nero* 19.2. • 27. Tacitus, *Histories* 2.81–2; CAH (1936) 10, p.558. • 28. Dio 67.3.7. • 29. ILS 9200; CAH 10 (1936), pp.168–78; Garzetti, *From Tiberius* op. cit., pp.290, 482. • 30. Suetonius, *Domitian* 6.1; Dio 67.7.3–4. • 31. Tacitus, *Annals* 1.3; cf. C. Wells, *The German Policy of Augustus* (Oxford 1972). • 32. H. Schönberger, 'Die Römischen Truppenlager der frühen und mittleren Kaizerzeit zwischen Nordsee und Inn', *Bericht der Römische-Germanischen Kommission des Deutschen archäologischen Instituts* 66 (1985), pp.321–497. • 33. Tacitus, *Histories* 1.55.5. • 34. B.W. Jones, *The Emperor Domitian* (1992), pp.144–50. • 35. Tacitus, *Germania* 37; C. Ruger, 'Roman Germany', CAH 11, pp.501–3. • 36. J. Sasel, 'Trajan's canal at the Iron Gate', JRS 63 (1973), pp.80–5; J. Mitova-Dzhonova, 'Stationen und Stützpunkte der Römischen Krieg und Handelsflotte am Unterdonaulimes', *Limeskongress* 13 (1986), pp.504–9. • 37. S. Dušanić, 'Aspects of Roman Mining in Noricum, Pannonia, Dalmatia and Moesia Superior', ANRS 2.11.6 (1977), pp.52–94; S. Mrozek, 'Die Goldbergwerke im Römischen Dazien', ANRW 2.11.6 (1977), pp.95–109; M. Werner, 'The Moesian *limes* and the imperial mining district', *Limeskongress* 13 (1986), pp.561–4; cf. G. Alföldy, *Noricum* (1974). • 38. Malcolm Todd, *The Northern Barbarians 100 BC–300 AD* (1975), p.19. • 39. Strabo 7.1.3. • 40. Tacitus, *Germania* 16; Thomson, *Early Germans* op. cit., pp.6–7. • 41. Caesar, *De Bello Gallico* 6.22.1; 6.29.1; cf. M.I. Finley, *Slavery in Classical Antiquity* (Cambridge 1960), pp.191–203. • 42. Tacitus, *Germania* 12; 21. • 43. Tacitus, *Germania* 8; 17–18. • 44. Tacitus, *Germania* 37. • 45. Caesar, *De Bello Gallico* 6.18.2; Tacitus, *Germania* 11; 13–15; 23–4. • 46. Dio 53.26.4; R.E.M. Wheeler, *Rome beyond the imperial frontiers* (1954), pp.11–13. • 47. Thompson, *Early Germans* op. cit., pp.21–4. • 48. ibid., pp.87–9; Ursula-Barbara Dittrich, 'Die Wirtschaftsstruktur der Quaden, Markomannen und Sarmaten im mitteleren Donauraum und ihre Handelsbeziehungen mit Rom', in *Münstersche Beiträge zur Antiken Handelsgeschichte* 6 (1987), pp.9–19. • 49. Tacitus, *Annals* 1.59.6–8. • 50. Strabo 7.1.3. • 51. Tacitus, *Germania* 42.2. As Thompson rightly comments: 'It is scarcely a coincidence that the Germanic autocrat made his appearance in exactly that part of the Germanic world where Roman influence was most intense, where the private ownership of property was most highly developed, and where a colony of Roman traders was continuously engaged in commerce and lending money to the native population' (*Early Germans* op. cit., p.69). • 52. Tacitus, *Annals* 12.29.2; Pliny, *Letters* 2.7.2; Dio 67.5.2. • 53. Suetonius, *Tiberius* 37; Tacitus, *Annals* 2.63.5; Velleius Paterculus, *Compendium* op. cit., 2.129.3. • 54. Tacitus, *Annals* 12.29.1; 2.63.7; HA Hadrian 12.7; Ammianus Marcellinus 29.4.7; Dio 66.18.2–4; Tacitus, *Germania* 43.2. • 55. 'Without a popular power base and with only symbolic support from Rome, these rulers found themselves in a state of paralytic tension, at the mercy of both parties, suspicious of all and trusted by none' (Herbert Schutz, *The Romans in Central Europe* (1985), p.35). • 56. Thompson, *Early Germans* op. cit., pp.72–108. • 57. Syme, 'Domitian, the last years', RP iv, pp.252–77; cf. also Syme, *Tacitus* (1958), pp.30–44. • 58. Dio 68.8–13; I.A. Richmond, 'Trajan's Army on Trajan's Column', PBSR 13 (1935), pp.1–40. • 59. Dio 68.14.3; Mrozek, 'Die Golbergwerke im Römischen Dazien op. cit., pp.95–109; D. Benea & R. Petrovszky, 'Werkstätten zur Metallverarbeitung in Tibiscum im 2. und 3. Jh. n. Chr.', *Germania* 65 (1987), pp.226–39. For the 'financial disaster' thesis, see Miriam Griffin, 'Trajan', CAH 11, p.114. • 60. F. Lepper & S. Frere, *Trajan's Column* (Gloucester 1988); J.E. Packer, *The Forum of Trajan in Rome; A Study of the Monuments* (Berkeley 1997). • 61. L. Rossi, *Trajan's Column and the Dacian Wars* (1971); J. Bennett, *Trajan Optimus Princeps. A Life and Times* (1997). • 62. Josephus, *Jewish Wars* 6.420; Joannes Laurentius Lydus, *Mag.* 2.2.8; *Chronicon Pascale* 1.474; Lydus (ed. R. Wunsch, 1903), *De magistratibus republicae Romanae*. • 63. C.C. Petrolescu, 'L'organisation de la Dacie sous Trajan et Hadrian', *Dacia* 29 (1985), pp.43–55; N. Gudea, 'Der Limes Dakiens und die Verteidigung der obermoesischen Donaulinie von Trajan bis Aurelian', ANRW 2.6 (1997), pp.849–87; B. Catanacia, *Evolution of the system of defensive works in Dacia* (1981), pp.11–20; C. Daicoviciu, 'Dakien und Röm in der Prinzipatzeit', ANRW 11.6 (1977), pp.889–918. • 64. A. Mocsy & D. Gabler, 'Alte und neue Probleme am Limes von Pannonien', *Limeskongress* 13 (1986), pp.369–76; D. Gabler (ed.), *The Roman Fort at Acs-Vaspuszta (Hungary) on the Danubian Limes* (Oxford 1989); K. Genser, *Der österreichische Donaulimes in der Römerzeit: Ein Forschungsbericht* (Vienna 1986); Z. Visy, *Der pannonische Limes in Ungarn* (Budapest 1988); V. Popović (ed.), *Sirmium. Archaeological Excavations in Syrmian Pannonia* (Belgrade n.d.), pp.5–90. • 65. H. & H. Polenz (eds), *Das römische*

Budapest: Neue Ausgrabungen und Funde in Aquincum (Munster 1986); K. Poczy et al., 'Das Legionslager von Aquincum: Ergebnisse der Ausgrabungen 1973–83', *Limeskongress* 13 (1986), pp.398–408; A. Neumann, *Vindobona; die römische Vergangenheit Wiens* (Vienna 1980); H. Stiglitz et al., 'Carnuntum', ANRW 2.6 (1977), pp.583–730; W. Jobst, *Provinzhauptstadt Carnuntum* (Vienna 1983); M. Kandler, 'Die Legio I Adiutrix und Carnuntum', *Limeskongress* 15 (1991), pp.237–41. • 66. M. Werner, 'The Moesian *limes* and the imperial mining districts', *Limeskongress* 13 (1986), pp.561–4; A.G. Poulter (ed.), *Ancient Bulgaria*, 2 vols (Nottingham 1983), pp.74–118; A.G. Poulter, 'The lower Moesian *limes* and the Dacian wars of Trajan', *Limeskongress* 13 (1986), pp.519–28. • 67. I. Mikl-Curk, 'Natives, Romans and newcomers in the Eastern Alps during the second century. The role of the army in ethnic interaction', *Limeskongress* 15 (1991), pp.248–51; J. Wilkes, 'The Danube Provinces', CAH 11, p.591. • 68. Tacitus, *Germania* 42. • 69. A. Mocsy, *Pannonia and Upper Moesia. A History of the Middle Danube Provinces of the Roman Empire* (1974), pp.102–3. • 70. HA Hadrian 6.6–8. • 71. J. Wilkes, 'The Danube Provinces', CAH 11, p.583. • 72. L.F. Pitts, 'Rome and the German "Kings" on the Middle Danube', JRS 79 (1989), pp.54–6; Klein, *Marc Aurel* op. cit., pp.389–99. • 73. Pitts, 'Rome and the German "Kings"' loc. cit., pp.54–6; V.A. Maxfield & M.J. Dobson, *Roman Frontier Studies* (Exeter 1991), pp.432–4; Klein, *Marc Aurel*, pp.389–99; R. Noll, 'Zur Vorgeschichte der Markomannenkriege', *Archaeologica Austriaca* 14 (1954), pp.43–67; P. Kos, *Monetary Circulation in the Southeastern Alpine region c.300 BC–AD 1000* (Ljubljana 1986), pp.81–91. • 74. HA Antoninus 5.4; Appian, *Praef*. 7.25–8; H. Mattingly & R.G. Carson, *Coins of the Roman Empire in the British Museum*, 6 vols (1962), iv. 124; H. Mattingly & E.A. Sydenham, RIC (1930), iii.620; J. Wilkes, 'The Roman Frontier in Noricum', *Journal of Roman Archaeology* 2 (1989), pp.347–52; G. Alföldy, *Noricum* (1974), p.145; E. Swoboda, 'Rex Quadis Datum', *Carnuntum Jahrbuch* 11 (1956), pp.5–12; D. Planck, 'Neue Forschungen zum Obergermanischen und Ratischen Limes', ANRW 2.5 (1976), pp.404–20; W. Wagner, *Die Dislokation der römischen Auxiliarformationen in den Provinzen. Noricum, Pannonien, Moesien und Dakien von Augustus bis Gallienus* (Berlin 1938), pp.95–193. • 75. Aelius Aristides, *Oration* 26.70; A.R. Birley, 'Die Aussen- und Grenzpolitik unter der Regierung Marc Aurels', in Klein, *Marc Aurel* op. cit., pp.82–3. • 76. Birley, *Fasti Romani Britanniae* op. cit., p.123; Birley, *Marcus Aurelius* op. cit., pp.113–14. • 77. G. Alföldy, *Römische Heeresgeschichte. Beiträge 1962–1985* (Amsterdam 1987), pp.394–410; G. Ulbert & T. Fischer, *Der Limes in Bayern* (Munich 1983), p.24; Birley, *Marcus Aurelius* op. cit., p.277. • 78. HA Antoninus 12.8. • 79. Gerhard Dobesch, 'Aus der Vor und Nachgeschichte der Markomannenkriege', in *Anzeiger der Österreichischen Akademie der Wissenschaften. Philosohie-Historische Klasse* 131 (1994), pp.67–125; S. Frere, *Britannia: A History of Roman Britain* (1987), pp.133–41; D. Breeze & B. Dobson, *Hadrian's Wall* (1976), pp.105–24. • 80. I. Mikl-Curk, 'Les guerres contre les Marcomannes du 2e siècle et les trouvailles céramiques de la zone entre Pannonie et Italie', *Revue archéologique de l'Est et du Centre-Est* 28 (1987), pp.241–6; P. Oliva, 'Marcomannia provincia?', *Studii Classice* 24 (1986), pp.15–29; W. Eck, 'Provincial Administration and Finance', CAH 11, p.286. On the self-interest of the legions, see J. Wilkes, 'The Danube Provinces', CAH 11, p.584. • 81. HA Marcus 12.13. • 82. Dio 72.11.3; AE 1934, 155; AE 1957, 121; M.M. Roxan, *Roman Military Diplomas*, 2 vols (1985), ii, pp.125–6; W. Eck, *Die Statthalter der germanischen Provinzen vom 1–3 Jahrhundert* (1985), pp.67–8. Some say the Chatti's raid was further north, in Lower Germany, possibly when Legio 1 Minervia was transferred thence to the Parthian front, but the archaeological evidence does not support this idea (Zwikker, *Studien zur Marcussaule* (Amsterdam 1941), p.53; H. Schönberger, 'Die Römischen Truppenlager', loc. cit., p.405). • 83. CIL iii, 3744, 3748, 7616, 12514, 13757, 10615, 10632, 10638, 10653. See also J. Sasel, *Opera Selecta* (Ljubljana 1992), pp.227–30. • 84. C.C. Petrolescu, 'L'organisation de la Dacie sous Trajan et Hadrian', *Dacia* 29 (1985), pp.45–55. • 85. C.C. Petrolescu, 'Die reorganisation Dakiens unter Marcus Aurelius', *Germania* 65 (1987), pp.123–34. • 86. K. Dietz, 'Zur Verwaltungs geschichte Obergermaniens und Rätiens unter Mark Aurel', *Chiron* 19 (1989), pp.407–48. • 87. Alföldy, KS, p.222. • 88. HA Marcus 21.7. • 89. B. Overbeck, 'Raetien zur Prinzipatzeit', ANRW 11.5.2 (1976), pp.658–89; T. Fischer, 'Neues zum Römischen Regensburg', *Limeskongress* 13 (1986), pp.146–51; H. Vetters, 'Lauriacum', ANRW 11.6 (1977), pp.355–79; K. Kneifel, *Lauriacum: Führer durch die Abteilung Römerzeit* (Ems 1984); C.R. Whitaker, *Frontiers of the Roman Empire* (Baltimore 1994), p.20; Mark Hassall, 'The Army', CAH 11, p.323. • 90. Dio 55.24.2–4; Suetonius, *Nero* 19; J.C. Mann, 'The Raising of New Legions during the Principate', *Hermes* 91 (1963), pp.483–9. • 91. For details of these tactics, see Alföldy, KS, pp.86, 99, 174, 184, 227, 232–37, 245, 325, 329–32. 'The Marcomanni, for example, were too amorphous for Roman commanders to try to deploy them against others even after their long involvement with Rome' (Burns, *Rome and the Barbarians* op. cit., pp.173–4). • 92. Here I must acknowledge the brilliant and invaluable work by William George Kerr, 'A Chronological Study of the Marcomannic Wars of Marcus Aurelius', PhD thesis, Princeton (1995), on which I have drawn heavily – hereinafter Kerr, 'Chronology'. • 93. AE 1956, 123; G. Winkler, 'Legio II Italica: Geschichte und Denkmaler', *Jahrbuch der Oberösterreichischen Musealvereines* 116 (1971), pp.85–138. • 94. J. Sasel, *Opera Selecta* op. cit., pp.388–93. • 95. Eutropius 8.8.3. • 96. D.R. Walker, *The Metrology of the Roman Silver Coinage, Vol. 2 From Nero to Commodus* (Oxford 1977) ii, pp.55–60. • 97. HA Marcus 7.9. • 98. Szaivert, *Die Münzprägung* op. cit., p.200; Mattingly & Carson, *Coins of the Roman Empire* op. cit., iv.433, 435, 439, 445, 447, 589, 598. • 99. HA Marcus 8.4.5; 11.3; Kerr, 'Chronology' loc. cit., pp.13–14. • 100. Philostratus, VS 2.1.9; Dio 71.1–2. • 101. For Marcus's bellicose intentions towards Germany, interrupted by factors like famine, plague, Parthia and financial stringency, there are extended discussions in A. Mocsy, 'Das Gerücht von neuen Donauprovinzen unter Marcus Aurelius', *Acta classica universitatis scientairum Debreceniensis* 7 (1971), pp.63–9; Mocsy, *Pannonia and Upper Moesia* op. cit., pp.183–5; Kerr, 'Chronology' loc. cit., pp.12–27. Debate about whether Marcus's intentions were offensive or defensive recalls the similar debate about Trajan's invasion of Dacia (Miriam Griffin, 'Trajan', CAH 11, p.112). • 102. Dio 71.12.1; 71.13.1; 72.1; Alföldy, KS, pp.371–2. These tribes are identified by Tacitus in *Germania* 40. See also G. Schindler-Horstkotte, *Der 'Markomannenkrieg' Mark Aurels und die Kaiserliche Reichsprägung* (Cologne 1985); G. Langmann, 'Die Markomannenkriege 166/167 bis 180', in *Militarhistorische Schriftenreihe* 43 (Vienna 1981). • 103. G. Walser, *Die römischen Strasse und Meilensteiner in Raetien* (1983), p.22; M. Ichikawa, 'The Marcomannic Wars: A reconstruction of their nature', in T. Yuge & M. Doi (eds), *Forms of Control and Subordination in Antiquity* (Tokyo 1988), pp.253–5. • 104. For the career of Macrinius Avitus Catonius Vindex, see H. Devijver, *Prosopographia Militiarum Equestrium Quae fuerunt ab Augusto ad Gallienum* (Leuven 1987), pp.550–1. Burns, *Rome and the Barbarians* op. cit., p.236, unaccountably ties himself in knots over Vindex's identity. He is, however, correct that the Vindex who defeated the Germans was not Macrinius Vindex the praetorian prefect, who died in 171 (see Boissevain, *Cassii Dionis Cocceiani historiarum Romanarum que supersunt* (Berlin 1901) iii, p.251. • 105. HA Marcus 8.7; H.J. Kellner, 'Raetien', in Klein, *Marc Aurel* op. cit., pp.243–4; B. Overbeck, 'Raetien zur Prinzipatzeit', ANRW 2.5 (1976), pp.677–8; Schönberger, 'Die Römischen Truppenlager' loc. cit., p.403. • 106. Dio 71.13.1. • 107. CIL iii.921–60. • 108. Ammianus Marcellinus 29.6.1; HA Marcus 22.1. The *Historia Augusta*, so far as it goes, is generally considered a good source for the German wars. See T. Burns, 'The Barbarians and the Scriptores Historiae Augustae', *Studies in Latin Literature and History*, *Latomus* 164 (Brussels 1979) i, pp.521–40. Some scholars think the Marcomanni devolved the task of seizing the gold mines of Dacia to a tribe known as the Victuali (see Ammianus Marcellinus 17.12.19; Kerr, 'Chronology' loc. cit., p.105). • 109. Todd, *Northern Barbarians* op. cit., p.36. • 110. G. Alföldy, *Noricum* op. cit., pp.152–7. • 111. Herodian 8.4.5; Pliny, NH 3.18.127; Strabo 4.208; Alföldy, *Noricum*, pp.153–4; J. Fitz, 'Der Markomannische-Quadische Angriff gegen Aquileai und Opitergium', *Historia* 15 (1966), pp.336–64. For the wealth of Aquileia, see especially A.J. Parker & J.A. Painter, 'A computer-based index of ancient shipwrecks', *International Journal of Nautical Archaeology* 8 (1979), pp.69–70. • 112. Fitz, 'Der Markomannische-Quadische Angriff' loc. cit., pp.348–51; Kerr, 'Chronology' loc. cit., p.105. • 113. P. Cos, *Monetary Circulation in the Southeastern Alpine region c.300 BC–AD 1000* (1986), pp.86–91; C.H. Dodd, 'Chronology of the Danubian Wars of the Emperor Marcus Aurelius', 2 *Numismatic Chronicle*, 4th series (1913), pp.162–276 (at pp.166–71); R. Duncan-Jones, *Structure and Scale in the Roman Economy* (Cambridge 1990), pp.73–6. •

114. There is a substantial body of thought that maintains that the raid on Aquileia took place three years later, in 170. However, my reasons for opting for 167 as the most likely date are fourfold: 1) Marcus went with Lucius Verus to Aquileia as a preliminary to his German campaign (in late 168). This makes no geographical, military or logistical sense in terms of a Danube campaign. It is fairly evident that he went there to restore morale, implying that the raid had already happened. 2) In 170 the Quadi and Marcomanni would have been checked by the *praetentura*, not in place in 167, yet the classical sources speak of a walkover victory. 3) Scholars have been led to opt for 170 by Lucian's testimony regarding Alexander of Abonoteichos. But this can easily be read as poetic licence or 'expedient exaggeration' on Lucian's part, designed to fasten the blame for the Aquileia debacle on Alexander. It is unlikely that Alexander was still alive by this date and, anyway, it would be unwise to rely on Lucian for exact chronology. 4) The sources do not speak of the emperor as being at the front during the disaster at Aquileia, which they would surely have done if it had in fact occurred in 170 rather than 167. The panic in Rome in the years 167–8 makes no sense if the German tribes were still on the other side of the Danube. Among the many scholars opting for 167 as the true date for Aquileia are A. Mocsy, *Pannonia and Upper Moesia* op. cit., p.187; Sasel, *Opera Selecta* op. cit., pp.388–9, 394–5; Kerr, 'Chronology', pp.57–8; Klaus Rosen, 'Der Einfall der Markomannen und Quaden in Italien 167', in Barbara and Piergiuseppe Scardigli (eds), *Germani in Italia* (Rome 1994), pp.87–104. • 115. P. Oliva, 'Zur Bedeutung der Markomannenkriege', *Altertum* 16 (1960), pp.53–61; H.W. Böhme, 'Archäologische Zeugnisse zur Geschichte der Markomannenkriege 166–180 n. Chr., *Jahrbuch des Römisch-Germanischen Zentralmuseums Mainz* 22 (1975), pp.153–216 (esp. pp.212–13); Zwikker, *Studien zur Markussaule* op. cit., p.37; H.J. Kellner, *Die Römer in Bayern* (Munich 1978), pp.71–3. • 116. For the *mfecane* controversy, see Carolyn Hamilton (ed.), *The Mfecane Aftermath* (Witwatersrand 1995); Norman Etherington, *The Great Treks: The Transformation of Southern Africa, 1815–1854* (2001). • 117. R. Syme, *Emperors and Biography* (Oxford 1971), p.182. See also Herwig Wolfram, *History of the Goths* (Los Angeles 1988); Peter Heather, *The Goths* (Oxford 1996); A. Bell-Fialkoff, *The Role of Migration in the History of the Eurasian Steppe* (2000). • 118. There are circumstantial mentions of the Alans in the sources in connection with the Marcomannic wars (e.g. HA Marcus 22.1), but no more than at any other time and with other emperors (e.g. HA Antoninus 5.5; Dio 69.15.1). Some have even tried to bring the Vandals into the act (again anachronistically), identifying them with the Asdingi or Astringes (Zwikker op. cit., p.17). For the circumstantial evidence on this, see HA Marcus 22.1; 17.3; Dio 71.12.1; Ammianus Marcellinus 17.12.19; L. Schmidt, *Geschichte der Vandalen* (Munich 1942); E. Schwarz, *Germanische Stammeskunde* (Heidelberg 1956). • 119. HA Marcus 22.1; Ammianus Marcellinus 31.5.13. Among modern advocates of a

conspiracy one might mention Zwikker, *Studien* op. cit., pp.77–87; Mocsy, *Pannonia and Upper Moesia* op. cit., pp.185–6; Kerr, 'Chronology'. • 120. The modern idiom would be 'good cop, bad cop'. • 121. Böhme, 'Archäologische Zeugnisse' loc. cit., pp.213–15. • 122. As mentioned in Tacitus, *Annals* 11.18. For the Chatti, Chauci and Hermunduri, see also Tacitus, *Germania* 29–31, 36–7. For the sucking into the vortex of the Rhine, see Schönberger, 'Die Römischen Truppenlager' loc. cit., pp.402–3. For the role of the Rhine tribes in the war, see HA Marcus 22.1; HA Julianus 1.7–8. On the Rhine-Weser tribes in general, see G. Mildenberger, *Sozial- und Kulturgeschichte der Germanen* (Stuttgart 1972); Todd, *Northern Barbarians* op. cit., pp.39–76. Dio distinguishes three types of Germanic tribe: the Celtic or western ones living along the Rhine; the Suebi of the Elbe-Danube lands; and the Dacians and others around the mouth of the Danube (Dio 51.22.6; 53.12.6; 55.1.2; 56.23.4; see also Zwikker op. cit., pp.155–7). • 123. The *Historia Augusta*'s famous list of tribes is at HA Marcus 22.2. For the Naristae, see Dio 71.12.1; H. Bengston, 'Neue zur Geschichte der Naristen', *Historia* 8 (1959), pp.213–21; also Klein, *Marc Aurel* op. cit., pp.248–51. For the Buri, see Todd, *Northern Barbarians* op. cit., pp.62, 70–1. • 124. Dio 71.20.1; HA Marcus 24.5–6. For the Marcomanni, see Böhme, 'Archäologische Zeugnisse' loc. cit., pp.184–6; Todd, *Northern Barbarians*, pp.73–4. • 125. Tacitus, *Germania* 42. • 126. For the Quadi, see Strabo 7.1.3; Caesar, *De Bello Gallico* 4.1.3. • 127. Rémy, *Antonin le Pieux*, p.244. • 128. Tacitus, *Germania* 43; M. Stahl, 'Zwischen Abgrenzung und Integration: Die Verträge der Kaiser Mark Aurel und Commodus mit den Völkern jenseits der Donau', *Chiron* 19 (1989), pp.289–317; Gerhard Wirth, 'Rome and its Germanic Partners in the Fourth Century', in Walter Pohl, *Kingdoms of the Empire: The integrations of barbarians in late antiquity* (Leiden 1997), pp.13–56. • 129. Velleius Paterculus, *Compendium* op. cit., 2.109; J. Eadie, 'Civitates and Clients: Roman frontier policies in Pannonia and Mauretania Tingitana', in D. Miller & J. Steffen, *The Frontier: Comparative Studies* (Norman, Oklahoma 1977), pp.57–80. • 130. H. Böhme, 'Archäologische Zeugnisse' loc. cit., pp.153–217. • 131. Tacitus, *Germania* 45.1–9; 46.1–6. • 132. Dio 72.11.1–5, 11–15; Mocsy, *Pannonia and Upper Moesia* op. cit., pp.186–7. One can see analogies with the desperate, clamorous and ultimately successful attempts by 'incubus' nations like Romania and Bulgaria (interestingly also Danubian nations) to get inside the EU today. • 133. Burns, *Rome and the Barbarians* op. cit., pp.230–1. • 134. W.V. Harris, 'Trade', CAH 11, p.738. • 135. HA Marcus 14.1; Arrian *Praef* 7.25–8. • 136. Dio 71.12.1; Zosimus, *Historia Nova* 1.68.3; G. Vitucci, *L'Imperatore Probo* (Rome 1952), p.41; G. Kerler, *Die Aussenpolitik in der Historia Augusta* (Bonn 1970), p.243. • 137. Burns, *Rome and the Barbarians*, p.236. • 138. Wirth, 'Rome and its Germanic Partners' loc. cit., p.28. • 139. C. Ruger, 'Roman Germany', CAH 11, pp.506–7. • 140. F. Hampl, 'Kaiser Marc Aurel und die Völker jenseits der Donaugrenze: Eine quellenkritische Untersuchung' *Festschrift für R. Heuberger* (Innsbruck

1960), pp.33–40; D. Van Berchem, 'Les Marcomans au service de l'empire', *Carnuntina* (1955), pp.12–16. • 141. Wirth, 'Rome and its Germanic Partners' loc. cit.; Harris, 'Trade' loc. cit.; Wilkes, 'Danube Provinces' loc. cit.; Brent D. Shaw, 'Rebels and Outsiders', CAH 11, pp.378–9. • 142. Eutropius 8.12. • 143. Livy 7.22; 7.27.1; 22.10.9. • 144. HA Marcus 12.13.1–6; Zwikker, *Studien zur Markussaule* op. cit., p.63. For the necromancers and magicians used by Marcus, see HA Heliogabulus 9.1. • 145. HA Verus 8.3; Ammianus Marcellinus 23.6.4. • 146. Pausanias 8.43.6.

Notes to Chapter Fourteen   *pp. 336–369*

• 1. HA Marcus 17.4–5; 21.6; 21.9; Eutropius 8.13; 13.2; Zonaras 12.1; Dio 71.32.2. • 2. CIL iii.14507. • 3. HA Marcus 21.7; C.P. Jones, 'The levy at Thespiae under Marcus Aurelius', *Greek, Roman and Byzantine Studies* 12 (1971), pp.45–65; Zwikker, *Studien* op. cit., pp.105–6; Mocsy, *Pannonia and Upper Moesia* op. cit., pp.154, 196. • 4. Michael Fulford, 'Britain', CAH 11, p.566. • 5. HA Marcus 17.7. • 6. HA Marcus 14.5; Zwikker op. cit., p.66; HA Marcus 13.6. • 7. ILS 8977; Sasel, *Opera Selecta* op. cit., pp.388–94. • 8. Syme, RP v, p.695. • 9. Herodian 2.11.8; 8.11; Ammianus Marcellinus 31.11.3; 21.12.21; Sasel, *Opera Selecta*, p.390; N. Christie, 'The Alps as a Frontier (AD 168–774)', *Journal of Roman Archaeology* 4 (1991), pp.413–25. • 10. For Fronto, see Alföldy, KS, pp.223, 235, 246; PIR2, p.203; A.R. Birley, 'The Status of Moesia Superior under Marcus Aurelius', *Acta Antiqua Philippolitana Studia Historica et Philologica* (Sofia 1963), pp.109–19; Birley, *Marcus Aurelius* op. cit., p.157; Zwikker, *Studien*, p.92. • 11. Kerr, 'Chronology', p.110. • 12. For Valerius Maximianus, see G. Alföldy, *Römische Heeresgeschichte. Beiträge 1962–1985* (Amsterdam 1987), pp.326–7; H. Devijver, *Prosopographia Militiarum Equestrium* op. cit., pp.820–1. • 13. HA Pertinax 4.9–10; HA Julianus 8.3. • 14. *Fragmenta Vaticana* No.195; S. Riccobono, G. Baviera et al., *Fontes Iuris Romani Anteiustiniani*, 3 vols (1943) ii, p.503. • 15. HA Marcus 2.14. • 16. Dio 71.3.2; Ammianus Marcellinus 29.6.1; Lucian, *Alexander* 48. That the trip to Aquileia made no strategic sense and was purely for psychological effect, see Kerr, 'Chronology', pp.70,109. • 17. HA Marcus 14.5. • 18. HA Verus 9.7–10. • 19. Galen K.14.7–8; 649–50; 19.18; HA Verus 9.8. • 20. HA Marcus 14.7–8; Galen K.14.650; 19.18; PIR 2, p.140. • 21. Aurelius Victor 16.8. • 22. HA Marcus 15.5–6. • 23. HA Verus 9.1; 10.11. • 24. HA Verus 10.1–4. • 25. Philostratus VS 2.560; Dio 71.3.1. • 26. HA Verus 10.3–4. • 27. HA Marcus 20.3–4. • 28. HA Marcus 15.6. • 29. HA Marcus 20.1–4; 16.3. • 30. HA Marcus 15. • 31. HA Marcus 15.1–2; HA Verus 9.3; 9.5–6. • 32. HA Marcus 15.3–4; 20.1.7; 20.6–7; HA Pertinax 2.4; Dio 71.3.2. • 33. Pflaum, 'Les gendres de Marc Aurèle' loc. cit. • 34. Meds 9.2.4. • 35. Mocsy, *Pannonia and Upper Moesia* op. cit., pp.99, 188. • 36. Dio 71.11. It must be pointed out that, unless the Germans had invaded in 167 (not the later date of 170 insisted on by some historians), such an offer makes no sense. The Germans could not be offering to return captives that it was impossible for them to have in the first place. • 37. HA Marcus 23.5. • 38. HA Marcus 22.5. • 39. Aurelius Victor 16.9–10. Rutherford (p.235) is adamant that this never happened. • 40. HA Avidius Cassius 3.6. • 41. Meds 10.36. • 42. Galen K.9.6–7; HA Marcus 21.5; Zwikker, *Studien* op. cit., pp.108–9. • 43. Dio 71.11.1; Eutropius 8.13.1. Such an offer would of course have been impossible if the Marcomanni and Quadi had not staged their raid on Aquileia until 170, as some historians would have it. • 44. Dio 71.11.2. • 45. André Chastagnol, *Histoire Auguste* (Paris 1994), pp.249–75. • 46. HA Pertinax 1.1–4; A.R. Birley, *The African Emperor. Septimius Severus* (1988), pp.63–7. • 47. Dio 73.3.1; HA Marcus 8.6; HA Pertinax 1.6; Alföldy, *Römische Heeresgeschichte* op. cit., pp.326–48. • 48. Birley, *The Fasti of Roman Britain* op. cit., pp.126–7; E. Birley, *Roman Britain and the Roman Army* (Kendal 1953), p.142; E. Birley, 'Promotions and Transfers in the Roman Army. The centurionate', *Carnuntum Jahrbuch* (1964), pp.21–33. • 49. AE 1956, 124; HA Pertinax 2.2–3. • 50. Alföldy, *Römische Heeresgeschichte* op. cit., p.328. • 51. Vivian Nutton, 'The Chronology of Galen's Early Career', *CQ* 23 (1973), pp.158–71. • 52. D.E. Eichholz, 'Galen and his environment', *GR* 20 (1951), pp.60–71. • 53. Galen K.5.112; 10.609; 16.223. • 54. For Hippocrates's influence on Galen and Galen's hypertrophied enthusiasm for his great Greek predecessor, see K.14.684; K.18.13; W.D. Smith, *The Hippocratic Tradition* (1979), pp.60–196; G.E.R. Lloyd, 'Galen on Hellenism and Hippocrateans', in J. Kollesch & D. Nickel (eds), *Galen und das Hellenistische Erbe* (Stuttgart 1993), pp.125–44. • 55. Galen K.12.60. Some idea of his range can be gathered from the following secondary works: G. Strohmaier, 'Galen's Commentary on Airs, Waters and Planes', in Hollersch & Nickel op. cit., pp.157–64; P. Manulli & M. Vegetti, *Le opere psicologiche di Galeno* (Naples 1988); O. Temkin, *Galenism: Rise and Decline of a Medical Philosopher* (1973); G.E.R. Lloyd, *Greek Science after Aristotle* (1973), pp.136–53; R.J. Hutchinson (ed.), *Galen on Antecedent Causes* (Cambridge 1998); Robert Blair Edlow, *Galen on Language and Ambiguity* (Leiden 1977). • 56. V. Nutton, 'Galen and Egypt', in Kollesch & Nickel op. cit., pp.11–32. • 57. A range of titles makes clear Galen's importance in the history of Greek philosophy: M. Frede, 'On Galen's epistemology', in V. Nutton (ed.), *Galen. Problems and Prospects* (1981), pp.279–98; J. Barnes, 'Galen in Logic and Therapy', in F. Kudlien & R.J. Durling (eds), *Galen's Method of Healing* (Leiden 1991), pp.50–102; R.J. Hankinson, 'Galen's philosophical eclecticism', *ANRW* 2.36 (1992), pp.3484–522; P.L. Donini, 'Galeno e la filosofia', *ANRW* 2.36 (1992), pp.3484–504; John Spangler Kieffer, *Galen's Instituto Logica* (Baltimore 1964); S. Gero, 'Galen on the Christians: A reappraisal of Arabic evidence', *Orientalia Christiana Periodica* 56 (1990), pp.371–411. Galen's basic philosophical stance was eclectic. His father had deliberately chosen teachers from the different philosophical schools (K.5.41–3). He used to say that people opted for the four great philosophical schools not after a period of profound study, but because their father or teacher was, say, a Platonist or their city was a centre of Platonism (K.19.50.4–13; K.2.82.24). He scathingly remarked that he knew nothing of the immortality of the soul or the eternity of the world, as there was no scientific evidence either way (K.19.255). Galen's eclecticism resulted in an olio that was Aristotelian in its methodology, but Platonic in its ethical approach – Plato was his father's favourite philosopher (K.5.17; 6.755; 8.587; 10.609; 19.59). Although Galen claimed to believe in God's providence, which might have aligned him with the Stoics (K.19.241–52), he overwhelmingly preferred Platonism and Aristotelianism to Stoicism and Epicureanism. But he was adamant that truth, not adherence to any one school, should be the aim of the true philosopher (K.5.97; 19.22). The Stoic he most admired was Posidonius, who was great enough of spirit to use Aristotelian insights. Alongside him, most of Stoicism and Epicureanism could be regarded as uncritical dogmatism (K.4.819–20; 19.227). He quoted Posidonius approvingly to the effect that it would be better to abandon Stoicism completely rather than the truth (K.19.262). Given Galen's attitude, the discussions with Marcus at Aquileia must have been lively. Galen also had little time for the notion of God and said that 'divine revelation', as opposed to logic and science, was so worthless that not even a book written by the Muses themselves would have any greater value than one written by the uneducated, if it relied simply on revelation. • 58. Vivian Nutton, *From Democedes to Harvey. Studies in the History of Medicine* (1988), pp.158–71. • 59. ibid. • 60. 'His precipitate departure for Pergamum in AD 166, perhaps to avoid the outbreak of plague in Rome, probably saved his life in more ways than one' (Ralph Jackson, *Doctors and Diseases in the Roman Empire* (1988), p.61). Galen K.14.649–50. • 61. Galen K.14.663. See also Nutton, *Galen on Prognosis* op. cit., pp.210–11. • 62. Galen K.10.909–16; 14.663. • 63. Galen K.5.40.15. • 64. Galen K.5.18. • 65. Galen K.19.18–19. Also in *Corpus Medicorum Graecorum* (1907–), 5.8.1; 118.20–120. As one Galen scholar has remarked: 'The dream in question was certainly *ben trovato*' (R.J. Hankinson, *Galen on Antecedent Causes* (Cambridge 1998), p.172). • 66. He later effected a 'miraculous' cure on Commodus. This is hardly something for which history can commend him (Dio 71.32.1; *Corpus Medicorum Graecorum* 5.8.1; 130.11–132; Galen K.661–4; Nutton, *Galen on Prognosis* op. cit., p.224). • 67. Galen K.832–5. • 68. *Corpus Medicorum Graecorum* 5.8.1; 126.16–130. Galen K.14.201; 14.216; 12.750; 13.179; 13.973 Cf. also Jonathan Barnes, 'Galen, Christians and Logic', in T.P. Wiseman (ed.), *Classics in Progress. Essays on Ancient Greece and Rome* (Oxford 2000), pp.399–417 (at p.399). • 69. Galen K.14 (p.661). • 70. For his medical achievements, see David T. Furley & J.S. Wilkie, *Galen on Respiration and the Arteries* (Princeton 1984); Vivian Nutton, *The Unknown Galen* (2002); Peter Brain, *Galen on Bloodletting* (Cambridge 1986); M. Frede, *Galen. Three Treatises on the Nature of Science* (Indianapolis 1985); R.J. Hankinson, 'Galen's anatomical procedures', ANRW

2.37 (1994), pp.1834–55; Hankinson (ed.), *Galen on the Therapeutic Method* (Oxford 1991); Mark Grant, *Galen on Food and Diet* (2000); Margaret Tallmadge, *Galen on the Usefulness of the Parts of the Body* (Ithaca 1968); L.H. Toledo-Pereyra, 'Galen's contribution to surgery', *Journal of the History of Medicine and Allied Science* 28 (1973), pp.357–75; F. Kudlien & R.J. Durling, *Galen's Method of Healing* (Leiden 1991); V. Nutton, 'The Patient's Choice: A new treatise by Galen', CQ 40 (1990), pp.236–57. • 71. V. Nutton, *From Democedes to Harvey* op. cit., pp.3–16. • 72. Galen K.11.314–15; 12.786; 13.1036; 14.182. • 73. For Caesar's numbers, see Adrian Goldsworthy, *Caesar* (2006) op. cit., p.491. For Trajan, see N. Gostar, 'L'armée romaine dans les guerres daces de Trajan, 101–102, 105–106', *Dacia* 23 (1979), pp.115–22; K. Strobel, *Untersuchungen zu den Dakerkriegen Trajans. Studien zur Geschichte des mittleren und unteren Donauraumes in der hohen Kaizerzeit* (Bonn 1984), pp.153–4. For Septimius Severus at Lyons, see Dio 76.6.1. • 74. Adrian Goldsworthy, *Roman Warfare* (2000), p.127; Goldsworthy, *The Complete Roman Army* (2003), pp.136, 209; M.C. Bishop, *Lorica Segmentata, Vol. 1 A Handbook of Articulated Roman Plate Armour* (2002). • 75. Some general pointers are available in Anne Kolb, *Transport und Nachrichtentransfer im Römischen Reich* (Berlin 2000). One might possibly be able to extrapolate from the problems encountered by Duke William of Normandy's army in 1066, though this was only about 14,000 strong (see Frank McLynn, *1066* (1998) pp.192–3). But Marcus's army was *ten* times this size. • 76. Tacitus, *Germania* 5; T.C. Champion, *Prehistoric Europe* (1984), p.323. • 77. Maroboduus was said to have had 70,000 foot and 4,000 horse (Velleius Paterculus, *Compendium* op cit., 2.109.2). A modern estimate agrees that this would be roughly the correct figure for the Marcomanni (Goldsworthy, *Complete Roman Army* op. cit., p.45). • 78. Dio 72.11–12. • 79. Tacitus, *Germania* 4. • 80. Tacitus, *Germania* 18–20, 25.3; 26.1; 27.1; Brent D. Shaw, 'Rebels and Outsiders', CAH 11, pp.378–9. • 81. E. Luttwak, *The Grand Strategy of the Roman Army* (Baltimore 1976), pp.45–6. • 82. Dio 56.22.2; Ammianus Marcellinus 17.6.1; 29.6.12; Tacitus, *Annals* 12.45.4. • 83. Tacitus, *Germania* 6; *Annals* 2.14.4; 2.45.4; *Histories* 2.22; 4.17; 5.17; Plutarch, *Marius* 25.7; Ammianus Marcellinus 17.12.2; Dio 38.35.4; Caesar, *De Bello Gallico* 1.46.1. Cf. also Todd, *Northern Barbarians* op. cit., pp.163–70, 172–4; Thompson, *Early Germans* op. cit., pp.9, 111; Goldsworthy, *Complete Roman Army* op. cit., pp.48–50. • 84. Tacitus, *Germania* 6; *Annals* 2.14; Caesar, *De Bello Gallico* 1.52.3. • 85. Goldsworthy, *Complete Roman Army*, p.74. • 86. Tacitus, *Germania* 14.31. • 87. Tacitus, *Annals* 2.21.1; Thompson, *Early Germans* op. cit., p.63. • 88. Thompson, *Early Germans*, p.115. • 89. Tacitus, *Germania* 7; 30.2–4. • 90. Tacitus, *Germania* 6; *Annals* 1.68; *Histories* 4.60; Goldsworthy, *Complete Roman Army*, pp.52–3. • 91. Tacitus, *Annals* i.55. • 92. Caesar, *De Bello Gallico* 6.23. • 93. Thompson, *Early Germans*, pp.115–16. • 94. Tacitus, *Annals* 1.63.1; 2.11.3; 2.14.3; 1.64.3; 2.5.3; *Histories* 5.17. For an example of German frustration during the Marcomannic wars, see C. Caprino, *La Colonna di Marco Aurelio* (Rome 1955), Plate 34, Fig.68. • 95. Caesar, *De Bello*

Gallico 5.32; Tacitus, *Annals* 1.50, 63. • 96. Burns, *Rome and the Barbarians* op. cit., pp.189–90. • 97. Velleius Paterculus, *Compendium* op. cit., 2.109.1; Tacitus, *Annals* 2.45.3. • 98. Todd, *Northern Barbarians* op. cit., pp.175, 210. • 99. Dio 71.3.5; ILS 1098. • 100. Lucian, *Alexander* 48; L. Robert, *À Travers l'Asie Mineure* (Paris 1980), pp.393–421; Lane Fox, *Pagans and Christians* op. cit., pp.241–50. • 101. Those who credit the story include Keith Hopkins, *Conquerors and Slaves* op. cit., p.233; J. Ferguson, *The Religions of the Roman Empire* (1970), p.189; C.P. Jones, *Culture and Society in Lucian* (Cambridge, Massachusetts 1986), p.144; J. Beaujeu, *La religion romaine à l'apogée de l'empire* (Paris 1955) i, pp.347–9. Farquharson considers it a 'ridiculous tale' (Farquharson ii, p.440). A compromise view is advanced by Rutherford, p.224. • 102. Kerr, 'Chronology', pp.90–1. • 103. ibid. • 104. The Sarmatians subdivided into the two principal branches of the Iazyges and Roxolani (Pliny NH 4.12.80–2; 6.19; Ptolemy 3.5.9; Lucian, *Toxaris* 51–4). See also T.T. Rice, 'The Scytho-Sarmatian tribes of South-Eastern Europe', in F. Millar (ed.), *The Roman Empire and Its Neighbours* (1981), pp.288–92; A. Mocsy, *Pannonia and Upper Moesia* op. cit., pp.36–7, 94–5; R. Rolle (ed.), *Gold der Steppe. Archäologie der Ukraine* (Schleswig 1991); T. Sulimirski, *The Sarmatians* (1970). • 105. Dio 71.11.1; CIL iii. 1957, 8009, 8021; ILS 1098; Alföldy, KS, p.233; Zwikker op. cit., p.231. • 106. Pausanias 8.43.6; Aelius Aristides, Oration 22 in Wehr (ed.), *Complete Works* op. cit., pp.23–5; A. Von Premerstein, 'Untersuchungen zur Geschichte des Kaisers Marcus', *Klio* 12 (1912), pp.139–49. • 107. Pausanias 10.34.2–5; W. Scheidel, 'Probleme der Datierung des Costoboceneinfalls im Balkanraum unter Marcus Aurelius', *Historia* 39 (1990), pp.493–9; C.P. Jones, 'The levy at Thespiae under Marcus Aurelius', *Greek, Roman and Byzantine Studies* 12 (1971), pp.445–8. • 108. Kerr, 'Chronology', p.88. • 109. HA Julianus 1.6–8; Böhme, 'Archäologische Zeugnisse' op. cit., pp.164–5; Alföldy, KS, p.302. • 110. HA Pertinax 2.4–6: Alföldy, KS, pp.330–3. • 111. HA Pertinax 2.6–8; Dio 71.3.2. • 112. G. Alföldy, 'P. Helvius Pertinax und M. Valerius Maximianus', in Alföldy, *Römische Heeresgeschichte* op. cit., pp.326–41; J. Fitz, 'Claudius Pompeianus, gener Marci', *Alba Regia* 19 (1981), pp.289–300. • 113. HA Marcus 22.8. • 114. Meds 4.10.10. • 115. Dio 71.11.2–3; 71.13.2–3. • 116. Duncan-Jones, *Structure and Scale in the Roman Economy* op. cit., p.74; Walker, *Metrology* op. cit., p.58; Szaivert, *Die Münzprägung* op. cit., pp.119–20, 203–4; Mattingly, RIC iii, 270, 340. • 117. W. Scheidel, 'Der Germaneneinfall', *Chiron* 20 (1990), pp.10–15; Hans-Jörg Kellner, 'Raetien und die Markomannenkriege', *Bayerische Vorgeschichtsblätter* 30 (1965), pp.154–75; Kerr, 'Chronology', pp.77–9. • 118. Dio 72.11.1–5. • 119. Dio 71.12.1–2. • 120. Dio 71.12.3. • 121. Dio 67.7.1; 71.11.3; 71.15.1; 71.20.1; 72.2.1; Petrus Patricius, fragment 6. • 122. Dio 71.22.1. • 123. AE 1956, 24; L. Barkóczi, 'Die Naristen zur Zeit der Markomannenkriege', *Folia Archaeologica* 9 (1957), pp.92–9. • 124. HA Marcus 21.10. • 125. Dio 72.2.1. • 126. Eutropius 8.13.1. • 127. Mattingly, RIC iii, pp.234–9. • 128. ibid.; Dio 71.3.5; 71.11.2. • 129. Dio 71.15.1. • 130. Dio 71.3.3–4.

• 131. Szaivert, *Die Münzprägung* op. cit. pp.94–141 • 132. RIC iii. 1046; BMC iv.1425–6. • 133. Dio 72.9.3; Herodian 1.13.8; 1.15.1; 1.15.7–8; 1.17.12. • 134. HA Julianus 1.7; Alföldy, KS, p.253; E.M. Wightman, *Gallia Belgica* (1985), p.159. • 135. Dio 72.13.1–2; 72.16.1. • 136. A. Alfoldi, 'The moral frontier on Rhine and Danube', *Limeskongress* 1 (1952), pp.1–16; Josephus, *Jewish Antiquities* 18.275; Appian, *De bello civico* 11.90. • 137. Kerr, 'Chronology', p.160. • 138. Dio 71.7.1; Jeno Fitz, 'A military history of Pannonia from the Marcomannic wars to the death of Alexander Severus', *Acta Archaeologica Academiae Scientiarum Hungariae* 14 (1960), pp.25–112. • 139. Mattingly, RIC iii, pp.234–9. • 140. HA Marcus 14.3. • 141. Dio 71.13.3–4. • 142. Dio 71.7.1; 71.13.2. • 143. Dio 71.10.5; Kerr, 'Chronology', pp.160–3. • 144. Campbell, *The Emperor and the Roman Army* op. cit., p.124. • 145. Burns, *Rome and the Barbarians* op. cit., p.237. • 146. B. Andreae, *The Art of Rome* (1977), pp.432–3. For the Aurelian column in general and its manifold meanings, see C. Caprino et al., *La Colonna* op. cit.; Felix Piron, 'Style and message on the column of Marcus Aurelius', PBSR 64 (1996), pp.137–99; R. Brilliant, 'The Column of Marcus Aurelius Reviewed', *Journal of Roman Archaeology* 15 (2002), pp.499–506. For comparisons with Trajan's column, see Martin Beckmann, 'The Columnae Cochlides of Trajan and Marcus Aurelius', *Phoenix* 56 (2002), pp.348–57; D. Nardoni, *La Colonna Ulpia Traiana* (Rome 1986); S. Settis et al. (eds), *La Colonna Traiana* (Turin 1988). • 147. R.R.R. Smith, 'The use of images; visual history and ancient history', in T.P. Wiseman (ed.), *Classics in Progress: Essays on Ancient Greece and Rome* (Oxford 2002), pp.60–102 (at p.82). • 148. Caesar, *De Bello Gallico* 3.16; 4.14–15; 8.44. As Smith ('The use of images' loc. cit., p.82) says: 'The modern visual parallel is not *All Quiet on the Western Front*, but something more like *Robocop* or *Death Wish*.' • 149. Meds. 8.34. • 150. A.C. Levi, *Barbarians on Roman Imperial Coins and Sculpture* (New York 1952), pp.25–6. • 151. HA Marcus 24.4; Caprino, *La Colonna* op. cit., Scene 11; BMC iv.566–7. • 152. Szaivert, *Die Münzprägung* op. cit., pp.206–7; H. Wolff, 'Welchen Zeitraum stellt der Bilderfries der Marcus-Säule dar?', *Ostbairische Grenzmarken. Passauer Jahrbuch für Geschichte, Kunst und Volkskunde* 32 (1990), pp.9–29. • 153. Dio 71.8–10; Caprino, *La Colonna* op. cit., Scene 16; BMC iv.609–10; 1483–4. • 154. Dio 72.8.1–4; 72.10.1–3. • 155. A careful investigation of the evidence shows that the 'Rain Miracle' occurred in July 174. See H. Wolff, 'Welchen Zeitraum' loc. cit. (at pp.20–2); J. Morris, 'The Dating of the Column of Marcus Aurelius', *Journal of the Warburg Institute* 15 (1952), pp.33–47 (at p.38); Kerr, 'Chronology', pp.141, 187; Penelope E. Davies, *Death and the Emperor* (Cambridge 2000), p.47. But it is only fair to point out that other scholars have dated the 'Rain Miracle' to 172. See J. Guey, 'La date de la "pluie miraculeuse" et la Colonne Aurelienne', *Mélanges de l'École Française de Rome* 60 (1948), pp.105–27 and ibid. 61 (1949), pp.93–118; Guey, 'Encore la pluie miraculeuse, mage et dieu', *Revue Philologique* 22 (1948), pp.16–62; Birley, *Marcus Aurelius* op. cit., pp.172, 251–2; W. Jobst, 11

Juni 172 n. Chr. Der Tag des Blitz- und Regenwunders im Quadenlande (Akademie Wien 335, Vienna 1978), actually tries to pin the miracle down to the precise date of 11 June 172. Still others plump for the year 173 (Farquharson i, p.279; Garzetti, *From Tiberius to the Antonines* op. cit., pp.493–4). The entire argument ultimately revolves around the dating of the events depicted on the Aurelian column. The supposedly 'unshakeable' proposition about 172 is that if the column showed events later in the war, it would have to portray Commodus, who is absent. But Wolff, 'Welchen Zeitraum' loc. cit; Morris, 'Dating' loc. cit. and Kerr, 'Chronology', pp.142–3, 187–8, argue convincingly that the column deals with the years 174–5 and 177–80. So, Scenes 1–54 cover the years 174–6 and Scenes 56–116 represent the war in 178–80. The non-appearance of Commodus can be explained in a number of ways (Kerr, pp.142, 188). Previous scholars seem to have confused the Marcomanni and the Quadi and argue that 174 is impossibly late for the 'Rain Miracle', since by that time Marcus was fighting the Iazyges and not the Germans, ignoring the very late entry of the Quadi into the fray. Besides, in a column that goes out of its way to point up striking visual images, it seems inconceivable that, if it was dealing with the years 172–3, the stunning Roman victory on the ice would not have been included. One would have expected this event to have produced 'stills' like those from the 1938 Eisenstein film *Alexander Nevsky*. • 156. Eusebius 1.4; 5.5–6. As Birley (*Marcus Aurelius* op. cit., p.173) rightly remarks: 'It is difficult to see how such a detail could have been invented.' See also Alföldy, *Römische Heeresgeschichte* op. cit., pp.333–6; Alföldy, KS, p.246. For the smallness of the Roman force, see Orosius 7.15.10. • 157. Kerr, 'Chronology', pp.137–41, 183–6. • 158. Dio 71.8.1–71.8.4; 72.14; AE 1934, 245; Zwikker, *Studien* op. cit., p.214; Guey, 'Encore la pluie miraculeuse' loc. cit., pp.16–36; Wolff, 'Welchen Zeitraum' loc. cit., pp.9–10; G. Fowden, 'Pagan Versions of the Rain Miracle of AD 172', *Historia* 36 (1986), pp.83–95. • 159. E.R. Dodds, *The Greeks and the Irrational* (1951), pp.283–5; Ramsay MacMullen, *Enemies of the Roman Order* op. cit., pp.104, 107; H. Lewy, *Chaldaean Oracles and Theurgy* (Cairo 1956), pp.3–5; J.H. Liebeschuetz, *Continuity and Change in Roman Religion* (Oxford 1979), pp.210–13. For Julianus himself, see PIR2 J.91. • 160. Ovid, *Metamorphoses* i.264–9. • 161. For this, see Tertullian, *Apol.* 5.2.21; 5.6; Eusebius 5.54.6; A. Von Harnack, 'Die Quelle der Berichte über das Regenwunder im Feldzuge Marc Aurel's gegen die Quaden', *Sitzungberichte der Preussichsen Akademie der Wissenschaften* (1894), pp.835–52; Michael Sage, 'Eusebius and the Rain Miracle; some observations', *Historia. Zeitschrift für Alte Geschichte* 36 (1986), pp.96–111; cf. also Thomas Matthews, *The Clash of Gods. A Reinterpretation of Early Christian Art* (1993); Rodney Stark, *The Rise of Christianity* (1997). • 162. Birley, *Marcus Aurelius* op. cit., p.173. • 163. For this entire question, see J. Helgeland, 'Christians in the Roman Army, AD 173–337', ANRW 2.23.1 (1979), pp.724–834 (pp.766–73 deal with the 'Rain Miracle'). Garzetti, *From Tiberius* op. cit., p.494, remarks that Christian claims on the miracle had 'some foundation, for there must have been many of them in the army by now and they could certainly have raised their prayers to God at such a difficult moment'. Some Christian apologists claim that the pagan position was inherently problematical, since the official Roman religion was sceptical of actual miracles, as opposed to signs and portents (Tacitus, *Histories* 2.78). The hold of the 'Rain Miracle' on the Christian imagination is certainly tenacious. No less a figure than Cardinal Newman believed that there had been intervention from the Christian God that day (J.H. Newman, *Essays on Miracles* (1853), Essay 2.51). • 164. Dio 71.10.4; RIC iii.299–309; 1109–21. • 165. As Kerr wryly remarks: 'Although the Quadi were defeated, it took a "miracle" to accomplish it; the Romans had had a fright' (Kerr, 'Chronology', p.165). • 166. Dio 71.13.1. • 167. Dio 71.15.1; 71.16.1. • 168. Dio 71.16.1. • 169. For Marcus's intentions in 175, see G. Alföldy, *Die Krise des Römischen Reiches* (Stuttgart 1989), pp.25–37. • 170. Kerr, 'Chronology', pp.178–80, 198–9. • 171. Dio 71.16.1; 71.17. • 172. HA Marcus 24.5–6; 25.1. • 173. Dio 71.17; HA Marcus 4.24–5; CIL 8.2276; Farquharson ii, p.835. • 174. AE 1956, 24. • 175. Dio 71.15; 71.16.2. • 176. Dio 72.15–16; 73.3.2. • 177. Dio 71.13.1–71.14.2. • 178. In AD 50 Claudius allowed a Suebian king and his tribe to settle in Pannonia, and in 57 a governor of Moesia resettled within his province 100,000 Germans from across the Danube (Suetonius, *Augustus* 21.1; Tacitus, *Annals* 12.27.1; 13.30.2; Strabo 4.34; 7.3.10). See also Ste Croix, *Class Struggle* op. cit., pp.509–18. • 179. Dio 71.11.4; HA Marcus 21.10; 22.2; 24.3; Velleius Paterculus, *Compendium* op. cit., 2.106.1; 22.10; 24.3; W. Will, 'Römische Klientel-Randstaaten am Rhein? Eine Bestandsaufnahme', *Bonner Jahrbücher* 187 (1987), pp.1–62; E. Ewig, 'Probleme der fränkischen Frühgeschichte in den Rheinlanden', in H. Beumann (ed.), *Festschrift für W. Schlesinger* (Cologne 1974), pp.47–91. See in general W. Pohl, *Kingdoms of the Empire. Integration of barbarians in late antiquity* (Leiden 1997). • 180. Joseph Vogt, *The Decline of Rome* (1967), p.59. • 181. Dio 71.16.2. • 182. I.A. Richmond, 'The Sarmatae Bremetennacum veteranorum, and the Regio Bremetennacensis', JRS 35 (1945), pp.15–29. • 183. Dio 71.6.3; 71.24.4; 71.34.2; 71.36.3; Herodian 1.2.1. • 184. S.Frere, *Britannia. A History of Roman Britain* (1987), pp.143–6; see also Michael Fulford, 'Britain', CAH 11, p.566. • 185. Alföldy, KS, pp.189, 253. • 186. AE 1956, 24. • 187. Dio 71.10.5; BMC iv.609–11; 1483–5. • 188. HA Commodus 1.11; 2.2; 12.2–3.

Notes to Chapter Fifteen — *pp. 370–393*

• 1. AE 1920, 45. • 2. Dio 71.24–6; Garzetti, *From Tiberius to the Antonines* op. cit., pp.497–8. • 3. For confirmation, see AE 1944, 42; AE 1955, 133–4. • 4. The dangers of such men becoming too powerful was obvious. Domitius Corbulo had had similar powers in the East under Nero and was eventually eliminated by the emperor, who finally thought he had given him too much power. Marcus seems to have allowed himself to be persuaded by Pescennius Niger (later – in 193–4 – to be a short-lived emperor himself) that all proconsuls, legates and provincial governors should serve at least five years in a province, because it took that long to master the intricacies of administration, local conditions, folkways, etc. (HA Pescennius Niger 7.2–3). The role and rebellious contumacity of Avidius Cassius, eastern proconsul, irresistibly reminds one of another eastern Caesar, General Douglas MacArthur in Japan after 1945. That particular proconsular revolt (over Korea) was ended in 1951 by President Truman, who showed an Aurelian toughness and courage in dismissing his insubordinate generalissimo. • 5. N. Rosenstein, *Rome at War: farms, families and deaths in the Middle Republic* (Chapel Hill, North Carolina 2004), pp.107–40. • 6. W. Scheidel, 'Marriage, families and survival in the Roman imperial army', in P. Erdkamp (ed.), *The Blackwell Companion to the Roman Army* (2007). • 7. Pausanias 8.43.3; Pliny NH 5.1.17; J. Arce, 'Inestabilidad política en Hispania durante el siglo II d. C.', *Archivo Español de Arqueología* 54 (1981), pp.105–10; M. Euzennat, 'Les troubles de Maurétanie', *Comptes rendues de l'Académie des inscriptions et belles-lettres* (1984), pp.372–91; Rémy, *Antonin le Pieux* op. cit., pp.250–4. • 8. Pausanias 8.43.3. • 9. Pliny, NH. • 10. D. Kehoe, *The Economics of Agriculture on Roman Imperial Estates in North Africa* (Göttingen 1988). • 11. Strabo 142.3.2.6; 144.3.28; 146.3.2.14; Pliny NH 3.7; Martial 12.98; 9.61.3; 14.133; Silius Italicus 3.40.1; 1.16.468–70. See in general W. Haley, *Baetica Felix. People and Prosperity in Southern Spain from Caesar to Septimius Severus* (Austin, Texas 2003). • 12. HA Septimius Severus 2.2–4; HA Marcus 22.11. • 13. G. Alföldy, *Fasti Hispanienses* (Wiesbaden 1969), pp.38–42; M. Rachet, *Rome et les Barbares* (Collection Latomus 110, Brussels 1970), pp.203–11; J.M. Blazquez, 'Hispania desde el año 138 a 235', *Hispania* 132 (1976), pp.5–87 (at pp.70–7); Alföldy, *Römische Heeresgeschichte* op. cit., pp.463–81. The Senate was temporarily given Sardinia in exchange for the loss of Baetica. • 14. CIL viii.21567. • 15. ILS 1354, 13459; R. Le Roux, *L'Armée Romaine et l'Organisation des provinces ibériques d'Auguste à l'invasion de 409* (Paris 1982), pp.373–7; R. Thouvenot, 'Les invasions des Maures en Bétique sous le règne de Marc-Aurèle', *Revue des États Anciens* 41 (1939), pp.20–8. • 16. Szaivert, *Die Münzprägung* op. cit., pp.136–7. • 17. G. Alföldy, 'Spain', CAH 11, p.460. • 18. M.Rostovsteff, *Social and Economic History* op. cit., pp.157–70. • 19. J. Lesquier, *L'armée romaine d'Égypte* (Cairo 1918), pp.29–31, 391, 402. *Le Papyre Thmouis*, col. 104, 114.6–10; 116.2–11, is apparently the crucial source for the *boukouloi*, but, sadly, is not available to the non-papyrologist. Its contents are discussed in S. Kambitsis, *Le Papyrus Thmouis I. Colonnes 68–160* (1986) and Ann Ellis Hanson (ed.), *On Government and Law in Roman Egypt. Collected Papers of Naphtali Lewis* (Atlanta 1995). • 20. Eric Hobsbawm, *Bandits* (1969), pp.70–82, identifies the *boukouloi* as being similar to the Haiduks in the Balkans under Ottoman rule. • 21. Dio 72.4.1–2. • 22. J. Winkler, 'Lokianus and the Desperadoes', *Journal of Hellenic Studies* (1980), pp.155–81. • 23. Goldsworthy, *Roman Army* op. cit., pp.94–5. • 24. Dio 72.4.2–4;

HA Avidius Cassius 6.6; R. Alston, 'The Revolt of the Boukouloi: Geography, History and Myth', in K. Hopwood (ed.), *Organised Crime in Antiquity* (1999), pp.129–53; cf. also Alston, *Soldier and Society in Roman Egypt. A Social History* (1995). • 25. Dio 72.22.2; Syme, RP v, pp.548–9. • 26. HA Avidius Cassius 1.4–5; Dio 71.17.2; Syme, RP v, pp.687–701 (esp. pp.696–8). As mentioned before, Avidius Cassius vis-à-vis Marcus is often compared to Domitius Corbulo vis-à-vis Nero. • 27. HA Avidius Cassius 4.2; 4.6. • 28. HA Avidius Cassius 4.7–9. • 29. HA Avidius Cassius 4.3–5. • 30. Syme, RP v, p.699; cf. also W. Weber in CAH 11 (1936), p.346; A. Downey, *A History of Antioch in Syria* (1961), p.226. • 31. Syme, RP v, p.699; Alföldy, KS, pp.279–83. • 32. HA Avidius Cassius 3.4–5. • 33. HA Avidius Cassius 6.3–5. • 34. 'Thucydidean' in that the speeches in Thucydides are not verbatim shorthand accounts, but the historian's 'educated guess' as to what was likely to have been said. 'Aristotelian' in that Aristotle tells us that drama should be concerned not with what actually happened, but with what could have happened, might have happened and even should have happened. • 35. The apocryphal letters, Verus to Marcus and Marcus to Verus, bearing a date of 166, are in Haines ii, pp.308–10, and also at HA Avidius Cassius 1.7.9; 2.1–8. • 36. A.R. Birley, 'Hadrian to the Antonines', CAH 11, pp.132–94 (at pp.169–70). • 37. HA Avidius Cassius 14.1–8. • 38. Antonio Baldini, 'La rivolta bucolica e l'usurpazione di Avidio Cassio', *Latomus* 37 (1978), pp.634–78. • 39. HA Marcus 24.6; HA Avidius Cassius 7.1; Dio 71.22.3. The comparisons with the other rebellions are in Syme, RP v, p.700. 'Providing action against an emergency, a sagacious and resolute woman took action to preserve the succession for the boy Commodus (now aged 13) and safeguarded her own position by annexing a powerful ally as regent' (Syme, RP iv, p.19). • 40. 'Since Faustina had been on the Danube with her consort, next door to the headquarters frequented by the top-ranking generals, among whom she could easily have found a remedy for her possible worries without seeking one at the other end of the empire' (Garzetti, *From Tiberius* op. cit., p.501). • 41. Syme, RP iv, p.19; Syme, *Emperors and Biography* (1971), p.129. • 42. Philostratus, VS 2.1.13; Astarita, *Avidio Cassio* op. cit., pp.92–9. • 43. Cassius Dio, who was anti-expansionist, would certainly have mentioned the existence of such a party it if had existed, but there is no mention of it in Marcus's comprehensive speech in 175 (Dio 71.24–6). • 44. Syme, RP v, p.701. • 45. R. Remondon, 'Les dates de la révolte de C. Avidius Cassius', *Chronique d'Égypte* 26 (1951), pp.364–71. • 46. Dio 71.27.12. • 47. It was a fixed axiom of Marcus's that such actions harmed the doer more than the victim (Meds 9.38). Moreover, the whole of Meds 9.42, referring to vicious, untrustworthy or shameless actions, can be read as a disguised comment on the Avidius Cassius revolt. • 48. Dio 71.24.1. • 49. Thoughts of suicide may have been on Marcus's mind at this point. Some commentators claim that Marcus was initially so depressed by news of the rebellion that he briefly contemplated suicide (Birley, *Marcus*

Aurelius op. cit., p.185). • 50. Dio 71.24.1–4; 71.25–71; 71.27.1. • 51. HA Marcus
25.5–6; Dio 71.30. • 52. HA Avidius Cassius 11.1–8; 12.1–6; 12.6–10; Dio 71.27.1.
• 53. HA Avidius Cassius 8.2–5. • 54. HA Avidius Cassius 8.6–7. • 55. Faustina
asked for the physician Soteridas to be sent to Formiae, as she had no confidence in Pisitreus, the doctor currently attending Fadilla (HA Avidius Cassius
10.10). • 56. The Marcus–Faustina correspondence, which some think apocryphal, can be found at Haines ii, pp.314–19; HA Avidius Cassius 10.1–9. • 57.
HA Marcus 24.9; HA Avidius Cassius 7.5; Plutarch, *Galba* 5. Nero was the only
emperor before Galba to suffer this ignominy (Suetonius, *Nero* 49), but it was
also the fate that lay in wait for Commodus (Dio 74.2.1). • 58. HA Avidius
Cassius 9.2–4. • 59. Dio 71.24.3–4; 71.26.2; HA Avidius Cassius 7.9; Astarita,
Avidio Cassio op.cit., pp.102–3. • 60. A.K. Bowman, 'A letter of Avidius Cassius's?',
JRS 60 (1970), pp.20–5. • 61. Dio 71.27.2–3; 71.28.1; HA Marcus 25.2–3; HA Avidius
Cassius 8.1. • 62. HA Avidius Cassius 7.9–8.1. • 63. Dio 71.31.1. • 64. CIL xiii.
1680, 6768. • 65. Dio 71.29.1; 71.28.2–3; 71.30.2; HA Marcus 25.5–7; HA Avidius
Cassius 12.3–4; Ammianus Marcellinus 21.16.11; Astarita, *Avidio Cassio*, pp.100–18.
Some say Commodus later reversed his father's policy of clemency and exter-
minated all the scions of the Cassius family he could lay hands on, but scholars
differ on this point (see HA Avidius Cassius 14.7; J.E. Trapman, 'The Life and
Reign of Commodus', PhD thesis, Princeton (1964), p.43; F. Grosso, *La lotta
politica al tempo di Commodo* (Turin 1964), pp.134–360. • 66. Dio 71.7.4. • 67.
Theodoret of Cyrrhus, *Letters* 42. • 68. John Eadie, 'One hundred years of
rebellion: The eastern army in politics, AD 175–272', in David Kennedy (ed.),
The Roman Army in the East (Ann Arbor 1966), pp.135–51. • 69. HA Marcus 26.4;
Alföldy, *Römische Heeresgeschichte* op. cit., pp.326–35; O. Hekster, *Commodus. An
Emperor at the Crossroads* (2002), p.38. • 70. Szaivert, *Die Münzprägung* op. cit.,
p.125. • 71. Ammianus Marcellinus 31.5.14; Alföldy, *Römische Heeresgeschichte*,
p.335. • 72. Dio 71.16.2; AE 1956, 122. For the pan-imperial project, see Kerr,
'Chronology', p.205. • 73. H. Halfmann, *Itinera Principum: Geschichte und
Typologie der Kaiserreisen im Römischen Reich* (Stuttgart 1986), pp.213–15. • 74.
HA Pertinax 2.10; HA Marcus 26.4; Alföldy, *Römische Heeresgeschichte*, pp.326–35.
• 75. Philostratus, VS 2.9.2; Dio 71.33.1; Alföldy, KS, pp.221, 260–2, 368. • 76. For
Bassaeus Rufus, see H.G. Pflaum, *Les carrières procuratoriennes équestres sous le
Haut-Empire*, 3 vols (Paris 1961), No.162; PIR 2, B.69. The snobbery was not
confined to Roman times. Instancing other 'upstarts', such as Vespronius
Candidus and Ulpius Marcellus, who came to prominence under Marcus,
Syme says: 'Those who in retrospect or from a safe distance admire low-born
generals devoid of education or social graces, and ferocious in warfare or
discipline, may contemplate the fearsome collection which Marcus bequeathed
to his son' (Syme, RP v, p.687). • 77. From where he wrote letters to the shrine
at Delphi (A. Plassant, *Fouilles de Delphe* (Paris 1970) iii.4, pp.323–6). For further
details on the landscape through which Marcus travelled, see Pliny, NH 3.24–6;

4.12; 4.75–9; 6.15–17. • 78. Halfmann, *Itinera Principum* op. cit., pp.215–16; Astarita, *Avidio Cassio*, pp.155–62; HA Commodus 2.3. • 79. Dio 71.5.1–2. • 80. HA Marcus 26.4–9; Philostratus, VS 2.1.12. • 81. Dio 71.29.1; 71.31.1–2. • 82. Astarita, *Avidio Cassio* op. cit., pp.137–53. • 83. Meds 9.3.1; 9.42. • 84. Meds 1.17.18. • 85. Philostratus, VS 2.560–1. • 86. This is the line taken by Syme in RP v, pp.687–701. • 87. For this version of Xanthippe, see Xenophon, *Symposium* 2.10. But she has always had her defenders, most famously Robert Graves. See also Eileen Ebert Smith, *Xanthippe* (1994). • 88. R. Brilliant, *Roman Art from the Republic to Constantine* (1974), p.52. • 89. I. Tontain, 'Réflexions sur une monnaie romaine', in *Hommages Bidez-Cumont* (Brussels 1949), pp.331–8. • 90. Renan, *Marcus Aurelius* op. cit., p.232; cf. also Renan, *Mélanges d'histoire et des voyages* (Paris n.d.), pp.169–95. • 91. Pliny NH 21.9.12. • 92. Dio 71.22; 71.29–30; 71.34.3. • 93. HA Marcus 29.1. • 94. Syme, *Emperors and Biography* op. cit., p.131. • 95. HA Marcus 29.2–3. • 96. HA Marcus 19.2–5. • 97. HA Marcus 19.7–8. • 98. Renan, *Marcus Aurelius* op. cit., pp.232–3. • 99. See Antonia Fraser, *Marie Antoinette. The Journey* (2002). • 100. HA Marcus 26.2; 26.19; E. Fantham et al. (eds), *Women in the Classical World* (1994), p.335; J.R. de Serviez, *The Roman Emperors* (New York 1913) ii, pp.47–91; S. Perowne, *The Caesars' Wives* (1974). • 101. AE 1956, 232; RIC iii.274.75; 346.1659; 115.678; H. Mattingly, 'The Consecration of Faustina the Elder and her Daughter', *Harvard Theological Review* 41 (1948), pp.147–51. • 102. RIC iii.349.1702; D.E. Kleiner & S.B. Matheson, *I, Claudia* (Yale 1996), p.80. • 103. For a wide range of views, see Gibbon, *Decline and Fall* op. cit., iv.1.83–4; Farquharson i, pp.263–7; Mary T. Boatwright, 'Faustina the Younger, Mater Castrorum', in Regula Frei-Stolba, Anne Bielman & Olivier Bianchi (eds), *Les femmes antiques entre sphère privée et sphère publique* (Berne 2003), pp.249–68. For Faustina's social rank, see M.T. Raepset-Charlier, *Prosopographie des femmes de l'Ordre Sénatorial, 1er–2er Siècles* (Louvain 1987). • 104. HA Marcus 29.10. • 105. R. Saller, 'Family and Household', CAH 11, pp.862–3. • 106. Philostratus, VS 2.1.12. • 107. HA Marcus 25.8–26.1; HA Avidius Cassius 9.1; Astarita, *Avidio Cassio*, p.56; Elizabeth Jeffreys, Michael Jeffreys, Roger Scott et al. (eds), *The Chronicle of John Malalas of Antioch* (Sydney 1956), pp.283–90. For Antioch, see also Pliny, NH 6.30; Warwick Ball, *Rome in the East* op. cit., pp.150–6. • 108. Ammianus Marcellinus 22.5.4–5; Astarita, *Avidio Cassio*, pp.118–19. • 109. Luitpold Wallach, 'The Colloquy of Marcus Aurelius with the Patriarch Judah I', *Jewish Quarterly Review* 31 (1941), pp.259–86; Astarita, *Avidio Cassio*, pp.119–22. Cf. also M. Avi-Yonah, *The Jews under Roman and Byzantine Rule* (1984). • 110. Motschmann, *Die Religionspolitik*, pp.263–9, 272–3. • 111. Diodorus Siculus 17.52.6; Pliny NH 5.11.62–3. See also D. Delia, 'The Population of Roman Alexandria', *Transactions of the American Philological Association* 118 (1988), pp.275–92; R.S. Bagnall & B.W. Frier, *The Demography of Roman Egypt* (Cambridge 1994). Alexandria was also a major Jewish centre (H.I. Bell, 'Antisemitism in Alexandria', JRS 31 (1941), pp.1–18). • 112. There is a vast literature on Roman

Alexandria. A few representative titles are D. Sly, *Philo's Alexandria* (1955); N. Lewis, *Life in Egypt under Roman Rule* (Oxford 1983); Judith Pollard & Howard Reid, *The Rise and Fall of Alexandria, Birthplace of the Modern World* (2006); P.M. Fraser, *Ptolemaic Alexandria*, 3 vols (Oxford 1972); R. Alston, *Soldier and Society in Roman Egypt. A Social History* (1995); D. Delia, *Alexandrian Citizenship during the Roman Principate* (Atlanta 1991); R. Alston, 'Trade and the City in Roman Times', in H. Parkins & C. Smith (eds), *Trade, Traders and the Ancient City* (1998), pp.168–202; Alston, 'Conquest by Text: Juvenal and Plutarch on Egypt', in J. Webster & N. Cooper (eds), *Roman Imperialism. Postcolonial Perspectives* (Leicester 1996), pp.99–110; Alston, 'Philo's *In Flaccum*: Ethnicity and Social Space in Roman Alexandria', GR 44 (1997), pp.165–75; A.K. Bowman, 'Cities and Administration in Roman Egypt', JRS 82 (1992), pp.107–27. • 113. HA Caracalla 3.8; 4.8; 6.3. • 114. HA Marcus 25.4–5; 26.1–3; Dio 71.28.2–4. • 115. Some say he went by sea from Alexandria to the mouth of the Orontes, but the sources do not allow us to be definite. • 116. R. Pack, 'Two Sophists and Two Emperors', *Classical Philology* 42 (1947), pp.17–20. • 117. Peter Brown, *The Making of Late Antiquity* (Princeton 1978), pp.40–5. • 118. For an exhaustive study of Aristides's career, see C.A. Behr, *Aelius Aristides and the Sacred Tales* (Amsterdam 1968). • 119. E.R. Dodds, *Pagan and Christian in an Age of Anxiety* (1965), pp.39–45 (at p.41). • 120. J. Dierkens, *Les rêves dans les 'Discours sacrés' d'Aelius Aristide, IIe siècle ap. J.C. – Essai d'analyse psychologique* (Mons 1972). Both Dodds and Dierkens have received strong support for their analyses in D.A. Russell, 'Aelius Aristides', *Proceedings of the British Academy* 67 (1981), pp.357–70. For a different view, see Peter Brown, *Religion and Society in the Age of St Augustine* (1972), pp.74–81. • 121. Sacred Tales 2.1. in A. Behr, *The Complete Works of Aelius Aristides* (Leiden 1981) ii, p.293. • 122. Behr, *Aelius Aristides and the Sacred Tales* op. cit., pp.27–9. • 123. ibid., pp.34–5; Behr, *Complete Works* op. cit. ii, p.298. • 124. The 'patients' at Asklepeion remind one of nothing so much as C.G. Jung's wealthy analysands, all suffering from nothing more serious than some vague 'individuation' problem. • 125. Galen K.176; K.137. • 126. Behr, *Complete Works* ii, pp.300, 309. • 127. Behr, *Aelius Aristides*, p.162. • 128. Behr, *Complete Works* ii, pp.278–91, 293, 300–6, 308–17, 320–5, 332–7, 340–52. • 129. ibid., pp.87, 292, 304, 417; Behr, *Aelius Aristides*, pp.166–7. • 130. Behr, *Complete Works* ii, pp.318–19; Behr, *Aelius Aristides*, pp.77–86. • 131. Meds 5.8. • 132. Meds 1.17.17. See also S.R.F. Price, 'Dreams: Freud to Artemidorus', PP 113 (1986), pp.3–37. • 133. Philostratus, VS 2.9.582–3.

Notes to Chapter Sixteen   *pp. 394–419*

• 1. For an over-sympathetic view of Herodes Atticus, see W. Ameling, *Herodes Atticus*, 2 vols (Hilversum 1983). • 2. Lucian, *Demonax* 33. • 3. For a full investigation of this cause célèbre, see Sarah Pomeroy, *The Murder of Regilla. A Case of Domestic Violence in Antiquity* (Harvard 2007). There are curious similarities between Regilla's case and that of Amy Robsart, supposed to have been murdered by Elizabeth I's agents to clear the way for her to marry the Earl of Leicester. • 4. ibid., pp.130–3. • 5. For details of the trial, see Philostratus, VS 2.555–556; Ameling, *Herodes Atticus* op. cit., i, pp.100–20; ii, pp.7–10. Ameling defends Herodes and Marcus from this charge by claiming that she died in 157, and that Marcus had nothing to do with the case, which was overseen by Antoninus Pius (ibid., i, p.118). • 6. Pomeroy, *Murder of Regilla* op. cit., p.124. • 7. J.H. Oliver, *Marcus Aurelius. Aspects of Civic and Cultural Policy* (Princeton 1970), pp.33–5. • 8. Philostratus, VS 2.1.11–12; Ameling, *Herodes Atticus* op. cit., i, pp.136–8. • 9. Oliver, *Marcus Aurelius* op. cit., p.83. • 10. Philostratus, VS 2.1.11; Pflaum, 'Les gendres de Marc-Aurèle' loc. cit., pp.37–8; K. Fittschen, *Die Bildnistypen* (Göttingen 1982), pp.31–2. • 11. Ameling, *Herodes Atticus* i, pp.63–76, 136–51. • 12. Philostratus, VS 2.1.561. • 13. Millar, *Emperor in the Roman World* op. cit. • 14. Philostratus, VS 2.1; G.W. Bowersock, *Greek Sophists in the Roman Empire* (Oxford 1969), pp.93–100. • 15. Philostratus, VS 2.1. • 16. Philostratus, VS 2.1.12. • 17. Quoted in Millar, *Emperor in the Roman World* op. cit., p.7; see also Oliver, *Marcus Aurelius. Aspects* op. cit., pp.3–5; C.P. Jones, 'A New Letter of Marcus Aurelius to the Athenians', ZPE 8 (1971), pp.161–83; W. Williams, 'Formal and historical aspects of two new documents of Marcus Aurelius', ZPE 66 (1976), pp.37–76. • 18. Philostratus, VS 2.1.562–3; Simon Swain, 'The Promotion of Hadrian of Tyre and the Death of Herodes Atticus', *Classical Philology* 85 (1990), pp.214–16. There are some who claim, unconvincingly, that Herodes was excluded from the list of dead people as he was still alive when Marcus wrote (S. Follet, 'Lettre de Marc Aurèle aux Athéniens: nouvelles lectures et interprétations', *Revue de philologie* 53 (1979), pp.29–43; Bowersock, *Greek Sophists* op. cit., pp.94–100. • 19. Astarita, *Avidio Cassio* op. cit., pp.142–4. • 20. There are some pointers in Pausanias 1.38.1–7; see also S. Alcock, J. Cherry & J. Elsner (eds), *Pausanias: Travel and Memory in Roman Greece* (Oxford 2001). On the mysteries in general, see R. Gordon Wasson, Carl Rusk & Albert Hoffman (eds), *The Road to Eleusis: Unveiling the Secret of the Mysteries* (1978); George Emmanuel Mylonas, *Eleusis and the Eleusinian Mysteries* (Princeton 1961). • 21. Carl Kerényi, *Eleusis: Archetypal Image of Mother and Daughter* (Princeton 1991); cf. also Erwin Rohde, *Psyche* (1925). • 22. Cicero, *Laws* 2.14.36. • 23. Mylonas, *Eleusis* op. cit., pp.231–3. • 24. HA Marcus 27.1; Philostratus, VS 1.12; 2.1. See also J. Beaujeu, *La religion romaine à l'apogée de l'empire* op. cit. • 25. C.P. Jones, 'A New Letter' loc. cit.; S. Follet, 'Lettre de Marc-Aurèle' loc. cit.; Oliver, *Marcus Aurelius. Aspects* op. cit. • 26. Dio 72.3.1; *Digest* 27.1.6.7; Lucian, *Eunuchus* 3; J.H. Oliver, 'Roman Emperors and Athens', *Historia* 30 (1981), pp.412–23. • 27. Philostratus, VS 2.566. • 28. Galen K.2.218, 627. • 29. J.M. Dillon, *The Middle Platonists* (1977), pp.247–62; J.M. André, 'Les écoles philosophiques aux premiers siècles de l'empire', ANRW 2.36.1, pp.5–77 (at p.53); J.P. Lynch, *Aristotle's School:*

A Study of a Greek Educational Institution (Berkeley 1972), p.190; H.B. Gottschalk, 'Aristotelian Philosophy in the Roman World from the time of Cicero to the end of the second century AD', ANRW 2.36.2, pp.1079–174. • 30. Philostratus, VS 2.2.1; I. Avotins, 'The holders of the chairs of rhetoric at Athens', *Harvard Classical Philology* 79 (1975), pp.313–23. Marcus also overruled the Athenians when they wanted Chrestus of Byzantium appointed to a chair. At first the Athenians threatened to appeal over the emperor's head to the Senate in Rome, but were 'persuaded' not to (Philostratus, VS 2.11–12, 30). • 31. HA Marcus 27.2–3. • 32. Dio 71.32.1. • 33. HA Marcus 16.1–2; 27.4–5; HA Commodus 2.3–5. • 34. Suetonius, *Nero* 14; HA Commodus 1.10–12. • 35. HA Marcus 29.10; HA Commodus 12.4–6. • 36. HA Commodus 1.7–8. See also Falko von Saldern, *Studien zur Politik des Commodus* (Rahden 2003), pp.9–13. • 37. HA Commodus 1.9; 2.8. • 38. Renan, *Marcus Aurelius* op. cit., p.233. • 39. AE 1948, 221. • 40. Dio 73.1.1. • 41. Hekster, *Commodus* op. cit., pp.117–18. • 42. Birley, *Marcus Aurelius* op. cit., p.198. • 43. Kerr, 'Chronology' loc. cit., pp.249–50. • 44. 'If he did stand at his father's feet in the base frieze, Commodus's position as heir would have been made explicit and his legitimation implied through the dynastic heritage expressed in the column's topographical ties' (Penelope J.E. Davies, *Death and the Emperor* (Cambridge 2000), pp.170–1). See also M. Hammond, 'The Transmission of the Powers of the Roman Emperor from the death of Nero in AD 68 to that of Alexander Severus in AD 235', *Memoirs of the American Academy in Rome* 24 (1956), pp.61–133. • 45. Julian, *Caesars* 312A–B, 334B. • 46. Dio 72.14.7. • 47. Galen K.14.661–3. • 48. V. Nutton, *Galen on Prognosis* (Berlin 1979), pp.126, 130–2, 218. • 49. Galen K.9.10–10.21; Nutton, *Galen* op. cit., pp.120–2. • 50. O. Hekster, 'All in the Family: The appointment of emperors designate in the second century AD', in L. de Blois (ed.), *Administration, Prosopography and Appointment Policies in the Roman Empire* (Amsterdam 2001), pp.35–49; Brian K. Harvey, 'Two Bases of Marcus Aurelius and the Roman Imperial Succession', *Historia* 53 (2004), pp.46–60. • 51. P. Grimal, *Marc Aurèle* (Paris 1991), p.216. • 52. Jane Gardner, *Family and Familia in Roman Law and Life* (Oxford 1998), p.115. • 53. Hekster, *Commodus* op. cit., pp.28–9. • 54. ibid., p.18–21. • 55. J. Keil, 'Kaiser Marcus und die Thronfolge', *Klio* 31 (1938), pp.293–300. • 56. For Pompeianus's marriage to Lucilla Augusta, Verus's widow, and the effect this had on Marcus's calculations, see J. Aymard, 'Lucilla Augusta', *Revue Archéologique* 35 (1950), pp.58–66. • 57. Herodian 1.8.3; HA Marcus 20.6–7; Astarita, *Avidio Cassio* op. cit., pp.75–6, 110. • 58. Meds 10.36. • 59. HA Marcus 27.11–12. • 60. Lucilla's daughter was later (182) involved in a plot against Commodus (Dio 72.4.4). For Lucilla, see Fittschen, *Die Bildnistypen* op. cit., pp.23–32; H.G. Pflaum, 'Les gendres de Marc-Aurèle' loc. cit., pp.28–41 (at pp.33–4). • 61. W. Ameling, 'Die Kinder des Marc Aurel und die Bildnistypen der Faustina Minor', ZPE 90 (1992), pp.147–66; Fittschen, *Die Bildnistypen*, p.27; Pflaum, 'Les gendres' loc. cit., pp.29–30. • 62. AE 1939, 127;

Fittschen, *Die Bildnistypen*, p.29; Pflaum, 'Les gendres' loc. cit., pp.34–5. • 63. Cornificia had the most interesting later life. Her first husband was murdered by Commodus (*c.* 190–1). She had an affair with Pertinax, remarried an equestrian procurator in Severus's reign and was put to death under Caracalla in 213 (Pflaum, 'Les gendres' loc. cit., pp.36–7). • 64. ibid., pp.37–8. • 65. A.R. Birley, 'Hadrian to the Antonines', CAH 11, pp.132–94 (at pp.169–70). • 66. Dio 71.33.1. • 67. HA Marcus 27.8. For Brutta Crispina, see PIR2 B.165, 170. For Pollux, see Philostratus, VS 2.12.2. • 68. Nutton, *Galen on Prognosis* op. cit., pp.126–7. • 69. Galen K.14.658–65. • 70. ibid. • 71. Dio 71.3; 71.6.1. • 72. Galen K.14.3–4. • 73. *Digest* 36.1.23. • 74. *Digest* 29.5.2. • 75. *Digest* 11.4.1.2–4. • 76. J.E. Spruitt, 'The penal conceptions of the emperor Marcus Aurelius in respect of lunatics', *International Journal of Law and Psychiatry* 21 (1998), pp.315–34. • 77. *Digest* 1.18.14. • 78. P.A. Brunt, 'The Roman Mob', PP 35 (1966), pp.3–27. Historians of Rome differ widely in their perceptions of the mob. In some quarters there is a wish to move away from the conception of *canaille* and more towards the nuanced 'crowd' treatment used by George Rudé in his studies of the French Revolution. Alan Cameron, for one, thinks the common people have been unjustly maligned: 'That notorious idle mob of layabouts sponging off the State is little more than a figment of middle-class prejudice, ancient and modern alike' (*Bread and Circuses: The Roman Emperor and his people* (1973), pp.2–3). • 79. AE 1977, 801. J.H. Oliver & R.E.A. Palmer, 'Minutes of an Act of the Roman Senate', *Hesperia* 24 (1955), pp.329–49. • 80. Talbert, *The Roman Senate* op. cit., p.291. • 81. Dio 71.28.2–3. • 82. *Digest* 23.2.59–60; 23.2.64; 23.2.67; 30.128; 48.5.7. • 83. *Digest* 38.17;26.7; 29.2.6.2; 32.7.2.4. • 84. *Digest* 23.1.16. • 85. HA Pertinax 1.4. See also Syme, *Emperors and Biography* op. cit., p.132. For the proposition in general, see D.A. Potter, 'Procurators in Asia and Dacia under Marcus Aurelius: A Case Study of Imperial Initiative in Government', ZPE 123 (1998), pp.270–94. 127 equestrians achieved the rank of procurators – a record (H.G. Pflaum, *Procurateurs équestres sous le Haut Empire Romain* (Paris 1950), p.105). • 86. HA Didius 5.6; Dio 72.8.5; 73.17.1. • 87. Dio 71.33.2. • 88. C.A. Behr, *Complete Works of Aelius Aristides* (Leiden 1981) ii, pp.7–13. • 89. Philostratus, VS 2.9. Philostratus, however, manages to contradict himself. First he says that Aelius Aristides was responsible for the rebuilding of Smyrna, then he states that Marcus would have rebuilt it anyway. This is typical of the way Philostratus always puts the best possible gloss on his beloved Sophists. • 90. Behr, *Complete Works* op. cit., pp.14–22; C.J. Cadoux, *Ancient Smyrna* (1938), pp.279–83. • 91. Dio 71.32.3. • 92. Dio 71.33.1; Alföldy, KS, pp.237–8, 261–2; BMC iv, pp.cxxx, cxliii. • 93. For some examples earlier in Roman history, see Pliny, *Letters* 6.25; Seneca, *Letters* 57; Epictetus, *Discourses* 4.1.94–5. • 94. HA Julianus 1.9; AE 1956, 124; BMC iv.1632–4; Alföldy, KS, pp.190, 226. • 95. Alföldy, *Römische Heeresgeschichte* op. cit., pp.326–7. • 96. HA Marcus 27.10. The Hermunduri were identified by Tacitus (*Germania* 41).

- 97. Szaivert, *Die Münzprägung* op. cit., pp.136–7; Kerr, 'Chronology', p.208.
- 98. HA Marcus 29.4. For the feeling that this might be a final departure, see HA Marcus 16.2; HA Commodus 12.4–5; Szaivert, *Die Münzprägung*, pp.209–10; D. Kienast, *Römische Kaisertabelle* (Darmstadt 1990), pp.147–8. • 99. Albert Camus, *La Chute* (final words). • 100. Dio 71.33.2–3. • 101. Dio 71.33.3.
- 102. Aurelius Victor, *De Caesaribus* 16.9–10. • 103. ILS 1112, 1117. • 104. Alföldy, *Römische Heeresgeschichte*, pp.203–4. • 105. Dio 71.33.3. • 106. For the contemporary sources, see HA Marcus 24.5; 27.10; Dio 71.33.4. There is a very able discussion of Marcus's annexation policy in Kerr, 'Chronology' loc. cit., pp.219–21. See also Gerhard Dobesch, 'Aus der vor- und nachgeschichte der Markomannenkriege', *Anzeiger der Österreichischen Akademie der Wissenschaften. Phil-Hist* 131 (1994), pp.67–125. • 107. G. Alföldy, *Die Krise des Römischen Reiches* (Stuttgart 1989), pp.35–8. • 108. Dio 71.11.4–5; 71.20.2; 71.33.4. • 109. Hans Jörg Kellner, *Die Römer in Bayern* (Munich 1978), pp.73–5. • 110. Kerr, 'Chronology', pp.216–17, 236. • 111. For the 'straight guy' persona, see Meds 1.15.8; 3.5.4; 7.12; 11.15. For the Machiavellian aspect of Marcus, see HA Marcus 29.6. Some go so far as to accuse him of listening to the ancient equivalent of 'focus groups' and framing his policies accordingly (HA Marcus 20.5). • 112. HA Marcus 24.5; 27.10; Dio 71.33.4. • 113. Dio 71.18–19; Hans Ulrich Instinsky, 'Cassius Dio, Mark Aurel und die Jazygen', *Chiron* 2 (1972), pp.475–82. • 114. Dio 71.18–19. • 115. Kerr, 'Chronology', p.234. • 116. Mocsy, *Pannonia and Upper Moesia* op. cit., pp.190, 199, 248. • 117. Dio 71.12.3. • 118. Dio 71.21. • 119. Dio 71.20.2. Here is a huge difference between Marcus and Trajan. Many Dacians, after Trajan's conquest, chose to trek out of Dacia and settle beyond the confines of the Roman empire (Eutropius 8.6.2). Now, when the Quadi tried to do the same thing, Marcus blocked them. • 120. Dio 71.20.1. • 121. Kerr, 'Chronology', p.207. See also G. Langmann, 'Die Markomannenkriege 166/167 bis 180', *Militärhistorische Schriftenreihe* 43 (Vienna 1981). • 122. Dio 71.33.3–4; Szaivert, *Die Münzprägung* op. cit., pp.138–9. • 123. Dio 71.20.1. • 124. Wolff, 'Welchen Zeitraum' loc. cit., p.22; Morris, 'Dating' loc. cit., pp.40–3. For comparisons with Trajan's column, see R. Brilliant, 'The Column of Marcus Aurelius reviewed', *Journal of Roman Archaeology* 15 (2002), pp.499–506; Martin Beckmann, 'The Columnae Cochlides of Trajan and Marcus Aurelius', *Phoenix* 56 (2002), pp.348–57. • 125. Dio 71.10.4. • 126. Dio 71.34.4. • 127. AE 1956, 124. • 128. HA Marcus 28.1. • 129. Herodian 1.4.1; E. Groag & A. Stein (eds), *Prosopographia* (Berlin 1936), p.973; G. Alföldy, *Fasti Hispanienses* (Wiesbaden 1969), p.38. • 130. HA Marcus 28.2–7. • 131. HA Marcus 28.10. • 132. Herodian 1.4.3–6. • 133. Dio 71.33.4. • 134. Dio 71.34. It is overwhelmingly probable – approaching certainty as a limit – that Marcus died of smallpox. This placed him as one of the first among many other rulers who would succumb to this disease, including Czars Peter II and Peter III of Russia, Elizabeth I of England, Louis XV of France, George Washington of the USA, Queen Mary

of England, the Incan emperor Huayna Capac (in 1527), to say nothing of Rameses V of Egypt and three emperors of China (Kangxi, Shunzhi and Tongzhi). Many other minor princelings were also victims: Maximilian III of Bavaria, Guru Kar Krishan, ruler of the Sikhs (in 1664), and so on. Perhaps the most famous escapee – he contracted the disease, but survived, albeit scarred – was Joseph Stalin. • 135. Aurelius Victor, 16.4, 12, 14, 17, opts for Vindobona, but Tertullian, writing less than twenty years after Marcus's death, says Sirmium and his accuracy is enhanced by his having the date right (Tertullian, *Apol.* 25). Herbert Bannert, in the best summary of the controversy so far, endorses Tertullian ('Der Tod des Kaiser Marcus', in Klein, *Marc Aurel* op. cit., pp.459–72. See also Ortolf Harl, *Vindobona, das Römische Wien* (Vienna 1979); G. Alföldy, 'Herodian über den Tod Mark Aurels', *Latomus* 32 (1973), pp.345–53. • 136. Dio 71.34.4.

Notes to Chapter Seventeen   *pp. 420–451*

• 1. Herodian 1.5.5–6. • 2. Dio 71.3.3; HA Commodus 12.6; L.F. Fitts, 'Relations between Rome and the German "kings" on the Middle Danube in the First to the Fourth Century AD', JRS 79 (1989), pp.45–58. • 3. HA Verus 2.9–10; 4.4.8.8; HA Marcus 19.1–11; HA Antoninus 3.7; M. Gherardini, *Studien zur Geschichte des Kaiser Commodus* (Vienna 1974). • 4. HA Commodus 3.5; Dio 73.1. • 5. HA Commodus 3.5; Dio 72.1–2; Herodian 1.1–6. • 6. Talbert, *The Senate of Imperial Rome* op. cit., pp.490–1. • 7. G. Alföldy, 'Die Friedensschluss des Kaisers Commodus mit den Germanen', in Klein, *Marc Aurel* op. cit., pp.389–428. • 8. HA Commodus 3.5; Herodian 1.6.8–9; Dio 73.2.3. • 9. Herodian 1.6.4–7. • 10. Susan P. Mattern, *Rome and the Enemy. Imperial Strategy in the Principate* (Berkeley 1999), pp.1–20. • 11. Herodian 1.6.3; 1.6.6. • 12. M. Sasel Kos, *A Historical Outline of the Region between Aquileia, the Adriatic and Sirmium in Cassius Dio and Herodian* (1986), pp.320–34. • 13. Hekster, *Commodus* op. cit., p.44. • 14. Galen K.19.8. • 15. D.B. Shaw, 'Rebels and Outsiders', CAH 11 (2000), pp.361–403. • 16. M.T. Schmitt, *Die Römische Aussenpolitik des 2. Jahrhunderts n. Chr. Friedenssicherung oder Expansion?* (Stuttgart 1997), pp.185–6. • 17. See especially G. Alföldy, *Die Krise des Römischen Reiches* (Stuttgart 1989), pp.25–68; Michael Stahl, 'Zwischen Abgrenzung und Integration: die Verträge der Kaiser Mark Aurel und Commodus mit den Völkern jenseits der Donau', *Chiron* 19 (1989), pp.289–317. Stahl argues that Marcus's treaties do not look like harbingers of annexation – there is no mention of Romanisation, citizenship, marriage, alliances, client kingdoms, etc. • 18. Eutropius 8.15; Dio 72.3.1–2; CIL iii.5937; Stahl, 'Zwischen Abgrenzung und Integration' loc. cit., pp.301–7; R.J.A. Talbert, 'Commodus as diplomat in an extract from the *Acta Senatus*', ZPE 71 (1988), pp.137–41. • 19. Aurelius Victor 17.2; Eutropius 8.15.1; Dio 72.20. Kerr, 'Chronology', pp.252–3, argues that the war with the Marcomanni and Quadi was hard fought by Commodus's commanders and concluded only in early 181, long after the peace with the Buri. See also Alföldy, *Die Krise* op. cit., pp.389–405; Schmitt, *Die Römische Aussenpolitik* op. cit., pp.190–6. • 20. Dio 72.2–4. • 21. Dio 71.18; 72.2.4; M.P. Speidel, 'Commodus and the king of the Quadi', *Germania* 78 (2000), pp.193–7. • 22. Dio 71.19.2; 72.2.4. • 23. Dio 73.3.3. • 24. Dio 78.13.4–6; Herodian 4.7.2–3; Burns, *Rome and the Barbarians* op. cit., pp.274–9. See also L. Okamura, 'Allamannia Devicta: Roman–German conflicts from Caracalla to the First Tetrarchy (AD 213–305)', PhD thesis, University of Michigan (1984). • 25. Dio 76.9.10; H. Wolfram, *The Roman Empire and its Germanic Peoples* (Berkeley 1997). • 26. HA Marcus 17.2; 28.4. • 27. K. Dietz, 'Zur Verwaltungsgeschichte Obergermaniens und Rätiens unter Mark Aurel', *Chiron* 19 (1989), pp.407–35 (esp. pp.426–35). • 28. Szaivert, *Die Münzprägung* op. cit., pp.142–53. • 29. Philostratus, *Vita Apollonii* ii.26. • 30. Herodian 1.7.1–5; HA Commodus 17.3. • 31. Dio 73.4.2; HA Commodus 3.6; Talbert, *Senate of Imperial Rome* op. cit., p.422. • 32. Hekster, *Commodus* op. cit., p.47. • 33. RIC iii.337, 264, 441, 654, 366; iii.401.292; 402.296; 401.294–5. • 34. Herodian 1.5.5–6. • 35. HA Commodus 14.4–7. • 36. HA Commodus 1.7–8; Herodian 14.8; Cassius Dio 72.1.1; 73.1.1; 73.4.1. • 37. HA Commodus 1.7. Cassius Dio reported that from early in his reign observers noted the parallels with Nero – a young, debauched, insane emperor, destined to be the last of his line – and both hoped and expected that the same fate would befall Commodus (Dio 71.33.42). • 38. Julian, *Caesars* 312C. • 39. HA Avidius Cassius 13.7. • 40. Dio 73.7.4; Traupman, *Commodus* op. cit., p.42. • 41. Herodian 1.7.5. • 42. HA Commodus 13.1–2; Hekster, *Commodus* op. cit., p.128. • 43. Birley, *Septimius Severus* op. cit., p.58. • 44. HA Commodus 14.16. • 45. R. Mortimer Wheeler, *Roman Art and Architecture* (1964), p.170. See also R. Hannah, 'The emperor's stars. The Conservatori portrait of Commodus', *American Journal of Archaeology* 90 (1986), pp.337–42. • 46. RIC iii.395.248; 433.631. • 47. HA Commodus 5.1; Dio 73.12.2; Traupman, *Commodus* op. cit., p.41; F. Grosso, *La lotta politica al tempo di Commodo* (Turin 1964), pp.113–16. In terms of sexuality, Commodus appears to have been the active partner and Saoterus the passive one (sodomite and catamite, respectively, in the old pre-PC terminology). I am told by one who knows about these things that in American usage Commodus would be 'top' and Saoterus 'bottom'. • 48. Grosso, *La lotta* op. cit., pp.99–120; Von Saldern, *Studien* op. cit., pp.52–4. • 49. Herodian 1.8.4; A. Bianchi, 'Lucilla Augusta: una rilettura delle fonti', *Miscellanea greca e romana* 13 (1988), pp.129–44. • 50. HA Commodus 4.1–2; Dio 73.4.5; Herodian 1.8.5. • 51. Herodian 1.6.6; HA Commodus 4.3; Dio 73.4.4; Ammianus Marcellinus 29.1.17; Falko von Saldern, *Studien zur Politik des Commodus* (Rahden 2003), pp.45–6. • 52. HA Commodus 4.4; 5.7; Dio 73.20.1; Herodian 4.6.3; Traupman, *Commodus* op. cit., p.50. • 53. Dio 73.3.2. • 54. J. Aymard, 'La conspiration de Lucilla', *Revue des États Anciens* 57 (1955), pp.85–91. • 55. Grosso, *La lotta* op. cit., pp.145–52. • 56. Dio 73.5.1–4; HA Commodus 4.7–11; Traupman,

Commodus, pp.50–1. • 57. HA Commodus 4.14.8. Still others claim that Paternus was actually innocent, on the alleged grounds that, when commander of the praetorians, he could easily have had Commodus killed. Another view is that Paternus knew about the plot, but was not an active participant; nevertheless he was guilty of 'sins of omission'. • 58. HA Didius Julianus 1.9–2.2. • 59. Dio 72.5.1–2; 73.11.2; HA Commodus 4.1.7–10; HA Didius Julianus 2.1.2. • 60. Grosso, *La lotta* op. cit., pp.153–63; Traupman, *Commodus*, p.53. • 61. Dio 72.6.1–72.7.2; HA Commodus 4.9. • 62. HA Pertinax 3.3; Birley, *Septimius Severus* op. cit., pp.67, 73. • 63. Dio 74.11.2. • 64. HA Septimius Severus 5.8; HA Pescennius Niger 2.6; HA Didianus 5.8. • 65. Traupman, *Commodus*, pp.89–91; Hekster, *Commodus* op. cit., p.59. • 66. HA Commodus 2.6–9; 5.4. • 67. HA Commodus 5.7; 5.10–11. • 68. HA Commodus 3.2. • 69. HA Commodus 6.2; 6.9. • 70. Herodian 1.8.2. • 71. Dio 73.10.1; HA Commodus 5.2–3; 6.13. The efficiency is also reflected in inscriptions (ILS 395, 396, 5849). • 72. AE 1953, 79; AE 1957, 203; HA Pertinax 4.2; Dessau, *Inscripta Selecta* 386; Henry Cohen *Description historique des monnaies frappées sous l'Empire romain*, 8 vols (Paris 1882) iii, p.337. • 73. Dio 72.8; RIC iii.377, 110. • 74. HA Pertinax 3.5–8; HA Commodus 8.4. • 75. Mattingly, BMC iv, p.153. • 76. HA Commodus 6.1–2; Dio 73.8–9. • 77. P.A. Brunt, 'The Fall of Perennis: Dio-Xiphilinus 79.9.2', CQ 23 (1973), pp.172–7. • 78. Birley, *Septimius Severus* op. cit., pp.74, 77. • 79. A canard that was nonetheless accepted as true by Herodian 1.9.1–7. • 80. Dio 73.10; Brunt, 'The Fall of Perennis' loc. cit. • 81. Herodian 1.10.2. • 82. HA Pertinax 3.10–11; HA Commodus 6.11–12. • 83. Herodian 1.3; 1.6–7; 1.10; 1.11.5. • 84. HA Pescennius Niger 3.3–5; HA Commodus 16.2. • 85. Alföldy, *Die Krise* op. cit., pp.69–80; Grosso, *La lotta* op. cit., pp.235–8. For the festival of Hilaria, see M.J. Vermaseren, *Cybele and Attis. The Myth and the Cult* (1977), pp.119–21. For the Maternus revolt as an inspiration to bandits everywhere, see Brent Shaw, 'Bandits', CAH 11, p.365. It should be noted, however, that some severe scholars say that, although the story of revolts in Gaul and Spain is factual, Paternus's antics in Rome are apocryphal (see G. Alföldy, 'Bellum desertorum', *Bonner Jahrbücher* 171 (1971), pp.367–76). • 86. Von Saldern, *Studien* op. cit., pp.190–216. • 87. Dio 73.12.1–5. • 88. HA Pertinax 6.2; HA Commodus 3.3, 6.9; Dio 73.12.3. • 89. L.L. Howe, *The Praetorian Prefect from Commodus to Diocletian AD 180–305* (Chicago 1942). • 90. HA Commodus 9.1. • 91. HA Commodus 6.10–12; 7.1; 8.4. • 92. HA Pertinax 3.5. • 93. Syme, *Emperors and Biography* op. cit., p.132. • 94. Dio 72.9.2; 73.4.1; 73.15.4; B.E. Thomasson, *Laterculi Praesidium* (Gothenburg 1984), pp.232, 384. • 95. HA Commodus 5.8. • 96. HA Commodus 12.8; Dessau, *Inscripta Selecta* 1574. For an exhaustive examination of Commodus's German policy, see Von Saldern, *Studien* op. cit., pp.76–89, 101–9, 135–7. • 97. 'It likely reflects either popular rumour or, if the *Historia Augusta* is correct in stating that Commodus was dissuaded from it by the Senate and people, a stage-managed ceremony designed to deflect general dissatisfaction and assuage the emperor's conscience' (Kerr, 'Chronology', p.249). For the bogus claims relating to Germany on Commodus's coinage see RIC iii.366.3; 401.292; 402.296. • 98. Hekster, *Commodus* op.cit. pp.168–77. • 99. J.H. Oliver, 'Three Attic Inscriptions concerning the emperor Commodus', *American Journal of Philology* 71 (1950), pp.170–9; R.L. Scranton, 'Two Temples of Commodus at Corinth', *Hesperia* 13 (1944), pp.315–48; Von Saldern, *Studien* op.cit., pp.266–88. • 100. HA Commodus 11.9; Hippolytus, *Refutations of All Heresies* 9.7; P. Keresztes, 'A Favourable Aspect of Commodus's Rule', in *Hommages à Marcel Bernard* (Brussels 1969), pp.368–77; H. Chantraine, 'Zur Religionspolitik des Commodus imSpiegel seiner Münzen', *Römische Quartalschrift für Christliche Altertumskunde und Kirchengeschichte* 70 (1975) pp.1–31; see also Keresztes, *Imperial Rome and the Christians* (Lanham, Maryland, 1989), and Keresztes, 'The Imperial Roman Government and the Christian Church', ANRW 2.23.1, pp.247–315 (at pp.304–8). • 101. B. Baldwin, 'Commodus the good poet and good emperor: Explaining the inexplicable', *Gymnasium* 97 (1990), pp.224–31; F.M. Clover, 'Commodus the Poet', *Nottingham Medieval Studies* 32 (1988), pp.19–33; Paul Zanker, *Augustus und die Macht der Bilder* (Munich 1987); Tonio Hölscher, *Römische Bildsprache als semantischer System* (Heidelberg 1987); J. Eisner, *Art and the Roman Viewer. The Transformation of Art from the Pagan World to Christianity* (Cambridge 1995). • 102. HA Commodus 12.12; 13.3. • 103. HA Commodus 10.6–7. • 104. HA Commodus 11.7. • 105. HA Commodus 10.5; 10.9. The mutilations are also detailed in Dio 72.17.2. • 106. HA Commodus 10.4. • 107. HA Commodus 11.1–2. • 108. Dio 72.20; HA Commodus 9.6. • 109. HA Commodus 11.5. • 110. Dio 72.15.3; HA Commodus 11.8. • 111. Syme, RP v, pp.668–9. • 112. Dio 76.5.3–4; Herodian 1.8; 3.10.6–3.11.3. • 113. Grosso, *La lotta* op. cit., pp.539–43. • 114. Dio 72.14.1–3; HA Commodus 8.3. • 115. Hekster, *Commodus* op. cit., pp.164–8; cf. also M. Hammond, *The Antonine Monarchy* (1959), pp.168–70. • 116. HA Pertinax 10.10; 14.6; 15.7. • 117. Dio 72.16.1. • 118. Von Saldern, *Studien* op. cit., pp.162–7. • 119. Dio 72.14.3; Herodian 1.12.1–2. • 120. Von Saldern, *Studien* op. cit., pp.161–2. • 121. Dio 72.24; Herodian 1.14.2–6; Cohen, *Descriptions historiques* op. cit. iii.251. • 122. HA Commodus 14.1–2. • 123. Hekster, *Commodus* op. cit., p.71. • 124. Dio 73.9.4–5; Herodian 1.12.3; HA Commodus 6.10. • 125. HA Pertinax 4.2. • 126. Dio 72.12.14; Alföldy, *Die Krise* op. cit., pp.255–62; C.R. Whitaker, 'The Revolt of Papirius Dionysius in AD 190', *Historia* 13 (1964), pp.348–69. • 127. Dio 72.13; 73.12.1–5; Ammianus Marcellinus 26.6.9. • 128. Dio 73.13.1–6; HA Commodus 7.1; Herodian 1.12.3–1.13.6. • 129. Hekster, *Commodus* op. cit., p.75; Von Saldern, *Studien* op. cit., pp.190–216. • 130. RIC iii.388.201. • 131. HA Commodus 11.3. • 132. HA Commodus 7.4; 11.7.4; Dio 72.14.1. • 133. Von Saldern, *Studien* op. cit., pp.110–11, 193, 249–53. • 134. HA Commodus 7.5–8. • 135. Dio 72.14.3–4. • 136. Herodian 1.1.6; 1.6.1. • 137. Dio 73.16.1; 73.21.1–2. • 138. Herodian 1.15.8; Dio 73.19.5. • 139. HA Commodus 11.10–11; 15.5–6; Dio 73.19.2; 73.20.1; Herodian

1.15.9; Aurelius Victor 17.4.6. • 140. Juvenal, *Satires* 11.8; Petronius, *Satyricon* 117.5; Seneca, *Letters* 4.33.7; Tacitus, *Histories* 11.62.5. It was the infra-dig aspect of patricians becoming gladiators that offended the Roman sense of gravitas and decorum. For the individual gladiator, a slave who knew no better, there could be admiration, particularly from the Stoics, for his courage and indifference to death (M. Wistrand, 'Violence and entertainment in Seneca the Younger', *Eranos* 88 (1990), pp.3–46). • 141. Von Saldern, *Studien* op. cit., pp.180–8. • 142. Dio 73.17.2; 73.20.2. • 143. Hekster, *Commodus* op. cit., pp.8, 158–60; J. Gagé, 'La mystique impériale et l'épreuve des jeux. Commode-Hercule et l'anthropologie herculéenne', ANRW 2.17.2 (1981), pp.663–83. • 144. C. Barton, *The Sorrows of the Ancient Romans. The Gladiator and the Monster* (Princeton 1993), p.34. • 145. Keith Hopkins, *Death and Renewal. Sociological Studies in Roman History* (Cambridge 1983) ii, pp.1–30. • 146. T. Wiedemann, *Emperors and Gladiators* (1992), p.179. • 147. P. Plass, *The Game of Death in Ancient Rome. Arena Sport and Political Suicide* (Wisconsin 1995); K. Coleman, 'Fatal Charades: Roman Executions Staged as Mythological Enactments', JRS 80 (1990), pp.44–73. • 148. Wiedemann, *Emperors and Gladiators* op. cit., pp.110–11. • 149. Michael Grant, *The Antonines* op. cit., p.4; J.H.W.G. Liebeschuetz, 'Religion', CAH 11, p.1001. • 150. J. Beaujeu, *La religion romaine à l'apogée de l'Empire* (Paris 1955), pp.369–412. • 151. Juvenal, *Satires* vi.534. • 152. HA Commodus 9.5–6. • 153. W. Weber, 'Commodus', CAH 11 (1936), p.392. • 154. Dio 72.15.4. • 155. HA Commodus 11.9; ILS 400; BMC iv, p.clxiii; RIC iii. 381.138; 396.255–6; 434.596–7. • 156. RIC iii.392.230; 433.595; 390.221; 432.581; 433.591. • 157. For an analysis of the impact of Hercules on the ancient world, see Alastair Blanshard, *Hercules. A Heroic Life* (2005). For the influence on Alexander the Great, see ibid., pp.89–90. See also C.C. Vermeule, 'Commodus, Caracalla and the Tetrarchs. Roman Emperors as Hercules', in U. Höckmann & A. Krug (eds), *Festschrift für Frank Brommer* (1977), pp.289–94. • 158. RIC iii.379.119; 457.628; 397.261; 282.146; 430.561; BMC iv, pp.xii, clxxiv; CIL iii.395.250; 394.249. • 159. Ralf von den Hoff, 'Commodus als Hercules', in Luca Giuliani (ed.), *Meisterwerke der Antiken Kunst* (Munich 2005), pp.114–35; Michael Stahl, 'Commodus', in Manfred Clauss (ed.), *Die Römischen Kaiser* (Munich 2001) ii, pp.159–69. • 160. M.P. Speidel, 'Commodus the God-Emperor and the Army', JRS 83 (1993), pp.109–14. • 161. Hekster, *Commodus* op. cit., pp.103, 199–202. • 162. ibid. But, as Hekster adds, Hercules was really an ambiguous image to use, as the hero himself was often drunk, lustful and irresponsible (ibid., p.12). • 163. F. Millar, *The Roman Empire and its Neighbours* (1996), p.127. • 164. Dio 72.22.3. • 165. Artemidorus 2.37 (White (ed.), *Dream Interpretation* op.cit., p.119). • 166. Grosso, *La lotta* op. cit., pp.360–9. • 167. Dio 72.24.1–3; Herodian 1.14.1–6; Galen K.2.216; 13.362. • 168. Dio 72.15.1; HA Commodus 8.5–9; 11.8–12.9. And indeed that the epithet Commodianus be applied to everything: the Senate, the people, the fleet, the individual legions, even Carthage (ILS 400). • 169. Herodian 1.16.3–5; F. Kolb, *Literarische Beziehungen zwischen Cassius Dio, Herodian und der Historia Augusta* (Bonn 1972), pp.25–37; Grosso, *La lotta* op. cit., pp.399–405; H. Sidebottom, 'Herodian's historical methods and understanding of history', ANRW 2.34.4 (1998), pp.2775–2836. • 170. Kolb, *Literarische Beziehungen* op. cit., pp.38–47; A.R. Birley, 'The coups d'état of the year AD 193', *Bonner Jahrbuch* 169 (1969), pp.247–80. • 171. HA Commodus 8.6; 17.1.2; Dio 72.22.3; 73.1.1–3; 73.22.4; 73.4.7. • 172. Herodian 1.15.1–6. • 173. Dio 72.20.1; 72.18.1–4. • 174. HA Pertinax 4.4; HA Commodus 16.3; Herodian 1.16.17; 2.1.3; 2.26; 2.1.5–7; Dio 74.1.1–2; F. Cassola, 'Pertinace durante il principato di Commodo', PP 20 (1965), pp.451–77. • 175. Dio 72.19.1–72.21.2; 72.22.1–6; 73.4.3–4; J. Gagé, 'L'assassinat de Commodus et les "sortes Herculis"', *Revue des Études Latines* 46 (1968), pp.280–303. • 176. Dio 72.22.3; 73.1.1–3; HA Pertinax 4.7; 12.1. • 177. HA Commodus 12.10; Dio 72.36.4. • 178. HA Pertinax 10.10; 14.6; 15.7; Dio 74.8.1. • 179. Herodian 2.6.4–5; Dio 74.11.2. • 180. HA Pertinax 4.9–10; Dio 73.3.2–3; Birley, *Septimius Severus* op. cit., p.144; John F. Oates, 'A Sailor's Discharge and the Consuls of 209', *Phoenix* 30 (1976), pp.282–7; E. Champlin, 'Notes on the heirs of Commodus', *American Journal of Philology* 100 (1979), pp.288–306. • 181. HA Caracalla 3.8. • 182. HA Caracalla 5.5. • 183. HA Commodus 18.3–19.3. • 184. Herodian 1.2.1.

Notes to Chapter Eighteen   *pp. 452–493*

• 1. Matthew Arnold, 'Marcus Aurelius', in R.H. Super (ed.), *The Complete Prose Works of Matthew Arnold* (Ann Arbor 1962), iii, pp.134–56. • 2. C. Parain, *Marc-Aurèle* (Paris 1957), p.304. • 3. Frank McLynn, *Robert Louis Stevenson* (1993), p.203. • 4. Edward Gibbon, *Decline and Fall of the Roman Empire* (1776), Chapter Three. • 5. Galen K.6.749–52. In a reverse sense this has become almost as well known as Gibbon's effusion. It is quoted also in Geoffrey de Ste Croix, *The Class Struggle in the Ancient Greek World* (1981), pp.13–14, and by Michael Grant, *The Antonines* op. cit., p.151. • 6. Apuleius, *Metamorphosis* (*The Golden Ass*) 9.12. • 7. Quoted in Ramsay MacMullen, *Corruption and the Decline of Rome* (Yale 1988), p.85. • 8. See Frank McLynn, *Crime and Punishment in Eighteenth-Century England* (1989), *passim*. • 9. Ste Croix, *Class Struggle* op. cit., p.380. • 10. ibid., p.375. • 11. Tertullian, *De Anima* 30. • 12. Ammianus Marcellinus 31.5.14. • 13. Dio 71.36.3; Pescennius Niger, imperial pretender, contrasted Marcus as a kind of combination of Trajan and Antoninus Pius with Commodus, a combination of Lucius Verus and Hadrian or, in other words, a meld of 'puppet and monster' (HA Pescennius Niger 12.1). • 14. Gabor Barta, 'Legende und Wirklichkeit – das Regenwunder des Marcus Aurelius', in Klein, *Marc Aurel* op. cit., pp.347–58; Ste Croix, *Class Struggle* op. cit., p.468; Roger Remondon, *La crise de l'empire Romain de Marc Aurèle à Anastase* (Paris 1964); Rostovsteff (1957), pp.532–41. • 15. Keith Hopkins, *Conquerors and Slaves* op. cit., p.2. • 16. Remondon, *La crise* op. cit., p.71. • 17. E.R. Dodds, *Pagan* and Christian in an Age of Anxiety (Cambridge 1965), p.137; Frend, Martyrdom and Persecution op. cit., p.389. It is only fair to add that this view has been criticised by Peter Brown in The Making of Late Antiquity op. cit., pp.2–4, who claims that Rome was still a 'knowable community' and that neurosis can be explained more simply by urban claustrophobia than by any general systemic angst. • 18. P. Slack, The Impact of Plague in Tudor and Stuart England (1975), p.25. • 19. R. Jackson, Doctors and Diseases in the Roman Empire (1988), pp.179–85; W.S. McNeill, Plagues and Peoples (1994), pp.202–3; P.A. Brunt, Italian Manpower (1987), pp.611–24. • 20. R. Duncan-Jones, 'The Impact of the Antonine plague', Journal of Roman Archaeology 9 (1996), pp.108–36 (at pp.109–13). • 21. Dio 53.33.4; 54.1.2; 66.23.5; 67.11.6; Tacitus, Annals 16.13; Suetonius, Nero 39; HA Hadrian 21.5; HA Antoninus 9.4. • 22. Orosius 7.7.10–11; 7.15.4–6; 7.21.5–6. • 23. Galen K.7.435; 7.467–8; K.17A. 121–2, 235. • 24. Galen K.11.18, 23, 114; 7.468; 17B.642. • 25. See Horace, Epistles 1.7.8–9; Juvenal, Satires 4.56–7; 10.21; Martial 2.16; 2.40; 3.93; 4.80. • 26. Orosius 15.5–6; R. Sallares, Malaria and Rome: A history of malaria in ancient Italy (Oxford 2002), pp.64, 86, 219–22. See also W. Scheidel, 'Germs for Rome', in C. Edwards & G. Woolf (eds), Rome the Cosmopolis (Cambridge 2003), pp.158–76. • 27. Dio 77.13.2. • 28. Sallares, Malaria op. cit., pp.101–3. • 29. Pliny, NH 19.58.180. As Sallares points out, one of the key factors in the elimination of malaria from Rome at the end of the nineteenth century was the destruction of these irrigated gardens (Malaria op. cit., p.211). • 30. Strabo 5.3.5–12. • 31. Livy 32.26; 33.36.1–3. • 32. There is a huge literature on the plague of Justinian, which has been conclusively identified as bubonic plague. For an excellent introduction, see William Rosen, Justinian's Flea (New York 2006). • 33. Thucydides 2.48–65; K.H. Leven, 'Thukydides und die "Pest" in Athen', Medizinhistorisches Journal 26 (1991), pp.128–60. • 34. K.J. Ryan & C.G. Ray (eds), Sherris Medical Microbiology (2004), pp.525–8; J. Longrigg, 'The Plague of Thucydides', Historical Science 18 (1980), pp.209–25; Z. Jezek et al., 'Facial scarring after varicella', American Journal of Epidemiology 114 (1981), pp.798–803; Leven, 'Thucydides' loc. cit., pp.142–4; R. Sallares, The ecology of the ancient Greek world (1991), pp.248–50. • 35. Patrick Olson, 'The Thucydides Syndrome: Ebola Déjà Vu? (or Ebola Reemergent)', Emerging Infectious Diseases 2 (1996), pp.1–23; Alison Bragg, 'Ancient Ebola Virus?', Archaeology, Nov.–Dec. 1996, p.28; Bernard Dixon, 'Ebola in Greece?', British Medical Journal 313 (17 August 1996), p.430; Constance Holden, 'Ebola: Ancient History or New Disease?', Science 272 (14 June 1996), p.1591. • 36. Duncan-Jones, 'Impact' loc. cit., p.136. • 37. ibid., pp.117, 136. • 38. HA Verus 8.1.1–2; Ammianus Marcellinus 23.6.24; 31.6.24; Herodian 1.12.1–2. • 39. Duncan-Jones, 'Impact' loc. cit., pp.135–6; Eutropius 8.12.2. • 40. C. Wells, Bones, Bodies and Disease (1964), p.87; W.H. McNeill, Plagues and Peoples (1977), p.116; P. Armitage, B. West & K. Steadman, 'New Evidence of the Black Rat in Roman London', London Archaeologist 4 (1984), pp.375–83; A.J. Parker, *Ancient Shipwrecks of the Mediterranean and Roman Provinces* (1992), p.551. • 41. W.V. Harris, 'Trade', CAH 11, p.740. • 42. Aurelius Victor 16. • 43. Lucian, *Alexander* 36. • 44. Meds 9.2. • 45. HA Marcus 13.3–6. • 46. *Digest* 11.7.39; 11.7.14.14; 11.7.6.1; 47.12.3.4; 2.4.3. • 47. Thucydides 2.47–8; Livy 8.18; 17.4; 39.41; 40.43; Orosius 3.10. • 48. Paul du Chaillu, *A Journey to Ashango-land* (1867), p.134. • 49. Lucretius, *De Rerum Natura* 6.1116–1286. • 50. For the implausible malaria thesis, see J.C. Russell, *The control of late ancient and medieval population* (Philadelphia 1985), pp.88–9. For exanthematic typhus or bubonic plague (also implausible), see A. Catiglioni, *A History of Medicine* (New York 1941), p.244. • 51. A.M. Behbehani, 'The smallpox story: Life and death of an old disease', *Microbiology Review* 47 (1983), pp.455–509. The reference to 'death' is because the World Health Organisation declared the disease extinct in 1979. This was the first major disease to have been eliminated by the ingenuity of mankind. • 52. W. Atkinson et al. (eds), 'Smallpox', *Epidemiology and Prevention of Vaccine-Preventable Diseases* (2005), pp.281–306. • 53. David A. Koplow, *Smallpox: The fight to eradicate a global scourge* (Berkeley 2003); D.R. Hopkins, *The greatest killer: Smallpox in history* (Chicago 2002); Jonathan B. Tucker, *The Once and Future Threat of Smallpox* (New York 2001). • 54. Galen K.10.360–7; 9.357; 5.115; 17.1.709; 17.2.683. • 55. R.J. Littman & M.L. Littman, 'Galen and the Antonine plague', *American Journal of Philology* 94 (1973), pp.243–55. • 56. Galen K.17.1.882; 7.290; 12.191; 16.106; 17.2.16; 17.2.402. He also explicitly links the Antonine plague with that of Pericles in 431–29 BC (K.12.191). • 57. Behr, *Aelius Aristides* op. cit., pp.96–103. Also in Behr (ed.), *Complete Works* op. cit., pp.289–300. • 58. McNeill, *Plagues and Peoples* op. cit., pp.113–14. • 59. Sallares, *Malaria* op. cit., p.273. • 60. The *locus classicus* for the low estimate of 1–2 per cent is J.F. Gilliam, 'The Plague under Marcus Aurelius', *American Journal of Philology* 82 (1961), pp.225–51. This has attracted the influential support of Ste Croix, *Class Struggle* op. cit., p.648. Cf. also P. Salmon, *Population et dépopulation dans l'empire romain* (1974), pp.133–9. A middling position is taken up by Littman, 'Galen and the Antonine plague' loc. cit., pp.254–5, who estimates a loss of 7–10 per cent in general, with maybe 13–15 per cent in cities and army camps. On this 'middle' position, see also D.W. Rathbone, 'Villages, land and population in Graeco-Roman Egypt', *Proceedings of the Cambridge Philological Society* 216 (1990), pp.103–42 (at pp.114–19). But the overwhelming consensus is that the loss of life was truly catastrophic, maybe at the level of 25 per cent. See Duncan-Jones, 'The Impact of the Antonine plague' loc. cit, p.116; McNeill, *Plagues and Peoples* op. cit., p.113; B. Ebbel, *Beitrage zur ältesten Geschichte einiger Infektionskrankheiten* (Oslo 1967), pp.53–9; Sallares, *The Ecology of the Ancient Greek World* op. cit., p.465; A.E.R. Boak, 'Egypt and the Plague of Marcus Aurelius', *Historia* 8 (1959), pp.248–50; J. Wiseman, *Studies in the Antiquity of Stobi* (Belgrade 1973). Then there is the hugely impressive *oeuvre* of Walter Scheidel, not just the brilliant article 'A model for demographic and economic change in Roman Egypt after the Antonine plague', *Journal of Roman Archaeology* 15 (2002), pp.97–114, but also his other works. It is significant, too, that the most recent scholarly study establishes a mortality rate of 25 per cent (Yan Zelener, 'Smallpox and the disintegration of the Roman economy after 165 AD', PhD thesis, University of Columbia 2003). I quote from the abstract as, sadly, I have been unable to see the original. • 61. Scheidel, 'A model for demographic and economic change' loc. cit. • 62. Duncan-Jones, 'Impact' loc. cit., pp.116–17, 127–9. • 63. W. Scheidel, *Death on the Nile: Disease and the demography of Roman Egypt* (Leiden 2001), pp.20–1, 78–9. • 64. For the numismatic evidence, see Gerald D. Hart, 'The Diagnosis of Disease from Ancient Coins', *Archaeology* 26 (1973), pp.123–7; Hart, 'Disease in the Ancient World; The Numismatic Evidence', *Cornucopiae* 1 (1973), pp.51–66. On army discharge lists, see Gilliam, 'The Plague' loc. cit., pp.236–8, 250, and Duncan-Jones, 'Impact' loc. cit., pp.124–6. For the epigraphic evidence in Rome, see Christer Bruun, 'The Antonine plague in Rome and Ostia', *Journal of Roman Archaeology* 16 (2003), pp.426–34. • 65. See Duncan-Jones, 'Impact' loc. cit., p.121; Scheidel, *Death on the Nile* op. cit.; S. Kambitsis (ed.), *Le Papyrus Thmouis* (Paris 1985), with special reference to coll. 68–169; N. Lewis, 'The Tax Concession of AD 168', ZPE 38 (1980), pp.249–54; Lewis, *On Government and Law in Roman Egypt: Collected Papers of Naphtali Lewis* (Atlanta 1995), pp.244–9, 357–74. R. Bagnall, 'P. Oxy 4527 and the Antonine plague in Egypt: Death or flight?', *Journal of Roman Archaeology* 13 (2000), pp.288–92, suggests that the declining agricultural productivity in Egypt may be the result of panicked flight by the peasantry, rather than mortality. But as Scheidel shrewdly retorts ('A model' loc. cit., p.111), where could they flee to, since there was no employment elsewhere? P. van Minnen has also challenged Bagnall's ideas, especially that of a wheat recovery in Egypt (P. van Minnen, 'P. Oxy. LXVI, 4527 and the Antonine plague in the Fayyum', ZPE 135 (2001), pp.175–7). • 66. And so we return in effect to the older (classic?) historians: B. Niebuhr, *Lectures on the History of Rome*, ed. L. Schmitz (1873), p.733, and O. Seeck, *Geschichte des Untergangs der antiken Welt* (Stuttgart 1923), pp.398–405, who both argue for the views held by Scheidel, Duncan-Jones, McNeill, Zelener and others in our own time. • 67. This is the main thesis of the (to me) convincing account by A.E.R. Boak, *Manpower Shortage and the Fall of the Roman Empire in the West* (Ann Arbor 1955). See also A. Landry, 'Quelques aperçus concernant la dépopulation dans l'antiquité gréco-romaine', *Revue Historique* 77 (1936), pp.1–33. Boak's book attracted surprisingly harsh criticism from M.I. Finley in JRS 48 (1958), pp.156–64, and from Ste Croix in *Population Studies* 10 (1956), pp.118–20. But we should remember that Ste Croix subscribed to the impossibly low figures for the Antonine plague advanced by J.F. Gilliam, 'The Plague' loc. cit. (Ste Croix, *Class Struggle* op. cit., p.648).

• 68. For the location of the *latifundia*, see K.D. White, 'Latifundia', *Bulletin of the Institute of Classical Studies* 14 (1969), pp.62–79. Cf. Garnsey, 'The Land', CAH 11, p.703. We should remember that Pudentilla had 400 slaves on an estate in Tripolitania (R. MacMullen, 'Late Roman Slavery', *Historia* 36 (1987), pp.359–82). R. Martin, 'Les sources littéraires de la notion de latifundium', *Du Latifundium au latifondo? Un héritage de Rome, une création médiévale ou moderne?* (Paris 1995), pp.97–106, takes a sceptical attitude, arguing that there is no real evidence outside the first century AD and that, anyway, the term *latifundium* is too vague. This view has rightly been criticised as 'an excessive preoccupation with legal issues' (Sallares, *Malaria and Rome* op. cit., p.241). Whether you call them *latifundia*, estates or plantations, there is no doubt that huge land holdings still existed as late as the end of the fourth century.
• 69. René Martin, *Recherches sur les agronomes latins et leurs conceptions économiques et sociales* (Paris 1971). • 70. Pliny, NH 18.35. Pliny is a prime source for the *latifundia*. It was he who pointed out that they were more widely scattered through the empire than was conventionally thought, and that just six landlords owned half of all Roman Africa until Nero put them to death (NH 18.35). • 71. Columella, *Rustica* 1.8.16; 3.3.8; 11.1.22; 1.3.12; Pliny, *Letters* 3.19.7; Martial 9.22.4; Juvenal, *Satires* 8.180; Suetonius, *Augustus* 32; Suetonius, *Tiberius* 8. The cheapness of such slaves was what appealed, as many Romans noted (Pliny, *Letters* 3.19.7; Seneca, *De Ben* 7.10.5; Martial 9.22.5). See also R. Martin, 'Pline le jeune et les problèmes économiques de son temps', *Revue des Etudes Anciennes* 69 (1967), pp.62–97. This was no mean consideration in an era when it has been estimated that it cost eight to ten times more per annum to keep a slave in Rome than in Periclean Athens (A.H.M. Jones, 'Slavery in the Ancient World', *Economic History Review* 9 (1956), pp.185–99 (at p.194)). • 72. Pliny, NH 18.21; 18.36–7; cf. also Martial 9.22.5. • 73. Columella, *Rustica* 1.7.6–7; 1.3.12. • 74. Ancient slavery is an academic minefield and even the most harmless-sounding propositions are regarded as controversial. For some different views, see W.V. Harris, 'Towards a Study of the Roman Slave Trade', in J.H. d'Arms & E.C. Kopff (eds), *The Seaborne Commerce of Ancient Rome* (1980), pp.117–40; K.R. Bradley, 'On the Roman slave supply and slave breeding', in M.I. Finley (ed.), *Classical Slavery* (1987), pp.42–64; R. MacMullen, 'Late Roman Slavery', *Historia* 36 (1987), pp.359–82; P.D.A. Garnsey & R. Saller, *The Roman Empire. Economy, Society and Culture* (1987), pp.60–2. But see the robust defence of the thesis of declining slave numbers in the classic account by Max Weber (who characterises this as 'the turning point of ancient civilisation') in his essay 'The social causes of the decline in ancient civilisation', in J.E.T. Eldridge, *Max Weber: The Interpretation of Social Reality* (1971), pp.254–75. • 75. Rostovsteff (1957), pp.194–5. • 76. R.P. Duncan-Jones, 'Some configuration of land holding in the Roman Empire', in M.I. Finley (ed.), *Studies in Roman Property* (Cambridge 1976), pp.7–34. • 77. Pliny, NH 13.92;

Seneca, *De Ben* 7.9.2. • 78. Rostovtzeff (1926), p.298. • 79. Sallares, *Malaria* op. cit., pp.241–2, 244–5. • 80. Ste Croix, *Class Struggle* op. cit., pp.453–503; Perry Anderson, *Passages from Antiquity to Feudalism* (1974). Of course, as Ste Croix has pointed out, the concepts of serfdom and feudalism are logically independent (*Class Struggle*, pp.267–9). • 81. R. Purcell, 'Rome and Italy', CAH ii, p.433. • 82. On the population implosion, see Tertullian's remark 'the city is everywhere' (*De Anima* 30.3) and, in general, Boak, *Manpower Shortages* op. cit., pp.48–54, 120. • 83. A. Carandini, 'Sviluppo e crisi dell manifatture rurali e urbane', in A. Giardina & A. Schiavone (eds), *Società Romana e produzione schiavistica*, 3 vols (Rome 1981) ii, pp.249–60. • 84. W.V. Harris, 'Trade', CAH ii, p.723. • 85. John Charles Edmondson, 'Roman Mining', in S. Hornblower & A.J.S. Spawforth (eds), *The Oxford Companion to Classical Civilisation* (Oxford 1998); J.A. Woods, 'Mining', in J. Wacher (ed.), *The Roman World* (1987) ii., pp.611–34. • 86. Pliny, NH 33.21; 33.66–7; 33.70; 33.95; 33.98; 34.3–9; 34.1–2. Cf. J.F. Healy, 'Pliny on mineralogy and metals', in R. French & F. Greenaway (eds), *Science in the Early Roman Empire: Pliny the Elder, his sources and influence* (1986), pp.111–46; J.F. Healy, 'Mines and Quarries', in M. Grant & R. Kitzinger (eds), *Civilisation of the Ancient Mediterranean. Greece and Rome*, 2 vols (1988) ii, pp.779–93; J.F. Healy, *Mining and Metallurgy in the Roman World* (1978). • 87. C.E. Conophagos, *Le Laurium antique et la technique grecque de la production de l'argent* (Athens 1980); S. Lauffer, *Die Bergwerkssklaven von Laureion*, 2 vols (Munich 1979); P.R. Lewis & G.B.D. Jones, 'The Dolaucothi Gold Mines. The Surface Evidence', *Antiquarian Journal* 49 (1969), pp.244–72; A.E. Aurels & B.C. Burnham, *The Dolaucothi Gold Mines: Geology and Mining History* (Lampeter 1986); O. Davies, *Roman Mines in Europe* (Oxford 1935). • 88. P.A. Brunt, 'Free labour and public works at Rome', JRS 70 (1980), pp.81–100. • 89. Diodorus Siculus 3.12–13; 1.5.36; Pliny, NH 33.98; 31.49; Strabo 12.3.40; Vitruvius 8.6.12; Lucretius, *De Rerum Natura* 6.808–15. • 90. Eusebius HE 8.13–15; Eusebius, *On the Martyrs of Palestine* 5.2; 7.2.4; 8a.1.13; 8.1; 9.1; 8.13; 9.10; 11.6. • 91. Tertullian, *Apol.* 12.5; 29.2. • 92. CIL iii.948–9; F. de Martino, *Storia economica di Roma antica* (Florence 1979), p.316; Rostovsteff (1957), pp.340–3. • 93. Kevin Green, 'Industry and Technology', CAH ii, p.749. • 94. Pliny, NH 23.97; 38.78; 34.49; Strabo 3.2.10; Robert Shepherd, *Ancient Mining* (1993), pp.114–15. • 95. C. Domergue & G. Herail, *Mines d'or Romaines d'Espagne* (Toulouse 1978); D.G. Bird, 'The Roman Gold Mines of North-West Spain', *Bonner Jahrbücher* 172 (1972), pp.36–64; B. Rothenburg & A. Blanco-Freijero, *Studies in Ancient Mining and Metallurgy in South-West Spain* (1982); C. Domergue, *Catalogue des mines et des fonderies antiques de la péninsule Ibérique*, 2 vols (Madrid 1987); G. Gondineau, 'Gaul', CAH ii, p.467. • 96. Diodorus Siculus 5.36–8; 3.12–13. I find unconvincing the arguments of those scholars who seek to diminish the importance of slavery in the mines on the grounds that mining requires skilled labour (see S. Mrozek, 'Die Golbergwerke im Römischen

Dazien', ANRW 2 (1977), pp.102–9; H.C. Noeske, 'Studien zur Verwaltung und Bevölkerung der dakischen Goldbergwerke in römischer Zeit', *Bonner Jahrbücher* 177 (1977), pp.386–415). • 97. Epictetus, *Discourses* 4.1.33–7; Ste Croix, *Class Struggle* op. cit., p.148. For slavery as being like death, see *Digest* 50.17.209. • 98. Wilkes, 'The Danube Provinces', CAH 11, p.595. • 99. John Charles Edmondson, 'Mining in the later empire and beyond: Continuity or disruption?', JRS 79 (1989), pp.84–102; Rostovsteff (1957), p.691. • 100. HA Marcus 11.7; Syme, RP ii, pp.626–8. • 101. Pliny, NH 33.1–5; 33.13. Pliny adds, in a remarkably Aurelian sentiment *avant la lettre*, that the lust for wealth is absurd, as there's always someone richer: 'What badness is it . . . to covet a thing in our lifetime that has either fallen to the lot even of slaves or has reached no limit even in the desires of kings!' (NH 33.47). • 102. Pliny, NH 33.14; 33.5; 33.17. • 103. Ball, *Rome in the East* op. cit., pp.123–33; K.S. Painter, 'Gold and Silver in the Roman World', in W.A. Oddy (ed.), *Aspects of Early Metallurgy* (1977), pp.135–48. • 104. Pliny, NH 19.7–8; Juvenal, *Satires* 8.101; J. Thorley, 'The Silk trade between China and the Roman Empire at its height, circa AD 90–130', GR 18 (1971), pp.71–80. • 105. Tacitus, *Annals* 3.53. • 106. Pliny, NH 9.117; 23.79. • 107. Tertullian, *De Cultu Feminarum* 1.9.3. • 108. Pliny, NH 23.79; 6.101; 12.84; 6.26; 12.41; 19.2.7. • 109. For critics of Pliny's figures, see M.G. Rashke, 'New studies in Roman commerce with the East', ANRW 2.11.9 (1978), pp.604–1378 (at pp.634–7); P. Veyne, 'Mythe et réalité de l'autarcie à Rome', *Revue des Études Anciennes* 81 (1979), pp.261–80. • 110. V. Begley & R.D. de Puma (eds), *Rome and India. The Ancient Sea Trade* (1991), pp.10, 26–31; J.I. Miller, *The Spice Trade of the Roman Empire* (Oxford 1969), pp.223–30; R.E.M. Wheeler, *Rome Beyond the Imperial Frontiers* (1954), p.142; R.M. Cimino, *Ancient Rome and India. Commercial and Cultural Contacts between the Roman World and India* (1994), pp.17–18, 141. • 111. C. Howgego, 'The Supply and Use of Money in the Roman World, 200 BC to AD 300', JRS 82 (1992), pp.1–31. • 112. Gary K. Young, *Rome's Eastern Trade. International Commerce and Imperial Policy, 31 BC–AD 305* (2001), p.77. This was also against all the tenets of Republican 'virtu'. Plutarch said that the only justification for debt was physical survival, and he loathed the idea of incurring debt to buy luxuries (Plutarch, *De vit. aere alieno* 7). • 113. See Jean Andreau, *La vie financière dans le monde romain: les métiers de manieurs d'argent* (Rome 1987); Andreau, *Banking and Business in the Roman World* (1987). • 114. Kevin Greene, 'Industry and Technology', CAH 11, p.751. • 115. Michael Grant, *Roman Imperial Money* (Edinburgh 1954), pp.241–8; R.P. Duncan-Jones, 'Weight loss and circulation patterns in late Roman gold hoards', in François Chausson & Etienne Wolff (eds), *Consuetudinis Amor* (Rome 2003), pp.251–62. • 116. These general remarks are drawn from a reading of: William Carroll Bark, *Origins of the Medieval World* (1958); Donald Kagan, *The End of the Roman World. Decline or Transformation?* (1992); and Bryan Ward-Perkins, *The Fall of Rome and the End of Civilisation* (2005). • 117.

Ball, *Rome in the East* op. cit., p.127. • 118. R. Bland, 'The changing patterns of precious metal hoards in the late empire', *L'Antiquité Tardive* 5 (1997), pp.29–55. • 119. T. Pekary, 'Studien zur Römischen Währungs- und Finanzgeschichte von 161 bis 235 n. Chr.', *Historia* 8 (1959), pp.443–89. • 120. Alexander Demandt, *Der Fall Roms: Die Auflösung des Römischen Reiches im Urteil der Nachwelt* (Munich 1984). • 121. For the controversy over lead poisoning, see John Scarborough, 'The myth of lead poisoning among the Romans: An essay review', *Journal of the History of Medicine and Allied Sciences* 39 (1984), pp.469–75; L. & D. Needleman, 'Lead poisoning and the decline of the Roman aristocracy', *Classical Views* 4 (1985), pp.63–94. The high incidence of suspected poisoning was because wine-makers in Rome insisted on lead pots, as the sweet flavour of lead was thought to enhance food and wine. The latest research shows high levels of atmospheric pollution in lead mining from the first to the end of the second centuries. The findings are part of an examination of the ecology of the ancient world via the Greenland ice cap (see Andrew Wilson, 'Machines, Power and the Ancient Economy', JRS 92 (2002), pp.1–32 (at pp.25–7); also S. Hong, 'Greenland ice evidence of hemispheric lead pollution', *Science* 265 (1994), p.1841; Hong, 'History of Ancient Copper Smelting. Pollution in Greenland Ice', *Science* 272 (1996), p.246; H. Shotyk, 'History of atmospheric lead deposition from a peat bog, Jura mountains, Switzerland', *Science* 281 (1998), p.1635. Of course lead was not the only source of pollution. The air of Rome was unhealthy not only because of mosquitoes and airborne pathogens such as tuberculosis, but also as a result of high levels of pollution from the burning of wood, oil and other materials, causing anthracosis and other diseases (L. Capasso, 'Indoor pollution and respiratory diseases in ancient Rome', *Lancet* 356 (2000), p.1774). • 122. A. Bernardi, 'The economic problems of the Roman Empire at the time of its decline', in C. Cipolla (ed.), *The Economic Decline of Empires* (1970), pp.16–83; T. Pekary, 'Die Staatsfinanzen unter M. Aurelius und Commodus', *Historia* 7 (1958), pp.448–72. • 123. The subject is discussed exhaustively in Graham Webster, *The Roman Imperial Army of the First and Second Centuries* (Oklahoma 1998). • 124. Rostovsteff (1957), pp.354–5. • 125. M.A. Speidel, 'Roman Army pay scales', JRS 82 (1992), pp.87–106. • 126. Campbell, *The Emperor and the Roman Army* op. cit., pp.163–4. • 127. Brent Shaw, 'War and Violence', in G.W. Bowersock, Peter Brown & Oleg Grabar (eds), *Interpreting Late Antiquity* (Harvard 2001), pp.130–69. • 128. HA Marcus 7.9; HA Pertinax 15.7. • 129. HA Didius Julianus 3.2; Herodian 2.7.1. • 130. HA Septimius Severus 5.2; Dio 46.46. • 131. Herodian 3.8.5. • 132. Although the move to military dictatorship can in no sense be blamed on Marcus Aurelius. This was entirely the responsibility of Septimius Severus (Rostovsteff (1957), p.710). • 133. And Marcus repeatedly made it clear that in any conflict between the interest of the state and the entrepreneurial zeal of individual capitalists, the state must always prevail

(Meds 6.44; 4.29; 7.55; 11.4). • 134. Rostovsteff (1926), p.201. • 135. And it got much worse. See the grim struggle unfolded in Ste Croix, *Class Struggle* op. cit., pp.219–21. • 136. A.R. Birley, 'The Third Century Crisis in the Roman Empire', *Bulletin of the John Rylands Library* 58 (1976), pp.253–81. • 137. Campbell, *The Emperor and the Roman Army* op. cit., pp.243–54. • 138. N. Lewis & M. Reinhold, *Roman Civilisation* (New York 1955), pp.183–4; R. MacMullen, *Roman Social Relations 50 BC to AD 284* (Yale 1974), pp.5–12. • 139. Tertullian, *Apol.* 7.3. • 140. Epictetus, *Discourses* 4.1.79; 3.24.117. • 141. A.H.M. Jones in *Proceedings of the British Academy* 5 (1952), pp.347–61; G.W. Bowersock, 'Rostovsteff', *Daedalus* 5 (1974), pp.15–23; Arnaldo Momigliano, *Studies in Historiography* (1985), pp.98–101. • 142. See, for example, on the aftermath of eighteenth-century wars, McLynn, *Crime and Punishment in Eighteenth-Century England* op. cit., pp.323–6. • 143. Barbara Levick, 'Greece and Asia Minor', CAH II, p.632. • 144. Garzetti, *From Tiberius* op. cit., pp.454–5, 457, 466. • 145. Galen K.2 (pp.221–2); A. Mocsy, 'Latrones Dardaniae', *Acta Antiqua Academiae Scientiarum Hungaricae* 16 (1968), pp.351–4; Mocsy, *Gesellschaft und Romanisation in der Römischen Provinz Moesia Superior* (Amsterdam 1970), pp.194–8. • 146. Pliny, *Letters* 6.25. • 147. B. Isaac, 'Bandits in Judaea and Arabia', *Harvard Studies in Classical Philology* 88 (1984), pp.171–203. • 148. A.H.M. Jones, *The Greek City* (1971), pp.211–13. • 149. Campbell, *The Emperor and the Roman Army* op. cit., pp.307–14. • 150. Dio 75.2.5 (cf. Dio 56.4.3); Philostratus VS.2,534; CIL viii.2728; HA Commodus 16.2; HA Pescennius Niger 3.3; Herodian 1.10. • 151. HA Marcus 11.7. • 152. T. Grünewald, *Räuber, Rebellen, Rivalen, Rächer. Studien zu Latrones im Römischen Reich* (Stuttgart 1999), pp.157–95; T. Pekary, 'Seditio, Unruhen und Revolten im Römischen Reich von Augustus bis Commodus', *Ancient Society* 18 (1987), pp.133–50. • 153. *Digest* i.18.13. • 154. Haines op. cit. i., pp.236–7. • 155. *Digest* 47.14.1–2. • 156. *Digest* 49.15.6. • 157. Brent D. Shaw, 'Bandits in the Roman Empire', in Robin Osborne (ed.). *Studies in Ancient Greek and Roman Society* (Cambridge 2004), pp.326–74; R. MacMullen, *Enemies of the Roman Order* (Cambridge, Massachusetts 1967), pp.255–68. • 158. Brent Shaw, 'Rauerbraude', in *Der Neue Pauly: Enzyklopädie der Antiken* (Berlin 2001) 10, pp.758–63; W. Riess, *Apuleius und die Räuber. Ein Beitrag zur historischen Kriminalitätsforschung* (Stuttgart 2001). • 159. Dio 74.2.4–6; 76.6.2; 76.10.1–7; 77.10. • 160. K. Hopwood, 'Bandits, Elites and Rural Order', in A. Wallace-Hadrill (ed.), *Patronage in Ancient Society* (1989), pp.171–87. See also the outstanding summary in Brent Shaw, 'Bandits' loc. cit., pp.366–8. • 161. HA Septimius Severus 18.6; Dio 74.2.5–6; 75.2.4. To appreciate the escalating bandit problem one can 'contextualise' from Dio's earlier remarks on banditry (Dio 56.4.3). • 162. And by the early fourth century brigandage was commonplace in the environs of Rome itself (Symmachus, *Epistulae* ii, p.22). • 163. Richard Saller, 'Status and Patronage', CAH II, p.852. • 164. *Digest* 48.5.398; Rémy, *Antonin le Pieux* op. cit., p.168. • 165. *Digest* 48.3.1.3; 22.5.3. • 166. Ste Croix,

Class Struggle op. cit., pp.455–62. G. Gardascia, 'L'apparition dans le droit des classes d'honestiores et d'humiliores', *Revue du Droit Français et Étranger* 28 (1950), pp.305–37, 461–85; P. Garnsey, *Social Status and Legal Privilege in the Roman Empire* (Oxford 1970), pp.141–7, 213–16; V. Marotti, '*Multa de iure sanxit*'. *Aspetti della politica di Antonio Pio* (Milan 1988) pp.209–17. • 167. Dio 76.9.10; 78.9.5. • 168. For complaints about 'uppity' freedmen, see Tacitus, *Annals* 13.26; Pliny, *Letters* 7.29; Seneca, *Moral Epistles* 47.9. Surprisingly, even Epictetus, an ex-slave, joined in this chorus, lamenting that senators had become 'slaves of slaves' (*Discourses* 4.1.148). • 169. P.R.C. Weaver, 'Social mobility in the early Roman empire: The evidence of the imperial freedmen and slaves', PP 37 (1967), pp.3–20. • 170. H.G. Pflaum, 'Titulaire et rang social sous le Haut-Empire', in C. Nicolet (ed.), *Recherches sur les structures sociales dans l'antiquité classique* (Paris 1970), pp.159–85. • 171. R. MacMullen, *Corruption and the Decline of Rome* (Yale 1988), p.7. • 172. Ste Croix, *Class Struggle* op. cit., pp.492–3. • 173. Saller, 'Status and Patronage' loc. cit., pp.853–4. • 174. Farquharson i, p.264. • 175. Peter Brown, *The World of Late Antiquity* (1971), p.34. • 176. Peter Garnsey, 'Aspects of the decline of the urban aristocracies in the empire', ANRW 2.1. (1974), pp.229–52. • 177. Garnsey & Saller, *The Roman Economy* op. cit., pp.51–2; Rostovsteff (1926), pp.298, 343; Grant, *The Antonines* op. cit., p.151. • 178. See, for example, Pliny, *Letters* 3.19.6. • 179. Ste Croix, *Class Struggle* op. cit., pp.49–69, 179–204, 445, 502. • 180. Rostovsteff (1926), p.333. • 181. For this, see A.H.M. Jones, *The Later Roman Empire* (1964), *passim*. • 182. Keith Hopkins, 'Rome, Taxes, Rent and Trade', in W. Scheidel & S. von Reden (eds), *The Ancient Economy* (Edinburgh 2002), pp.190–230. • 183. Miriam Hopkins, 'Trajan', CAH 11, pp.118–22. • 184. MacMullen, *Corruption* op. cit., p.135. • 185. Grant, *The Antonines* op. cit., pp.66–77. • 186. Dio 68.9.5–6. • 187. For this flight phenomenon in general, see Ste Croix, *Class Struggle* op. cit., p.470. For the detail of some of Marcus's taxes, see *Digest* 50.6.6.5. • 188. Rostovsteff (1926), p.591. • 189. ibid., pp.302–5. • 190. Some of the greatest achievements included the giant bridge at Alcantara in Spain, spanning the Tagus, built by Trajan (C. O'Connor, *Roman Bridges* (1993), pp.109–11). Also the new hexagonal harbour at Ostia, which eclipsed Puteoli in importance (as also those at Terracine, Ancona and Centumcellae – modern Civitavecchia – for which see R. Meiggs, *Roman Ostia* (1973)). For the marble industry, see John Ward-Perkins, 'The Marble Trade and Its Organisation', in J.H.D. Arms & E.C. Kopff (eds), *The Seaborne Commerce of Ancient Rome* (1980), pp.326–8. For the brick industry, see Jean-Jacques Aubert, *Business Management in Ancient Rome* (Leiden 1994), pp.227–39; cf. also CAH 12, pp.232–81; W.V. Harris, 'Roman Terracotta lamps: The organisation of an industry', JRS 70 (1980), pp.126–45; A.H.M. Jones, 'The Cloth Industry under the Roman Empire', *Economic History Review* 13 (1960), pp.183–92. • 191. Andrew Wilson, 'Machines, Power and the Ancient Economy', JRS 92 (2002), pp.1–32. • 192. Keith Hopkins,

Conquerors and Slaves op. cit., is careful to argue that military conquest and its spin-off wealth had the same effect on technological innovation, but only when Rome was still expansionist. • 193. A.H.M. Jones, *The Later Roman Empire* op. cit., p.465. • 194. Pliny the Elder noted that Chinese and Parthian iron was superior to anything Rome could produce (NH 34.41). • 195. Nagayama, *Tamil Culture* op. cit., pp.156–8, 162–80. • 196. *Digest* 7.1.273; 50.4.25. • 197. Suetonius, *Vespasian* 18; Suetonius, *Domitian* 7. Domitian's actions were anyway pointless, as Italian wine could never compete with that from the Greek islands, Asia Minor, Syria or Palestine (Rostovsteff (1926), pp.194–5. • 198. *Digest* 48.13.8.2. • 199. Rostovsteff (1957), p.157; Richard Daniel de Puma, *Rome and India. The Ancient Sea Trade* (Madison, Wisconsin 1991), pp.8–11; R. Mortimer Wheeler, *Rome Beyond the Imperial Frontiers* (1954), pp.138–53; Casson, *Mariners* op. cit., pp.226–7. • 200. Young, *Rome's Eastern Trade* op. cit., pp.53–5. • 201. CIL ii.6278; ILS 5163. • 202. Juvenal, *Satires* 3.305–8. • 203. Ste Croix, *Class Struggle* op. cit., pp.243–9, 511–18. • 204. ibid., pp.247–8. • 205. *Digest* 30.112. • 206. Otto Seeck, *Geschichte des Untergangs der antiken Welt*, 5 vols (Stuttgart 1921) i, pp.404–7; ii, pp.585–90. • 207. 'Looking at the age of the Antonines we find that the role of the individual in relation to the divine is distinctly subdued . . . in the next [*sc.* 3rd] century, the individual will leap into focus' (Brown, *The World of late Antiquity* op. cit., p.26). • 208. Dodds, *Pagan and Christian in an Age of Anxiety* op. cit., p.100; cf. Ramsay MacMullen, *The Roman Government's Response to Crisis, AD 235–337* (Yale 1976). • 209. S. Mazzarino, *The End of the Ancient World* (1966), p.130. • 210. Plutarch, *Themistocles* 18.1. For *philotimia* in Christian thought, see Romans 15.20; 2 Corinthians 5.9; 1 Thessalonians 4.11. • 211. Brown, *The World of Late Antiquity* op. cit., pp.15, 24–5, 27–8, 31, 35–6, 38. • 212. HA Septimius Severus 15.1–2; 16.1–5. • 213. Dio 75.9.4; 75.3.2–3. • 214. Peter Heather, *The Fall of the Roman Empire* (2005), pp.56–63. • 215. Dio 71.36.2; 75.3.2; 76.11.2; 76.121.1; 76.13.2; 78.1.1.

Notes to Chapter Nineteen   *pp. 494–536*

• 1. HA Pescennius Niger 12.1; Syme, *Emperors and Biography* op. cit., p.111. • 2. HA Marcus 19.12. • 3. Julian, *Caesars* 333C; 334A; 328D; 333B; 317C. • 4. ibid. 312; 334–5. • 5. Ammianus Marcellinus 22.14.3. • 6. Julian, *Caesars* 317B; 324D; 328. • 7. J. Bonffartigue, *L'Empereur Julien et la culture de son temps* (Paris 1992), pp.73–6. It has to be said that this is a minority opinion. Those convinced of Julian's sincere admiration for Marcus include Polymnia Athanassiadi, *Julian. An Intellectual Biography* (1992), pp.197–200; J. Matthews, *The Roman Empire of Ammianus* (1989), pp.137–8; B. Baldwin, 'The *Caesares* of Julian', *Klio* 60 (1978), pp.449–66 (esp. pp.453–61); G.W. Bowersock, 'The Emperor Julian and his Predecessors', *Yale Classical Studies* 27 (1982), pp.159–72. • 8. David Hunt, 'Julian and Marcus Aurelius', in D. Innes, H. Hine & C. Pelling (eds), *Ethics and Rhetoric* (Oxford 1995), pp.288–98; Gavin Kelly, 'Constantius II, Julian and the

Example of Marcus Aurelius', *Latomus* 64 (2005), pp.409–16. • 9. Athanassiadi, *Julian* op. cit. • 10. Ammianus Marcellinus 22.14.3; 25.4.22; Julian, *Misopogon* 338B–9B. • 11. Hunt, 'Julian and Marcus Aurelius,' loc. cit. • 12. For further pointers, see Eutropius, *Breviarium* 10.16.3; Ammianus Marcellinus 21.16.11; 31.5.13–14; 31.10.19; 27.6.16. Some modern scholars, indeed, claim that Julian is a surer guide to the 'real' Marcus Aurelius than Marcus's contemporary Lucian. See Howard D. Weinbrot, *Menippean Satire Reconsidered. From Antiquity to the Eighteenth Century* (Johns Hopkins 2005). • 13. By, for example, Gilbert Murray in *Five Stages of Greek Religion* (1935), pp.213–14. • 14. See, for example, the passages in *Confessions* 8.8. on the struggle between reason and desire, which irresistibly recall Marcus in Meds 11.20. • 15. Peter Brown, *Augustine of Hippo* (1967), p.173. • 16. Augustine, *Confessions* 2.4. • 17. *Confessions* 11.20. • 18. Michael L. Humphries, 'Michel Foucault on Writing and the Self in the *Meditations* of Marcus Aurelius and the *Confessions* of St Augustine', *Arethusa* 30 (1997), pp.125–38. • 19. Augustine, *City of God* 22.24. • 20. *Confessions* 10.57; *De Ordine* 1.25. • 21. *Confessions* 1.23. By contrast he was an enthusiastic Latinist and adored Virgil (*City of God* 1.3). • 22. Although some passages of the *Confessions* can be cited showing a Pauline concern with 'God within' or Man as part of the divine body (*Confessions* 4.16). • 23. *Confessions* 4.16; *City of God* 8.5. • 24. Augustine also thought Stoicism was misled by astrology. For the most recent thinking on this subject, see Gareth B. Matthews, *Augustine* (Oxford 2005), and James O'Donnell, *Augustine. A New Biography* (2005). • 25. Henry Chadwick, *The Early Church* (1993), pp.232–3. • 26. *Confessions* 2.2; 3.1; 4.2. • 27. *Confessions* 6.15. • 28. *Confessions* 8.7. • 29. Meds 2.15 is the most obvious source. See above • 30. Ammianus Marcellinus 5.4.2. • 31. Henry Chadwick, *Boethius. The Consolations of Music, Logic, Theology and Philosophy* (Oxford 1981); John Marenbon, *Boethius* (Oxford 2003). • 32. *Consolations* 2.41. • 33. *Consolations* 2.44; 3.58. • 34. *Consolations* 4.117. • 35. *Consolations* 4.127; 5.141–3. • 36. *Consolations* 3.93. • 37. *Consolations* 1.8. • 38. Chadwick, *The Early Church* op. cit. • 39. Henry Corbin, *History of Islamic Philosophy* (1993). L.E. Goodman, *Avicenna* (Cornell 2006); Barry S. Kogan, *Averroes and the Metaphysics of Causation* (1985). • 40. Meds 7.44–6; 7.48; 9.29; 10.23. • 41. This is not the place to revive the ancient Plato-versus-Aristotle controversy, which will always to some extent be a dialogue of the deaf or, to cite the old joke, 'Fishwives who bawl at each other through windows across the street will never agree that they're arguing from different premises'. Philosophical temperament will always decide the outcome. For example, for A.N. Whitehead, modern philosophy was 'a series of footnotes to Plato' (*Process and Reality* (1929), p.39) whereas for Geoffrey Ste Croix, Aristotle was incomparably the superior thinker (*Class Struggle* op. cit., pp.68–80). • 42. Respectively, Thomas à Kempis, *Imitation of Christ* 2.1; 2.5; 1.20; 1.22; 1.13; 3.11; 1.7; 3.24; 3.41; 1.9; 1.10; 1.12; 1.6; 1.3; 2.10; 2.6; 1.11; 1.14; 1.8. The similarities between the *Meditations* and the *Imitation of Christ* were also pointed out by Matthew Arnold in 'Marcus Aurelius', *The Complete Prose Works of Matthew Arnold*, ed. R.H. Super (Ann Arbor 1962) iii, pp.133–4. • 43. *Imitation* 1.23. This closely follows what Marcus has to say in Meds 2.5; 4.17; 4.48. • 44. *Imitation* 2.3; 3.53; cf. Meds 8.48; 7.29. • 45. *Imitation* 2.6; 1.21; cf. Meds 4.20; 7.24. • 46. *Imitation* 3.32; 3.12; 3.37; 3.43; 3.18–19. • 47. *Imitation* 4.7. • 48. *Imitation* 1.23. • 49. *Imitation* 3.54. • 50. Montaigne, *Essays* 2.2. • 51. Montaigne, *Essays* 1.19; 2.17; 3.1; 2.12; 3.13. • 52. Farquharson i, pp.xiii–xxii. • 53. Michael P. Mezzatesta, 'Marcus Aurelius, Fray Antonio de Guevara and the Ideal of the Perfect Prince in the Sixteenth Century', *The Art Bulletin* 66 (1984), pp.620–33; David A. Lupher, *Romans in a New World: Classical Models in Sixteenth Century Spanish America* (Ann Arbor 2003), pp.50–6. • 54. Thomas Gataker, *M. Antonini imp. de rebus suis* (Cambridge 1652), praeloquium p.18. • 55. A.A. Long, 'Stoicism in the Philosophical Tradition', *The Cambridge Companion to the Stoics* op. cit., pp.365–92 (esp. pp.369–79). • 56. For example, Browne was a convinced believer in witches and witchcraft (*Religio Medici* 1.47). • 57. *Religio Medici* 1.47. • 58. Browne, *Pseudoxica Epidemica* 6.1. • 59. *Religio Medici* 2.12; 1.15; Frank Livingstone Huntley, *Sir Thomas Browne. A Biographical and Critical Study* (Ann Arbor 1962), pp.228–9; Olivier Leroy, *Le Chevalier Thomas Browne* (Paris 1931), pp.345–6. • 60. *Religio Medici* 1.55. • 61. Blaise Pascal, *Pensées* 7.453. • 62. *Pensées* 6.387. • 63. *Pensées* 3.220; 1.18; 2.80; 2.63–5; 5.325; 7.466–7; 13.814; 6.350; 7.431. • 64. *Pensées* 2.73; 2.150–1; 6.404; 6.412. • 65. *Pensées* 7.451; 1.44; 2.101; 2.171; 6.345; 6.379; 3.199. • 66. *Pensées* 6.394. • 67. *Pensées* 6.360. • 68. *Pensées* 7.481. • 69. Hadot, *Inner Citadel* op. cit, pp.124–5. • 70. Compare, for instance, Meds 3.10 with *Pensées* 2.72. • 71. *Pensées* 2.172. • 72. *Pensées* 2.176. • 73. *Pensées* 2.132. • 74. *Pensées* 2.148. • 75. *Pensées* 6.386. • 76. Joseph Butler, *Analogy of Religion, Natural and Revealed* (1736) 1.1.15; Butler, *Two Dissertations* ii.4. Butler quotes Meds 9.3–4, 9.16 and 9.19. See also A.A. Long, 'Stoicism in the Philosophical Tradition' loc. cit., pp.382–9; E.C. Mossner, *Bishop Butler and the Age of Reason* (1936). • 77. See Robert Voitle, *The Third Earl of Shaftesbury 1671–1713* (Baton Rouge, Louisiana 1984); Stanley Grean, *Shaftesbury's Philosophy of Religion and Ethics* (Athens, Ohio 1967). • 78. Alexander Pope, *An Essay on Criticism* ll.68–9. • 79. Alexander Pope, 'The Temple of Fame' ll.165–7. • 80. Alexander Pope *An Essay on Man* iv.ll.233–6; i.ll.267–8, 289–94. • 81. Christopher Brooke, 'How the Stoics became Atheists', *Historical Journal* 49 (2006), pp.387–402; Jill Kraye, '"Ethnicorum omnium sanctissimus": Marcus Aurelius and his *Meditations* from Xylander to Diderot', in Jill Kraye & M.W.F. Stone (eds), *Humanism in Modern Philosophy* (2000), p.114. • 82. Voltaire, 'Humility', *A Philosophical Dictionary*, trans. E.R. Dumont (1901). • 83. Montesquieu, *Considérations sur les causes de la grandeur des Romains et leur décadence* (1734), Chapter 16. • 84. See Alexander Broadie (ed.), *The Cambridge Companion to the Scottish Enlightenment* (Cambridge 2003); William R. Scott, *Francis Hutcheson* (Cambridge 1990); Lisa Hill, *The Passionate Society. The Social, Political and Moral*

Thought of Adam Ferguson (2006). • 85. P. Minowitz, *Profits, Priests and Princes: Adam Smith's Emancipation of Economics from Politics and Religion* (Stanford, California 1993), p.154; P.H. Clarke, 'Adam Smith, Stoicism and Religion in the Eighteenth Century', *History of Human Sciences* 13 (2000), pp.49–72; Athol Fitzgibbons, *Adam Smith's System of Liberty, Wealth and Virtue* (Oxford 1995), p.34. • 86. Adam Smith, *The Theory of Moral Sentiments* (1759), Part 7, Section 2, Chapter One. • 87. Victor Goldschmidt, *Le système stoïcien et l'idée de temps* (Paris 1979), pp.120–1; Martha Nussbaum, 'Kant and Stoic Cosmopolitanism', in J. Bohman & M. Lutz-Bachmann (eds), *Kant's Idea of Perpetual Peace* (Cambridge, Massachusetts 1997). • 88. Charles Darwin, *The Descent of Man*, Part One, Chapter Four, pp.149, 188–9 (1922 edn). • 89. Arnold, 'Marcus Aurelius' loc. cit. iii, p.156. • 90. ibid., pp.134–5, 136, 144, 156. • 91. ibid., p.149. • 92. John M. Robson et al. (eds), *The Complete Works of John Stuart Mill* (1981) viii, p.1073; cf. vii, p.197. • 93. ibid. i, p.532. • 94. John Stuart Mill, 'On Liberty', ibid. xv, p.602. • 95. ibid. xviii, p.236. • 96. ibid. xviii, p.237. • 97. John Coates, 'Renan and Pater's *Marius the Epicurean*', *Comparative Literary Studies* 37 (2000), pp.402–22. • 98. Bryan Magee, *The Philosophy of Schopenhauer* (Oxford 1997); Christopher Young & Andrew Brook, 'Schopenhauer and Freud', *International Journal of Psychoanalysis* 75 (1994), pp.101–18. • 99. Harry J. Ausmus, 'Schopenahauer and Christianity', *Illinois Quarterly* 36 (1974), pp.26–42. • 100. Meds 6.46. • 101. For the most explicit statement by Marcus on eternal recurrence, see Meds. 7.49.2. For Lucretius's view, see *De Rerum Natura* 3.944. • 102. Arthur Schopenhauer, *The World as Will and Representation*, trans. E.F.J. Payne, 2 vols (New York 1966) ii, p.444. • 103. See in general Curtis Cate, *Friedrich Nietzsche* (2002); B. Magnus & K. Higgins, *The Cambridge Companion to Nietzsche* (Cambridge 1996). • 104. Friedrich Nietzsche, *The Antichrist*, trans. L. Mencken (1920) (esp. Sections 5, 7, 15, 22, 23, 51, 57). • 105. ibid., Section 11. • 106. Nietzsche, *Zweite Abteilung: Der Wanderer und sein Schatten* (1880), Section 185; R.J. Hollingdale, *Nietzsche. The Man and His Philosophy* (Cambridge 1999), pp.145–6, 164–6, 224–5. • 107. Nietzsche, *Ecce Homo*, ed. & trans. Walter Kaufmann (New York 1967) p.258; 'Nietzsche contra Wagner', in W. Kaufmann (ed.), *The Portable Nietzsche* (New York 1954), p.680; Nietzsche, *The Will to Power*, ed. & trans. W. Kaufman (New York 1968), pp.532–3, 536–7; Nietzsche, *Die Fröhliche Wissenschaft* (1882), p.276. • 108. See Matthew Arnold's remarks in 'Marcus Aurelius' op. cit., p.140. • 109. G.W. Allen, 'Walt Whitman and Stoicism', in D.J. Macmillan (ed.), *The Stoic Strain in American Literature* (Toronto 1979), pp.43–60. • 110. Brand Blanshard, *Four Reasonable Men* (1984). For Blanshard himself, see P.A. Schilpp (ed.), *The Philosophy of Brand Blanshard* (La Salle, Illinois 1980). • 111. Henri Bergson, *Time and Free Will* (1910); J.M.E. McTaggart, *The Nature of Existence* (1927). • 112. Bart Schultz, *Henry Sidgwick. Eye of the Universe* (Cambridge 2004). See also Blanshard, *Four Reasonable Men* op. cit. It must be conceded that the Epicureans may have been an even bigger influence on

Sidgwick than the Stoics (Schultz, *Sidgwick* op. cit., pp.142, 688). • 113. Here the key texts are A.N. Whitehead, *Process and Reality* (1929) and S. Alexander, *Space, Time and Deity* (1920). • 114. For the 'heirs of Freud' view, see Richard Wollheim, *The Thread of Life* (1984), p.163; L.H. Martin, G. Gutman & P.H. Hutton (eds), *Technologies of the Self: A Seminar with Michel Foucault* (Amherst 1988), pp.37–8. • 115. Stoicism is well to the fore in both Theodore Dreiser's *Sister Carrie* and Tom Wolfe's *A Man in Full*. Joseph Brodsky has written a long essay on Marcus in *On Grief and Reason* (New York 1995). Maurice Maeterlinck is fascinated with (though ambivalent about) Marcus. He quotes him approvingly in *Le Temple Enseveli* (1902), to the effect that a man cannot retire better than to his own soul, but in *La Sagesse et La Destinée* (1898) argues that both Marcus and Jesus Christ did not suffer as much as Hamlet or Oedipus. In *Le Trésor des Humbles* (1896) he claims that the silence of a child is wiser than the speech of Marcus Aurelius. Anatole France was particularly drawn to Marcus's analytical-synthetic method, first stripping down everything to its essential elements, then seeing how all the parts relate to the whole – a classical summary of the 'whole greater than the sum of its parts' proposition (Meds 3.11; 11.2). He explicitly used the method when describing Madame Gance in *Le Livre de mon ami* in *Oeuvres* i, p.515 (Pleiade edn, Paris 1994). • 116. For the issues thrown up by autobiography in general I have used Roy Pascal, *Design and Truth in Autobiography* (Harvard 1960); James Olney, *Memory and Narrative* (Chicago 1998); Jerome Hamilton Buckley, *The Turning Key* (Harvard 1984); and Carolyn A. Barros, *Autobiography: Narrative of Transformation* (Ann Arbor 1998). The great disappointment was Philippe Lejeune, *On Autobiography* (Minneapolis 1989), which was no help at all, quite apart from the fact that nearly all his examples are drawn from twentieth-century literature. This is a typical product of French academe, over-theoretical, over-conceptual, hypertrophied in every sense, exhibiting the usual Gallic obsession with dissolving the concrete into the abstract and the abstract into the even more abstract. For the neurotic and mendacious element in autobiography, see J. Strachey (ed.), *Standard Edition of the Works of Sigmund Freud*, 24 vols (1974), Vol. 21, p.182. Freud's point is made more pithily and in typical crackerjack fashion by the American humorist Will Rogers: 'When you put down the good things you ought to have done, and leave out the bad ones you did do – well, that's memoirs' (*The Autobiography of Will Rogers* (1949). • 117. Pascal, *Design and Truth in Autobiography* op. cit., p.8. • 118. Gilbert Murray, *Five Stages of Greek Religion* (1935), pp.213–14. • 119. J.S. Mill, *Autobiography* (New York 1924), pp.3–4, 6–7, 12, 19–20, 21. • 120. ibid., pp.22–4, 27–9, 32–4. • 121. ibid., p.94. • 122. ibid. • 123. Buckley, *The Turning Key* op. cit., p.80. • 124. Mill, *Autobiography* op. cit. • 125. ibid., p.100. • 126. Buckley, *The Turning Key* op. cit., p.79. • 127. Pascal, *Design and Truth* op. cit., p.22. • 128. ibid., p.29. • 129. Carolyn A. Barros, *Autobiography* op. cit., pp.85–116. • 130. J.H. Newman, *Apologia pro Vita Sua*

(1864), p.42. • 131. Sheridan Gilley, *Newman and his Age* (1990), p.325. • 132. Herbert Paul (ed.), *Letters of Lord Acton to Mary, daughter of the Right Honourable W.E. Gladstone* (1904), p.lx. • 133. J.E.C. Bodley, *Cardinal Manning* (1912), p.22. • 134. Barros, *Autobiography* op. cit., pp.51–83. • 135. Newman, *Apologia pro Vita Sua*, p.216. • 136. ibid., pp.15–16. • 137. ibid., pp.217–18. • 138. Jean Starobinsky, *Jean-Jacques Rousseau, Transparency and Obstruction* (Chicago 1988), p.115. • 139. Delusional incidents: S. Elosu, *La maladie de Rousseau* (Paris 1929). Paranoia: A. Chatelain, *La Folie de Jean-Jacques Rousseau* (Neuchâtel 1890); P. Sérieux & P. Capgras, *Les folies raisonnantes* (Paris 1909). Latent homosexuality: 'Étude sur Jean-Jacques Rousseau', *Psychopathologie de l'échec* (Paris 1944). • 140. Starobinsky, *Jean-Jacques Rousseau* op. cit., p.371. • 141. Jean-Jacques Rousseau, 'Émile', *Oeuvres Complètes de Rousseau* (Pleiade) iv, p.268. • 142. Starobinsky, *Jean-Jacques Rousseau* op. cit., p.167. • 143. Jean-Jacques Rousseau, *Confessions* (1892). • 144. ibid., pp.68–70. • 145. ibid., p.167. • 146. ibid., p.207. • 147. ibid., pp.302, 355, 513. • 148. ibid., p.300. • 149. ibid., p.309. • 150. ibid., p.306. • 151. ibid., pp.508–36. • 152. Starobinsky, *Jean-Jacques Rousseau* op. cit., p.48. • 153. *Confessions* op. cit., p.296. • 154. ibid., p.343. • 155. Starobinsky, *Jean-Jacques Rousseau* op. cit., pp.33–64. • 156. Quoted in ibid., p.61. • 157. *Confessions*, p.341; also *Oeuvres Complètes* op. cit., i., pp.386–8. • 158. *Confessions*, p.343. • 159. For example, Meds 11.22; 4.48. • 160. *Confessions*, p.14. • 161. ibid., pp.45, 72, 119, 343, 352. • 162. ibid., p.9. • 163. For this entire issue, see David Reynolds, *In Command of History. Churchill Fighting and Writing in the Second World War* (2004). • 164. Andrew M. Riggsby, *Caesar in Gaul and Rome* (Austin, Texas 2006). • 165. Kathryn Welch & Anton Powell (eds), *Julius Caesar as Artful Reporter: The War Commentaries as Political Instruments* (Swansea 1998). • 166. Riggsby, *Caesar in Gaul and Rome* op. cit., pp.207–13. • 167. J.E. Lendon, 'The Rhetoric of Combat', *Classical Antiquity* 18 (1999), pp.273–329. • 168. U.S. Grant, *Personal Memoirs* (1885), pp.175–8. • 169. ibid., p.60. • 170. ibid., pp.197–9. To say nothing of the measles and smallpox he observed among the Indians of the Columbia River (ibid., pp.205–6). • 171. ibid., p.182. • 172. ibid., p.68. • 173. ibid., p.165. • 174. ibid., p.248. • 175. ibid., p.521. • 176. ibid., p.213. • 177. For the construction of the myth, see David Horspool, *Why Alfred Burned the Cakes* (2006). • 178. Malcolm Godden, 'The player king: identification and self-representation in King Alfred's writings', in Timothy Reuter (ed.), *Alfred the Great* (2006), pp.137–50; cf. also, for Alfred as philosopher-king, Richard Abels, *Alfred the Great. War, Kingship and Culture in Anglo-Saxon England* (1998). • 179. Godden, 'The player-king' loc. cit., p.149. • 180. By far the best book on St Louis is Jacques Le Goff, *Saint Louis* (Paris 1996). Amazingly erudite and scholarly, it has just one flaw: the astonishingly exiguous space given to the Mongols (whom Goff dismisses cavalierly as *L'Illusion Mongole* on pp.552–5). For Louis's anti-body prudishness, see ibid., pp.860–1; for his saintliness ibid., pp.827–86; and for his attitude to the Jews ibid., pp.793–814. • 181. Giles MacDonough,

Frederick the Great (1999), pp.121–3. • 182. There is no satisfactory biography in English of Benedict XIV. Renee Haynes's *Philosopher-King* (1970) is a very superficial and unsatisfactory sketch. Those wishing to get a flavour of the man's thought and personality should consult Emilia Morelli, *Le lettere di Benedetto XIV al Card. de Tencin* (Rome 1955). • 183. The definitive Smuts biography is by W.H. Hancock in two volumes (1968). • 184. Epictetus, *Discourses* 4.76. • 185. Meds 6.4.5. • 186. Galen K.19.263–70. • 187. Meds 4.33; 4.40; 6.38; 7.9; 7.54; 8.7; 9.6–7. Cf. Hadot, *Inner Citadel* op. cit., p.44. • 188. Pope, *An Essay on Man* i.237. • 189. Oliver Lodge, *Modern Scientific Ideas* (1927), p.13. • 190. Edward Young, *Night Thoughts* (1745), Book One. • 191. William Blake, 'Auguries of Innocence'. • 192. Francis Thompson, 'The Mistress of Vision' (1897). • 193. J.C. Smuts, *Holism and Evolution* (1926), pp.92–5. • 194. ibid., pp.268–70. • 195. ibid., pp.158–61. • 196. ibid., pp.2–5. • 197. ibid., pp.11–15. • 198. ibid., pp.32–4. • 199. ibid., pp.59–61; 182–223. • 200. ibid., pp.88–9. • 201. This idea, that philosophers had ignored the body, was later taken up with gusto by Maurice Merleau-Ponty. See M.R. Barral, *Merleau-Ponty. The Role of the Body-Subject* (Pittsburgh, Pennsylvania 1965). • 202. Smuts, *Holism and Evolution* op. cit., p.139. • 203. ibid., pp.1–2, 17, 31, 336–8. • 204. ibid., pp.116, 260, 239. • 205. ibid., pp.341–2. • 206. ibid., p.92. • 207. ibid., p.317. • 208. ibid., p.301. • 209. ibid., p.337. • 210. ibid., pp.106–7. • 211. ibid., pp.110, 184, 343.

Notes to Appendix One   *pp. 538–554*

• 1. For Zeno, see Gilbert Murray, *The Stoic Philosophy* (1915); Barth, *Die Stoa* (Stuttgart 1922). • 2. Alexander Jones, 'The Stoics and the Astronomical Sciences', in Brad Inwood (ed.), *The Cambridge Companion to the Stoics* (Cambridge 2003), pp.328–44. • 3. F.H. Sandbach, *The Stoics* (1975), pp.82, 111–15; Seneca, Letter 102; R.J. Hankinson, 'Stoicism and Medicine', *The Cambridge Companion to the Stoics* op. cit., pp.295–309 (at pp.299–301). But see Galen's idiosyncratic view of *pneuma* in K.5.281; 287–9; 4.674. • 4. This was a very influential part of Stoic doctrine and was even accepted by some Christians (Tertullian, *De Carne Christi* 11). • 5. W. Tarn, *Hellenistic Civilization* (1927), p.287; J. Gernet, *Chine et Christianisme* (Paris 1991), p.192. • 6. A.A. Long, *Hellenistic Philosophy* (1974), pp.197–8. • 7. A.A. Long & D.N. Sedley (eds), *The Hellenistic Philosophers* (Cambridge 1987), *passim*. • 8. A.A. Long, *Epictetus* (Oxford 2002), p.14. • 9. L. Kolakowski, *Main Currents of Marxism* (Oxford 2005), pp.254–5. • 10. Sandbach, *The Stoics* op. cit., p.59. • 11. Hume, *A Treatise of Human Nature* (1740), 2.3.3.4. • 12. T.H. Irwin, 'Stoic Naturalism and its critics', *The Cambridge Companion to the Stoics* op. cit., pp.345–64. • 13. Epictetus, *Discourses* 1.17.27; Michel Foucault, *Histoire de la Sexualité, Vol.3 Le Souci de Soi* (Paris 1984), pp.101–17. • 14. Seneca, Letter 92. • 15. Seneca, Letter 8; Keimpe Algra, 'Stoic Theology', *The Cambridge Companion to the Stoics* op. cit., pp.153–78 (at p.171). • 16. Diogenes Laertius, 7.177. • 17. There is a huge literature in

Stoicism on the 'representations', as we note below (pp.221–5) in our discussion of Epictetus. Two handy references in Marcus Aurelius's own work are at Meds 7.68 and 8.50. • 18. Seneca, Letter 53. • 19. Hahn, *Der Philosoph und die Gesellschaft* (Stuttgart 1989); J.M. Rist, 'Are you a Stoic? The Case of Marcus Aurelius', in B.F. Meyer & E.P. Saunders (eds), *Jewish and Christian Self-Definitions* (1983) iii, p.23. • 20. Hadot, *The Inner Citadel* op. cit., *passim*. One can well understand why R.B. Rutherford remarks that Stoicism was 'never a popular or an easy doctrine' (Rutherford, p.180). • 21. Seneca, Letters 70, 8–12, 18; M.D. Griffin, *Seneca. A Philosopher in Politics* (Oxford 1976). • 22. 'Marcus Aurelius writes to himself; Seneca writes to an alter ego' (C.D.N. Corta (ed.), *Seneca* (1974), p.75). • 23. Seneca, Letters 77, 86; Seneca, *Cons. Helv.* 14.3; Seneca, *Nat. Quaest* 3.7.1; Tacitus, *Annals* 13.42; 14.57; Juvenal, *Satires* 5.109; Martial 12.36; Columella, *Rustica* 3.3. • 24. Keimpe Algra et al. (eds), *The Cambridge History of Hellenistic Philosophy* (2006), p.734. • 25. ibid., pp.735–6. • 26. Seneca, Letter 71; Paul Veyne, *Seneca. The Life of a Stoic* (2003), p.85. • 27. Hadot, *Inner Citadel* op. cit., p.192. Stoicism's air of self-confidence is predicable only of the sage who may never exist, nor ever have existed. But once you remove the aplomb, you are back with ordinary hunches and probability and, even, tea-chest philosophy. • 28. Cicero, *De Finibus* 3.60; J.M. Rist, *Stoic Philosophy* (1969), p.233 (on Chrysippus); Diogenes Laertius 7.130; Epictetus, *Discourses* 1.9.2–6; 2.1.19. • 29. Seneca, Letter 71. • 30. Rist, *Stoic Philosophy* op. cit., pp.231–55. • 31. Veyne, *Seneca* op. cit., pp.103, 110. • 32. Seneca, Letters 108, 83, 87, 123; Tacitus, *Annals* 15.64; Dio 62.25–30. • 33. Sandbach, *The Stoics* op. cit., p.155. • 34. Dio 62.2. • 35. Veyne, *Seneca*, op. cit., p.138, • 36. Seneca, *On Benefits* 3.20–1; H. von Arnim (ed.), *Stoicorum Veterum Fragmenta* (1905) iii, pp.351–7. • 37. Veyne, *Seneca*, p.141. • 38. Musonius, *Diatribes* 19.108; Veyne, *Seneca*, p.14 • 39. Seneca, Letter 95; Veyne, *Seneca*, p.144. • 40. ibid., p.146. • 41. H.R. Neuenschwander, *Mark Aurels Beziehungen zu Seneca und Poseidonios* (Berne 1975), pp.7, 10, 97. • 42. Haines ii, pp.100–8. • 43. Seneca, *On Benefits* 2.27. • 44. Lucian, *Philopseudus, passim; Hermotimus* 4–7. • 45. Dio 71.35.1–2. • 46. Epictetus, *Discourses* 1.13.3; Seneca, *On Constancy* 14.1; Seneca, *Cons. Helv.* 16–17. • 47. J.M. Rist, *The Stoics* (Berkeley 1978), p.263. • 48. Musonius, *Fragment* 17. This is a curious pre-echo of the twentieth-century theorist Ernst Bloch's notion in *Das Prinzip Hoffnung* that God does not yet exist, but he will in the future. • 49. Cicero, *De Officiis* 3.6. • 50. Julia Annas, *The Morality of Happiness* (New York 1993), pp.306–11. • 51. *Stoicorum Veterum Fragmenta* op. cit. iii, pp.314–26. • 52. S. Bobzien, *Determinism and Freedom in Stoic Philosophy* (Oxford 1998). • 53. Ted Honderich, *A Theory of Determinism: The Mind, Neuro-Science and Life Hopes* (Oxford 1988). • 54. Cicero, *De Officiis* 1.107–15. • 55. Meds 10.33. • 56. Hadot, *The Inner Citadel* op. cit., p.209. • 57. For this reason it is probably a mistake to count Galen as a Stoic. He locates the centre of the self in the brain, not the heart, as most mainstream Stoics do (Galen K.3.20; 3.641;

4.347). • 58. Matthew 6.3. • 59. Seneca, Letter 92. • 60. Christopher Gill, *Marcus Aurelius's Meditations* (1997), pp.xi–xii. • 61. See, for example, Epictetus, *Discourses* 1.14.13–14; 2.8.10–11. • 62. Long, *Epictetus* op. cit., pp.147–8. • 63. John Stuart Mill, 'Three Essays on Religion', in Mill, *Collected Works* (Toronto 1969) x, p.369. • 64. A.Bodson, *La morale sociale des derniers stoïciens: Sénèque, Épictète et Marc Aurèle* (Paris 1967); E.V. Arnold, *Roman Stoicism* (1911). • 65. Epictetus, *Discourses* 3.21.4–6. • 66. M.T. May, *Galen on the Usefulness of the Parts of the Body*, 2 vols (Ithaca 1968); D.E. Eichholz, 'Galen and his environment', GR 20 (1951), pp.60–71. • 67. Hume, *Dialogues Concerning Natural Religion* (1779), Part Five. • 68. One could, of course, spend an entire volume discussing Stoicism – many eminent writers have done so. But even its most elementary propositions always seem to generate confusion or paradox. Take Epictetus's proposition that intention is everything and consequences nothing in the contemplation of a moral action (Epictetus, *Discourses* 2.16.5). The morality is supposed to lie in the intention, for the end is decreed by Providence. But then, to escape the free-will/determinism dilemma a distinction is introduced between 'goals' and 'ends'. Goals are what we aim for probabilistically, as when an archer aims at a target, while the end is directed by Providence. Then Epictetus muddies the waters by telling us that attaining a goal is important only for gaining a moral end. This, then, seems to make *consequences*, not intention, the most important aspect of morality. • 69. Veyne, *Seneca*, p.34. • 70. Quoted in ibid., p.39. • 71. See Frank McLynn, *Robert Louis Stevenson* (1993), pp.254–66; Karl Miller, *Doubles* (1985). • 72. P.H. Clarke, *Adam Smith and the Stoics* (1996). • 73. Epictetus, *Discourses* 3.24.2.

Notes to Appendix Two   *pp. 555–564*

• 1. V. Marotti, *'Multa de iure sanxit'* op. cit., pp.66–70. • 2. R. Syme, 'The Proconsuls of Asia under Antoninus Pius', in Syme, RP iv, pp.325–46. • 3. Rémy, *Antonin le Pieux* op. cit., pp.144–7. • 4. G. Alföldy, KS, p.64. • 5. HA Antoninus 6.2; 6.4; 11.1. • 6. CIL ix.2828. • 7. Rémy, *Antonin le Pieux*, pp.177–84. • 8. HA Antoninus 8.7. Syme (RP v, p.673) denies that Antoninus kept his governors in office for a long time, but his counter-arguments are unconvincing. • 9. HA Pescennius 7.2. • 10. HA Antoninus 5.3; 8.6; H.G. Pflaum, *Les carrières procuratoriennes équestres sous le Haut Empire romain* (Paris 1961), pp.264–71. • 11. HA Antoninus 6.5; 11.6. • 12. P. Lambrechts, *La composition du sénat romain de l'accession au trône d'Hadrien à la mort de Commode (117–192)* (Anvers 1936), pp.191–5; H. Halfmann, *Die Senatoren aus dem östlichen Teil des Imperium Romanum bis zun Ende des 2. Jahrhunderts n. Chr.* (Göttingen 1979), pp.173–4, 182–3, 191–2. • 13. CIL vi.1001; ILS 341; Rémy, *Antonin le Pieux*, pp.138, 147–50. • 14. HA Antoninus 8.10. • 15. HA Antoninus 7.3; Vidman, *Fasti Ostienses* op. cit., pp.49–51. • 16. ILS 5878, 2666A; CIL viii.10237–8; ix.670. • 17. Meds 1.16; Rémy, *Antonin le Pieux*, pp.216–17, 221–2. • 18. Malcom A.R. Colledge, 'Art and Architecture', CAH 11, pp.972–4.

• 19. Dio 69.4.1; HA Hadrian 19.9–13. • 20. HA Antoninus; H. Mattingly, BMC, pp.549–52, 916, 938–43, 1718, 2063–6, 2098; Digest 1.10.7. • 21. Ramsay MacMullen, Corruption, p.197. • 22. J.H. Oliver, Greek Constitutions of the Early Roman Emperors (Philadelphia 1989), pp.300–6, 327–9. • 23. ILS 334, 336, 337, 6309; HA Antoninus 9.1–3. • 24. Dio 70.1.4; Aurelius Victor 16.12; CIL x.6891; 6664; Vidman, Fasti Ostienses, pp.207, 236–7. • 25. Pausanias 8.43.4. • 26. Richard J.A. Talbert, The Senate of Imperial Rome (Princeton 1984), pp.444–7. • 27. A scholarly study of the reign identifies one mandatum, 165 rescripts, eighty-six letters to magistrates, thirty-one letters to communities, fourteen decrees, three senatus consulta (as against twenty-six in Hadrian's reign, hence, presumably, the accusation of laziness) plus twenty-two various texts to officials (Marotti, 'Multa de iure sanxit' op. cit., pp.357–80). • 28. Garzetti, From Tiberius op. cit., pp.456–60. • 29. Digest 49.16.13.6. • 30. Rémy, Antonin le Pieux op. cit., p.172. • 31. Digest 1.6.2. • 32. Digest 11.4.3–5; cf. Rémy, Antonin le Pieux, pp.50–1, 158. • 33. Rémy, Antonin le Pieux pp.158–9. • 34. Digest 40.2.9.1; 40.5.26.2; 48.10.15.3. • 35. RIC 33.107; 37.94; 110.624; Richard D. Weigel, 'The Commemorative Coins of Antoninus Pius Re-examined', in W. Heckel & R. Sullivan (eds), Ancient Coins of the Graeco-Roman World; The Nickle Numismatic Papers (Waterloo, Ontario 1984), pp.187–200. • 36. Aurelius Victor, Epitome 15.2–3; Champlin, Fronto op. cit., pp.84–5; Farquharson ii, p.475. • 37. HA Antoninus 11.5; Dio 70.5; Eutropius 8.8.; RIC 104.574; Mattingly, BMC, iv, p.xcv; J. Beaujeu, La religion romaine à l'apogée de l'Empire. La Politique religieuse des Antonins (Paris 1955), pp.279–330; W. Hüttl, Antoninus Pius, Vol.2 Römische Reichsbeamte und Offiziere unter Antoninus Pius. Antoninus Pius in den Inschriften seiner Zeit (New York: 1975), pp.130–6. • 38. Rémy, Antonin le Pieux, pp.258–74. • 39. Pausanias 8.3.4. • 40. Aurelius Victor, Epitome 15.4. • 41. RIC iii.9.14; BMC iii.37.100. • 42. HA Antoninus 9.10. • 43. HA Antoninus 13.4. • 44. Aurelius Victor, Epitome 15.1–5; Pausanias 8.43.8; HA Antoninus 5.4–5. • 45. RIC iii.121.742; B. Dobson, Hadrian's Wall (1987); J.C. Mann, The Northern Frontier of Britain from Hadrian to Honorius. Literary and Epigraphic Sources (1969). • 46. AE 1936, 75; Rémy, Antonin le Pieux, pp.234–5. • 47. Pausanias 8.43.3; AE 1931, 36–8; AE 1957, 176; AE 1954, 51; J. Baradelle, 'Les nouvelles familles de Tipas et les opérations d'Antonin le Pieux en Mauretaine', Libya 11 (1954), pp.89–148. • 48. HA Antoninus 5.4–5; 9.6–7. • 49. Rémy, Antonin le Pieux, p.240. • 50. Eutropius 8.3; RIC iii.108.604; 111.6349; 119.721. • 51. Though some claim the speech was delivered in 155, on the grounds that Aelius Aristides was too ill in the mid-140s (C.A. Behr, Aelius Aristides and the Sacred Texts (Amsterdam 1968), pp.88–90). • 52. C.A. Behr, Complete Works of Aelius Aristides (Leiden 1981), 2 vols, ii, pp.73–97 (Oration 26). • 53. ibid. (Oration 33); Syme, RP ii, p.548; iii, p.1441; iv, p.344; v, pp.546–55. • 54. Garzetti, From Tiberius op. cit., p.444. • 55. M. Hammond, 'Imperial Elements in the Formula of Roman Emperors during the first two and a half centuries of Empire', Mem. American Academy at Rome 25 (1957), pp.17–64. • 56. Rostovsteff, pp.130–1, 153. One can push this 'envelope' even further. If we accept Herodotus's story of the circumnavigation of Africa by the Carthaginians – as famously provided by Herodotus in his *History* 4.42 – one can include southern Africa in the known world. Even more amazing possibilities have been suggested. See Maria Giulia Amadasi Guzzo, 'Did the Phoenicians land in America?', in Sabatino Mosca (ed.), *The Phoenicians* (New York 1999), pp.657–60; cf. also Barry Fell, *Saga America* (1980), pp.51–7.

Notes to Appendix Three   *pp. 566–567*

• 1. Thoreau, *Walden*: respectively 'Economy' (1906 edn, p.5), 'Solitudes' (p.117), 'The Pond' (p.170); 'Higher Laws' (pp.197–9); 'Conclusion' (pp.296–7). • 2. Richard Byrd, *Alone* (1938), pp.111, 164, 302. • 3. ibid., pp.122–3. • 4. ibid., pp.85–6. • 5. ibid., p.86. • 6. For Byrd's career, see Simon Nash, *The Last Explorer* (2005). • 7. Robert Louis Stevenson, *Familiar Studies of Men and Books* (1911), Vol.3, p.105.

INDEX